DUN & BRADSTREET

GUIDE TO
$YOUR INVESTMENTS$™: 1993

NANCY DUNNAN

HarperPerennial

A Division of HarperCollins *Publishers*

Dedication: To Jay J. Pack, a Wall Street perennial.

Grateful acknowledgment is made for permission to reprint:

"Calculating Growth Rates" table from *Security Analysis,* Fourth Edition, by Benjamin Graham et al. Copyright © 1962 by McGraw-Hill, Inc. Reprinted by permission of McGraw-Hill, Inc.

Material from *Donoghue's Moneyletter, Donoghue's Money Fund Report,* and *The Treasury Manager* reprinted by permission of The Donoghue Organization, Inc., Holliston, MA 01746.

"Top Performers" table reprinted by permission of *The Hulbert Financial Digest,* 643 South Carolina Avenue SE, Washington, DC 20003.

"Dun & Bradstreet" is a registered trademark of The Dun & Bradstreet Corporation and is used under license. The title *$Your Investments$*™ is a registered trademark of HarperCollins Publishers, Inc.

Designer: Gayle Jaeger

ISSN   73-18050
ISBN   0-06-271538-0
ISBN   0-06-273119-X (pbk.)

CONTENTS

ACKNOWLEDGMENTS

American Stock Exchange, New York, NY: Judy Chuisano
Bankcard Holders of America, Herndon, VA: Gerry Detweiler
Burnham Securities Inc., New York, NY: Jay J. Pack
Dow Theory Forecasts, Hammond, IN: Charles B. Carlson
Dow Theory Letters, San Diego, CA: Richard Russell
Federal Reserve Bank, New York, NY: Barton R. Sotnick
Investment Company Institute, Washington, DC: Betty Hart
KPMG Peat Marwick, New York, NY: Thomas Hakala, David Damon
NASDAQ, New York, NY: Joan Ward
National Association of Investment Clubs, Royal Oak, MI: Ken Janke
New York Stock Exchange, New York, NY: Judy Poole
Shearman Ralston, Inc., New York, NY: Thomas B. Shearman
Standard & Poor's Corp., New York, NY: Arnold Kaufman, Jon Diat

Special thanks to:
  Robert Wilson, HarperCollins Publishers
  Marcy Ross
  Joseph Spieler

This book offers only general investment observations based on the author's experience and makes no specific recommendations.

It is intended and written to provide the author's opinions in regard to the subject matter covered. This book is prepared solely by Nancy Dunnan and not by The Dun & Bradstreet Corporation and its subsidiaries; The Dun & Bradstreet Corporation does not give out investment advice. The author, the publisher, and The Dun & Bradstreet Corporation are not engaged in rendering legal, accounting, or other professional advice, and the reader should seek the services of a qualified professional for such advice.

The author, the publisher, and The Dun & Bradstreet Corporation cannot be held responsible for any loss incurred as a result of the application of any of the information in this publication.

Every attempt has been made to assure the accuracy of the statistics that appear throughout *$Your Investments$*.™ In some cases, data may vary from your reports because of interpretations or accounting changes made after the original publication. In others, there may be errors—for which we apologize. Please remember that *$Your Investments$*™ is a *guide,* not a definitive source of financial information. When you have a question, check with your broker's research department.

ABOUT THE AUTHOR

NANCY DUNNAN is a financial analyst. She hosts a regular call-in radio program on WNYC in New York. In addition to *Dun & Bradstreet Guide to $Your Investments$*™, she is the author of *How to Invest $50 to $5000* (4th edition), *How to Invest in Real Estate, Your Year-Round Investment Planner, How to Save on Your Taxes if You Make $30,000 or Less,* and *Financial Savvy for Singles.* She writes a monthly column, "Smart Investor," for *Lear's* magazine.

In 1991, Ms. Dunnan was awarded the Distinguished Service Award in Investment Education from the Investment Education Institute, an affiliate of the National Association of Investors Corporation.

GETTING STARTED ON YOUR INVESTMENT PORTFOLIO

Sophie Tucker put it well when she said, "I've been rich and I've been poor, and believe me, rich is better." You too can start on the road to riches or increase the riches you already have during 1993 by heeding the suggestions/advice in this year's edition of *Dun & Bradstreet Guide To $Your Investments$™ 1993*. It doesn't matter whether you have $5,000, $50,000 or $550,000. At all three levels and those in between there are many investment choices, so many in fact you may have difficulty deciding where to put your money. That is what this section, Part One, will help you sort out. It will simplify what can otherwise be a tough decision-making process. Gathering and understanding the information needed to make those decisions is your first step in building up your riches and becoming at ease in the financial world.

BEGINNING INVESTORS
Please start by reading *all* of Part One, "Getting Started on Your Investment Portfolio." Here you will find information on basic, time-tested smart choices, as well as on:

- How to pick a money market fund
- How to get the best deal at your bank
- The advantages of a credit union
- When to move into mutual funds, and which ones
- How to protect and insure your money
- Sound financial opportunities for unsound times

Then move on to the "Investors Almanac" and Part Two to size up the risks and rewards of more sophisticated investments.

SEASONED INVESTORS
Begin by reading the first 11 pages of Part One, which contain new and timely advice on:

- Alternatives to CDs and money market funds
- Where to invest as we come out of the recession

INTRODUCTION:
Special Advice for 1993

The summer of 1992 saw short-term interest rates fall to their lowest levels in two decades, putting many Americans on the prowl for alternatives to low-yielding money market funds, CDs and Treasury bills. Others are reluctantly accepting these lower returns because they don't want to take on the risks that come with stock and bond investments.

ALTERNATIVES TO CDs AND MONEY MARKET FUNDS

If you do not wish to accept the greater risk that accompanies the stock market or other investments offering higher yields than today's Certificates of Deposit (CDs) and money market funds, then switch only a portion of your money in these "safe havens" into one or more of these higher-yielding choices:

- Longer-term CDs. Going farther out in terms of time increases your yield. Bear in mind, however, that your money will be tied up and when rates rise again you will want to reinvest at the new rates—one reason for not putting all your money in long-term instruments.
- Treasuries. Again, consider going out five or ten years to get higher yields.
- Corporate bonds. Although Treasuries are safer since they are backed by the full faith and credit of the U.S. government, corporate bonds offer better yields. There are a number of A-rated corporates with yields ranging from 7% to 8½%. Locking in such yields when rates on other types of investments are much lower, is a smart move. Confine purchases to bonds listed on the New York or American exchanges so price quotes can readily be checked and so you can find a market should you wish to sell. One particularly sound category to consider: Bonds issued by public utility companies. The overall creditworthiness of utility bonds is typically high because they provide a needed service in an almost monopolistic setting.
  Examples of public utility bonds:
  1 Commonwealth Edison, rated A-, 8¾% coupon rate, due 2005
  2 Ohio Edison, rated BBB, 8½% coupon rate, due 2006
  3 Cleveland Electric, rated BBB-, 9¼% coupon rate, due 2009
  Examples of non-utility corporate bonds, rated A or better:
  1 American Brands, 7.50%, due 1999
  2 John Deere Capital, 7.20%, due 1997
  3 General Electric, 7.17%, due 1997
  4 Bell Telephone of Pennsylvania, 8½%, due 2017

5 Exxon, 6½%, due 1998

6 Dow Chemical, 8½%, due 2005

- High-yield stocks. Check yields on electric and gas utility and oil company stocks in particular (see list on page 185).

- Closed-end bond funds. Many investors shy away from these funds because they don't understand how they work. Read the details in Chapter 7 first. Ignoring them means ignoring a good investment opportunity because a number are relatively high in safety and have better than average yields, especially those that invest in U.S. and foreign government debt.

  Examples of closed-end bond funds:

1 Putnam Intermediate Government Income Trust (NYSE:PGT), $9.25/ share, yielding 7.8%

2 Dreyfus Strategic Government Income Fund (NYSE:DSI), $12/share, yielding 8.7%

3 Dreyfus Closed-end Strategic Municipal Bond Fund (NYSE:DSM), $10.50/share, yielding 6.8%. This stock has the advantage that the interest earned is free from federal income tax.

AN INVESTOR'S ROADMAP FOR THE RECOVERY

Compounding the problem of low interest rates is the fact that the recession seems to linger on forever. These two factors mean it's time to revamp your investment program and to evaluate the benefits of a long-term, diversified investment portfolio rather than simply reacting in a knee-jerk fashion to the existing market situations.

If you hold a mixture of stocks, bonds, and money market securities you will earn higher returns over time than if you simply stick to very conservative investments. If you find this hard to believe, consider this fact: Although common stocks tend to fluctuate the most in price from one year to the next, they have over time given the best long-term returns and they also provide the best hedge against inflation. In fact:

Over the past 20 years, stocks, as measured by Standard & Poor's 500 Stock Index gave investors an annualized return of 11.9% compared to 9.4% for 10-year Treasury bonds and 7.7% for 90-day Treasury bills. During this time period, inflation averaged 6.3%.

As you put together your portfolio, bear in mind that:

- Risk and return go hand-in-hand: The greater the risk the greater the potential return.

- The longer the investment time period, the higher the yield but the longer your money is tied up.

- Check the customized sample portfolios in Part 8 for specific suggestions.

Then, as the recession ends, or winds down, be prepared to take advantage of the investment opportunities that will inevitably occur.

Economists agree that the recovery will be in fits and starts and vary by industries and geographical regions of the country.

Generally speaking, the Midwest has recovered the fastest. At the top of the list of recovery stocks is *Norwest Corporation,* a financial services company whose regional banking division has 339 offices in 12 midwestern states. The company's fees for mortgages and trusts are on the rise with business conditions improving. A St. Louis company, *Emerson Electric* manufactures a wide range of electrical and electronic goods. It has had 34 consecutive years of increased earnings. Demand for its consumer tools, appliance parts, and industrial motors is on the rise. *G&K Services* of Minneapolis is a major supplier of rental uniforms, linens, and custodial textiles. Its business is expected to be profitable as the economy recovers.

Other companies likely to benefit from the end of hard times are (1) *Waste Management,* an Oak Brook, Illinois, company that is the nation's largest collector of household and industrial products. It also manages air-pollution and water treatment projects. (2) *Werner Enterprises,* a trucking company headquartered in Omaha with some 2,500 trucks and 5,000 trailers. (3) *Black & Decker,* best known for its power tools and accessories, has also developed a large line of household appliances, electric lawncare equipment, and plumbing fixtures. A solid bank in the southeast to consider: (4) *NationsBank Corporation.* Rapidly growing business in this region plus the strong balance sheets of both banks bodes well for these two stocks. (5) *H.F. Ahmanson & Co.,* the country's largest thrift-holding company, has had its price knocked down by public fears surrounding the S&L debacle. However, this particular stock is likely to benefit from anticipated price increases and it offers a solid dividend.

KNOWING WHEN THE RECESSION WILL END: THE DUNNAN INDICATORS

Although there are many official government statistics that help us determine when a recession is drawing to a close, such as unemployment figures, new

---

STOCKS POISED FOR THE RECOVERY

STOCK	BUSINESS	PRICE	DIVIDEND YIELD
H.F. Ahmanson	Savings institution	$18¼	4.8%
Black & Decker	Manufacturer	22	1.8
Emerson Electric	Manufacturer	49	2.8
G&K Services	Uniform rental	14	0.7
NationsBank	Bank	46	3.2
Waste Management	Garbage collector	35	1.5
Werner Enterprises	Trucking	33	0.5

housing starts, and increased manufacturing, sometimes these figures, although extremely useful in making investment decisions, seem remote from everyday life. Here are ten indicators that everyone can relate to.

The recession is winding down when:

1 it's tough to get a ticket to a Broadway play.
2 cruise lines stop discounting prices.
3 you have trouble getting a taxi cab.
4 sales of men's suits pick up.
5 help wanted ad pages in the newspaper increase.
6 boat sales increase.
7 it's hard to get a reservation at a good restaurant.
8 you start saving mail order catalogues instead of throwing them out.
9 your dry cleaning bill goes up.
10 pennies appear on the street again.

You can also find clues to the economy's direction by watching the earnings growth and stock prices of the nation's major retailers. When the recession began, their businesses took a nose dive along with their stock prices. In turn, they are likely to lead the way out of the doldrums. Among those to track are: Wal-Mart, Sears Roebuck, J.C. Penney, K Mart, Limited, Gap, Dayton-Hudson, Filene's Basement, and Federated Department Stores.

LOW-DEBT INVESTING

Another investment area to focus on in the post–recession economy is that of low-debt companies. During the 1980s, the decade of excess, in which the United States tripled its debt, corporations thought nothing of borrowing billions. RJR Nabisco, Union Carbide, Holiday Inns, Philips Petroleum, and Federated Department Stores are just a few of many that took on heavy debt. When the recession set in, in late 1990 and early 1991, however, consumer spending slowed, corporate income slid, and interest bills became tougher to pay. Many highly leveraged companies were forced to go further into debt, and some have declared bankruptcy.

Today, companies with little or no debt are solid investments. Their strong balance sheets enable them to expand—to buy stores and factories from owners who are cash strapped—and, if the need arises, to borrow money at a reasonable cost.

A DEBT PRIMER

There are two basic types of debt—short term and long term. Short-term debt signifies what a company owes its bankers, and since this must be paid on demand, it is the more onerous. Long-term debt, meaning corporate bonds that don't mature for at least 10 years, is more manageable because only interest must be paid until the principal comes due at the end of the term, when new debt can be issued.

A company's debt load can be found in its balance sheet. An excess of current assets over current liabilities is the company's working capital—the money it has to run the business. As a rule of thumb, it's best if current

CASH COWS

COMPANY NAME	LINE OF BUSINESS	SYMBOL	PRICE*
Abbott Laboratories	Health care products	ABT	$ 33
Bristol-Myers Squibb	Drugs	BMY	73
Calgon Carbon Corp.	Activated carbons	CCC	17
Dun & Bradstreet Corp.	Business publisher	DNB	50
A.G. Edwards & Sons	Securities broker	AGE	21
Family Dollar Stores	Retail stores	FDO	17
Federal Signal Corp.	Signal manufacturer	FSS	22
Gibson Greetings Inc.	Greeting cards	GIB	9
Int'l. Flavors & Frag.	Perfumes, cosmetics	IFF	106
Jean Philippe Fragrances	Perfumes	JEAN	14
Lawson Products Inc.	Fastener distributor	LAWS	26
Long Drug Stores Corp.	Drugstore chain	LDG	34
Luby's Cafeterias	Restaurants	LUB	16
Merck & Co., Inc.	Drugs	MRK	145
Michael Baker Corp.	Engineering consultant	BKR	28
Quality Food Centers	Food distributor	QFCI	35
Raytheon Co.	Missiles, appliances	RTN	45
Rollins Inc.	Pest control	ROL	29
A. Schulman Inc.	Plastics, resins	SHLM	30
J. M. Smucker Co.	Jams, jellies	SJM	28
Tootsie Roll Industries	Candy	TR	66

* Prices as of May 1992

assets are twice as large as current liabilities. Utilities, supermarkets, and other businesses that generate immediate cash payments, however, are an exception to this rule.

SOUND FINANCIAL OPPORTUNITIES IN UNSOUND TIMES

Although predictions about the length and depth of the recession vary widely, there is no question that we are living in a less than robust economy, regardless of whether it's officially labeled a recession. This situation is not all bad, however. In fact, it offers several excellent investment opportunities and unique personal perks. So, if your job is secure or you have independent income, and you've saved nine months of living expenses, you can take advantage of a number of investment situations offered by our weakened economy.

- *Buy retirement property.* Prices for land and houses in many resort and retirement areas are low. Distress sales are not uncommon.

- *Refinance your mortgage.* If you purchased your home when fixed-rate mortgages were 11% and higher, consider refinancing as long as the current rate is at least 2 percentage points less and if you plan to remain in your home three years or longer. This will free up cash that you can invest elsewhere.
- *Buy distressed property.* Many houses and business properties are up for sale because their owners cannot meet mortgage payments. Check your newspaper for local auctions or call the Resolution Trust Corp. for a listing of properties for sale (1-800-431-0600). If it's a rental property, buy within a day's drive so you can easily oversee its use.
- *Take a vacation.* Airlines, hotels, and cruise lines, hard hit by the recession, are offering good deals to woo passengers. To find the best prices, subscribe to "Travel Smart," a monthly newsletter that tracks the best in fares, packages, hotels, and unique vacations. Subscribers are entitled to book the best in tickets through the newsletter's special travel agency. Call: Travel Smart, 1-800-FARE-OFF or 1-914-693-8300; 12 issues plus special reports for $44.
- *Buy a new car.* Dealers are under pressure and willing to negotiate as never before. Shop around and take your time.

☐CAUTION: Financing a car with a consumer loan is no longer tax deductible. Try to finance with home equity credit, where interest payments are tax deductible.

- *Buy other items.* If you need a major item—an appliance, TV, video player, for example—check troubled retailers for low prices.

WHAT ELSE YOU CAN DO TO IMPROVE YOUR FINANCIAL LIFE

1 *Be aware.* Take time to learn how to handle your money. It is a fact that a stock market crash, a recession, high unemployment, or generally hard times are at one time or another part of our lives. Therefore, to put your trust in time or your spouse or parents, or even the corporation you work for, to take care of your present and future financial needs is childlike and unrealistic. Although many regulatory agencies, as well as the Securities and Exchange Commission, the stock exchanges, and the Federal Reserve Board, make every effort toward maintaining an orderly market and stable economy, you too should take certain steps to protect yourself in this fully globalized investing world. To choose to remain uninvolved or ignorant about the stock market, the direction of the economy, and the workings of the entire financial world is not only to court disaster but to invite financial loss.

2 *Be informed.* The two best defenses you have against trouble are relatively simple: The first is *information,* and the second is *diversification.* After taking time to learn how the economy, individual companies, the banks, interest rates, the dollar, and inflation affect your

YOUR FINANCIAL LIBRARY

Read one of these publications each week. They are arranged by approximate level of sophistication, beginning with the most elementary. Subscriptions are available for each one.

- *USA Today*
- Your local newspaper
- *Bottom Line Personal*
- *U.S. News & World Report*
- *Better Investing* (National Association of Investment Clubs)
- *Consumer Reports*
- *Money*
- *Your Money*
- Standard & Poor's *The Outlook*
- *New York Times*
- *Investors Daily*
- *Wall Street Journal*
- *Business Week*
- *Barron's*
- *Value Line*

investments, you may still lose money some of the time, but you will win far more often if you are both diversified and informed.

Begin by reading at least one intelligent financial publication each week. Select one that matches your level of sophistication. Carry it with you (see the box). Watch the market news on CNN, CNBC, or PBS television or listen to broadcasts on public radio. Know what's happening in this country and abroad.

3   Then, *diversify*—among types of investments and risk levels. Check your holdings against the investment pyramid on page 17. Make certain you have dollars invested in several levels.

HOW TO PICK WINNERS

There was a time when all an investor had to do was pick attractive stocks or bonds. Now you're faced with a bewildering variety of choices, often involving hefty commissions. It's important to determine if they are speculations or investments. To boost your success ratio:

- **Don't become involved with special "opportunities"** until you've developed a balanced portfolio. Stay away from futures, indexes, most new issues, and other complicated investments. These are dominated by the professionals, who have more skill, knowledge, and money than most individuals—and even they get hurt.
- **Don't follow the crowd.** The majority opinion is often wrong. Every major market advance has begun when pessimism was loudest and prices lowest.

HOW TO CALCULATE THE EFFECT OF INFLATION

YEARS FROM NOW	4%	5%	6%	7%	8%
5	1.22	1.28	1.34	1.40	1.47
10	1.48	1.63	1.79	1.97	2.16
15	1.80	2.08	2.40	2.76	3.17
20	2.19	2.65	3.21	3.87	4.66
25	2.67	3.39	4.29	5.43	6.85
30	3.24	4.32	5.74	7.61	10.06

SOURCE: Reprinted with permission from *Encyclopedia of Banking and Financial Tables,* copyright © 1980, 1986, Warren, Gorham & Lamont, Inc., Boston, Mass. All rights reserved.

- **Don't dash in and out of the market.** You'll find your profits are eaten up by commissions.
- **Don't be in a hurry to invest your money.** If you miss one opportunity, there will be another just as good and possibly better along soon.
- **Don't fall in love with your investments.** There is always a time to be in a stock, a bond, a money market account, and a CD and a time to be out. Remember, with few exceptions most investments become overpriced, and no tree ever grows to the sky.

THE POWER OF COMPOUND INTEREST

A REGULAR INVESTMENT OF $100 PER YEAR, INVESTED AT:	WILL, COMPOUNDED ANNUALLY AT THE END OF EACH YEAR, GROW TO THIS SUM AFTER THIS NUMBER OF YEARS:							
	5	10	15	20	25	30	35	40
6%	$564	$1,318	$2,328	$3,679	$5,486	$7,906	$11,143	$15,476
8	587	1,449	2,715	4,576	7,311	11,328	17,232	25,906
10	611	1,594	3,177	5,727	9,835	16,449	27,102	44,259
12	635	1,755	3,728	7,205	13,333	24,133	43,166	76,709
14	661	1,934	4,384	9,102	18,187	35,679	69,357	134,202
16	688	2,132	5,166	11,538	24,921	53,031	112,071	236,076

To get the corresponding total for any other annually invested amount (A), multiply the dollar total given above for the yield and the number of years by $\frac{A}{100}$. Example: You plan to invest $75 per month, $900 a year. What capital sum will that provide after 35 years, at 12% compounded annually? Check where the lines cross for 12% and 35 years: $43,166 $\times \frac{900}{100}$ = $388,494. Note: The totals will be greater if: (1) the deposits are made at the beginning of the year; (2) compounding is more frequent.

SOURCE: Reprinted with permission from *Encyclopedia of Banking and Financial Tables,* copyright © 1980, 1986, Warren, Gorham & Lamont, Inc., Boston, Mass. All rights reserved.

THE MAGIC OF COMPOUNDING

In view of our renewed emphasis on safe investing during troubled times, one point that's worth repeating is the positive impact of compounding, or earning income on income, by prompt reinvestment of all interest, dividends, and realized capital gains. As shown in the accompanying tables, savings can mount at an astonishing rate over the years.

➤ THE RULE OF 72 For a quick calculation on how long it takes to double your money, use *the rule of 72*: divide 72 by the yield. Thus, at 9%, it will take 8 years; at 10% about 7 years; at 12%, 6 years to double your money.

LISTENING TO THE PROS

John Kenneth Galbraith, in his book *The Great Crash*, reminds us that John D. Rockefeller told the press after the crash of October 29, 1929, "Believing that fundamental conditions of the country are sound, my son and I have for some days been purchasing sound common stocks." To this Eddie Cantor replied, "Sure, who else had any money left?"

After reading the *Dun & Bradstreet Guide to $Your Investments$*™ and becoming an informed investor, you too will be able to decide if you wish to follow Rockefeller's notion or side with Mark Twain, who said, "October. This is one of the peculiarly dangerous months to speculate in stocks. The others are July, January, September, April, November, May, March, June, December, August, and February."

If not all your investment decisions turn out to be spectacular, and no one's ever are, and if at the same time you have adequately diversified, the worst scenario will still leave you upright and in good shape. But then, cut your losses. As Warren Buffett, the chairman of Berkshire Hathaway, Inc., said in one of his annual reports, "Should you find yourself in a chronically leaking boat, energy devoted to changing vessels is likely to be more productive than energy devoted to patching leaks."

ANOTHER VIEW OF COMPOUNDING

RATE OF RETURN	AVERAGE ANNUAL RETURN ON ORIGINAL INVESTMENT				
	5 YEARS	10 YEARS	15 YEARS	20 YEARS	25 YEARS
6%	6.8%	7.9%	9.3%	11.0%	13.2%
7	8.1	9.7	11.7	14.3	17.7
8	9.4	11.6	14.5	18.3	23.4
9	10.8	13.7	17.6	23.0	30.5
10	12.2	15.9	21.1	28.6	39.3
11	13.7	18.4	25.2	35.3	50.3
12	15.2	21.0	29.8	43.2	64.0

Personally, I like Mae West's attitude best: "Too much of a good thing can be wonderful." May 1993 be a wonderful year for you and your investments.

FOR FURTHER INFORMATION

Jonathan Pond, *Safe Money in Tough Times* (New York: Dell Publishing Co., 1991).

Nancy Dunnan and Jay J. Pack, *How To Survive and Thrive in the Recession* (New York: Avon Books, 1991).

2

BUILDING YOUR OWN INVESTMENT PYRAMID

A few years ago, the world of investing was a far simpler one than it is today: Investment choices were pleasantly limited, and only a few basic concepts governed the ways in which you could make (or lose) money. If you were terribly conservative, you put your hard-won earnings in the local bank where you earned 5%; or perhaps your family broker bought some stock in AT&T or a carefully selected public utility company. If you were willing to assume a little more risk, you might have moved out of the blue chip arena into more speculative growth stocks. If you wanted a steady stream of income, you merely purchased high-quality corporate or government bonds and waited for the interest to roll in. But the only choices available for the general investor were basically stocks, bonds, and the bank.

But it's 1992 and no longer quite so easy. The banking crisis, recession, and unprecedented market volatility now affect every investor, large or small. Not only must you decide what to invest in and when, but realize you are also competing with highly sophisticated institutions. In addition, lower interest rates have made conservative investments less appealing. And you face a bewildering array of products and institutions: certificates of deposit (CDs), money market funds, interest-bearing bank accounts, options, and index futures, as well as the traditional stocks, bonds, and savings accounts.

The proliferation of investment choices has made wise decision making far more complicated, and now more than ever before, information and knowledge are absolutely essential. In fact, the world of finance is changing so rapidly that unless you are up to date and well informed, you'll be left in the dust. That is why *$Your Investments$*™ can make the difference between a well-informed decision and pure guesswork. It helps you determine if you're better off buying a bank CD or a Treasury bond, making a play in commodity futures or looking for takeover targets, using your broker's research or following the charts.

Whether you're a new investor or a sophisticated money manager who has weathered numerous bull and bear cycles, this vital reference brings you more data on the more familiar vehicles, introduces you to new products, and, finally, offers you the best in smart money-making strategies as followed by the professional investment community.

BECOMING A SAVVY INVESTOR

Before you plunge into your pocket and buy 100 shares of a reportedly "hot stock" or set up a personally tailored investment program with a stockbroker or financial planner, it's wise to take a few moments to decide your answers to three key questions:

1   What do I want to derive from such a move or investment?
2   How much can I sensibly afford to invest?
3   What are my major financial goals?

Random purchases of stocks, bonds, and mutual funds may initially seem rewarding but are unlikely to fulfill your long-range goals. To get the most out of your investment dollar, the answers to these three questions and some background preparation are essential. The four homework assignments below can produce large benefits in the long run, enabling you to make better investment decisions whether you make them on your own or with professional guidance.

KNOW THY WORTH

Before making any type of investment expenditure, whether it's buying a stock, a bond, or a house, you must know your net worth. This is one of the first questions most stockbrokers, money managers, and bank mortgage officers ask. If, like most people, you're uncertain of the precise answer, don't panic. Figuring out your net worth is easy. All you need is a free evening, a calculator, your checkbook, bills, and a record of your income. Then follow these two easy steps:

1   Add up the value of everything you own (your assets).
2   Subtract the total of all you owe (your liabilities).

The amount left over is your net worth. You can use the worksheet on the following page as a guide for arriving at the correct amount. When figuring your assets, list the amount they will bring in today's market, which could be more or less than you paid for them originally. Assets include cash on hand, your checking and savings account balances, the cash value of any insurance policies, personal property (car, boat, jewelry, real estate, investments), and any vested interest in a pension or retirement plan. Your liabilities include money you owe, charge account debts, mortgages, auto payments, education or other loans, and any taxes due.

KNOW WHERE THY WORTH IS GOING: BUDGETING

A budget, like braces on the teeth, is universally unappealing. It's a very rare person who likes either one, yet each has its place. Some form of budgeting should be part of your overall investment plan. It's not only a good way of knowing how much you're spending and on what, but it is also a sensible means of setting aside money for investing, our primary concern in this book. If you need help in establishing a budget for investing, use the worksheet on page 16. In order to budget dollars for investing, try setting aside a certain dollar amount on a regular basis, even if it's not an impressively large number. Mark it immediately for "savings/investing." Ideally you should try to save 5% to 10% of your annual income; if you make more than $70,000 a year, aim for 15%. Don't talk yourself out of budgeting for investing simply because it is a nuisance to keep track of what you spend. You'll be convinced of the wisdom of saving and the

FINDING YOUR NET WORTH

ASSETS as of _____ (date)		LIABILITIES as of _____ (date)	
Cash on hand	$_____	Unpaid bills	
Cash in checking accounts	_____	Charge accounts	$_____
Savings accounts, money market fund	_____	Taxes, property taxes, and quarterly	
Life insurance, cash value	_____	income taxes	_____
Annuities	_____	Insurance premiums	_____
Retirement funds		Rent or monthly mortgage payment	_____
IRA or Keogh	_____	Utilities	_____
401(k) plan	_____	Balance due on:	
Vested interest in pension or		Mortgage	_____
profit-sharing plan	_____	Automobile loans	_____
U.S. savings bonds, current value	_____	Personal loans	_____
Investments		Installment loans	_____
Market value of stocks, bonds,		Total liabilities $_____	
mutual fund shares, etc.	_____		
Real estate, market value of real			
property minus mortgage	_____		
Property			
Automobile	_____		
Furniture	_____		
Jewelry, furs	_____		
Sports and hobby equipment	_____	Assets $_____	
Equity interest in your business	_____	Minus liabilities _____	
Total assets $_____		Your net worth $_____	

advantages of compound interest if you take a look at the table below, which shows what happens to $1,000 over 20 years when you put it in an investment yielding 5¼% and the income earned is reinvested or compounded.

KNOW THY GOALS AND PRIORITIES   After you've accumulated money to invest, your next homework assignment is to decide what you want to accomplish by investing. If you were to take a trip to Europe or travel by car across the country, you would bring along a good road map. This should also be the case with investing, only the road map would consist of financial, not geographic, destinations. When you travel

WHAT HAPPENS TO A $1,000 INVESTMENT AT 5¼%

FREQUENCY OF COMPOUNDING	1 YEAR	5 YEARS	10 YEARS	20 YEARS
Continuous	$1,054.67	$1,304.93	$1,702.83	$2,899.63
Daily	1,054.67	1,304.90	1,702.76	2,899.41
Quarterly	1,053.54	1,297.96	1,684.70	2,838.20
Semiannually	1,053.19	1,295.78	1,679.05	2,819.21
Annually	1,052.50	1,291.55	1,668.10	2,782.54

through Italy, you decide what towns, cathedrals, or monuments you want most to visit; how long it will take you to get from one to the next; and approximately what it will cost. The same procedure should be applied to your financial journey through life. Your highlights or destination points may include some of these:

- Building a nest egg for emergencies
- Establishing an investment portfolio
- Reducing taxes
- Preparing for retirement
- Paying for a college education
- Buying a house, car, or boat
- Traveling or taking a cruise
- Investing in art or antiques
- Adding on a room or installing a swimming pool
- Setting up your own business

Goal setting, you will discover, enables you to take firm control of your financial life, especially if you actually write your goals down. The process of listing goals on paper, perhaps awkward at first, forces you to focus on how you handle money and how you feel about risk versus safety. Divide your goals into two sections: immediate goals (those that can be accomplished in a year or less) and long-range goals.

If you're unmarried, your immediate goals could be:

- Obtain a graduate degree
- Join a health club
- Save for summer vacation
  Longer-term goals:
- Buy a car
- Set up a brokerage account or buy shares in a mutual fund
- Purchase a co-op or condo with a friend
  If you're married and raising a family, the goals might shift to include:
- Buying a house
- Setting up educational funds for children
- Building a growth portfolio
  Singles and marrieds closer to retirement tend to seek other goals:
- Shift bulk of portfolio to safe income-producing vehicles
- Increase contribution to retirement plan
- Find appropriate short-term tax shelters
- Set up a consulting business; incorporate

Regardless of your age or income, individual goals make it easier and more meaningful to stick to a budget and to save for investing. Putting aside that 5% to 15% every month for an investment program suddenly has a very tangible purpose—one that you personally decided on.

BUILDING YOUR INVESTMENT PYRAMID

Once you know why you want to invest, you are ready to think about your investments as part of a pyramid in which each level builds on the earlier ones. This approach to investing offers a carefully designed, diversified system that provides for financial growth and protection regardless of your age, marital status, income, or level of financial sophistication. As you can see by looking at the illustration, you begin your financial program on the pyramid at Level 1. It is the lowest in terms of risk and the highest in safety. As your net worth grows, you automatically move up to the next level, increasing both the amount of risk involved and the potential for financial gain.

Level 1 covers life's basic financial requirements and includes:

- An emergency nest egg consisting of cash or cash equivalents such as savings account, CDs, money market funds
- Health, life, and disability insurance
- A solid retirement plan, including an IRA, Keogh, or 401(k)

YOUR CASH FLOW

WHERE IT COMES FROM

INCOME	ANNUAL AMOUNT
Take-home pay	$_____
Bonus and commissions	_____
Interest	_____
Dividends	_____
Rent	_____
Pensions	_____
Social Security	_____
Annuities	_____
Tax refunds	_____
Other	_____
Total	$_____

WHERE IT GOES

EXPENSES	ANNUAL AMOUNT
Income taxes	$_____
Mortgage or rent	_____
Property taxes	_____
Utilities	_____
Automobile maintenance	_____
Commuting or other transportation	_____
Insurance	
Homeowner's or renter's	_____
Life	_____
Disability	_____
Child care	_____
Education	_____
Food	_____
Clothing	_____
Household miscellaneous	_____
Home improvements	_____
Entertainment	_____
Vacations, travel	_____
Books, magazines, club dues	_____
Contributions to charities or organizations	_____
Total	$_____
Surplus or deficit	$_____

Before leaving this level, you will have saved enough cash or cash equivalents to cover a minimum of 3 to 9 months' worth of living expenses. This minimum is your emergency reserve, and when you've achieved this goal, you're financially solid enough to advance to Level 2.

Level 2 is devoted entirely to safe income-producing investments such as corporate or municipal bonds; Treasury securities; longer-term CDs; zero coupon bonds; and real estate (your primary residence)—all of which are described in this book.

Although safety is key at this step, the liquidity factor emphasized in Level 1 is now traded off for a higher return or yield. And because some of these items, notably zero coupon bonds and CDs, are timed to mature at a definite date, they provide ideal means to meet staggering college tuition bills and retirement costs.

Money to buy real estate is also included, not only because it gives you a place to live, but also because historically real estate has appreciated significantly in value. At the same time, it offers tax benefits in the form of deductions for mortgage interest payments and real estate taxes.

Level 3 involves investing for growth. At this point you can afford to

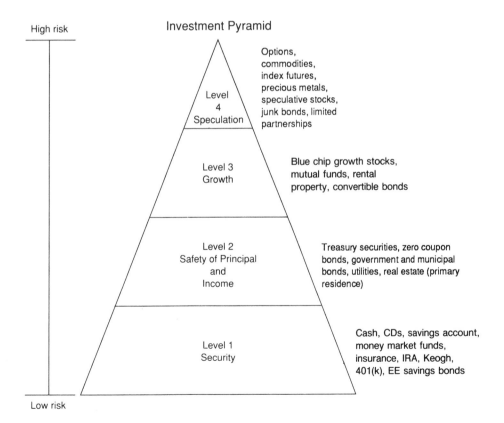

Investment Pyramid

High risk

Level 4 Speculation — Options, commodities, index futures, precious metals, speculative stocks, junk bonds, limited partnerships

Level 3 Growth — Blue chip growth stocks, mutual funds, rental property, convertible bonds

Level 2 Safety of Principal and Income — Treasury securities, zero coupon bonds, government and municipal bonds, utilities, real estate (primary residence)

Level 1 Security — Cash, CDs, savings account, money market funds, insurance, IRA, Keogh, 401(k), EE savings bonds

Low risk

HINTS FOR THE BEGINNING INVESTOR

- Don't think you're going to get rich immediately. It takes time and wisdom to become a winning investor.
- Start by investing only in stocks or bonds of leading companies. They have proven track records, a lot of research on them is available, and there will always be a buyer if you should wish to sell.
- Buy a stock *only* if you can state a reason why it will appreciate in price or pay high dividends; merely feeling good about an issue is not a solid enough reason to justify purchase.
- Don't churn your own account so that commissions eat up any profits. Even if the average commission is only 5%, your stock will have to move up at least 10% to be even.
- Spread out your risks. Every company has the potential to be a loser some of the time.
- Decide on the maximum amount that you're willing to lose and stick to it.
- When you lose, if you do, try to determine why your security went down.
- Read about investing and investments regularly.

be more adventuresome, more risk-oriented, and less conservative; and this book shows you how to turn away from liquidity and assured income and toward growth and blue chip stocks, conservative mutual funds, convertible bonds, and rentable property. If you find you're interested in the stock market, this is the ideal time to join an investment club and learn by doing so.

FINANCIAL RESOLUTIONS FOR 1993

I resolve to:
- Pay myself first every month—to make savings the first paid bill
- Live within my income
- Organize my financial papers
- Review or write my will
- Subscribe to a financial publication . . . and read it
- Be an informed investor, not a speculator
- Spend half an hour each day listening to or reading about financial matters
- Invest only in things I understand and learn about those I don't
- Read most of this book

Level 4, the pinnacle of the pyramid, is given over to the riskiest investments, which may or may not yield spectacular returns. These include speculative stocks, stocks in new companies, takeover candidates, options, commodities, index futures, gold and precious metals, junk bonds, and limited partnerships, all vehicles discussed in detail in the following chapters.

3

FINDING SAFE PLACES FOR YOUR MONEY:
Banks, Money Market Funds, CDs,
and Credit Unions

Throughout your investment life there will be many times when varying portions of your assets should be kept liquid; that is, readily available. The traditional savings account simply won't do anymore; the interest rate is far too low. Fortunately, you have an abundance of other options.

Interest-bearing accounts are best for the portion of your money that calls for sure income and preservation of capital, as illustrated on Level 1 of your investment pyramid. Reserves for unexpected emergencies, such as interest-bearing accounts—safe places while you're looking for more rewarding opportunities, call them what you will—are available through banks, savings and loans, credit unions, brokerage firms, and even mutual funds. Many are insured by the federal government.

Whether you invest in savings accounts, certificates of deposit, or money market funds, you will always get back the same number of dollars you put in plus interest, unless, of course, you make an early withdrawal, in which case you may be penalized. The income earned is taxable along with your salary, wages, and other earnings, which means that if inflation advances more rapidly than interest rates, the purchasing power of both the principal and the interest will decrease every year (an exception: tax-free money market accounts).

FLIGHT TO SAFETY

The October 19, 1987, market crash, the insider trading scandals, the 1990 collapse of junk bonds, and the more recent savings and loan debacle, have forced even the highest of the high rollers to consider what was once a wallflower concept: safety.

The key players in the flight to safety are money market mutual funds, bank money market accounts, certificates of deposit, Treasury bills and notes, EE savings bonds, and select mutual funds. The table on page 21 shows their current yields as we went to press as well as their average minimum requirements for investment. We don't by any means suggest that you put all your money in these safe havens—their yields are too low—but you should certainly earmark at least one-quarter of your assets for this category. Investors—amateur and pro—have come to realize that the stock market is indeed unpredictable, and diversification is not just mumbo jumbo from the mouths of conservative financial advisers and writers; it is the basis of protecting one's investments in economic climates of all kinds.

The best way to decide which safe haven is for you is to determine how long you would like to invest this portion of your money. Suggested designations are given in the table below.

AT YOUR BANK

Banks now offer a wide variety of accounts with varying interest rates, so it pays to check several in your area before making a decision. Although it's time-consuming, it can mean as much as a 1% to 2% difference in the interest earned on your account. Select an institution that will tell you about a bounced check ahead of time and that offers an automatic credit line, which will help eliminate the expense of bounced checks.

PASSBOOK SAVINGS

Fewer and fewer banks are offering the old-fashioned passbook savings account to their new customers. Most have replaced it with a *statement account,* which provides a monthly or quarterly computerized update of your savings transactions. A statement

SAFE HAVENS

INVESTMENT	YIELD	AVERAGE MINIMUM INVESTMENT
1 to 3 Months		
Money market mutual funds	3.32%	$1,000
Bank money market accounts	3.08	1,000
Super NOW bank accounts	2.45	2,500
Short-term CDs	3.34	500
3-month Treasury bills	3.23	10,000 initial; 5,000 thereafter
Passbook savings account	3.12	50
Credit union sharedraft	3.50	50
3 Months or Longer		
12-month CD	3.68	500
3-month Treasury bills	3.23	10,000 initial; 5,000 thereafter
5-year Treasury notes	5.70	5,000 (1- to 4-year maturities) 1,000 (4- to 10-year maturities)
10-year Treasury bonds	6.80	1,000
Short-term closed-end government bond funds	9.00	$8 per share 500
EE savings bonds	5.58	25

SOURCE: Barron's, July 27, 1992.

account typically has a higher minimum deposit requirement than the $1 to $100 required to open a passbook account. Most such savings accounts still pay 5¼%. However, banks can pay whatever they like. The total yields will be based on (1) the starting date set by the bank, sometimes the day of deposit but more often the first of the succeeding month, and (2) the method of compounding. Faster reinvestment makes a difference: At 12%, $1,000 savings earns $175 more in a year when compounded daily than when compounded annually.

Unless you have a very small amount to save or are opening an account for a child, avoid savings accounts; better interest rates and returns are available through the other accounts described below.

NOW ACCOUNTS

A NOW (negotiable order of withdrawal) account is an interest-bearing checking account in which the rate of return is the same as with passbook accounts. They may involve a monthly service charge and a computerized printout of transactions rather than a return of canceled checks.

By selecting the right NOW account, you can earn interest on idle money, but only if you select the right bank and understand the rules and the fee structure. To earn interest on your NOW account, you are required to maintain the minimum balance set by the bank. If you fall below this amount, you will lose interest and in some cases be subject to additional charges. Fees range from $5 per month and 15¢ per check to $12 to $20 and 25¢. Rates also vary, with the average 4.6% at banks and 5¼% at most savings and loans.

Geography may determine whether or not you should have a NOW account. In smaller cities and towns, required balances tend to be lower: $250 to $1,000. Major city banks often require $2,500. If you are a member of a credit union or can join one easily, open a sharedraft account: Over 85% of credit unions offering this type of account do not have service fees.

FINDING YOUR TRUE YIELD

To find out which NOW account offers the best deal, use this simple formula:

1 Take the minimum deposit and multiply it by the interest rate:

$$\$2,500 \times 6\% = \$150$$

2 Then multiply the monthly service fee by 12 and subtract the total from your annual interest income:

$$\$4 \times 12 = \$48$$

$$\$150 - \$48 = \$102$$

3 $102 ÷ $2,500 = 4.1%. This is your true yield.

Dividends (the credit union equivalent of interest) on sharedrafts vary, too, but in many cases are higher than interest on NOW accounts (see page 21).

$ HINT: "Daily" interest does not mean that the bank compounds interest daily. It means that the interest is compounded quarterly or semiannually based on the average of your daily balance. Select a bank that *compounds* interest daily.

$ HINT: Ask for overdraft checking privileges. This is a permanent line of credit that prevents you from bouncing a check. The bank will automatically cover your check even if you don't have money in the account—for up to a predetermined dollar amount. You will have to pay back the loan plus interest.

$ HINT: Once you have more than $2,500 in your NOW account, move the excess into a money market deposit account or a money market mutual fund where rates and terms are better.

☐ CAUTION: The Consumer Federation of America has discovered that a number of banks overstate the rates they are paying on interest-bearing checking accounts. They may advertise, for instance, that they are paying 5% on NOWs, yet not all your money is actually earning that amount—only the so-called investable balance is. The bank may pay no interest on, say, 12% of the money in your account, thus effectively reducing the rate from 5.0% to 4.4%.

The basis for the term "investable balance" is that government regulations require banks to keep 3% to 12% of their assets in reserve at all times. However, that does not mean they are prohibited from paying interest on all of your deposit. Read the fine print before opening any interest-bearing checking account.

Example: If you kept a $3,000 balance all year in a NOW account that paid 5% interest, you'd earn $150 before compounding. But if that bank deducted a 12% reserve, meaning that interest was calculated on a balance of $2,640, you'd earn only $132 in interest before compounding, for a 4.4% yield.

BANK MONEY MARKET DEPOSIT ACCOUNT

The counterpart of a money market mutual fund at a bank is a money market deposit account. Offered by most of the nation's banks, such accounts provide competitive interest rates as well as liquidity and, like all bank accounts, including the NOW and SuperNOW, are insured up to $100,000 by the FDIC or, at a savings and loan, by the FSLIC. They tend to pay slightly lower yields than money market mutual funds and Treasury bills (T-bills). The rates change daily or weekly along with changes in short-term interest rates. There's no guarantee that the rate quoted one day will be the same the next.

Yields and penalties for falling below the required minimum vary from bank to bank.

Find out if your bank avoids paying interest on a money market deposit account if the balance drops below a certain minimum, often $2,500 or $5,000.

$ HINT: Interest rates for money market deposit accounts vary as much as 3 percentage points between banks. Take time to call several to find the best deal.

As holder of a money market account, you are allowed to write only three checks per month to a third party and to make three preauthorized transactions (as might occur when you arrange in advance to pay a specific bill such as a mortgage payment). You may withdraw cash in person generally as often as you like. Some banks also allow use of ATMs for transfer of money, but money market deposit accounts are not intended to replace checking accounts. If you try to do that, you'll encounter extremely high fees.

CERTIFICATES OF DEPOSIT (CDs)

CDs, also officially known as time certificates of deposit, are safe, reliable saving instruments available at every local bank. The certificate indicates that you have deposited a sum of money for a specified period of time at a specified rate of interest. Their low risk level, the fact that they're insured up to $100,000, and their current high yields make them especially appealing.

Although CD rates, terms, and size vary from bank to bank, the following varieties are generally available:

- 7- to 31-day CD with the yield tied to that of a 13-week T-bill
- 91-day CD with interest rate tied to that of a 13-week T-bill

---

METHODS OF COMPUTING INTEREST

This affects earnings as much as the frequency of compounding. The methods are listed in order of preference.

- *Day of deposit to day of withdrawal.* Money earns interest as soon as it is deposited. It keeps earning interest until, but not including, the day it is withdrawn.
- *Daily collected balance or investable balance.* Cash and checks from your bank begin to earn interest as soon as deposited; checks from other banks do not earn interest until officially cleared, 1 to 3 business days later, generally.
- *Low balance.* Interest is paid only on the lowest balance during the time period covered.
- *Last in, first out.* Withdrawals are deducted from the last deposit. For example, you deposit $3,000 on the 10th and then withdraw $2,000 on the 30th. The $2,000 withdrawal is deducted from the $3,000. No interest is earned on the $2,000 that was in your account from the 10th to the 30th.
- *First in, first out.* Withdrawals are deducted first from your initial deposit and then from subsequent deposits. For example, you have a balance of $5,000. You then make a $3,000 deposit on the 10th and a $1,000 withdrawal on the 20th. You earn interest on $4,000 from the 1st to the 10th and on $7,000 the rest of the month.

BANK CDs VS. T-BILLS

If you can afford to invest $10,000, compare the 6-month money market certificates with Treasury bills. In most cases (especially in states where income is taxed), the T-bills will be a better deal. Here's the calculation:

1 Since T-bills are sold at a discount, use this formula:

$$D = \frac{L}{360} \times SY$$

D = discount per $100 face value
L = life span of security
360 = number of days in financial year
SY = stated yield

With a 180-day T-bill and a 9% yield:

$$D = \frac{180}{360} = .5 \qquad .5 \times 9 = 4.5$$

Subtract the 4.50 ($450) from $10,000 to get $9,550 cost.

2 The true yield of the T-bill is more, because T-bill trading uses a 360-day year, but your money works 365 days and the stated yield is based on the cost.

$$TY = \frac{D}{C} \times \frac{365}{L}$$

TY = true yield
D = discount
C = cost
L = life span of security

With that 180-day T-bill, a yield of 9%, and a cost of $9,550, the true yield is 9.56%.

$$TY = \frac{450}{9550} \times \frac{365}{180}$$

$$4.71 \times 2.03 = 9.56\%$$

3 Interest on T-bills is exempt from state and local income taxes. Interest on the certificate is fully taxable.

4 If the certificate is cashed in early, there's a penalty. With T-bills, there's an active aftermarket, so you will get more than you invested since the sales price includes accumulated interest—unless there's a sharp rise in interest rates.

- 6-month CD to yield about ¼% above the average T-bill rate for the most recent 4-week period
- 30-month CD with a fixed rate, typically 1% higher than that of shorter-maturity accounts

In most cases, the big type in the ads shows the compounded yield, which will, of course, be paid only when the CD is held to maturity. There are penalties for early withdrawal, but these are usually waived in three instances:

- If the owner dies or is found to be mentally incompetent
- If the time deposit is in a Keogh or IRA retirement plan and the depositor is over 59½ years old
- If the bank offers penalty-free early withdrawals

Many banks offer adjustable-rate CDs, in which case the interest rate fluctuates weekly along with the average T-bill rate. For CDs of 32 days or more, issued after October 1983, there is no federally imposed ceiling on either the interest rate or the minimum size of the deposit. Banks are free to set their own numbers. CD minimums range from $500 to $5,000 and more. Those that are $100,000 or over are called "jumbo CDs" and often pay a slightly higher yield. A number of banks will let you buy a "designer CD," one in which you set your own maturity date, so that you can time it to come due when your child goes off to college, when you retire, or when you will need a lump sum.

$ HINT: Before you buy a long-term CD, check out the Treasury note
        interest rate. T-note interest is exempt from state and local taxes, but
        you must pay taxes on CD interest.

When buying any CD, take the time to find out how frequently the bank compounds the interest and ask what the effective annual yield is. It can make an important difference.

To maximize your return, buy a CD in which interest is not actually paid out until maturity. This gives you the benefit of compounded interest. *Caution:* Interest is taxable in the year it is available for withdrawal without penalty.

UNDERSTANDING
CDs

To remain competitive with money market funds and each other, a handful of banks are marketing CDs that feature an added element of speculation. These CDs have yields tied to the S&P 500 index, to the price of gold, even to the cost of college tuition. But before rushing out to buy one of these CDs, find out precisely how the yield is calculated, whether it is tiered (the larger your deposit, the greater the interest rate), if it is automatically renewed upon maturity, and if so, whether at the same rate or a new one. You should also ask if your principal is in jeopardy, if

---

HOW COMPOUNDING AFFECTS RETURNS ON A $1,000 CD OVER A 1-YEAR PERIOD

RATE	DAILY	MONTHLY	QUARTERLY	ANNUALLY
5%	$1,051.27	$1,051.16	$1,050.95	$1,050.00
6	1,061.83	1,061.69	1,061.37	1,060.00
7	1,072.50	1,072.28	1,071.86	1,070.00
8	1,083.28	1,083.00	1,082.44	1,080.00

SOURCE: Carteret Savings Bank, Morristown, NJ.

CDs WITH A TWIST

BANK	SPECIAL FEATURE
American Charter, Omaha, NE (1-402-390-5000)	Rises with interest rates every 6 months
College Savings Bank, Princeton, NJ (1-800-888-2723)	Rises with college tuition
Northeast Savings Bank, Hartford, CT (1-203-280-1110)	One-year tax advantage
Wells Fargo Bank, San Francisco, CA (1-415-396-3188)	Continual deposits; expandable CDs

---

your interest rate could fall to zero, if there's a minimum interest rate floor, if there are up-front costs. If you cannot do the necessary calculations yourself (and they can be complex), ask your accountant to help out. You should be familiar with two terms:

➤ BUMP-UP Bump-up CDs give you one or two opportunities to get higher returns if the bank raises its CD rates after you purchase yours.

➤ STEP-UP The rates on step-up CDs, also called "rate builders," move up at a set pace at a predetermined time, say, every 3, 6, or 12 months. Check the initial rate. Many step-up CDs start off about 1% lower than the going rate.

$ HINT: If you have $50,000 to $100,000 or more to invest, negotiate your rate. Many banks will pay between ¼% and 1% more on large deposits.

ZERO CDs

Some brokerage firms offer zero coupon CDs in a variety of maturities. This type of CD does not pay interest on a regular basis. Instead it is sold at a discount from face value. The interest accrues annually until the CD matures. You must report the income for tax purposes each year as it accrues.

$ HINT: Zero CDs are more volatile in price than regular CDs, so plan to hold them until maturity.

OUT-OF-STATE CDs

If you're seduced by ads for the higher yields available at out-of-state banks, remember that the grass isn't always greener. Proceed with caution and steer clear of troubled savings and loans. Even though your money is insured up to $100,000, if the institution is closed, there may be delays in getting your money out, and there have been cases where high yields have been reduced.

$ HINT: Know the difference between interest rate and yield. Interest rate is the annual return without compounding. The effective yield reflects compounding—daily, monthly, quarterly, annually. Compare bank *yields* if you plan to leave your earned interest in the bank. Compare bank *rates* if you are taking out your earned interest.

$ HINT: Robert Heady, publisher of *100 Highest Yields,* suggests purchasing CDs only from institutions whose net worth exceeds 5% of assets and has recorded a profit for the previous two quarters. (*100 Highest Yields,* P.O. Box 088888, North Palm Beach, FL 33408; 1-800-327-7717; 8 issues, $34; 52 issues, $98).

The Friday issue of the *Wall Street Journal* lists the top-yielding CDs in the country for 1-, 2-, 3-, and 6-month and for 1-, 2-, and 5-year maturities.

JUNK CDs

During 1990, some banks started pushing a new type of investment popularly known as junk CDs.

☐ CAUTION: They're actually subordinated notes and are *not* insured by the FDIC or FSLIC. Although they have high yields, 3 percentage points above Treasuries, they are not high enough to compensate for the fact that they are uninsured and that there's almost no secondary market. In addition, banks can call many of these notes prior to maturity. Denominations are as little as $1,000.

WHAT IS THE TRUE RATE?

Bank CD ads are often very confusing, with two rates given: fixed rate and yield. The yield figure is always higher, but to earn it, you must have your CD at the bank for one full year at the same annual rate. For example, if your bank advertises a fixed rate of 6.5% and a yield of 6.75%, and you buy a 6-month CD and take it out at maturity, you will earn only the 6.5% fixed rate.

$ HINT: Roll over your 6-month CD so that it is on deposit the full year in order to earn the effective annual yield. In most institutions, the original yield is applicable even if the yield falls.

BROKERED CDs

Buying a CD through your stockbroker is often a better deal than buying it through a bank, because yields tend to be higher. That's because brokers have access to CDs from banks across the nation and are not limited to just one institution. Merrill Lynch, for example, can tap 160 banks, which gives investors more choices in terms of maturity, yield, and risk factor. And since brokered CDs are still bank CDs, they are insured up to $100,000.

Stockbrokers usually do not charge fees for CDs because they receive their commission from the issuing bank. Brokered CDs are also more liquid than their bank counterparts, because they can be sold by your broker in a "secondary market." And there's no penalty for selling prior to maturity as there is with a bank CD.

☐ CAUTION: The value of CDs, just like bonds, rises and falls in direct relationship to interest rates: if interest rates rise, the price of your CD will fall and you'll receive less than face value if you sell. If interest rates fall, you may be able to sell your CD at a premium because it's worth more, since its rate is higher than that being paid on newly issued certificates.

FOUR WAYS TO MAKE MORE MONEY AT YOUR BANK

- *Stagger your maturities.* Mix your CD maturity dates, say, for 6 months, 12 months, and 15 months. If interest rates rise, you can reinvest CDs that mature at the new rate. If rates fall, your longer-term CDs will be earning the old, higher rate.
- *Invest your CD interest.* Ask your bank to invest your CD interest automatically in a money market deposit account. You'll earn interest on your interest yet have access to the money without incurring a withdrawal penalty.
- *Snowball a CD.* If your bank offers higher rates on larger CDs, it may pay to roll over several small CDs into one big one. Select a target date, say 1 month after your longest-term CD matures. When you renew your smaller CDs, have them mature on that date. Then all your CDs will mature on the same day and you can reinvest in one large CD with a high rate.
- *Establish your own interest-bearing checking account.* Instead of depositing your paycheck into your checking account, put it in your money market deposit account. Several times during the month, transfer money to cover your checks. You will earn money market rates and be less tempted to spend without thinking about it first.

$ HINT: Some brokers sell CDs of troubled S&Ls in order to get higher yields. Make sure the CD you're buying is from a federally insured institution. The broker must tell you the name of the bank.

☐ CAUTION: Your interest may not compound with a brokered CD as it does with a bank CD. Check with your broker. Some brokered CDs pay out on maturity, especially if they come due in 1 year or less; others

BROKERED CDs

FIRM	MINIMUM	6-MONTH	1-YEAR	2-YEAR	5-YEAR
A. G. Edwards (1-800-999-4448)	$1,000	5.5%	5.75%	6.0%	6.5%
Fidelity (1-800-544-6666)	5,000	4.0	4.25	5.25	6.25
Edward D. Jones (1-314-851-2000)	5,000	4.25	4.60	5.25	6.75
Merrill Lynch* (any local office)	1,000	4.1	4.4	NA	6.6
Piper Jaffray & Hopwood (1-612-342-6000)	1,000	4.1	4.6	NA	NA
Prudential-Bache (local office)	1,000	4.3	4.4	4.85	NA
Charles Schwab (1-800-435-4000)	5,000	4.25	4.4	4.85	NA
Quick & Reilly (1-800-221-5220)	10,000	4.25	4.0	NA	6.6
Quick & Reilly (1-800-522-8712 in NY)					

* Merrill Lynch's CDs are rated by Standard & Poor's.
Data current May 1992.

TAKE ADVANTAGE OF INTEREST RATE CHANGES

1   When rates are low: buy short-term CDs.
2   When rates begin to rise: put more money into your money market account so you can ride up with the rates.
3   When rates are high: lock in yields with long-term CDs. Move money out of money market accounts into higher-yielding CDs.
4   When rates are falling: immediately lock in with a CD before they fall further.
5   When rates are low: invest over the short term and add to your money market account so that your cash will be available for reinvesting when rates begin to rise.

---

pay interest quarterly or annually. Many brokerage firms will automatically "sweep" these interest payments into a money market account if you so request.

$ HINT: The best indicator of trends in CDs and money accounts is the federal funds rate—the rate banks charge each other for overnight loans. If a bank has to pay more itself for money, it will try to raise money by offering higher yields to depositors. The federal fund rate is listed in the financial pages of major newspapers.

CREDIT SERVICES

Banks offer a number of credit-related services and loans. Loans are classified as either secured or unsecured.

➤ SECURED LOANS With a secured loan, you offer something of value as collateral. Should you not pay back the loan, the bank can take possession of the item or account. Secured loans are auto loans, residential mortgage loans, and home equity loans. Home equity lines of credit allow homeowners to write checks against the equity or value of their homes up to an amount determined by the bank. These loans can be repaid in monthly installments and may carry fixed or variable interest rates. Home equity borrowers pay interest only on the funds actually drawn against the equity line of credit that have not been repaid.

$ HINT: Although interest on these loans is generally fully tax deductible, use with great caution. Home equity loans can be seductive. Use only for big-ticket items such as college education.

➤ UNSECURED LOANS Unsecured loans are usually personal loans for which no collateral is put up. Interest rates on these loans are higher than on secured loans.

Guaranteed education loans, designed for students or parents who need money for education, are also unsecured. They are guaranteed by the federal government and administered by each state's higher education assistance agency. Interest rates and repayment terms may be more favorable than for other types of unsecured loans.

Overdraft checking, another form of unsecured loan, allows you to write a check for more money than is in your checking account. The bank will credit your account to cover the difference and charge a transaction fee (possibly) and interest on the overdraft. You can pay the loan back in one installment or over time. If you pay it back over time you pay interest on the outstanding balance.

➤ CREDIT CARDS Bank cards, such as VISA and MasterCard, are issued by individual banks. VISA and MasterCard provide the advertising, credit authorization, and record keeping for the banks. Most bank cards charge an annual fee and they can, within broad terms, charge whatever interest they like on unpaid balances. They are issued with a preset spending limit. This figure, determined by the bank that issues the card, is also referred to as a line of credit. It is based on your income and your credit history.

$ HINT: If you pay your bill in full within the stated time period, the interest rate a bank charges is not a crucial factor in selecting a card, but the annual fee is. Therefore, select a low- or no-fee card. If you pay your bill in installments over time, select a card with low rates. Bankcard Holders of America, a nonprofit consumer organization, continually surveys credit card issuers and makes the results available to the public through these pamphlets:

- For a list of credit cards with low interest and no annual fee, request "Low Rate/No Fee" List, $4.
- For a copy of "How To Choose a Credit Card," send $1.
  Bankcard Holders of America
  560 Herndon Parkway
  Suite 120
  Herndon, VA 22070
  1-800-553-8025

Credit unions also offer credit cards, usually with lower interest rates on unpaid balances. In 1992, their average rate was 15%, compared with more than 18% for banks. And two-thirds of credit unions do not charge an annual fee for their cards.

➤ GOLD CARDS Gold cards carry higher credit limits than standard cards and therefore require a higher level of creditworthiness, often including a $35,000 minimum annual income. Card issuers generally charge a lower interest rate on gold cards—about 1 percentage point lower. Annual fees

TOP CREDIT UNION CREDIT CARDS

Boeing Federal Employees Credit Union	Seattle, WA
San Antonio Federal Credit Union	San Antonio, TX
Alaska USA Federal Credit Union	Anchorage, AK
Security Service Credit Union	San Antonio, TX
Travis Federal Credit Union	Vacaville, CA

LOW-RATE CREDIT CARDS FOR BORROWERS

ISSUER/TELEPHONE	ANNUAL FEE	INTEREST RATE
Arkansas Federal Savings Little Rock, AR/1-800-477-3348	$35	8.5%
Simmons First National Pine Bluff, AR/1-501-541-1304	35	8.5
Wachovia Wilmington, DE/1-800-842-3262	39	9.4
People's Bank Bridgeport, CT/1-800-423-3273	25	11.9
Bank of Montana System Great Falls, MT/1-800-735-5536	19	12.25
Bank One, Cleveland Cleveland, OH/1-800-395-0010	20	13.2

NO-FEE CREDIT CARDS FOR OTHERS

ISSUER/TELEPHONE	INTEREST RATE
Bank of New York Newark, DE/1-800-942-1977	11.9%
USAA Federal Savings Bank Tulsa, OK/1-800-922-9092	12.5
Union Planters Bank Memphis, TN/1-800-628-8946	15.25
Abbott Bank Omaha, NE/1-800-999-6977	16.3

SOURCE: RAM Research & Publishing Co., 905 West 7th Street, Frederick, MD 21701; April 1992; $5 per copy for "Cardtrak," which covers 500 cards in four categories: low interest rate, no annual fee, gold cards and secured cards.

NO-FEE GOLD CARDS

INSURER	RATE	INCOME REQUIRED	TELEPHONE
Amalgamated of Chicago Chicago, IL/1-800-365-6464	11.00%	$40,000	1-800-365-6464
AFBA Industrial Park Alexandria, VA	12.50	35,000	1-800-776-2265
Oak Brook Bank Oak Brook, IL	12.90	35,000	1-800-666-1011
Union Planters National Memphis, TN	13.50	35,000	1-800-628-8946
Security Bank & Trust Southgate, MI	13.50	50,000	1-800-443-5465

SOURCE: RAM, see above.

range from zero (very rare) to $75. Many gold cards offer extras, such as purchase protection, extended warranty coverage, rental car insurance, legal referrals, medical assistance, and travel accident insurance.

➤ SECURED CARDS Secured means the card issuer requires you to make a deposit into a savings account to collateralize the credit line. The collateral is usually equal to the credit limit on the card. Secured cards are suitable for consumers establishing or rebuilding credit. If you are new to the world of credit, you may find it difficult to qualify for an unsecured credit card. Students, divorcees, widows, retirees, and immigrants are often turned down by credit card issuers for insufficient credit history. This is usually not an obstacle with secured card issuers. Or, if you have a poor credit history or have declared bankruptcy at some time in your life, you may be able to get a secured card. Most secured cards have higher interest rates (as much as 22%) and higher, nonwaivable annual fees than unsecured cards and, in addition, charge an application fee ranging from $30 to $75.

$ HINT: When shopping for a secured credit card, deal only with banks. Avoid unscrupulous marketers charging extremely high fees for a "guaranteed" bank credit card.

➤ AFFINITY CARDS An affinity card is one affiliated with an outside sponsoring organization. It can be a profit or nonprofit group. Often the annual fee or interest rate is lower as an incentive to use. There are over 2,000 affinity programs in the United States. Most are alumni, fraternal, and professional organizations. Check with any organization you belong to to determine if such an affinity program is available. For example, the National Football League and American Airlines have their affinity cards through Citibank, while US Sprint uses State Street Bank.

➤ ENHANCEMENTS To help win bank customers, issuers are offering a smorgasbord of features to entice customers:

- Citibank, the nation's largest issuer, rolled out its "price protection" service in the spring of 1990. It guarantees cardholders the lowest available price for the purchases. The difference between the price charged on a customer's card and a lower advertised price for the same product is credited.
- Sears' Discover Card offers yearly cash rebates of up to 1% on each year's purchases (check with the retailer).

TOP SECURED CREDIT CARDS

American National Bank (New York)	1-800-234-8472
Bank of Hoben (South Dakota)	1-818-880-2290
Central National Bank (Illinois)	1-217-234-6434
Dreyfus Thrift & Commerce (New York)	1-800-727-3348
Farrington Bank (New Jersey)	1-609-665-0400

SOURCE: RAM Research (see above).

■ The AT&T Universal Card combines a phone credit card with a VISA or MasterCard and gives members a discount on AT&T calls.

TAKING A LOOK AT YOUR CREDIT REPORT

How you handle your payments on credit cards, mortgages, and other loans is reported to one or more of the nation's credit bureaus. Take time to get a copy of your credit report once a year. You may never be affected by what's in your file, but if you plan to take out a mortgage or a loan, say to finance a new car or meet college bills, it could be important. Knowing what data credit agencies have collected on your financial habits can prevent headaches later on, especially if there are errors in your file or if it's out of date. Until these errors are corrected, you may have trouble borrowing money or getting a credit card with more favorable terms. Most people don't realize they have negative information in their files until they're denied credit.

A credit report can contain data on unemployment history, loans outstanding, types of credit cards held, payment patterns, and the dollar amount of credit available (i.e., credit lines). It can also include information about bankruptcies, foreclosures, tax liens, and judgments in court.

Contrary to popular opinion, there is no actual credit rating in an individual file. Decisions about creditworthiness are made by the lenders—bankers, retail merchants, and others—not by the credit agencies, which merely collect the data.

One late VISA card payment won't make the difference between getting a mortgage or not, but a pattern of late payments may, and personal bankruptcy almost certainly will. Although almost any payment that is 30 days late can be reported as a delinquency, most merchants wait at least an additional 30 days before reporting an account as overdue. Delinquencies remain on file for up to 7 years; bankruptcies for 10.

HOW TO FIND YOUR CREDIT FILE

Getting a copy of your file is not difficult. The three major credit agencies are:
- Equifax   1-800-685-1111
- TRW   1-714-991-6000
- Trans Union   1-312-645-6000

There are also regional and local firms. Each has different rules and procedures to obtain information. Call for instructions. Most agencies require that you send in a written request, including your name, address, date of birth, and Social Security number. If you cannot locate the correct credit agency, call the credit department of your bank or a major department store to get the names of the agencies serving your area. If you've been denied credit within the last 60 days, you can get a copy of your report for free. Otherwise, there's a fee, usually around $15.

When you get your report, look for inaccuracies such as bad debts of another person with a similar name, tax liens that have been satisfied, or disputes with merchants that have been resolved. If there's something in your file you believe is inaccurate, ask the credit bureau, in writing, to investigate. If you are not satisfied with the results, under federal guidelines you may write a statement of up to 100 words giving your side of the story, and ask that it be included in your file. If, on the other hand, an error is found, an updated and corrected report will be sent to any business that has requested your file within the past 6 months.

$ HINT: For further help, order a copy of "Understanding Credit Bureaus" for $1 from Bankcard Holders of America (see page 31).

TRUST SERVICES

Trust services involve the bank managing property for someone else. Property may be assets or funds, real estate, or investments, for example. A bank may manage a trust established to provide a college education or to support your favorite charity. A bank may also be named executor for probate of a will and administrator of the estate. In this role, the bank takes over settlement of a deceased person's estate, locates relatives and witnesses to the will, presents the will for probate, collects any debts due the estate, and pays debts.

Banks also help in setting up trusts. The two basic types are a testamentary trust and a living trust. A testamentary trust is established by your will and becomes effective upon your death. With a living trust, the bank manages some or all of your property while you are living. It is often used to pay bills should you become seriously ill or incapacitated. They also invest money or advise individuals about investing. Fees for these services are high.

➤ TRUST ACCOUNTS   Savings accounts can be opened by someone for someone else, which is called "in trust for." The typical example is an adult opening an account for a minor. The person for whom the account is opened is known as the beneficiary. The account owner, the one funding the account, is the only one who can make withdrawals. When that person dies the money passes on to the beneficiary. The account owner can change that beneficiary at any time by signing a change-of-beneficiary form at the bank. This type of account is sometimes called a "Totten trust."

➤ UNIFORM GIFTS TO MINORS ACCOUNTS   This account, often called a custodial account, also permits transfer of money to someone else. However, it is less flexible than the Totten trust, because once it is set up, the money in the account legally belongs to the person named, frequently a minor. In other words, the gift of money is irrevocable. The custodian or person who opens and funds the account can determine how the money is invested but cannot withdraw the funds except to use them to benefit the child.

$ HINT: When the child reaches legal age, full control of the money in the account must be turned over to the then-adult recipient by the custodian.

OTHER
SERVICES   Banks have a number of other services available. Not
▬▬▬▬▬▬▬▬▬   all are advertised, so be certain to ask about those that
interest you.

➤ AUTOMATED TELLER MACHINES (ATMs) The electronic age makes it possible
to move money instantly, 24 hours a day, through ATMs. To use an ATM
you need a plastic card and a personal identification number, issued by the
bank. Both are required to make deposits, transfer money, make cash
withdrawals, or check on your balance. Select an identification number you
can remember so you won't have to write it down. Do not carry the number
in your wallet. Check with your bank to see whether it charges for ATM
transactions. Many cards, issued by one bank, may be used in the ATMs of
another bank, but often for a fee. Ask if your bank is part of an ATM
network such as MAC, MOST, NICE, STAR, or CIRRUS. These machines
work for people out of state and sometimes overseas. VISA and MasterCard
can be used in many ATMs for cash advances. You pay interest on these
advances from the minute you receive the advance.

$ HINT: Each bank sets a limit on how much cash you can withdraw on
      any one day. If you're planning to get cash for a trip, check the daily
      limit first.

➤ TIMESAVERS To avoid a trip to the bank or a long wait in line when you
get there, use these timesavers.

- *Make deposits by mail.* Use the preprinted envelopes designed for this
  purpose. Use only for checks. Never send cash in the mail. The bank
  will mail you a record of the transaction.

- *Use deposit boxes.* These express payment boxes are as safe as a teller
  transaction. You put your money into a locked box and at the end of
  the day the envelopes are opened. Always use your preprinted deposit
  slips and the special envelopes designed for this purpose. In some
  banks you must keep one copy of the deposit slip; in others, the bank
  will mail back one copy.

- *Have checks deposited directly into your account.* You may arrange
  for direct deposit of Social Security, pension, government, and a great
  many payroll checks. It saves time and, if put into an interest-earning
  account, enables you to earn interest sooner than if the check is
  mailed to you and then you take it to the bank. Checks cannot be lost
  or stolen, and deposits are made on time, even if you are on vacation,
  traveling, or ill.

- *Have bills paid.* If you make regular payments, such as rent,
  mortgage, or utility bills, you can authorize your bank to pay these
  bills and deduct the amount from your checking or savings account.
  The bank makes the payment by either check or electronic funds
  transfer and records all payments on your monthly statement.

- *Use POS.* Point-of-sale (POS) terminals are electronic terminals placed
  by the bank in retail stores to allow you to pay for goods through a
  direct debit to your account at the bank. They also allow merchants to
  get authorizations or bank guarantees that your personal check is
  covered by funds in your account.

- *Use home banking.* Available at some of the nation's larger banks, this service, which operates through home computers and telephones, is still in the formative stages. Customers dial the bank's computer and then get a display on their home TV screen or computer monitor, showing their bank account balance and/or the amount of credit available. Some systems enable subscribers to pay bills.

    Prodigy, a videotex service launched by IBM and Sears, Roebuck & Co. in 1988, is a leader in the field. Using personal computers, Prodigy subscribers have access to hundreds of data bases and features, including home banking. Over 2 million people had subscribed by 1992. About 15 other financial institutions around the country, including Wells Fargo, First Interstate Bank of Denver, and Manufacturers Hanover, have bought the right to bank through the system.

➤ SENIOR CITIZENS' PROGRAMS Low-cost banking accounts are available to older Americans at an increasing number of institutions. Through these "lifeline" accounts, banks assure that all people can have access to the basic banking services. Their programs have such names as Years Ahead Club, 50 Plus, and Advance 50. Their biggest appeal is higher interest rates on CDs and money market accounts. Some offer free safe deposit boxes. Others waive credit card fees or provide free traveler's checks. A few organize packaged travel tours. To qualify, sizable deposits are usually required.

➤ PRIVATE BANKING Major banks and some smaller ones operate private banking divisions and trust departments for wealthy clients. Minimum requirements vary, but one must have at least $100,000 in annual income, often three to five times that much, plus substantial net worth. Private bankers attend to the needs of busy executives, professionals, and others on an individual basis. Among the specific services available are fast mortgages, quick loan approvals, immediate deposits and withdrawals, and house or office calls. Tickets to the theater, concerts, and games and other perks are often thrown in.

➤ OTHER PERKS Many banks offer attractive extras, so if you can use them, do so. For example, Citibank will credit $10 to your Citi-One checking account for every person you refer to the bank who opens a Citi-One account. If five or more referrals sign up, you'll get $100. Banks have recently been offering EE savings bonds, money off airfares, and other perks to customers.

MONEY MARKET MUTUAL FUNDS

Money market funds are pooled investments offered by mutual funds, insurance companies, and brokerage firms. Basically, they invest your money in high-yielding short-term financial instruments—Treasury bills, CDs, commercial paper, repurchase agreements, bankers' acceptances, etc.

Money market mutual funds have three objectives: (1) preservation of capital, (2) liquidity, and (3) highest possible yields.

Yields on money market funds fluctuate daily. Your interest is compounded by immediate reinvestment. Yields in July 1992 ranged from about 3% to 3¾%.

$HINT: Money market funds are best as parking places while deciding on more rewarding holdings. They are not a true investment except when rates are high.

There are three types of money market funds: general, government-only, and tax-free. They are listed in the financial pages of most newspapers (see example, page 43).

THE PLUSES OF MONEY MARKET FUNDS

- *Daily income.* Dividends are credited to your account each day, which means that your money is always working for you.
- *Liquidity.* There is no minimum investment period, and there are no early withdrawal penalties. Money can be withdrawn quickly by telephone, mail, wire, or check.
- *Stability of principal.* Most money market funds have a constant share price of $1. This makes it easy to determine the value of your investment at any time. Earnings are also paid in shares, so the value of a share never increases above $1. For example, if your interest in a money market mutual fund averaged 8% and you invested $1,000, at the end of 1 year you would have 1,080 shares worth $1,080.
- *No fees or commissions.* When you open your account, all your money goes to work immediately.
- *Small minimum investment.* Some funds require as little as $500 to open; most minimums are between $1,000 and $2,000. In general, funds do not require shareholders to maintain the minimum investment as an average balance.
- *Safety.* Your money is used to buy prime debt of well-rated corporations or the U.S. government and its agencies. If you choose a fund that invests only in U.S. government securities, your yield will be ½% or so lower, but you can count on Uncle Sam's guarantee. Money market funds bought through your stockbroker are protected by the SIPC. This is because shares of money market funds are in fact securities (not cash). When held by a SIPC member in a customer's securities account, they are protected by the SIPC against the brokerage firm's failure but *not* against declines in the value of the securities (or shares) themselves. (See page 52 for details on SIPC.)
- *Checkwriting.* Most funds offer this service free, although some require that checks written be for at least $250 or $500.
- *Continual high yields.* If rates drop, you will receive the higher interest rate for about a month afterward until the high-yielding securities are redeemed. With a bank, the yield changes more frequently, usually on a weekly basis.

THE TRUTH ABOUT YIELDS

The yield of a money market fund changes on a daily basis and is never fixed or guaranteed, because it reflects the current money market rates earned by the underlying securities that make up the fund's portfolio. The yield that you receive as an investor in the fund is net of the expenses of the fund; in other words, the costs of running the fund (management fees and administrative expenses) are subtracted from the daily gross.

Money market funds price their shares at $1 each. The stated yield, as reported regularly in the financial press, reflects the interest earned on investments. The base is the net asset value (NAV) per share. The NAV is determined by subtracting all liabilities from the market value of the fund's shares and dividing the result by the number of shares outstanding.

Money market mutual funds lend your money for short periods of time, and the fund collects interest on these loans, paying it out to you, the shareholder. The money you deposit in a bank money market account, by contrast, is not invested in any one area; it becomes part of the bank's general assets. Money market mutual funds are required to pay out all their earnings after expenses to shareholders and tend to pay higher rates than banks. Banks are required to pay only the rate that they decide on and advertise. The more competitive the banking atmosphere, of course, the higher the interest rate will be.

THE MONEY MARKET: WHAT IT IS

Contrary to popular belief, the money market does not exist in the heart of Wall Street, or in London, Brussels, or even Washington, DC. Nor is it housed in an impressive Greek revival building. The money market runs throughout the country and is made up of large corporations, banks, the federal government, and even local governments.

When any of these institutions need cash for a short period of time, they borrow it from this seemingly elusive money market by issuing money market instruments. For example, the U.S. government borrows through Treasury bills, large corporations through commercial paper, and banks via jumbo CDs.

MAJOR USES OF MONEY MARKET FUNDS

- As a place to accumulate cash for a large expenditure, such as a house, a car, taxes, or a vacation
- As a temporary place to deposit large amounts of cash received from the sale of a stock or a property, an inheritance, an IRA rollover, etc.
- As a parking place until you find a desirable stock, bond, or other investment
- As a resting place for funds when switching from one mutual fund to another within a family of funds

---

WHAT THE MONEY MARKET MUTUAL FUNDS BUY

- *Bankers acceptances:* drafts issued and sold by banks with a promise to pay upon maturity, generally within no more than 180 days
- *Certificates of deposit:* large-denomination CDs sold by banks for money deposited for a minimum time period (14 days, 91 days, etc.)
- *Commercial paper:* unsecured IOUs issued by large institutions and corporations to the public to finance day-to-day operations, usually in amounts of $100,000 for up to 91 days
- *Eurodollar CDs:* dollar-denominated certificates of deposit sold by foreign branches of U.S. banks or by foreign banks; payable outside the United States, the minimum is generally $1 million, with maturities of 14 days or more
- *Government-agency obligations:* short-term securities issued by U.S. government agencies
- *Repurchase agreements ("repos"):* short-term buy/sell deals involving any money market instrument (but usually Treasury bills, notes, and bonds) in which there is an agreement that the security will be resold to the seller on an agreed-on date, often the next day. The money market fund holds the security as collateral and charges interest for the loan. Repos are usually issued as a means for commercial banks and U.S. government securities dealers to raise temporary funds.

These instruments are purchased by other large corporations, banks, and extremely wealthy investors. The instruments pay high interest rates because the dollar amounts involved are so large, the maturity lengths are so short (1 year or less), and the borrowers are well known and considered excellent risks. These money market instruments, not stocks and bonds, constitute a money market mutual fund's portfolio.

THE ISSUE OF SAFETY

All investors want to know how safe their money market fund or account is. It's very safe. But every investment has some degree of risk. Money market funds have an excellent safety record, primarily because they invest in short-term securities of the government, large institutions, and corporations. However, on April 12, 1990, Mortgage and Realty Trust declared bankruptcy, affecting $150 million in outstanding commercial paper. About half that paper was owned by a number of money market funds, including T. Rowe Price and Alliance. In each case, the parent companies of the affected funds bought back the defaulted paper, thus preventing any losses to investors. That event underscored a fact that had largely been ignored—that money market funds, while very safe, are not totally risk free.

The basic principle to keep in mind is: The shorter the maturity of an investment, the lower the risk.

Short portfolio maturities keep a fund's risk level to a minimum, because a bank or corporation whose securities are sold in the money markets is not very likely to default in such a short time. In addition, securities that mature so quickly seldom fluctuate in value. A money market mutual fund's securities must mature in 1 year or less, and no one individual security may make up more than 5% of a fund's assets.

$ HINT: The average maturity is about 40 days. You can check maturities in the financial section of your newspaper.

For the ultimate in safety, select a fund that invests only in Treasury issues (see list on page 43). These are backed by the full faith and credit of the U.S. government. They are called "government" or "Treasury-only" funds. The yields are about 1% lower than nongovernment money market funds.

Several other factors contribute to the superior safety of money funds: (1) Money fund managers continually analyze and compile ratings of the strength of the issuers of money market instruments. Whenever an issuer's credit rating declines, the name is deleted from the acceptable list. (2) The SEC regulates the funds, requiring annual independent audits, detailed data in the fund's prospectus, and making other disclosure requirements. Money market funds must have:

- Ninety-five percent of their assets in the highest-grade commercial paper. The other 5% can be held in second-tier paper, such as A-2 or P-2, but no more than 1% of this can come from the same issuer.

- No more than 5% of a fund's total assets can be invested in the securities of a single issuer, except for those of the U.S. government.

- The average maturity of a fund's portfolio can be no more than 90 days, down from the previous requirement of 120 days.

☐ CAUTION: If your account is with a bank that has FDIC or a savings and loan that has FSLIC, it is insured up to $100,000 per account name. Money market mutual funds with your stockbroker are protected by SIPC. Money market mutual funds purchased directly from the fund are not insured unless the fund itself indicates that they are. Be sure to ask.

SELECTING THE RIGHT MONEY MARKET FUND

Although there are several hundred money market mutual funds, they fall into four basic categories. Knowing which one is best for meeting your investment goals will help narrow the search.

- *General funds.* Available from your stockbroker or directly from the fund itself, general funds invest in nongovernment money market securities.

- *Government-only funds.* Also available directly or from a broker, government-only funds limit their investments to U.S. government or federal agency securities. Because their portfolios are backed by the "full faith and credit" of the U.S. government, they are regarded as less risky; consequently, they have lower yields than general funds.

- *Tax-free funds.* Available directly or from a broker, tax-free funds restrict their portfolios to short-term tax-exempt municipal bonds. Their income is free from federal tax but not necessarily from state and local taxes. These are generally advisable only for investors in the 28% tax bracket. Their yields are, of course, much lower, sometimes about half those of a regular money market fund.

Even though their yields are lower, tax-free money market funds are more appealing now that other ways of sheltering income are limited by the 1986 Tax Reform Act.

■ *Triple tax-exempt money funds.* Designed for residents of high-income-tax states, such as New York, California, Massachusetts, and Connecticut, these invest in short-term tax-exempt municipals and are free from federal, state, and local taxes for residents of the states and localities that issue them.

By shopping around you will find that some funds have higher yields than others (see the table on page 43). At various times the yield discrepancy has been as much as 3% to 3½% on taxable funds. But the current yield is not the only factor to consider; look also at the 12-month yield and the character of the fund's holdings.

➤ MATURITY The risk factor—even though it's quite minimal with money market funds—rises with the portfolio's maturity. By law, any money market fund that says it keeps its net asset value at $1 per share is required to limit its average portfolio maturity to 90 days. If you're a conservative investor, select a fund with maturities of 90 days or less. If you're willing to assume more risk, you may get a slightly higher yield.

➤ QUALITY Lower-quality portfolios lead to higher yields but also higher risk.

➤ EXPENSES Money market funds take an annual management charge, called the *expense ratio,* from the investor's assets. These fees range from about 0.48% to 0.80%.

Funds that have the highest yields are often those with fewest expenses deducted from the portfolio's earnings. According to *Donoghue's Money Fund Report,* expense charges generate nearly two-thirds of the discrepancy in yields. You can actually boost your returns by switching to a fund with lower expenses. Among the funds whose expenses have been low for a number of years are Vanguard and Kemper. Some funds actually waive fees. According to Sheldon Jacobs, editor of *No-Load Fund Investor* newsletter, Dreyfus Worldwide Dollar, the Flex-Fund, and Fidelity Spartan have guaranteed fee waivers seemingly for an indefinite time.

$ HINT: The average money fund's expense ratio as a percentage of assets is about 0.75%. Therefore, a fund earning 10% gives a yield to investors of 9.25%.

SYSTEMATIC WITHDRAWAL PLANS (SWPs)

SWPs, long a favorite with retired people, are also ideal for making mortgage payments, paying insurance premiums, or other regular commitments. SWPs are an alternative to traditional written or telephone requests for withdrawal of your money from a mutual fund. Under an SWP, the fund periodically redeems the dollar value or percentage you request. Payment is made by check to you, to a third party, or to your bank account.

MONEY MARKET FUNDS WITH CONTINUALLY HIGH YIELDS

Alger Fund	1-800-992-3863
Dreyfus Liquid Assets	1-800-645-6561
Dreyfus Worldwide Dollar Fund	1-800-645-6561
Evergreen Fund	1-800-235-0064
Fidelity Spartan	1-800-544-8888
Flex-Fund	1-800-325-FLEX
Vanguard Prime Portfolio	1-800-662-7447

☐ CAUTION: Fidelity Spartan charges $2 per check.

The amount required to maintain an SWP varies with each fund, but typical SWPs require a $5,000 or $10,000 minimum opening balance and a minimum $50 per month withdrawal. You can withdraw money monthly, bimonthly, or quarterly. Some funds permit you to withdraw only on the same day each month; others permit withdrawals on any day.

ULTRASAFE MONEY MARKET FUNDS

	YIELD (MAY 1992)
Mutual Funds Specializing in U.S. Treasury Securities	
Capital Preservation Fund (1-800-321-8321)	3.56%
Fidelity Government Reserves (1-800-544-8888)	3.91
Fidelity U.S. Treasury Money Market (1-800-544-8888)	4.08
Vanguard U.S. Treasury Money Market Portfolio (1-800-662-7447)	3.80
Tax-free Money Market Funds	
Calvert Tax-free Reserves (1-800-368-2748)	3.57
Dreyfus Tax-exempt Money Market (1-800-645-6561)	2.80
Franklin Tax-exempt Money Fund (1-800-342-5236)	2.62
Lexington Tax-free Money Market (1-800-526-0056)	2.94
USAA Tax-exempt Money Market (1-800-531-8000)	3.49
High-Income States: Triple Tax-exempt	
Fidelity Massachusetts Tax-free MM Portfolio* (1-800-544-8888)	3.10
Prudential-Bache New York Money Market Fund (call local office)	2.67
Seligman California Money Market Fund (1-800-221-2783)	5.97

* Double-exempt.

SWPs offer several advantages:

- Steady stream of controlled income prevents overspending.
- Paperwork is reduced.
- Plan eliminates telephoned withdrawal requests.

And some disadvantages:

- You may draw out more money than you need or than you earn on the principal.
- May lead to apathetic attitude about saving.

Funds offer one or more of four types of withdrawals: (1) straight dollar amounts, (2) a fixed number of shares, (3) a fixed percentage, and (4) a declining balance based on your life expectancy.

$ HINT: If you don't wish to tap your principal, remove your money at a lower rate than the fund's increase in net asset value.

Keep in mind that withdrawing a regular dollar amount is in effect reverse dollar cost averaging. In dollar cost averaging (see page 261), you invest an equal dollar amount every month and in this way buy more fund shares for the same amount when the market is down and fewer shares when it's up. In a fixed-amount withdrawal plan, you are forced to redeem more shares when the market is down to meet the set dollar amount and to sell fewer shares when the market is up.

If you use a percentage plan, the number of shares you need to sell in a down market will tend to be less.

$ HINT: Another way to withdraw money regularly is to keep your dividends and capital gains distributions from stock and bond funds instead of reinvesting them. This way, you won't need to sell shares. If your dividends and capital gains distributions add up to more money than you need, reinvest the excess in a money market fund.

Remember, too, that the day you pick to redeem your shares is not the day you'll receive your check. Ask the fund how soon checks are mailed out, and ask your bank how long it will take for checks to clear.

□ CAUTION: Each withdrawal of funds is a taxable event, usually because of capital gains. Keep records of your withdrawals to simplify year-end tax calculations.

USES FOR SWPs

- To pay your mortgage
- As a monthly living allowance for college students
- As income while on maternity leave
- For retirement
- To provide care for someone in a nursing home
- To meet insurance premiums
- As income while on sabbatical
- For alimony or child support payments

BANK DEPOSIT ACCOUNTS
VS. MONEY MARKET FUNDS

Competition between money market funds and bank deposit accounts is reflected in the extra services they advertise, such as free checking, discounts on brokerage services, no-fee credit cards and debit cards, extended lines of credit, and direct deposit of pension and dividend checks. Both institutions are vying for your dollars.

The key benefits of a bank account are these:

- Easy access at a number of local offices.
- Instant interest, as new deposits are credited immediately. With money market mutual funds, it takes a couple of days for the mail to get through and up to 5 days or more for the check to clear.
- Instant credit, as local merchants will accept checks drawn against your bank account but may balk at cashing one from a mutual fund's bank, especially if it is an out-of-state bank.

CREDIT UNIONS

A credit union is a cooperative, not-for-profit financial institution organized to promote savings among its members. Membership is limited to those having a common bond—occupation, association, etc.—and to groups within a community or neighborhood. Many credit unions allow members to remain members even if they move away or change jobs.

Credit unions are member owned and controlled, with each member having an equal vote and the opportunity to serve on the board of directors. The board, elected by the membership, sets dividend and interest rates. Board members are volunteers, except for the treasurer, and they may not receive payment for their services.

Credit unions are either state or federally chartered. State-chartered unions are supervised by a state regulatory agency. Federally chartered ones are supervised by the National Credit Union Administration, an independent agency in the executive branch of the federal government. Member share accounts are insured up to $100,000 per account by the National Credit Union Share Insurance Fund.

There are approximately 13,890 credit unions representing more than $241.9 billion in assets and over 62.6 million individual member-owners.

Credit union CDs, sharedraft accounts (interest-bearing checking accounts), and money market deposit accounts pay extremely competitive rates, often ½% higher than banks. Loans may be ½% lower. Credit unions can afford to undercut their competitors because they are nonprofit corporations, don't pay taxes, and are essentially volunteer directed.

Credit unions are also available for students. The Credit Union National Association Foundation, Inc., offers a training manual for student credit unions entitled *Handbook for College Student Credit Unions.*

$ HINT: To find a credit union near you, check the yellow pages under "Credit Unions" or write: Credit Union National Association (CUNA),

CREDIT UNION AND BANK CHECKING SERVICES

	CREDIT UNION	BANK
% charging per check fee	20%	45%
Average monthly service charge	$4.32	$7.29
% of accounts earning interest	83%	48%

SOURCE: Credit Union National Association, April 1992.

P.O. Box 431, Madison, WI 53701. Many credit unions have modified their membership requirements and now allow members with different common bonds, such as employees of several different companies, to join.

4

PROTECTING ALL YOUR INVESTMENTS

The ongoing wave of complex failures of financial institutions has caused even the most trusting investors and savers to question how safe their securities and cash are in the nation's banks, savings and loans, mutual funds, and brokerage firms—and rightly so.

AT YOUR BANK

Over the past several years, more banks and savings and loan associations have been liquidated or merged than at any time since the Great Depression. The number of commercial and savings banks on the FDIC's trouble list now numbers some 975. The troubled banks hold $400 billion—more than 10% of the banking industry's total assets.

THE FACTS

Most of the country's commercial banks are insured by the Federal Deposit Insurance Corporation (FDIC), an independent government agency. To be eligible for membership in the FDIC, a bank must meet certain standards and be regularly examined by both federal and state agencies. Member banks pay insurance fees, which are in turn invested in federal government securities. This constitutes the FDIC's insurance fund. In addition, the FDIC may borrow several billion dollars from the U.S. Treasury, even though it has never had to do so in the more than 50 years since it was established.

Most savings and loan associations (also known as thrifts), which prior to August 9, 1989, were insured by the Federal Savings & Loan Insurance Corporation (FSLIC), are now insured by a new government entity, the Savings Association Insurance Fund (SAIF), which is administered by the FDIC. Some S&Ls are insured by state insurance, and a very few are privately insured. A handful of savings and loan associations have absolutely no insurance at all.

Most credit unions (95%) are insured by the National Credit Union Administration (NCUA); others, by state agencies.

The FDIC and NCUA are backed by the federal government, and money insured by them is considered safe since the government would presumably come to their rescue. Banks that are insured by a state or privately, however, do *not* have the backing of the federal government. The FDIC reserves were down to $11 billion as of September 1990, which provides about $60 of coverage for every $100 of insured deposits. The FSLIC was in such sorry shape that it was declared insolvent by the General Accounting Office. The parent of FSLIC, the Federal Home Loan Bank Board, was abolished in the summer of 1989 under the Financial Institutions Reform

---

GOVERNMENT PROTECTION

FEDERAL DEPOSIT INSURANCE CORPORATION
- Guarantees depositors for up to $100,000
- Consumer hotline: 1-800-424-5488
- Address for more information on evaluating your bank: 550 17th Street NW, Washington, DC 20429

SAVINGS ASSOCIATION INSURANCE FUND
- Guarantees depositors for up to $100,000
- Consumer affairs: 1-800-424-5488
- Address for more information on evaluating your S&L: 550 17th Street NW, Washington, DC 20429

NATIONAL CREDIT UNION SHARE INSURANCE FUND
- Guarantees depositors for up to $100,000
- Telephone: 1-202-682-9640
- Address for more information on your credit union: 1776 G Street NW, Washington, DC 20456

Recovery & Enforcement Act. This act created the Office of Thrift Supervision as a bureau of the Treasury Department and the Resolution Trust Corporation (RTC) to deal with the crisis of failing S&Ls.

The solution is not to tuck your money under the mattress but to get information about your bank.

- Bank only at federally insured institutions.
- Keep in mind that individual depositors, not accounts, are insured up to $100,000, including interest and principal. That means that if you have four accounts in the same name in one institution, you are insured only for a total of $100,000, not $400,000.
- Cut back each account to under $100,000 to leave room for earned interest.
- If you are married, you and your spouse can insure up to $500,000 at one bank by establishing several types of accounts: two individual accounts, one for each of you; a joint account; and two testamentary revocable trusts, to be set up for each of you (this type of account pays the balance to the beneficiary upon the death of the trustee).

$ HINT: Five types of accounts are insured separately from other accounts that you may have in one institution. Each is insured individually for $100,000: money market accounts, IRAs, Keoghs, testamentary accounts, and irrevocable trusts.

If a federally insured institution fails, regulators will liquidate the assets, and insured depositors will be paid usually in 5 business days. If you have money in excess of the $100,000 insured limit, however, you will have a pro rata stake for that portion in excess of $100,000, along with other creditors, and you may or may not get that portion of your money back.

BANK
CHECKUP

You can protect your money by taking these steps:

1   Get a copy of your bank's annual report and financial statements.

2   Request and read the "Report of Condition" on your bank (not available for branches, only main banks). It will tell how much the bank is making, what its loan portfolio is made up of, and what percentage of loans is nonperforming. The FDIC will bill you $6. Do not send cash. Order from:

FDIC
M.I.S.B. Disclosure Group
Room F-518
550 17th Street NW
Washington, DC 20429
1-202-898-7112; 1-800-843-1669

3   Request and read "Uniform Bank Performance Reports," which compare banks within a certain state or county. They cost $40 each. Order from:

Federal Financial Institutions Examination Council
U.B.P.R.
Dept. 4320
Chicago, IL 60673
1-800-843-1669

4   Evaluate the safety of your bank. David C. Cates, president of Cates (Bank) Consulting Analysts, Inc., in New York, gives these guidelines for determining a bank's safety:
    - Excessively rapid growth of commercial loans indicates a bank that hasn't enough expert people to check credit ratings and make loan assessments.
    - Unusually high loan portfolio yields indicate that the bank may be making risky loans.
    - Increased reliance on funds outside the bank's natural market suggests lack of client support and a pulling out of outsiders at the first sign of trouble.
    - How solid is the bank's loan portfolio? Determine by comparing nonperforming assets (loans that are 90+ days overdue or are no longer accruing interest) to total loans, the FDIC bank standard being 1%.
    - Could the bank handle a run? Look for a loan-deposit ratio of no more than 70% and a minimum of 5% in cash or short-term investments.

5   Keep all your bank records; many failed institutions have been guilty of sloppy record keeping.

6   Give your bank this three-step test.
    - *Step one.* Does the bank have enough equity? This determines whether it has a cash cushion to cover big losses. The bank's total

---

HELP FROM REGULATORS

If you're having a problem with your bank, call one of the regulatory authorities listed below. They are surprisingly accessible, often more so than your local bank official. If you need to file a written complaint, include a brief statement describing the problem and a list of the steps you've taken to try to resolve it. Include your bank account number and copies of all documents.

Ask the customer service department which regulator oversees your bank—they are legally obligated to tell you.

FDIC
Office of Consumer Affairs
550 17th Street NW
Washington, DC 20429
1-800-424-5488

Federal Reserve Board
Consumer & Community Affairs
Mail Stop 198
20th and C Streets NW
Washington, DC 20551
1-202-452-3946

Office of Thrift Supervision
Consumer Affairs Division
1700 G Street NW
Washington, DC 20552
1-202-906-6237 or
1-800-842-6929

U.S. Comptroller of the Currency
Compliance Management
Mail Stop 642-C
490 L'Enfant Plaza SW
Washington, DC 20219
1-202-622-2000

---

assets and its total equity, also known as shareholder's equity, are on the statement of condition in the annual report. Divide assets into equity and express the result as a percentage. Beware if equity is below 5% of assets.

- *Step two.* Does the bank have too many "problem" loans? Problem loans or notes are those that are 3 months or longer past due or that are unlikely to ever be paid—these are noted in the section called "past due and nonaccrual loans." Look at the bank's loan-loss reserve balance; this is money on hand to cover problem loans. If problem loans are greater than loan-loss reserves, the bank could be headed toward insolvency.
- *Step three.* Check the bank's profitability. If its net income—listed in the call report—is positive, it's okay. If it's negative, then the bank is losing money, and you should divide the latest year's loss by the months of red ink. The result is the average monthly loss rate. Then divide the bank's equity by the average monthly loss rate to find out how long the bank can keep losing money at the current rate before it runs out of equity.

IF YOUR BANK OR S&L FAILS

Should the unthinkable happen and a federally insured bank or S&L fail, the Savings Association Insurance Fund (SAIF) will either liquidate the institution's assets to pay off depositors or transfer assets to a healthy institution. You may have to wait, but you will receive your principal and interest, up to $100,000.

In most cases, in fact, a solvent institution takes over the failed institution's assets and liabilities. For example, the April 1990 collapse of Seamen's Bank for Savings in New York, the largest bank failure of the year, was estimated to cost the FDIC $2.8 billion. Seamen's 13 branches, valued at $2.1 billion, were sold to Chase Manhattan Bank for $5 million.

☐CAUTION: When accounts of a failed institution are transferred, the new management can lower the interest rate being paid on CDs or increase the rate you pay on a home-equity loan or other credit line. However, you must be given prior notice and time to make penalty-free switches to another institution that has more favorable rates. If bank officials won't let you know whether they are honoring your existing terms, take it as a warning and begin looking for a new bank or S&L.

If you have a loan, the loan cannot be called in by the new bank under any conditions not spelled out by the original loan agreement. Check your agreement for loopholes.

If regulators are not able to arrange a transfer of accounts to a solid bank, they will liquidate and pay off depositors from the insurance fund. You will get back your principal and interest earned up until the takeover date. It is possible you could lose access to your money for several days.

IN A MUTUAL FUND

Since the 1987 stock market crash, questions that were once unthinkable— Could a mutual fund close down? Could it cancel the investor's right to redeem shares? Could it run out of cash to meet shareholders' demand?— are unthinkable no longer.

The mutual fund industry is governed by the Investment Company Act of 1940—but that doesn't guarantee total protection. Here are the facts:

➤ BANKRUPTCY The assets of a mutual fund belong to the shareholders, and all securities are held in trust by a third party. A fund's directors can theoretically ask shareholders to allow the fund to close down if assets have dwindled away and it is no longer profitable to operate, for example, but to date this has not happened.

It's far more likely that a troubled fund will merge into a larger, healthier one; this often happens when a bank, S&L, or brokerage firm goes bankrupt. However, a very small fund that is poorly managed might be unable to attract a merger candidate.

If a fund were to liquidate, the shareholders' fortunes would depend on market conditions and the quality of the fund's holdings. The SEC would oversee the sale and subsequent distribution of assets. A small fund with large holdings of thinly traded securities or little cash on hand could be in for losses if the market were down.

➤ SUSPENSION OF TRADING Trading can be suspended only in national emergencies—closing of the New York Stock Exchange, presidential assassination, war, etc. However, even under these circumstances, you still have the right to place a redemption order—and such an order would lock in the price at the end of the day.

➤ CASH RESERVES The fund managers hold cash and Treasury securities in their reserves, plus proceeds from security sales. Funds also have bank credit available to them: they can borrow $1 for every $3 of assets. Yet a heavily invested fund, when faced with a barrage of redemption requests, might have to sell stocks even when it would prefer not to.

$ HINT: Invest only in a fund that has at least 10% or more in cash reserves.

➤ PROTECTING YOURSELF IN THE FUTURE (1) Find out if your fund has an office locally; if so, keep some of your money there, so you can have access to it in person. (2) Prepare the fund's official redemption form or letter, and be prepared to send it by Express Mail if the telephone systems are overloaded.

$ HINT: It doesn't matter what time of day you put in your mutual fund buy or sell order; as long as it's in before 4 P.M., you're guaranteed the closing share price that day. Phones are busiest in the morning.

AT A BROKERAGE FIRM

The Securities Investor Protection Corporation is a $691 million fund supported by nearly 8,100 member brokerage firms. It also has a $1 billion credit line with the government that can be activated only by the SEC. The SIPC is not a government agency, nor is it a regulatory agency. Rather, it is funded through assessment of dealer members. All brokers and dealers registered with the SEC and national stock exchanges must contribute. The rate as of spring 1992 was .065% of annual revenues. If a member brokerage firm fails, the SIPC appoints a trustee to liquidate the firm and perhaps transfer customer accounts to another broker. (If the firm is small, the SIPC may decide to cover losses from its funds immediately.)

If it has the securities on hand, the liquidating firm will send the securities registered in customers' names directly to them. If it does not have enough securities to meet all customer claims, the customers will receive them on a pro rata basis, and any remaining claims will be settled in cash. However, this ties up your money for several months.

If the brokerage house in liquidation does not have enough securities or funds to settle all claims, the rest will be met by the SIPC—up to $500,000 per customer, including $100,000 for any cash held in the brokerage account.

The SIPC covers only cash and securities, that is, stocks, bonds, CDs, notes, and warrants on securities. Commodities and commodity options are *not* covered. Shares in money market mutual funds *are* covered by the SIPC.

$ HINT: Extend your coverage by opening a second account as a joint account with your spouse, as a trustee for a child, or as a business account. Each account receives full protection—$500,000.

Keep in mind that the SIPC covers losses due to the failure of the firm, not losses because investments turned out to be of poor quality or because securities fell in price. And many brokerage firms carry additional insurance, about which you can ask your broker. In the past 21 years, SIPC has liquidated about 228 firms, more than half in their first 4 years.

Burned by the poor performance of the stock market in 1987 and the American investors' subsequent flight to safety, brokerage firms and sponsors of various investment products have added a new enticing feature to their advertisements, touting them as "guaranteed" or "insured." The idea, of course, is to make high-risk investments appear safe. Many of these guarantees have questionable value and are being investigated by the SEC. Ask your broker or financial planner these questions when you're faced with what appears to be a come-on:

- How much of my money is being invested in the primary product? Where will the rest be invested?
- How long is the guarantee or insurance good for?
- Am I protected against market loss?
- If the project or investment fails, who is responsible for covering the losses?
- Who backs the insurance or guarantee?

IN A PENSION PLAN

Think of pension plans like any other investment—one that requires safeguarding.

- Defined benefit plans promise a set amount upon retirement, usually a percentage of earnings multiplied by the number of years you worked at the company. Most are insured by the Pension Benefit Guaranty Corporation, "an FDIC-like agency that will pay each employee up to about $28,000 a year if the company fails.

□CAUTION: A company can terminate a fully funded pension plan at any time and pay benefits in a lump sum or buy annuities from insurance companies to take over monthly benefit payments. When that happens you have lost your protection.

- Defined contribution plans, which include 401(k)s, profit sharing plans, and employee stock option plans, include more than 80% of all private pensions. The amount contributed to the plan by you and by your employer is typically a percentage of your pay or the company's profits.

□CAUTION: You are not guaranteed a specific amount upon retirement. You get the contributions plus any earnings. And, this type of plan is not insured by the PBGC.

About one-third of the money in defined contribution plans is invested in GIC contracts, which, like bank CDs, pay a guaranteed interest rate for a set time. GICs are sold by insurance companies; if you do not live in one of the states that insures these plans, your money is backed by the insurer only. If the insurance company is in bad shape, then so is the GIC it sells.

$HINT: Ask your company's plan administrator for a copy of Form 5500, the financial report the plan is required to file with the Labor Department. For help in understanding the form and your retirement plan in general, send $6 to Pension Publications, 918 16th Street NW, Washington, DC 20006 for a copy of "Protecting Your Pension Money."

If your pension money is invested with an insurance company, read that section in this chapter for safety tips.

AT AN INSURANCE COMPANY

In recent years, several life insurance giants became insolvent. Heavy investments in junk bonds brought Executive Life Insurance Company to its knees and Mutual Benefit Life Insurance was seized by New Jersey regulators, making it the largest insurance failure in the nation's history.

Consumers have less protection when life insurers fail than they do when banks tumble. Insurance companies are regulated by state commissioners, not by federal authorities, and there is no national fund to cover losses. Instead, when an insurer fails, state regulators collect assessments from other insurers operating in the same state to pay off policyholders. Rules regarding who is eligible for reimbursement vary from state to state.

Until policies can be transferred to another company or some other arrangements are made, insurers typically lose access to the cash value of their contracts, sometimes for periods of a year or more. It is possible that, in the final analysis, they may get less than the contract's full value.

§ HINT: Call your state insurance commission to make certain you would be covered under the state guaranty system if your insurer became insolvent. Some state plans cover contract holders of companies headquartered in that state regardless of where they live; others guarantee only their own residents and only if they are insured by companies licensed in that state.

FOR FURTHER INFORMATION

For information about the SIPC and what it covers:

SIPC
805 15th Street NW, Suite 800
Washington, DC 20005
1-202-371-8300

If you have a complaint or a question about your bank, write to the Consumer Services Division of your State Banking Commission or Department in your state capital. If you live in New York, write to:

Consumer Services Division
New York State Banking Department
2 Rector Street
New York, NY 10006
1-212-618-6445

An overview of the financial condition of many commercial banks, savings and loans, and credit unions is available for a modest fee from:

Veribanc, Inc.
P.O. Box 461
Wakefield, MA 01880
1-617-245-8370; 1-800-442-2657

For information about a brokerage firm and its insurance:

Office of Consumer Affairs
Securities & Exchange Commission
450 Fifth Street NW
Washington, DC 20549
1-202-272-7440

"How to Get Safety Information from Your Financial Institution"

Weiss Research
2200 North Florida Mango Road
West Palm Beach, FL 33409
1-800-289-9222
$2

Booklet includes postcard questionnaires you can send to your bank, S&L, or stockbroker, along with simple instructions on how to interpret the answers.

5

MOVING FROM SAVER TO INVESTOR

TRUE GRIT

Now that you have set aside money in several safe places where it is earning well above the savings account rate, you are ready to stretch your wings and move into the arena of the true investor. Incidentally, before you leap from saver to investor you should have a minimum of 3 and preferably 6 months' worth of living expenses in one of the safe havens discussed in the previous chapters. That means if you need $4,000 per month to operate comfortably, set aside $12,000 to $24,000 in a combination of CDs, Treasuries, and money funds. Then if you are hit with a financial emergency, such as losing your job or getting a serious illness, you will have immediate liquid resources to draw upon.

$ HINT: If you feel your job may be in jeopardy, set aside at least 9 months of expenses—it's taking longer for people to find new jobs in these hard times.

Moving from saver to investor is a step many people, especially those with a conservative bent, find difficult to take. Some, in fact, never manage to make the move at all. Although there's nothing inherently wrong with leaving your money in a safe haven, during inflationary periods you may actually lose money, and during a bull market, even a moderate one, you'll be on the sidelines. And, for those facing high taxes, these safe investments are not truly safe at all, for instead of reducing your federal income tax bite, they add to it.

Of course, no investment is for all seasons. Review the tables on pages 64–65 to help you determine what vehicles are best during various economic periods. Keep in mind that the greater the risk you take, the greater the potential return.

MUTUAL FUNDS VS. INDIVIDUAL SECURITIES

One of the first key decisions you will have to make as you move from saver to investor is whether to select your own stocks and bonds or to buy shares in a mutual fund. Mutual funds, in which professional portfolio managers make all the buy and sell decisions, are described in Chapter 6. There are more mutual funds than stocks trading on the New York Stock Exchange. By reading the chapters on mutual funds, stocks, and bonds, you can arrive at portfolio conclusions that suit your investing temperament and income level.

MOVING FROM SAVER TO INVESTOR

INVESTMENT	WHERE TO FIND	FACTS TO KNOW
Savings account	Bank, credit union	What is the interest rate? How often is it compounded? Is it federally insured?
Money market deposit account	Bank, credit union	What is the interest rate? How often does it change? Are there withdrawal penalties/limitations?
Certificate of deposit (CD)	Bank, credit union	How much money will I have at maturity? Can I roll it over at the same or a higher rate? Are there withdrawal penalties?
Brokered CD	Stockbroker	Will my interest compound? If I sell my CD back to you before maturity, will I lose money? Is the originating bank sound?
Money market mutual fund	Brokerage firm, mutual fund	What is the yield? What is the fund's average maturity?
EE savings bonds	Bank, Federal Reserve, Bureau of Public Debt	What is the current rate? When do the bonds mature?
Treasury issues	Bank, Federal Reserve, Bureau of Public Debt	What is the current rate? If I redeem early will I lose money? Is there a fee?
Stocks	Brokerage firm, investment club	What is the commission? Is there a dividend? What is the *Value Line* rating?
Bonds	Brokerage firm	What is the commission? Can the bond be called? What is the yield? What is the rating?
Mutual funds	Mutual fund, brokerage firm	What is the total return for 6 months, 1 and 5 years? Are there fees?

If you are interested in stocks, a good place to begin is in your own backyard. Investigate your local utility company or a corporation headquartered in your area. Call for the annual report and ask a local broker for additional research information. Another easy way to dip into the market is by purchasing shares in the company you work for or one whose products or services you use and like. If you are wedded to your Reeboks or if you love Kellogg cereals, you might like to start down the investor's path by purchasing stocks in those companies.

HOW TO SET UP A MONEY-MAKING PORTFOLIO

The world of finance is complex, competitive, subject to economic and political pressures, and dominated by shrewd, powerful people who control billions of dollars. For most Americans who can save only a few thousand dollars a year, making money in such an arena sounds difficult, if not impossible.

Yet everyone can be a successful investor if he or she takes time to set specific objectives, to learn the facts, to adhere to proven profitable rules, to be patient, and, most important, to use common sense. Sometimes success comes quickly, but over the long term, making money requires careful planning and conscientious management.

You may feel that the index arbitrageurs, institutional managers, huge fund managers, and program traders control the game. To a large extent they do—yet market crashes take them down too, in many cases more than the smaller individual investors who don't panic and don't sell out at overwhelming losses.

If you proceed with caution and gather sound information, you have one major advantage over the big guns: You care more about your money than any stockbroker, fund manager, or financial adviser ever will.

PREVENTIVE PORTFOLIO MANAGEMENT

If you are averse to risk or want to reduce your risk quotient, here are seven easy preventive techniques that will enable you to maintain a healthy portfolio and weather any future declines in the market.

- *Diversify.* To some extent you can protect yourself from market swings by owning a mixture of stocks, bonds, precious metals, real estate, and other investments, because seldom does everything decline at the same time.
- *Buy for the long haul.* If you plan in general to hold your stocks 1 to 3 years, day-to-day and month-to-month fluctuations can largely be ignored.
- *Select investments on the basis of quality.* Take advantage of low-priced high-quality stocks. Ignore rumors and study the fundamentals.
- *Include high-yield investments.* Common stocks with high dividends, preferred stock, high-yielding bonds, and CDs all help cushion dips in the market.

- *Investigate convertibles.* Their yields are higher than the underlying stock of the same company, and should the stock fall in price, the convertible (CV) will fall less.
- *Use dollar cost averaging.* With both mutual funds and stocks, this approach enables you to buy more shares at lower prices and fewer shares at higher prices, as well as to ignore short-term market gyrations. (See page 261 for more on dollar cost averaging.)
- *Don't buy on margin.* You will be able to hold your stock through all kinds of weather if you buy for cash. With a margin account, you are subject to margin calls from your broker. (For more information on margin accounts, see pages 265–267.)

How you manage your money is largely determined by your personality, your specific financial goals, and your tolerance for risk. In the broad sense, your choices are (1) between sleeping well and lying awake worrying, (2) between managing your money and letting someone else do it, and (3) between income and growth. For most people, the first choice is the most important: Don't make investments that keep you awake at night—money by itself is never as important as peace of mind. It's absolutely impossible to be a successful investor when you're fearful!

WHAT TYPE ARE YOU?

Investors fall into three broad categories: *conservative, aggressive,* and *speculative.* By and large, your portfolio should reflect some of each, the emphasis shifting with market conditions, how much money you have, your age, and family responsibilities.

➤ CONSERVATIVE The conservative investor seeks safety and income and aims to preserve capital. In most cases, conservative investors look at an investment's yield and pay little heed to the impact of taxes and inflation on their money.

Investment choices are (1) fixed assets such as CDs and short-term Treasury bills, notes, or bonds and (2) solid, income-producing stocks such as utilities and real estate investment trusts.

☐ CAUTION: Avoid taking the path of least resistance—that of being an ultraconservative investor who stashes large amounts of money in savings accounts or money market funds or, even worse, buys stocks and holds them until forced to sell because of the need for cash or money to live on.

The conservative approach provides peace of mind, but it's very poor protection against inflation and low interest rates. If, for instance, the cost of living rises 4% a year, and your conservative investments don't keep pace, you will actually lose. With a 4% rise, the real purchasing power of every $1,000 is cut to $822 in 5 years and to $703 in 10 years.

Conservative investments should, of course, constitute a portion of everyone's portfolio, but they are most appropriate for people who are retired or soon to be, are on fixed incomes, or earn low to modest salaries.

➤ AGGRESSIVE The aggressive investor is more comfortable moving money about and is interested in total return; that is, income plus price appreciation. Such an investor does not hesitate to sell in order to take profits.

Although some of this investor's money is in conservative holdings, the bulk is spread between quality growth stocks, corporate and municipal bonds, convertibles, and real estate.

The aggressive investor is likely to have substantial income, be at least a decade away from retirement, and not need investment income for day-to-day living.

➤ SPECULATIVE Speculative investors may not always be gambling Las Vegas style, but they often try to outwit the market and the pros. As long as speculators research their choices carefully and use only money they can afford to lose, they may very well make money—lots of it. However, they are just as likely to lose everything unless they force themselves to sell when their investments attain specific levels.

Speculative investors favor takeover candidates, junk bonds, precious metals, and leveraged real estate. Such investors should be well off, with steadily increasing sources of income.

For additional suggestions on equating your appetite for risk with your investment choices, see the pyramid on page 17.

FINDING MONEY TO INVEST

Saving is essential for achieving your personal economic goals, security, and a carefree life when it comes to money. But it is not enough to set aside money sporadically. You must save regularly.

$ HINT: Make your first monthly check out to yourself; earmark it for investments or your IRA, Keogh, or money market account. Then begin paying your bills!

Other painless sources of money to invest:

- Dividend checks
- Gifts
- Bonuses
- A raise
- Tips
- Automatic payroll deduction plan

CHARGE YOUR SAVINGS
■■■■■■

In May 1990, American Express launched a new way to save money painlessly, called "Membership Savings." If you have an American Express card you can call 1-800-225-SAVE and tell them how much you'd like to save. The minimum is $50. The amount then appears on your monthly statement. When you pay your bill, the money is put in a federally insured savings account. Money can be withdrawn by calling American Express. This type of account pays a variable rate that is 0.5% above the average for bank savings accounts as reported by *Bank Rate Monitor*.

- Inheritance
- Free-lance activities
- Company savings plans
- Tax refunds

Much of the information you need to analyze the wide range of investments and develop your own personal strategy is readily available from annual reports, investment services, and financial newspapers and magazines. Investment newsletters are also helpful. See Appendix A.

Most portfolios consist of stocks, bonds, U.S. Treasury obligations, real estate, precious metals, and limited partnerships. No one portfolio should consist of only one type of investment—diversification is one of the best lines of defense against losses. We will introduce the various types of stocks, bonds, and other securities in the following chapters.

SPOTTING ECONOMIC TRENDS

To build and maintain a profitable portfolio, you must develop a sense of the country's economic strength or weakness. By following these key short-term indicators, all of which are reported in the media, you can take the pulse of the nation.

- *Capacity utilization.* Measures the activity of U.S. manufacturers and the percentage rate at which factories are operating. A healthy rate is about 85%. When it drops, unemployment is high.
- *Consumer price index.* Also known as the cost-of-living index (COLA), it measures price changes for goods and services. Its components include housing, food, transportation, clothing, medical care, and electricity.
- *Gross domestic product.* The GDP measures the total value of all goods and services produced and sold in the United States over a particular time period. It tells whether the U.S. economy is expanding or contracting. Less than 2% is regarded as slow growth; over 5% is a boom. When the GDP declines two quarters in a row, it indicates that a recession has begun.
- *Index of leading economic indicators.* This index represents 11 components of economic growth, ranging from stock prices to housing permits. If it falls for 3 or 4 consecutive months, an economic downturn is likely.
- *New car sales.* Consumer buying trends are reflected in this purchase pattern, reported every 10 days. Keep track over a minimum of 2 months.
- *Retail sales.* Compare monthly sales with those of the previous month, 6 months, and 1 year.
- *Department store sales.* These reflect both regional and seasonal trends but can be an accurate indicator if they confirm other trends.
- *Housing starts.* Any improvement indicates optimistic consumer attitudes and, quite often, lower interest rates.

- *Unemployment.* This statistic reflects the overall status of the country's economy. Watch it regularly.
- *Federal funds rate.* This figure, which fluctuates daily, tracks the interest rate banks charge each other overnight.
- *Prime rate.* Interest rate banks charge their most creditworthy customers. Follow at least 3 months.
- *Broker loan rate.* Interest rate for brokers borrowing money from banks.

DOS FOR SUCCESSFUL INVESTING

DO investigate BEFORE you invest. Do not buy on impulse, hunch, or rumor. Make all investments according to your goals for income and/or growth. Take nothing for granted. Get the facts lest the lack of facts get you.

DO limit your purchases until your forecast is confirmed. When you feel you have latched onto a winner, buy half the amount of shares you have money for even if it means buying less than a round lot. You may lose a few points' profit by waiting, but you will also minimize your losses. Watch the action in the marketplace, and when your judgment appears accurate, buy the other half of your position.

DO focus on the downside risk. An important aspect of buying stocks is not how much you can make but how much you can lose. If a stock's dividend, asset value, or price history clearly indicates a limited downside risk, it's probably a good investment.

DO buy only stocks quoted regularly in the *Wall Street Journal*, the *New York Times*, or *Barron's*. You want a ready market that will attract other investors when you sell.

DO investigate AFTER you invest. There is no such thing as a permanent investment. (Even IBM has bounced up and down over the years.) This caveat applies especially to small companies that show great promise at the outset but all too soon fall by the wayside.

DO watch trends: of the economy, of the stock market, of industry groups, and of the stocks in which you are interested. Stock market leaders change almost monthly, so what was favorable in January may be sliding in June.

DO set realistic goals and target prices when you make the original commitment. Roughly, these should be 35% to 50% higher than your cost, and the time frame should be 24 to 36 months. Once in a while, a stock will zoom up fast, but investments usually move up slowly and steadily, with interim dips, to new highs.

DO diversify, but carefully. As a rule of thumb, a $100,000 portfolio should have no more than 10 securities, with no more than 20% in any one company or industry. However, you can put as little as 5% of your assets in special high-risk situations. Above $100,000, add one new security for each additional $10,000.

DO stay flexible. This will let you make the most profitable use of your money during any specific period. When yields on bonds, CDs, money market funds, and Treasuries are 8% or more, move part of your savings into these areas. When the yield drops, take your profits and invest the proceeds in quality common stocks where the chances of appreciation are greater.

DO keep a list of 10 "future" investments. Review them periodically to determine whether any offer greater prospects for faster rewards than the holdings you now have. This list should include stocks, convertibles, bonds, and, when appropriate, limited partnerships. Don't switch as long as your original investments are profitable and appear to have reasonable prospects of reaching your goals.

DO watch market timing, and never be in a hurry to spend your money. If you miss one opportunity, there will be another soon.

- *When trading is active,* buy at the market price. If you're dealing with a stock that is beginning to attract attention, you may save a point or two by waiting for a temporary dip. But if you are convinced that this is a wise investment, make your move, even if there is a decline later.

- *When trading is slow,* place your order at a set price and be willing to wait a while.

DO be patient. Never flit from one stock to another. This will make your broker rich, but it will cut your potential profits and, unless you are very wise and very lucky, will not increase your capital. Four trades a year, at an average cost of 1% of stock value, equals 4% of income. (You may save a few dollars by using a discount broker.)

In normal markets, it takes a quality stock 2 to 3 years to move from undervaluation to overvaluation. Always remember that by definition, investments are long-term commitments and rarely create millionaires overnight.

DO upgrade your portfolio periodically. Review all holdings quarterly and plan to sell at least one security every 6 months. Replace the weakest securities with those on your "futures" list. Be slow to sell winners, because this will leave you with less profitable holdings. On the average, a successful portfolio will be turned over every 5 years, about 20% annually.

DO average up when you choose well. Buy more shares as the price of the stock rises.

DO set selling prices, preferably stop-loss orders at 15% to 20% below your cost or the recent high. This is discussed in greater detail in Chapter 25, but it is a key factor in successful investing. It is just as important to keep losses low as to keep profits high. At times, this can be a tough decision, so action should be taken only after you have learned the real reason for the price decline. If the company runs into temporary difficulties, don't panic. But if research concludes that profits will be below projections, it's usually smart to sell now. You can always buy back later.

DO stand by your investment rules. Once in a while, it will pay to make exceptions, but in successful investing, rules should seldom be broken.

DON'TS FOR SUCCESSFUL INVESTING

DON'T invest in a vacuum. You must have a systematic, sensible, long-range plan for your personal, business, and retirement savings. Wise planning is easy, enjoyable, and rewarding. Lack of planning leads to mistakes that can be more costly than spending the time to understand the fundamentals of investing.

DON'T be overly conservative. This means limiting the portion of your savings allocated to fixed asset or income investments, such as money market accounts, CDs, preferred stocks, and Treasuries. These are safe, but they rarely grow in value. Most of these holdings should be viewed as temporary parking places while you wait for more rewarding opportunities, or as a segment of your total portfolio.

DON'T be overly optimistic or pessimistic about the market or the securities that you own. Even the best corporations falter now and then: Their growth slows or their markets change. Smart professionals recognize when this occurs and also when the stock price soars to an unrealistic level. When any stock becomes clearly overvalued by your standards, sell or set stop-loss orders.

DON'T be lured by the "greater fool theory": that the price will keep rising because someone else will be foolish enough to pay far more than the stock is worth. When you have a pleasant profit, cash in.

DON'T rush to buy bargains, regardless of the pressure from your adviser or broker. When a stock is at a low price, there is usually a reason.

REVIEW YOUR PORTFOLIO WHEN . . .

- there's a significant move up or down in the stock market.
- prime and other bank interest rates change.
- a new tax law is passed.
- the dollar becomes substantially stronger or weaker in the international market.
- there's been a major scientific breakthrough.
- regulatory agencies adopt a new policy.
- the inflation rate changes.
- there's a change in political leadership.
- foreign-trade restrictions are put into effect.
- a new international trade agreement is reached.
- new rules are passed on margin accounts.
- war begins or ends.
- the economy changes from boom times to recessionary times, or vice versa.
- bond interest rates change.
- there's a shortage in a key commodity or energy source.

It may not appear to be logical, but major investors are either skeptical or uncomfortable. They will not start buying until their peers do so. Once you spot a bargain, wait until the price and volume start to rise, and then proceed cautiously, buying in small lots even if it costs more money.

DON'T average down. A stock that appears to be a good buy at 20 is seldom more attractive at 15. When there's a serious decline in your current favorite, either your research is inaccurate or your access to the latest information is inadequate. Ask your broker to check with the research department. If you are wrong and keep buying as the price declines, you'll only compound your mistake.

DON'T assume that a quality rating will continue. With cost squeezes, foreign competition, governmental regulations and edicts, and fast-changing

---

AND THEN TAKE THESE STEPS:

- Buy more stock of a proven company when the market falls and prune out losers when it rises.
- As rates move up, lock in higher yields in CDs and longer-term bonds; as rates fall, start short term—under 2 years—and look to stocks.
- Determine your new tax bracket and talk to your accountant about ways to cut taxes.
- When the dollar is stronger, go to Europe on vacation; when it weakens, buy foreign currencies.
- Select one or two stocks within the industry to buy.
- Look for investments that will benefit, such as environmental mutual funds, waste and hazardous waste removal stocks, engineering companies, and water purification stocks.
- If inflation increases, interest rates will rise, so turn to money market funds and high-yielding CDs. If inflation decreases, stocks will do well.
- Read the newspaper to determine the current administration's priorities—military buildup or reduction; concern about education, the environment, or health care; protection of the rich—and position on taxes. Invest in areas where there's likely to be increased spending.
- Reduce holdings in companies or mutual funds heavily dependent on foreign sales.
- Look for corporations already operating or prepared to operate in that country.
- Call your broker to discuss implications for your account.
- If war starts, buy military stocks or investigate which commodities may be in short supply, depending on location of the conflict—copper, gold, wheat, oil. If war ends, decrease military holdings.
- If the economy is booming, take profits. If a recession starts, build up cash reserves and buy stocks at their lows.
- If rates go up, buy longer-term bonds. If rates decline, keep shorter term.

financial and market conditions, even stable corporations can become less attractive in a few months.

DON'T heed rumors. Wall Street is a center of gossip, hopes, and fears, but a rumor is *never* a sound reason for investment decisions. By the time you hear or read it, the professionals have made their move.

DON'T forget that a stock does not care who owns it. The price per volume of the trading of its shares is the result of forces far stronger and wealthier than you are or probably ever will be.

DON'T look back. There's no way that you can reverse your decision. If your judgment was wrong, there's nothing that you can do about it except learn from it.

REDUCING FEES: A PAINLESS WAY TO BOOST YOUR RETURNS

By reducing your investing costs, you can painlessly raise the returns you make on stocks, bonds, mutual funds, and other investments. The impact of these fees and other charges on your profits can be impressive.

There are three basic types of investing costs: (1) sales commissions, which you pay when you buy stocks, bonds, and load mutual funds; (2) mutual fund expenses; and (3) the spread: the difference between the ask price at which dealers sell a security to the public and the bid price at which they buy it back. Spreads are particularly heavy in purchasing zero coupon bonds, municipals, and over-the-counter stocks.

U.S. TREASURIES

Banks and brokerage firms charge sales commissions for buying and selling Treasury securities, which range from $25 to $50+ for up to $10,000 worth of securities. Ask before you buy.

$ HINT: Avoid commissions by purchasing direct from the Treasury through its Treasury Direct system. For a free brochure call your Federal Reserve Bank. (See page 127.)

MONEY MARKET FUNDS

These mutual funds are sold without any sales charge or commission; however, their management expenses can take a bite out of your yield. (See page 43 for a list of money funds with the highest yields.)

$ HINT: Call several funds or read their prospectuses to find a fund with an expense ratio below 0.6%. But remember, an extremely low expense ratio often means that management is absorbing some of the costs to push up the fund's yield and attract customers. This is often the case with new funds. Once the fund has new investors, it may raise expense charges.

MUTUAL FUNDS

Funds sold by brokers, called load funds, charge front-end loads or fees of as much as 8.5%. Many funds have back-end loads of up to 1.5%, which go into effect when you sell your shares. Still others have 12b-1 fees—an annual fee of up to 1.25% to cover marketing costs to bring in new shareholders. These 12b-1 fees are on top of annual management fees, which range from 0.3% to 1.5%. (Management fees are highest for international stock funds, which must be actively managed.)

The SEC passed a ruling in the spring of 1988 that all sales charges and fees must be listed in the fund's prospectus accompanied by a table showing their precise effect on a $1,000 investment after 1, 3, 5, and 10 years.

$ HINT: Select no-load funds; check the fund's expenses for the year.

STOCKS

The lower the number of stocks you buy and sell, the wider the spread. With actively traded stocks, which includes most blue chips, the spread is typically narrow—say 12¢ per share. Yet a thinly traded stock that sells over the counter (OTC) could have an ask price of $5 and a bid price of just $4.50. Another point to keep in mind with OTC stocks: if you buy from the market maker (a broker/dealer firm that keeps the stock in its inventory), then you pay only the spread. On the other hand, if you buy through a broker who must in turn get the shares from a market maker, you wind up paying the spread plus the broker's commission.

If you buy less than 100 shares of any stock (100 shares being a round lot), you pay an odd lot charge, typically 12½¢ per share.

$ HINT: Buy in round lots; buy OTC stocks from the market maker, listed in the "pink sheets" directory available from most brokers. (See page 181 for more on pink sheet listings.)

DISCOUNTERS

You can cut sales commissions by buying through discount brokerage firms, although you have to give up the research and personal feeding and care you get from a full service firm. Yet you'll save as much as 50% to 80%. (See Chapter 25 for more on discount firms.)

Discounters also relieve you of another fairly new expense: annual fees for customers who do not actively trade their accounts. The leader of this charge, Merrill Lynch, charges $30 a year for accounts that generate less than $100 a year in commissions. Other firms have similar charges.

MUNICIPAL BONDS

Spreads, which are built into the bond's price, are higher for odd lot purchases. With munis, an odd lot is less than $25,000. If you buy a municipal bond in the secondary or aftermarket from a broker who does not have it in inventory, your yield is further reduced by about an eighth of a percentage point to cover the broker's costs in getting the bonds from another dealer.

$ HINT: Buy actively traded bonds, and new issues in particular. Spreads are typically 0.75%, compared to as much as 4% to 5% for odd lots. Try to pick bonds from your broker's inventory.

ZERO COUPON BONDS

The pricing of zeros tends to be confusing, and hefty spreads are not uncommon. Some brokers have been known to charge as much as 5%.

$ HINT: Shop among several brokers, asking how much you must invest per $1,000 face value for the particular zero you want. Then ask what the effective yield to maturity is. Buy from the broker with the lowest price and the highest yield.

KNOWING WHEN TO GO LONG

Interest rates, like women's hemlines, are constantly moving up and down. Rate changes impact directly on the appeal of certain investment choices that are popular with conservative investors such as Treasury bills and notes, money market funds, and CDs. When rates peak, and start to head down, high yields are suddenly history. When that happens, you want to be locked in, not only to profit from high rates but also to benefit from rising bond prices that always accompany falling rates. Use the box on page 69 as a guideline for timing your investments with changing rates.

There's no magic formula for knowing when to go long (for knowing when interest rates have topped out), but these four common indicators provide an accurate view of interest rate trends:

- *Money market maturities.* The average maturity on money market funds reveals the direction the fund managers think rates will take. This figure, available from the funds and also reported in many newspapers, tells the maturity of Treasury bills, CDs, and other short-term securities in a fund's portfolio. Short maturities allow fund managers to capture high rates more immediately and also indicate that they think rates will climb even higher. Rates tend to turn downward when maturities reach 39 or 40 days.
- *Gold prices.* The price of gold is traditionally an indication of the direction of inflation. Rising metal prices mean rising inflation, which in turns signals rising interest rates.
- *Prime rate.* A drop in prime usually occurs after other short-term rates have fallen, indicating that banks anticipate the downward spiral to continue. When prime drops, investors should lock in high yields.
- *Yield curve.* This illustrates the relationship between short- and long-term interest rates (see page 127). Usually long-term rates are higher than short-term rates to reward investors for tying up their money for many years. When short-term rates are higher, the yield curve is "inverted." An inverted yield curve generally indicates that interest rates have not peaked.

INVESTMENT CLUBS

If you're skittish about picking your own stocks or nervous about working with a stockbroker, you can circumvent these problems by purchasing

WHEN INVESTMENTS PERFORM BEST

INVESTMENT	ADD TO YOUR PORTFOLIO	RISK LEVEL
Growth stocks	When economy is growing at above average rate When interest rates are stable	Medium to high
Blue chip stocks	During slow to moderate growth periods When interest rates are falling	Medium
Utility stocks	When interest rates are falling When energy costs are falling	Low to medium
Long-term bonds	When interest rates are falling	Low to medium
Short-term notes and bills	When interest rates are stable or falling	Low
Money market funds and CDs	When interest rates are rising	Low

stocks through an investment club, a team approach that is used by thousands of Americans.

An investment club is a group of individuals, often neighbors, co-workers, or friends, who meet once a month, contribute a set dollar amount, and invest the common pool in stocks. Every member is responsible for doing research on individual stocks on a rotating basis. They then report their findings to the club, and members debate the risks and rewards of each stock and finally take a vote on which ones to buy.

Much of the guidance for clubs comes from the National Association of Investors Corporation (NAIC), a nonprofit organization operated by and for the benefit of member clubs. This association, which has been the force behind the investment club movement in the United States since the 1950s, has about 150,000 individual and 7,600 club members. Membership is $30 for clubs plus $10 for each club member and $32 for individuals. The association offers detailed information on how to start a club, how to analyze stocks, and how to keep records.

Clubs and individual members of NAIC can also dispense with brokerage commissions by participating in NAIC's "Low-Cost Investment Plan." Under this program, clubs can buy as little as one share directly from about 50 major participating companies, such as Disney, Kellogg, McDonald's, Mobil, and Quaker Oats, for a one-time charge of $5 per firm. Most of these corporations do not charge a commission, although some have a nominal fee ($3 to $5) for each transaction to cover their expenses. All of these

---

JOIN AN INVESTMENT CLUB

If you'd like to start building a portfolio of stocks but feel uncertain about making your own selections, join an investment club in your area. By pooling your money with that of 15 to 20 other people and sharing research, you can comfortably begin to develop investment savvy.

Kenneth S. Janke, president of the National Association of Investors Corporation, says the following three guiding principles followed by clubs enable them to frequently outperform the S&P 500:

1   Invest a fixed amount regularly to eliminate the guesswork of trying to time the market.
2   Reinvest earnings to take advantage of the magic of compounding.
3   Invest in stocks growing faster than the economy.
    For details on joining a club, contact:

National Association of Investors Corp.
1515 East Eleven Mile Road
Royal Oak, MI 48067
1-313-543-0612

---

companies also have dividend reinvestment programs, so instead of taking dividends in cash, the club or individual members automatically reinvest the dividends in additional shares of the company's stocks.

Of the 500 clubs surveyed in April 1991, the average club was 8½ years old, had a compound annual growth rate of 10.8%, compared with 10.6% for the S&P 500 stock index, and its average portfolio was worth $69,000.

HELP FROM THE NEW YORK STOCK EXCHANGE

Several years ago, individual investors across the United States felt they could no longer be successful players in the stock market. They were driven away in droves by the huge institutional investors—mutual funds, pension funds, and so on—and by computerized program trading. Yet there's been a significant change in attitude, and Wall Street is trying to woo back those who want to select their own stocks, bonds, commodities, and other investments.

Symbolizing this shift is the Individual Investors Advisory Committee to the New York Stock Exchange (NYSE). It serves as a liaison between individual shareholders and the NYSE Board, advising the Board on policies and programs that affect individual investors in equities, options, futures, and fixed-income securities. In addition, it reviews the impact of proposed rules and related matters on individual shareholders and recommends additional ways to provide fair and open markets for investors of all kinds. The committee is made up of members of the public.

Another step taken by the NYSE is the Individual Investor Express System (IIES). This system provides priority delivery via electronic means of round lot and odd lot orders up to 2,099 shares *if* the broker has identified these individual investor orders with an "I." These orders then get priority routing so they reach the floor of the exchange ahead of other orders.

KEEPING GOOD RECORDS

Most of us realize that good records are essentially for cutting tax bills, but proper documentation of investments can also improve profits and make estate planning less onerous. By keeping track of investments' performance, you can weed out those that are poor performers or no longer meeting your financial goals. Records are also critical to your family's financial security should you become ill or die. Here's a look at the documents you need to keep:

- *Stocks.* Keep all confirmation slips of trades plus the most recent quarterly dividend reinvestment statements and year-end dividend reinvestment statements. When you sell you can minimize taxes by selling the high-cost shares first. Give your broker the purchase date and cost of the shares you want to sell. Follow this up with a written note in case you need it for the IRS. Documentation of stock transactions should be kept for 6 years.
- *Bonds.* The same record-keeping rules that apply to stocks also apply to bonds. In other words, keep the confirmation slips if you are buying a bond for which you have to pay some accrued interest to the seller at the time of purchase. For example, if the last interest payment was 2 months ago and the next one is 4 months in the future, you must pay the seller the 2 months' interest due him or her, since you will be receiving the full payment. This amount returned to the seller can be subtracted from your taxable income. This amount should be noted on your confirmation slip.

RECORD-KEEPING TERMS

- *Cost basis.* The original price of an investment.
- *FIFO.* A way to calculate the cost basis of an asset that is part of a larger holding purchased at various prices. With first in, first out, securities are sold in the order in which they were bought.
- *Dividend reinvestment.* Automatic investment of cash dividends in additional stocks or mutual fund shares.
- *Accrued interest.* The portion of interest on a bond due for the time period between the last interest payment and the sale date. The buyer pays the seller this dollar amount in addition to the purchase price.

- *Mutual funds.* With mutual funds, as with stocks and bonds, you must pay taxes on any price appreciation when you sell your shares. Therefore, when you buy shares in a mutual fund, save the confirmation slip indicating the number of shares you bought and what you paid for them.

Certain funds pay interest or dividends. In addition, you may get distributions of capital gains from the sale of investments held in the fund's portfolio. Taxes are due on these payouts in the year in which you receive them. Should you reinvest this money in more fund shares, save the statements recording this reinvestment transaction. Otherwise you may forget to include these distributions as part of your "cost basis" when you sell. Some firms send out cumulative statements, in which case you need to save only the December one, which lists all transactions for the year.

If you decide to sell only some of your shares, your records will help you decide which ones to unload. The IRS assumes that you are selling the first shares you purchased *unless* you specify to the contrary. This is called "first in, first out" (FIFO), and can be unnecessarily costly if you have regularly purchased shares in a fund that has continually increased in value.

There are two other options besides FIFO: the identifiable-cost and average-cost approaches. With the identifiable-cost approach, you specify to the fund that you are selling a certain number of shares

18 WAYS TO EARN INTEREST

Part of your money should be put to work earning money. Here are 18 ways to do just that. (Data as of July 1992.)

INVESTMENT	RISK LEVEL	YIELD
Bank money market accounts	Low	3.08%
Money market funds	Low	3.32%
Treasury bills (3 month)	Low	3.23%
Certificates of deposit (6 month)	Low	4.00%
Savings bonds (minimum, 5 year)	Low	5.58%
Treasury bonds (10 year)	Low	6.80%
Treasury zeros	Low to moderate	7.30%
Ginnie Mae certificates	Low to moderate	7.40%
CMOs	Moderate	8.04%
Utility stocks	Moderate to medium	6–8%
Utility bonds	Moderate to medium	7–9%
Closed-end bond funds	Moderate to medium	9%
Municipals	Medium	6.10%
Municipal zeros	Medium	6.00%
REITs	Medium to high	6.20%
Convertible bonds (new)	Medium to high	6.00%
Junk bonds	High	9–11%

purchased on a particular date or dates. With a rising fund, this approach enables you to sell the most costly shares—those purchased most recently—and postpone taxes on the cheaper shares purchased earlier. If you sell by phone, send the mutual fund a letter confirming this fact. Keep a copy of your letter plus the transaction statements for 6 years.

With the average-cost method, you find the total cost of all shares ever purchased, including reinvestments, and divide by the number of shares you own to arrive at the cost per share. Then, multiply this by the number of shares you plan to sell to find your total tax cost. This method must be entered on tax Schedule D when you report the sale, and you must use the same method for future sales.

FOR FURTHER INFORMATION

NEWSLETTERS
Call or write for sample issues if you are interested in receiving continual data on the funds.

Income & Safety
Institute for Econometric Research
3471 North Federal Highway
Fort Lauderdale, FL 33306
1-800-327-6720; 1-305-563-9000
Monthly; $49 per year
Covers money market funds, Ginnie Maes, and tax-free bonds.

100 Highest Yields
P.O. Box 088888
North Palm Beach, FL 33408
1-800-327-7717; 1-407-627-7330
Monthly; 8 issues for $34; 52 issues for $98

PAMPHLETS

Money Market Mutual Funds
Publications Division
Investment Company Institute
1600 M Street NW, Suite 600
Washington, DC 20036
1-202-293-7700
Free; explains how money market funds are regulated.

Why Save and Invest at Your Credit Union
National Credit Union Association, Inc.
P.O. Box 431
Madison, WI 53701
1-608-231-4000
Free; explains benefits of using a credit union.

New York Stock Exchange Investors Information Kit. Contains:

- *NYSE: A Basic Guide*
- *Understanding Stocks and Bonds*
- *Understanding Financial Statements*
- *Getting Help When You Invest*
- *Glossary*
- *Margin Trading Guide*

$12; prepay by check or money order. Send to:

New York Stock Exchange
P.O. Box 5020
Farmingdale, NY 11736
1-516-454-1800

6 | INVESTING WITH MUTUAL FUNDS

Although there's no one ideal investment for everyone, mutual funds come closest for many of us. A mutual fund is an investment company in which an investor's dollars are pooled with those of thousands of others; the combined total is invested by a professional manager in various securities. Their popularity is unrivaled. According to the Investment Company Institute, the industry trade group, $21.5 billion poured into stock funds in just three months—the three-month period ended February 1992.

Bond funds and other types of income funds likewise have received enormous infusions of cash during this same period, primarily from investors who saw yields on money market funds and new bank CDs wilt to half the returns they had been getting.

ADVANTAGES OF MUTUAL FUNDS

➤ DIVERSIFICATION Unless you have $50,000, it is almost impossible to have a properly diversified portfolio. It's costly to buy in odd lots, and if you buy round-lot shares of quality corporations, your average per-share cost will be about $40, so you can own only about 12 stocks—the minimum for a cross section of securities. Mutual fund portfolios, on the other hand, provide excellent diversification.

➤ SYSTEMATIC SUPERVISION Mutual funds handle all details of stock transactions efficiently, mail dividend checks promptly, provide accurate year-end summaries for income tax purposes, and are always ready to answer questions on their toll-free phone lines.

➤ PROFESSIONAL MANAGEMENT Mutual fund managers are professionals with experience and a wealth of research to assist them in managing their portfolios. If their fund's performance falters in comparison with its peers', the fund manager may be replaced.

➤ SWITCHING PRIVILEGES When a management company sponsors more than one type of fund (and most do), shareholders may switch from one fund to another as the market changes. Most funds offer free switching; some impose nominal fees.

$ HINT: Select a fund that permits the portfolio manager to shift out of stocks and into U.S. Treasury bills, jumbo CDs, and other higher-yielding cash instruments if it looks like the stock market may decline. This gives you added protection when the market or interest rates change.

HOW FUNDS WORK

All mutual funds operate along the same lines. They sell shares to the public at net asset value (NAV) price. (NAV per share equals the total assets of the fund divided by the outstanding shares minus liabilities.) The money received is then pooled and used to buy various types of securities. So when you buy into a fund, you are really buying shares in an investment company, but the assets of this company consist not of a plant or equipment but of stocks, bonds, and cash instruments. The price of your shares rises and falls every day with the total value of the securities in the fund's portfolio.

As the owner of mutual fund shares, you receive periodic payments, provided your fund does well. Of course, if the fund has a poor year, you stand to lose money; that is, your NAV will fall. Most funds pay dividends every quarter and capital gains distributions annually. Capital gains distributions result when a fund sells some of its securities at a profit. You may elect to have your earnings reinvested automatically in additional fund shares, usually at no cost.

➤ OPEN VS. CLOSED Funds are either open- or closed-ended. In an *open-end fund,* shares are continually available to the public at NAV. The fund's shares are always increasing or decreasing in number depending on sales to the public.

A *closed-end fund* has fixed capitalization and makes one initial issue of shares. After that it trades as a stock on the major stock exchanges or over the counter. In other words, it closes its doors to new investors, and shares can be purchased only by buying the stock. Prices are determined by supply and demand: When buyers are plentiful, the price of the stock rises, and vice versa. Depending on market conditions, the price will be above or below NAV. When a closed-end fund is selling at a discount from NAV, the investor has an opportunity to see profits from price appreciation. (See Chapter 7 for more on closed-end funds.)

➤ LOAD VS. NO-LOAD Mutual funds can also be categorized as load or no-load. *No-load funds* are sold directly by the fund and not by stockbrokers. Since no broker is involved, there is no commission, which is known as a "load" (or burden). Money market mutual funds are virtually all no-load. However, all other funds charge a management fee of about 0.5% of the fund's total assets per year. This covers the fund's administration. These expenses are paid from the fund's assets and are reflected in the price of fund shares.

Load funds are sold by stockbrokers or financial planners, who charge a commission every time you buy new shares. The highest load allowed by the National Association of Security Dealers is 8.5%. This amount is deducted from the amount of your initial investment. Thus, on a $10,000 purchase, the dollars that go to work for you are reduced by the 8.5% load to $9,150 ($10,000−$850).

§ HINT: The formula for determining the load: Subtract the net asset value from the offering price and divide the difference by the offering price. There are also *low-load funds,* which charge only 2% to 3%.

§ HINT: There is no evidence that load funds perform better than no-loads, so if you don't need help in selecting a fund, go with a no-load and save the fee. And if you plan to invest for 1 year or less, always select a no-load. One year is seldom long enough to make up an 8.5% commission.

➤ OTHER FEES Until relatively recently the choices were simple: load or no-load. But today new fees keep coming out from under the rug. Not only are there the usual fees for management and operating expenses, but there are other charges—for redeeming shares, for example. These *redemption fees,* also called back-end loads or contingent deferred sales charges, may be a flat percentage of the share price or may be based on a sliding scale, usually 6% the first year, moving down to 0% in year 6. Sometimes a redemption fee applies only to your initial investment.

Worst of all are the so-called hidden fees, which aren't even called fees. They're called *12b-1 plans,* after the SEC regulation that authorized them in 1980. Under this ruling, funds that do not have their own salespeople can deduct up to 1.25% of their assets to pay for advertising and marketing expenses. Unlike front- and back-end loads, which come directly out of your investment, 12b-1 fees are generally subtracted from the fund's assets. The only way to find out about a 12b-1 plan is in the fund's prospectus under "Distribution Charges." According to Norman Fosback, editor of the newsletter *Mutual Fund Forecaster,* any such fee over 1% is "abusive to the investor."

§ HINT: A redemption fee is slightly better from an investor's viewpoint than a sales charge, because you can earn income on that amount until you sell your shares.

HOW MUTUAL FUND SHARES ARE QUOTED

	NAV	OFFER PRICE	NAV CHANGE
Dreyfus Funds			
Cap V p	12.35	12.93	+.12
Index	17.21	NL	−.14
Interm	13.93	NL	−.02
Levge	17.63	18.46	−.14

p—distribution costs apply
NAV—net asset value
NL—no-load

SOURCE: *Wall Street Journal,* May 15, 1992.

Reloading charges are levied by a few funds on reinvestment of capital gains distributions and are described in the prospectus. The maximum is 7.25% of the total investment. For example, if you receive a capital gains distribution of $100 and you automatically reinvest these gains, the fund can retain $7.25 as a selling fee and reinvest only $92.75 in new fund shares.

➤ HOW TO READ FUND QUOTES You will find a listing of mutual funds in the financial pages of the newspaper (see the accompanying example). Funds are listed under the sponsor's name, such as Vanguard or Fidelity. The first column is the name of the fund, then the NAV, or "Bid" as it may be called. (The NAV is the price at which fund shareholders sold their shares the previous day.) The next column, "Offer Price," is the price paid by new investors the previous day. When the offer price is higher than the NAV there is a load: The difference between the NAV and the offer price is the sales commission. Funds with "NL" in the offer column are no-loads. A small "r" next to a fund's name indicates that a redemption charge may apply. Funds do not always have an "r" when they should, according to a study done recently by the American Association of Individual Investors. (Redemption fees are also called back-end loads.) The "p" denotes that a fund charges a fee from assets for marketing and distribution costs, also known as a 12b-1 plan.

$ HINT: When a distribution is made to shareholders, the NAV is reduced by the amount of the distribution per share. So, buy shares just after a distribution to save paying tax on the distributed amount. Call the fund to get exact dates.

Keep in mind that the NAV column states the price the fund will pay to buy back its shares; but from your viewpoint, it's the price at which your shares can be sold. The offer price is the price you will have to pay to buy shares in the fund.

$ HINT: Don't panic if a fund's quoted price doesn't change much over the year. You may buy shares at $10 per share and find them the same a year later. That's because 90% of income and capital gains have been distributed to shareholders. Instead, judge the fund's total performance (capital appreciation plus dividend income) as a percentage gain or loss. This figure is available by calling the fund.

FUND SERVICES

Not all funds offer all services, but here are some of the extras frequently available:

➤ AUTOMATIC REINVESTMENT This means that all dividend and capital gains disbursements will be automatically reinvested to compound your earnings. With a total average annual return of 10%, for example, your money will double in a little over 7 years. Automatic reinvestment is also a form of dollar cost averaging. By investing the same dollar amount on a regular basis, regardless of the stock's price, you buy more shares when the price is down and fewer shares when the market rises. To determine the average per-share price, add up all the prices and divide by the number of shares. Dollar cost averaging tends to reduce the average per-share price.

$ HINT: Automatic reinvestment may be a form of dollar cost averaging, but it may not always be in your best interests. Mutual funds pay their largest distributions when the stock market is relatively high. Instead of reinvesting at the high level, you may do better to take the cash and wait for the market to decline, when your cash will buy more shares.

➤ BENEFICIARY DESIGNATION You can name your beneficiary by means of a trust agreement so that your investment goes directly to your designated heir when you die, with none of the delays and expenses of probate. Consult your lawyer, because some states prohibit this transfer.

➤ REGULAR INCOME CHECKS Set up monthly or quarterly income in several ways: (1) by buying shares in several funds, each with different dividend months; (2) by arranging for regular quarterly dividends to be paid out; (3) by arranging to redeem automatically the dollar value of the number of shares you specify (there's usually a $50 minimum per month). The fund will mail a check to you monthly, quarterly, or annually.

➤ INFORMATION AND SERVICE Almost all investment companies provide toll-free numbers. You can call to learn about prices, minimum investments, charges, and types of other funds available for switching. You can also ask for forms for setting up automatic withdrawals and switching into other funds.

➤ DISTRIBUTION OF INCOME Mutual funds distribute money to investors in two ways: income dividends and capital gains distributions. *Income dividends* represent the interest and/or dividends earned by the fund's portfolio, minus the fund's expenses. *Capital gains distributions* represent a fund's net realized capital gains—when there are profits in excess of losses on the sale of the portfolio securities. Both income dividends and capital gains distributions can be reinvested in the fund automatically, usually at no cost.

Most funds operate as "regulated investment companies" so they can qualify for an exemption from corporate income taxes. A fund must meet these tests:

- Distribute at least 90% of its investment company taxable income to its shareholders each year. Thus, a shareholder receives dividends and capital gains distributions from a qualifying fund without any tax being levied on the fund. Instead, shareholders report these payments on their own tax returns.

- Distribute 97% of its income from dividends and interest and 98% of its net realized capital gains with respect to the calendar year in which they are earned or realized.

A summary of the distributions made to each shareholder annually, called a Form 1099, is sent to the shareholder and to the IRS.

TYPES OF FUNDS

Mutual funds come in all sizes, shapes, and combinations. It is extremely important that you match your personal investment objectives with those

TYPES OF MUTUAL FUNDS

FUND	OBJECTIVE
Aggressive growth funds	Seek maximum capital gains, not current income. May invest in new companies, trouble firms. Use techniques such as option writing to boost returns. Highly risky.
Balanced funds	Aim to conserve principal, generate current income, and provide long-term growth. Have portfolio mix of bonds, preferred stocks, and common stocks.
Corporate bond funds	Seek high level of income. Buy corporate bonds, some U.S. Treasury bonds or bonds issued by federal agencies.
Flexible portfolio funds	May be 100% in stocks or bonds or money market instruments. Have the greatest portfolio flexibility of all funds.
Ginnie Mae funds (GNMAs)	Invest in mortgage-backed securities. Must keep majority of portfolio in these securities.
Global bond funds	Invest in debt of companies and countries throughout the world, including the United States.
Global equity funds	Invest in securities traded worldwide, including the United States.
Growth funds	Invest in common stock of well-established companies. Capital gains, not income, is primary objective.
Growth and income funds	Invest in common stock of dividend-paying companies. Combine long-term capital gains and steady stream of income.
High-yield bond funds	Keep two-thirds of portfolio in lower-rated corporate bonds (junk bonds) to achieve high income.
Income bond funds	Invest at all times in corporate and government bonds for income.
Income equity funds	Invest in companies with good dividend-paying records.
Income mixed funds	Seek high current income by investing in equities and debt instruments.
Index funds	Buy stocks to match an index such as the S&P 500.
International funds	Invest in equity securities of companies located outside the United States.
Long-term municipal bond funds	Invest in bonds issued by states and municipalities. In most cases, income earned is not taxed by the federal government.
Money market mutual funds	Invest in short-term securities sold in the money market. Safe, relatively high yields.
Option/income funds	Seek high current return by investing in dividend-paying stocks on which call options are traded.
Precious metals/gold funds	Keep two-thirds of portfolio in securities associated with gold, silver, platinum, and other precious metals.

TYPES OF MUTUAL FUNDS (*Cont.*)

FUND	OBJECTIVE
Sector funds	Concentrate holdings in a single industry or country.
Short-term municipal bonds	Invest in municipals with short maturities; also known as tax-exempt money market funds.
Single-state municipal bond funds	Portfolios contain issues of only one state so that income is free of both federal and state taxes.
Socially conscious funds	Avoid investments in corporations known to pollute, to have poor records in hiring minorities, and to be involved in the military, tobacco, and liquor industries.
U.S. government income funds	Invest in a variety of government securities, including U.S. Treasury bonds, mortgage-backed securities, and government notes.

of the fund. The accompanying list summarizes the broad objectives and should be read carefully in order to familiarize yourself with the various terms or bits of jargon the funds use to describe what they do with your money.

Keep in mind that there are scores of other mutual funds, many of which are described in chapters relating to specific types of securities. Before you commit any money to a fund, do your homework and make certain you understand exactly what you are investing in.

HOW TO SELECT MUTUAL FUNDS

As with all types of investments, the number one factor is the competency of management, as measured by its ability to meet or surpass stated goals fairly consistently over a fairly long period of time: at least 5 and preferably 10 years.

Be wary of highly publicized, aggressively promoted funds, especially those with a "gimmick." You can judge a fund's future performance by checking the stocks shown in the last quarterly report. Watch to see if they rise or fall in price.

Study the performance in both up and down markets. Several major funds have never been first in any one year, but they do better than the market in good periods and lose less in bear markets. One of the best guides is the annual *Forbes* magazine report in the late August issue. This rates funds on the basis of performance in both rising and falling markets. To get a high score, the fund must perform consistently, in relation to other funds, in both up and down periods. Adjustments are made to prevent exceptional performance (good or bad) in any one period from having undue

---

BLUE SKY LAWS

Laws have been passed in various states to protect individual investors against securities fraud. The law requires sellers of new stocks or mutual funds to register and provide financial data, usually with the state attorney general's office. The term "blue sky law" originated when a judge reportedly said that a new stock issue was about as valuable as a patch of blue sky.

Most funds register in all states, but occasionally one will not because of excessive paperwork or delays. Always buy into a fund that is registered in the state of your legal residence.

---

influence on the fund's average performance—calculated separately for both up and down markets. Popular periodicals such as *Money*, *Your Money*, and *Forbes* also track fund performance. *Morningstar*, a weekly update of mutual funds and their performance, is the most thorough in coverage.

Here are some points to keep in mind in selecting funds:

➤ TURNOVER This shows the dollar amount of stocks sold in relation to total assets. Thus if a fund had assets of $100 million and sold $75 million in stocks in one year, the turnover would be 75%. This is high and may indicate that the fund managers are speculating for short-term profits or are not making successful choices.

$ HINT: Set a stop-loss figure, say, 10%, 15%, or 20% below current NAV. That way you'll keep your losses small, even if you misjudge market trends.

➤ YIELD VS. TOTAL RETURN It is important to know the difference between yield and total return when evaluating a fund. Yield is the income per share paid to the shareholder. It is derived from dividends and interest and is expressed as a percentage of the current offering price per share.

Total return measures the per-share change in the total value of a fund, from the beginning of the year to any given date. Total return is derived from dividend and interest income, capital gains distributions, and any unrealized capital gains or losses.

➤ SIZE The larger the assets of a mutual fund, the smaller the amount each investor pays for administration.

Stay away from funds whose assets have been under $50 million for over 10 years. If a fund hasn't grown, its performance must have been so poor that new shares could not be widely sold.

Conversely, when a fund becomes huge, there's a tendency for the managers to confine their investments to a relatively few major corporations that have millions of shares outstanding. In order not to upset the market, large commitments must be purchased or sold over a period of time and so may not always be traded at the most advantageous prices. (A fund with $2 billion is regarded as medium in size. Fidelity's Magellan Fund has assets of $19 billion.)

LOW-COST FUND FAMILIES

FUND	EXPENSE RATIO
Vanguard	0.45%
Dreyfus	0.71
Federated	0.73
Merrill Lynch	0.74
USAA	0.78
T. Rowe Price	0.92

Some lack of agility makes it difficult for major funds to beat the averages. In a sense, they are the market. By contrast, smaller funds can score welcome gains if they pick three or four winners. But large funds are likely to be more consistent in their returns.

➤ COST Some funds, like some people, are more frugal than others. According to a study by Financial Planning Information of Cambridge, Massachusetts, several fund families have lower than average expenses. Although frugality should not be more important than performance in selecting a fund, begin your search by reviewing the information in Chapter 7.

THE PROSPECTUS

You must read the prospectus before investing in a fund. Although it may appear formidable at first glance, a half-hour with this step-by-step guide will crystallize the entire process and enlighten you about the fund. Here's what to look for:

- What the fund's investment objectives are. These will be spelled out at the beginning.
- A risk factor statement.
- What strategies will be used to meet the fund's stated goals.
- The degree of diversification. How many issues does it hold?
- What is the portfolio turnover? A low rate, below 75%, reflects a long-term holding philosophy, whereas a high rate indicates an aggressive strategy.
- Fees and expenses. Check in particular the cost of redeeming shares, which should not exceed 1% per year.
- Rules for switching within a family of funds and fees, if any.
- Restrictions. Will the fund sell securities short, act as an underwriter, engage in selling commodities or real estate? What percentage of total assets is invested in any one security? Be wary of a fund that is not adequately diversified.
- How much the fund has gained or lost over 1, 5, and 10 years.

FOUR AGGRESSIVE GROWTH FUNDS

ASSETS MIL.$	FUND	5-YEAR TOTAL RETURN TO 12/31/91	TELEPHONE
$ 224	Founders Special	143%	1-800-525-2440
2,993	Janus Fund	152	1-800-525-3713
403	Oppenheimer Time Fund	104	1-800-525-7048
205	Sit New Beginning Growth	154	1-800-332-5580

Other findings: International and precious metals funds usually have the highest expense ratios and fixed-income funds the lowest.

$ HINT: To determine any fund's expense ratio: divide operating expenses (management's fees, etc.) by the average net assets.

FUND NAMES AND CATEGORIES

In May 1992, the *Wall Street Journal* and *Morningstar, Inc.,* a mutual fund evaluative service (similar to *Value Line* for stocks), questioned the widespread practice in the mutual fund industry of using misleading names, making it difficult for investors to judge the purpose and risk level of a fund. In other words, some funds claim one style of investing while practicing another. Their wish to be ranked number one in the performance rankings published by Lipper and others has apparently led to this trend. For instance, an aggressive growth fund may call itself "balanced" or "equity income" when in reality it is aggressive.

Investors willing to spend a little time sorting out this issue will be well rewarded. The key comparison to make is that of the P/E ratio. (See 360–362 for details on the P/E ratio.) The Standard & Poor P/E, listed regularly in the financial press, gives the average P/E at which stocks are currently selling. As we went to press it was 19. This figure can be used as a rough benchmark: stocks selling around 19 are considered average; those under 19 conservative and those over 19 more growth oriented and

---

THREE WINNING FUNDS

Balanced or total return stock funds that seek both dividends and capital gains have outdistanced the average equity fund in recent months.

- Wellington (1-800-662-7447)   23.7% 1991 return
- Fidelity Balanced (1-800-544-8888)   26.8% 1991 return
- Lindner Dividend (1-314-727-5305)   27.4% 1991 return

---

speculative. The key then is to find out the mutual fund's price/earnings ratio. If it's way above the S & P average, then it's an aggressive fund, no matter what its stated category. For example, the 20th Century Balanced Investors Fund officially calls itself a balanced fund, yet its P/E ratio in May 1922 was 33, hardly balanced. To obtain any fund's P/E ratio, call the fund; you may have to be aggressive to get it, but if you're concerned, do it. If that fails, read about the fund in *Morningstar*, available at most libraries and brokerage firms.

FOUR THINGS YOU CAN LEARN FROM YOUR MUTUAL FUND STATEMENT

1   *What you own*. When you own shares in a fund, you also own a portfolio of individual securities. The fund provides a snapshot of its holdings as of the statement date. If it's a stock fund, you'll find the actual names of the stocks you owned on the statement date.

2   *How well it's performing*. The section with "Per Share Data" shows the change in the fund's market value by giving the price of a fund share, usually called the "net asset value," for the beginning and end of the reporting period. The section called "Distributions to Shareholders" includes both dividend income and capital gains distributions.

$ HINT: To figure the total return, take the amount of the distributions to shareholders and add the amount of share price gain, or subtract the amount of share price loss, during the period. To get the total return as a percentage, divide the result by the share price at the beginning of the period.

3   *How much it cost*. A summary of expenses is found in the "Statement of Operations." This includes the fee paid to the fund's management company as well as other expenses to operate the fund.

$ HINT: To see how these expenses affected your investment, multiply the value of your shares, found in "Per Share Data," by the expense ratio. For example, if total expenses were 1.3% and your shares were worth $5,000, you paid $65 for one year of your fund's services.

4   *Do other investors like this fund*? In the "Notes to Financial Statements" there is a section called "Capital Share Transaction" that shows the amount of fund shares purchased and sold, expressed in both dollars and number of shares.

Mutual fund statements reflect history. Since it takes a month or so to prepare, audit, print, and mail these statements, they are not right up to the minute.

$ HINT: If there's anything you don't understand, call your fund and ask for the answer. It's a competitive business, and most funds are service oriented, even on the telephone.

TAXES AND MUTUAL FUNDS

Each time you touch your mutual fund shares there are tax implications that must be reported to the IRS, including these:

■ When you switch from one fund to another within a family, the IRS considers this a sale in one fund and a purchase in another. You must report your profit or loss.

■ When your fund earns dividends and taxable interest and passes them on to you, you must pay taxes on this distribution.

■ When your dividends are automatically reinvested in more shares, you must report this as dividend income.

■ When there are capital gains distributions, these must also be reported.

For further information, read IRS booklet No. 564, "Mutual Fund Distributions," and contact T. Rowe Price for a free copy of "Calculating Taxes on Mutual Funds," 100 East Pratt Street, Baltimore, MD 21202; 1-800-638-5660.

$ HINT: If you buy shares in a fund just prior to its annual earnings distribution, you will be taxed on this distribution even though the value of your new shares drops to reflect this distribution. Buy just after distribution.

TAX-FREE FUNDS

Should you be in a tax-free mutual fund? To compute how much you need to earn on a taxable investment to equal a tax-free one, use the following formula:

$$\frac{\text{tax-exempt yield}}{1 \text{ minus your tax bracket}} = \text{equivalent yield of a taxable investment}$$

For example, if you're in the 28% tax bracket and a tax-exempt bond is yielding 10%, you would have to receive a yield of 13.8% on a taxable investment to be equivalent:

$$\frac{.10}{1 - .28} = .138$$

In the 31% bracket, a tax-exempt bond yielding 7% is the equivalent of a 10.14% yield on a taxable investment:

$$\frac{.07}{1 - .31} = .1014 = 10.14\%$$

$ HINT: In all states, dividends from U.S. Treasury money funds or bond funds are also tax-free, even though you have to pay federal tax on them. And you may be eligible for a foreign tax credit if you own a mutual fund that invests in stocks or securities of foreign corporations. Watch for an indication on your 1099-DIV form of foreign tax paid on your behalf.

MARKET TIMERS

The continuing popularity of mutual funds has given birth to an interesting side industry—market timers. The majority are publishers of newsletters who also offer, at additional cost, hotline telephone services that update their published recommendations. Subscribers are given a special number.

There are two basic systems: (1) timers who actually designate specific mutual funds and (2) timers who let you do the fund selection. Timers focus primarily on the stock market, although some deal with bonds, gold, international funds, and commodities.

EVALUATING THE TIMERS

In deciding whether or not to use a timer, take a long-term position. Hulbert's *Financial Digest* says that since 1980, when the publication began following timers, about 50% of the time they have beaten the various averages. Too much short-term switching runs up transaction costs, and even if you use no-load funds, you may run into an obstacle: Many have imposed limits on the number of switches you can make each year.

TIMERS VS. THE MARKET

A study done recently by United & Babson Investment Co. concluded that during the past 40 years, stocks went up in 26, were even in 3, and fell in 11. Translated into action that suggests two rules of thumb: (1) ride out the bear markets, and (2) stick to the time-honored buy-and-hold theory. That doesn't mean you should ignore your investments, but it does indicate that in certain cycles, timers have to be very good to beat the market. And you must select as good a timer as you do a stockbroker or even individual funds. In the final analysis, there is no magical, surefire, winning system.

EASY ALTERNATIVE: DOLLAR COST AVERAGING

A simple and widely used alternative to following a professional timer is dollar cost averaging. This involves regularly investing a set dollar amount in a fund—say, $150 to $500 per month. This system provides a steady

---

BUYING ON MARGIN

If you're an aggressive trader, you can buy mutual funds on margin. You must pay 50% of the total cost of your transaction up front. The rest you borrow from your broker. Before doing so, see pages 265–267 on how a margin account works, and beware of the pitfalls.

Among the brokerage firms offering mutual fund shares on margin are these:

- Charles Schwab & Co. (1-800-435-4000)
- Jack White (1-800-233-3411)
- Quick & Reilly (1-800-221-5220; 1-800-522-8712 in NY)

LEADING FUND TIMERS

	ANNUAL FEE
Fund Exchange Report (1-800-423-4893)	$ 99
Investors Intelligence (1-914-632-0422)	156
Marketarian Letter (1-800-658-4325)	175
Dow Theory Letters (1-619-454-0481)	250
Elliot Wave Theorist (1-800-336-1618)	233
Investech Mutual Fund Advisor (1-800-955-8500)	175

way to save, and it also means you must buy when the market is down, thereby pushing down your average cost per share. You buy more shares for each dollar invested. Many funds will automatically transfer money from your bank account to the fund every month. Let's say you put $100 into a mutual fund every 3 months. The shares sell at $10 per share. You invest $100 and receive 10 shares. Then the market drops. You invest your $100 the next quarter, and at $5 per share you receive 20 shares. The next quarter the market returns and your fund is again selling at $10 per share, so you now receive 10 shares for your $100. *The bottom line:* You own 40 shares after a total investment of $300. However, with an ending market price of $10 per share, your shares are actually worth more than you paid for them.

$ HINT: For a free brochure on "Dollar Cost Averaging," contact T. Rowe Price Associates, 100 East Pratt Street, Baltimore, MD 21202; 1-800-638-5660.

HOW DOLLAR COST AVERAGING PAYS OFF

	REGULAR INVESTMENT	SHARE PRICE	SHARES ACQUIRED
	$100	$10	10
	100	5	20
	100	10	10
TOTAL	$300	$25	40

Average share cost: $7.50 ($300 ÷ 40)
Average share price: $8.33 ($25 ÷ 3)

BOSTON COLLEGE'S PORTFOLIO MODEL

Boston College, with its $327 million endowment, uses seven advisory firms to manage its money. Its low-risk portfolio earns at least 10% a year versus 7.4% for the average college endowment. Individuals can invest in mutual funds run by four of the school's advisors:

- Gabelli Asset (Mario Gabelli)   1-800-422-3354
- Mutual Beacon (Peter Lynch)   1-800-553-3014
- Putnam Convertible Income/Growth (Tony Kreisel)   1-800-225-1581
- Enterprise Capital Appreciation (Jeff Miller)   1-800-432-4320

SECTOR FUNDS

If you're confident about what industry or industries will do well during 1993 and 1994, consider a sector fund, one that invests in a single industry. Keep in mind, however, that although such funds offer greater profit potential than broader-based funds, they're also far riskier. This risk factor is reflected in their great price volatility.

☐CAUTION:

- Stocks in a given group tend to fall in unison.
- Most sector funds stay fully invested or nearly so even when their industry has a slide. They are less likely to switch portfolios into Treasuries or cash equivalents. Select a fund that's part of a family of funds so you can switch out when your industry turns sour.
- It's difficult to use past performance to predict future performance in this group.

TYPES OF SECTOR FUNDS

Agriculture	International
Chemicals	Leisure
Computers	Precious metals/gold
Defense/aerospace	Real estate
Energy	Service
Environment	Socially responsible
Financial services	Technology
Foreign countries	Transportation
Health care	Utilities

- Read one or two of the newsletters listed at the end of this chapter, plus *Value Line Investment Survey* and Standard & Poor's *Outlook* to keep up to date on industry developments.

$ HINT: Limit your investment in sector funds to 10%. Since they focus on one economic area, you'll reduce your chances for loss if that particular sector experiences a downturn.

INVESTING IN GOOD CAUSES

Earth Day, held in April, heightens the country's awareness of the urgent need to save our environment, specifically, the importance of developing better methods of energy conservation, waste management, and pollution control. Wall Street offers ways to invest in the emerging business of environmental housecleaning.

➤ SOCIALLY RESPONSIBLE MUTUAL FUNDS Socially responsible investing is not a new phenomenon. Several such mutual funds have been around for years, but they're now getting more attention. The goals of these funds range from avoiding firms that deal in liquor, tobacco, or military weapons to championing the environment. Others look for companies that are involved in community development and low-income housing projects.

The granddaddy of socially responsible investing, *The Pax World Fund* of Portsmouth, New Hampshire, is a balanced stock and bond fund that was started in 1971. The fund, which has $326 million in assets, will not buy companies in the liquor, tobacco, or gambling industries, and it emphasizes health care and education stocks. For the 12 months that ended in March 1992, it was up 10.5%.

The Dreyfus Third Century, started a year later in 1972, is a much larger fund with $424 million in assets. It invests in companies that protect or improve the environment, that make careful use of our natural resources, and that are involved in occupational health and safety and consumer protection. All companies must be equal opportunity employers. Dreyfus will, however, invest in firms with military sales. For the 10-year period through March 1992, the fund chalked up an annual return rate of 14.61%.

The Parnassus Fund in San Francisco was named for a sacred Greek mountain overlooking the oracle at Delphi. It follows a contrarian philosophy, investing only in stocks that are out of favor with the investment community. Among the factors used in building its portfolio: Companies must produce a product or service of high quality, be sensitive to the communities where it operates, and treat its employees fairly and well.

The Calvert Social Investment Fund invests in companies that make quality products and environmentally responsible goods. They must be equal opportunity employers, promote women and minorities, and provide safe workplaces. The fund will not buy companies primarily engaged in the production of nuclear energy or weapons systems, or those doing business in South Africa.

The nine funds operated by *The Pioneer Group* rule out investments in liquor, tobacco, or gambling.

SOCIALLY RESPONSIBLE EQUITY FUNDS

FUND	TELEPHONE	TOTAL RETURN/1991
Calvert Social Investment	1-800-368-2748	21.73%
Dreyfus Third Century	1-800-645-6561	38.06
Parnassus Fund	1-800-999-3505	52.00
Pax World Fund	1-800-767-1729	20.08
Pioneer Fund (stocks)		22.75
Pioneer II (stocks)		25.75
Pioneer III (stocks)	1-800-225-6292	36.46
Pioneer Bond Fund		15.54
Pioneer Muni Bond Fund		11.17
Pioneer U.S. Government Trust		12.03

SOCIALLY RESPONSIBLE MONEY MARKET FUNDS

FUND	TELEPHONE	YIELD AS OF APRIL 1992
Calvert Money Market Fund	1-800-368-2748	3.58%
Pioneer Cash Reserves		3.40
Pioneer U.S. Government	1-800-225-6292	3.44
Pioneer Tax-Free Money Fund		2.79
Working Assets Money Fund	1-800-533-3863	3.38

➤ SOCIALLY RESPONSIBLE MONEY MARKET FUNDS In addition to these stock funds, there are several socially responsible money market funds for those who want a parking place for their cash. The largest, *Working Assets Money Fund,* was started in 1983 with $100,000 by a group of 8 Bay Area people interested in educating the public on social issues. It invests in money market instruments that help finance housing, small businesses, family farms, higher education, and certain types of energy.

INDEX FUNDS

It's not easy to beat the various market indexes year after year, but if you want to bet on the averages, you can do so with an index fund. These funds buy the same securities that make up an index, and therefore their performance mirrors that of the index, such as the S&P 500, the S&P 100, the NASDAQ 100, the Wilshire 5000, or the Small Cap Index. One fund even buys the Morgan Stanley's Europe, Australia, Far East Index. Many institutional investors subscribe to the efficient market theory that trying to surpass the averages is not possible in the long run. These funds, on the other hand, at least keep pace with the market.

☐ CAUTION: If the market declines, so will the value of your shares.

These funds provide excellent diversification and, of course, you know exactly what stocks you're invested in at all times.

INDEX MUTUAL FUNDS

FUND	TELEPHONE
Colonial Funds (load)	1-800-426-3750

International Equity Index (5.75%)
(Morgan Stanley's Europe, Australia, Far East
Index)

Small Stock Index Trust (5.75%)
(smallest companies on the NYSE)

U.S. Equity Index (5.75%)
(S&P 500 Index)

Gateway Option Index Plus (no-load)	1-800-354-6339

(S&P 100 Index)

Principal Preservation S&P 100+ (4.5%)	1-800-826-4600

(S&P 100 Index)

Rushmore Funds (5 redemptions/year)	1-800-343-3355

OTC Index Plus (no-load)
(NASDAQ 100 Index)

Stock Market Index Fund (no-load)
(S&P 100 Index)

Vanguard Funds ($10 annual fee)	1-800-662-7447

Bond Market Fund (no-load)
(Salomon Bros. Broad Investment-Grade
Bond Index)

S&P Index-500 (no-load)
(S&P 500 Index)

Extended Market Portfolio (no-load)
(Wilshire 4500 Index)

Sheldon Jacobs, publisher of the *No-Load Fund Investor*, says that there are two criteria for selecting an index fund: (1) pick the lowest cost and (2) pick one that is tracking an index you think will be a top performer.

WHEN TO SELL YOUR MUTUAL FUND

Unquestionably, the toughest decision mutual fund investors face is when to sell. It's particularly difficult when the market and your fund are doing well. Here are some objective sell signals. Consider selling if:

- The portfolio manager quits
- The economy shifts
- The fund's performance ranks in the bottom fifth of funds of its type for over a year

A FUND IS NOT FOREVER

You revise your stock and bond portfolios; you should do the same with mutual funds. They should be evaluated periodically and weeded out. No fund is perfect for your needs forever. Switch out of a fund when:

- The market shifts dramatically. Equity funds generally suffer during bear markets. Bond funds tend to be hurt when interest rates rise. You can't hope to avoid short-term corrections, but plan to miss the longer-term ones.
  1. Switch from stocks to money market funds at the beginning of a bear market.
  2. As a bull market begins, move into conservative blue chip funds.
  3. As the bull begins to roar, put more dollars into aggressive growth funds.
  4. When interest rates rise, put cash into money market funds.
- Your fund lags the market averages, such as the S&P 500.
- Your fund consistently underperforms other similar funds.

- Your investment objectives change
- Your stock fund gets too big or more than doubles in size

WHEN A MUTUAL FUND MANAGER LEAVES

Just when you've found a fund that's making money, the portfolio manager suddenly leaves to run another fund. Do you stay or follow him to his new

NEW, CREATIVE FUNDS

These funds, which started up in late 1991 and early 1992, aren't old enough to have established a long-term track record, but their investment philosophies are intriguing. Track performance carefully before buying shares.

FUND	TYPE	TELEPHONE
Dreyfus Edison Electric Index	Electric utilities index	1-800-373-938
Gabelli Equity Income	High-yielding stocks	1-800-422-355
Janus Worldwide	International stocks	1-800-525-371
Montgomery Emerging Markets	Emerging country stocks	1-800-428-187
Strong Insured Municipal Bond	Insured municipal bonds	1-800-368-386
T. Rowe Price Japan	Japanese stocks	1-800-638-566
Vanguard Total Stock Market	Wilshire 5000 index	1-800-257-999

home? Generally you're all right to stay put, at least for 6 months, during which time you can see how the new manager is performing. This is particularly true if switching means paying high redemption fees. If it's a money market fund or an index fund, the manager has relatively little to do with performance so there's no need to change. However, consider following the manager to his or her new fund after 6 to 12 months if:

1   its investment goals match yours;
2   your current fund, under the new manager, is underperforming in its category 6 to 12 months after the changeover;
3   the new manager revises the fund's strategies so it no longer fits your needs—it becomes too conservative or too aggressive, for example.

FOR FURTHER INFORMATION

GENERAL DIRECTORIES

Individual Investor's Guide to No-Load Mutual Funds
American Association of Individual Investors
625 North Michigan Avenue
Chicago, IL 60611
1-312-280-0170

An annual guide with evaluative data on 500 funds; $24.95.

Donoghue's Mutual Fund Almanac
Donoghue Organization
P.O. Box 91004
Ashland, MA 01721
1-508-429-5930 (in MA); 1-800-343-5413

Annual with data on more than 2,100 funds; $31.95 + $3 shipping.

The Handbook for No-Load Fund Investors
P.O. Box 283
Hastings-on-Hudson, NY 10706
1-914-693-7420; 1-800-252-2042

An annual directory with useful ideas on how to pick a no-load fund; $49.

Wiesenberger's Investment Companies
CDA/Wiesenberger Investment Companies Service
210 South Street
Boston, MA 02111
1-800-232-2285
$395

Mutual Fund Fact Book
Publications Division
Investment Company Institute
1600 M Street NW, Suite 600
Washington, DC 20036
1-202-293-7700
$15

BOOKS AND PAMPHLETS

Warren Boroson, *Keys to Investing in Mutual Funds* (Hauppauge, NY: Barron's Educational Publishing, Inc., 1992), $4.95.

Sheldon Jacobs, *How to Pick the Best No-Load Mutual Funds for Solid Growth and Safety* (Homewood, IL: Business One Irwin, 1992), $12.95.

The pamphlets below are free from:
Publications Division
Investment Company Institute
1600 M Street NW, Suite 600
Washington, DC 20036
1-202-293-7700

A Close Look at Closed-End Funds
What Is a Mutual Fund?
Discipline: Dollar Cost Averaging

NEWSLETTERS

The No-Load Fund Investor
P.O. Box 283
Hastings-on-Hudson, NY 10706
1-800-252-2042

A monthly analysis of the no-load funds; $105.

No-Load Fund X
235 Montgomery Street, Suite 662
San Francisco, CA 94104
1-415-986-7979; 1-800-323-1510

Monthly; lists top performers by investment goals; $114.

Mutual Fund Forecaster
3471 North Federal Highway
Fort Lauderdale, FL 33306
1-305-563-9000; 1-800-327-6720

Monthly; ranks funds by risk and profit potential; $100.

Mutual Fund Letter
680 North Lake Shore Drive
Tower Suite 2038
Chicago, IL 60611
1-312-649-6940

Monthly; excellent evaluation of mutual funds and various industries; $120.

Telephone Switch Newsletter
2100 Main Street
Huntington Beach, CA 92647
1-714-536-1931; 1-800-950-8765

Monthly; gives timing and switching advice; $137.

United Mutual Fund Selector
Babson-United Investment Advisors, Inc.
101 Prescott Street
Wellesley Hills, MA 02181
1-617-235-0900

Twice a month; tracks major funds; $125 annually.

Sector Fund Newsletter
P.O. Box 270048
San Diego, CA 92198
1-619-748-0805

Bimonthly; tracks the sector funds; $157.

For sampling of newsletters:

Select Information Exchange
244 West 54th Street
New York, NY 10019
1-212-247-7123

SIE is a financial publications subscription agency providing a group of trial subscriptions to various investment newsletters. One trial group comprises 25 different mutual fund services for $19.

The Clean Yield Newsletter
Box 1880
Greensboro Bend, VT 05842
1-802-533-7178
Monthly; $85/year

Written for concerned individual investors and financial professionals, this stock market newsletter profiles 2 stocks per month and updates 8 others. It screens companies for their environmental practices and weapons production and presents a monthly model stock portfolio.

The Social Investment Forum
430 First Avenue North
Suite 290
Minneapolis, MN 55401
1-612-333-8338

Associated membership in this nonprofit coalition that promotes ethical investing is $65. Membership includes the *Forum Guide*, which provides information on mutual funds, money managers, newsletters, and organizations involved in ethical investing.

7

USING CLOSED-END FUNDS

Many investors shy away from closed-end funds because they simply don't understand how they work. Yet overlooking them means missing a good investment opportunity. Closed-end funds, also called Publicly Traded Investment Companies, are similar to open-end mutual funds, described in the previous chapter. Officially, both are investment companies: companies that invest in various securities for their shareholders—individuals and institutions—having a common investment objective. They provide their shareholders with professional management through money managers who decide what to buy and sell, and when. Most open-end and closed-end funds reduce the risk to investors through diversification, by holding a wide range of securities that meet the fund's investment goal.

However, there are some very major differences between open-end mutual funds and closed-end funds:

- Unlike open-end mutual funds, which issue new shares for new investors and buy back or redeem shares from existing investors when they want to leave the fund, closed-end funds, with very rare exceptions, issue a set number of shares only once. Then, after the initial public offering (IPO), the fund is "closed," hence its name. The fund shares are traded on one of the major stock exchanges or over the counter, like regular stocks. That is why they are sometimes called "publicly traded" funds.

- Fund shares cannot be purchased directly from the fund itself as is the case with an open-end, no-load mutual fund. Instead, they are bought and sold through a broker and you pay a commission, just as you do when trading most other securities.

- Because they are traded on the exchanges, their shares fluctuate in price based upon demand, just as with any stock.

- Closed-end funds have a different price structure from open-end funds. Open-end fund prices are based on their net asset value (NAV)—the fund's investment portfolio divided by the total number of shares outstanding. The open-end fund's portfolio value changes daily, based on prevailing market conditions. The number of shares in open-end mutual funds fluctuates daily, depending on shareholder sales and purchases.

Although the price of closed-end funds is also based upon supply and demand in the marketplace, the price changes occur regardless of the NAV per share. In fact, the price of a closed-end fund's shares may sell at a premium to or a discount from its NAV, depending upon investor interest in the fund. It depends upon investor sentiment and it moves independently of the portfolio value. When buyers of the fund outnumber sellers, the price rises, and when sellers outnumber buyers, the price declines.

For example, if a fund has a NAV per share of $15, based on the current value of its portfolio, but is priced at $12, it is selling at a 20% discount. Or, to look at it another way, when a share of a closed-end fund is selling at a 20% discount, every $12 invested in a share puts $15 in assets to work for you.

- The NAV for each fund, its weekly closing share price as well as its premium or discount from NAV (expressed as a percentage), are listed once a week in the financial press. However, closing share prices are quoted daily on the stock exchange. (See box on page 101.)

TYPES OF CLOSED-END FUNDS

- Balanced funds. These invest in common and preferred stocks and bonds. Because they are so diversified, they are usually more conservative than common stock funds.
- Closed-end bond funds invest in a range of bonds, including high quality corporates, low-rated or junk bonds. Some invest only in U.S. government bonds, municipal bonds, or bonds of foreign governments. As with any fixed-income investment, the price of closed-end bond funds move in opposite directions from interest rates. They also offer the liquidity of holding a security listed on an exchange, plus professional management at relatively low costs. Examples: 1838 Bond-Debenture Fund, Montgomery Street Fund, Fort Dearborn Income Fund.

$ HINT: Two government bond funds that have high yields yet have relatively safe portfolios are given in the box below.

- Closed-end convertible bond funds have portfolios that consist of bonds that can be converted into common stock (see box). Convertibles offer relatively high yields in comparison to some other investments, plus they have a potential for capital gains.
- Closed-end stock funds, sometimes referred to as equity funds, invest primarily in common stocks, although some may hold cash or bonds under certain conditions. They also may specialize in stocks of an industry, such as the Duff & Phelps Select Utilities Fund, or be more general in approach such as the Gabelli Equity Fund or Blue Chip Value Fund.
- Specialty or single country funds are a type of closed-end stock fund that specializes in stocks of a given country or geographical area, such as the New Germany Fund, the Asia Pacific Fund, or the Irish Investment Fund.
- Dual-Purpose Funds. These funds have two classes of shares. The income shares are entitled to all of the dividends or interest earned. The capital shares receive all capital gains. Dual-purpose funds usually end 10 to 15 years after being launched. When they are terminated, income shares are redeemed at a specific price. Owners of capital shares divide up the fund's remaining assets, either by liquidating the

---

GOVERNMENT CLOSED-END BOND FUNDS

- ACM Government Income Fund   NYSE:ACG   Price: $10¾
  Yield: 8.9%
      Portfolio consists primarily of U.S. government and agency debt
  and some foreign government debt. Managed by Alliance Capital of
  New York.
- Putnam Intermediate Government Income Trust   NYSE:PGT   Price:
  $8⅞   Yield: 8.1%
      Has most assets in U.S. government securities, some in debt of
  foreign governments, and cash. (May 1992).

---

fund or by converting it to an open-end status and permitting
investors to sell shares at NAV.

YOUR RETURN

There are three basic kinds of return for investors in
closed-end funds:

- *Dividend income.* Funds receive interest and dividend income from
  the securities in their portfolios. This income, minus fund operating
  costs, is distributed to shareholders as dividends.
- *Capital gains distributions.* Most funds buy and sell portfolio securities
  throughout the year. If a net gain is realized from these sales, most
  funds pay all or most of this money to shareholders as a capital gains
  distribution.
- *Capital gains.* If you sell shares in the fund for more than you paid
  for them, you then make your own capital gain through the sale.

PROS AND CONS

➤ ADVANTAGES There are two key advantages to closed-end funds: (1)
Since the portfolio managers are not involved in buying and selling in order
to accommodate new investors or old investors selling shares, they can trade
at times they deem best and not upon investor demand. (2) Shares can often
be purchased at a price that is below NAV, apparently because the public
mistakenly feels that fixed capitalization limits management's ability to
take advantage of profitable market opportunities. If you buy at a discount
and the NAV rises, you'll have a profit. For example, if a fund has a net
asset value per share of $15, but based on the current value of its portfolio,
it is priced at $12, it is selling at a 20% discount. To look at it another way,
when a fund is selling at a 20% discount, every $12 invested puts $15 in
assets to work for you.

With income funds, the yield is determined by dividing the annual
dividend by the price of the stock. Thus if the dividend is $1 and shares
with a $10 NAV are selling at $9, that $1 dividend yields 11.1%.

CHECKING CLOSED-END FUND PRICES

The *Wall Street Journal* has two categories for closed-end funds. One is called "closed-end bond funds" and the other "publicly traded funds."

PUBLICLY TRADED FUNDS

FUND NAME	STOCK EXCHANGE	N.A. VALUE	STOCK PRICE	% DIFF.
Diversified Common Stock Funds				
Adams Express	NYSE	19.63	19	−3.21
Blue Chip Value	NYSE	7.81	7⅞	+0.83
Zweig Fund	NYSE	11.20	12⅞	+14.96
Specialized Equity and Convertible Funds				
American Capital Conv	NYSE	21.97	19	−13.52
Austria Fund	NYSE	9.34	8⅜	−10.33
Duff & Phelps Utility	NYSE	9.22	10	+8.46
Petrol & Resources	NYSE	27.48	25½	−7.21

CLOSED-END BOND FUNDS

FUND NAME	STOCK EXCHANGE	N.A. VALUE	STOCK PRICE	% DIFF.
Bond Funds				
1838 Bond-Deb Trade	NYSE	21.47	23¼	+8.29
MFS Special Value	NYSE	14.95	16½	+7.86
First Commonwealth	NYSE	14.26	14¾	+3.44
Global Income Plus	NYSE	9.79	9¾	−0.41
Dreyfus NY Muni Income	AMEX	9.76	9⅞	+1.18
Nuveen CA Muni Income	NYSE	11.99	12⅞	+7.38

SOURCE: Wall Street Journal, May 15, 1992.

➤ DISADVANTAGES Keep in mind that the value of closed-end fund shares often moves quite independently of the value of the securities in the portfolio. This may lead to shares trading at a discount to NAV, a distinct disadvantage if you are selling.

FOR FURTHER INFORMATION

Investor's Guide to Closed-End Funds
Thomas J. Herzfeld Advisors
Box 161465
Miami, FL 33116
1-305-271-1900

$325/year or $60 for 2-month trial

Monthly

Also publishes: *The Annual Encyclopedia of Closed-End Funds,* which has one page each on over 300 funds; $140 for the 1992–1993 edition.

The Value Line Investment Survey (available at most libraries and brokerage offices) reports on 40 closed-end funds.

THE INVESTOR'S ALMANAC

Do you love to rummage through flea markets and antique shops and visit auctions? Or perhaps you're looking for an exciting, less traditional way to spend your bonus, small inheritance, or profit from sale of a stock.

There are endless numbers of "offbeat" investment choices if you are willing to be experimental. The Investor's Almanac highlights three of the most timely such choices. These do not come with a guarantee that you'll make a huge killing, but you certainly will have fun learning about a new field, and, of course, you may see a solid return on your investment over the long term.

Before you invest in any one of the three Investor's Almanac selections, spend some time doing background preparation. A suggested reading list is provided. If you know experts in these areas, ask them for advice and additional suggestions. In terms of collectibles in general:

- **Buy only what you like.** If later on the value should fall or if you decide to sell only part of your collection and keep this particular item, you should be left with something you cherish.
- **Focus on something.** Random collecting tends to be less valuable over the years. Decide on an art form or category. Then try to specialize in an artist, period, craftsman, or country. Unrelated individual pieces have less marketability than a cohesive collection.
- **Set aside a limited dollar amount.** You can revise this amount annually. Don't take all your money out of your money market fund or sell your IBM stock to move into exotic investments. If you should suddenly need cash when everything you have is tied up in baseball cards, farmland, or estate jewelry, you will be forced to sell, and if at the time

prices are low, you will have made a poor investment decision. It's always best to diversify.
- **Buy in your price range.** If your resources are modest to start with, begin small. As circumstances and finances improve, you can always go after more elaborate and expensive items. It is unwise to take a second mortgage to make your first purchase.

HOW TO PROTECT YOURSELF

Many collectibles, including the model trains, furniture, and marbles described on the following pages, are found at antique shops, galleries, through dealers, and at shows and flea markets. When you buy from these sources, you have enough time to study each object. But when making a bid at an auction, the gavel swings fast and decisions must be made almost instantly. In this pressurized atmosphere, keep these points in mind to protect yourself from "auction fever" and buy the right thing at the right price.

➤ DO YOUR HOMEWORK Study up on the item. Know the price range.

➤ READ THE CATALOG Purchase the catalog in advance of the auction. It will give dollar estimates as well as a description of the items for sale. During the auction, write down what each item sold for and use these figures as price guidelines in the future.

➤ ATTEND THE PREVIEW Study the lots on display and make notes in the catalog regarding their size, age, condition, etc. Take a pen, pad of paper, small flashlight, magnifying glass, and a tape measure with you. At the preview open drawers, look for cracks, plug in lamps, look for identifying marks, signatures, initials, etc.

➤ MAKE A LIST OF THE ITEMS YOU REALLY WANT A list will help you avoid auction fever and buying everything in sight.

Then, at the auction:

- After registering, you will be given a number and something to bid with, most likely a paddle.

- Next, find out what the incremental dollar amounts are. Some auctioneers move up by $10; others by $100. Ask, or check in the catalog.

- If you don't want your bidding noticed, sit either near the front, a little to the side so you can see others bidding, or in the back rows.

- Listen to the bidding terminology. "Silver looking" is NOT the same as "sterling silver." Wait to place a bid after you have become at ease with the auctioneer's patter. Know if you are bidding by the piece or by the lot.

- Get a feel for the timing of the auction. The most important items are generally brought out toward the middle of the sale, when the crowd is largest and has been "warmed up." After the major items have been sold, the crowd may thin out, leaving less competition for the remaining items. This is an excellent time to bid, provided, of course, the items you're interested in have not been auctioned off.

- Never be the first to bid on an item you want. Auctioneers often set an arbitrary opening price which may turn out to be artificially high. If so, it will drop in price if there are no bidders. Watch who else is bidding. You certainly want to avoid bidding against yourself. Bid as you sense the price rising or when it's near the top.

2 *Policy on reserves.* Although all items are sold to the highest bidder, in practice it may be somewhat different. Some lots have a "reserve" or minimum price. If a lot does not actually bring this price, it can be withdrawn. Some auction houses use an "R" to designate that a lot has a reserve price.

3 *Descriptive statements.* These are usually given to aid the bidder if the piece is by a well-known artist, craftsman, or designer. Be aware of such phrases as "attributed to" and "in the school of," which indicate that the experts are not absolutely certain that the work is indeed by a certain person.

4 *Descriptive information.* Catalogs often tell the style, patterns, colors, ounces, measurements. The term "style" may signal a reproduction. For example, a Queen Anne table means the piece is from the chronological period of Queen Anne; on the other hand, a Queen Anne Style chair means it is a reproduction of that style and may have been made yesterday.

5 *Guarantees or warranties.* Catalogs are not perfect. Neither are experts and appraisers. If you purchase an item described as silver and it turns out to be silver plate, or mahogany that is really walnut, you may have a claim against the auction house.

6 *Presale estimates.* Estimates represent the auctioneer's opinion based on the current market. If you're interested in an item and it seems way above your price limit, don't despair. The estimate may be too high or interested people may not show up at the auction—any number of circumstances can reduce that sale price.

DECIPHERING AUCTION CATALOGS

Auction catalogs are excellent resources and should be read carefully. Often they are available well in advance of the auction, giving you time to comparison shop and study various subject areas. Catalogs spell out:

1 *Terms of the sale,* including deposit requirements, method of payment, how to place absentee bids, buyer's fees or premiums, and when and how purchased items should be picked up.

GETTING AN APPRAISAL

To get an official evaluation or appraisal of your collectible you need to hire an appraiser. An appraisal, which is a statement of an accurate and realistic value of a possession made by a knowledgeable person, can be used for establishing an item's worth, either for insurance coverage or to determine the price to ask when selling. Appraisals are also required by the IRS when something of value is donated to a charity and you wish to declare a deduction.

An official appraisal must be written, dated and signed. It should also indicate whether the appraisal is the fair market value (used for selling the item, dividing an estate, or donating it to charity), or replacement value (for insurance reimbursement). The object appraised should be described in as much detail as possible and the number of pieces being appraised should be made clear. For example, if the value given is for a pair of vases, a set of 12 water goblets, etc., these numbers should be given.

Before hiring an appraiser, ask what he or she charges and for an estimate regarding how long it will take. Some charge a flat fee; others an hourly rate.

$ HINT: Never hire an appraiser who asks to be paid a percentage of the dollar value of the appraisal.

Although there are no licensing or educational requirements for becoming an appraiser, you can find a reliable one through the International Society of Appraisers. This group grants associate membership to appraisers who have 5 years of experience, and full membership to those who have completed a training course given by Indiana University at various continuing education sites across the country. Recommendations from a bank's trust department, a lawyer, or a museum or gallery are also suggested.

FOR FURTHER INFORMATION

Indiana University
Independent Study Program
School of Continuing Studies
Bloomington, IN 47405
1-800-457-4434; 1-812-335-5323

International Society of Appraisers
485 West Berkley
Hoffman Estates, IL 60194
1-708-882-0706

American Society of Appraisers
Box 17265
Washington, DC 20041
1-703-478-2228

ANTIQUE FOUNTAIN PENS

Take a look in your attic, an old desk or forgotten trunk. You're just likely to find a fountain pen left there years ago by an aunt or uncle. And, it may be worth more than you think.

The fountain pen is pretty much an American invention. The first ones, produced in the early 1880s, were the "dip and drip" type, modeled closely after old quills. This pretty messy number was replaced in 1884 when Lewis Edson Waterman, a New York insurance salesman, obtained a patent for what became the first modern working fountain pen. It is said that he lost a client when his dip pen splashed ink all over an insurance contract. Whether the story is true or not, his invention caught on quickly, primarily because it did not cause an inky mess. Soon after getting his patent, Waterman founded the Ideal Pen Company, which later became the L. E. Waterman Company.

These first fountain pens were made of hard rubber or *gutta percha*, and were gold-tipped with iridium as the nib. The points were fashioned by hand and made only in black. Waterman pens were guaranteed by the company and endorsed by many notables, including Oliver Wendell Holmes. Later on, with the advent of plastic, swirls and marbleized effects were incorporated into the design.

By the early 20th century, three other companies joined Waterman in making pens: Sheaffer, Wahl-Eversharp, and Parker. Together they are known as the Big Four. In 1908, Sheaffer invented the lever-filling mechanism that did away with the need for filling the pen with a messy eyedropper. Around this time, the clip was added so the pen could be carried in a jacket or shirt pocket.

Fountain pens manufactured between 1900 and World War II are quite ornate, often silver- or gold-plated, with intricate designs. Makers tended to come out with new designs on a regular basis, much the way Detroit produces new car models. Many of these pens were sold then for less than $10. This trend continued until the introduction of the ballpoint pen around 1944–45, which virtually closed the door on the era of the fountain pen until its 1980s revival as a luxury item.

TODAY'S PRICES

Ten or more years ago, fountain pens were a regular item at flea markets and yard sales—and if they went for $100, it was big news. Some dealers even sold bags of them for that price! Yet, within the past few years, three leading penmakers—Waterman, Parker, and Montblanc—have brought back the fountain pen as a luxury item. Their huge advertising campaigns have boosted the sales of these new pens. Consequently, today's so-called "power pens" have become a popular item in the executive's life, along with power breakfasts. At the same time interest in old pens has been revived. This new enthusiasm for pens has led Christie's in London to hold regular fountain pen auctions.

Prices for the new pens start at $200 and go up and up. Old ones now command even more: A silver Parker "Swastika" pen, manufactured about 1910, sold in August 1991 for $28,000. Other pens that have sold recently for $1,000 and more include the 1916 Waterman gold-filled pens, one of the first lever pens made; the giant-sized Waterman's #20; the Parker Black Giant of 1918; and the Waterman's Patrician, a marbleized model popular in the late 1920s and early 1930s, which originally sold for $7. The Lady Patrician, smaller in size, is worth several hundred dollars less in today's market.

A favorite of collectors with deep pockets is the Parker "Snake" pen. Fewer than 100 are believed to exist. One prominent collector reportedly turned down an offer in 1991 for $25,000 for his perfect condition "snake" pen.

However, not all antique fountain pens cost thousands of dollars. Lovely smaller versions, not made by the Big Four, can be found in the $75 to several hundred dollar range. Among the less well known companies are: Swan, John Holland, Conklin, Moore, Paul Wirt, LeBoeuf, Dunn, Cary, Edison, and A. A. Waterman. Most of these companies did not make it through the depression. Those that did were then crippled by the introduction of the ballpoint pen around 1944–45.

WHAT TO FOCUS ON

In assembling a collection, it pays to concentrate on a particular manufacturer, a year, a style, or color. Make certain before buying any fountain pen that it is in good working condition and clean. Collectible antique pens can be repaired, but if they are totally reconstructed they lose their value.

THE WRITE STUFF: POINTS TO CONSIDER

A collectible pen is more valuable if it:
- has an imprint of the name brand
- has a gold nib
- has no noticeable wear
- is ½ inch or greater in diameter (oversized)
- has gold or silver filigree or trim
- is in working condition

FOR FURTHER INFORMATION

Pen World
Bimonthly; $42/year
Articles about vintage pens

PenFinder
Bimonthly; $70/year
Consists only of pictures of pens for sale; on consignment
Runs about 135 pens per issue

Collectible Fountain Pens ($21.95) and *Annual Price Guide* ($9.95)

All available from:
World Publications
2240 North Park Drive
Kingwood, TX 77339
1-713-359-4363

Also will appraise pens: $25 for up to six; mail photo
Pen Fancier's Magazine
Pen Fancier's Club
1169 Overcash Drive
Dunedin, FL 34698

The club also publishes *The 1992 Official P. F. C. Pen Guide* by Cliff and Judy Lawrence; $24.95. This book lists prices with photographs of hundreds of pens.

One-year membership plus the book is $54.95
One-year membership only, $45
Six-month membership, $25

Repairs and information:
Fountain Pen Hospital
10 Warren Street (across from City Hall)
New York, NY 10007
1-212-964-0580

Parker Pen History
Free folder with good reference material
from:
The Parker Pen Company
1400 North Parker Drive
Janesville, WI 53547
1-608-755-5000

POPULAR VINYL RECORDS

Today many music lovers own CD players, relegating their old turntable and records to the garage or closet. And so, as compact discs increase in popularity, vinyl records are joining the endangered species lists—a process that in this case has created a collectible.

When vinyl LPs were introduced in 1948, they immediately put the kibosh on the older disks, which were made of shellac and played at 78 revolutions per minute (rpm). The new LPs were an overnight success, reaching a high point in 1977, when 344 million of them were sold. Then in 1990, as new polycarbonate and aluminum CDs became the rage, LP sales fell to 11.7 million disks per year. In fact today LPs are outsold by CDs by about 124 to 1.

WHAT TO LOOK FOR

Among the LPs worth collecting are:

1 debut albums by artists who went on to stardom
2 albums with distinctive sleeve cover art
3 albums dealing with controversy (those with songs about social and political topics of the time, for example)
4 LPs from the 1950s and 1960s, including all rock 'n' roll
5 LPs issued with the Blue Note jazz label
6 Frank Sinatra's Capitol LPs
7 Elvis records

In order to build a sound investment in vinyls you must study the field closely and be able to recognize the unusual. For example, Bob Dylan's original releases are all highly regarded as collectibles, but some command higher prices than others. On the earliest release of his second album, *Freewheelin,* there are several political songs, one of which is titled, "John Birch Society Blues." These songs were pulled by Dylan from later releases, some say because he had an offer to appear on the *Ed Sullivan Show,* where such songs were unacceptable. Mono LPs with these political songs are now worth $8,000 to $10,000. Last year a collector found the one known stereo copy in a Greenwich Village charity shop in New York for about $2; he sold it for around $15,000.

The same principle of finding the unique applies to Beatles' albums. The Beatles' *Yesterday and Today* album with its famous butcher cover, which shows the boys from Liverpool in white smocks and covered with broken doll parts, pieces of meat and blood, is worth up to $10,000 if in good condition. This original butcher cover stereo album was later replaced by a cover showing the Beatles standing near an open trunk; this second version is worth considerably less, about $1,000 to $1,500. A stereo version of *The Beatles and Frank Ifield on Stage,* an early album, has sold for $6,000 in recent months.

With the shrinking number of new releases on LPs, the value of the existing ones rises. Yet many are still available for reasonable prices. For instance, Fats Domino's early hits bring anywhere from $20 to $100.

☐CAUTION: The field is full of forgeries. The Beatles, one of the most sought-after groups, for example, is also one of the most popular groups with counterfeiters. Their first U.S. album, *Introducing the Beatles,* was released by Vee Jay Records, an American company in 10 variations between 1963 and 1964. The first release commands the highest price, assuming all to be in equal condition. On it, the Vee Jay's name appears in an oval on the record label and it includes the songs "Love Me Do" and "P.S. I Love You." Then, after a copyright dispute with Capitol Records, Vee Jay replaced these two songs with "Please Please Me" and "Ask Me Why." These are worth less. And, *Introducing the Beatles* (not to be mistaken for Capitol's *Meet the Beatles*) is one of the music world's most counterfeited albums.

107

If you decide to collect vinyls, keep in mind that in order for an LP to be worth a great deal as a collectible investment it must be in pristine condition. You must also devote care to your collection: Records must be properly cleaned and stored like wine. Sunlight, humidity, and heat wreak havoc with vinyls.

FOR FURTHER INFORMATION

Goldmine
700 East State Street
Iola, WI 54990
1-715-445-2214

Biweekly; $2.50/copy or $35 for one year
This periodical is the bible of the recording industry. Not only are its articles helpful, readers can also use it to locate a dealer to verify authenticity of an album, to place an ad, to find a buyer, or to respond to ads. Also available: *Annual Price Guides,* $19.95.

FINE ARTS: MARITIME PAINTINGS

The recession caused art sales to slump in 1991 and the early part of 1992 to about half of what they were in 1990. This, of course, pushed prices of many fine arts items way down, particularly Impressionist and contemporary paintings. Interestingly enough, most of the Old Masters seemed to have held their own, with Titian's *Venus and Adonis* recently fetching £7.5 million. While this level may be beyond your personal budget for collectibles, there are fine arts categories where prices are more reasonable. One such area where it's still a buyer's market is that of ship paintings, a subject matter that seems to hold permanent appeal.

Before you buy, take time to visit some of the museums that have first-rate maritime collections (see box). Study their works, attend any lectures being given on the topic, and visit the museum bookshop or library for more information.

A number of points add value to any maritime painting, although, of course, it must be a well-executed work to begin with. Here are seven points to look for in testing the waters:

1 Paintings showing several boats engaged in an activity, which could be hauling goods, participating in a flotilla, etc.
2 Battle scenes add to a painting's worth.
3 Paintings of ships which also include human figures are prized.
4 A painting of a ship done at the time. For example, a naval battle from the War of 1812 painted by an artist who was present is more valuable than the same scene painted years later.

MUSEUMS WITH LARGE MARITIME ART COLLECTIONS

■ Peabody Museum	Salem, MA	1-508-745-9500
■ Mystic Seaport Museum	Mystic, CT	1-203-572-0711
■ Philadelphia Maritime Museum	Philadelphia, PA	1-215-925-5439
■ Mariner's Museum	Newport News, VA	1-804-595-0368
■ Columbia River Museum	Astoria, OR	1-503-325-2323
■ National Museum	San Francisco, CA	1-415-556-8177

SPECIALIZED ART GALLERIES

■ Marine Arts Gallery	Salem, MA	1-508-745-5000
■ Vose Gallery	Boston, MA	1-617-536-6176
■ Smith Gallery	New York, NY	1-212-744-6171

LEADING U.S. AUCTION HOUSES

Christie's
  502 Park Avenue
  New York, NY 10022
Sotheby's
  1334 York Avenue
  New York, NY 10021
Phillips
  405 East 79th Street
  New York, NY 10021
C. G. Sloan & Co.
  919 E Street, N.W.
  Washington, DC 20004
Richard W. Skinner, Inc.
  585 Boylston Street
  Boston, MA 02116
DuMouchelle's
  409 Jefferson Avenue
  Detroit, MI 48226
Garth's Auctions
  2690 Stratford Road
  Delaware, OH 43015

5 If the ship did something important, such as transporting a famous person or changing the course of a battle, it is regarded as a more important investment.

6 The paintings may be more valuable if they are accompanied by pertinent memorabilia, such as the ship's log book, the captain's personal letters or diary, papers documenting who owned the ship, and what its itinerary or history was.

7 If the ship was featured in a novel, movie, or play.

MARITIME ARTISTS

There are a number of well-known maritime artists to look for:

- Early 19th-century painters: FitzHugh Lane, who worked in Boston; Robert Salmon of New York; and Thomas Birch of Philadelphia. Their paintings run from $7,500 to $25,000 and up. Sketches by these three painters are often available for $5,000 and under.

- Ship portraits: Several mid-19th century painters specialized in painting ship portraits. Smaller sized paintings sell in the neighborhood of $3,000, while larger works go for $8,000 to $12,000. Among the artists to look for: S. F. M. Badger, Wesley Webber, and J. G. Tyler.

- Three Philadelphia painters who shared a shop in the 1880s were Edward Moran, James Hamilton, and George Bonfield. Larger works by Moran now command $25,000, but smaller works by all three can be found for $5,000, sometimes less.

- Frederik Cozzens, a New Jersey watercolorist, specialized in painting yacht scenes. His work spans from the 1880s through the 1920s. Smaller paintings sell for less than $3,000.

- Antonio Jacobsen, a contemporary of Cozzens, lived in Hoboken, New Jersey. His early works are his most valuable and are priced in the $20,000 to $35,000 range, but later works are sometimes found for under $5,000.

$ HINT: You can track prices of ship paintings through the catalogs of the major auction houses, such as Christie's and Sotheby's in New York (see box for addresses). Auctions devoted solely to maritime paintings are rare; instead, ship paintings are generally included in larger auctions of American paintings.

WHEN THE BEARS ARE OUT OF THE CAVE

Most people initially feel more at ease with bonds than stocks, perhaps because they know bonds provide fixed income, during any kind of market. Yet bonds in recent years have become almost as volatile as stocks. So, even if you have always looked upon bonds as your safe investment, take time to read Part Two and update your position. You'll learn about the safest bonds (those issued by the government) as well as the riskiest (junk or high-yield bonds). In between there is information on how to evaluate bonds, use the rating services, read the quotes in the newspaper, and get call protection.

Part Two covers these broad categories:

- Corporate bonds
- Bond mutual funds
- U.S. Treasury issues
- Savings bonds
- Convertibles
- Municipal bonds
- Junk bonds
- Ginnie Maes and Ginnie Mae funds
- Zero coupon bonds
- CMOs

8

BOND BASICS:
How Corporate Bonds Work

If you want to protect your principal and set up a steady stream of income, corporate bonds, rather than stocks, are the answer. Income is traditionally the most important reason people own bonds, which generally generate greater returns than CDs, money market funds, and stocks. They also offer greater security than most common stocks, since an issuer of a bond will do everything possible to meet its bond obligation. Interest on a corporate bond must be paid before dividends on common or preferred stocks of the same corporation, and it's payable before federal, state, and city taxes. This senior position helps make your investment safer. By contrast, a corporation can and often does decide to cut back or eliminate the dividend on its common stock.

HOW BONDS WORK

Bonds, unlike stock, are debt. They can best be described as IOUs, or as contracts to pay money. When you buy a bond, you loan money to the issuer and in return receive a certificate stating that the issuer will pay a stated interest rate on your money annually until the bond matures. The date of maturity is predetermined and ranges from 1 to 40 years. The interest rate received is called the *coupon rate* and is usually paid twice a year. At the date of maturity you get back the full purchase price, or face value, which is also called *par* and is usually $1,000.

Many investors think of bonds as being stable in price, almost stodgy. Not true. When they are first issued, they are sold at face value, but afterward they move up and down in price, trading in the secondary market either above par at a premium or below par at a discount in response to changes in interest rate markets. Rates and prices move in opposite directions: When rates move down, prices move up. You

can therefore make money with bonds in two ways: (1) by earning a fixed rate of interest or (2) by selling at a higher price than you paid.

Note: Although bonds are issued at par ($1,000), in the financial pages of newspapers they're quoted on the basis of $100, so always add a zero to the price; for example, a bond quoted at $108 is really selling at $1,080.

Bonds are issued by corporations, by the U.S. government and its agencies, and by states and municipalities. The latter, also called "munis," are discussed in Chapter 11, high-yield or junk bonds appear in Chapter 12, and Treasuries in Chapter 9.

In the last few years, the proliferation of new bond products has kept investors and brokers on their toes. New products such as zero coupon bonds, zero convertibles, and delayed payment bonds (which pay no interest for the first 5 or 6 years), among others, have all been used to raise capital in innovative ways.

Adding to the excitement, the introduction of bond futures, and options on these futures, has turned the traditionally conservative bond markets into areas of intense speculation. For the average investor, this host of new and fascinating products provides endless opportunities, and as long as you exercise caution and investigate carefully, you can make money. The increased action in bonds also opens the door to trading these securities for appreciation, as well as investing for income.

BOND YIELDS

Like stocks, bonds fluctuate in price, their market value changing any number of times a day in reaction to interest rate movements. This is because the only way the bond market can accommodate the changes in interest rates is by changing the price of bonds. If you buy a bond at par ($1,000) and its coupon rate (the annual interest rate bondholders receive) is 10%, you will receive $100 each year in interest payments. If interest rates move up, the same corporation will issue new bonds yielding a higher rate, say 10.5%. The older bonds then fall in price, perhaps to $960, in order to keep the yield competitive. (The yield is the equivalent of 10.5% on the new bond because of the $40 saved when buying it at $960.) If new bonds pay less interest, older bonds rise in price, because they immediately become more desirable due to their higher coupon rates.

Yield is a matter of definition and objective.

➤ COUPON YIELD   This is the interest rate stated on the bond: 8.75%, 9%, etc. It is determined by the issuing corporation and depends on the prevailing cost of money at the time the bond is issued.

➤ CURRENT YIELD ON THE PURCHASE PRICE   This is the rate of return per year that the coupon interest rate provides on the *net* price (without accumulated interest) at which the bond is purchased. It is *higher* than the coupon yield if you buy the bond below par and *lower* if you buy the bond above par.

➤ YIELD TO MATURITY   Since maturities vary and the current yield measures only today's return, the bond market relies on the yield to maturity (YTM). This is the total return, comprising both interest and gain in price. Put another way, it is the rate of return on a bond when held to maturity. It includes the appreciation to par from the current market price when bought at a discount or depreciation when bought at a premium. To approximate the YTM for a discount bond:

1   Subtract the current bond price from its face value.
2   Divide the resulting figure by the number of years to maturity.
3   Add the total annual interest payments.
4   Add the current price to the face amount and divide by 2.
5   Divide the result of step 3 by the result of step 4.

   Example: A $1,000 7% coupon bond due in 10 years is selling at 72 ($720). The current yield is 9.7% ($70 ÷ $720). The YTM is about 11.4%.

$$1,000 - 720 = 280$$
$$280 \div 10 = 28$$

$$28 + 70 = 98$$
$$720 + 1,000 = 1,720 \div 2 = 860$$
$$98 \div 860 = 11.4\%$$

The YTM is the yardstick used by professionals, because it sets the market value of the debt security. But to amateurs, the spread—between the current and redemption prices—is what counts, because this appreciation will be added to your income. You get a competitive return while you wait—usually over 8 years, because with shorter lives, the current yield is modest: for example, AT&T 5½, 97 at 88. That's a current yield of 6.3%, but each year there will be an additional $24 price appreciation per $1,000 bond *if* the bond is held to maturity in 1994.

➤ DISCOUNT YIELD   This is the percentage from par or face value, adjusted to an annual basis, at which a discount bond sells. It is used for short-term obligations maturing in less than 1 year, primarily Treasury bills.

It is roughly the opposite of YTM. If a 1-year T-bill sells at a 6% yield, its cost is 94 ($940). The discount yield is 6 divided by 94, or 6.38%.

WHY BUY BONDS

➤ CURRENT RETURN   Annual interest payments must be made to bondholders at the stated fixed rate unless the company files for bankruptcy or undergoes a restructuring of its debt. In the latter case, the corporation will issue new securities in exchange for existing bonds. In other words, you are guaranteed an annual income.

➤ SENIORITY   Interest on a corporate bond must be paid before dividends on common and preferred stocks.

➤ CAPITAL GAINS   If you buy a bond at discount (below $1,000 face value) and you either sell or redeem it at a profit, this gain is taxed.

➤ SAFETY   Ratings are available on corporate bonds that help determine how safe they are as an investment. Both Moody's and Standard & Poor's rate bonds on a continuing basis, as explained below.

UNDERSTANDING RISKS

As with all securities, there are some disadvantages to bonds, especially when purchased at par, which is the usual price when a bond is first sold to investors.

➤ LIMITED APPRECIATION Bond values move in the opposite direction to interest rates: up when interest rates fall and down when rates rise. The recent rises and falls in interest rates have sent bond prices moving like yo-yos, so the bond market is no longer the safe harbor it once was. If you buy a bond today and interest rates fall, you'll make a profit if you sell. However, if rates climb back up, you'll lose if you have to sell your bond before maturity.

➤ EROSION BY INFLATION Since bonds have set interest rates and pay back the principal at a future date, they do not offer a hedge against inflation.

➤ CORPORATE REVERSES Corporate financial woes can hurt bonds. Two prime examples: Chrysler and Navistar. Stick with high-rated companies, A or above (see table to right for bond ratings).

➤ FIXED RATE OF RETURN Stockholders have an opportunity to enjoy increased dividends, but bondholders do not receive interest rate increases unless they hold special floating-interest notes.

➤ CALLS Most corporate bonds are sold with a "call" feature that allows the issuer to redeem the bond before maturity. The conditions of a call are set when the bonds are first sold to the public. Bonds are not usually called in if the current rate of interest is the same as the bond's coupon rate or higher.

However, if interest rates fall below the bond's coupon rate, it is likely to be called in, because the issuer can now borrow the money elsewhere at a lower rate. When this happens, you lose your steady stream of income. You can protect yourself from early calls by purchasing bonds with "call protection," a feature that guarantees the issue will not be called in for a specific number of years, often 10. The call protection date is listed in the prospectus and in both Moody's and Standard & Poor's bond guides, available at your library or any brokerage firm.

➤ DIFFICULTY REINVESTING INTEREST Unless you buy zero coupon bonds or shares in a bond mutual fund, automatic reinvestment of interest is seldom available, as with stock dividend reinvestment plans. Therefore, you must find ways to reinvest your coupon payments as you receive them. One partial solution is, instead of

HOW BONDS ARE RATED

GENERAL DESCRIPTION	MOODY'S	STANDARD & POOR'S
Best quality	Aaa	AAA
High quality	Aa	AA
Upper medium	A	A
Medium	Baa	BBB
Speculative	Ba	BB
Low grade	B	B
Poor to default	Caa	CCC
Highly speculative default	Ca	CC
Lowest grade	C	C

Ratings may also have + or − sign to show relative standings in class.

depositing interest checks in a low-yielding savings or NOW account, to add to your shares of your money market fund. As long as the return is close to that of the bonds, you'll be OK. But if the fund pays 7% vs. 11% for the bonds, accumulate enough money to buy zeros or other high-yielding bonds.

➤ LIMITED MARKETABILITY With taxable bonds, there are two major markets: (1) the New York Stock Exchange, where a relatively small number of debt issues of major corporations are traded with daily quotations, and (2) the over-the-counter market, dominated by bond dealers who handle U.S. government bills, notes, and bonds; debt of smaller companies; and special offerings and packages via bid and asked prices.

With small lots (under 25 bonds), the prices can fluctuate widely from day to day or even during a given trading day. The spreads between the offers by the buyer and seller normally run from ⅜% to ½% in strong markets, up to 3% in weak markets, and even more with little-known issues.

$ HINT: Unless you have special knowledge, buy only bonds or debt issues whose trading is reported in the financial press.

WHAT TO LOOK FOR

Determining a corporate bond's value depends on two factors: the credit quality of the bond and the rate of interest. Bonds of a solid, successful corporation are certainly a better investment than bonds of a weaker firm. The interest rate factor must also be considered: If you buy a bond with a fixed rate of interest, say 8%, and rates rise to 10% or 11%, the bond will decline in value. There are three areas to consider when selecting bonds:

➤ QUALITY RATINGS Examining ratings is essential in choosing bonds for investments. Most investors should stick to A-rated bonds or better. True, you can get extra interest each year with lower-quality bonds, but your risks are greater.

The ratings are made by independent research services that analyze the financial strength of the corporation, project future prospects, and determine how well the corporation is prepared to cover both interest and principal payments. By and large, the two top services, Moody's Investors Service and Standard & Poor's, reach the same conclusions about each bond.

Watch for changes in bond ratings. When a bond is upgraded, its market price will probably rise (and the yield dip) a bit; downgrading signals possible trouble, so the value will decline. Slight shifts are not too important so long as the rating is A or better.

➤ TERMS Most bonds issued by the federal government and corporations carry a fixed coupon as well as a fixed date of maturity. But there are occasionally serial bonds in which a portion of the issue will be paid off periodically. Usually, the earlier the redemption date, the lower the interest rate, by ¼% to ½% or so. These can be useful if you have a target date for need of money. Serial bonds are widely used

HOW TO MEASURE BOND QUALITY

A handy formula for determining investment-grade bonds is the number of times total annual interest charges are covered by pretax earnings for a period of 5 years.

	BEFORE FEDERAL INCOME TAXES	AFTER FEDERAL INCOME TAXES
Industrial bonds	5×	3×
Public utility	3×	2×

with tax-exempt issues, and CMOs, which are discussed in Chapter 12.

➤ TYPE OF COLLATERAL This is the property behind each bond. There are two basic types: secured bonds and debentures, or unsecured bonds. Secured bonds are backed either by the company's real estate—these are mortgage bonds—or by equipment—called equipment certificates. Unsecured bonds are backed only by the promise of the issuer to pay interest and principal. The seniority ranking becomes most important when default or insolvency occurs. Secured, or senior obligation–backed bonds, receive preferential treatment.

Unsecured bonds or debentures are backed only by the general credit standing of the issuing company. The investor should assess the company's ability to pay annual interest plus the principal sum when due. The projection should consider recent historical ratios and trends and should apply to the *total* debt.

In practice, the ability of the corporation to pay is much more important than theoretical security, because legal obstacles to investors' collecting a bond's security in the event of insolvency are often formidable and time-consuming and can require litigation.

HOW TO READ BOND QUOTES

Unlike most stocks, many bonds have thin markets, trading only now and then. That means that quotes for these issues may not be listed in the newspaper. The trading trans-

CHANGES IN BOND RATINGS

UP:	Century Communications B to B+
	Cooper Industries A− to A
	Continental Telephone of CA A+ to AA−
DOWN:	Borden, Inc. A+ to A
	El Paso Power CCC to D

SOURCE: Standard & Poor's, May 1992.

actions of bonds that you should consider owning are listed in financial publications: daily in major newspapers, weekly in *Barron's* and other specialized publications.

The table on page 117 shows a listing for AA-rated AT&T with a coupon of 7⅛% and a 2002 maturity date. The last quotation was 96¾ ($967.50), and during the week, the high price was 101⅞ and the low 101⅛, with the last sale at 101⅜, down ¼ from the price of the last sale on the previous day. Altogether, 1,468 $1,000 bonds changed hands.

Each bond paid $87.50 annual interest, so the current yield was 8.6%. In the year 2002, each bond can be redeemed at 100 ($1,000) for a loss of 1.375 per bond. The yield to maturity was competitive with that of new issues.

BOOSTING YOUR SAFETY

The key point to keep in mind about investing in bonds is that the longer the maturity, the greater the susceptibility to price advances or declines. If long-term interest rates rise substantially (2 points or more), existing long-term bonds (10–30 years) will drop in price to a point where their yields are comparable to those on bonds issued at the new higher rates. The same process can work in reverse if interest rates drop.

- In general, the shorter the term of a bond, the lower the yield but the smaller the price swings.
- You can protect yourself against price declines to some extent by purchasing high-grade bonds at discount; that is, below face value. This is especially true if their maturity is not far away.
- Rather than having all bonds come due at the same time, own a spread of bonds to come due every year or so. That way you'll periodically receive cash, which you can reinvest to keep the cycle going. Spreading out maturities also tends to average out the effects of price changes.
- Diversify through a bond mutual fund or unit investment trust, which will also help reduce risk.

$ IF YOU DARE: To get the highest yields, invest for the shortest time possible while rates are rising. When rates have peaked, sell and buy longer-term bonds to lock in those higher yields.

THE BOND PROSPECTUS

In addition to using the S&P and Moody ratings and your stockbroker's research, you can evaluate bonds on your own by looking at the bond's prospectus. This document details the issue's financial features, the means of payment, what the money raised will be used for, and what analysts think about the issuer's creditworthiness.

The two key points to look for are:

- *The amount of debt the company has already issued.* Heavy debt means that much of the money raised by this issue could go toward interest payments on the company's debt.
- *The bondholder's claim on the company's cash flow.* Is it a first claim or subordinated? You want one with first claim. Often the employee pension plan has a higher claim on revenues than bondholders should there be a default. Note, too, whether the pension plan is funded or unfunded; if a large part is unfunded, discuss the appropriateness of the investment with your broker.

WHAT TO BUY

It is probably safe to purchase bonds of our largest corporations, such as IBM, Exxon, and DuPont. Bonds of most utilities are also considered safe from leveraged buyouts (LBOs). Look into the so-called supranational issuers, such as the World Bank and the issues of Yankee bonds (dollar-denominated bonds sold in the United States by foreign governments). The safest bonds of all, of course, are U.S. Treasury issues.

$ HINT: If you own bonds of an LBO company and you have no appetite for risk, take your losses. Up to $3,000 in losses can be used to reduce your taxable income. If you can bear to wait it out, continue to hold for the high yields.

SPECIAL TYPES OF BONDS

The variety of bonds is almost endless, far too great to cover in a general investment guide such as this. Some of the more interesting ones are described below; foreign bonds are discussed in Chapter 20. The leading sources for in-depth bond research are given under "For Further Information" at the end of this chapter.

HOW CORPORATE BONDS ARE QUOTED

STANDARD & POOR'S RATING*	ISSUE	CURRENT YIELD	SALES ($1,000s)	HIGH	LOW	CLOSE	CHANGE**
AA	AT&T 7⅛, 2002	7.4%	972	96¾	96	96½	+$^5/_8$

* The rating is not shown in the press.
** From previous day.

SOURCE: Barron's, May 1992.

➤ DEEP-DISCOUNT BONDS This type of bond sells at a price substantially below par ($1,000), which means that the bond buyer receives not only the coupon rate but also the dollar appreciation to par at maturity. Some deep-discount bonds are initially offered at discounts; others drop in price because of credit uncertainties or changes in interest rates. These bonds can be extremely profitable, but those selling at a discount in the secondary market because their credit rating has deteriorated are highly speculative.

Example: Reliance Group, 9⅞%, due 1998, 94, for a yield to maturity of 11.28%.

➤ EQUIPMENT CERTIFICATES This classical type of bond is issued by airlines, railroads, and shipping companies to finance the purchase of new equipment. The certificate gives bondholders first right to the airplane, railroad car, etc., in the event that the interest and principal are not paid, thereby providing the investor with an added element of security.

Example: Seaboard Coastline Railroad Equipment Trust, 11⅜%, due 1995, 110.

➤ FLOATING-RATE NOTES These are notes on which the interest rate changes periodically, often as frequently as every 6 months. The rate is tied to a money market index such as T-bills. This variable interest rate enables investors to participate in rising interest rates, but it is far less appealing when rates are falling. Floating-rate notes, which usually have a 5-year maturity, tend to pay lower yields than fixed-rate notes with the same maturity.

Example: Citicorp Floating Rate Notes, 6.5%, due 1998, 90.

➤ FLOWER BONDS Flower bonds, issued between 1953 and 1963 at rates that today are no longer competitive, now are available *only* in the secondary market. They were designed to pay estate taxes after the death of the bondholder. The bonds today sell at a deep discount. You'll have to ask your broker for quotes.

The appeal of flower bonds is that they are valued at full face value at any time even prior to maturity provided they are used to pay estate taxes. To qualify, the bonds must have been purchased by the deceased; they cannot be purchased by the estate and used retroactively. If the portfolio of the deceased, for instance, contains $50,000 worth of par face value flower bonds, they will pay $50,000 worth of estate taxes, *even* if the market price at the time of death is only $25,000.

Note: Consult your accountant prior to purchasing flower bonds in the secondary market.

➤ OPTIONAL MATURITY These bonds can be redeemed by the investor at specified times, frequently after the first 5 years.

➤ YANKEE BONDS These dollar-denominated bonds are issued in the United States by foreign governments, banks, and institutions. When market conditions are better here than abroad, these bonds tend to pay higher interest than other bonds of comparable credit quality.

Example: Kingdom of Sweden, 8⅛%, due 1996, AAA-rated, NYSE, selling at 102.

➤ CREDIT CARD SECURITIES A relatively new type of bond, these are backed by credit card debt. In May 1990, Citicorp issued a record $1.4 billion of credit card debt. Investors are almost entirely institutions, not individuals. Most credit card securities are rated AAA.

INTEREST

This is the interest a bond earns between one coupon date and the next.

When a bond changes hands between coupon dates, the buyer pays the seller all interest the bond has earned from the last coupon date up to the time of ownership transfer.

Example: 10 corporate bonds are sold at 79¾. The seller receives $8,046.67: the $7,975 price plus $71.67 interest (not counting commissions).

Alternatives:

1 Schedule your savings so that you will have enough extra money to add to the interest to buy additional bonds or stocks.

2 Buy shares of a bond mutual fund that provides automatic reinvestment of interest earned.

GET CALL PROTECTION

To attract investors for long-term commitments, corporations usually include call protection when they issue new bonds.

When a bond is called, the issuer exercises a right (which will appear in the prospectus) to retire the bond, or call it in, before the date of maturity. This right to call gives the issuing corporation the ability to respond to changing interest rates. If, for example, a corporation issued bonds with an 11½% rate when rates were high and then rates dropped to 7%, it would be to the issuer's advantage to call in the old bonds and issue new ones at the lower prevailing rate. In fact, it is often so advantageous that a corporation is willing to pay a premium over par to call its bonds.

There are three types of call provisions you should know about:

- *Freely callable:* Issuer can retire the bond at any time; therefore, it has no call protection.
- *Noncallable:* Bond cannot be called until date of maturity.
- *Deferred call:* Bond cannot be called until after a stated number of years, usually 5 to 10.

The call price is the price the issuer must pay to retire the bond. It's based on the par value plus a premium, which in theory often works out to be equal to 1 year's interest at the earliest call date. For example, an 8% bond would theoretically have an initial call of $1,080—the $80 being the premium. However, there are many variations. For example, the call price can be specified, or it can be based on a declining scale, with greater premiums given for calling in during the earlier years.

REFUNDING PROVISIONS

This feature permits a company to call in or redeem its old, high coupon rate debt in order to reduce its interest expenses by issuing new bonds at a lower interest rate. Some bonds offer refunding protection. The new bonds will pay a lower interest rate, a negative for the investor.

A call on a bond is nearly always bad news for the investor. That's because issuers seldom call a bond when interest rates are rising and when getting your money out would enable you to reinvest at the higher rates. On the contrary, bonds are generally called when rates are declining and you would prefer to lock in your higher yield by keeping the bond. So try to purchase bonds with call protection. Check the prospectus or ask your broker.

In effect, call protection guarantees a minimum period of investment income at the stated coupon rate.

Example: Viacom International, 10¼% debentures, due 2001, are noncallable to maturity. This means that an investor who buys these bonds in 1993 can look forward to 8 years of receiving a 10¼% coupon.

PICKING THE RIGHT BOND OR NOTE

If you want to invest $10,000 in bonds for 10 years, you have these choices:

- A 6-month T-bill that will be rolled over at each maturity.
- A 2- to 3-year Treasury note that at maturity will be turned into a 7- to 8-year note at a somewhat more rewarding yield *if* interest rates go up.
- A 10-year bond to be held to redemption. This would be best if you expect interest rates to decline or stay about the same.
- A 15- to 20-year bond to be sold at the end of 10 years, best if you expect rates to fall, but the longer the maturity, the greater the risk if rates climb.

CALL ALERT

Your broker should advise you about the call status of any bond; otherwise, be certain to ask. Calls are also listed in the bond's prospectus and in Standard & Poor's and Moody's bond guides, available from your broker or at your library. Here's how it looks in the bond dealer's guides or on quote sheets:

Corporate bond: "NC" means noncallable for life.

Government bond: "8½ May 1994–99" means the bond matures in May 1999, but is callable in 1994.

If you pay any premium above par in buying these bonds, you must understand that this premium reduces your overall yield to the call date (see "Yield to Maturity," page 113).

SINKING FUND PROVISIONS

Often a corporation borrows millions of dollars in any one bond issue, so quite obviously that amount of money must be available when the bond matures and the bondholders are paid back the full face value. In order to retire a portion of that enormous debt, some issuers buy back part of it, leaving less to be paid off at one time in a lump sum. In the process they shrink the debt. The money used to do this repurchasing is called a sinking fund. When a corporation sets up a sinking fund, it means that it must make periodic predetermined cash payments to the custodial account set up for this purpose.

With a sinking fund, the corporation pays less total interest. With a 25-year issue set up to buy back 3.75% of the debt annually, for example, 75% of the bonds will be retired before maturity. This means that the average life of the bonds will be about 17 years, not the 25 years anticipated by the investor.

A sinking fund adds a margin of safety for investors: The periodic purchases provide price

support and enhance the probability of repayment when the bond matures. But it also narrows the time span of the bond, so that there will be less total income for the long-term investor. Sinking funds benefit the corporation more than the bondholder.

▢CAUTION: Watch out for call provisions on high-coupon utility bonds. An example is the case of Niagara Mohawk Power 10.20% of 2005. These are callable from March 1, 1993, at a price of 103.27. Ask your broker to check the prospectus or call the company's investor relations division to inquire about possible call dates before buying any utility bond.

SWAPPING BONDS

To the serious (and affluent) investor, swapping bonds can be profitable: A loss can reduce taxes; a higher yield can boost income; a wise switch can raise quality and extend the maturity of the debt.

Example: Investor X owns 25 ABC Bonds, 9%, due in 1996—at par ($25,000). They drop in price to 85 (25M × $850 = $21,250). He gets an annual income of $2,250 with a 10.6% annual yield (9 ÷ 85 = 10.6).

Seeking a tax loss, he sells them, for a $3,750 loss ($25,000 − $21,250 = $3,750). This loss can be used against any capital gains he

THE SINKING FUND

A sinking fund specifies how certain bonds will be paid off over time. If a bond has a sinking fund, the company must redeem a certain number of bonds annually before maturity to reduce its debt.

- *Advantage:* Bondholders get their principal back earlier than the maturity date.
- *Disadvantage:* If the coupon rate is high, bondholders will not want to retire the bond early.

If your bond is called in, you will be notified by mail and in the newspaper. You *must* take your money, because interest will cease at the specified time.

may have. If he has no capital gains, he is limited to a $3,000 capital loss against ordinary income.

He then buys 25 XYZ 10¾s, due 2013, at 82 and thus replaces his bonds with a better-quality investment while establishing a tax loss.

If you have a sizable loss in bonds, consider swapping if the results are beneficial and help you to meet your investment objectives.

BOND MUTUAL FUNDS

Many of the negatives of bonds can be eased, if not eliminated, by buying shares of bond funds. (See Chapter 6 for details on mutual funds.)

Shares can be purchased for as little as $250 to $1,000, with smaller increments thereafter. Most funds encourage automatic reinvestment of interest for compounding—something that individuals rarely do on their own.

The yields may be a bit less than those available from direct investments, but you get diversification, convenience, and the opportunity to switch to other funds (bond, stock, or money market) under the same sponsor.

- *Evaluate the portfolio.* For safety, choose funds with the most A- or better-rated holdings. For good income, look for those with lower-quality issues (but not too low). The highest yields are available from junk bonds—but they are also highest in risk, as explained in Chapter 12.
- *Check the performance.* Follow

PROS AND CONS OF CLOSED-END FUNDS

PROS
- ↑ Closed-end funds do not have to sell off their portfolios when the market declines as open-end funds must do in order to meet redemption demand by investors.
- ↑ The managers tend to have greater flexibility in portfolio composition. A fund selling at a discount is sometimes a takeover candidate.

CONS
- ↓ Funds react very quickly to interest rate changes: When rates rise, bond prices fall, and vice versa.
- ↓ Many funds buy lower-quality bonds to boost yields and to compete with older funds that sell at a discount.

---

performance over at least 5 years, long enough to include both bad and good years for debt securities.

- *Look for frequent distributions.* A mutual fund that pays monthly ensures a steady cash flow. If this is reinvested, compounding will be at a more rewarding rate. Buy right before the distribution declaration date.

Open-end bond funds, commonly called mutual funds, continually issue new shares to sell to investors. They are available directly from the fund or through your stockbroker.

DEBT FOR EQUITY

A variation on the sinking fund is **defeasance,** which is used by corporations to discharge debts without actually paying them off prior to maturity. The company arranges for a broker to buy a portion of the outstanding bond issues for a fee. The broker then (1) exchanges the bonds for a new issue of corporate stock with a market value equal to that of the bonds and (2) sells the shares at a profit. The corporate balance sheet is improved without harming operations or prospects.

CLOSED-END BOND FUNDS

FUND	YIELD	PRICE	SYMBOL
High Yield Income	10.5%	$8½	HYI
MFS Gov't. Markets	10.8	8¼	MGF
Putnam Master Inc. Trust	10.3	8	PMT
First Boston Income	10.2	8¾	FBF
ACM Gov't. Income	8.9	10	ACG
John Hancock Inc. Sec.	8.4	16¾	JHS
Ft. Dearborn Inc.	8.0	15	FTD

SOURCE: Standard and Poor's, *Stock Guide,* May 1992.

THREE WAYS TO MAKE MONEY IN BONDS

- *Recognize a bull market in bonds.* It usually takes place before a recession when interest rates begin to drop because the demand for credit is easing up.
- *Recognize when to sell.* Sell just before an inflationary spell when interest rates climb because the demand for money is up.
- *Understand event risk.* Bonds tend to lose their value if their issuer is taken over or if the company is restructured. Buy only those new bonds that have protective provisions.

Closed-end bond funds do not issue new shares or units after their initial offering. Instead they trade on one of the exchanges or over the counter. The capitalization of this type of fund is fixed at the outset, and investors must buy shares either at the initial offering or later in the secondary market or aftermarket. This means that the price of a closed-end fund is determined by two variables: (1) the public's demand for its shares and (2) the value of its portfolio. Therefore, such funds sell either at a premium or at a discount from the portfolio's net asset value. Like their open-end cousins, closed-end funds are professionally managed, contain a wide variety of bonds, and make monthly distributions. (See Chapter 7 for more on closed-end bond funds.)

$ HINT: New funds often have high sales fees, as much as 7%—which is part of the offering price. So wait and buy in the secondary market, where you'll pay only your broker's commission. Select a fund selling at a discount.

Closed-end bond funds are listed each Wednesday in the *Wall Street Journal.*

FOR FURTHER INFORMATION

BOOKS AND PAMPHLETS

Marcia Stigum and Frank J. Fabozzi, *The Dow Jones–Irwin Guide to Bond and Money Market Investments* (Homewood, IL: Dow Jones–Irwin, 1987).

> *The Investor's Guide to Bonds* ($29)
> by Robert B. Taylor
> KCI Communications, Inc.
> 1101 King Street, Suite 400
> Alexandria, VA 22314
> 1-703-548-2400

NEWSLETTERS AND NEWSPAPERS

The Bond Buyer
One State Street Plaza
New York, NY 10004
1-212-943-8200
Published daily; $1,897/year; $15 per copy

Investor's Guide to Closed End Funds
Thomas J. Herzfeld, Editor
P.O. Box 161465
Miami, FL 33116
1-305-271-1900
Monthly; $60 for 2-month trial; $325/year

9

U.S. GOVERNMENT TREASURIES: NOTES, BILLS, AND BONDS

There are no safer securities than U.S. Treasury obligations, which are backed by the full faith and credit of the U.S. government. So, if you're looking for a risk-free investment, invest in the federal government. Uncle Sam is continually borrowing money, and he has an excellent reputation for paying back his debts.

In addition to safety and affordability, Treasuries provide interest that is exempt from state and local income taxes—a plus for anyone, but especially those who live in high-tax states. And if interest rates fall, you can sell your Treasury for more than you paid.

Treasuries are also easy to unload because of the enormous size of the government bond market. In fact, the Treasury market is the world's largest securities field, with average trading volume in excess of $100 billion annually.

So, are there any disadvantages? Yes. If interest rates rise after your purchase, the value of that Treasury will fall because new issues will pay a higher annual interest; to make up for that, buyers will pay only a discounted price for the older issues. Of course, if you hold your Treasuries until maturity, you're guaranteed to get the full face value.

☐ CAUTION: The government also has the right to call its bonds prior to maturity, as it did in 1991, although this very rarely happens.

BUYING TREASURIES

Buying Treasuries is not difficult. You can, of course, buy them from a broker, but you'll pay a minimum commission ranging from $25 to $100. Since fees vary, call several full-service and discount brokers.

You can sidestep the commission by buying them yourself at one of the 37 Federal Reserve Banks or branches, or by mail. To do so, you

need to understand the auction system. There are two kinds of bids:

- *Competitive* These bidders must state not only the amount they want to buy but also what yield they will accept. Competitive bidders risk getting shut out if the yield they bid is too high. Institutions and anyone wanting to buy $1 million or more at a Treasury auction must submit a competitive bid.

- *Noncompetitive* Most individuals take this path because you don't have to try to outguess the big bidders. And you're guaranteed to get the average yield from the competitive bidders.

➤ FOR FIRST-TIME INVESTORS If you have not purchased Treasuries directly, send for the booklet listed at the end of this chapter offered by the Federal Reserve Bank of Richmond. Or, follow these instructions: You can use the official tender form, available from the Federal Reserve Banks, or you can write a letter stating how many securities you want (the dollar amount), your name, telephone number, Social Security number, and the name under which the securities are to be registered. You also need to give the name and account number of the bank to which you want your dividends sent. If you're sending a letter instead of the tender form, you must also include a W-9 form from the IRS. (Call 800-TAX-FORM to order the W-9, or pick one up at your bank.)

➤ PURCHASING BY MAIL If you are purchasing Treasuries by mail, write TENDER FOR TREASURY SECURITIES in large letters on the envelope and enclose a check for the face value of the notes. You need a certified check only if you are buying Treasury bills. For notes and bonds, a personal check is acceptable.

Bids sent by mail must be postmarked no later than the day before the auction. Bids must be submitted in person at the Federal Reserve Bank or branch by 1 P.M. eastern time.

You will not receive the Treasury itself. The government, through its Treasury Direct system, will set up an account for you and then send a statement each time there is activity in your account, such as an interest payment or when money is received upon maturity of a security. (T-notes and bonds pay interest twice a year.)

$ HINT: Buying Treasuries directly at auction works best for those who plan to keep them until they mature. You can sell Treasuries on the secondary market, but only through a broker or bank, which again entails paying a commission.

If you are already holding Treasuries in your bank or brokerage account and wish to transfer them to the Treasury Direct system, submit New Account Request Form PD 5182, available from a Federal Reserve Bank.

HOW TO READ THE QUOTES

After a Treasury issue is first sold, it then trades in the secondary or aftermarket—not on the major exchanges but over the counter. The issues are quoted in dollars plus units of $1/32$ of a dollar (0.03125), with bid and asked prices daily. (*Barron's* lists the high, low, and last price; volume; and yield.) The quotations are per $1,000 face value. The first line in the table at the top of page 124 shows notes due in 1994 with a coupon of 9%, a bid price of 101–12 ($1,013.75), and an asked price of 101–22 ($1,016.88) with a yield of 8.46%. An investor who held these notes for four years until maturity will get $90 per year less the premium of $16.88, for a yield to maturity of 8.46% when redeemed in February of 1994.

The 12% bond due to mature in 2008–2013 has what is known as a double maturity, sometimes referred to as a call date. Its yield is calculated on the earlier maturity, 2008; however, at the Treasury's choice, the maturity may be extended to 2013. Notification appears in the newspaper, and in some cases by letter. All Treasury issues with this modified call feature can be identified in the paper by the hyphenated listing. A small "n" indicates that the issue is a note rather than a bond.

TREASURY BILLS

Treasury bills mature in 3 months, 6 months, or 1 year. T-bills, as they are often called, are issued in minimum denominations of $10,000, with $5,000 increments. They are sold at a discount from face value and are redeemed at full face value upon maturity. Because they are guaranteed by the full faith and credit of the U.S. government, investors have no risk of default. In fact, if the federal government goes into bankruptcy, it won't matter what types of investments you have!

T-bills constitute the largest part of the government's financing. They are sold by the Treasury at regular auctions where competitive bidding by major institutions and bond dealers takes place. Auctions are held weekly for 3- and 6-month maturities, monthly for 1-year bills. (Occasionally the government issues a 9-month T-bill.) The yields at these auctions are watched very carefully as indications of interest rate trends. Floating-rate loans, variable-rate mortgages, and numerous other investments tie their rates to T-bills.

➤ FIGURING YIELDS Because T-bills are sold at auction at a discount from face value, there is no stated interest rate. You can determine their yield by using the formula in this box:

DETERMINING THE YIELD ON A 1-YEAR T-BILL

$$\frac{\text{Face value} - \text{price}}{\text{price}} = \text{``annual interest rate''}$$

$$\frac{10,000 - 9,100}{9,100} = \frac{900}{9,100} = 9.9\%$$

Thus a 1-year 9.9% bill will be purchased for $9,100 and redeemed 12 months later at full face value, or $10,000. This gain of $900 is interest and subject to federal income tax but is exempt from state and local taxes.

➤ TO DEFER INCOME WITH T-BILLS Since Treasury bills are sold at a discount price—that is, at less than face value—and are redeemed at

HOW GOVERNMENT NOTES AND BONDS ARE QUOTED

ISSUE	BID	ASKED	CHANGE	YIELD
Feb. 94, 9	101–12	101–22	+04	8.46
Aug. 08–13, 12	127–22	127–28	−09	8.88
May 16, 7¼	84–27	84–31	−07	8.72
May 18, 9⅛	104–05	104–09	−06	8.71

SOURCE: Wall Street Journal.

maturity at full face value, they do not pay an annual interest. Therefore, in the following example, you would not have to pay taxes until your T-bill matured in 1992. This is to your advantage if you expect your income to be lower in 1992.

Example: You buy a $10,000 1-year bill in February 1993 for $9,380. Your real yield is 6.6% ($10,000 − $9,380 ÷ $9,380). When you cash in the bill in February 1994, you will receive $620 on a cash investment of only $9,380.

$ HINT: Use T-bills as a short-term parking place for money received in a lump sum, say from the sale of a house or yacht, as a bonus, or from a royalty check. Think of them as interest-bearing cash.

TREASURY NOTES

These intermediate-term securities mature in 2 to 10 years. They are issued in $1,000 and $5,000 denominations. The $1,000 minimum is usually available only on notes of 4 to 10 years. Notes maturing in 2 to 3 years are issued in $5,000 denominations. The interest rate is fixed and determined by the coupon rate as specified on the note. It is calculated on the basis of a 365-day year. Interest earned is paid semiannually and is exempt from state and local taxes. Two-year notes are issued monthly; 3-year notes, quarterly; and 4- to 10-year notes, also quarterly.

T-notes are growing in popularity with investors, primarily because they are more affordable than T-bills (which have hefty $10,000 minimums), but also because their longer maturities usually give investors a higher yield. Another plus is the fact that they are not callable, so you are guaranteed a steady stream of income until maturity.

TREASURY BONDS

These long-term debt obligations are also issued in $1,000 minimums, with $5,000, $10,000, $50,000, $100,000, and $1 million denominations also available. They range in maturity from 10 to 30 years. A fixed rate of interest is paid semiannually. The interest earned is exempt from state and local taxes. Unlike T-notes, these bonds are sometimes subject to a special type of call. If a specific bond is callable, its maturity date and call date are both listed in hyphenated form in the newspaper. In the example described on this page, the 12% bond due to mature in 2013 could be called in at any time starting in 2008.

$ HINT: Because government bonds come in so many maturities, stagger your portfolio to meet future needs and to take advantage of any rise in interest rates.

SAVINGS BONDS

Savings bonds are a safe and extremely easy way to save, and thanks to the upgrading of

A POTPOURRI OF RATES

INVESTMENT	YIELD/ RATE
6-month CD	3.50%
1-year CD	3.68
Money market mutual fund	3.32
Money market deposit account	3.96
1-year Treasury bill	3.51
5-year Treasury note	5.70
10-year U.S. government bond	6.80
30-year U.S. government bond	7.50
AA-rated 10-year corporate bond	7.50
A-rated 20-year corporate bond	8.00
High-yield (junk) corporate bond	10.00
Ginnie Mae certificate	7.40
Federal Home Loan Agency notes	7.82

SOURCE: Barron's, July 27, 1992.

WHERE TO BUY U.S. TREASURIES

U.S. T-BILLS
NEW ISSUES (PRIMARY MARKET)
- Through a commercial bank or brokerage firm. Commissions range from $39 to $75 per T-bill; bank fees are usually in the neighborhood of $50.
- Through a "noncompetitive" bid in the Treasury's weekly auction at any of the Federal Reserve Banks. There are no fees.
- Through the Bureau of Public Debt Securities Transaction Branch, Dept. A, Room 429, Washington, DC 20239. Call: 1-202-874-4000.

EXISTING T-BILLS (SECONDARY MARKET)
- Through a brokerage firm. Minimum purchase is $10,000 with multiples thereafter of $1,000.

U.S. TREASURY NOTES AND BONDS
- NEW ISSUES: Directly from Federal Reserve Banks as described above.
- EXISTING ISSUES: From brokerage firms. Minimum purchase is $1,000, although $10,000 is regarded as a round lot. The secondary market for government issues is over the counter.

---

interest rate formulas, they are a better investment than they were a decade ago. They are backed by the full faith and credit of the U.S. government, are inexpensive, entail no commissions, and permit postponement of taxes. Their yields, compounded semiannually, are flexible. They can be bought at banks, at savings and loans, through payroll deduction plans, and through the Bureau of Public Debt.

From 1941 until 1979 the government issued Series E bonds. Starting in 1980 both Series EE and Series HH bonds were issued.

▶ SERIES EE SAVINGS BONDS These pay no coupon interest. Instead they sell for one-half their face value and are redeemed at full face value upon maturity. These are "accrual-type" bonds, which means that interest is paid when the bond is cashed in on or before maturity and not regularly over the life of the bond.

Denominations range from $50 to $10,000. A $50 bond costs $25; a $10,000 bond costs

$5,000. The maximum annual investment in EE bonds is $30,000 face value per calendar year per person.

The interest on EE bonds purchased after November 1, 1986, is 4.16% for the first 6 months, 4.27% for the first year, and then moves up $\frac{1}{4}$% every 6 months until the fifth year, when it reaches 6%. (EE bonds purchased before November 1, 1986, retain the old 7.5% minimum.) After the fifth year, the interest rate is equal to 85% of the average yield paid on 5-year Treasury notes. On May 1, 1992, the rate was 5.58%. If your state and local taxes come to 10%, then this 5.58% yield equals 6.2% return on an investment subject to taxes. In addition, the government guarantees a minimum of 6% on bonds held 5 years or longer, which protects you against sharp drops in interest rates. You receive the accrued interest as the difference between the purchase price and the face value when you hold the bond to maturity. Interest is exempt from state and local taxes and deferred from federal tax until cashed in. Even then you can further delay paying federal taxes by swapping Series EE bonds for Series HH bonds.

$ HINT: Because their interest is credited only twice a year, redeem EE bonds right after their 6-month anniversary; if you redeem prior to that date, you will lose several months' interest.

If you still hold Series E and H savings bonds, cash them in or roll them over into EEs or HHs. On the old issues, no interest will be paid 40 years after the original date: before April 1952 for Es, before May 1959 for Hs.

$ HINT: To determine the average rate that applies to a bond, you must add up the different rates for all the periods you have held the bond and divide by the number of periods. Round that number off to the nearest quarter of a percentage point.

▶ SERIES HH BONDS These are available only through an exchange of at least $500 in Series E or EE bonds. They are issued in denominations from $500 to $10,000 and pay 6% over a 10-year period to maturity. Unlike EEs, they pay interest semiannually and are sold at full face value. You get the interest twice a year by Treasury check and, at redemption, receive only your original purchase price. There's a penalty for early redemption when bought for cash but not when exchanged for E or H bonds.

➤ AS A TAX SHELTER When you swap EEs for HHs, the interest—unlike that from savings accounts, money market funds, bonds, and many other investments—does not have to be reported to the IRS annually until you cash them in. By swapping, you can postpone the tax on the accumulated interest for as long as 10 years. At that time, the amount of the accrued income is stamped on the face of the HH bonds, and from then on, you must pay taxes on the semiannual payments. Fill out form PD 3523 to make the transfer.

$ HINT: Buy bonds at the end of the month to gain more income, because the interest is credited from the first day of the month.

➤ LOCATING LOST SAVINGS BONDS If you've lost your savings bonds, get form PD 1048, an Application for Relief, from the U.S. Treasury. Write down as much information as you have: serial number; issuance date; name, address, and Social Security number of the original owner. To obtain a form, call Bureau of Public Debt, 1-202-447-1775. Even with the partial data, the bureau may be able to locate or replace the bonds.

$ HINT: Use EE savings bonds to finance your child's education or other major expense.

HOW SAVINGS BONDS GROW

The more you can allot to savings bonds, the greater your total savings will be when you need them, and the faster you'll reach your savings goals.

SAVE EVERY 2 WEEKS	FOR 5 YEARS*	FOR 8 YEARS*	FOR 12 YEARS*
$7.50	$1,110.88	$1,962.68	$3,366.38
12.50	1,857.60	3,279.12	5,624.72
25.00	3,719.74	6,565.98	11,263.18
50.00	7,439.48	13,131.96	22,526.36
100.00	14,878.96	26,263.92	45,052.72

* Assumes an annual interest rate of 6% (current minimum rate). Rate could be higher.

Target your bonds to come due in tandem with tuition bills. Until a child reaches 14, investment income earned from assets given by parents to the child is taxed at the parents' rate. However, there is no tax on income below $1,000 per year. After the child turns 14, the income is taxed at the child's lower rate. Consult an accountant about your personal situation.

EE SAVINGS BONDS

PROS
↑ Safe; principal and interest guaranteed
↑ No fees or commissions
↑ If lost, replaced free of charge
↑ If held 5 years or more, get floating rate of interest with minimum of 6% guaranteed
↑ Federal taxes deferred
↑ No state or local taxes
↑ Market value does not drop when interest rates rise as with other bonds

CONS
↓ Floating rate minimum available only if bond held 5 years
↓ Cannot be used as collateral
↓ Limited purchase: $30,000 face value in 1 year per person
↓ Other vehicles may pay higher rates

ISSUES OF FEDERAL AGENCIES

Numerous other federal agencies also issue securities—notes, bonds, and certificates—in order to finance their activities. The agencies most popular with investors are those that promote home building and farming, such as the Federal Home Loan Bank System, the Government National Mortgage Association (Ginnie Mae), the Banks for Cooperatives, and the Federal Farm Credit Bank.

Some are guaranteed by the U.S. government, but most are considered only obligations of the government. Even so, they are regarded as akin to U.S. Treasury bills, notes, and bonds, the highest-quality securities available.

Yields on agency issues are generally slightly higher than Treasuries (because they are not considered quite as safe) but lower than most Aaa- or Aa-rated corporate bonds.

YIELD CURVES OF TREASURY SECURITIES

This illustration shows the yield curve for Treasury securities of all maturities from 3 months to 30 years. Three yield curves, each for 3 different dates, are indicated by the different types of lines. Note that the yields for shorter term Treasuries have fallen considerably more than those with 10 to 30 year maturities. For example, the yield for 5 year notes fell from about 7.5% in April of 1991 to nearly 6% in April of 1992.

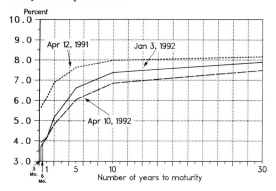

SOURCE: The Federal Reserve Bank of New York, 1992.

THE YIELD CURVE

A yield curve is a diagram that illustrates the relation between bond yields and maturities on a particular day. Use it to decide which type of bond to buy at a certain period. It is published daily in the *Wall Street Journal.*

To draw a yield curve, professionals set out the maturities of like bonds—all Treasuries or all AA rated corporates, on graph paper on a horizontal line, from left to right, starting with the shortest maturities (30 days) and continuing over days or years to the longest (30 years). Then they plot the yields on the vertical axis and connect the dots with a line that becomes the yield curve.

$ HINT: When short-term rates are more than a percentage point above long-term rates, the yield curve is inverted. A recession typically follows, usually within 6 months.

The curve is used to tell if short-term rates are higher or lower than long-term rates. When short-term rates are lower it is called a "positive yield curve." When short-term rates are higher, it's a "negative" or "inverted yield curve." If there is only a modest difference between the two, it's known as a "flat yield curve."

Generally, when the yield curve is positive, investors who are willing to tie up their money long term are rewarded for their risk by getting a higher yield.

Although any fixed-income securities can be plotted on a yield curve, the most common one illustrates Treasuries, from a 3-month T-bill to a 30-year bond.

FOR FURTHER INFORMATION

Free pamphlets, "The Savings Bonds Question and Answer Book," "U.S. Savings Bonds Buyer's Guide," and "U.S. Savings Bonds: Now Tax-Free for Education," are available from:

Department of the Treasury
U.S. Savings Bond Division
Washington, DC 20226
1-202-377-7715

Basic information on Treasury bills is free from your nearest Federal Reserve Bank or:

Federal Reserve Bank of New York
Issues Division, 1st floor
33 Liberty Street
New York, NY 10045
1-212-720-6619

For material on the Treasury Direct program, call or write your area Federal Reserve Bank or write:

Bureau of Public Debt
Department A, Room 429
1300 C Street SW
Washington, DC 20239-1000
1-202-874-4000 (recorded message)

Buying Treasury Securities is available for $4.50 from:

Federal Reserve Bank of Richmond
Public Services Department
P.O. Box 27471
Richmond, VA 23261

These bonds and preferred stocks can be exchanged for a specified number of common shares—almost always those of the issuing company. So investors can have their cake and eat it too. Generally, convertibles (CVs) trade at prices that are 5% to 20% or even 25% above that of the common stock into which they can be converted. The reason behind this premium over the conversion price is that CVs tend to yield 3% to 5% more than common stock dividends. Thus these hybrids combine the safety and fixed income of bonds or preferred stocks with the potential price appreciation of common stock. They pay higher income than common stock and have greater appreciation than regular bonds. CVs pay a fixed rate of interest or a preset dividend and can be exchanged for shares of common stock of the same company, at a specific price.

There are two types of CVs: *Bonds*, secured by the overall credit of the corporation, or *debentures*, corporate bonds that are not secured by specific property, are generally sold at $1,000 each, and are redeemable at par. They pay a fixed rate of interest, which as a rule is less than the interest on straight or nonconvertible bonds of equivalent quality and maturity.

What makes CVs unique is that you can redeem them for the company's underlying stock at a fixed price. This means that CVs offer appreciation possibilities linked to the growth of the company, because as the common stock rises in price, the price of the CV also increases. More often than not, however, the issuing company calls the convertible bonds, forcing a conversion—but never below their conversion value. Bonds are generally called when interest rates fall so the corporation can save money by issuing new bonds at a lower rate.

$ HINT: If the CV is called when the market value of the stock is greater than the conversion value of the bond, you should opt to convert.

HOW CONVERTIBLES WORK

Company ABC needs to raise capital for expansion but does not want to dilute the value of its common stock by issuing new shares at this time. It also rejects selling a straight bond since it would be forced to pay the going interest rate, which for this example is 12%. Instead, management offers a bond that can be "converted" into its own common stock. Because of this desirable conversion feature, investors are willing to buy the CV bond at a lower rate of only 10%. Bonds are quoted as a percentage of par, or face value, which is $1,000, so this bond is listed as 100. This is the *market price*, the price at which the CV can be bought and sold to investors.

When Company ABC issues the CV bonds, its common stock is selling at $32 per share. Management decides its offering will be attractive to the public if each $1,000 bond can be converted into 25 shares of common. This is the *conversion ratio*—the number of shares of common stock you receive by converting one bond. The *conversion price* of the ABC bond is $40 (divide 25 into $1,000). The current value of the total shares of ABC Corp. to which a bond can be converted is the *conversion value*. With ABC stock trading at $32 and a CV ratio of 25, the conversion value is $800.

On the day of issue, the difference between $40 (the conversion price) and $32 (the current market price) is $8. To determine the *conversion premium*, $8 is divided by $32 to yield 0.25, or a 25% CV premium. Another way to figure the conversion premium is to take the price of the bond ($1,000), subtract the CV value ($800), and divide the remainder ($200) by the CV value.

CONVERTIBLE BONDS

COMPANY/BOND	CV PRICE OF BOND*	PRICE OF COMMON	PRICE OF BOND	S&P RATING
Anadarko Petroleum 6¼, 2014	$34.20	$20	$92	BBB+
Browning Ferris 6⅛s, 2012	41.00	21	86	A
Hechinger 5½s, 2012	27.84	12	72	BBB−
Potomac Electric Power 7s, 2018	27.00	23	98	A+
Tele-Communications 7s, 2012	17.00	16	103	B+

* CV price of the bond is equal to the price at which you can convert the bond into stock.

SOURCE: Standard & Poor's Bond Guide, April 1992.

The *investment value* of ABC's CV is an estimated price, usually set by an investment advisory service, at which the bond would be selling if there were no conversion feature. For ABC it is 75.

The *premium-over-investment value* is the percentage difference between the estimated investment value and the market price of the bond. Here the investment value is 75 and the market price is 100, so the difference is 25, or 33% of 75. The premium-over-investment value is therefore 33.

TIPS FOR INVESTING IN CVs

- Buy a CV only if you like the common stock.
- Avoid CVs of potential takeover companies; you may be forced to convert early.
- Buy only high-rated issues—BB or above as rated by Standard & Poor's or Ba by Moody's
- Know the call provisions; if a CV is called too early, you may not recover your premium.

HOW TO MAKE A PROFIT

IF THE STOCK GOES UP

In general, a CV's price will accompany the rise in price of the company's common stock, although it never rises as much. For example, let's say the underlying stock rises by 50%, from $32 to $48. To find the value of the CV bond, multiply the higher price by the conversion ratio: $48 × 25 = $1,200 (or 120, as bond prices are expressed). During the time in which this rise has taken place, the investor has received 10% interest on the bond and has participated in the appreciation of the common stock by seeing the value of the CV bond appreciate by 20%, from $100 to $120.

IF THE STOCK GOES DOWN

If the underlying stock falls in price, the CV may also fall in price, but less so. Let us assume that the price of ABC, instead of appreciating by 50% to $48, drops by 50% to $16 per share. Its conversion value is now only $400 ($16 × the CV ratio of 25). What happens to the price of the CV? The senior position of the bond as well as the 10% interest rate payable to bondholders serve as a brake on its decline in price. Somewhere between $100 and $40 the safety features inherent in a CV bond become operative, usually at the investment value, which in this case is 75. At 75 the bond's yield will rise to 13.33%.

§ HINT: When you want to make an investment but you fear that the company's common stock is too volatile and therefore risky, check to see if there are any convertible bonds or preferreds outstanding.

TO CONVERT OR NOT TO CONVERT

By and large, holders of CVs should stay with the security of the CV and not convert. Stock markets are uncertain, and prices of individual stocks have been known to fall 50% or even more. Therefore, the holder of a CV, which is senior to the common stock, should surrender or convert only under certain circumstances such as these:

- The company, in a restructuring, makes a tender offer for a large percentage of its outstanding common stock at a price well above the market price. The CV bondholder must convert to common stock in order to participate in this tender offer.
- In another type of restructuring, the company pays stockholders a special dividend equal to most of the price of the common stock. Here again, the CV bondholder must convert in order to receive this special dividend. In July 1988, USG Corp. paid for each common share outstanding $37 in cash, plus other securities, in a corporate restructuring.
- Corporations in cyclical businesses pay oversized year-end dividends. General Motors, for instance, did this for many years. To receive a special dividend, CV bondholders must convert prior to the ex-dividend date.

CV MUTUAL FUNDS

If you have limited capital or prefer to let someone else make the selections, there are mutual funds that use a substantial portion of their assets to buy CVs and, in some cases, to write options.

When considering CV mutual funds, keep these tips in mind:

- Usual minimum investment is $1,000.
- Shares can be purchased directly from the fund or from a stockbroker.
- Read the fund's prospectus before investing.
- Check the quality of the fund's underlying stocks.
- Convertibles offer a hedge against volatile changes in the stock market.
- Automatic reinvestment of distribution into additional fund shares is available.
- If you invest in a family of funds and your yield declines, you can switch to higher-yielding funds within the family.

HEDGING WITH CVs

For experienced investors, CVs offer excellent vehicles for hedging—buying one security and simultaneously selling short its related security. The hedge is set up so that if the market goes up, one can make more money on the purchase than one can lose on the sale, or vice versa if the market goes down. Such trading is best in volatile markets (of which there have been plenty in recent years).

Here's an example cited by expert Thomas

CONVERTIBLES

PROS

↑ When the stock market falls, CVs do not fall as much as the underlying stock.

↑ You can keep collecting regular income no matter what happens to the stock.

CONS

↓ You do not receive the full price gain when the stock goes up.

↓ You do not earn as much interest as you would had you bought the bond.

↓ When a takeover bid is made, the common stock usually soars in price.

↓ A proposed new takeover deal may eliminate CV holders' rights to exchange their bonds for stock.

↓ CVs are often issued by companies with poor ratings.

LEADING CONVERTIBLE BOND MUTUAL FUNDS

FUND	TOTAL RETURN, JANUARY 1 TO MARCH 31, 1992
Dreyfus Convertible Securities (1-800-645-6561)	+.44%
American Capital Harbor Fund (1-800-421-5666)	−13.0
Putman Convertible Income Growth (1-800-354-4000)	+6.92
AIM Convertible Securities (1-800-347-1919)	−6.0
Calamos Convertible Income Fund (1-800-323-9943)	+.38
Value Line Convertible Fund (1-800-223-0818)	+1.27
Phoenix Convertible Fund Series (1-800-243-1574)	+2.85

C. Noddings: The CV debenture carries a 10% coupon and is convertible into 40 shares of common stock. The CV trades at 90; the common at 20. *Buy* 10 CVs at 90 at a cost of $9,000; sell short 150 common at 20—$3,000. Since the short sale requires no investment, the cost is $9,000 (not counting commissions).

- *If the price of the stock falls to 10,* the CV's estimated price will be 72, so there will be a loss of $1,800 ($9,000 − $7,200). But 150 shares of stock can be acquired for $1,500, for a profit of $1,500. Add $500 interest (10% for 6 months), and the net profit is $200.
- *If the price of the stock dips to 15,* the CV will sell at 80 for a $1,000 loss, but this will be offset by the $750 profit on the stock plus $500 interest, for a return of $250.
- *If the price of the stock holds at 20,* the CV will stay at 90. There will be no profit on either, but the $500 interest will represent an annualized rate of return of 11%.

- *If the stock rises to 25,* the CV will be worth 104, for a $1,400 profit, but there will be a $750 loss on the shorted stock. With the $500 interest, there'll still be a $1,150 profit.
- *And if the stock soars to 40,* the CV will trade at 160, for a whopping $7,000 gain, which will be offset by a $3,000 loss on the stock but enhanced by the $500 income, for a total of $4,500 on that $9,000 investment—all in 6 months!

Says Noddings: "Selling short stock against undervalued CVs can eliminate risk while offering unlimited gains if the stock advances."

Best bet with hedges of CVs: Try out the "if projections" on paper until you are sure that you understand what can happen. By and large, the actual transactions will follow these patterns. At worst, the losses will be small; at best, the profits will be welcome.

WRITING CALLS WITH CVs

Noddings also shows how to write calls with CVs. This is a conservative way to boost income and, when properly executed, involves minimal risks and fair-to-good gains. Since the CVs represent a call on the stock, they provide a viable base. Let's say that a $1,000 par value CV debenture can be swapped for 40 shares of common; the CV is at 90, the stock at 20; the calls, exercisable at 20, are due in 6 months and carry a premium of 2 ($200) each.

Buy 10 CVs for $9,000 and sell 3 calls. (Since the CVs represent 400 shares of stock, this is no problem.) The $600 premium will reduce the net investment to $8,400. *If the stock jumps to 40,* the CV will sell at 160, for a $7,000 gain. Add $500 interest to get $7,500 income. But there will be a $5,400 loss because the calls will have to be repurchased with a (tax-advantaged) deficit of $1,800 each. The net profit will thus be $2,100.

Warning: Writing calls on CVs is *not* for amateurs. To be worthwhile, this technique should (1) involve a substantial number of shares (at least 300), (2) be done with the aid of a knowledgeable broker who watches for sudden aberrations in price spreads, (3) be initiated with adequate cash or margin reserves that may be needed to buy back calls early, and (4) be undertaken only by individuals in a high enough tax bracket to benefit from the short-term losses.

FOR FURTHER INFORMATION

BOOKS

Thomas C. Noddings, *Superhedging* (Chicago: Probus Publishing Co., 1985).

NEWSLETTERS

Value Line Convertibles
711 Third Avenue
New York, NY 10017
1-212-687-3965; 1-800-634-3583
48 times per year; $475

RHM Convertible Survey
172 Forest Avenue
Glen Cove, NY 11542
1-516-759-2904
50 times per year; $350

MUNICIPAL BONDS:
Last of the Tax Shelters

Tax-exempt bonds (also called municipals) are debt issues of states, local governments, and certain public authorities. Their interest is free of federal income taxes; if issued in the investor's state of residence, they are also exempt from local and state income levies. Debt issues of Puerto Rico, Guam, and the Virgin Islands are tax-exempt in all 50 states.

Because of their tax-exempt status, munis pay a lower interest rate than taxable bonds. They are issued in units of $5,000 or $10,000. Most brokers are reluctant to sell just one bond, and many have $20,000+ minimums.

Tax-free income has always been appealing, and municipal bonds are one of the few ways left to achieve this goal since the 1986 tax reform.

CATEGORIES OF MUNICIPAL BONDS

In broad terms, the 1986 Tax Reform Act divides municipals into four categories.

➤ GENERAL OBLIGATION BONDS (GOs) Also known as public-purpose bonds, these have not been touched much by reform. The Act maintains the historic tax-exempt status for these bonds, which are sold to finance roads, schools, and government buildings. However, these issues, which are the most conservative of the municipals, are now tax-exempt only when no more than 10% of their proceeds is used by a private entity. Under the old rules, GOs were tax-exempt unless more than 25% of the proceeds benefited a private entity.

General obligation bonds are the most common and generally the safest municipals. They are backed by the full taxing power of the issuer. The payment of their interest and redemption is a primary obligation, so they usually have the highest safety ratings but often the lowest yields.

➤ INDUSTRIAL DEVELOPMENT BONDS (IDBs) As soon as more than 10% of the dollars raised by the sale of a muni is used by a private entity, the bond is classified as an industrial development bond. IDBs are issued by states or authorities to finance construction of plants, buildings, and facilities that are then leased to private firms such as Exxon, RCA, General Motors, or McDonald's. Because of the backing by major firms, many of these issues carry top ratings.

To permit small investors to participate, brokerage firms offer packaged industrial development bonds in limited partnerships at $5,000 per unit. The income increases with the gross revenues from the tenant. The aftermarket is limited, there's little diversification, and costs and fees tend to be high. Investigate carefully before purchasing.

☐ CAUTION: If you buy an IDB issued after August 7, 1986, beware: The interest earned is treated as a "preference" item and must be added to your taxable income *if* you are required to calculate the alternative minimum tax (AMT). This means that IDBs are suitable for people not likely to be subject to the AMT. The one exception: bonds issued by private, nonprofit hospitals and universities; these so-called 501(c) bonds are not taxable.

$ HINT: As compensation for the fact that the interest income, by its nature as a "tax preference," may be subject to the 21% alternative minimum tax, industrial development bonds pay a slightly higher yield than general obligation or public-purpose bonds.

➤ TAXABLE MUNICIPALS The tax law eliminates issuance of tax-exempt bonds for what Congress

---

PRE–AUGUST 7, 1986, BONDS

PROS
↑ Virtually the only tax shelter available
↑ Higher yields than Treasury bonds in many cases
↑ Excellent ratings
↑ Especially valuable in states with high local taxes
CONS
↓ Dominated by institutional investors
↓ Limited market if selling bonds before maturity
↓ Lower tax rates reduce attractiveness

STRIPPED MUNIS

PROS
↑ Can time your balloon payment
↑ No problem of where to reinvest income
↑ Noncallable
↑ Know exactly what you will receive
↑ Shorter maturity dates than regular munis
CONS
↓ Interest is locked in; yield could rise
↓ Should be held to maturity
↓ Slim secondary market at present

---

deems nonessential purposes, such as pollution control facilities, sports stadiums, convention and trade shows, industrial parks, and parking facilities. For the most part, these bonds continue to be exempt from state and local taxes where issued, even though they are now subject to federal taxes.

To win over investors who traditionally purchased Treasury and corporate bonds, the new taxable municipals, or "private-activity bonds" as they're also called, are being conservatively designed to assure top rankings from Moody's and Standard & Poor's. Yields so far are generally 2 to 3 percentage points higher than fully tax-exempt municipals.

➤ PRE–AUGUST 7, 1986, BONDS You can avoid the problems that accompany newly issued municipals by purchasing in the secondary market bonds issued prior to August 7, 1986. These are generally not taxable. A number of firms packaged pre–August 7 bonds, but the supply of older bonds is dwindling now because of aggressive purchases by both bond mutual funds and trusts. As is always the case, the demand is boosting prices and lowering yields.

ZERO COUPON MUNIS

Thanks to the 1986 Tax Reform Act, a variation on municipal bonds was introduced for the small investor that enables smaller investors to participate for a relatively low dollar amount.

"Stripped munis," as the product is called, remove or strip off the semiannual coupons from a municipal bond and then sell both parts separately—the principal and the series of coupon interest payments. By dividing the bond into two pieces, maturities are created that never existed before in the municipal bond market. Before, bondholders had to wait 20 to 40 years for a muni to mature; zeros mature in less than half that time.

When you buy a stripped muni, you are in essence buying a couponless bond with zero interest, hence the name "zero coupon." You will never receive interest on this bond, but to offset this disadvantage, the zero coupon muni sells at a discount (below par). You receive the full face value ($1,000) at maturity.

And there are tax advantages: If, for example, you buy a zero at $800, when it matures you'll receive $1,000, but there will be no federal tax due on the $200—the profit made during the holding period.

Alternatively, you can buy one or a whole series of coupons. The coupon, of course, costs far less than the bond. And again there will be no federal tax on the earned interest.

$ HINT: Use zero munis to pay for college or plan for retirement or other distant obligations. Place them in your child's name. There is no federal tax on zero munis.

Bonds used for stripping are noncallable, so you are assured of your position. But to reap full benefits, you should plan to hold these securities until maturity. Talk to your accountant or broker first—the details vary from issue to issue. Strips are sold by Salomon Brothers as M-Cats, by Goldman Sachs as Municipal Receipts, and by Morgan Stanley as MBears.

CONVERTIBLE MUNICIPALS

You're now familiar with zero coupon munis—STRIPS—yet there is another variation on the theme—zero coupon convertible municipal bonds. Like other zeros (see Chapter 12), they sell at a deep discount to face value. Their unique feature, however, is that at a certain time they convert into regular interest bonds.

For example, a 25-year zero muni bond pays out no interest during the first 10 years. Then in the tenth year it converts into a regular bond. At that point the investor starts to receive 10% interest (in cash) and continues to receive it for the remaining 15 years. At maturity, the bond returns the full face value of $1,000. Both appreciation and income are free of federal income tax.

There are two major drawbacks, however: States may impose tax on the imputed interest, and a zero muni can be called in early.

$ HINT: Buy only zero munis that are issued in your own state, so that interest is tax-free, and that are noncallable or can be called only *after* they start paying out cash interest. This way you'll capture the most interest.

PREREFUNDED BONDS

These are high-quality, triple-A rated bonds that are guaranteed by U.S. Treasury obligations until the first date of call—that is, the earliest time the issuer can redeem the bonds before maturity. They come into being when a state or municipality refinances an existing bond issue that it cannot yet call. This is usually done to take advantage of lower interest rates. A new bond is issued to raise money to pay off the old one, and the proceeds are invested in enough Treasuries to cover interest and principal payments until the call date.

Example: New York State Urban Development 8⅞s, yield 7.3%, due to be called in 1996.

SINGLE-STATE BONDS

If you live in a high-tax state, look for munis issued by your own state and local governments. You can add as much as 1½ percentage points to your yield. Among the highest-taxed states are California, Connecticut, Massachusetts, Minnesota, and New York. Single-state unit trusts and mutual funds are listed in the box below.

Funds that specialize in single-state bonds must purchase bonds from a smaller pool than regular bond funds and consequently have less choice when it comes to bond grade, type, and maturity. This adds an element of risk to these bonds.

$ HINT: If you pay high state and/or local income taxes, look into single-state bond funds that invest only in your state.

LEADING SINGLE-STATE MUNICIPAL BOND FUNDS

STATE	MUTUAL FUND	YIELD (MAY 1992)	TOTAL RETURN (MAY 1992)
Minnesota	Franklin Minnesota Insured (1-800-632-2180)	5.78%	8.83%
New York	Putnam New York (1-800-225-1581)	6.03	10.39
West Virginia	MFS Managed West Virginia (1-800-225-2606)	5.86	9.5
California	MFS Managed California (1-800-225-2606)	6.04	10.5
Oregon	Oregon Municipal Bond Fund (1-503-295-0919) (1-800-541-9732)	4.86	8.35

Whether you select a bond mutual fund or a unit trust, read the prospectus first and determine the minimum rating set by management. Beware of any fund with a large portion of its holdings in issues with a B rating.

☐ CAUTION: Munis rated below A (muni-junk bonds) are regarded by many bond experts as risky. (The ratings are behind the true credit risk—they're a lagging indicator.) But because there is a shortage of municipals, many fund managers and others buy them anyway. Certain housing and health care bonds fall into this risk category. When buying a muni fund, trust, or individual bond, check the exact ratings.

YOUR TAXES AND MUNICIPALS

One of the unfortunate fallouts of tax reform that affects a great many investors stems from the provisions covering the alternative minimum tax (AMT). According to the terms of the 1986 Tax Reform Act, interest earned on all newly issued IDBs, with the sole exception of those issued by private, nonprofit hospitals and universities, called 501(c) bonds, is subject to a 21%

AMT for individuals and a 20% AMT for corporations, if, of course, they are subject to the AMT. Check with your accountant.

💲 HINT: Municipal bond income is taxable under certain circumstances for some retirees. Up to half of a retiree's benefits can be taxed if municipal bond interest income plus adjusted gross income plus half of Social Security payments is more than $32,000 for couples or $25,000 for singles. Ask your accountant.

■ In a state that has local or state income taxes, the interest on municipal bonds issued in that state is exempt from these taxes as well as the federal income tax. Thus if you live in New Jersey, buy bonds issued there.

A FREEBIE

The Franklin fund family has a free slide rule that lets you figure out your combined state and federal marginal income tax rate. The data are available for every state and for both the 28% and 31% tax brackets. Call 1-800-342-5236.

FEDERAL EQUIVALENT YIELDS FOR 1992

Tax Bracket	Joint Return	Single Return	AND...	5.5%	6.0	6.5	7.0	7.5	8.0	8.5
	If your 1992 Federal tax bracket is...			you have a tax exempt investment yielding:						
				Then you'll be earning the equivalent of a taxable investment paying:						
28%	$35,801–86,500	$21,451–51,900		7.64%	8.33	9.03	9.72	10.42	11.11	11.81
31%	Over $86,500	Over $51,900		7.97%	8.70	9.42	10.14	10.87	11.59	12.32

This chart is for illustrative purposes only. Both the Fund's net asset value and yield will vary, and there can be no guarantee that the Fund will achieve any particular tax exempt yield. Income may be subject to some state or local taxes. Some income may be subject to the Federal alternative minimum tax for certain investors. This material must be preceded or accompanied by a current Prospectus.

SOURCE: U.S. Treasury, 1992.

BUYING MUNICIPAL BONDS

- If, after calculating your tax rate, you find that municipals turn out to be advantageous, start with general obligation bonds. These bonds typically yield less than riskier municipals because they are the most conservative.

- All municipals are sold with legal opinions attached to their offering circulars. These will tell you if the issue is tax-free or not.

- As with all investments, the number one checkpoint is *quality,* best indicated by the ratings set by Moody's and S&P.

  For investments, buy only bonds with A ratings. They are safe, and in most cases their yields will be only slightly lower than those of poor-quality bonds.

  For speculations, a Baa rating involves as much risk as anyone seeking income should take. If you want to gamble, do not buy tax-exempt bonds unless you are very experienced and very rich.

  Once in a while, you may be asked to buy unrated issues: those from municipalities that are so small or have such modest debt that they have never been rated. If you personally know the community and its officials, these can be viable investments, but keep the maturities short, because you will have difficulty selling in a hurry.

TURBULENT TIMES FOR MUNICIPALS

Many state and local governments are facing financial difficulties and, in fact, as of mid-1992, about 35 states were in the red. The cause: big cutbacks in federal grants to states as well as the economic slowdown, which has lowered tax revenues. Due to the budget crunch, the credit ratings of some municipalities are likely to be lowered. This doesn't mean you should shy away from munis altogether. They remain one of the few ways to lower your federal taxes and even state taxes in some cases.

➤ MUNIS TO BE CAUTIOUS ABOUT Beware of most general obligation (GO) bonds. These are backed by state and local tax revenue and not by money from a specific project. As a group, they are the most likely to be downgraded. However, those likely to remain solid are munis of strong midwestern cities such as Columbus, Ohio, Indianapolis, Indiana, Milwaukee, Wisconsin, and Minneapolis, Minnesota. Also beware of some revenue bonds. These are supported by income from specific projects, not by taxes in general, therefore they tend to be safer than GOs. But many are backed by projects that could run into trouble, such as housing, hospital, airport, and toll road revenue bonds.

➤ MUNIS TO CONSIDER The safest munis, again in general, are revenue bonds backed by highly steady streams of income, such as utility bills.

10 TAX-EXEMPT BOND FUNDS

FUND	YIELD (MAY, 1992)
Calvert Tax-free Long Term (1-800-368-2748)	5.65%
Dreyfus Intermediate Tax-exempt (1-800-645-6561)	5.89
Fidelity Municipal Bond (1-800-544-8888)	5.76
Financial Tax-free Income (1-800-525-8085)	5.94
New York Muni Fund (1-800-225-6864)	5.31
T. Rowe Price Tax-free Intermediate (1-800-638-5660)	4.92
Scudder Managed Municipal (1-800-225-2470)	5.57
Stein Roe Intermediate Municipal (1-800-338-2550)	4.94
Value Line Tax-exempt Fund (1-800-223-0818)	6.02
Vanguard Long-Term Municipal (1-800-662-7447)	6.00

WATER REVENUE BONDS

ISSUER	MOODY'S RATING	APPROXIMATE YIELDS
Seattle, WA, Water System	Aa	6.35 to 7.00%
New York City Municipal Water Financial Authority	A	7.50 to 7.75
DuPage, IL, Water Commission	A1	6.40 to 7.00
Kansas City, MO, Water System	Aa	6.25 to 6.75
Birmingham, AL, Water & Sewer	Aa	6.30 to 6.80
South Central CT, Water Authority	A	6.50 to 7.00

Among these, water revenue bonds are probably the best bet. Electric revenue bonds are also solid choices, especially those issued by utilities with new coal plants and few nuclear operations. Because of the export boom in this country, revenue bonds for ports are also relatively safe. And keep in mind bonds of the Commonwealth of Puerto Rico. Their income is free from state, local, and federal taxes no matter where you live in the United States. To date, Puerto Rico has never defaulted on a bond issue. The economy is improving, with unemployment dropping from about 20% to around 10%.

$ HINT: Look for "escrowed to maturity with Treasury bonds." Nicknamed ETMs, these bonds were issued in the early 1980s and have been refunded now that interest rates have come down. This means that the issuers have taken some of the proceeds of the new issue and bought Treasury bonds that are in an escrow account and guarantee both the interest and principal payments of the original issue. Therefore, it is a municipal issue guaranteed with U.S. Treasury bonds.

CHECKPOINTS FOR TAX-EXEMPTS

➤ MATURITY DATE   For bonds with the same rating, the shorter the maturity, the lower the yield and the greater the price stability. Unless you plan to buy municipals regularly, it is usually prudent to stick to those with maturities of less than 10 years. In many cases, these will be older bonds selling at a discount. Select maturities according to your financial needs and

ELECTRIC REVENUE BONDS

ISSUER	MOODY'S RATING	APPROXIMATE YIELDS
South Carolina Public Service Authority	A1	6.60 to 7.05%
Intermountain Power Agency (UT)	Aa	6.50 to 7.00
Austin, TX, Combined Utility	A	6.50 to 6.95
New York State Power Authority	Aa	6.15 to 6.90
Indiana Power Agency	A	6.25 to 6.90
Orlando Utilities Commission (FL)	Aa	6.30 to 7.00

PUERTO RICO MUNICIPAL BONDS

ISSUER	MOODY'S RATING	APPROXIMATE YIELDS
Puerto Rico Electric Power	Baa1	6.75 to 7.25%
Puerto Rico Highway Authority	Baa1	6.80 to 7.30
Puerto Rico Telephone Authority	A	6.50 to 7.05
University of Puerto Rico	A	6.40 to 7.05
Commonwealth of Puerto Rico	Baa1	6.80 to 7.30

time schedule. If you plan to retire 8 years from now, pick a discount bond that will mature at that time. Munis range from 1 month (notes) to 30 years.

➤ MARKETABILITY The most readily salable municipals are general obligation bonds of state governments and revenue bonds of large, well-known authorities. Smaller issues have few price quotations, and the cost of selling, especially in odd lots, can be high.

➤ CALL PROVISION Larger issues usually permit the bonds to be called—redeemed before maturity—at a price above par. With older low-coupon issues, there's no problem, because they will be selling below par. But with high-coupon issues, when interest rates decline, watch out. If a bond is trading at 115, it will be callable at 105, and it will pay the issuer to retire the bonds and refinance at a lower interest rate. Most municipals are issued with 10-year call provisions. Many issued in the early 1980s, when interest rates were much higher than they are now, are likely to be called between 1991 and 1995. People living off these dividends will have to reinvest at lower rates.

➤ YIELD DISPARITIES If you buy more than 10 bonds, shop around. It's best to buy from your broker's inventory; but even if you do, you will find wide differences among munis of comparable ratings.

➤ TYPES OF BONDS Prior to 1983 there were two types of tax-free bonds: *bearer, or nonregistered, bonds* whose holders detached coupons and sent them in or went through a bank to receive the interest, and *registered bonds* with the name and owner identified on the face of the certificate or, more likely, in a central filing system of the issuer. Today, all munis are issued in registered form. They therefore cost less to handle and usually eliminate printed certificates. A registered bond can be transferred to another owner *only* when endorsed by the registered owner. Bearer bonds are actually nonnegotiable instruments and payable only to the bearer or holder. They do not require a legal endorsement.

➤ BROKER'S REPUTATION If you get a hard sell on tax-exempts, especially by phone, be *very* cautious. Do business only with your regular broker, or one you trust.

➤ SERIAL MATURITIES Unlike most corporate bonds, which usually have the same redemption date, municipals often mature serially: A portion of the debt comes due each year until the final redemption. Select maturities to fit future needs: college tuition, retirement, etc.

$ HINT: If you're in the 28% tax bracket, an 8% tax-free municipal is equal to an 11% federally taxed bond.

➤ BUYING AND SELLING MUNIS You must shop around for the best price. In May 1992, the *Wall Street Journal* reported that an investor contacted eight securities firms regarding sale of a $10,000 face value Port Authority of New York and New Jersey bond. He was given prices ranging from $9,500 (Charles Schwab & Company) to $9,865 (Roosevelt & Cross). Several firms raised their bids when given competitive quotes. Moral: Don't take the first price offered. It's like selling jewelry or fine art—prices vary from dealer to dealer.

BONDS SUBJECT TO PERSONAL
ALTERNATIVE MINIMUM TAX

- General obligation issues in which more than 10% of the proceeds is used by a private entity
- Single- and multifamily housing bonds
- Student loan bonds
- Bonds financing small industrial development projects
- Bonds for airports and other ports not owned by local governments

---

MUNICIPAL BOND MUTUAL FUNDS

For small investors, one of the best ways to buy municipals is through a mutual fund. Mutual funds provide diversification (by type, grade, coupon, and maturity), continuous professional management, the opportunity to add to your portfolio with relatively small dollar amounts, the ability to switch to other funds under the same sponsorship, and, most important, prompt reinvestment of interest to buy new shares and benefit from compounding.

Unless you have over $10,000 and can watch the market, a fund is the best way to invest in munis. The yields may be lower than you could obtain with individual bonds, but you won't be tempted to spend the income if you

have the fund automatically reinvest it. Minimum investments are generally $1,000. (See Chapter 6 for details on selecting mutual funds.)

In a fund that is open-ended the portfolio contains bonds with varying maturities. The manager continually buys and sells bonds in order to improve returns, switching from short- to long-term maturities when yields are high and doing the opposite when yields decline. When interest rates shift quickly, some funds do extremely well; some do not. Keep in mind that your income from the fund will fluctuate, unlike that from an individual bond or a unit trust, where the yield is locked in.

MUNICIPAL BOND UNIT TRUSTS

These are closed-end funds with fixed portfolios of municipal bonds that remain in the trust until maturity, unless they are called. The trust aims to lock in the highest yield possible with good-quality issues at the time of the initial offering. Each trust has a limited number of shares for sale, but new trusts are continually being brought to the market. Sponsors also buy back existing units from investors who want to sell before the trust matures. The units are registered in the name of the investor, and monthly, quarterly, or semiannual checks are mailed out to the holder. A handful of unit investment trusts have reinvestment privileges. Most provide income for a limited period—3, 5, 10, 20, or 30 years.

When the bonds mature, are sold (rarely),

INSURED MUNICIPAL BOND MUTUAL FUNDS

FUND	YIELD (MAY 1992)
Vanguard Muni Bond Insured Long Term (1-800-662-7447)	6.06%
Merrill Lynch Muni Insured Portfolio (1-609-282-2800)	6.26
American Capital Tax-exempt Insured (1-800-421-5666)	6.12
Dreyfus Insured Tax-exempt Bond Fund (1-800-645-6561)	5.54
Fidelity Insured Tax-free (1-800-544-8888)	5.89

MUTUAL FUND VS. UNIT TRUST

- A managed mutual fund is generally a better investment for people who expect to sell in less than 10 years. The shares react quickly to fluctuating interest rates. Check the 1-, 5-, and 10-year performance records of several before investing.
- Unit trusts are best for long-term holdings, especially when the initial yield is high enough that you want to lock it in.

INTEREST RATE RISK

Interest rate risk is a greater problem than defaults for municipal bonds. According to the Value Line Investment Service, a 20-year bond with an interest coupon of 9% that is trading at par declines in value by 8.6% when interest rates rise 1 percentage point; it rises in value by 9.9% when rates decline 1 percentage point. This volatility increases as the bond's maturity lengthens and its coupon rate declines.

or are called, the principal is returned to the unit holders as a return of capital. If the sponsor feels a bond is endangering the trust's interest, it can be sold and proceeds paid out. Unit trusts, of course, are vulnerable to the risks of rising interest and early call on bonds in the portfolio.

Units can be sold in the secondary market, but doing so entails a commission. If interest rates have fallen, you could make a profit, but if they've gone up, you may not get back your original investment. Unit trust prices are based on the price of the securities in the portfolio and are determined either by the sponsor or by an independent evaluator. Nuveen, for instance, which has a number of trusts, sets the price on a daily basis. Although unit prices are not given in the newspaper, you can call the sponsor for up-to-date quotes.

There are two kinds of trusts: general and state. General trusts include bonds from various states and territories, while state trusts have bonds only from a single state, hence the name "single-state unit trusts." Income is generally free from state and local taxes in the issuing state as well as from federal taxes.

Unit trusts are usually sold in $1,000 units and have a one-time sales charge that typically ranges from 2% to 5% plus annual fees in the neighborhood of 0.15%. Both these costs are factored into the yield. Mutual funds, by contrast, may be subject to a sales charge ("load") or not ("no load").

MUNICIPAL BOND INSURANCE

Years ago, investors never doubted that a municipal bond issuer would pay the annual interest and pay back the principal. Then along came the default of the Washington Public Power System. Now an increasing number of tax-free issues, as well as mutual funds and trusts, offer insurance for additional peace of mind. According to the Chicago-based bond counsel firm of Chapman & Cutler, fewer than 1% of the municipals issued since the Great Depression have defaulted. Of those defaults, approximately 77% occurred with bonds issued to finance revenue-producing facilities such as utilities, bridges, and nuclear power plants.

To insure its bonds, the issuer pays an insurance premium ranging between 0.1% and 2% of total principal and interest. In return, the insurance company will pay the principal and interest to the bondholders should the issuer default. Generally, policies for new issues cannot be canceled, and the insurance remains active over the lifetime of the bond. With a bond fund or unit trust, the insurance is generally purchased for the entire portfolio. The oldest insurers are the American Municipal Bond Assurance Corp. (AMBAC) and the Municipal Bond Insurance Association (MBIA). Both are rated Aaa by Moody's and AAA by Standard & Poor's.

Once a bond is insured, it is given an AAA rating by S&P *even if the bond originally had a BBB rating.* So remember that if you are purchasing an AAA insured bond, it may really be a BBB bond with insurance.

Insured municipal bonds pay lower yields, usually 0.1 to 0.5 percentage points less than comparable uninsured bonds. If the insurer's rating drops, so do the ratings of all the issues that the company has insured.

$ HINT: Insurance does not protect you against market risks: If interest rates go up, the value of bonds still goes down.

FOR FURTHER INFORMATION

Muni Week
1 State Street Plaza
New York, NY 10004
1-212-943-8200
Weekly; $597 per year; $10 per copy

David L. Scott, *Municipal Bonds: The Basics and Beyond* (Chicago: Probus Publishing Co., 1992).

12 NONTRADITIONAL BONDS: Maes, Junk, and Zeros

THE MAE FAMILY

High yields, safety, and convenience—that's what the various mortgage-backed securities in the Mae family offer. These securities, which are shares in pools of secured mortgages, are often called *pass-throughs* because the sponsor who packages the loans passes through the income (minus a modest fee) directly to investors. Payments are monthly, and yields tend to be 1.5+ points higher than those on comparable Treasury bonds, largely because the monthly payments include principal as well as interest. In this respect the Mae family does not behave like regular bonds, which provide a return of principal upon maturity. Instead you receive monthly checks that reflect both interest *and* principal. It is important to understand this distinction. Many investors mistakenly believe that these monthly checks are interest only. They are both interest *and* part payment of principal.

The pass-through technique allows individual investors to share the income derived from monthly mortgage payments and prepayments. They are similar to mutual funds in that investors do not own one particular mortgage but pieces of many mortgages.

Ginnie Maes are the only securities, other than U.S. Treasury issues, that carry the direct full faith and credit guarantee of the U.S. government. Others in the Mae group, to be described shortly, carry an indirect guarantee.

GINNIE MAEs

"Ginnie Mae" stands for the Government National Mortgage Association (GNMA), a wholly owned corporation of the U.S. government that functions as part of the Department of Housing and Urban Development. The objective of Ginnie Mae is to stimulate

housing by attracting capital and guaranteeing mortgages. A GNMA certificate represents a portion of a pool of 30-year FHA- or VA-insured mortgages. The GNMA provides payment of interest and principal on a monthly basis.

When a homebuyer takes out a mortgage, the house is pledged as collateral. The bank or savings and loan pools this loan with others of similar terms and rates, thus creating a package of mortgages worth $1 million or more. Ginnie Mae reviews the mortgages to make certain they meet certain standards and then assigns a pool number. Stockbrokers and others sell pieces of this pool, called certificates, to the public.

Homebuyers then make their payments (interest and principal) to the bank, which deducts a handling fee as well as a Ginnie Mae insurance fee. The rest of the money is "passed on" to the investors from the mortgage bankers.

Because GNMA certificates carry the guarantee of the U.S. government, they have made mortgage investments especially safe. And since certificates can be traded in the secondary market, they also offer liquidity.

The minimum investment for a GNMA is $25,000, with $5,000 increments thereafter. Monthly interest is considered ordinary income and is taxed, whereas monthly principal payments are considered a return of capital and are exempt from taxes. Monthly payments are *not* uniform—they are based on the remaining principal in the pool. As homeowners make their mortgage payments, the mortgage pool gets paid down, and although you receive the stated coupon interest, it is on a declining amount of debt. In other words, each month the proportion of interest received is slightly less and the proportion of principal slightly more. Over the long term, GNMAs are therefore self-liquidating. When the pool of mortgages is paid in full by homeowners, that's it. You don't receive a lump payment or a return of face value as you do with a zero or straight bond. *Note:* When interest rates fall, homeowners pay off their mortgages and refinance at lower rates. This means your Ginnie Mae is "called in" quickly.

You can purchase Ginnie Maes for less than $25,000 through mutual funds (discussion follows), or you can buy older Ginnie Maes in the secondary market. Older Ginnie Maes have been partially paid down and are usually bid down in value to compensate for the declining stream of income.

☐ CAUTION: Ads for Ginnie Maes and their mutual funds often claim they are totally safe and 100% government guaranteed. This is not true. Ginnie Maes are *not* completely risk-free.

- The government does *not* guarantee the yield.
- The government does *not* protect investors against declines in either the value of the fund's shares or the yield.
- The government, however, *does* indeed protect investors against late mortgage payments as well as foreclosures. If homeowners default, you will still receive payments on time.

$ HINT: If you're considering Ginnie Maes, bear in mind that the average 30-year Ginnie Mae is repaid in about 12 years.

GINNIE MAE MUTUAL FUNDS

For investors who don't want to invest $25,000, Ginnie Maes are available through unit investment trusts and mutual funds for as little as $1,000. In a unit trust, once the trust's portfolio is assembled, it's set. The portfolio manager cannot make adjustments, so if interest rates drop, you face exactly the same dilemma you do in owning a GNMA certificate. Unit investment trusts are explained in greater detail on page 140.

A Ginnie Mae mutual fund is not a pass-through security like the certificates. The fund itself receives interest and principal payments from the certificates in its portfolio. You then own shares in the fund, which in turn pays you dividends. The market value of your shares fluctuates daily, and the interest rate does, too.

☐ CAUTION: The fund's yield is not fixed, nor is it guaranteed. If interest rates fall, as

GNMA MTGE. ISSUES   A-BOND

RATE	MAT.	BID	ASKED	YLD.
7.00	30 Yr	94:28	95:04	7.92
7.50	30 Yr	97:14	97:22	8.00
8.00	30 Yr	100:15	100:23	8.00
8.50	30 Yr	103:02	103:10	8.03
9.00	30 Yr	105:18	105:26	7.98
9.50	30 Yr	107:12	107:20	7.90
10.00	30 Yr	108:29	109:05	7.60
10.50	30 Yr	110:00	110:08	7.44
11.00	30 Yr	111:15	111:23	7.12
11.50	30 Yr	114:09	114:17	7.47
12.00	30 Yr	116:00	116:08	7.29
12.50	30 Yr	116:22	116:30	6.61

SOURCE: *Wall Street Journal,* May 15, 1992.

mortgages are paid off, principal payments are received by the mutual fund. The manager then must reinvest this money, usually in lower yielding certificates. So, if interest rates are declining, your fund yield will fall also.

$ HINT: Because of this volatility, John Rekenthaler, editor of *Morningstar Mutual Funds,* says investors should hold fund shares at least three to five years.

One advantage of a fund over a unit trust is that portfolio managers can shift the maturities of the certificates in the fund to reflect changing economic conditions. For example, if it appears that inflation is returning, they will

---

HIDDEN RISKS IN GINNIE MAEs FOR RETIREES

- If you spend each monthly check, you are using up both interest and principal.
- You may want to reinvest your monthly payments. Finding a better rate with equal safety is often difficult.
- Monthly checks are not all the same, which is worrisome if you need a set dollar amount to live on.

move to shorter maturities to protect the return. And in certain types of funds, part of the portfolio can be shifted into other types of investments. The Kemper U.S. Government Securities Fund, for instance, also invests in intermediate Treasury bonds.

An advantage the funds have over straight Ginnie Mae certificates is that they will reinvest the principal payments received from homeowners in more fund shares if you so request.

Funds are best for investors who want high current income rather than capital appreciation. Plan on a long-term play, since these funds are volatile and subject to market risks.

☐CAUTION: In seeking high yields, many GNMA funds use almost speculative strategies, investing in put and call options, interest rate futures contracts, etc. Others invest in mortgage-related securities that do not carry the full government guarantee. Check the prospectus, and remember that a fund's shares may go down in value as well as its yield.

Ginnie Mae funds are offered by many of the large family funds, including Vanguard, Lexington, Franklin, Kemper, Fidelity, and Shearson. Their yields ranged from 6.9% to 7.94% as of May 1992.

For every 1% change in interest rates, the value of the average Ginnie Mae fund will move in the opposite direction almost 6%. Therefore, Ginnie Maes are well suited to tax-deferred portfolios, where regular contributions over a period of time cushion the negative effect of price swings.

FREDDIE MACs

The Federal Home Loan Mortgage Corp., known as Freddie Mac, issues its own mortgage-backed securities, which are called participation certificates, or PCs. Freddie deals primarily in conventional single-family mortgages, which are backed by the Veterans Administration, but it also resells non-government-backed mortgages. If homeowners do not make their mortgage payments on time, you will receive your monthly payment on time, but you may have to wait several months to a year to receive your share of the principal. A key difference between Freddie and Ginnie is that Ginnie Maes are backed by the U.S. government; Freddies are guaranteed by private mortgage insurance. Even though they're not quite as secure as GNMAs, they are considered very safe. Because of the discrepancy in safety, Freddie often pays slightly higher yields.

Freddie Mac PCs are sold for $25,000. Since the market is dominated by institutional investors, there are fewer mutual funds: Vanguard and Federated Investors are two. The US AA Income Fund divides its assets between Ginnie and Freddie.

FANNIE MAEs

The Federal National Mortgage Association (FNMA, or "Fannie Mae") is a private shareholder-owned corporation that buys conventional mortgages, pools them in $1 million lots, and sells them in $25,000 units. Although not backed by the full faith and credit of the U.S. government, Fannies are AAA-rated by both S&P and Moody's. Fannie Mae shares also trade on the NYSE.

ESTIMATING A FANNIE MAE'S YIELD TO MATURITY

A Fannie Mae with: 10% coupon
price of 85 (85% of par)
11.76% current yield
25 years to maturity

1 Divide the amount of the discount by the number of years to maturity.

$$\frac{100 - 85 = 15}{25} = 0.60$$

2 Divide the result by 2 to factor in discounting.

$$0.60 \div 2 = 0.30$$

3 Add this number to the current yield.

$$0.30 + 11.76 = 12.06$$

4 This is your approximate current yield: 12.06%.

SOURCE: Fact magazine, February 1985.

Both Freddie Mac and Fannie Mae are corporations chartered by Congress and are *not* officially part of the federal government. Therefore, they do not carry the unconditional guarantee of Ginnie Mae. One advantage of this discrepancy in safety is a slightly higher yield. Another is that the mortgage pools are larger than the Ginnie Mae pools. The more mortgages, the more accurately you can predict how fast the principal will be returned.

After their initial offering, both Freddie and Fannie PCs trade in the secondary market.

CMOs

Collateralized mortgage obligations (CMOs) were introduced in 1983 by the Federal Home Loan Mortgage Corp. Their advantage is a more predictable payout of interest and principal than with Ginnie Maes. Instead of buying mortgage securities directly, you buy a AAA-rated bond. These bonds are sold against mortgage collateral comprised of GNMA- and FNMA-guaranteed mortgages. Each bond is divided into four classes, or tranches, having different dates of maturity ranging from 3 to 20 years. Each CMO has a fixed coupon and pays interest like a traditional bond—monthly or quarterly—but, and here's the difference, principal payments are initially passed through only to investors in the shortest maturity class, class A. Once that group has been paid in full, principal payments go to the next class. In the fourth and final class, investors get all interest and all principal in one lump sum.

These certificates generally have slightly lower yields than the regular pass-throughs, because the size and length of payments can be more accurately determined and you have some protection against prepayments. CMOs are available from larger brokerage firms in $5,000 units.

☐CAUTION: Although CMOs improve on traditional mortgage securities by smoothing the rate of early principal payments, they are less liquid, more expensive to trade, and harder to track. They also entail record-keeping and reinvestment problems that most individuals want to avoid.

SALLIE MAEs

Created in Congress in 1972 to provide a nationwide secondary market for government guaranteed student loans, Sallie Mae (the Student Loan Marketing Association) is to students what Ginnie Mae is to homeowners. It issues bonds, rather than certificates, based on a pool of loans. Each bond is backed by Sallie Mae, and since its assets are made up of loans that have a government guarantee, these bonds are regarded as almost as safe as Treasuries. However, and this is key, this federal backing is only implied, not explicit. They yield about ¼% more than equivalent Treasury bonds.

Student Loan Marketing is a publicly owned company chartered by the government. Its stock trades on the New York Stock Exchange. Originally issued at $20 per share, it split a 2.5 for 1 in 1988; as of July 1992 it was selling at $65/share. It also issues floating-rate notes and convertible bonds. The need for student loans is expected to continue into the 1990s.

GOVERNMENT AGENCY BONDS

Despite lowered interest rates, there are still some bonds that are almost as safe as U.S. Treasuries and have respectable yields—government agency bonds. They are either affiliated with or owned by the government and so are mostly insured against default by some type of federal guarantee. No agency has defaulted on its debt. The distinguishing feature of government agency bonds is whether they are guaranteed by the government. Here's a guide to who's who in agency bonds:

- *Fully guaranteed agencies.* Their bonds are guaranteed against default by the U.S. government:
1   Federal Housing Administration (FHA). Insures mortgages made by private lending firms to individual homebuyers, thus lowering the costs.
2   Government National Mortgage Association (GNMA). Ginnie Mae improves liquidity of the mortgage trading market by guaranteeing securities backed by pools of federally insured mortgages, for example, by the FHA.
3   Tennessee Valley Authority (TVA). U.S. government–owned utility providing electricity to the Tennessee River valley and area. Created in 1933 to promote regional growth.

- *Unguaranteed agencies.* These do not carry an unconditional guarantee. They are stockholder owned:

1 Federal Home Loan Mortgage Corporation (FHLMC or Freddie Mac). Increases liquidity of mortgage market by buying mortgages from lending institutions and selling them to individual investors.
2 Federal National Mortgage Association (FNMA or Fannie Mae). Performs same function as Freddie Mac.
3 Student Loan Marketing Association (SLMA or Sallie Mae). Improves liquidity of student loan market by providing financing to state student loan agencies and buying loans made by private sources.

- *Partially guaranteed agencies.* The United States and most other industrialized nations are obligated to contribute funds to these agencies:

1 Asian Development Bank. Makes loans to developing countries in Asia.
2 Inter-American Development Bank. Makes loans to developing nations in Latin America.
3 World Bank. Makes loans to developing countries throughout the world.

JUNK BONDS

If you're looking for very high yields, a solution is the so-called high-yield or junk bond, which yields substantially more than higher-quality bonds. With the economy picking up, these could be one of 1993's best investments.

Junk bonds are those rated BB or lower by Standard & Poor's and Ba or lower by Moody's. Some have no ratings at all. The world of junk bonds comprises new or old companies with uncertain earnings coverage of their fixed obligations (bond interest payments) along with blue chip companies that have been forced into heavy debt in order to fend off a takeover or to finance an acquisition or a buy-back of their own stock. For example, Kroger Co., in an effort to avoid a takeover attempt, paid its shareholders a special distribution of $40 per share and financed it by raising its debt level to $4.6 billion.

When these situations occur in a blue chip company, a new set of circumstances comes into being:

A TWO-TIER SYSTEM

In 1992–1993, the market shifted to a two-tier system and a recognition that not all junk is equal junk. This applies to mutual funds as well, as portfolio managers try to lure back investors by upgrading their holdings. For example:

HIGH RISK	
Loehmanns	13.75%
American Standard	14.25
Cullum	16.00
Stone Container	10.75
LOWER RISK	
Kroger	12.875%
Embassy Suites	10.875
Safeway Stores	9.65
Viacom Int'l.	10.25

- Low-earning or unprofitable assets are sold off.
- Costs are cut, reflecting corporate efforts to become "lean and mean."

The credit rating gradually improves as these changes are implemented. Thus a good junk bond is always one in which the coverage of fixed charges increases with time.

$ IF YOU DARE: An astute investor can find the amount of projected cash flow and future asset sales for a corporation and thus identify bonds with substantial prospects for improvement.

However, default is not out of the question, which is why, unless you have sufficient money with which to speculate, you should invest in junk bonds only through a mutual fund, where the element of risk is diversified.

JUNK BOND MUTUAL FUNDS

High-yield junk bond mutual funds offer professional management plus portfolio supervision. As with other mutual funds, track records vary, so care must be exercised. The publicity attached to the Ivan Boesky insider trading scandals sent shock waves through the junk bond markets, but junk bonds have fared

HOW JUNK BONDS FARED IN 1992

COMPANY	S&P RATING	1986 HIGH	PRICE (SPRING 1992)
Coastal Corp. 11¾%; 2006	BBB−	$104	$111
Nat'l. Medical Enterp. 12%; 2000	BBB	107⅞	called
Occidental Petrol. 11¾%; 2011	BBB	105	117
Safeway Stores 11¾; 1996	B	N.A.	called
Showboat 13%; 2004	CCC−	N.A.	102

SOURCE: Standard & Poor's, April 1992.

well despite the adverse publicity provoked by these and other notorious cases (see table above).

The sponsors of junk bond funds, of course, are quite apt to play up the diversification point and de-emphasize the risks involved. They make much of the fact that their portfolios are diversified and continually monitored so that issues in trouble can be jettisoned. This is, of course, absolutely true *if* the portfolio manager is astute. But there's another risk involved—the risk of changing interest rates. Like any fixed-income security, junk bond funds are vulnerable to broad changes in interest rates, and as those rates rise, the value of the fund falls.

HIGH-YIELDING JUNK BOND MUTUAL FUNDS

FUND	YIELD (MAY 1992)
Oppenheimer High Yield (1-800-525-7048)	10.05%
T. Rowe Price High Yield (1-800-638-5660)	10.22
American Capital High Yield (1-800-421-5666)	10.38
Prudential-Bache High Yield Corp. Fund (1-800-648-7637)	9.94
Fidelity Spartan High Income (1-800-544-8888)	10.46

Some of the top-yielding junk bond funds in the first five months of 1992 are listed in the table. If one bond in a fund defaults, it means a decrease in the overall fund yield, certainly less of an impact than if you owned the bond directly. However, if several bonds default, the fund share price will suffer.

MUNICIPAL JUNK BONDS

High-yield municipal bond funds are another matter altogether, since tax revisions have made some municipals taxable. Check each fund's prospectus for its policy on taxable munis. Some of the best performers among the high-yield municipal funds for the first quarter of 1992 are listed in the table below.

Junk bond munis are regarded as riskier than corporates. Corporates are frequently issued by new companies without a past history of earnings. Theoretically, these companies are on their way up. Munis that are low rated are more often than not the result of a fundamentally risky situation that is unlikely to improve.

Fund managers try to cut risks primarily by diversifying their portfolios according to both bond type and bond rating. A number of them limit their holdings of any one issue to 5% of the fund's total assets. Others offset risk by adding a mixture of investment-grade bonds. More frequent review of the portfolio—monthly or quarterly—is another risk-cutting technique. In selecting a junk bond fund, if you're concerned with risk, call the fund and inquire about the portfolio mix and management's position. Don't shy away solely because there are nonrated

HIGH-YIELDING MUNICIPAL BOND FUNDS

FUND	YIELD (MAY 1992)
Franklin High Yield Tax-free Income (1-800-342-5236)	7.28%
Fidelity Aggressive Tax-free Portfolio (1-800-544-8888)	7.0
Stein Roe High Yield Muni (1-800-338-2550)	6.45
T. Rowe Price Tax-free High Yield (1-800-638-5660)	6.88

issues: Some smaller municipalities have local appeal although they do not request a rating from S&P or Moody's.

If you own shares in a high-yield bond fund, find out:

1 *Is the fund cutting its dividend?* This is not a bad sign, but instead indicates that the manager is raising cash and diversifying into higher-quality issues.

2 *What's the total return?* Don't gauge everything by yield. Get the fund's total return (income plus appreciation) and compare it to the group average.

3 *What's in the portfolio?* A fund that owns recession-resistant and noncyclical bonds is less at risk because these bonds are likely to meet their payments. (Noncyclical industries include health care, food, drug, and utilities.)

JUNK BOND UNIT INVESTMENT TRUSTS

Unit investment trusts are closed-end investment companies. Because they have fixed portfolios, their yields are more predictable than those of a mutual fund. However, they have far less flexibility in terms of adjusting the portfolio and getting rid of poor bonds. Since they are not actively managed, *investors are at risk* should there be a default. "The unit investment trust is fine for quality bonds but should be avoided for junk issues," warns Peter Hegel, bond expert at Van Kampen Merritt.

ADVICE FOR 1993

Junk bonds can be a mine field for the unsophisticated investor. Yet it's hard to say no to a 9% to 10% yield. Here are nine ways to protect yourself if you decide to take the risk.

- Put no more than 10% of your portfolio in junk bonds.
- If you want to buy individual bonds, use a broker who knows the area well.
- Watch the market closely and be prepared to sell quickly and swallow losses.
- If you buy individual bonds, diversify among types: fallen angels (companies facing difficulties), emerging growth (companies that have yet to achieve quality ratings), and LBO bonds (companies going through restructuring and/or a leveraged buyout). LBO bonds are the riskiest, since they involve massive debt.
- Buy only publicly listed bonds—they are quoted daily and somewhat easier to sell.
- Avoid bond issues under $75 million; they tend to be illiquid.
- Buy bonds with a protective covenant so that if a hostile takeover occurs, bondholders can sell the bonds back to the corporation at par. This is called a "put feature"—you put the bonds to the issuer.
- Use a mutual fund for diversification unless you can afford to buy 10 to 15 bonds.
- If you buy a mutual fund, select it based upon total return, not just yield. A solid fund should generate capital gains along with income. Also, pick a well-diversified fund with no more than 2% to 3% of its assets in any one company's bonds. This broad base helps the fund to weather any adverse situations.

ZERO COUPON BONDS

Zero coupon bonds ("zeros") are an excellent choice if you know you will be needing a lump sum of money at a certain date in the future. These bonds, offered by both corporations and the U.S. government, are sold at a deep discount from face value ($1,000) and pay no interest. Worthwhile? Yes, as long as you understand the facts. These bonds are "stripped" of their interest coupons and, instead of being paid out, this interest is added to the principal every 6 months. So when zeros mature, you get this interest back in a balloon payment. In this respect they are much like EE savings bonds. In other words, they are fully redeemed at par or face value. The difference between the fractional price paid initially and the value at maturity is the return on your investment, that is, the yield to maturity. For example, a zero coupon Treasury selling for $121 will be worth $1,000 at maturity in 2004. That is a yield to maturity of 11.25%.

➤ TAXATION The annual appreciation (or undistributed interest) is subject to tax. *You must pay taxes* annually all along the way, just as if you had actually received the interest payments. Zeros tend to be volatile in price because of this compounding effect; in fact, since there are no interest payments to cushion market swings, zeros can fall dramatically in price when interest rates rise. Therefore, if you buy zeros, plan to hold them to maturity.

➤ WAYS TO USE ZEROS Zeros are tailor-made for retirement accounts, such as IRAs and Keoghs, so you can avoid paying taxes every year on interest you don't actually receive. For example, a BankAmerica zero due 1994 sold at 76 ($760 per bond) with a yield of 9.58%. In June 1994, bondholders will receive $1,000 per bond.

Zeros are also ideal for saving for a specific goal, such as college tuition payments or a vacation home. If you use zeros to finance a child's college education, have your broker select ones that come due in the years your child will be in school. Better yet, put them in your child's name; when they mature, they'll be taxed at the child's lower rate after age 14.

➤ AVOIDING THE NEGATIVES Locking in your yield can turn out to be a disadvantage if interest rates rise over the life of your zero so that other investments are offering higher yields. To tackle the dual problem of rising interest rates and increasing inflation:

- Select zeros with medium-term maturities—3 to 7 years, possibly 10—and avoid being committed to an interest rate over the long term.
- Purchase zeros continually—say every year—as part of your IRA, to take advantage of changing rates.
- Purchase zeros with varying maturities to cover yourself in case interest rates decline.

$ HINT: Zero coupon Treasuries are backed by the full faith and credit of the U.S. government and are one of the safest and simplest ways to invest for your retirement. You lock in a fixed rate of return, thus eliminating unpredictability.

TYPES OF ZEROS

➤ GOVERNMENT ZEROS In 1982 Merrill Lynch devised the idea of Treasury zeros by purchasing long-term government bonds, placing them in an irrevocable trust, and issuing receipts against the coupon payments. This created a series of zero coupon Treasuries, one for every coupon date. In other words, Merrill "stripped" the interest coupons from the principal of the Treasury bond and sold each portion separately. Merrill called these TIGRs (Treasury Investment Growth Receipts). Then along came Salomon Brothers with their version—CATS (Certificates of Accrual on Treasury Securities). All are certificates held in irrevocable trust in a custodial bank.

➤ CORPORATE ZEROS These are not generally suggested for individual investors because of their potential credit risk: If the issuer defaults after you've owned the bond for some time, you've more to lose than with a straight bond since you've received no interest along the way.

➤ DINTS Deferred Interest Securities, also known as DINTS, are unique corporate zero coupon bonds that were issued by Exxon Shipping Company and General Motors Acceptance Corporation before the IRS ruled in 1983 that corporate zero interest was taxable. Their yields range between 8% and 9% with maturities in 2012 and 2015.

➤ TREASURY STRIPS In 1985 the government entered the act, introducing its own coupon-stripping program called STRIPS (Separate Trading of Registered Interest and Principal Securities). Because they are issued directly by the Treasury, they are safer than all other types of zeros. Yields are slightly less than those of TIGRs, LYONs, and CATS, because of the greater degree of safety. Treasury STRIPS must be purchased from a stockbroker.

Example: A 20-year bond with a face value of $20,000 and a 10% interest rate could be stripped into 41 zero coupon instruments: the 40 semiannual interest coupons plus the principal. The body upon maturity is worth the $20,000 face value. The other coupon zeros would be worth $1,000 each, or half the annual interest of $2,000 (10% of $20,000) on the payment date.

☐ CAUTION: Brokers and others may fail to emphasize that the price volatility of long-term Treasury zeros is above average. In fact, zero coupon Treasuries run a greater interest rate risk than straight Treasury coupon bonds of the same maturity.

➤ MUNICIPAL ZEROS Issued by state and local governments, these are exempt from federal taxes and generally also from state taxes in the state where issued. They are suggested for investors in high tax brackets. An A-rated muni zero

THE POWER OF COMPOUNDING:
How Much $1,000 in Zeros Will Grow, before Taxes, at Various Compounding Rates

	SEMIANNUAL COMPOUNDING RATE				
MATURITY	6%	7%	8%	9%	10%
5 Years	$1,343	$1,410	$1,480	$1,553	$1,629
10 Years	1,806	1,990	2,191	2,412	2,653
15 Years	2,427	2,807	3,243	3,745	4,322
20 Years	3,262	3,959	4,801	5,816	7,040
30 Years	5,892	7,878	10,520	14,027	18,679

SOURCE: Merrill Lynch.

issued by the New York State Local Government Assistance Agency, due 2007, with a yield of 7%, recently sold for $335.27. That means that in the year 2005 you would receive $1,000 for each $335.27 invested.

☐CAUTION: Zeros issued with call features should be shunned.

➤ MORTGAGE-BACKED ZEROS These are backed by securities issued by Ginnie Mae, Fannie Mae, and Freddie Mac (see pages 144–146). The securities are secured by AAA-rated mortgages. You'll see some of them referred to as ABCs (agency-backed compounders).

☐CAUTION: You may not get to hold your mortgage-backed security until maturity if mortgages are paid off early.

➤ ZERO COUPON CONVERTIBLES This hybrid vehicle allows you to convert the bond into stock of the issuing company. Merrill Lynch, the leading marketer of zero CVs, calls them LYONs (Liquid Yield Option Notes). Conversion premiums on LYONs are generally lower than on traditional coupon issues; therefore, they offer potential appreciation if the underlying stock moves up in price. LYONs are sold at a substantial discount from par. They give the holder the right, after a certain date, to sell the issue back to the issuer at the original issue price plus accrued interest. This so-called "put" feature can reduce some of the market risk that accompanies convertibles. (See Chapter 10 on convertibles.) For example, a Merrill Lynch LYON sold for $280 for a yield of 8.28%. It converts into 5.31 shares of common at $42.61.

➤ ZERO COUPON CERTIFICATES OF DEPOSIT These are really CDs but sell at discount and do not pay current interest. They are sold by banks and stockbrokers.

$HINT: Buy zeros that are the last callable issues in a particular series to partially protect yourself against call provisions.

ZERO COUPON TREASURY BONDS

PROS
↑ Lock in fixed yield
↑ Maturity dates can be tailored to meet future needs
↑ Call protection available
↑ Predictable cash payment
↑ Guaranteed by U.S. government
↑ Tax-deferred in retirement accounts
↑ No reinvestment decisions
↑ Less expensive than most bonds

CONS
↓ If interest rates rise, you're locked in at a lower yield
↓ Inflation erodes purchasing power of the bond's face value
↓ Commissions and/or sales markups not always made clear
↓ Many zeros have call provisions permitting issuer to redeem them prior to maturity

ZERO COUPON FICO STRIPS

These zero coupon obligations derived from bonds issued by the federally sponsored agency FICO, the Financing Corp., first appeared on the scene in May 1988. They were the first zeros created from the bonds of a federally sponsored agency.

FICO was created by Congress to raise money for the ailing Federal Savings & Loan Insurance Corp. (FSLIC). FICO was authorized to raise about $11 billion over a 3-year period. The lead underwriter, Salomon Brothers, purchased $750 million of 10% bonds maturing in 30 years. It then stripped all 60 interest coupons from the bonds, creating 61 separate entities. Investors can purchase either the coupon strip or the principal strip.

The principal of these bonds is secured by U.S. Treasury securities that match the maturities on FICO bonds. Interest on the bonds is paid from assessments made on the S&L industry.

FICO zeros have higher yields than Treasury bonds. The longest-maturing FICOs pay the highest returns.

Although S&P does not assign credit ratings to FICOs, it has stated that it believes these bonds are "very high quality, the equivalent of AAA issues, based on a commitment of Congress to both FICO and FSLIC."

FICO strips trade over the counter and can be purchased from a stockbroker. Like other bonds, when interest rates rise, their value drops, and vice versa. The minimum face value of a FICO coupon strip is $1,000; of a principal strip, $20,000.

HOW TO BUY BONDS

A recent survey revealed the fact that brokers' fees for trading bonds can vary by as much as 7%. And sometimes discount brokers are more expensive than full-service brokers, particularly for over-the-counter bonds, and less so for corporate and U.S. Treasury issues. (The vast majority of zero coupons trade over the counter.) In many cases the brokers did not charge a commission but instead added a fee to the price of the bond, ranging from $1.50 to $12 per bond. The more thinly traded the bond, the more the fee.

ZERO COUPON BOND MUTUAL FUNDS

Zeros, like straight bonds, rise in price when interest rates fall and fall when rates rise. And since they are even more sensitive to interest rates, they should be held until maturity. If this is not your plan, use a mutual fund. You'll avoid both being forced to sell early and paying a broker's commission.

Benham Target Maturities Trust (1-800-4 SAFETY)

Scudder U.S. Government Zero Coupon Target Portfolio (1-800-225-2470)

$ HINT: To make certain you're getting a fair price when buying or selling bonds:

1 Find the price of the bond in the newspaper.
2 Call several brokers. Get the bid and asked price and what fees this includes. Find out if there are also commissions involved. If the bond is not listed in the paper, you'll have to call several more brokers to ascertain the true price range.
3 Try to negotiate with a full-service broker—if there's a discrepancy in the prices you're quoted.

FOR FURTHER INFORMATION

THE MAE FAMILY

Investor Relations Department
Federal Home Loan Mortgage Corp.
8200 Jones Branch Drive
McLean, VA 22102
1-800-424-5401

Investor Relations
Student Loan Marketing Association
1025 Thomas Jefferson Street NW
Washington, DC 20007
1-202-333-8000

CMOs

Pension Investment Memorandum: CMOs
  (free)
Research Division

Gabriele, Hueglin & Cashman
44 Wall Street
New York, NY 10005
1-212-607-4100; 1-800-422-7435

WHEN THE BULLS ARE RUNNING

At the heart of every portfolio are, of course, stocks. Whether you have only dreamed about owning a stock or whether you and your money manager are trading hundreds of shares every morning and afternoon, we suggest you read this entire section. The basic information is essential to the beginner and the lists of suggested stocks and the tips on trading options, getting in on new issues, and ways to make money with rights and warrants can help even the most wizened investor.

In Part Three you will learn about:

- Common and preferred stocks
- How to pick winners
- When to buy and when to sell
- Over-the-counter stocks
- Electric utilities and water company stocks
- High-dividend stocks
- Low-debt companies
- Options
- Stock rights and warrants
- New issues

13 | FINDING QUALITY INVESTMENTS: Your Key to Making Money

QUALITY RANKINGS

The number one criterion for successful investing is always *quality*. In the stock market, quality is determined by a corporation's investment acceptance, financial strength, profitability, and record of growth. *Standard & Poor's Stock Guide, Value Line Investment Survey,* and *Moody's Handbook of Common Stocks* each assign quality ratings to companies on the basis of past performance in earnings and dividends, corporate creditworthiness, and the growth and stability of the company.

STANDARD & POOR'S

The Standard & Poor's categories range from A+ (highest) to A (high), A− (above average), B+ (average), B (below average), B− (lower), to C (lowest). With the exception of banks and financial institutions, which are rated NR (no ranking), most publicly owned corporations are listed. *Never invest in any company rated below B+,* and always check recent earnings to make certain that the quality rating is still deserved.

VALUE LINE

The *Value Line Investment Survey* is a weekly service that reports on 1,700 stocks classified into 94 industry groups. A report on each industry precedes the individual stock reports. Each stock is given two rankings: one for "timeliness" (the probable relative price performance of the stock within the next 12 months) and one for "safety" (the stock's future price stability and its company's current financial strength). Within these two categories each stock is assigned a rank from 1 (the highest) to 5 (the lowest). Here's what the rankings mean:

➤ VALUE LINE TIMELINESS

RANK 1   (highest)   Expect the stock to be one of the best price performers relative to

the 1,700 other stocks during the next 12 months.

RANK 2   (above average)   Expect better than average price performance.

RANK 3   (average)   Expect price performance in line with the market.

RANK 4   (below average)   Expect less than average price performance.

RANK 5   (lowest)   Expect the poorest price performance relative to other stocks.

➤ VALUE LINE SAFETY

RANK 1   (highest)   This stock is probably one of the safest, most stable, and least risky relative to the 1,700 other stocks.

RANK 2   (above average)   This stock is probably safer and less risky than most.

RANK 3   (average)   This stock is probably of average safety and risk.

RANK 4   (below average)   This stock is probably riskier and less safe than most.

RANK 5   (lowest)   This stock is probably one of the riskiest and least safe.

PICKING GROWTH STOCKS

It sounds as though it is easy to pick growth stocks, but true growth equities are relatively rare, because their companies must combine growth with profitability.

Example: In base year 1, on a per-share basis, the stock's book value is $10.00; earnings $1.50; dividends 50¢; leaving $1.00 for reinvestment. This boosts the book value, in year 2, to $11.50 per share. At the same 15% return on equity, the per-share earnings will be $1.75 and dividends will be 60¢, leaving $1.15 for reinvestment. And so on.

At the end of only 4 years, on a per-share basis, the book value will be $15.25; earnings, $2.30; dividends, 90¢; with $1.40 put back into

HOW A QUALITY INVESTMENT GROWS

	PER SHARE			
YEAR	BOOK VALUE	EARNINGS	DIVIDENDS	REINVESTED
1	$10.00	$1.50	$.50	$1.00
2	11.50	1.75	.60	1.15
3	13.25	2.00	.76	1.25
4	15.25	2.30	.90	1.40

the business. Thus the underlying worth of this quality company is up 52.5%, and in normal markets, such profitable growth will bring a much higher valuation for the stock.

Compare these projections with the past records of several of your most successful holdings and you'll see why quality stocks are always worth more in the long run. The truest, most valuable growth companies are those that continue to report ever-higher revenues and earnings and, as a result, greater book values.

So, in choosing growth stocks, weigh carefully the record, over at least 5 years, and then project a realistic future.

GUIDELINES FOR SELECTING GROWTH FIRMS

Throughout this book, you'll find checkpoints to help you make money with your investments. With small, unseasoned companies, you are always taking extra risks, but the reward can

UPTRENDING PROFITS

	STARS	QUALITY RANK	EARNINGS $ PER SHARE			PRICE DATA			
			5-YEAR GROWTH RATE (%)	1991	EST. 1992	CUR-RENT	% BELOW 1991–92 HIGH	P/E RATIO	YIELD %
Abbott Laboratories	4	A+	17	2.55	2.95	66	5	22.4	1.8
Albertson's Inc.	4	A+	21	1.94	2.25	43	16	19.1	1.5
Block (H&R)	5	A+	15	1.31	1.60	32	22	20.0	2.8
Coca-Cola	5	A+	17	2.43	2.90	82	3	28.3	1.4
Cooper Tire & Rubber	4	A	28	1.92	2.15	49	9	22.8	0.6
General Electric	4	A+	17	5.10	5.65	76	6	13.5	2.9
Interpublic Group	4	A+	16	2.60	3.10	57	3	18.4	1.5
Johnson & Johnson	5	A	29	4.39	5.10	100	15	19.6	1.6
Kimberly-Clark	5	A+	16	3.18	3.50	52	4	14.9	3.2
MAPCO	5	B+	24	4.20	5.25	57	10	11.0	1.8
McDonald's Corp.	4	A+	14	2.35	2.60	42	7	16.2	0.9
Medtronic Inc.	4	A	14	2.25	2.67	74	25	27.7	0.6
Merck & Co.	5	A+	27	5.49	6.60	152	10	23.0	1.8
Nalco Chemical	4	A−	18	1.82	2.00	32	24	16.0	2.6
Newell Company	4	A+	29	1.81	2.10	47	11	22.4	1.3
NIKE Inc. Cl. B.	4	B+	51	3.77	4.35	66	15	15.2	0.9
Novell Inc.	5	NR	51	1.10	1.55	55	15	35.5	Nil
Philip Morris	5	A+	24	4.24	5.60	77	7	13.8	2.7
Sara Lee	4	A+	18	2.15	3.05	51	12	16.7	2.0
Schering-Plough	4	A	23	3.01	3.60	56	18	15.6	2.4
St. Jude Medical	4	B	44	1.75	2.15	48	14	22.3	0.8
Stride Rite	4	A−	28	1.28	1.45	25	22	17.2	1.2
Student Loan Marketing	4	A	23	3.55	4.10	67	12	16.3	1.5
U.S. Surgical	4	B+	36	1.58	2.20	111	17	50.5	0.3
UST Inc.	5	A+	21	1.18	1.40	30	12	21.4	2.7

SOURCE: The Outlook, April 15, 1992.

often be worthwhile. To keep the odds in your favor, use these guidelines:

- **Read the annual report backward.** Look at the footnotes to discover whether there are significant problems, unfavorable long-term commitments, lawsuits, etc.
- **Analyze the management's record** in terms of growth of revenue and earnings and, especially, return on stockholders' equity.
- **Find a current ratio of assets to liabilities of 2:1 or higher.** This indicates that the company can withstand difficulties and will probably be able to obtain money to expand.
- **Look for a low debt ratio with long-term debt no more than 35% of total capital.** This means that the company has staying power and the ability to resist cyclical downturns.
- **Compare a stock's price-earnings ratio** to those of other companies in the same industry. If their ratios are higher, this may be a sleeper. If the P/E multiple is above 20, be wary. Such stocks tend to be volatile.
- **Look for stocks with strong management,** little debt, and a return on investment high enough to generate internal growth.
- **Concentrate on companies whose earnings growth rate has been at least 15%** annually for the past 5 years and can be projected to be not much less for the next 2 years.

Keep in mind that (1) you are buying the future of the company, (2) increasing revenues are not enough (the real test is increasing profits), and (3) the stock market is built on hype, and that's easy with new companies that do not have a long, successful record.

ESTABLISHED COMPANIES

The corporation does not have to be young to have growth potential. There are opportunities with old companies where there's new management, a turnaround situation, or R&D-based developments. Analyst James Wolpert lists these ever-important developments:

- **Strong position in an evolutionary market.** Find an industry or market that is bound to move ahead and check the top

CALCULATING GROWTH RATES

ANNUAL RATE OF EARNINGS INCREASE PER SHARE	JUSTIFIED P/E RATIOS			
	5 YEARS	7 YEARS	10 YEARS	15 YEARS
2%	15	15	13	12
4	17	17	16	16
5	18	18	18	18
6	19	19	20	21
8	21	22	24	28
10	23	25	28	35
12	25	28	33	48

Note that there should be only a small premium when a low growth rate remains static over the years. A 5% annual gain in EPS justifies the same P/E no matter how many years it has been attained. But when a company can maintain a high rate of earnings growth, 10% or more, the value of the stock is enhanced substantially.

SOURCE: Graham and Dodd, *Security Analysis*, 4th ed. (New York: McGraw-Hill, 1962).

half dozen corporations. The leaders are probably the best bets, but do not overlook the secondary companies. They may provide a greater percentage gain on your investment.

- **Ability to set prices at profitable levels.** This is important in service industries where greater volume can bring proportionately higher profits as overhead remains relatively stable. The same approach applies to companies making or distributing branded merchandise.
- **Adequate funds for R&D.** With few exceptions, future growth of any corporation is dependent on finding new and better products, more efficient methods of doing business, etc. Look for a company that is building for that sort of future.
- **Control of a market.** For example, IBM is in a dominant position, not because of price but because of its ability to engineer new computers and office equipment and to provide good, continuing service at reasonable cost to the customer.

- **Strong technology base.** This is a valuable, but not essential, asset. Growth companies usually start with expertise in specific areas and then move out into other products and markets.
- **Growing customer demand.** This means a total market that is growing faster than the GNP. In the early years of new items, almost any company can prosper, because the demand is greater than the supply. Later, when production has caught up, the strong, better-managed firms will survive and expand their positions.
- **Safety is always important,** but with common stocks, the foremost consideration should be profitable growth: in assets, revenues, and earnings.

RISING EARNINGS AND DIVIDENDS

Despite some temporary setbacks, American business continues to make more money and to pay out higher dividends.

In selecting stocks, check the growth of earnings and dividends. Select companies that have posted rising earnings and dividends not for just a year or two but fairly consistently over a 5-year period.

- **Look for a high compound growth rate:** at least 15% to 20% annually.
  Compounding means that every year earnings are 20% higher than in the prior year. The table below shows a theoretical example of earnings growth of 20% compounded annually.

  Example: To find earnings growth for any one year, subtract the earnings per share of the prior year from the earnings per share of the year in question. Then divide the difference by the base year (i.e., the prior year) earnings.

  For example, a company earned $1.20 per

EARNINGS GROWTH RATE

Year 1	$1.00 × 20% = 0.20 = $1.20
Year 2	$1.20 × 20% = 0.24 = $1.44
Year 3	$1.44 × 20% = 0.29 = $1.73
Year 4	$1.73 × 20% = 0.35 = $2.08

WHAT ARE EARNINGS WORTH?

ANNUAL GROWTH RATE	WHAT $1.00 EARNINGS WILL BECOME IN 3 YEARS AT GIVEN GROWTH RATE	THE P/E RATIO YOU CAN PAY TODAY TO MAKE 10% ANNUAL CAPITAL GAIN AND EXPECT P/E RATIO IN 3 YEARS TO BE	
		15×	30×
4%	$1.12	12.6	25.3
5	1.16	13.1	26.2
6	1.19	13.4	26.8
7	1.23	13.9	27.7
8	1.26	14.2	28.4
9	1.30	14.7	29.3
10	1.33	15.0	30.0
12	1.40	15.8	31.6
15	1.52	17.1	34.3
20	1.73	19.5	39.0
25	1.95	22.0	44.0

SOURCE: Knowlton and Furth, *Shaking the Money Tree* (New York: Harper & Row, 1979).

share this year and, in the prior year, it earned $1.00 per share.

$$\begin{array}{r} \$1.20 \\ -\ 1.00 \\ \hline 0.20 \end{array} \div \$1.00 = 20\% \text{ growth rate}$$

In the next year, in order to maintain a 20% growth rate, it would have to report an increase of 20% of $1.20, or $1.20 × 0.20% = 24¢. Therefore, earnings expectations are $1.44 per share in the third year ($1.20 + 24¢ = $1.44). Tables for compound growth rates are available from your stockbroker.

- **Look for the earnings trend as reported for two consecutive quarters:** If profits fall, find out why. The decline may be temporary and reflect heavy investments in new products or markets. But if the drop indicates real trouble, consider selling.

  Similarly, if profits rise, be just as curious. If they are the result of higher sales and lower costs, this could be the

PROFITS: PHANTOM OR REAL?

It sounds great when a company reports debt reduction, but the wise investor should check to see how this is accomplished. One of the newest methods is to swap bonds for stock. This is like buying back the mortgage on your home. You save current dollars but lose the benefit of the old low interest rate.

Example: A wily investment banker accumulates large amounts of old low-coupon bonds that have been selling at deep discounts, say, 70¢ on the dollar. The banker then swaps this debt for shares of common stock, which are then sold to the public . . . at a modest profit. On its books, the corporation shows a "profit" because the price of the bonds was far below the face value that would have to be paid at the future redemption date.

Similarly, watch out when a company keeps reducing its debt by new stock offerings. Since the interest is a business expense, the net cost is about half that of the same dollars paid out in dividends. When debt is repaid from the proceeds of new common stock, the same dividend rate requires greater after-tax profits.

start of something big. But if the improvements come from accounting changes, it's far less impressive and probably temporary.

$ HINT: *Never fall in love with any stock.* If the corporate prospects are dim, why hang on? If you are convinced that it is still a quality company, you can buy back at a lower price.

HOW TO DETERMINE REAL GROWTH AND PROFITABILITY

Two fundamental measures of corporate growth and profitability are *earned growth rate* (EGR) and *profit rate* (PR). These reveal the ability of management to make the money entrusted to

THE GROWTH STOCK PRICE EVALUATOR
How to Weigh Prices of Growth Stocks in Terms of Their Future Gains in Earnings or Cash Flow

IF— A STOCK NOW SELLS AT THIS MANY TIMES ITS CURRENT EARNINGS OR CASH FLOW:	—AND YOU BELIEVE ITS AVERAGE ANNUAL GROWTH IN EARNINGS OR CASH FLOW PER SHARE (COMPOUNDED) WILL BE: THEN—HERE IS HOW MANY TIMES ITS PROJECTED EARNINGS OR CASH FLOW PER SHARE 5 YEARS HENCE THE STOCK IS CURRENTLY SELLING AT:						
12	7.5	6.0	4.8	3.9	3.2	2.2	1.6
14	8.7	7.0	5.6	4.6	3.8	2.6	1.8
16	9.9	8.0	6.5	5.2	4.3	3.0	2.1
18	11.2	9.0	7.3	5.9	4.9	3.3	2.4
20	12.4	10.0	8.1	6.6	5.4	3.7	2.6
22	13.7	10.9	8.9	7.2	5.9	4.1	2.9
24	14.9	11.9	9.7	7.9	6.5	4.5	3.2
26	16.1	12.9	10.5	8.5	7.0	4.8	3.4
28	17.4	13.9	11.3	9.2	7.5	5.2	3.7
30	18.6	14.9	12.1	9.8	8.1	5.6	3.9
32	19.9	15.9	12.9	10.5	8.6	5.9	4.2
34	21.1	16.9	13.7	11.1	9.2	6.3	4.5
36	22.4	17.9	14.5	11.8	9.7	6.7	4.7
38	23.6	18.9	15.3	12.5	10.2	7.1	5.0
40	24.8	19.9	16.1	13.1	10.8	7.4	5.3
42	26.1	20.9	16.9	13.8	11.3	7.8	5.5
44	27.3	21.9	17.7	14.4	11.9	8.2	5.8
46	28.6	22.9	18.5	15.1	12.4	8.6	6.1
48	29.8	23.9	19.4	15.7	12.9	8.9	6.3
50	31.1	24.9	20.2	16.4	13.5	9.3	6.6

This evaluator can be used to make your own projections. It is most useful when studying fast-growing companies with above-average growth rates and cash flow, because it shows that if your growth assumptions are correct, the P/E ratio based on your cost today will be more modest.

Example: The stock of a small high-technology corporation is selling at 30 times current earnings. You estimate that over the next 5 years, earnings will grow at an average annual compound rate of 20%. The table shows that if this projection is correct, the stock will be selling at 12.1 times its anticipated 5-years-hence profits.

This evaluation technique can be reversed. Today the stock is selling at a multiple of 30, but you are not so sure about its future profits. From experience, you are willing to pay no more than 12 times future 5-year earnings for any growth stock. Checking the table, you find that the average annual growth rate must be 20% compounded annually to meet your investment standards. This stock just meets your criteria.

The Growth Stock Price Evaluator does *not* show the *future* price-to-earnings multiple or cash flow. They might be lower than, the same as, or greater than they are today.

them by stockholders grow over the years. You can use the same technique.

➤ EARNED GROWTH RATE   The EGR is the annual rate at which the company's equity capital per common share is increased by net earnings after payment of the dividend—if any. *It is a reliable measure of investment growth because it shows the growth of the capital invested in the business.*

$$EGR = \frac{E - D}{BV}$$

E = earnings
D = dividend
BV = book value

The book value is the net value of total corporate assets, that is, what is left over when all liabilities, including bonds and preferred stock, are subtracted from the total assets (plant, equipment, cash, inventories, accounts receivable, etc.). It is sometimes called stockholders' equity and can be found in every annual report. Many corporations show the book value over a period of years in their summary tables. A good growth company will increase its equity capital at a rate of at least 6% per year.

To determine the EGR for a company, take the per-share earnings, say $5.73, and subtract the $3.34 dividend to get $2.39. Then divide

COMPANIES THAT HAVE INCREASED CASH DIVIDENDS EACH OF LAST TEN YEARS

ISSUE	QUALITY RANK	DIVIDENDS CURRENT INDIC. RATE	DIVD. PAID 1981	% CHANGE '81 TO DATE	YIELD %
American Home Products	A+	$2.60	$1.08	142	3.5
AMP Inc.	B+	1.52	0.47	226	2.4
Block (H&R)	A+	0.88	0.24	267	2.5
Borden Inc.	A−	1.14	0.36	214	3.5
Bristol-Myers Squibb	A+	2.76	0.51	443	3.5
Central & South West	A	3.08	1.68	83	6.0
Chubb Corp.	A−	1.48	0.65	128	2.2
Clorox Co.	A	1.56	0.45	247	3.4
Deluxe Corp.	A+	1.28	0.27	383	3.3
Dun & Bradstreet	A+	2.16	0.67	225	3.9
Emerson Electric	A+	1.38	0.68	104	2.6
Engelhard Corp.	B−	0.80	0.37	114	2.3
GTE Corp.	A−	1.70	0.95	78	5.5
General Electric	A+	2.20	0.83	167	2.8
General Mills	A	1.48	0.44	240	2.2
Humana Inc.	A−	0.90	0.25	260	3.3
K mart	A−	1.76	0.66	167	3.5
Kimberly-Clark	A+	1.64	0.49	236	3.3
Masco Inc.	A−	0.60	0.20	200	2.1
May Dept. Stores	A+	1.62	0.60	172	2.8
Morgan (J.P.)	B+	2.18	0.85	156	3.7
PPG Industries	A	1.84	0.59	212	3.2
Pfizer Inc.	A	1.48	0.46	222	2.1
Philip Morris	A+	2.10	0.29	630	2.8
Quaker Oats	A	1.72	0.46	272	2.6
Tambrands Inc.	A−	1.36	0.66	105	2.1
UST Inc.	A+	0.80	0.12	586	2.9
V.F. Corp	A	1.08	0.33	232	2.5

SOURCE: The Outlook, February 26, 1992.

SEVEN STOCKS WITH HIGH DIVIDENDS

Stocks with comparatively high dividends give income plus some protection against a falling stock market. Dow Chemical, for instance, has paid a dividend every year since 1911 and increased it over the past five years at a compound annual rate of 13%.

COMPANY	BUSINESS	PRICE	YIELD
National City	banking	$42	4.5%
Cincinnati Bell	telecomm	18	4.4
Dow Chemical	chemicals	59	4.3
Simpson Indus	auto parts	13	4.2
First of America Bank	banking	30	4.2
Hartford Steam Boiler	insurance	48	4.1
JC Penney	retail	66	4.0

SOURCE: Quotron, May 1992.

---

this by the book value at the *beginning of the year*. Let's say it was $17.42. Thus, the EGR for that year was 13.7%:

$$EGR = \frac{5.73 - 3.34}{17.42} = \frac{2.39}{17.42} = 13.7\%$$

➤ PROFIT RATE The PR is equally important in assessing real growth, because it measures the ability of the corporate management to make money with your money; it shows the rate of return produced on shareholders' equity at corporate book value. It is calculated by dividing the earnings per common share by the per-share book value of the common stock, again at the *beginning of the year*.

Continuing the example above:

$$PR = \frac{5.73}{17.42} = 32.8\%$$

CHECKPOINTS FOR FINDING QUALITY COMPANIES

- **Improving profit margins.** This is an excellent test, because wider PMs almost always indicate increased earnings per share within a short period of time.

  The gross profit margin (sometimes

called the operating profit margin) shows a company's operating income, before taxes, as a percentage of revenues. It is listed in many annual reports and most statistical analyses. It can be calculated by dividing the operating income (total revenues less operating expenses) by the net sales. Generally, a gross PM of 12% indicates a company that deserves further study. Anything below that, especially when it is lower than the previous year, is a danger signal.

  The gross profit margin is useful in comparing companies within a given industry. However, since it varies widely among industries, avoid interindustry comparisons. For example, supermarket stores have lower gross PMs than many others.

- **Plowed-back earnings.** The fastest-growing companies will almost always be the stingiest dividend payers. By reinvesting a substantial portion of its profits, preferably 70% or more, a company can speed expansion and improve productive efficiency. Any corporation that plows back 12% of its invested capital each year will double its real worth in 6 years.

- **Strong research and development.** The aim of research is knowledge; the aim of development is new or improved products

STOCKS SELLING AT MODEST P/E RATIOS

COMPANY	PRICE	P/E
American Greetings Cl.A	$38	11.7
Avnet Inc.	27	16.9
Bell Atlantic	45	12.2
Belo (A.H.)	37	16.4
Boeing Co.	50	10.0
Chemical Waste Management	21	23.3
Coastal Corp.	24	9.8
Eastern Enterprises	27	10.6
Eastman Kodak	47	10.8
Hanson plc ADR	19	9.3
Humana Inc.	28	11.2
Raytheon Co.	86	8.8

As of May 1992.

and processes. A company that uses reinvested earnings largely for new plants and equipment will improve its efficiency and the quality of its products, but it may not grow as fast in the long run as a company that spends wisely to develop new and better products.

A prime test for aggressive growth management is whether the company is spending a higher than average percentage of its revenues for research and new process and product development. *With good management, dollars spent for R&D constitute the most creative, dynamic force for growth available for any corporation.* It is not unusual for the thousands of dollars used for research to make possible millions of dollars in additional sales and profits.

WHAT TO AVOID

To spot the nonachievers among companies in a growth industry, look for these danger signals:

- **Substantial stock dilution.** This means that a company repeatedly and exclusively raises funds through the sale of additional common stock, either directly or through convertibles. There's no harm in small dilution, especially when there are prospects that the growth of earnings will continue. But beware of any company with heavy future obligations. Too much dilution merely enlarges the size of the company for the benefit of management and leaves stockholders with diluted earnings.

- **Vast overvaluation as shown by price-earnings ratios of 30 or higher.** This is a steep price to pay for potential growth. Take your profits, or at least set stop-loss prices. When any stock sells at a multiple that is double that of the overall market (usually around 14.56), be cautious.

DISCOVERING BARGAINS

Benjamin Graham, in his book *Security Analysis,* looks for bargains in stocks, which he defines as the time when they trade at:

- A multiple of no more than twice that of the prevailing interest rate: that is, a P/E ratio of 16 vs. an interest rate of 8%
- A discount of 20% or more from book value
- A point where current assets exceed current liabilities and long-term debt combined
- A P/E ratio of 40% less than that of the S&P index P/E. Some examples of stocks with low P/Es as of early 1992 are listed above.

FOR FURTHER INFORMATION

Michael B. Lehman, *The Dow Jones–Irwin Guide to Using the Wall Street Journal* (Homewood, IL: Dow Jones–Irwin, 1990).

Charles D. Ellis, ed., *Classics: An Investor's Anthology* (Homewood, IL: Dow Jones–Irwin, 1989).

STOCKS:
Common and Preferred

WHY STOCKS?

The two basic tools of investing are stocks and bonds, or equity and debt, to use a little Wall Streetese. Bonds have been discussed. The first part of this chapter is devoted to common stocks; then we describe preferred stocks. There are several truly compelling reasons for investing in stocks, and one or two reasons why you shouldn't—at least at certain times, in certain stocks. Sorting out the who, what, where, when, and how of making money in stocks hinges on two simple concepts that are frequently ignored in the excessively technical discussions of financial wizards and pundits.

- *Over the long run, stocks outperform bonds*—although sometimes it may indeed be a very long run. Both trade in the marketplace, which historically rewards risk rather than caution. There are, of course, periods when you're better off in T-bills or corporate bonds, but the fact that stocks are better profit-makers remains a truism of investing.
- *Stocks tend to keep pace with inflation.* With stocks, at least you have a fighting chance of staying even. Not so with bonds: Once you buy a bond, the interest rate is locked in. If, for example, oil prices go up, it doesn't matter—your bond will pay exactly the same whether crude is at $18 or $35 a barrel. (Bonds do compensate for this factor by moving up or down in price, however.) If you own shares in Exxon or Occidental Petroleum, however, you'll participate in the increase in oil prices through higher dividends *and* a rising price for your shares. Stocks, in fact, respond directly to inflation: If the buying power of your dollar is reduced to 50¢ by rampant inflation, you and everyone else

buying Exxon will have to pay more for the company's shares. At the same time, inflation will eat away at interest earned on fixed-income securities.

SUCCESS WITH STOCKS

Over the past 20 years, stocks, as measured by the S&P 500 Stock Index, provided an annualized return of 11.9% compared to 9% on 10-year Treasury bonds and 7.7% for 90-day Treasury bills. Inflation averaged 6.3% during this period.

TYPES OF STOCKS

There is no such thing as a stock that's always an excellent holding. It's a mistake to expect all things from any stock. A great number of investors are unaware of the fact that stocks are *not* all designed to do the same thing. In fact there are two distinct types of stocks: those that generate income and those that appreciate in price. Income-oriented stock, such as utility stocks, real estate investment trusts (REITs), and closed-end funds that trade on the exchanges, should be held primarily for income; you should not also expect appreciation from these issues, or at least not very much.

Stocks selected for appreciation are an entirely different matter. Within this growth category you must narrow your selection even further: to low-risk growth stocks or speculative stocks. Throughout this book you will find var-

BLUE CHIP—STOCKS
Standard & Poor's List: in 1992
All ranked A or A+

Apparel
Nordstrom, Inc.
V.F. Corp.

Beverages
Anheuser-Busch Co.
Coca-Cola

Chemicals
Betz Labs
Lilly (Eli)

Diversified
MMM
National Service
  Industries

Drugs, Cosmetics
Bard (C.R.) Inc.
Becton Dickinson
Gillette Co.
Pfizer, Inc.
Upjohn Co.

Electrical
Emerson Electric
General Electric

Electronics
IBM

Food
Dean Foods
General Mills
Quaker Oats
Sara Lee

Health
Manor Care

Printing, Publishing
Dun & Bradstreet
Dow Jones & Co.
Knight-Ridder

Restaurants
McDonald's Corp.

Retailers
Dayton Hudson
Maytag Co.
Melville Corp.
Walgreen Co.
Winn-Dixie Stores

Tobacco
American Brands

Utilities
Central & South West
Consolidated Edison
Texas Utilities

Miscellaneous
Rubbermaid, Inc.

SOURCE: Standard & Poor's, May 1992.

ious lists of stocks suggested for growth, income, or total return.

- *Blue chip stocks* represent ownership in a major company that has a history of profitability and continual or increasing dividends with sufficient financial strength to withstand economic or industrial downturns. Examples: IBM, General Electric, Exxon, Du Pont, Procter & Gamble.

- *Growth stocks* represent ownership in a company that has had relatively rapid growth in the past (when compared with the economy as a whole) and is expected to continue in this vein. These companies tend to reinvest a large part of their earnings in order to finance their expansion and growth. Consequently, dividends are small in comparison with earnings. Examples: Cascade Corp., Tonka Corp., Brown & Co., Reader's Digest, and UST, Inc.

- *Cyclical stocks* are common stocks of companies whose earnings move with the economy or business cycles. They frequently have lower earnings when the country is in a slump and higher earnings when the economy is in a recovery phase. Examples of cyclical industries: aluminum, steel, automobiles, machinery, housing, paper, airlines, and travel and leisure.

- *Income stocks* have continually stable earnings and high dividend yields in comparison with other stocks. Income stocks generally retain only a small portion of earnings for expansion and growth, which they are able to do because there is a relatively stable market for their products. Examples: public utility companies, international oil companies, closed-end bond funds, and REITs.

Now you're ready to start selecting stocks for your own personal portfolio, keeping the following key consideration in mind: *Every investment involves some degree of risk.* Stocks vary in their degree of risk, depending on the stability of their earnings or dividends and the way they are perceived in the marketplace.

$ HINT: The general rule is that return is correlated to risk: The greater the risk, the greater the expected return.

HOW STOCKS WORK

When you buy shares in a company, you become part owner of that company, and you can make money in one of two ways: through dividends

CASH GENERATORS
(Stocks of companies that earned more cash than was needed to pay dividends and build plants)

STOCK	SYMBOL	PRICE	ACTIVITY
Durr-Fillauer	DUFM	$22	Medical supplies
Kellwood	KWD	25	Apparel
Loews	LTR	108	Financial services
Seagram Co.	VO	119	Beverages
Stride Rite	SRR	22	Shoes
Tootsie Roll	TR	66	Candy

SOURCE: Value Line, May 1992.

or through price appreciation when you sell your shares at a profit.

Dividends, a distribution of earnings, are generally declared when the company is comfortably profitable. The dollar amount is decided by the board of directors and is traditionally paid to shareholders quarterly.

A stock may appreciate for a variety of reasons, not all of which are completely rational:

- The company is profitable.
- It has an exciting new product.
- It is part of an industry that is performing well.
- It is the subject of takeover rumors or actual attempts.
- Wall Street likes it.

If a corporation earns 15% on stockholders' equity (the money invested by shareholders), it ends the year with 15¢ per dollar more. After payment of a 5¢-per-share dividend, 10¢ is reinvested for future growth: research and development, new plants and equipment, new products and markets, etc. Thus the underlying value of the corporation doubles in about 7½ years. Eventually, these gains will be reflected in the price of the common stock. That's why the best investments are shares in companies that continue to make the most money!

As you might expect, it can fall in price for similar reasons and others: a poor earnings report, ineffective management, negative publicity, or even a mass dumping that feeds on itself, perhaps unrelated to the performance of the company.

Timing is an important factor in stock selection. In general there are times when you should move out of the market and times when you should be in high-yielding fixed-income securities. Just think about the world around you: Industries change with the times, and so do common stocks. Utilities face nuclear problems; the electronics and computer field has become overbuilt and competition is tough; the Koreans now make cheaper steel; the Japanese and Germans, better cars. Woe to the investor who psychologically locks into a stock as though it were a CD. To make a profit, always be prepared to sell your stock when the time is right.

$ HINT: The single most common mistake of investors is *inertia.* The market constantly changes, and no one stock (or any other investment) is right for all seasons. Do not buy a stock, even a solid blue chip, and then never look at it again. While your back is turned the company could be taken over, enter bankruptcy, or just have a bad year. In each case, you should be ready to

FOUR STOCKS WITH LONGEST RECORD OF DIVIDENDS

Bank of Boston	1784
Fleet/Norstar Financial	1791
Midlantic	1805
First Maryland Bancorp	1806

SOURCE: Standard & Poor's Corp.

take some form of action—buy more shares, sell all your shares, or sell some of your shares.

ADVANTAGES OF COMMON STOCKS

➤ GROWING VALUES Stocks are *live* investments. The market value of a common stock grows as the corporation prospers, whereas the face value of bonds remains the same, so that over the years, their real value, in terms of purchasing power, decreases.

The prices of bonds are almost completely controlled by interest rates and change almost immediately when rates do. When the cost of money rises, bond values drop to maintain competitive returns; when interest rates decline, bond prices rise. Bonds, therefore, are traded by yields; stocks, by what investors believe to be future corporate prospects.

➤ SAFETY Quality stocks are often as safe as corporate bonds. As long as the corporation meets quality standards—financial strength, growth, and profitability—your money is safe. The company will continue to pay dividends, usually with periodic increases; and with higher earnings, the value of its shares will increase. If a well-known corporation pays dividends for more than 40 years, its stock is certainly as durable as its bonds.

➤ GROWING DIVIDENDS This is important for investors who want ever-higher income. Almost all quality companies keep boosting their payouts because of higher earnings.

➤ LIQUIDITY Common stocks traded on major stock exchanges can be quickly bought or sold at clearly stated prices, the ranges of which are quoted in the financial press. You can instruct your broker to buy or sell at a specific price or at "market," which will be the best price attainable at that time. The complete transaction will take 5 working days, but immediately after the transaction, you can get exact data from your broker.

RISKS OF COMMON STOCK OWNERSHIP

There are, of course, risks associated with ownership of common stocks. The risks are far less with quality corporations and, to a large degree,

---

DIVIDENDS EVERY MONTH

You can receive a dividend check every month of the year by purchasing a group of stocks with different dividend-payment dates. The following is a list of issues broken down by payout dates. By purchasing stocks from each of the groups, you will have a portfolio of stocks producing dividend checks every month of the year.

January, April, July, October

Burlington Northern	Morgan (J.P.) & Co.
CIGNA	Northern States
Dexter	Power
Dow Chemical	Ogden
Eastman Kodak	Philip Morris
General Electric	Companies
Genuine Parts	SCEcorp
Heinz (H.J.)	Sears, Roebuck &
Kimberly-Clark	Co.
McKesson	Thomas & Betts

February, May, August, November

American Tel. &	Lincoln National
Tel.	Orange & Rockland
BellSouth	Utilities
Betz Laboratories	Penney (J.C.) Co.
Bristol-Myers	Procter & Gamble
Squibb	Rochester
Brooklyn Union Gas	Telephone
Clorox	Southwestern Bell
Colgate-Palmolive	TECO Energy
Consolidated	WPL Holdings
Natural Gas	

March, June, September, December

American Brands	K mart
American Home	Minnesota Mining
Products	& Mfg.
Amoco	Norfolk Southern
Atlantic Richfield	Potomac Electric
Deluxe	Power
Du Pont (E.I.)	South Jersey
Dun & Bradstreet	Industries
Exxon	Southern Indiana
General Motors	Gas & Electric
Indiana Energy	
International	
Business Machines	

SOURCE: Dow Theory Forecasts, 7412 Calumet Avenue, Hammond, IN 46324; 1-219-931-6480; 1992.

can be controlled by setting strict rules for selling and by using common sense. As long as the company continues to make more money, its stock price is likely to rise, but this may take time, often longer than you are prepared to accept financially or mentally.

➤ PERMANENT LOSS OF CAPITAL You may lose all your profits and some of your capital. When you speculate in high-flying stocks that are temporarily popular, the odds are against success. Only a few strong-minded people have the courage to sell such stocks when they become overpriced. When such equities start down, many people hang on in hope of a comeback that seldom materializes.

> HINT: *Speculation in stocks should be limited to half the money you can afford to lose.*

➤ STOCK MARKET RISK Regardless of whether you opt for income or appreciation, you certainly want all your stocks to be winners. This means avoiding ridiculous risks and instead incorporating *realistic risk* into your selections. A totally riskless portfolio is by its very nature doomed to mediocrity, since nothing exciting will happen to it. For risk-free investments, turn to EE savings bonds, bank CDs, or money market accounts.

You can, however, reduce your risk quotient and still make a profit with common stocks. Here are the best ways: (1) buy stocks with low betas (see page 169 for a full explanation of how beta works), (2) diversify by type of stock and industry, (3) spread out your risk over a number of stocks and industry groups, and (4) be defensive by moving in and out of the market when appropriate.

➤ INTEREST RATE RISK Certain stocks are "interest-sensitive," which means they are directly affected by changes in interest rates. These stocks include utilities, banks, financial and brokerage companies, housing and construction, REITs, and closed-end bond funds. You can cut your risk in these stocks by moving to other investments when interest rates are high or on the way up. The reason why these industries suffer during high-interest-rate seasons is because:

1 Utility companies have to pay more on monies borrowed for expansion or upgrading of facilities.
2 Banks and finance companies are forced to pay more on money deposited in their

institutions as well as for money they borrow.
3 Building falls off because of higher interest rates.

WAYS TO SELECT STOCKS

Eight analytic tools are used most often in stock selection and appraisal.

➤ EARNINGS PER SHARE For the average investor, this figure distills the company's financial picture into one simple number. Earnings per share is the company's net income (after taxes and preferred stock dividends) divided by the number of common shares outstanding. When a company is described as growing at a certain rate, the growth is then usually stated in terms of earnings per share.

Look for a company whose earnings per share have increased over the past 5 years; 1 down year is acceptable if the other 4 have been up. You will find earnings per share in *Moody's, Value Line, Standard & Poor's,* or the company's annual report.

➤ PRICE-EARNINGS RATIO (P/E) This is one of the most common analytic tools of the trade and reflects investor enthusiasm about a stock in comparison with the market as a whole. Divide the current price of a stock by its earnings per share for the last 12 months: that's the P/E ratio, also sometimes called the "multiple."

You will also find the P/E listed in the daily stock quotations of the newspaper. A P/E of 12, for example, means that the buying public is willing to pay 12 times earnings for the stock, whereas there is much less interest and confidence in a stock with a P/E of 4 or 5. A company's P/E is of course constantly changing and must be compared with its own previous P/Es and with the P/Es of others in its industry or category.

It is important to realize that the P/E listed in the paper is based on the last 12 months' earnings; however, Wall Street professionals refer to the earnings of the current year. So when considering a stock to buy or sell, remember to focus on its future, not its past.

Although brokers and analysts hold varying views on what constitutes the ideal P/E, a P/E under 10 is regarded as conservative. As the P/E moves above 10, you start to pay a premium. If the P/E moves below 5 or 6, it tends to signal uncertainty about the company's prospects and balance sheet.

Try to buy a strong company with favorable prospects and a conservative P/E *before* other investors become interested in it and run it up in price. Sometimes growth industries—for example, cellular telephones—fall into economic slumps and may provide this type of investment opportunity.

➤ BOOK VALUE This figure, also known as stockholders' equity, is the difference between a company's assets and its liabilities, in other words, what the stockholders own after all debts are paid. That number is then divided by the number of shares outstanding to arrive at book value per share. The book value becomes especially important in takeover situations. If book value is understated—that is, if the assets of the company are worth substantially more than the financial statements say they are—you may have found a real bargain that the marketplace has not yet recognized. (This is often true with in-the-ground assets such as oil, minerals, gas, and timber.)

➤ RETURN ON EQUITY (ROE) This number measures how much the company earns on the stockholders' equity. It is a company's total net income expressed as a percentage of total book value and is especially useful when comparing several companies within one industry or when studying a given company's profitability trends. To calculate a "simple" ROE, divide earnings per share by book value. A return under 10% is usually considered poor.

➤ DIVIDEND Check the current and projected dividend of a stock, especially if you are building an income portfolio. Study the payouts over the past 5 years as well as the current dividend. There are times when a corporation reinvests most of its earnings to ensure its future growth, in which case the dividend will be small. Typically, the greater the current yield, the less likelihood there is of stock price appreciation. However, it's best if a company earns $5 for every $4 it pays out.

➤ VOLATILITY Some stocks go up and down in price like a yo-yo, while others trade within a relatively narrow range. Those that dance about obviously carry a greater degree of risk than their more pedestrian cousins.

The measurement tool for price volatility, called *beta*, tells how much a stock tends to

STOCKS FOR SUPERIOR LONG-TERM TOTAL RETURN

EARNINGS PER SHARE ($)							DIVIDEND HISTORY			
1991	EST. 1992	1990–92 PRICE RANGE	RECENT PRICE	P/E RATIO	YIELD %	QUALITY RANK		5-YEAR GROWTH RATE %	NO. OF ANN. INCR. 1986–91	5-YEAR AVG. PAYOUT %	LATEST INCREASE (EFFECTIVE DATE)
2.34	2.50	43¼–24¾	$39	15.6	3.8%	A	ALLTEL Corp.	10	5	53	1-3-92
4.39	4.85	69¾–52½	60	12.4	5.9	A−	■ Ameritech	7	5	66	2-1-92
							Atlanta Gas Lt.				
2.07	↓2.25	37⅝–26½	32	14.2	6.4	A−	(Sep.)	8	5	90	12-1-90
							Bklyn. Un. Gas				
2.18	2.45	32¼–25	29	11.8	6.7	A−	(Sep.)	3	5	76	2-1-92
2.60	2.70	35 –25½	32	11.9	5.4	A	■ Duke Power	5	5	65	9-16-91
2.58	3.05	51½–36¼	40	13.1	5.4	A−	■ Pacific Telesis	7	5	72	5-1-91
1.87	2.00	25⅛–18	23	11.5	7.0	A	Potomac Elec. Pwr.	6	5	74	3-31-92
3.85	4.10	66 –47¼	60	14.6	4.7	A−	■ Southwestern Bell	6	5	70	5-1-91
2.55	↓2.70	41¾–26¼	37	13.7	4.6	A	TECO Energy	6	5	66	5-15-91
2.81	↓3.00	39⅝–26⅝	37	12.3	5.0	A+	Wisconsin Energy	7	5	59	6-1-91

SOURCE: The Outlook, March 4, 1992.

move in relation to changes in the Standard & Poor's 500 stock index. The index is fixed at 1.00, so a stock with a beta of 1.5 moves up and down $1\frac{1}{2}$ times as much as the Standard & Poor's index, whereas a stock with a beta of 0.5 is less volatile than the index. To put it another way, a stock with a 1.5 beta is expected to rise in price by 15% if the Standard & Poor's index rises 10% or fall by 15% if the index falls by 10%. You will find the beta for stocks given by the investment services as well as by good stockbrokers.

➤ TOTAL RETURN Most investors in stocks tend to think about their gains and losses in terms of price changes, not dividends, whereas those who own bonds pay attention to interest yields and seldom focus on price changes. *Both approaches are mistakes.* Although dividend yields are obviously more important if you are seeking income, and changes in price play a greater role in growth stocks, the total return on a stock is extremely important. It makes it possible for you to compare your investment in stocks with a similar investment in corporate bonds, municipals, Treasuries, mutual funds, and unit investment trusts.

To calculate the total return, add (or subtract) the stock's price change and dividends for 12 months and then divide by the price at the beginning of the 12-month period. For example, suppose you buy a stock at $42 a share and receive $2.50 in dividends for the next 12-month period. At the end of the period, you sell the stock at $45.00. The total return is 13%.

Dividend	$2.50
Price appreciation	+ 3.00
	$5.50 ÷ $42 = 13%

➤ NUMBER OF SHARES OUTSTANDING If you are a beginning investor or working with a small portfolio, look for companies with at least 5 million shares outstanding. You will then be ensured of both marketability and liquidity, because the major mutual funds, institutions, and the public will be trading in these stocks. You are unlikely to have trouble buying or selling when you want to. In a smaller company, your exposure to sharp price fluctuations is greater.

FINDING WINNERS

➤ CONTINUITY For investors who place safety first, the best common stocks are those of companies that have paid dividends for 20 years or more. Many have familiar names: Abbott Labs, Bristol-Myers, H. J. Heinz, Olin Corp., Philip Morris, Wells Fargo, and Woolworth.

Always check a company's annual report to see if (1) the dividends have increased fairly consistently as the result of higher earnings and (2) the company has been profitable in recent years and appears likely to remain so in the near future. It's great to do business with an old store, but only if the merchandise is up to date and priced fairly.

➤ INSTITUTIONAL OWNERSHIP Pick stocks chosen by the "experts"—managers of mutual funds, pension plans, insurance portfolios, endowments, etc. With few exceptions, these are shares of major corporations listed on the New York Stock Exchange.

Institutional ownership is no guarantee of quality, but it does indicate that some professionals have reviewed the financial prospects and for some reason (not always clear) have recommended purchase or retention. Without such interest, stocks are slow to move up in price.

In most cases, these companies must meet strict standards of financial strength, investment acceptance, profitability, growth, and, to some extent, income. But institutions still buy name and fame and either move in after the rush has started or hold on after the selling has started.

Institutions are not always smart money managers, but since they account for nearly three-fourths of all NYSE transactions (and a high percentage of those on the AMEX and OTC), it's wise to check their portfolios when you consider a new commitment.

$ HINT: Every investment portfolio should contain at least three stocks whose shares are owned by at least 250 institutions.

If you want to track portfolio changes, watch for reports on actions of investment companies in *Barron's*.

☐ CAUTION: Public information comes months after decisions have been made. By the time you get the word, prices may have risen so much that your benefits will be

INDUSTRY LEADERS

	QUALITY RANK	EARNINGS $ PER SHARE 5-YEAR GROWTH RATE	CURRENT PRICE	P/E RATIO	YIELD %
BEVERAGES					
Anheuser-Busch	A+	14%	$ 55	14.9	2.0
Coca-Cola	A+	17	81	27.9	1.4
PepsiCo	A	19	34	18.9	1.4
Seagram	A	12	115	13.3	1.7
DEPARTMENT STORES/ GENERAL MERCHANDISE					
Dillard Dept. Stores	A+	19	124	19.7	0.2
Kmart	A−	3	51	11.3	3.6
May Dept. Stores	A+	10	58	12.9	2.9
Nordstrom	A+	11	35	16.7	0.9
Penney (J.C.)	B+	def.	67	13.4	3.9
Sears, Roebuck	B+	def.	45	10.0	4.4
Wal-Mart	A+	29	52	30.6	0.4
HOUSEHOLD FURNISHINGS & APPLIANCES					
Armstrong World Industries	A−	def.	32	18.3	3.8
Ladd Furniture	B−	def.	11	36.7	Nil
Masco Corp.	B+	def.	27	18.0	2.2
Maytag	B	def.	19	17.9	2.9
Shaw Industries	A−	7	25	25.8	1.2
Whirlpool	B+	def.	45	15.0	2.4
POLLUTION CONTROL					
Ogden Projects	NR	N.A.	21	15.6	Nil
Rollins Environmental	B	19	12	21.8	0.8
Waste Management	A	12	38	20.0	1.2
Wheelabrator Tech.	NR	N.A.	31	23.0	0.3
SEMICONDUCTORS					
Altera Corp.	NR	N.M.	22	20.0	Nil
International Rectifier	B−	N.M.	11	22.0	Nil
Linear Technologies	NR	39	35	26.9	Nil
LSI Logic	C	def.	7	17.5	Nil
TELECOMMUNICATIONS					
American Tel. & Tel.	A−	51	41	14.1	3.2
MCI Communications	B	N.M.	33	14.0	0.3
Sprint Corp.	B	N.M.	22	11.3	4.5
TOBACCO					
Philip Morris	A+	24	76	13.6	2.8
UST Inc.	A+	21	29	20.7	2.8

SOURCE: The Outlook. April 8, 1992.

comparatively small. Or you may be buying just before the portfolio managers on Wall Street, realizing their mistake, start selling.

➤ MOST PROFITABLE COMPANIES An important standard of safety is high and consistent profitability. It can be determined by calculating the rate of return on shareholders' equity, a minimum annual average of 11%. By sticking to these real winners, you will always make a lot of money—in time.

The tables on page 169 show one investment advisory firm's projected winners in the next couple of years, listing companies that are expected to achieve high total returns because of higher profits and current undervaluation.

➤ INDUSTRY LEADERS Companies that capture the business within their industry are creative, and well managed (See list on page 171).

CALCULATING YOUR RETURN

To know when to sell a stock, you should monitor your rate of return on each investment. To make this calculation, divide the total end value by the starting value, subtract 1, and multiply by 100:

$$R = \left(\frac{EV}{BV} - 1\right) \times 100$$

where R = rate of return
EV = value at end of period
BV = value at beginning of period

For example, in early January you bought 100 shares of OPH stock at a cost of $3,315 (price plus commissions and fees). During the year, OPH pays dividends of $3 per share. In December, the stock is at 45. For that year, the rate of return is 45%.

$$R = \frac{4,500 + 300}{3,315} = \frac{4,800}{3,315} = 1.45$$

The gain is 1.45 − 1 = 0.45 = 45%.

If you had held the stock for 2 years and the dividends rose in the second year to $3.50 per share but the stock price stayed at 45, the rate of return would be 55% over 2 years, or 27.5% per annum.

SELECTED LOW-RISK STOCKS

COMPANY	INDUSTRY GROUP
Abbott Laboratories	Medical supplies
American Home Products	Drugs
Boeing	Aircraft
Bristol-Myers Squibb	Drugs
Coca-Cola	Beverages
Consolidated Edison	Electric utility
Dun & Bradstreet	Publishing
Exxon Corp.	Petroleum
General Mills	Food processing
Genuine Parts	Manufacturing
Hanson PLC	European cos.
IBM	Computers
Johnson & Johnson	Drugs
Kellogg	Food
McDonald's	Restaurants
Procter & Gamble	Drugs
Ralston Purina	Food processing
Royal Dutch Petroleum	Petroleum
Sara Lee	Foods
Weis Markets	Grocery
Winn-Dixie Stores	Grocery
Wisconsin Energy	Electric utility

SOURCE: Value Line, May 15, 1992.

$$\frac{4,500 + 300 + 350}{3,315} = 1.55$$

The gain is 1.55 − 1 = 55% ÷ 2 = 27.5%.

To make similar calculations with a time-weighted rate of return (where the rates of return vary and there are additional investments over a period of time), use the same general formula but calculate each time frame separately.

For example, you started the year with a portfolio worth $10,000 and reinvested all income. At the end of March, your portfolio was worth $10,900; on June 30, it was up a bit to $11,100. On July 1, you added $1,000. At the end of the third quarter, the value was $13,500, and $15,000 at year-end. Here's how to determine the return.

March 30: $\dfrac{10,900}{10,000} = 1.09$, or 9%

June 30: $\dfrac{11,100}{10,900} = 1.01$, or 1%

September 30: $\dfrac{13,500}{12,100} = 1.12$, or 12%

December 31: $\dfrac{15,000}{13,500} = 1.11$, or 11%

Now use the quarterly figures according to the formula:

$$1.09 \times 1.01 \times 1.12 \times 1.11 = 1.37$$

The gain is $1.37 - 1 = 0.37 = 37\%$.

Thus 37% is the time-weighted rate of return, but the average rate of return is much lower.

WHEN TO SELL A STOCK

Financial whiz kids and Wall Street gurus are always weaving complex theories about when to buy a stock. That's the easy part. They shy away from explaining when to sell, which is a much trickier business.

Although there's no foolproof system for making certain you always buy low and sell high, you can make an educated decision.

- You should consider selling when you think the market is headed for a serious setback. But, of course, not all stocks react to a declining market to the same degree. So to judge how much an individual stock fluctuates against broad market drops, check its beta in *Value Line Investment Survey.* The higher the beta, the more it moves and the faster you should sell (see list on next page).

- You should also consider selling if you think the company is in serious trouble and its earnings prospects are poor and not likely to recover quickly.

- If your stock suddenly drops in price by 20% or more within a short period—a month or less—you need to find out why and then consider selling.

- If your stock has become overvalued—you can tell if its P/E suddenly moves up and is way above the average P/E of the S&P 500—find out if it's soared because of good news, in which case hold, or because it's out of line, in which case sell and take your profit.

> **CONSIDER INCREASING OR DECREASING YOUR POSITION IN AN INDIVIDUAL STOCK WHEN . . .**
>
> - The price changes substantially.
> - New management takes over.
> - Earnings increases or decreases are announced.
> - A new product comes on line.
> - A merger or acquisition takes place.
> - The company is listed on or unlisted from one of the exchanges.
> - Substantial legal action is brought against the company.
> - Dividends are increased, cut, or canceled.
> - The P/E multiple changes dramatically.
> - The stock is purchased or sold by the institutions.
> - The company spins off unprofitable divisions or subsidiaries.

These four indicators, all reported in the *Wall Street Journal* as well as most major newspapers, should be your signposts for selling.

- *Stock prices are inflated.* This is indicated by a high P/E ratio for the S&P 500. In August 1987, just before the crash, it hit 23. Check the ratio regularly. In July 1992, it was 15.38.

- *There's a rise in interest rates.* Escalating interest rates hurt stocks as money moves to CDs and bonds. Watch the 3-month T-bill rate and the Federal Reserve discount rate. The market tends to fall when the Fed has raised the discount rate three or four consecutive times. It also falls if the T-bill rate is double the S&P 500 dividend yield. In July 1992, the T-bill rate was 3.23% and the dividend yield on the S&P 500 was 3.03%.

- *A recession is in the wings.* The market tends to decline 6 to 9 months before an economic slump. Watch the Department of Commerce's leading economic indicators, which are reported monthly. If they are down for three consecutive months, the market may soon follow.

- *The market breadth is narrowing.* Often a group of stocks pushes the Dow Jones

Industrial Average (or some other indicator) higher even though most other stocks are declining. This is called a narrowing of the market's breadth. You can spot this trend by following the advance/decline line that is reported in *Investor's Daily* and *Barron's*. It reflects the difference between the number of stocks that gain and lose each day. In August 1987 the market was moving up but the advance/decline line was moving down. In fact, the Dow reached a high of 2722 during that period.

HOW HIGH DIVIDENDS PAY

Dividend-paying stocks are not just for retirees and ultraconservative investors. They are important to everyone because they both boost the value of a stock and generally indicate that the company is a mature one, no longer in the throes of expensive expansion. A company that can afford to pay high dividends is no longer reinvesting all its profits in the company.

Another reason why high-dividend stocks are looked upon with such favor is that the dividend is likely to increase if the company's earnings grow—unlike a bond, whose coupon rate remains the same throughout its life.

$ HINT: Dividend-paying stocks fall less in price when the market falls. A study by Avner Arbel, professor of finance at Cornell University, shows that high-dividend stocks fell only 21% in the 1987 crash while nondividend payers dropped 32%.

To determine if a company is likely to continue making dividend payouts:

- Check the dividend-payout history for the past 10 years in *Standard & Poor's Stock Guide* or *Value Line Investment Survey*. Those with uninterrupted payouts are your best bet.
- Check the company's payout ratio: total dividends paid divided by net operating income. If the payout ratio is less than 50% the company will probably continue to pay dividends.
- Check the company's cash flow per share. If cash flow is three times the dividend payout, dividends will probably continue to be paid.
- Avoid or invest very carefully in stocks

that have extraordinarily high yields for the industry group. Extremely high yields can signal trouble.

- Don't buy a high-yield stock near the ex-dividend date. That is the beginning of the time period during which purchasers of the stock cannot receive the next quarterly dividend, generally paid 3 to 4 weeks later. Usually stock prices are inflated just before the ex-dividend date, and on that date they tend to fall. If you buy the stock at an inflated price in order to receive the dividend, you may not break even since you'll be paying tax on the dividend income.

$ HINT: Sign up for a company's dividend reinvestment plan so your dividends will automatically be reinvested in additional shares of stock. Most companies do not charge a brokerage fee for these purchases, and some companies offer a 5% discount off market price for shares purchased through dividend reinvestment. Approximately 1,000 companies have dividend reinvestment plans.

$ HINT: Call the investor relations division of any company you own shares in to see if it has a dividend reinvestment plan, or obtain a list by sending $2 to:
Standard & Poor's Corp.
Direct Marketing
25 Broadway
New York, NY 10004

HEDGING GAINS

Of course the most obvious way to keep your gains is simply to sell your investment when you've made a profit. This approach has several drawbacks—you have to pay taxes on the gain, and if the market goes up you won't benefit. Here are four ways to protect your position on the downside and profit on the upswings.

- *Enter stop orders.* Have your broker sell your stock if it drops to a particular price. This protects you against major declines.
- *Sell into strength.* Each time the market makes a major move on the up side, sell a portion of your holdings. For example, if you own 500 shares of Xerox and you have big gains, sell 100 shares each time it appreciates 10%. You reduce your risk,

WHERE 5% PLUS DIVIDEND HIKES ARE EXPECTED

	QUALITY RANK	DIVIDEND		CURRENT STOCK PRICE	YIELD (%)	
		CURRENT ANNUAL RATE	PROBABLE NEW ANNUAL RATE		ON CURRENT RATE	ON PROB. NEW RATE
Allegheny Ludlum	NR	$0.88	$0.94	34	2.6	2.8
ALLTEL	A	1.48	1.56	37	4.0	4.2
American Home Products	A+	2.60	2.88	78	3.3	3.7
AMP Inc.	B+	1.52	1.60	63	2.4	2.5
Anheuser-Busch	A+	1.12	1.28	55	2.0	2.3
Aon Corp.	A	1.60	1.68	43	3.7	3.9
Block (H&R)	A+	0.88	1.00	34	2.6	2.9
Borden	A−	1.14	1.25	32	3.6	3.9
British Gas	NR	3.06	3.40	44	7.0	7.7
Bristol-Myers Squibb	A+	2.76	3.00	79	3.5	3.8
Brown-Forman Corp.	A−	2.44	2.60	77	3.2	3.4
Burlington Northern	NR	1.20	1.30	40	3.0	3.3
Clorox	A	1.56	1.66	48	3.3	3.5
Crane Co.	B	0.75	0.80	28	2.7	2.9
Deluxe Corp.	A+	1.28	1.40	42	3.0	3.3
Engelhard	B−	0.80	0.88	37	2.2	2.4
Freep't-McMoRan Copper & Gold	NR	1.20	1.40	43	2.8	3.3
General Electric	A+	2.20	2.42	78	2.8	3.1
General Public Utilities	B	1.50	1.60	25	6.0	6.4
Great A&P	B+	0.80	0.90	31	2.6	2.9
GTE Corp.	B+	1.70	1.80	30	5.7	6.0
Harland (John)	A	0.86	0.96	24	3.6	4.0
Houghton Mifflin	A	0.78	0.82	31	2.5	2.6
Humana	A−	0.90	1.00	25	3.6	4.0
Kellwood	A−	0.80	0.88	31	2.6	2.8
Lilly (Eli)	A+	2.20	2.44	72	3.1	3.4
Long Island Lighting	B	1.70	1.80	23	7.4	7.8
Loral Corp.	A+	0.96	1.04	34	2.8	3.1
Marion Merrill Dow	A+	0.92	1.04	35	2.6	3.0
Maytag	B	0.50	0.60	18	2.8	3.3
Monsanto	B+	2.08	2.20	69	3.0	3.2
Nalco Chemical	A−	0.84	0.88	35	2.4	2.5
National Med. Enterprises	A−	0.46	0.50	15	3.1	3.3
Niagara Mohawk	B	0.64	0.80	18	3.6	4.4
NIPSCO Industries	B	1.24	1.34	23	5.4	5.8
Perkin-Elmer	B−	0.68	0.75	33	2.1	2.3
Penney (J.C.)	B+	2.64	3.10	62	4.3	5.0
Philadelphia Electric	B	1.30	1.40	24	5.4	5.8
Philip Morris	A+	2.10	2.50	75	2.8	3.3

WHERE 5% PLUS DIVIDEND HIKES ARE EXPECTED

	QUALITY RANK	DIVIDEND		CURRENT STOCK PRICE	YIELD (%)	
		CURRENT ANNUAL RATE	PROBABLE NEW ANNUAL RATE		ON CURRENT RATE	ON PROB. NEW RATE
Potlatch	B+	1.40	1.50	45	3.1	3.3
Procter & Gamble	A	2.00	2.24	102	2.0	2.2
PSI Resources	B	1.00	1.20	16	6.3	7.5
Questar	A−	1.02	1.08	19	5.4	5.7
Rockwell Int'l.	A	0.92	1.00	26	3.5	3.8
SAFECO Corp.	A−	1.48	1.60	48	3.1	3.3
Schering-Plough	A	1.32	1.48	59	2.2	2.5
Stanley Works	A	1.24	1.32	46	2.7	2.9
Textron Inc.	A	1.12	1.18	37	3.0	3.2
Thiokol Corp.	NR	0.36	0.40	16	2.3	2.5
Torchmark Corp	A+	1.60	1.80	59	2.7	3.1
Union Pacific	A−	1.36	1.44	48	2.8	3.0
Upjohn	A	1.36	1.52	41	3.3	3.7
USLIFE Corp.	B+	1.64	1.76	45	3.6	3.9
UST Inc.	A+	0.80	0.95	27	3.0	3.5
VF Corp.	A	1.08	1.16	42	2.6	2.8
Whirlpool	B+	1.10	1.32	44	2.5	3.0
Wisconsin Energy	A+	1.86	1.96	37	5.0	5.3

SOURCE: The Outlook, March 11, 1992.

and at the same time you're selling your stock at higher prices.

■ *Buy put options.* This gives you the right to sell 100 shares of a stock at a particular price within a certain time period, up to 9 months. These options set a selling floor. For example, if you own a $50 stock, you buy a put allowing you to sell 100 shares for $45 at any time within the next 6 months. The put costs about 75¢ per share and it limits your loss to $5 per share.

■ *Switch to convertibles.* Move out of common stock into convertibles to lower your risk and still profit from a rise in the market.

Buy stocks for the long term. Suggested companies are listed below.

PREFERRED STOCK

Individual investors usually gravitate toward preferred stocks because of their high, secure dividends. Many are issued by utilities.

As their name implies, preferred stocks enjoy preferred status over common stocks. Preferred shareholders receive their dividend payments after all bondholders are paid and before dividends are paid on common shares. Like bonds, preferreds have a fixed annual payment, but it's called a dividend. It is set at a fixed dollar amount and is secure for the life of the stock. If a payment is skipped because of corporate losses, it will be paid later when earnings recover. That's why preferreds are sometimes

CORE STOCKS FOR LONG-TERM CAPITAL APPRECIATION

	EARNINGS PER SHARE ($)		INDICATED DIVD. $	RECENT PRICE	P/E RATIO	YIELD %	QUALITY RANK
	1991	EST. 1992					
Abbott Laboratories	2.55	2.95	1.20	63	21.4	1.9	A+
Block (H&R)	1.30	1.50	0.88	35	23.3	2.5	A+
Bristol-Myers Squibb	3.95	4.65	2.76	80	17.2	3.5	A+
ConAgra	1.42	1.60	0.54	28	17.5	1.9	A+
CPC Int'l	4.80	5.80	2.20	85	14.7	2.6	A
CSX Corp.	0.75	4.60	1.52	60	13.0	2.5	B
Emerson Electric	2.83	3.10	1.38	53	17.1	2.6	A+
Federal Home Loan	9.25	10.50	2.00	120	11.4	1.7	NR
General Electric	5.10	5.65	2.20	80	14.2	2.8	A+
Int'l Business Machines	0.99	7.20	4.84	88	12.2	5.5	A—
Merck & Co.	5.49	6.60	2.52	159	24.1	1.6	A+
Procter & Gamble	4.92	5.20	2.00	102	16.9	2.0	A
Waste Management	1.23	1.95	0.44	43	22.1	1.0	A

SOURCE: *The Outlook,* Spring 1992.

called *cumulative,* because the dividends accumulate and must be paid out before common. Most preferreds are cumulative and are indicated by the initials "cm" in the stock guides.

There are also *noncumulative preferreds:* If a dividend is skipped, it is not recovered. It's best to avoid this type of preferred.

➤ PROS Although there have been a few incidents of corporations skipping preferred dividends, on the whole these securities have an excellent safety record. And if the yield is high, it remains permanently high.

➤ CONS Inflation and high interest rates can have a large negative impact on preferreds. That's because the dividend is fixed, and when rates rise, holders are locked in at the old lower rate. Not only are they shut out of rising interest rates, but the opportunity for substantial price appreciation of their shares is limited.

Although preferreds trade like bonds on the

LOW- OR NO-DEBT COMPANIES

SYMBOL	COMPANY	PRICE	YIELD	ACTIVITY
AGE	A. G. Edwards	$21	2.4%	Brokerage firm
IFF	Int'l. Flavors & Fragrances	106	2.5	Food flavoring
Ldg	Longs Drug Stores	34	3.1	Drugstore chain
LUB	Luby's Cafeterias	15	3.1	Restaurants
WMK	Weis Markets	26	2.5	Supermarket
WWY	Wm. Wrigley Jr.	72	1.3	Chewing gum

SOURCE: *Quotron,* May 1992.

basis of their yields, unlike bonds they have no maturity date. With a bond you know that at a specified time you will get back your initial investment, the face value. There is no such assurance with a preferred. Market conditions are the sole determinant of the price you will receive when you sell.

SELECTING PREFERREDS

The basic criteria for selecting preferreds are *quality* of the issuing corporation, as shown by financial strength and profitability; *value,* as indicated by the yield; and *timing,* taking into account the probable trend of interest rates. Then:

- **Deal with a brokerage firm that has a research department that follows this group of securities.** Not every broker is familiar with preferreds, and many will not be able to provide enough pertinent information.

- **Recognize the inherent volatility because of limited marketability.** Preferreds listed on a major stock exchange may drop (when you want to sell) or rise (when you plan to buy) 2 or 3 points the day after the last quoted sale. If you have to sell in a hurry, this can be expensive. Preferreds sold over the counter (OTC) may fluctuate even more because of their thin markets. As a rule, place your orders at a set price or within narrow limits.

[$] HINT: Ask your broker about *adjustable-rate preferreds.* The quarterly dividend fluctuates with interest rates and is tied to a formula based on Treasury bills or other money market rates.

[$] HINT: *Participating preferreds* entitle shareholders to a portion of the company's profits. In *nonparticipating preferreds,* shareholders are limited to the stipulated dividend.

➤ QUALITY Choose preferred stocks rated BBB or higher by Standard & Poor's or Baa or higher by Moody's if you are conservative. But if you are willing to take greater risks, you can boost your income by buying BB-rated preferreds, such as Philadelphia Electric 7.80% cm pfd selling at 89 with a yield of 9.2%.

Usually, but not always, the higher rating will be given to companies with modest debt. Since bond interest must be paid before dividends, the lower the debt ratio, the safer the preferred stock. For example, look for utilities with balanced debt and then check the preferred stocks. Buy several different preferreds so you can benefit from diversification.

➤ CALL PROVISION This provision allows the company to redeem or call in the shares of a preferred, usually at a few points above par (face value). When the original issue carries a high yield, say over 10%, the company may find it worthwhile to retire some shares (1) when it can float new debt or issue preferred stock at a lower rate, say, 8% or (2) when corporate surplus becomes substantial. In both cases, such a prospect may boost the price of the preferred by a point or two.

[□] CAUTION: Preferred stock, especially of small, struggling corporations, often has special call or conversion provisions. And utilities sometimes take advantage of obscure provisions in their charters to use other

SELECTED PREFERRED STOCKS

COMPANY	DIVIDEND	RECENT PRICE	RECENT YIELD
Alabama Power "F"	$9.00	$102	8.8%
Du Pont (E.I.) "A"	3.50	49	7.1
Georgia Power "B"	7.80	94	8.3
Mohawk Power "A"	1.70	22	7.6
Pennsylvania Power & Light "J"	8.00	99	8.1
Southern Calif. Edison "D"	1.08	14	7.5
Virginia Electric "H"	7.45	93	8.0

SOURCE: Quotron, prices, May 1992.

PREFERRED STOCK

PROS

↑ Generally pays higher dividends than common

↑ Receive your dividend before common stockholders

↑ Dividends generally cumulative; if dividend skipped, made up in future

↑ Know what your dividend income is

↑ Possibility of capital gain in price of stock

CONS

↓ If company's earnings rise, you don't share in increases unless it is a participating preferred

↓ Dividend fixed, with few exceptions

↓ Call provisions allow company to redeem your stock at stated price

↓ No protection against inflation

---

assets to call in their preferreds. You may end up with a modest profit, but if the redemption price is less than that at which the stock was selling earlier, you will lose money. Always check a preferred's call features.

➤ SINKING FUND Corporations use "sinking funds" to accumulate money on a regular basis in order to redeem the corporation's bonds or preferred stocks from time to time so that the entire issue is retired before the stated maturity date. For example, starting 5 years after the original sale, a company might buy back 5% of the stock annually for 20 years. The yields of such preferreds will usually be slightly less than those for which there is no such provision.

$ IF YOU DARE: Look for a company that has omitted dividend payouts for several years. It will probably be selling at a discount. Should earnings recover, it will pay off all accumulated dividends, and the price of the stock is likely to rise.

$ HINT: Buy participating preferreds to ensure receiving a percentage of any exceptional profit gain, as for example, if the corporation sells a subsidiary and has excess profits for the year.

CONTINUAL DIVIDENDS

Sharp investors may get as many as 12 dividends a year by rolling over preferred stocks. By buying shares just before the dividend date, they get the full payout. They sell the next day and buy another preferred with an upcoming dividend payment date. Because of the commission costs and need for constant checking, this technique is difficult for amateurs. Yet it can work well when it involves 500 shares or more and you work with a discount broker.

Timing is the key. After the payout date, the price of the preferred may drop almost as much as the value of the dividend. A 12% preferred thus might trade at 100 before the dividend date and drop back to just over 97 the next day. If you sell, you take a small loss. If you wait a week or so and are lucky in a strong market, you may be able to sell at 100. If you have the time, money, and a feel for this type of trading, you could make substantial profits.

$ HINT: You can also purchase preferreds through the Lindner Dividend Fund, which is about 50% invested in preferreds. Among its preferred holdings as of May 1992: Transco Energy, Variety Corp., (automotive/agricultural business), National Intergroup (retail distribution).

FOR FURTHER INFORMATION

Louis Engel & Brendon Boyd, *How to Buy Stocks* (Boston: Little, Brown & Co., 1982; New York: Bantam paperback, 1991).

Lawrence J. Gitman and Michael D. Joehnk, *Fundamentals of Investing* (New York: HarperCollins, 1990).

Benjamin Graham & David L. Dodd, *Security Analysis*, 5th ed. (New York: McGraw-Hill, 1988) (updated by S. Cotile).

Richard J. Teweles and Edward S. Bradley, *The Stock Market* (New York: John Wiley & Sons, 1992).

Andrew Tobias, *The Only Investment Guide You'll Ever Need* (New York: Bantam paperback, 1989).

Philip B. Capelle, *Investing in Growth* (Chicago: Probus Publishing Co., 1992).

15 OVER-THE-COUNTER STOCKS

A good investment is not always an obvious one, dancing in the limelight of the New York Stock Exchange. Even the venerable Benjamin Graham, father of security analysis, subscribed to this theory. He advised investors to consider making one out of three securities in their portfolios an over-the-counter (OTC) stock. (The term *over-the-counter* stems from the days when securities were sold over the counter in banks and stores, right along with money orders and dry goods.)

This is an area of the market traditionally dominated by individual investors rather than the institutions, and over 11,000 securities trade OTC. Of these, approximately 4,700 are listed on NASDAQ (National Association of Securities Dealers Automated Quotation system), more than twice the number on the American and New York exchanges.

Since requirements for listing on NASDAQ are less stringent than for either the New York or American exchange (see box on page 181), the OTC companies tend to be smaller, newer, and less well known. This is reflected in their lower prices but higher risk level. And since fewer OTC stocks are owned by institutions or closely followed by analysts, research is not abundant on many of these issues, a fact that can work to your advantage, since it means neither Wall Street nor the public has run up the prices.

THE OTC MARKET

Unlike the New York and American stock exchanges, the OTC does not have a centralized trading floor. Instead, stocks are bought and sold through a centralized computer-telephone network linking dealers across the nation. There are two "divisions" of the OTC market: NASDAQ, a self-regulated trade group, which publishes daily quotes; and the National Quotation Bureau, a private company, which distributes daily data to brokers about small, thinly traded stocks, on what Wall Streeters call the "pink sheets" (because the data are printed on pink paper).

OTC trading is sometimes an expensive proposition. On the major and regional exchanges, specialists (who concentrate on particular stocks) match buy and sell orders received from brokerage firms. If no match is possible, the specialist usually fills the order from a personally held inventory. But when you trade OTC, your broker will fill your order from his or her inventory if there is one. Otherwise, your broker will buy the stock from another broker who makes a market in it and will then in turn sell it to you. The price is determined by a number of factors: the amount of stock the market maker has, the prices of recent trades, the markup, and the level of demand.

When you read the quotes in the paper, remember that the bid (or lower price) is what brokers or dealers are offering to pay for the stock. The higher (or asked figure) is what they will sell it for. The difference between these two numbers is the spread. On most exchanges, the spread is just a few pennies, but on the OTC the market makers actually negotiate the prices, and spreads are typically larger because of the greater risks involved.

HINT: The SEC requires all brokers who make a market in a stock to state their markup to clients. Be sure you ask.

GUIDELINES FOR SELECTING OTC STOCKS

- Start in your own backyard. Do research on companies in your region. Check with a local stockbroker for ideas. Read annual reports and visit the company personally.

- Buy only companies with established earnings growth and, if possible, low debt. Ideally, the assets–to–current liabilities ratio should be 2:1.
- Study wide economic and industrial trends and select companies that have a timely product or service.
- Find companies that have a market niche.
- Allow 2 to 10 months for price and/or earnings movement.
- Avoid penny stocks (stocks that sell for less than 50¢); the bid/asked price spread is often over 25%.

USING THE KEY INDICATORS

If and when you believe the big stocks are overpriced, it's time to move some of your portfolio into smaller issues. To help you time your move, watch these key indicators:

➤ NASDAQ COMPOSITE INDEX Listed in the major newspapers, its direction and progress can be compared with those of other major indexes. If its trend is up, the environment is favorable.

➤ OTC VOLUME Volume tends to verify the direction, up or down, of a market or individual issue. If the market rises on low volume, for example, generally the rise will be short.

➤ NEW HIGHS AND LOWS A number of new highs over new lows is a positive buy sign.

➤ BLOCK TRADING When trades of 10,000 shares or more take place, it probably signals institutional participation and future interest in the stock.

➤ S&P OTC 250 INDEX Like the NASDAQ index, Standard & Poor's indicates the overall direction of secondary issues. It is especially valuable to compare it to the S&P 500. Since the beginning of 1988, many OTC stocks have recovered from their lows of October–November 1987.

➤ SHADOW STOCK INDEX In January 1986 the American Association of Individual Investors, a nonprofit educational organization, introduced this index, which covers less well-known stocks. The market value of a company's outstanding stock must fall between $20 million and $100 million to qualify for inclusion. This means that all companies in the Shadow Stock Index have some sort of track record. Most trade OTC.

REQUIREMENTS FOR LISTING OF STOCKS ON EXCHANGES

NEW YORK STOCK EXCHANGE
- Pretax income: $2.5 million for most recent year and $2.0 million for each of 2 preceding years
- Number of shareholders of 100 shares or more: 2,000
- Number of publicly held shares: 1.1 million
- Value of shares outstanding: $18 million

AMERICAN STOCK EXCHANGE
- Pretax income: $750,000 for previous year or 2 out of the last 3 years
- Number of shareholders: 800 (if 500,000 shares outstanding) or 400 (if 1 million shares outstanding)
- Value of shares outstanding: $3 million

NATIONAL ASSOCIATION OF SECURITIES DEALERS AUTOMATED QUOTATION SYSTEM (OVER THE COUNTER)
- Total assets: $4 million
- Number of shareholders: 300
- Number of publicly held shares: 100,000
- Stockholders' equity: $2 million

THE PINK SHEETS

This is also fertile territory for investors, but only for speculators, since these stocks are not listed on the NASDAQ electronic system, usually because of limited capitalization or the small number of shares outstanding. They are listed in *The Pink Sheets*, published daily by the National Daily Quotation Service. They give bid and asked prices for more than 11,000 OTC stocks. *The Pink Sheets* tells your broker who makes a market in the stock, although the prices are negotiable. These small and thinly traded companies offer high growth potential, which of course means high risk.

$ HINT: Look for local companies or firms that make products you like; chances are they will be trading over the counter.

▢ CAUTION: There are two key problems with pink sheet stocks: (1) The spreads between the bid and asked prices can be significant on thinly traded stocks, and (2) illiquidity is common.

OTC STOCKS FOR CONSIDERATION

- **Amgen Inc.** Leading biotech products
- **Apple Computer** Strong demand for new notebook computers
- **Food Lion** Expansion program boosts supermarket sales
- **Microsoft** Windows doing well, but legal problems exist
- **Nordstrom Inc.** Specialty retailer is expanding on East Coast
- **Price Co.** Wholesale clubs doing well and expanding
- **St. Jude Medical** Leading producer of mechanical heart valves

$ HINT: Don't buy a pink sheet stock unless you can find adequate information on the company from reliable sources. Even then, stick to the well-researched OTC stocks that trade frequently.

SMALL CAP STOCKS

Another area that is often overlooked by investors is small cap stocks, those with a limited number of shares outstanding and small capitalization. (Capitalization is determined by multiplying the number of shares by the current market value of one share.) These are discussed in Chapter 24.

OTC MUTUAL FUNDS

FUND	TOTAL RETURN JANUARY 1 TO APRIL 30, 1992
USF&G OTC Securities Fund (1-800-323-8734)	5.63%
Fidelity OTC Portfolio (1-800-544-8888)	1.17
T. Rowe Price New Horizon (1-800-638-5660)	−2.04
American Capital Emerging Growth Fund (1-800-421-5666)	−2.28

OVER-THE-COUNTER STOCKS

PROS
↑ In an OTC mutual fund, professional management, diversification, liquidity, possibility of switching into other funds within the same family
↑ Prices often low
↑ Potential capital appreciation
CONS
↓ May be thinly traded
↓ Can be difficult to sell when negative news appears
↓ Research difficult to find, sometimes nonexistent
↓ Losses can be large
↓ Value of fund shares can decline

USING MUTUAL FUNDS

If you want a professional to make the buying and selling decisions in the OTC market, you can invest in one of several mutual funds. These funds invest in stocks of small companies. But remember, higher interest rates and inflation will hurt stocks.

Tips for selecting a fund:

- Invest only in a fund that has $100 million or less in assets. A larger fund may have to buy stocks of larger companies, or its portfolio may become too unwieldy to manage effectively.
- Portfolio turnover should be 30% per year or less.
- Check the prospectus and quarterly reports to make certain the fund is indeed investing in small companies with capitalization below $100 million.

FOR FURTHER INFORMATION

The 1992 NASDAQ Company Directory and Fact Book
NASD
Book Order Department
9513 Key West Avenue
Rockville, MD 20850
1-202-728-8000
$15

Lists all NASDAQ stocks with their symbols, their addresses, and telephone numbers.

> *Equities* (magazine)
> 37 East 28th Street, Suite 706
> New York, NY 10016
> 1-212-685-6244
> Monthly; $42 per year

Contains studies of individual stocks.

> *Growth Stock Outlook* (newsletter)
> P.O. Box 15381
> Chevy Chase, MD 20825
> 1-301-654-5205
> Twice monthly; $195 per year

Published by Charles Allmon; covers stocks with potential appreciation.

> *The OTC Profiles*
> Standard & Poor's
> 25 Broadway
> New York, NY 10004
> 1-212-208-8000; 1-800-221-5277
> $79 per year

Published quarterly; lists historical data and prices for the larger OTC companies. Check your library.

> *OTC Insight* (newsletter)
> P.O. Box 127
> Moraga, CA 94556
> 1-510-376-1223
> Monthly; $190 per year

Scans data on 100 OTC stocks per month and provides sample portfolios.

> *Value Line OTC Special Situation Service*
> 711 Third Avenue
> New York, NY 10017
> 1-800-634-3583
> Bimonthly; $390 per year

Reliable coverage of OTC and small cap stocks.

16 UTILITIES

Immediately after the October 1987 crash, thousands of investors flocked to public utility stocks for safety and high yields—and with good reason. A study by Standard & Poor's in early 1992 revealed that over the last 20 years, shares of electric and gas utilities did better than the broader market. For the period beginning April 20, 1972, and ending February 28, 1992, the Dow Jones utility average increased at a compound annual rate of 12.1% while the S&P 500 rose 11.4% (both with dividends reinvested). Utilities also outperformed from 1982–1992, a period in which the stock market as a whole enjoyed a strong upturn, then crashed in 1987 before rebounding to new highs.

Why did they do so well? During periods of high inflation, utilities passed along much of their higher operating costs to customers. And, during recessionary periods, industrial and commercial demand for electricity and gas slowed, but not nearly as much as that for other cyclical industrial products.

As we go to press, the five highest yielding stocks in the S&P utility index are: American Electric Power, Commonwealth Edison, Ohio Edison, Public Service Enterprise Group, Texas Utilities.

GUIDELINES FOR SELECTION

In the past, utility stocks moved pretty much as a group, but today the difference between the best and the poorest has widened and skepticism should be your guiding principle. When making a utility selection you should ask:

- How good is management?
- Is the dividend safe?
- What is the nuclear situation?
- What is the regulatory environment?
- What is the reserve margin? (Reserve margin is power capacity above peak-load usage; if it is especially high, the company may have unused plants and high costs. (The industrywide average is around 25%.)

Moreover,

- Don't select a utility stock solely on the basis of its yield. (A high return often reflects Wall Street uncertainty about the safety of the dividend.)
- Do select stocks that have expectations for higher earnings and growth rates.
- If all other things are equal, select a utility that has a dividend reinvestment plan. You will save on commissions.
- Diversify. Buy utilities from several states, to avoid any one state's unfavorable regulatory policies.

With stocks of quality utilities, the wise investor can look for total returns of about 10.5%: 6.5% to 8.5% from dividends and the balance from appreciation. At some point, most shares will become fully valued and should be sold, typically after 2 or 3 years.

To achieve such returns, you must be selective and be armed with plenty of information such as:

- **Bond rating,** as determined by Standard & Poor's or Moody's. This is a measure of the company's financial strength.
- **Regulatory climate.** The attitude of state authorities toward permitting the utility to earn an adequate rate of return is an important factor.
- **Return on equity.** This is that basic standard of quality—the ability of management to make money with your money. It is often a reflection of the state authorities, who may or may not permit an adequate rate of return.
- **Main fuel.** This is a key criterion for many analysts. Utilities that use water (hydroelectric plants) have no cost worries;

184

those that use coal seldom have major problems with the supply or price of their fuel; those that rely on gas or oil are subject to conditions beyond their control; and those with nuclear plants are regarded as questionable to dangerous. This pessimism stems from huge overrun costs and standstills involving Public Service of New Hampshire and Long Island Lighting.

Note: With utilities, state laws often prescribe actions that in other industries would be management's prerogative.

$ HINT: Look for utilities with strong internal cash flow that have completed construction programs.

BRIGHT LIGHTS

There are a number of bright lights on the horizon.

- Construction programs have generally ended, which means stronger balance sheets.
- Many utilities are diversifying into nonutility areas, such as TECO Energy's move into shipping and transportation.
- Cash flows are up, thus enabling a number of companies to boost dividends, reduce high-cost debt, repurchase shares, or diversify.
- The group remains recession-resistant, since electricity, water, and gas are necessities. That means that in a recession, these stocks should suffer far less than most.

NINE UTILITIES WITH SECURE DIVIDENDS

COMPANY	YIELD
Allegheny Power	7.4%
Brooklyn Union Gas	7.1
Connecticut Natural Gas	7.0
Delmarva Power	7.2
FPL Group	7.0
Kansas Power & Light	6.7
Orange & Rockland	7.0
Public Service Enterprise	8.1
Union Electric	6.7

SOURCE: Quotron, May 1992.

THE BELL COMPANIES

As a result of the now historical AT&T breakup, there are eight different Bell companies. Shares of all are traded on the NYSE. Yields range from 6.2% to 3.6%.

Phone company stocks have changed little over the past year—some are slightly lower in price—yet they are much higher than after the 1987 crash.

SYMBOL	COMPANY	PRICE (MAY 1992)	P/E RATIO	YIELD
T	AT&T	$43	16	3.0%
AIT	Ameritech	63	13	5.5
BEL	Bell Atlantic	43	13	5.9
BLS	Bell South	48	14	5.7
NYN	NYNEX	78	13	5.9
PAC	Pacific Telasis	42	15	5.1
SBC	Southwest Bell	63	16	4.6
USW	U.S. West	35	12	5.8

SOURCE: Quotron, May 1992.

THE SAFEST COMPANIES

Some of the highest quality utilities are listed in the table on page 186—"Arranging Monthly Income." These companies are well able to cover their dividend earnings, even in a recession. They are suggested for conservative portfolios—and, in fact, a number are likely to increase their dividends over the next few years. Despite their high safety rankings, you should monitor their activities on a regular basis, and at the first sign of a problem, ask your broker for an up-to-date research report or check Value Line or Standard & Poor's coverage of the company.

BABY BELLS: MINOR GROWING PAINS

Domestic investments in nonutility businesses are starting to reap benefits. Since the 1980s, cellular phones, cable TV, digital equipment, and satellite networks have become

ARRANGING MONTHLY INCOME

If you're looking for steady income, you can invest in certain top-rated utilities and receive monthly income.

- Dividends paid in January, April, July, October: Northern States Power (NSP) $41—5.9%; SCE Corp. (SCE) 43—6.2%
- Dividends paid in February, May, August, November: Orange & Rockland Utilities (ORU) $36—6.7%; WPL Holdings (WPH) 34—5.4%
- Dividends paid in March, June, September, December: Potomac Electric Power (POM) $25—6.3%; Southern Indiana Gas & Electric (SIG) 32—4.8%

a major part of the operations of these companies. In fact, many have developed an edge over their foreign and domestic competitors. Now they're taking that advantage abroad.

UTILITY MUTUAL FUNDS

If you prefer professional management of your money and a broadly diversified utility portfolio, turn to one of the utility funds listed on page 187. However, select with care. All funds are not created equal—Fidelity's Select Utilities, for example, does not pay out dividends to investors but instead reinvests them in the fund.

WATER COMPANIES

Telephone and electric companies have always been in the spotlight, hogging center stage in the utility industry. Yet stocks of public water companies also deserve a place in the limelight. This group, which has low institutional ownership, over the years has turned in a solid performance.

- It provides a commodity everyone needs.
- It has no competition; there is no alternative to water.
- It has no nuclear exposure.
- Many water companies are profitably diversified.

Although there are an estimated 65,000 water companies in the United States, about 85% are municipally owned and regulated by city governments. That leaves about 350 investor-owned operations, and of these, only 17 have above $15 million in total capital. American Water Works is the largest. It serves over 1.4 million customers in 500 communities in 20 states. Its largest customer is Monsanto.

☐ CAUTION: If you decide to invest in a water company, keep in mind that rate increases are determined by area regulatory bodies and that various local situations, including the weather and the economy, have a major effect on earnings. Residential customers dominate the industry, and companies therefore tend to benefit from hot weather spells when Americans use more water. Companies must continually meet the water standards set by the Environmental Protection Agency.

WATER COMPANIES

COMPANY	EXCHANGE: SYMBOL	PRICE	YIELD
American Water Works	NYSE: AWK	$22	4.2%
Citizens Utilities (A)	OTC: CITU-A	39	Nil
Consumers Water	OTC: CONW	17	6.6
Philadelphia Suburban	NYSE: PSC	14	7.2
Southern California Water	OTC: SWTR	33	7.0
United Water Resources	NYSE: UWR	14	6.4

SOURCE: Quotron, May 1992.

UTILITY MUTUAL FUNDS

FUND	MINIMUM	TOTAL RETURN (1/1/92 TO 4/1/92)	CURRENT YIELD (MAY 1, 1992)
Fidelity Select Utilities (1-800-544-8888)	$2,500	−4.7%	DR*
Fidelity Utilities Income (1-800-544-8888)	2,500	−4.0	DR*
Franklin Utilities (1-800-342-5236)	100	−4.75	+5.88%
Stratton Monthly Dividend (1-800-634-5726)	2,000	−2.7	+6.32

* Dividends reinvested.

The larger, better-known water firms are listed in the table on page 186. You may also want to investigate your local water company—find out if it is publicly traded—but read the last two annual reports and the current quarterlies before purchasing shares.

UTILITY BONDS

When RJR Nabisco's CEO told the investment world that he planned to take his company private by floating new debt, the value of Nabisco's bonds immediately fell by nearly 20%. Suddenly investors in other high-grade corporate bonds were fearful, wondering if their bonds would do the same if a takeover or leveraged buyout came their way.

Certain bonds, however, are relatively free from takeover troubles: Treasury issues, for example, are not vulnerable to an LBO since it's unlikely anyone will try to take over the Treasury! Another fairly safe haven lies in high-rated utility bonds, whose yields tend to be slightly above those of Treasuries. Most utility bonds have high ratings because these corporations provide continually needed services and are recession-resistant. Bondholders receive interest semiannually, and as we go to press their yields ranged from 7½% to 9½% to 9¾%.

☐ CAUTION: Buy only bonds rated A or above and check the call feature. Most utilities have only 5-year call protection, whereas Treasuries are essentially noncallable.

Avoid bonds of companies with nuclear or regulatory problems.

Many high-yielding utility bonds have early redemption clauses built into their issues. These call provisions permit a utility to buy back its bonds at face value or even a bit higher, but more often than not at prices below the current market. Utility companies are allowed to use these special "calls" to cut expenses by retiring high-yield or high-coupon bonds.

17 OPTIONS

Everyone who owns securities should understand options and use them at times. They can produce quick profits with little capital, make possible protective hedges, and usually limit losses. But to make money with options, you must work hard, research thoroughly, review often, and adhere to strict rules. To be really successful, you should have ample capital and recognize that compared with stocks and bonds, the commissions as a percentage of the option prices are high.

Before you allocate savings to any type of options, discuss your plans with your broker, and test out your ideas on paper. If you are not willing to follow your hypothetical choices for several months, get quotations for the previous 13 weeks from newspaper files at your library.

With careful selections and constant monitoring, *selling* options can boost annual income by 15% or more; *buying* options can bring quick gains. With options, you have the power of leverage (a small sum can control a large investment), low costs, and a variety of choices (in types of underlying assets, strike prices, and time frames).

Options are a cross between trading in stocks and trading in commodities. They permit holders to control for a specified period of time a relatively large amount of stock with a relatively small amount of capital. An option represents the *right* to buy or sell a specific stock at a specific price (called the strike price) for a limited time. You do not need to own the stock to buy an option. If the stock rises, the option should rise too, giving you a profit if you sell. Of course, if the stock falls in price, so will the option, and you'll face a loss.

In effect, options have a limited life of 9 months. They pay no dividends and, by definition, are diminishing assets. The closer the expiration date, the less time there is for the value of the option to rise or fall as the buyer anticipates.

TERMS USED IN OPTION TRADING

➤ PUTS AND CALLS The most popular and widely used option is a *call*—the right to buy the underlying stock. A *put* is the opposite—the right to sell the stock. For sophisticated traders, there are complex combinations: *spreads, strips, straps,* and *straddles.*

➤ PREMIUM The cost of the option is called the *premium.* It varies with the duration of the contract, the type of stock, corporate prospects, and the general activity of the stock market. Premiums run as high as 15% of the value of the underlying stock; that is, for a volatile stock selling at 50 ($5,000 for 100 shares), the premium for a call to be exercised 9 months from now might be 7½ ($750) when the exercise price is also 50. Shorter-term options on more stable stocks carry smaller premiums: from 2% for those expiring in a month or so to 5% for those with longer maturities. Commissions will cut those returns.

➤ STRIKE PRICE This is the price per 100 shares at which the holder of the option may buy (with a call) or sell (with a put) the related stock.

For stocks selling under $100 per share, the quotations are at intervals of 5 points: 45, 50, 55, etc. For stocks trading at over $100 per share, the quotations are every 10 points: 110, 120, etc.

New listings are added when the stock reaches the high or low strike price; that is, at 40 when the stock hits 35, and at 25 when the stock falls to 30. When you see a long list of strike prices, the stock has moved over a wide range.

➤ EXPIRATION DATE The option expires the Saturday following the third Friday of the month in which it can be exercised. Maximum length is 9 months.

➤ DIVIDENDS AND RIGHTS As long as you own the stock, you continue to receive the dividends. That's why calls for stocks with high yields sell at lower premiums than those for companies with small payouts.

A stock dividend or stock split automatically increases the number of shares covered by the option in an exact proportion. If a right is involved (see Chapter 18), its value will be set by the first sale of rights on the day the stock sells ex-rights.

➤ COMMISSIONS These vary with the number of contracts traded: For a single call, the maximum is often $25; for 10 calls, about $4 each. As a guideline, make your calculations, in multiple units, at $14 per contract, less if you use a discount broker. Ask your broker his rates *prior* to trading.

You may be able to save on commissions when you write calls for a premium of less than 1 ($100). A call traded at $^{15}/_{16}$ ($93.75) will cost $8.39 compared with $25 for one priced at 1 or higher.

➤ RESTRICTED OPTION This may occur when the previous day's price closed at less than 50¢ per option and the underlying stock price closed at more than 5 points *below* its strike price for calls or more than 5 points *above* its strike price for puts. Opening transactions (buying or writing calls) are prohibited unless they are covered. Closing transactions (liquidations) are permitted. There are various exceptions, so check with your broker.

HOW PREMIUMS WORK

The cost of the option is quoted in multiples of $^{1}/_{16}$ for options priced below $3, ⅛ for those priced higher. To determine the percentage of premium, divide the current value of the stock into the quoted price of the option. When there's a difference between the exercise price of the option and the quoted price of the stock, add or subtract the spread.

Here's how options were quoted in the financial pages when EFG stock was at 32⅜ (see the table on page 190):

The April 30 call prices ranged from a high

RELATIVE PREMIUMS
As Percent of Price of Underlying Common Stock When Common Is at Exercise Price

MONTHS TO EXPIRATION	LOW	AVERAGE	HIGH
1	1.8–2.6	3.5–4.4	5.2–6.1
2	2.6–3.9	5.2–6.6	7.8–9.2
3	3.3–5.0	6.7–8.3	10.0–11.7
4	3.9–5.9	7.9–9.8	11.8–13.8
5	4.5–6.8	9.0–11.2	13.5–15.8
6	5.0–7.5	10.0–12.5	15.0–17.5
7	5.5–8.2	10.9–13.7	16.4–19.2
8	5.9–8.9	11.8–14.8	17.7–20.6
9	6.4–9.5	12.7–15.9	19.0–22.2

of 4¾ ($475) to a low of 2¾ ($275) and a closing price of 3⅛ ($312.50) for a net change from the previous week of −⅛ ($12.50). There were 1,317 sales of contracts for 100 shares each.

The second line lists the action with April 30 puts: a high of $^{9}/_{16}$ ($56.25), a low of ¼ ($25), and a closing price of ⅜ ($37.50). For the week, the net change was −$^{1}/_{16}$ ($6.25). There were 996 contracts traded.

Traders looking for quick profits were pessimistic, as shown by the heavy volume in puts: 1,422 contracts for the April 35s and 2,219 for the April 40s. But there were fairly sharp differences of opinion, as the April 35 puts were up $^{5}/_{16}$ and the April 40s up ⅜.

Investors were more optimistic and appeared to believe that EFG stock was ready for an upswing: April 40 calls, due in a few weeks, were quoted at ⅛, whereas the farther-out October 40s were quoted at 1⅝. Much of the spread, of course, was due to the time factor.

The prices of the options reflect temporary hopes and fears, but over a month or two they will tend to move with the underlying stock. But do not rely solely on this type of projection: Near the expiration date, the prices of options move sharply.

One key factor to keep in mind is that the premium at the outset reflects the time factor. This will fall rapidly as the expiration date nears. In the last 3 months of a call, the

HOW OPTIONS ARE QUOTED

NAME, EXPIRATION DATE, AND PRICE	SALES	HIGH	WEEK'S LOW	LAST	NET CHG.
EFG Apr30	1,317	$4^3/_4$	$2^3/_4$	$3^1/_8$	$-^1/_8$
EFG Apr30 p	996	$^9/_{16}$	$^1/_4$	$^3/_8$	$-^1/_{16}$
EFG Apr35	3,872	$1^1/_4$	$^3/_8$	$^1/_2$	$-^3/_{16}$
EFG Apr35 p	1,422	$3^1/_8$	$1^5/_8$	$2^{15}/_{16}$	$+^5/_{16}$
EFG Apr40	1,526	$^3/_{16}$	$^1/_{16}$	$^1/_8$	$-^1/_{16}$
EFG Apr40 p	2,219	$7^7/_8$	$5^7/_8$	$7^7/_8$	$+^3/_8$
EFG Jul30	426	6	$4^1/_2$	$4^1/_2$	$-^1/_2$
EFG Jul30 p	805	$1^3/_8$	$^7/_8$	$1^3/_8$	$+^1/_8$
EFG Jul35	1,084	3	2	$2^1/_{16}$	$-^3/_{16}$
EFG Jul35 p	870	$3^7/_8$	$2^3/_4$	$3^7/_8$	$+^1/_4$
EFG Jul40	1,145	$1^1/_8$	$^3/_4$	$^3/_4$	$-^1/_8$
EFG Jul40 p	523	$7^3/_4$	$6^1/_8$	$7^3/_4$	$+^3/_8$
EFG Oct35	346	$4^3/_8$	$3^1/_8$	$3^1/_4$	$-^1/_4$
EFG Oct35 p	261	$4^3/_8$	$3^1/_2$	$4^3/_8$	$+^3/_8$
EFG Oct40	137	$2^1/_4$	$1^5/_8$	$1^5/_8$	$-^1/_4$
EFG Oct40 p	326	$7^7/_8$	$6^1/_2$	$7^3/_4$	$+^1/_4$

Stock price: $32^3/_8$. Table does not show open interest because of space limitations.

premium can be cut in half because of the dwindling time.

WRITING CALLS

When you write or sell calls, you start off with an immediate, sure, limited profit rather than an uncertain, potentially greater gain, which is the case for puts. The *most* you can make is the premium you receive, even if the price of the stock soars. If you write calls on stock you own, any loss of the value of the stock will be reduced by the amount of the premium. Writing covered calls (on stock you own) is a conservative use of options. You have these choices.

➤ ON-THE-MONEY CALLS These are written at an exercise price that is at or close to the current price of the stock.

Example: In December, Investor One buys 100 shares of Company A at 40 and sells a July call, at the strike price of 40, for 3 ($300). He realizes that A's stock may move above 43 in the next 7 months but is willing to accept the $3 per share income.

Investor Two is the purchaser of the call. He acquires the right to buy the stock at 40 at any time before the expiration date at the end of July. He anticipates that A's stock will move up well above 43.

Investor One will not sustain a dollar loss until the price of A goes below 37. He will probably keep the stock until its price goes above 43. At this price, the profit meter starts ticking for Investor Two, so let's see what happens if company A's stock jumps to 50. At any time before late July, Investor Two can exercise his option and pay $4,000 for stock now worth $5,000. After deducting about $400 (the $300 premium plus commissions), he will have a net profit of about $600, thus doubling his risk capital.

Investor Two will sell the call at $2 and lose $1 per call. Investor One will end up with about $375: the $300 premium plus two dividends of $50 each minus the $25 commission for the sale of the call.

➤ IN-THE-MONEY CALLS In-the-money calls are those where the exercise price is below the price of the underlying stock. This is a more aggressive technique that requires close attention but can result in excellent profits.

Example: In January, Karen buys 300

shares of Glamor Electronics Co. (GEC) at 105 ($31,500) and sells three June 100 calls at 8 each ($2,400). If GEC stock drops below 100, she keeps the premiums and the stock. If it goes to 110, she can buy back the calls at, say, 11, $1,100 ($3,300 total), to set up a loss of $900.

➤ DEEP-IN-THE-MONEY CALLS These are calls that are sold at strike prices far *below* the current quotation of the stock—8 to 20 points below. Writing them is best when the investor is dealing in large blocks of stock because of the almost certain commissions that have to be paid when the underlying stock is called. With this approach, the best selection is a stable, high-dividend stock. Your returns may be limited, but they are likely to be sure.

The technique used by professionals is called *using leverage:* When the exercise price of the call is below that of the current value of the stock, both securities tend to move in unison. Since the options involve a smaller investment, there's a higher percentage of return and, in a down market, more protection against loss.

Example: Pistol Whip, Inc. (PWI), is selling at 97⅝. The call price at 70 two months hence is 28, so the equivalent price is 98. If PWI goes to 105, the call will keep pace and be worth 35.

If you bought 100 shares of the stock, the total cost would be about $9,800. Your ultimate profit would be about $700, close to a 7.1% return. If you bought one option, your cost would be $2,800 and you would have the same $700 profit. Your return would be about 25%.

Note: All too often, this is more theory than practice. When an option is popular, it may trade on its own and not move up or down with the price of the stock. This separate value will shift only when the expiration date is near.

When one volatile stock was at 41 in March, the November 45 call was trading at 2 1/16. Three weeks later, when the stock fell to 35 1/2 (−16%), the call edged down to 2: a 3% decline. The professionals had moved in and set their own terms.

But remember that at times the price of the call may drop further percentagewise than that of the stock.

A variation of this use of deep-in-the-money calls is to create cost by basing the return on the total income received from premiums plus dividends.

Example: In January, one professional money manager seeking extra income for his fund bought 1,000 shares of Wellknown Chemical at 39½. He then sold April 35 options for 6⅞ each, thereby reducing the price per share to 32⅝. He could count on a 45¢-per-share dividend before the exercise date.

When the call is exercised at $35 per share, the profit on the $32.625 investment will be $2.375 plus the 45-cent dividend, or $1.825 for a return of 8.66% in a four month period.

➤ OUT-OF-THE-MONEY CALLS This is when the strike price is above the market price of the underlying stock for a call or the strike price is below the market price of the underlying stock of a put.

WRITING NAKED CALLS

Some calls are sold by speculators or investors who do not own the underlying stock. This is referred to as writing a naked call. The writer is betting that the stock will either remain at its current price or decline. He receives a premium, which he pockets if the stock does not rise above the call price. But if it does, he then *must* buy back his call at a loss.

$ HINT: Don't get involved unless you maintain a substantial margin account, have

---

RULES FOR WRITING OPTIONS

- Define your goal.
- Work on a programmed basis.
- Concentrate on stocks that you would like to own.
- Set a target rate of return.
- Buy the stock first.
- Write long-term calls.
- Calculate your net return.
- Keep your capital fully employed.
- Be persistent.
- Watch the timing.
- Protect your capital.
- Use margin to boost profits.
- Watch the record date of high-dividend stocks.
- Keep a separate bookkeeping system.

considerable experience, and feel confident that the price of a stock will stay flat or decline. It's risky, because if the stock hits the strike price before or at the exercise date, you are obligated to deliver the shares you do not own.

You can, of course, cover your position by buying calls, but if the stock price soars, the loss can be substantial. At best, your premium income will be reduced.

One technique that works well is to write two out-of-the-money calls for every 100 shares you own. This gives you double premiums. Do not go too far out, because a lot can happen in a few months.

Example: You own 300 shares of Company XYZ at 32. The 35 call, due in 4 months, is 3, but you are not convinced that the market, or the stock, will rise soon. You sell six calls, pocket $1,800 (less commissions), and hope that the stock stays under 35. If it moves to 36, you can buy back three calls for, say, 1½ ($450) and let the stock go. But if the stock jumps to 40, you're in deep trouble.

BUYING CALLS

Investors buy calls in anticipation of an increase in the price of the underlying stock. If that happens, the call may also rise in price and you can sell at a profit. Buying calls means you can invest a fraction of the cost of the stock and obtain greater leverage. You also limit your risk since the most you can lose is the cost of the option.

§ HINT: The basic problem with buying options is that calls are wasting assets. At expiration date, their values can decline to zero if the stock price moves opposite to your expectations or stays fairly stable.

Example: On February 15, ABC's common is selling at $40 per share. An October 40 call can be purchased for $500 (100 shares at $5 per share). On April 15, ABC is selling at $46 per share and the October 40 call is trading at a value of $750. The investor, anticipating an increase in the value of ABC, had purchased the call for $500 and sold it for $750, realizing a $250 profit.

Here are the ways leverage works in this situation:

	STOCK	CALL
Bought—February 15	$4,000	$500
Sold—April 15	4,600	750
Profit	600	250
Return on investment	15%	50%

In this example, the call buyer can lose no more than the $500 he paid for the October 40 call, regardless of any decline in the stock, but he can lose the entire $500 if he is wrong. However, he may be able to resell his option in time to recover some of his cost. Keep in mind that if he had purchased the stock itself for $4,000 and it had gone down in price, he would have lost more than $500 if he had sold. If he decided to hold the stock and it appreciated, he would have another opportunity to make a profit.

A put buyer does not have to resell a profitable call but can instead exercise it and take delivery of the underlying stock. He can then sell the stock for a gain or hold it for long-term appreciation.

§ IF YOU DARE: In an up market, buy calls on up stocks on either of these terms:

- Long-term, out-of-the-money options at a low premium, typically 1 or less. By diversifying with four or five promising situations, you may be lucky enough to hit it big with one and make enough to offset the small losses on the others.

- Short- or intermediate-term in-the-money or close-to-the-money options of volatile stocks: 2 months to expiration date, a stock within 5% of the strike price, and a low time premium. If the price of the premium doubles, sell half your holdings. Advice from one expert: "Never pay a premium of more than 3 for a call on a stock selling under 50 or more than 5 for one trading over 60. Both prices should include commissions."

§ HINT: The strike price of the option and the market price of the stock should change by about half as many points as the change in the stock price: For example, if a 30 option is worth 5 when the stock is at 30, it should be worth 2½ when the stock falls to 25 and worth 8 when the stock moves up to 36.

PUTS FOR PROFIT AND PROTECTION

In a broad sense, a put is the opposite of a call: It is an option to *sell* a specified number of shares (usually 100) of a specified stock at a specified price before a specified date. Puts have the same expiration months and price intervals as listed calls. The put buyer profits when the price of the underlying stock declines significantly. Then he sells the put at a profit, with the holder buying the stock at the lower current market price and selling it at the higher exercise or striking price.

The value of a put moves counter to that of the related stock: *up* when the price of the stock falls, *down* when it rises. You buy a put when you are bearish and anticipate that the market or stock will decline. Vice versa with selling puts. As with all options, a put is a wasting asset, and its value will diminish with the approach of the expiration date.

Here again, the attraction of puts is *leverage*. A few hundred dollars can acquire temporary control of thousands of dollars' worth of stock. The premiums are generally smaller than those of calls on the same stock because of lower demand, reflecting the small number of people who are pessimistic. Sharp traders take advantage of this situation, because they realize that most people tend to be optimistic about the stock market.

➤ SELLING (WRITING) PUTS This provides instant income but involves your responsibility to buy the stock if it sells, before the expiration date, at or below the exercise price.

Example: Ed owns Xanadu stock, now selling at 53, well above the purchase price. He's hopeful that the market will keep rising but decides to write a put at 50 for 2 ($200).

As long as the stock stays above 50, the put will not be exercised and Ed keeps the $200 per contract. But once the stock falls below 50, Ed must buy the shares or buy back the put, thus cutting or eliminating the opening profit.

➤ BUYING PUTS These can be used to protect positions and, of course, to score a quick gain. The profits come when the price of the stock falls.

Example: In March, Ann becomes skittish about the stock now trading at 47. She buys a July put at the strike price of 50 for 4 ($400). This put has an intrinsic cash value of 3, because the stock is selling 3 points below the exercise price. In effect, she is paying 1 ($100) to protect her position against a sharp market or stock decline.

If Ann's prediction is right and the price of the stock drops, the value of the put will rise: to over 7 when the stock falls to 43.

In late July, the stock price is 45, so Ann sells the put for 5 for a $100 gross profit. If the price of the stock goes below 43, her profit will be greater.

As with calls, the important factor in profitable puts is the related stock. The best candidates for both writing and buying puts are stocks that:

- *Pay small or no dividends.* You are hoping that the value of the stock will decline. Dividends tend to set a floor because of their yields.

- *Sell at high price-earnings ratios.* These are more susceptible to sharp downswings than stocks with lower multiples. A stock with a P/E of 25 runs a greater risk of a quick decline than one with a P/E of 10.

- *Are historically volatile*—with patterns of sharp, wide swings in price. Stable stocks move slowly even in an active market.

- *Are unpopular with institutions.* At the outset, when selling starts, the price drops can be welcome. Later, however, when panic selling is over, there's likely to be minimal action, because there will be few buyers.

TECHNIQUES FOR HIGH ROLLERS

➤ SPREADS A spread is the dollar difference between the buy and sell premiums. Spreads involve buying one option and selling another short, both on the same stock. If the cost of the option is greater than the proceeds of the option sold, it is a "debit." If the reverse is true, it's called a "credit." If the costs and proceeds are the same, the spread is "even money." *Your goal:* to capture at least the difference in premiums—at least ½ point between the cost of options exercisable at different dates and/or at different prices. *Make your calculations on paper first*, and make no commitments until you are sure you understand the possibilities or probabilities.

Here's an example involving POP stock priced at 50 in April. The premiums for 50 calls are 3½ for July, 4 for October.

Sell July 50 for 3½	+$350
Buy October 50 for 4	− 400
Cash outlay	− 50
Commission	− 25
Total cost	−$ 75

If POP is below 50 in July, you keep $350 and still own an option worth $250 to $300.

If POP goes up by October, the option will be worth $500 or more, so you have a profit of $850.

If POP is at 60 at the end of July, that month's option will be worth 10, so you have to buy it back at a loss of about $650 plus in-and-out costs. But the October call might be at 14, so you could sell that for a gross profit of $1,000 to offset the July loss.

If the stock falls below 46½, you will lose money unless there's a recovery by October. But with such a stable stock in a rising market, this is not likely. The key factor is the small spread, which keeps the maximum loss low.

➤ PERPENDICULAR SPREAD Also called a price or vertical spread, it is based on buying and selling options with the same exercise date but different strike prices.

Example: Easy Rider (ER) is at 101¾. The market is moving up and you are bullish. Sell 10 ER October 100s at 12¼ and buy October 90s at 16⅞. This requires an outlay of $4,625. Your maximum loss will occur if ER plunges below 90.

If it goes to 95, you will still make $375. At 100 or higher, your profit will be a welcome $5,375, a 120% return on your investment.

If the market is declining, set up a bearish spread. Psychologically, the risk is greater, so it is best to deal with lower-priced stocks, selling at, say, 24⅝.

Buy 10 October 25s at 2⅛ and sell 10 October 20s at 5⅜. This brings in $3,250 cash. Since the October 20 calls are naked, you'll need

---

MAKING YOUR OWN PUT

Options are flexible and can be combined so that the stock purchases, sales, or short sales protect positions and make profits. Here's an example, by Max Ansbacher, of how to create your own put.

Assume that in late summer, your stock is at 69⅞ and the January 65 call is 9¼. You sell short 100 shares of the stock and buy the call. Here are the possibilities:

■ If the stock falls to 55 by the end of January, the call will be worthless, so you lose $925. But your profit from the short sale is $1,487.50 ($6,987.50 sale; $5,500 buy-back cost) for a net profit of $562.50 (not counting commissions and fees).

■ The option limits your risk of loss on the short sale even if the stock price should rise. Thus if the stock jumps to 100, an unprotected short sale would mean a loss of $3,012.50 ($10,000 purchase price minus $6,987.50 received from the short sale).

■ But with a short sale of the stock and a purchase of a call, the loss will be only $437: the purchase price of 9¼ ($925) minus $488 (the spread between the stock price of 69⅞ and the exercise price of 65)—again not counting costs.

$5,000 margin (but the premiums cut this to $1,750) to control nearly $50,000 worth of stock.

If the stock goes to 22, you will make $1,250. At 20 or below, your profit is $3,250 for a 180% return. With perpendicular spreads, you know results at any one time. With horizontal spreads, there's the added risk of time.

➤ STRADDLE A straddle is a double option, combining a call and a put on the same stock, both at the same price and for the same length of time. Either or both sides of a straddle may be exercised at any time during the life of the option—for a high premium. Straddles are profitable when you are convinced that a stock will make a dramatic move but are uncertain whether the trend will be up or down.

Traditionally, most speculators use straddles in a bull market against a long position. If the stock moves up, the call side will be exercised and the put will expire unexercised. This is more profitable than writing calls, because the straddle premiums are substantially higher than those of straight calls.

But this can be costly in a down market. If the underlying stock goes down, there's a double loss: in the call and in the put. Therefore, when a straddle is sold against a long position, the straddle premium received must, in effect, protect 200 shares.

In a bear market, it is often wise to sell straddles against a short position. The odds are better.

Here's how one self-styled trader did it:

"In January, QRS stock was at 100. This was close to the last year's high, and since the stock had bounced as low as 65, I felt the best straddle was short term, so I picked a February expiration date. Simultaneously, I bought a call and a put, both at 100: 5 ($500) for the call and 4 ($400) for the put. With commissions (for buying and selling) of about $100, my exposure was $1,000.

"To make money, QRS had to rise above 110 or fall below 90. I guessed right. The stock's uptrend continued to 112. I sold the call for $1,300 and was lucky to get rid of the put at $50: profit—$350 in one month!

"I would do OK if the stock fell to 88. Then the call would be worth ½ but the put would bring at least $1,200, so I end up with about $250.

"The risk was that the stock's price would hold around 100. This would mean an almost total loss. But from experience I know that I'll lose on about 25% of my straddles, so I have to shoot for a high return on the other deals."

➤ STRIP   A strip is a triple option: two puts and one call on the same stock with a single option period and striking price. A strip writer expects the stock to fall in the short term and rise over the long term. He offers to sell 100 shares that he owns above the market price or take 200 shares below the market. The premium is higher than for a straddle.

➤ STRAP   This is also a triple option: two calls and one put on the same stock. The writer gets top premium—bullish over the long term but more negative than the strip seller on short-term prospects.

➤ INSURANCE   To protect a profit, buy a put on stock you own. *Example:* Your stock has soared from 30 to 60, so you expect a setback. You buy a short-term put, at 60, for $400. If the stock dips to 50, the put will be worth 10 ($1,000), so you sell for a profit of $600 and still own the stock. If the stock keeps moving up to 70, the put expires worthless. You lose $400, but you have a paper profit of $1,000 on the stock, so you are $600 ahead.

➤ LOCK IN CAPITAL GAINS   The same technique can be used to lock in a capital gain. By buying the put at 60 for $400, you reduce the stock value to 56. If it falls to 50, you sell the stock at the exercise price of 60 for $6,000. Deduct the $400 premium from the $3,000 profit (from cost of 30) and you still have $2,600. That's $600 more than if you had held the stock until its price fell to 50.

FOR FURTHER INFORMATION

Kenneth H. Shaleen, *Technical Analysis & Options Strategies* (Chicago: Probus Publishing Co., 1992).

18 | STOCK RIGHTS AND WARRANTS

STOCK RIGHTS

Stock rights are a special type of option that permits current shareholders to buy more corporate securities, usually common stock, ahead of the public, without commissions or fees, and typically at a discount of 5% to 10%.

Most rights allow shareholders to buy new shares on the basis of the number of shares of common already held; therefore, two or more rights are often required to buy one new share. The price, given in the prospectus, is called the exercise or subscription price. It is always below the current market price.

Rights are a convenient way for corporations to raise additional capital at a modest cost. In a sense, they are a reward to shareholders. They are often used by utilities eager to issue more common stock to balance their heavy debt obligations. The discount makes it possible for investors (who obviously have confidence in the company) to acquire additional shares at a bargain price or to pick up a few extra dollars by selling the rights in the open market. But rights are worthwhile only when the additional money raised by the company can be expected to generate extra profits and eventually lead to higher dividends on the additional shares. This is an important aspect of judging rights, because essentially they represent a dilution of your ownership in the company.

To be eligible for rights, you must own the common stock on a stated date. Most offerings must be exercised within a short time, usually less than 30 days, so watch your mail, and if the shares are held by your broker, be doubly alert. Failure to take advantage of this opportunity is foolish and can be costly—causing loss of the actual value of the rights.

Rights have an intrinsic value, but they are also speculative because of the high leverage they offer: A 10% rise in the price of the stock can mean as much as a 30% jump in the value of the right. Or vice versa on the loss side.

Let's assume that the stock is trading at $28 per share, that shareholders get one right for every 5 shares, and that each right entitles the holder to buy 1 new share at $25 each.

$$VR = \frac{MP - EP}{NR + 1}$$

where VR = value of right
  MP = stock's market price
  EP = exercise price
  NR = number of rights needed to
    buy one share

To calculate the value of one right *before* the ex-date, add 1 to the number of rights:

$$VR = \frac{28 - 25}{5 + 1} = \frac{3}{6} = 0.50$$

Thus each right is worth 50¢, and the stock at this time is worth that much more to investors who exercise their rights.

After the stock has gone ex-right, there'll be no built-in bonus for the stock, and the right will sell at its own value, or possibly higher, if the price of the stock advances, lower if it declines.

ADVANTAGES TO SHAREHOLDERS

- **Maintenance of ownership position.** If you like a company well enough to continue as a shareholder, pick up the rights. Historically, 80% of stocks bought with rights have outperformed the market in the year following the issue. That's logical; management was optimistic.

HOW RIGHTS ARE QUOTED

52 WEEKS		STOCK	SALES 100s	YIELD	WEEK'S	
HIGH	LOW				HIGH	LOW
68	42	XYZ Corp.	132	3.7	64	62¼
1	⅜	XYZ Corp. rts	27		⅞	½

- **Bargain price.** When Southwestern Public Service issued 29.2 million rights, the offer permitted shareholders to buy one additional common share at $10.95 for each 10 shares already held. At the time, the stock was trading at $11.50, so the new shares were available at a 4.8% discount. If you owned 1,000 shares, you could save about $55 on the deal, because there were no transaction costs.
- **Profits from rights themselves.** If you do not want to acquire more stock, you can sell the rights in the open market: through your broker or through a bank designated by the company. With Southwestern, each right was worth 4⅝¢ ($4.625 for each 100 rights).
- **Trading rights.** You can buy rights either to exercise or to speculate. Trading in rights starts as soon as the offer is announced. For a while, the prices of both the basic stock and the rights are quoted— the latter on a "when issued" (wi) basis, as shown with XYZ Corp. in the table. As a rule, it's best to buy rights soon after they are listed in the financial press; it's best to sell a day or two before the lapse date.

SPECIAL BENEFITS

There are two other investment advantages with rights. These give you the opportunity to purchase:

1. The stock with a very low margin in a special subscription account (SSA). This is a margin account set up to use the rights to buy extra stock within 90 days after the rights issue. To open an SSA, deposit rights—your own or purchased—with your broker.

   In addition to no commission for exercising that purchase, the *advantages* are a 25% margin, compared with 50% for stocks, and a year to pay if you come up with 25% of the balance each quarter.

   Example: You have rights to buy Kwick Kick common, selling at 63, for 56 on the basis of 1 new share for 10 old shares. You acquire 100 rights, so you need $5,600 to complete the purchase. You can borrow up to 75% ($4,200), so you can make the deal with only $1,400 in cash or collateral. Every 3 months you must reduce the outstanding balance by 25%.

   The *disadvantages* of SSA are that the price of the stock may decline, so you will have to come up with more margin, and you cannot draw cash dividends or use the securities for collateral as long as they are in this special account.

   Neither the receipt nor the exercise of the right results in taxable income to the stockholder. But you will have to pay taxes on ultimate profits when the stock is sold.

2. Oversubscription privileges. Some shareholders will not exercise their rights, so after the expiration date, you can buy these rights, usually on the basis of your original allotment. You must indicate your wish to participate in the oversubscription early, preferably when you send in your check for the new shares.

   $ HINT: Rights offerings often put downward pressure on the price of the stock and therefore represent a good investment opportunity.

WARRANTS

Warrants are pure speculations. Their prices are usually low, so there can be high leverage if the value of the related stock rises.

A warrant is an option to buy a stated number of shares of a related security (usually common stock) at a stipulated price during a specified period (5, 10, 20 years, or, occasionally, perpetually). The price at which the warrant can be exercised is fixed above the current market price of the stock at the time the warrant is issued. Thus when the common stock is at 10, the warrant might entitle the holder to buy 1 share at 15. (This differs from a right, where the subscription price is usually lower than the current market value of the stock and the time period is typically several weeks.)

Since the two securities tend to move somewhat in parallel, an advance in the price creates a higher percentage gain for the warrant than for the stock.

Example: Let's say that the warrant to buy 1 share at 15 sells at 1 when the stock is at 10. If the stock soars to 20 (100% gain), the price of the warrant will go up to at least 5 (400% gain).

But the downside risk of the warrant can be greater than that of the stock. If the stock drops to 5, that's a 50% loss. The warrant, depending on its life span, might fall to ⅛, an 88% decline.

A warrant is basically a call on a stock. It has no voting rights, pays no dividends, and has no claim on the assets of the corporation. Warrants trade on the exchanges and are usually registered in the owner's name. Some warrants are issued in certificate form although most are not.

The value of a warrant reflects hope: that the price of the stock will rise above the exercise price. When the stock trades *below* that call price, the warrant has only speculative value: With the stock at 19 and the exercise price at 20, the warrant is theoretically worthless. But it will actually trade at a price that reflects the prospectus of the company and the life of the warrant. When the price of the stock rises above the specified exercise price, the warrant acquires a tangible value, which is usually inflated by speculation plus a premium, because it is a lower-priced way of playing the common stock. However, the closer a warrant gets to its expiration date, the smaller the premium it commands. Conversely, the longer the life of the warrant, the higher the premium if there is real hope that the price of the stock will rise. After expiration, the warrant is worthless.

$ HINT: The main advantage warrants have over options is that they run for much longer. The longest an option lasts is 9 months. Warrants, however, run for years and some in perpetuity, which gives the investor a chance to speculate on a company over the long term at a relatively low cost. This time frame makes warrants less risky than options.

CALCULATING THE VALUE OF A WARRANT

The speculative value of a warrant is greatest when the warrant price is below the exercise price. If the stock moves up, the price of the warrant can jump fast. The table below shows guidelines set by warrant expert S. L. Pendergast for the maximum premium to pay. For example, when the stock price is at the exercise price (100%), pay at most 41% of the exercise price. Thus with a stock at the exercise price of 30, the maximum price to pay for a warrant (on a one-for-one basis) would be about 12. In most cases, better profits will come when the warrant is bought at a lower price.

An actual example is Atlas Corp. warrants that are perpetual; that is, they do not expire. They trade on the ASE at $3, with an exercise price of $15.625. The market price of the stock, as of July 1992, was $5¾.

$$7 \div 15.625 = 46\%$$

$$3 \div 15.625 = 19\%$$

These percentages fall outside the acceptable buying range using the table.

HOW TO SELECT PROFITABLE WARRANTS

Warrants are generally best in bull markets, especially during periods of great enthusiasm. Their low prices attract speculators who trade for quick gains. At all times, however, use these checkpoints:

MAXIMUM PREMIUM TO PAY

STOCK PRICE AS PERCENT OF EXERCISE PRICE	WARRANT PRICE AS PERCENT OF EXERCISE PRICE
80	28
90	34
100	41
110	46

➤ BUY ONLY WARRANTS OF A COMMON STOCK THAT YOU WOULD BUY ANYWAY If the common stock does not go up, there's little chance that the warrant's price will advance.

The best profits come from warrants associated with companies that have potential for strong upward swings due to sharp earnings improvement, a prospective takeover, newsmaking products or services, etc. It also helps if they are temporarily popular.

In most cases, the warrants for fast-riding stocks, even at a high premium, will outperform seemingly cheap warrants for issues that are falling.

At the outset, stick with warrants of fair-to-good corporations whose stocks are listed on major exchanges. They have broad markets.

When you feel more confident, seek out special situations, especially warrants of small, growing firms. Many of these "new" companies rely on warrants in their financing. Their actual or anticipated growth can boost the price of their warrants rapidly.

But be wary of warrants where the related stock is limited or closely controlled. If someone decides to dump a block of stock, the values can fall fast.

➤ BUY WARRANTS WHEN THEY ARE SELLING AT LOW PRICES The percentages are with you when there's an upward move, and with minimal costs the downside risks are small. But watch out for "superbargains," because commissions will eat up most of the gains.

Also watch their values and be cautious when their prices move to more than 20% of their exercise figure.

➤ WATCH THE EXPIRATION OR CHANGE DATE After expiration, the warrant has no value. If you're conservative, stay away from warrants with a life span of less than 4 years. When you know what you are doing, short-life warrants can bring quick profits if you are smart and lucky. But be careful. You could end up with worthless paper.

➤ AVOID DILUTION If there's a stock split or stock dividend, the market price of the stock will drop but the conversion price of the warrant may not change. The same caveat goes for warrants subject to call. Warrants of listed companies will generally be protected against such changes, but take nothing for granted.

Once in a while, warrants will be reorganized out of their option value. This occurs with

SOME POPULAR WARRANTS

COMPANY	EXERCISE PRICE TERMS	RECENT PRICE OF COMMON STOCK	RECENT PRICE OF WARRANT
ADT Ltd.	$10	$8	$2
Atlas Corp.	15.625	6	2
BSN Corp.	10.15	7⅝	0.75
Mercury Air	3.50	2	0.25

SOURCE: Standard & Poor's *Stock Guide,* May 1992.

troubled corporations taken over by tough-minded operators who are unwilling to pay for past excesses or to provide profits for speculators.

➤ SPREAD YOUR RISKS If you have sufficient capital, buy warrants in five different companies. The odds are that you may hit big on one, break even on two, and lose on the others. Your total gains may be less than if you had gambled on one warrant that proved a winner, but your losses will probably be less if you're wrong.

➤ LOOK FOR SPECIAL OPPORTUNITIES SUCH AS "USABLE" BONDS WITH WARRANTS ATTACHED Some bonds are sold along with detachable warrants. In many cases the bonds can be used at par ($1,000) in paying the exercise price. In other words, they can be used in lieu of cash to pay for the stock at the specified warrant price.

Should the bond trade at 90, a discount to par, the discounted price of the bond also discounts the exercise price of the warrant.

Except in unusual situations, all warrants should be bought to trade or sell and not to exercise. With no income, usually a long wait for appreciation, and rapid price changes, warrants almost always yield quick gains to speculators who have adequate capital and time to watch the market.

10 POINTS FOR EVALUATING WARRANTS

1 *Underlying stock price.* The higher the stock price, all other things being equal, the higher the value of the warrant.

2 *Stock volatility.* The higher the volatility of the underlying stock, the higher the value of the warrant. Volatile stocks are more likely to appreciate or depreciate substantially. A warrant, too, will benefit from appreciation.

3 *Dividend.* The higher the dividend on the underlying stock, the lower the value of the warrant. Warrant holders are not entitled to receive dividends paid to stockholders.

4 *Strike price.* The lower the exercise price, all other things being equal, the higher the value of the warrant.

5 *Time to expiration.* The longer the warrant's life, the higher the value of the warrant.

6 *Interest rates.* Higher rates tend to increase the value of warrants.

7 *Call features.* Call features shorten the life of the warrant and detract from its value.

8 *Usable bonds.* A usable bond can be used at par to pay the exercise price of a warrant. This gives a warrant added value.

9 *Ability to borrow the underlying stock.* This tends to depress the warrant's value.

10 *Takeovers.* If the company is taken over at a high price, warrants will appreciate.

NIKKEI WARRANTS

Warrants that allow investors to bet on the Japanese stock market were introduced at the start of 1990. These eight warrants, which trade on the American Stock Exchange, have at various times accounted for as much as 40% of the AMEX's daily volume.

Six of the eight are put warrants, which pay off in dollars if the Nikkei index of 225 Tokyo stocks falls below specified levels within a stated time period. The two call warrants came out in April 1990. (Put warrants represent a bet on the market dropping.) Since the eight were issued, new warrants have been brought to market by several brokerage firms. Prices of the put warrants rose 200% as the Nikkei declined 25%.

The popularity of the Nikkei warrants led Wall Street and investment bankers to issue warrant offerings tied to the London stock market, and others are expected to follow.

☐CAUTION: Unless you have the time and expertise to follow foreign markets, this

---

WHERE TO FIND WARRANTS

WARRANTS ARE ISSUED:
- With bonds as a sweetener to buy them
- As part of initial public offering packages consisting of shares of common plus warrants
- In conjunction with mergers and acquisitions

WHERE TO FIND WARRANTS:
- Brokerage firm research lists
- Newspaper securities listings, where they are identified by the letters "wt"

---

investment doesn't warrant your time and is best left to the Wall Street pros.

SELLING WARRANTS SHORT

Selling short means selling a security you do not own, borrowing it from your broker to make delivery. This is done in anticipation of a decline in price. Later you expect to buy it at a lower price and make the profit between that lower price and your original short sale.

But short selling is always tricky, and with warrants there can be other problems: (1) limited markets because of lack of speculator interest; (2) exchange regulations—e.g., the American Stock Exchange prohibits short selling of its listed warrants several months before expiration date; (3) the possibility of a "short squeeze"— the inability to buy warrants to cover your short sales as the expiration date approaches; (4) the possibility that the life of the warrants may be extended beyond the stated expiration date, advancing the date when the warrants become worthless, so a short seller may not be able to cover a position at as low a price as was anticipated.

FOR FURTHER INFORMATION

R.H.M. Survey of Warrants (newsletter)
R.H.M. Associates, Inc.
172 Forest Avenue
Glen Cove, NY 11542
1-516-759-2904
Weekly; $280 per year or $150 for 6 months

19 NEW ISSUES

After the October 1987 crash, new issues, also known as initial public offerings (IPOs), plummeted and remained a small part of the market during the depths of the recession. As the economy began to recover in late 1992, so did the number of IPOs.

New issues continue to tempt many investors. If you're one of those, learn the facts and follow our guidelines for selecting fledgling companies to back. It is possible to make money in IPOs, but it requires far more research than most investments, as well as an understanding of the market. Norman G. Fosback, editor of *New Issues,* favors companies that have reported profits for at least 5 years and whose earnings are trending up.

If you don't buy an IPO when it's first issued, you can buy shares in the aftermarket when they trade OTC. If it's a weak market, chances are you won't pay much more, if anything; but in a hot market, expect a 20% to 25% increase in the aftermarket. If you are enamored of the issue but cannot buy at a reasonable price, follow the stock's progress carefully. Wait for the first blush to fade, and move in when it takes a tumble. Often a new company will lose its initial luster or report lower earnings, thus pushing the price down temporarily.

Learning about new issues is less difficult than you might think. A number of the larger brokerage firms publish a list of them on a regular basis, but unless you're a major client, you won't hear about them. Your broker or library may subscribe to the bible in the field, *Investment Dealer's Digest,* which lists all IPOs as they are registered with the SEC.

A good example of a successful IPO: Gaylord Entertainment Co., offered at $20.50 per share when it went public in October 1991. It was selling above $30 by May 1992. Gaylord owns Nashville Network, an ad-supported cable TV service with country-western music, talk shows, etc. It's leading the "country craze."

THE UNDERWRITER

Your chances for success will be increased if you select IPOs from reputable investment bankers. First-class underwriters will not allow themselves to manage new issues that are of poor quality or highly speculative. Moreover, if a fledgling company runs into a need for additional financing, a first-rate banker will be ready to raise more capital. Thus the prime consideration is the reputation of the underwriters. However, this is not written in stone.

THE PROSPECTUS

Once you learn about a new issue, your first investigative step is to read a copy of the prospectus, generally available when an offering is registered with the SEC. (It's also called a "red herring" because of the red-inked warning that the contents of the report are not final.) Despite its many caveats, the prospectus will help you form a rough opinion about the company and what it may be worth. Look for:

➤ DETAILS ABOUT MANAGEMENT The success of a company is often determined by the quality of the management team. The officers and directors should have successful experience in the company and/or similar organizations; they should be fully involved in the firm and should not treat it as a part-time activity.

➤ TYPE OF BUSINESS New ventures have the best chance of success in growth areas, such as electronics, specialty retailing, and biotechnology. Software companies, environmental cleanup, waste disposal stocks, and health care are expected to do well. The risks are greatest with companies in exciting but partially proven fields such as biotechnology, genetic engineering, and AIDS research. These companies are tempting but pay off only after heavy capital investments and successful R&D. Try to invest in an area you know something about or a business located near you. A good prospectus will also list some of the company's customers.

➤ FINANCIAL STRENGTH AND PROFITABILITY Apply the following criteria to the current balance sheet. Glance at the previous year's report to catch any major changes.

- Modest short-term debt and long-term obligations of less than 40% of total capital. With $40 million in assets, the debt should not be more than $16 million.
- Current ratio (of assets to liabilities) a minimum of 2:1 except under unusual, temporary conditions.
- Sales of at least $30 million to be sure that there's a market for products or services.

MUTUAL FUNDS THAT INVEST IN SMALL, EMERGING COMPANIES

Alliance Quasar Fund
500 Plaza Drive (3rd floor)
Secaucus, NJ 07094
1-800-247-4154

American Capital
  Emerging Growth Fund
P.O. Box 418256
Kansas City, MO 64141
1-800-231-3638

Fidelity Growth Co.
  Fund
21 Congress Street
Boston, MA 02109
1-800-544-8888

Keystone S-4 Fund
Box 2121
Boston, MA 02106
1-800-225-2618

The Nautilus Fund
24 Federal Street
Boston, MA 02110
1-800-225-6265

New Horizon Fund
T. Rowe Price Associates
100 East Pratt Street
Baltimore, MD 21202
1-800-638-5660

20th Century Ultra
  Investors OTC
P.O. Box 419200
Kansas City, MO 64141
1-800-345-2021

Vanguard Explorer Fund
P.O. Box 2600
Valley Forge, PA 19482
1-800-662-7447

Double-check if revenues exceed $50 million. That's the threshold for the big leagues, where competition is sure to heighten.

- High profitability: a return on equity of 20% annually for the past 3 years—with modest modifications if recent gains have been strong. This will assure similar progress in the future.

➤ EARNINGS The company should be able to service its debt. Look for the most recent P/E and compare it with P/Es of competitors, listed in the newspaper. If a P/E is significantly higher than the industry average of a similar-sized company, shares are overpriced. Robert S. Natale, editor of Standard & Poor's *Emerging & Special Situations* newsletter, states that a young company often hasn't had time to produce much in the way of earnings, so instead look for a ratio of total offering price to annual sales. On the whole, this market-capitalization-to-sales ratio should not be greater than 2:7.

➤ USE OF PROCEEDS Check out what the company plans to do with the newly raised capital. It should not be devoted to repaying the debt or bailing out the founders, management, or promoters. Most of it should be used to expand the business. If 25% or more is going toward nonproductive purposes, move on. Avoid firms whose management or a founding shareholder is selling a large percentage of the shares (30% or more).

§ HINT: Whenever the public is chasing after new issues beware of telephone solicitations from high-pressure salesmen who guarantee that you'll double your money once the company goes public. Careful: You're skating on thin ice.

FOR FURTHER INFORMATION

To help you spot the winners and avoid the losers when firms go public, you may want to read one of the following advisory newsletters for background data:

Emerging and Special Situations
Standard & Poor's Corp.
25 Broadway
New York, NY 10005
1-212-208-8000; 1-800-221-5277
Monthly; $223.50 per year

New Issues
Institute for Econometric Research
3471 North Federal Highway
Ft. Lauderdale, FL 33306
1-800-327-6720
Monthly; $95 per year

Ground Floor
The Hirsch Organization
6 Deer Trail

Old Tappan, NJ 07675
1-201-664-3400
Monthly; $115 per year

Investment Dealers Digest
2 World Trade Center (18th floor)
New York, NY 10048
1-212-227-1200
Weekly; $375 per year

PART FOUR

HIGH RISK FOR HIGH RETURNS

There are occasions when a portion of your savings can be used for speculations. Recognize the hazards and limit your commitments to 15% of your capital. If you are smart—and lucky—enough to score, put half your winnings into a money market fund or certificate of deposit to build assets for future risks.

Speculations are not investments. This statement sounds simple-minded, but most people fail to make the distinction. Investments are designed to preserve capital and to provide income. The decisions are made on the basis of fundamentals: the quality and the value of the investment.

Speculations involve risks and are profitable primarily because of market fluctuations. They should *never* be included in retirement portfolios. They should be entered into only when you understand what you are doing *and with money that you can afford to lose.* Before getting into details about speculations:

- Recognize that there is usually a sound reason why a security is selling at a low price or paying a very low yield. Investors are not interested, so you must be certain that there are facts to justify higher future values.
- In making projections, cut in half the anticipated upward move and double the potential downswing.
- Speculate only in a rising market unless you are selling short. Worthwhile gains will come when more people buy more shares—not likely in a down market.
- Be willing to take quick, small losses, and never hold on in blind hope of a recovery.
- When you pick a winner, sell half your shares (or set a protective stop-loss order) when you have doubled your money.
- *Most important, buy a rabbit's foot.*

On the next few pages you will read about:

- Foreign stocks, bonds, and currencies
- Commodities
- Precious metals
- Financial futures and market indexes
- Splits, spin-offs, small caps, stubs, and stock buy-backs

20 FOREIGN STOCKS, BONDS, CDs, AND CURRENCIES

The electronic age makes the flow of money and information almost instantaneous, so whatever happens on the Hong Kong stock exchange or to the price of gold in London impacts directly on investors in Des Moines, Duluth, and Davenport. As we draw closer and closer to one market, it is essential for investors also to widen their horizons. If you're not convinced, just consider this fact: The U.S. stock exchanges now account for about 30% of the world's equity capitalization. Until 1986 that figure was always 50% or more.

At various times and in certain economic cycles, astute investors are able to make substantial profits by "going global" because of the international ripple effect: Each country's economic cycle is a separate one, so when one nation is in the midst of a poor stock market, others are inevitably thriving. Wise investors realize the advisability of not locking themselves into a narrow geographical investment sphere.

The European Economic Community of 1992, combined with the reunification of Germany into a single nation and the meetings among the leaders of the world, have focused all eyes on the emergence of a world increasingly based on free enterprise.

Timing overseas investments is tricky. A strong dollar makes foreign investments less profitable for Americans—but as the dollar levels off, it is a good point to enter the global arena.

MAKING PROFITS

An investment in a foreign stock offers at least two ways to make a profit or loss:
- The price of the stock can go up (or down) in its local currency.
- The value of the foreign country's currency can rise (or drop) relative to the

U.S. dollar, thereby increasing or decreasing the value of your stock.

The best situation obviously exists when the price of the stock rises *and* the value of the country's currency likewise rises against the dollar. An important fact to keep in mind is that a rising currency can sometimes save you from the pitfalls associated with a poor or only mediocre foreign stock.

Despite these compelling reasons for international investing, many otherwise clever investors still remain unschooled in the mechanics of successful investing in foreign stocks. The necessary guidelines, given here, can be mastered by anyone with the time and inclination to do so. But first let's examine the key pros and cons of international investing.

UNDERSTANDING THE RISKS

With all companies that have substantial foreign interests, there are extra risks resulting from gains or losses through foreign exchange. Since the company's earnings are in local currencies, they can lose a portion of their value when transferred back into dollars. The stronger the dollar, the lower the net earnings reported by the parent company. The impact can reduce profits by as much as 10%. Some international or foreign companies try to hedge against these currency swings by geographical or product diversification, but this can be expensive and is not always effective.

Currency fluctuations also affect the value of a company's nonmonetary assets (plant, equipment, inventories). When the dollar's value rises, that of the foreign currency declines. But the assets are shown at the exchange rates that were in effect when these items were purchased.

That's why constant monitoring of the dollar's value is so important when going global. A good stockbroker or the international division of a large bank can keep you abreast of currency fluctuations and how they may affect your investments.

Although there are several methods for investing in foreign stocks, the three most popular are American Depository Receipts (ADRs), mutual funds, and multinational companies, which are discussed in the next chapter.

AMERICAN DEPOSITORY RECEIPTS (ADRs)

ADRs are negotiable receipts representing ownership of shares of a foreign corporation that is traded in an American securities market. They are issued by an American bank, but the actual shares are held by the American bank's foreign

---

FOREIGN INVESTMENT

PROS
↑ Provides diversification
↑ Provides additional investment opportunities not available in U.S. markets
↑ Provides hedge against U.S. monetary or economic troubles such as inflation, dollar depreciation, slump in stock market
↑ As vitality shifts from one country to another, foreign firms may represent attractive alternatives

CONS
↓ Currency fluctuations
↓ Local political situations
↓ Less information available on foreign companies than on U.S. firms
↓ Foreign firms not required to provide the same detailed type of information as U.S. firms
↓ Different accounting procedures, which can make accurate evaluation complex
↓ Foreign brokers and foreign exchanges seldom bound by regulations as strict as those imposed by the SEC (every country has its own set of regulations)
↓ Quotes sometimes difficult to obtain

---

depository bank or agent. This custodian bank is usually but not always an office of the American bank (if there is one in the country involved). If not, the bank selected to be custodian is generally a foreign bank with a close relationship to the foreign company for which the ADRs are being issued.

ADRs allow you to buy, sell, or hold the foreign stocks without actually taking physical possession of them. They are registered by the SEC and are sold by stockbrokers. Each ADR is a contract between the holder and the bank, certifying that a stated number of shares of the overseas-based company have been deposited with the American bank's foreign office or custodian and will be kept there as long as the ADR remains outstanding. The U.S. purchaser pays for the stock in dollars and receives dividends in dollars.

When the foreign corporation has a large capitalization, so that its shares sell for the equivalent of a few dollars, each ADR may represent more than 1 share: 10, 50, or even 100 shares in the case of some Japanese companies, where there are tens of millions of shares of common stock.

ADRs are generally initiated when an American bank learns that there is a great deal of interest in the shares of a foreign firm. Or a foreign corporation may initiate action if it wants to enter the American market. In either case, the bank then purchases a large block of shares and issues the ADRs, leaving the stock certificates overseas in its custodian bank.

The most important test in a foreign company's selection of an ADR is whether a market exists in the United States for the shares. In other words, the ADR process is not designed to make a market for the shares of a foreign company so much as it is to follow the market.

$ IF YOU DARE: For risk-oriented investors, ADRs offer excellent opportunities for *arbitrage* (the simultaneous purchase and sale of identical or equivalent investments in order to profit from the price difference). You can take advantage of the price differences between the stocks traded locally and the ADRs selling in New York. With gold shares, for example, there can be three different quotations: London, Johannesburg, and New York. A sharp trader, noting the wide spread, can buy

---

HOW ADRs ARE PURCHASED

1. Investors give a buy order to their broker.
2. Brokers place a buy order abroad.
3. Foreign brokers buy the stock.
4. The stock is deposited with the custodian banks in the foreign country.
5. Custodians instruct the American depository bank (Citicorp, Bank of New York, Morgan Guaranty, for example) to issue an ADR.
6. The ADR is issued to the American investors.

LEADING ADRs

ADR	SYMBOL	PRICE SPRING 1992
Barclays plc	BCS	$27
British Airways	BAB	51
British Gas	BRG	45
British Petroleum	BP	57
Glaxo Holding plc	GLX	27
Honda Motor	HMC	23
Imperial Chemical Ind.	ICI	98
National Westminster	NW	38
News Corp., Ltd.	NWS	32
Novo-Nordisk	NVO	87
Saatchi/Saatchi	SAA	1
Shell Transport	SC	55
Smithkline Beecham plc	SBH	79
Unilever	UN	102

SOURCE: Quotron, May 1992.

---

shares in London and sell short ADRs in the United States.

$ IF YOU DON'T: Stick with mutual funds specializing in foreign stocks and let someone else do the decision making and trading for you.

If you decide to buy ADRs, select those actively traded in the United States—i.e., listed on one of the exchanges. Of the 750 ADRs available in May 1992, about one-fourth were listed, because not all foreign companies want to meet the disclosure requirements of or for listing. Those that are not listed trade over the counter. Their prices are not given in the newspaper, but are available from traders.

MORE ABOUT DIVERSIFICATION

As with any investment, diversification greatly reduces the level of risk involved. With foreign stocks, it is especially important to avoid reliance on the performance of any one stock, one industry, or even one country. Risk reduction is best achieved by spreading out your investment dollars in at least one of the following ways:

- *By country.* When some foreign stock markets fall, it is inevitable that others will rise. Diversification by country offers a hedge against a poor economic climate in any one area. Keep in mind that the U.S. market tends to be an anticipatory one, reflecting what the American investor

thinks will happen in the forthcoming months.

- *By type of industry.* Buying shares in more than one industry—high-tech, computers, oil, automobiles, etc.—likewise provides protection.
- *By company within the industry.* For example, an energy portfolio could include stocks from a number of companies located in the North Sea area, Southeast Asia, Canada, the Middle East, and the United States.
- *By region.* Diversify among the regions of the world. Never become too dependent on any one area.

Buy stocks with P/E ratios that are lower than those of comparable U.S. companies. There should always be a compelling reason to purchase a foreign security, such as a low P/E or a unique industry position.

1993 OPPORTUNITIES IN FOREIGN STOCKS

The collapse of the Berlin Wall in 1989 brought about a burst of enthusiasm for German and other European stocks. But since then there has been much investor gloominess about the troubles in Russia and the problems facing the rebuilding of Eastern Europe. Some say it could take ten years to bring the economy of eastern Germany to western Germany's standards. And, of course, there's no guarantee that capitalism will improve the economics of the former East bloc countries.

However, European stock markets should be given serious investment consideration. There are rare buying opportunities here, especially for those who are willing to hold these securities long term.

In addition, Mexico and some other Latin American countries are making strong economic strides. Mexico, in particular, is serious about returning to private ownership and a more open trade policy.

Below are stocks to discuss with your stockbroker. But remember, all are above average in risk.

- *Antofagasta Holdings.* London Exchange. $10.25. A Chilean company with interests in railroads, water supply systems, banking, communications, and mining companies.
- *Attwoods plc.* New York Exchange. $11. Worldwide waste management company with thriving business in Germany.
- *Cemex.* Mexico Exchange. $33. A large Mexican producer and exporter of building materials.
- *CIFRA S.A.* Mexico Exchange. $1.56. The country's largest retailer; also owns restaurants.
- *Compania Naviera Perez Companc.* Buenos Aires Exchange. $11.10. An Argentinean conglomerate specializing in natural resources.
- *Compania Vale do Rio Doce.* Sao Paulo Exchange. $0.11. A Brazilian company that is the world's largest producer of iron ore.
- *Ipako S.A.* Buenos Aires Exchange. $26. An Argentinean petrochemical company.
- *Mannesmann.* ADRs on OTC. $185. A debt-free maker of steel tubing; controlling interest in Germany's cellular telephone franchise.
- *Rhone-Poulenc.* New York Exchange. $23. French chemical company with rapid growth.
- *Sandoz.* ADRs on OTC. $43. Swiss company is one of world's largest drug companies. Long-term prospects excellent.
- *Varig.* São Paulo Exchange. $0.13. Brazil's large travel company, noted for its airline and hotel divisions.

INVESTING IN ISRAEL

Because this country's fragile economy is being hurt by the large influx of Russian immigrants, the best stocks to consider are those whose revenues are largely foreign-derived. If you're in a position to assume some risk in your portfolio, here are five well-run companies:

■ *Scitex Corp.* This nearly debt-free company makes imaging equipment for the publishing industry.

■ *Lannet Data Communications.* Designs and manufactures computer networking systems; only 10% of revenues are Israeli-derived.

■ *ECI Telecom Ltd.* Producer of telephone circuit equipment for AT&T, British Telecom, MCI, etc.

■ *Israel Land Development.* In a country where land is not only in short supply but also very expensive, this company is well positioned. Its real estate portfolio includes over 100 acres in Eilat, Haifa, Jerusalem, and Tel Aviv, four resort hotels, plus assorted publishing and insurance interests.

THREE EUROPEAN MUTUAL FUNDS

These open-minded mutual funds focus on blue chip stocks:

■ *Financial Strategic European Portfolio.* 1-800-525-8085. A no-load fund that's ideal for small investors. It tends to favor British, German, and French stocks.

■ *Vanguard International Equity Index Fund/European Portfolio.* 1-800-662-7447. Portfolio matches the weightings of the Morgan Stanley European Index. Large

holdings in stocks traded on the largest European stock exchange, the London.

■ *T. Rowe Price European Stock Fund.* 1-800-638-5660. A no-load fund whose managers have an outstanding record with other international funds.

MUTUAL FUNDS

Perhaps the easiest way to go global, especially if you do not have the time or inclination to do your own research, is to purchase shares in one of the mutual funds specializing in foreign investments. In this way, you can participate in a diversified portfolio and, as with domestic mutual funds, you reap the advantages of professional management—in this case with foreign expertise. Although many of these funds are American owned and operated, they have foreign consultants providing up-to-date material on specific stocks as well as on the country's political situation and outlook.

Some funds consist entirely of foreign stocks; others mix foreign and American stocks. Most are members of a larger family of funds and thus offer the advantage of free switching from one fund to another (see boxes).

$ HINT: Before signing on with any of these mutual funds, write or call for a copy of the prospectus. Investment philosophies of the funds vary widely from conservative to very aggressive.

CLOSED-END COUNTRY FUNDS

These funds are an excellent way for investors to participate in foreign bull markets without having to select individual stocks. However, they are not risk-free and should not be confused with international mutual funds.

These funds for the most part are *closed-end*, which is part of the reason why they remained in relative obscurity until recently. They are still less popular than their close cousin, open-end mutual funds, and there are fewer to select from: 120 closed-end foreign country sector funds versus nearly 2,000 open-end mutual funds.

Unlike open-end funds, which continually issue new shares to the public, closed-end funds sell their shares just once, when they begin

---

FOUR WAYS TO MAKE A PROFIT IN OVERSEAS STOCKS

■ When the price of a stock rises
■ When a foreign currency rises against the U.S. dollar
■ When you buy shares in a closed-end investment company at a discount to NAV and the discount narrows because of increased demand
■ When both the stock and the foreign currency advance, creating a compounding effect

FOREIGN STOCK EXCHANGES

Amsterdam Stock Exchange
Bursplein 5
NL-1012 JW Amsterdam
Netherlands

Australia Stock Exchange
87-92 Pitt Street
Sydney, N.S.W. 2000
Australia

Frankfurt Stock Exchange
Frankfurter Wertpapierboerse
Boersenplatz 4
Postfach 100811
D-6000 Frankfurt ag Main 1
Germany

Hong Kong Stock Exchange
Exchange Square
GPO Box 8888
Hong Kong

Johannesburg Stock Exchange
17 Diagonal Street
Johannesburg 2001
South Africa

London Stock Exchange
Old Broad Street
London EC2N 1HP
England

Luxembourg Stock Exchange
11, Avenue de la Porte-Neuve
L-2227 Luxembourg

Milan Stock Exchange
Borsa Valori di Milano
Piazza degli Affari, 6
I-20123 Milan
Italy

Paris Stock Exchange
Bourse de Paris
4, place de la Bourse
F-75002 Paris Cedex 02
France

Singapore Stock Exchange
1 Raffles Place, 24-00
Singapore 0104

Tel Aviv Stock Exchange
54 Ahad Haam Street
Tel Aviv 65202
Israel

Tokyo Stock Exchange
Nihombashi-Kabuto-cho
2-1 Chuo-ku
Tokyo 103
Japan

Vienna Stock Exchange
Wiener Börsekammer
Wipplingerstrasse 34
A-1011 Wien 1
Austria

Zurich Stock Exchange
Bleicherweg 5
8021 Zurich
Switzerland

operating. After that shares can be bought or sold only on stock exchanges or over the counter through a broker. Their prices then move up and down with investor demand just like any stock. Consequently, their price is often above or below net asset value (NAV), the value of the holdings in the portfolio divided by the number of shares. When the price of a fund is above NAV, it is being sold at a "premium"; when it falls below NAV, it's at a "discount" (see box).

BUYING AT A DISCOUNT

Closed-end funds provide investors with the possibility of buying a dollar's worth of common stock for less than $1. This occurs if you buy shares at a

---

FOUR TOP INTERNATIONAL MUTUAL FUNDS

FUND	TELEPHONE	TOTAL RETURN (1/1/92 TO 4/1/92)
Fidelity Overseas Fund	1-800-544-8888	0.55%
G.T. Pacific Fund	1-800-824-1580	4.69
New Perspective Fund	1-800-421-0180	0.40
T. Rowe Price International Discovery Fund	1-800-638-5660	0.54

---

discount and thereafter the shares move up to or above NAV.

§ HINT: This can work negatively in reverse: If you're forced to sell your shares at the same or a lower discount, you'll lose money.

Most closed-end shares trade at a premium to NAV for a spell just after their initial public offering. Then, if they continue to sell at premium, it's often because they've cornered the market. Generally, however, closed-end funds trade at a discount to NAV, partly because there are no salespeople keeping them in the public eye.

§ IF YOU DARE: Purchase closed-end shares at a discount and hold until they are selling at or above NAV. When funds reach NAV, they may become takeover targets or be converted into a regular mutual fund, at which point they are automatically repriced at 100¢ on the dollar.

§ HINT: To find out if a fund has an official antitakeover provision, get a copy of the

CLOSED-END COUNTRY FUNDS

NAME	SYMBOL	PRICE/SPRING 1992
Asia Pacific	APB	$15
Austria	OST	8
Chile	CH	39
First Australia	IAF	9
First Iberian	IBF	8
First Philippine	FPF	11
Germany	GER	11
India Growth	IGF	19
Italy	ITA	8
Korea	KF	11
Malaysia	MF	13
Mexico	MXF	25
ROC Taiwan	ROC	10
Scudder New Asia	SAF	16
Singapore Fund	SGF	11
Spain	SNF	11
Swiss Helvetia	SWZ	15
Taiwan	TWN	23
Templeton Emerging Markets	EMF	24
Thai	TTF	15
Turkish Inv. Fund	TKF	6

SOURCE: Barron's, May 1992.

FOREIGN COUNTRY SECTOR FUNDS

PROS
↑ Professionally managed
↑ Offer diversification within a country, which reduces risk
↑ Provide a hedge against U.S. market
↑ Way to maintain position in overseas markets
↑ High liquidity
↑ May be able to buy shares at a discount

CONS
↓ If foreign currency declines, value of your investment drops
↓ Value of stocks in fund can fall
↓ May be special taxes for Americans
↓ Political uncertainty
↓ Price of funds subject to fluctuations, like any stock
↓ Foreign markets less well regulated than U.S. market

prospectus and check the section under "Common Stock," or call and ask the fund's manager.

FOREIGN BONDS

If you're income-oriented, you may want to own nondollar assets when the U.S. dollar is weak. Consider mutual funds that own foreign bonds. Your return is based on three factors: (1) the bond yields, (2) the price changes due to interest rate changes abroad, and (3) currency fluctuations. Since most individuals cannot monitor all three areas, mutual funds are the logical way to invest.

☐CAUTION: Although fund managers can move in and out of various countries, foreign bond funds are riskier than a U.S. one because of the myriad of economic and political variables. Therefore, put no more than 10% of your portfolio into one of these funds.

There are two kinds of funds: "international" bond funds with investments solely in foreign bonds; and "global" funds that hold positions in a variety of foreign and U.S. bonds. The ability to invest in U.S. as well as foreign bonds gives shareholders added protection because the fund manager can buy where yields and safety are highest.

☐CAUTION: A foreign bond is not an alternative to a U.S. government or corporate bond fund. It is riskier and subject to far greater price fluctuations. In a U.S. bond fund, an investor's total return

(income plus price appreciation of the fund's shares) involves only two factors: (1) interest payments received by the fund on its bonds and (2) changes in the prices of the bonds themselves. The total return for foreign bonds is more complex: It involves the third crucial factor of currency risk. Some funds aim to keep this risk factor as low as possible by purchasing bonds of governments they believe to be politically and economically stable, even though yields may be lower. Risk is further reduced when the average maturity of the bonds in the fund is relatively short. This gives the bonds less time in which to fluctuate in price. Short maturities—4 or fewer years—provide a quicker term payoff and the flexibility to buy or sell as interest rates or the economic situation in any one country changes.

HIGH YIELDS FROM GERMAN BONDS

As we go to press, German bonds are offering attractive yields; in fact, U.S. investors can lock in rates of around 9% while the same time yields in this country are falling. For example, the German government's three-year bond is yielding 8.73%, about 3.7% higher than U.S. government treasuries. German time deposits, which are the equivalent of our bank CDs, offer another option. Their 6-month time deposits are yielding 9.5% versus about 4% on U.S. CDs.

You can contact German banks on your own, or use one of the large U.S. retail securities firms. Most brokerage houses have a $25,000 minimum on purchases of individual bonds. Merrill Lynch also has a unit investment trust composed of German fixed-income securities; the minimum is $5,000 with units available now on the secondary market.

HOW TO CONTACT GERMAN BANKS

■ Commerzbank
Box 100505
6000 Frankfurt am Main 1
Germany
telephone: 011-49-69-1362-2099

MUTUAL FUNDS THAT INVEST IN FOREIGN BONDS

Fidelity Global Bond	1-800-544-8888
GT Global Government Income	1-800-824-1580
PaineWebber Master Global	1-800-457-0849
Scudder International Bond	1-800-225-2470
T. Rowe Price International Bond	1-800-638-5660
Templeton Income	1-800-237-0738

No opening minimum; 0.5% fee plus small annual custodial fee
- Deutsche Bank
  DWS Investment Division
  Gruneburgweg 113
  6000 Frankfurt am Main 1
  Germany
  telephone: 011-69-7190-9250

Minimum is 10,000 deutsche marks (about $6,600)

Mutual funds that invest exclusively in German bonds are available through German banks for a fee. The Commerzbank has the Adirenta Fund, and the Deutsche Bank has the Inrenta Fund.

☐CAUTION: Obviously you should use money you will not need immediately in German securities.

WHY EXCHANGE RATES FLUCTUATE

Exchange rates among currencies fluctuate for a number of reasons. Here are the key factors to watch.
- *Inflation.* Rates move to reflect changes in the currencies' purchasing power.
- *Trade deficits.* Countries with large trade deficits usually have a depreciating currency. Inflation is often a cause of this deficit, making a country's goods more expensive and less competitive, which in turn reduces demand for its currency abroad.
- *Budget deficits.* Countries with large deficits and low savings rates have to borrow to finance their deficits. The currency often depreciates as payments on the debt's interest flood the currency markets.
- *Interest rates.* High rates usually boost currency values in the short term by making these currencies appealing to investors. If high rates are the result of high inflation, in the long run the currency will fall in value.
- *Political instability.* Upheaval makes a country a less desirable place in which to do business.

INTERNATIONAL MONEY MARKET AND CURRENCY FUNDS

A more conservative way to invest overseas is through one of the handful of money market funds with portfolios denominated in foreign currencies. Like their domestic counterparts, these international money funds invest in short-term, top-quality money market instruments, such as foreign bank CDs, government issues, and high-quality corporate paper. They make money for investors by earning interest.

The best known among the international money funds is the Global Currency Portfolio, part of the International Currency Portfolio Group (ICP). This fund is able to profit from appreciation or depreciation of the dollar by moving its assets among CDs and other instruments in 16 different currencies, including that of the United States.

ICP runs two additional funds: the High Income Currency Portfolio, which invests in currencies of countries with the highest interest rates; and the Hard Currency Portfolio (1-800-354-4111).

Another foreign income fund that has posted impressive yields is Alliance Short-Term Multimarket Trust (1-800-221-5672).

FOR FURTHER INFORMATION

FOREIGN STOCKS

➤ BOOKS You can add to your list of multinationals by studying one of the standard reference books such as Moody's *Handbook* and *Standard & Poor's Stock Market Guide* or *Value Line.* All three give the percentage of a company's earnings and sales derived from foreign operations. You should also read various company annual reports to learn what areas their sales come from. Earnings from Western Europe and Japan are currently more stable than those from Latin America.

Moody's International Manual & News Reports

Moody's Investors Service
99 Church Street
New York, NY 10007
1-212-553-0300; 1-800-342-5647
2-volume annual; $1,995

Contains financial information on over 5,000 companies and institutions in 100 countries.

Thomas R. Keyes and David Miller,
The Global Investor: How to Buy Stocks Around the World
(Chicago: Dearborn Financial Publishing Co., 1990.)

➤ PERIODICALS The following periodicals provide coverage of foreign markets as well as individual stocks:

Wall Street Journal

Barron's National Business & Financial Weekly

The Economist

Investor's Chronicle and Financial World (London)

Far Eastern Economic Review

Japan Economic Review

The Financial Times (London)
14 East 60th Street
New York, NY 10022
1-800-628-8088
Daily; $420 per year

The Asian Wall Street Journal
Dow Jones & Company
200 Liberty Street
New York, NY 10281
1-212-416-2000
Weekly; $239 per year

Global Investor
Monthly; $255 per year

Euromoney (London)
Monthly; $330 per year

Both are available from:

Reed Business Publications
205 East 42nd Street, Suite 1705
New York, NY 10017
1-212-867-2080

➤ NEWSLETTERS The following newsletters regularly cover foreign stocks. Also see Appendix A on evaluating newsletters.

Capital International Perspective
Morgan Stanley
1251 Avenue of the Americas
New York, NY 10020
1-212-703-2965
Monthly and quarterly; $5,000 per year

Dessauer's Journal of Financial Markets
P.O. Box 1718
Orleans, MA 02653
1-508-255-1651
Bimonthly; $195 per year

International Bank Credit Analyst
BCA Publications Ltd.
3463 Peel Street
Montreal, Quebec H3A 1W7
1-514-398-0653
Monthly; $695 per year

CLOSED-END FOREIGN FUNDS

The *Wall Street Journal's* Monday issue lists closed-end funds under "Publicly Traded Companies." You'll find the NAV, share price, and discount or premium as of the preceding Friday.

Investor's Guide to Closed-End Funds
Box 161465
Miami, FL 33116
1-305-271-1900
Monthly; $325 per year

Listing of Closed-End Funds
Investment Company Institute
Publications Dept., Suite 600
1600 M Street NW, 6th floor
Washington, DC 20036
1-202-955-3534
Free

FOREIGN CDs

One of the more conservative ways to bet on the falling dollar is to buy foreign currency CDs—they're available at the large U.S. branches of overseas banks and the currency traders, such as Thomas Cook Foreign Exchange. Cook has a $50,000 minimum with 3- and 6-month maturities. Its product is called a "forward contract."

☐CAUTION: Foreign CDs are a good investment *only* if the dollar is weak and/or the foreign interest rate is higher than you can get at home. If the dollar rises, you could suffer significant losses.

In some cases, interest rates are above those paid on U.S. bank CDs. If the dollar falls, your gain will be even greater. Details are available from any Thomas Cook office.

A handful of banks now offer special accounts that allow depositors to easily invest in foreign CDs and foreign currency money market funds. Most banks offer these accounts primarily to business customers, with the exception of Citibank. Citibank offers two accounts: its Foreign Currency Money Market Deposit Account pays the overnight interest rate in each currency. Its Foreign Currency Time Deposit, like a CD, has maturities of 1 month to 1 year and pays a fixed rate. Both accounts are available in 7 currencies: British pounds, Japanese yen, Canadian dollars, Swiss francs, German marks, and New Zealand and Australian dollars. The minimum deposit is the equivalent of $25,000. These accounts are protected by federal deposit insurance—up to $100,000 each. Details: 1-800-321-CITI.

TRAVELER'S CHECKS

A low-cost way to play the game is to purchase traveler's checks in the currency you feel will rise against the dollar. Cash them in when that currency rises to pocket your gains.

The key disadvantage with traveler's checks is that you do not earn interest on your money.

CURRENCY OPTIONS

These operate like stock options (see Chapter 17). If you think a given currency will rise against the U.S. dollar, you buy a call. If you think it will fall, purchase a put.

Say you believe that the dollar will fall against the Japanese yen. By purchasing a call option on the yen, you gain the right to purchase a stated number of yen at a predetermined strike price in dollars. You have that right until the expiration date—usually at 3-month intervals.

☐ CAUTION: If the option exercise date comes up and the yen is below your strike price, your entire investment is lost.

The Philadelphia Stock Exchange trades op-

tions in 5 currencies. You can also buy options on the New York Commodity Exchange's U.S. Dollar Index, which contains a basket of 10 currencies. Generally, options on the index are less volatile than options on individual currencies; nevertheless, this is an area *for speculative investors only.*

$ HINT: Make certain you use a broker who specializes in foreign currency options—most do not.

HOW TO SPECULATE IN FOREIGN CURRENCIES

Trading in foreign currencies can be exciting and profitable.

Futures contracts of foreign currency are traded on the International Monetary Market Division (IMM) of the Chicago Mercantile Exchange. Basically, positions are taken by importers and exporters who want to protect their profits from sudden swings in the relation between the dollar and a specific foreign currency. A profit on the futures contract will be offset by a loss in the cash market, or vice versa. Either way, the businessperson or banker guarantees a set cost.

The speculation performs an essential function by taking opposite sides of contracts, but unlike other types of commodities trading, currency futures reflect reactions to what has already happened more than anticipation of what's ahead.

For small margins of 1.5% to 4.2%, roughly $1,500 to $2,500, you can control large sums of money: 100,000 Canadian dollars, 125,000 German marks, 12.5 million Japanese yen, etc.

The attraction is leverage. You can speculate that at a fixed date in the future, the value of your contract will be greater (if you buy long) or less (if you sell short).

The daily fluctuations of each currency futures contract are limited by IMM rules. A rise of $750 per day provides a 37.5% profit on a $2,000 investment. That's a net gain of $705 ($750 less $45 in commissions). If the value declines, you are faced with a wipeout or, if you set a stop order, the loss of part of your security deposit. Vice versa when you sell short.

One of the favorite deals is playing crosses, taking advantage of the spread between different currencies: buying francs and selling liras short, etc. For example, when the German mark was falling faster than the Swiss franc relative to the U.S. dollar, an investor set up this spread:

April 15: He buys a June contract for 125,000 francs and sells short a June contract for 125,000 marks. The franc is valued at .6664¢, the mark at .5536¢. Cost, not including commissions, is the margin: $2,000.

May 27: The franc has fallen to .6461, the mark to .5120. He reverses his trades, selling the June contract for francs and buying the mark contract to cover his short position.

Result: The speculator loses 2.03¢ per franc, or $2,537.50, but he makes 4.16¢ per mark, or $5,200.00. The overall gain, before commissions, is $2,662.50, a return of 133% on the $2,000 investment—in about 6 weeks.

Warning: IMM is a thin market. Small speculators may not be able to get out when they want to at the price they expect. On a one-day trade, the value of a currency can swing sharply, so that the pressure can be intense.

➤ CURRENCY OPTIONS According to some traders, currency options can be the fastest game in town (or perhaps they should say "in the free world"). The premiums are small, so the leverage is high.

The options, traded on the Philadelphia Exchange, are for five currencies: Deutsche mark (DM), pound sterling, Canadian dollar, Japanese yen, and Swiss franc. The premiums run from $25 for a short-life out-of-the-money option to $2,000 for a long-term deep-in-the-money call or put.

The option represents the currency value against the dollar, so traders buy calls when they expect the foreign money to gain ground against the dollar and puts when they anticipate the reverse. The options expire at 3-month intervals.

The quotations are in U.S. cents per unit of the underlying currency (with the exception of the yen, where it's $1/100$¢): Thus, the quote 1.00 DM means 1¢ per mark, and since the contract covers 62,500 DM, the total premium would be $625.

➤ OPTIONS ON FUTURES These are now available on the Chicago Mercantile Exchange, where the currency futures are already traded. They are similar to regular options except that they give the holder the right to buy or sell the currencies themselves, *not the futures.*

The CME rules permit the speculator to do the following:

- Generate extra income by writing calls or selling puts (but this can be very expensive if you guess wrong and the option is exercised).

- Exercise the option at any time. But once you do so, you may not liquidate your option position with an offsetting option as you can do in futures trading. So you have to sell to, or buy from, the other party the required number of currency units at the option exercise price.

These options on futures sound risky—but only for the speculator. Business firms use them to hedge the prices of foreign goods at a future delivery date.

FOREIGN CURRENCY WARRANTS

This is a relatively new investment item, one issued by corporations to raise money. Each warrant allows you to purchase $50 at a certain exchange rate. As the dollar moves up and down, so does the value of your warrant, or the right to buy the $50.

Most warrants have been issued against the Japanese yen and the German mark. They trade on the AMEX.

Most warrant holders, however, tend to sell when their warrants go up rather than hold until the expiration date.

FOR FURTHER INFORMATION

Michael Bowe, *Eurobonds* (Homewood, IL: Dow Jones–Irwin, 1988).

C. David Chase, *Chase Global Investment Almanac, 1989 edition* (Homewood, IL: Dow Jones–Irwin, 1989).

Frank J. Fabozzi, *The Japanese Bond Markets* (Chicago: Probus Publications, 1990).

Christian Dunis and Michael Feeny, *Exchange Rate Forecasting* (Chicago: Probus Publications, 1990).

21 COMMODITIES

FUTURES TRADING

The concept of buying or selling agricultural goods at a price agreed on today but with actual delivery of the goods sometime in the future is a time-honored practice dating back to the early 19th century. Today futures are traded in many areas: grain, meat, poultry, lumber, metals, foreign currencies, interest-bearing securities such as Treasury bonds and notes, and even stock indexes.

A futures contract is an obligation to buy or sell a commodity at a given price sometime in the future. If you buy a contract, you are betting that prices will rise. If you sell a contract, you are betting that prices will fall.

The theory behind futures is twofold: (1) they are supposed to transfer risk from one party to another, and (2) they are designed to even out price fluctuations. Although the theory tends to be true in agricultural markets, the proliferation of financial and stock index futures has led to increased volatility and speculation.

Trading futures is *not* an area for the novice, the conservative, or the timid. Proceed with great caution.

Futures contracts are closed by offsetting transactions. This is when you sell the contract before its expiration date, the date when the commodity must be delivered. For instance, if you had purchased a May 1993 wheat contract and you wanted to get out of the market, you would sell a May 1993 contract, thus closing out the position. The two positions cancel each other out. If you don't offset, you are obliged to take physical delivery. It's cumbersome and costly to have wheat unloaded into your living room.

COMMODITIES

During uncertain times in the stock market, diversification into nonequity areas with a portion of one's portfolio is often advantageous. The top commodity funds in 1989 had returns ranging from −20% to +40%.

Commodities include a variety of bulk products such as grain, metals, and foods, which are traded on a commodities exchange. The exchange deals in futures trading, for delivery in future months, as well as spot trading, for delivery in the current or "spot" month.

Futures contracts are agreements to buy or sell a certain amount of a commodity at a particular price within a stated time period. The price is established on the floor of a commodities exchange.

Note: A futures contract obligates the buyer to buy and the seller to sell *unless* the contract is closed out by an offsetting sale or purchase to another investor before the so-called settlement or delivery date.

Commodities are one of the quickest ways to get rich, but they can also be a fast way to lose money. These futures contracts are almost always 100% speculation because you must try to guess, months in advance, what will happen to the prices of food products, natural resources, metals, and foreign currencies.

Trading in commodities involves active, volatile markets, high leverage, hedging, and short selling. It's a game that requires ample capital, emotional stability, frequent attention to trends, and experience. Although everyone should understand trading in commodities markets, you should get involved only with money you can afford to lose.

In addition to the normal hazards of speculations, there are special risks beyond the ken or control of most participants. With skill and luck, an individual can score high on occasion, but the odds are always against the amateur. According to a recent study, *75% of all commodities speculators lose money.*

The great appeal of trading commodities lies in the impressive amount of leverage they provide. Your broker will require you to meet certain net worth requirements and make a margin deposit. Nevertheless, there are low cash requirements: 7% to 10% per contract, depending on the commodity and the broker's standards. That means that $2,000 could buy, say, $29,000 worth of soybeans.

HOW THE MARKET OPERATES

Commodity trading is different from investing in stocks. When you buy a common stock, you own a part of the corporation and share in its profits, if any. If you pick a profitable company, the price of your stock will eventually rise.

With commodities, there is no equity. You basically buy hope. Once the futures contract has expired, there's no tomorrow. If your trade turned out badly, you must take the full loss. And it's a zero sum game: For every $1 won, $1 is lost by someone else.

➤ HEDGING   Let's say a hog farmer has animals that will be ready for market in 6 months. He wants to assure himself of today's market price for these hogs, which he does by selling a contract for future delivery. When the hogs are ready for market, if the price has dropped, he will be forced to take a lower price on the actual hogs, but he will have an offsetting gain, because the contract he sold 6 months ago was at a higher price. In other words, he closes that contract with a profit.

- *The advantage to the sellers:* They have themselves locked in a price, thereby protecting themselves from any future fall in the price of hogs. In effect, they have transferred this price risk to the buyers.
- *The advantage to the buyers:* They also have locked in a price, thereby protecting themselves from any future rise in the price of hogs. The buyer in this

AGRICULTURAL COMMODITIES CONTRACTS

COMMODITY	SYMBOL	ONE CONTRACT EQUALS
Soybeans	S	5,000 bushels
Soybean oil	BO	60,000 pounds
Soybean meal	SM	100 tons
Oats	O	5,000 bushels
Wheat	W	5,000 bushels
Corn	C	5,000 bushels
Silver	AG	1,000 troy ounces
Gold	K	1 kilogram

SOURCE: Chicago Board of Trade.

hypothetical case might be a speculator, a meat packer, or a meat processor.

➤ MARGIN   Since payment is not received until the delivery date, a type of binder or good faith deposit is required. It is called "margin." The margin in the world of commodities is only a small percentage of the total amount due, but it serves as a guarantee for both buyer and seller. Unlike margin for stocks, which is an interest-bearing cost, margin for commodities is a security balance. You are not charged interest, but if the price of your futures drops by a certain percentage, more money must be deposited in the margin account or your position will be closed out by your broker.

In reality, most futures trading is not this simple. More often than not, the opposite side of each transaction is picked up by speculators who believe they can make money through favorable price changes during the months prior to delivery.

➤ TRADING LIMITATIONS   The commodity exchanges set "day limits," based on the previous day's closing prices, specifying how widely a contract's trading price can move. The purpose of these limits is to prevent excessive short-term volatility and therefore also to keep margin requirements low. But trading limits can also lock traders into positions they cannot trade out of because the contract held is either up or down to the daily limit.

For example, an investor buys one gold contract (100 ounces) at $500 per ounce on June

30. On July 1 gold falls to $470 an ounce. The trading limit on gold is $20 per day, which means that on that day gold can be traded anywhere from $480 to $520 per ounce. Since the price has dropped below $480, trading is halted and the investor is locked into his position, unable to sell on that day. On the next day, July 2, the trading limits change to $460 to $500.

➤ PRICE QUOTATIONS Commodity prices are printed in the papers in various ways. In general you'll find the "high" (highest price of the day), the "low," and the "close." "Net change" refers to the change from the prior day's settlement price. The final column gives the high-low range for the year. Grain prices are given in cents per bushel; for example, wheat for December may be listed at a closing price of 3.71 per bushel.

STEPS TO TAKE

➤ GET CURRENT INFORMATION There is no inside information about commodities. All statistics are available in government reports, business and agricultural publications, newsletters, and special services. Always check two or three for confirmation and then review your conclusions with your broker. It will help to become something of an expert in both the fundamental and technical aspects of a few major commodities. When you become experienced, you can move into other areas where information is not so widely available.

COMMODITIES

PROS
↑ Large potential capital gains
↑ High amount of leverage available
↑ Small initial investment
↑ High liquidity

CONS
↓ Extremely risky
↓ Requires expertise
↓ Highly volatile
↓ Must continually monitor position
↓ Could lose total investment

➤ CHOOSE AN EXPERIENCED BROKER Deal only with a reputable firm that (1) has extensive commodities trading services and (2) includes a broker who knows speculations and can guide you. Never buy or sell as the result of a phone recommendation until it has been confirmed in written or printed form.

➤ ZERO IN ON A FEW COMMODITIES Preferably those in the news. For instance, during the drought in the Midwest in spring 1988, soybeans and grains experienced wild price gyrations. Watch for such movements and remember that in commodities "the trend is your friend."

➤ AVOID THIN MARKETS You can score when such a commodity takes off, but the swings can be too fast and may send prices soaring or plummeting, and the amateur can get caught with no chance of closing a position.

➤ LOOK FOR A RATIO OF NET PROFIT TO NET LOSS OF 2:1 Since the percentage of losses will always be greater than that of profits, choose commodities where the potential gains (based on confirmed trends) can be more than double the possible losses.

➤ PREPARE AN OPERATIONAL PLAN Before you risk any money, test your hypothesis on paper until you feel confident that you understand what can happen. Do this for several weeks to get the feel of different types of contracts in different types of markets.

With an active commodity, "buy" contracts at several delivery dates and calculate the potential profits if the price rises moderately.

➤ NEVER MEET A MARGIN CALL When your original margin is impaired, your broker will call for more money. Except in most unusual circumstances, do not put in more money. Liquidate your position and accept your loss. This is a form of stop-loss safeguard. When a declining trend has been established, further losses can be expected.

➤ BE ALERT TO SPECIAL SITUATIONS Information is the key to profitable speculation. As you become more knowledgeable, you will pick up many points, such as these:

■ If there's heavy spring and summer rain in Maine, buy long on potatoes. They need ideal weather.

■ If there's a bad tornado over large portions of the Great Plains, buy wheat contracts. Chances are the wheat crop will be damaged, thus changing the supply and demand.

➤ TRADE WITH THE MAJOR TREND, AGAINST THE MINOR TREND With copper, for example, if you project a worldwide shortage of the metal and the market is in an uptrend, buy futures when the market suffers temporary weak spells. As long as prices keep moving up, you want to accumulate a meaningful position.

The corollary to this is never to average down. Adding to your loss position increases the number of contracts that are returning a loss. By buying more, you put yourself in a stance where you can lose on more contracts if the price continues to drop.

Generally, if the trend is down, either sell short or stay out of the market.

➤ WATCH THE SPREADS BETWEEN DIFFERENT DE-LIVERY DATES In the strong summer market, the premium for January soybeans is 8¢ per bushel above the November contract. Buy November and sell January.

If the bull market persists, the premium should disappear and you will have a pleasant limited profit. Carrying charges on soybeans run about 6½¢ per month, so it is not likely that the spread will widen to more than 13¢ per bushel. Thus with that 8¢ spread, the real risk is not more than 5¢ per bushel.

➤ NEVER SPREAD A LOSS Turning a long or short position into a spread by buying or selling another contract month will seldom help you and in most cases will guarantee a locked-in loss. When you make a mistake, get out.

$ HINT: If you don't dare play the commodities game yourself, invest in one of the publicly traded commodity funds. They're diversified and professionally managed. You could, of course, lose money if the fund performs poorly, but you'll never be subject to margin calls.

➤ WATCH THE PRICE PEAKS AND LOWS Never sell at a price that is near the natural or government-imposed floor, and never buy at a price that is near its high.

Similarly, do not buy after the price of any commodity has passed its seasonal high or sell after it has dropped under its seasonal low.

➤ RISK NO MORE THAN 10% OF YOUR TRADING CAPITAL IN ANY ONE POSITION And risk no more than 30% of all capital in all positions at

COMMODITY FUTURES OPTIONS

COMMODITY	SYMBOLS	ONE CONTRACT EQUALS
Options on T-bond futures	CG, PG	One T-bond futures contract
Options on soybean futures	CZ, PZ	One soybean futures contract
Options on corn futures	CY, PY	One corn futures contract
Options on silver futures	AC, AP	One 1,000-ounce silver futures contract
Options on 10-year Treasury futures	TC, TP	One 10-year Treasury futures contract

SOURCE: Chicago Board of Trade.

any one time—except when you have caught a strong upswing and can move with the trend. These limits will ease the effect of a bad decision. Few professionals count on being right more than half the time.

➤ BE SLOW TO LISTEN TO YOUR BROKER Unless the recommendations are backed by absolutely clear analyses. In most cases, by the time you get the word, smart traders have made their moves. To be successful, you must anticipate, not follow. The same caveat applies to professional newsletters.

➤ USE TECHNICAL ANALYSIS Especially charts, because timing is the key to speculative success, and with commodities, what has happened before is likely to be repeated.

COMMODITY FUNDS

Commodity funds offer an easier (but not risk-free) way to participate in the action. Professionals make the buy and sell decisions for you—and most guarantee that you won't lose more than half your investment. The typical minimum for a pool is $5,000.

These funds are a hybrid, a mix of mutual fund and limited partnership. Like mutual funds, they are professionally managed pooled investments. Most cover 20 to 30 different futures

SPECIAL TERMS IN COMMODITIES TRADING

- **Arbitrage** Simultaneous purchase and sale of the same or an equivalent security in order to make a profit from the price discrepancy.
- **Basis** The difference between the cash price of a hedged money market instrument and a futures contract.
- **Contract month** Month in which a futures contract may be fulfilled by making or taking delivery.
- **Cross hedge** Hedging a cash market risk in one financial instrument by taking a position in a futures contract for a different but similar instrument.
- **Forward contract** An agreement to buy or sell goods at a set price and date, when those involved plan to take delivery of the instrument.
- **Hedge** Strategy used to offset an investment risk that involves buying and selling simultaneously in the futures market.
- **Index** Statistical composite that measures the ups and downs of stocks, bonds, and commodities; reflects market prices and the number of shares outstanding for the companies in the index.
- **Long position** Futures contract purchased to protect the investor against a rise in cost of a future commitment or against a drop in interest rates.
- **Mark to the market** Debits and credits in each account at the close of the trading day.
- **Open interest** Contracts that have not been offset by opposite transactions or by delivery.
- **Physical** The underlying physical commodity.
- **Selling short** A popular hedging technique involving sale of a futures contract that the seller does not own. A commodity sold short equals a promise to deliver at a future date.
- **Spot market** Also known as the actual or physical market in which commodities are sold for immediate delivery.
- **Spread** Holding opposite positions in two futures contracts with the intent of profit through changes in prices.

markets, so they offer wide diversification. For example, a loss in gold could be offset by a gain in corn. Their performance is best when there is a long steady direction in prices.

They are also similar to limited partnerships in that as an investor, you are part of a corporation, and your losses are limited to the dollar amount you invest.

$ HINT: Although most commodity funds permit investors to get out, either monthly or quarterly, do not invest unless you plan to stay in for at least a year. On a short-term basis, commodities are more volatile than stocks, fluctuating as much as 5% to 10% per month. Funds also have hefty fees: Sales charges range from 5% to 8% of your initial investment plus an annual management fee.

The prospectus reports the month-by-month track record for traders for the last several years. Examine that record closely to help you determine how well the fund is run. Yet even with this data it's hard to pick winners. As with *all* investments, caveat emptor!

TIPS ON INVESTING IN COMMODITY FUNDS

Read the prospectus to determine:
- The average annual performance
- Rules regarding redeeming shares
- Net worth and income requirements for investing
- Fees
- If the adviser is registered with the Commodities Futures Trading Commission; if not, do business elsewhere

LEADING COMMODITY FUNDS

FUND	TELEPHONE
Cornerstone Fund (New York, NY)	1-212-392-8837
Tiverton Trading (Princeton, NJ)	1-609-921-3019
Trout Trading (Chicago, IL)	1-312-372-9262
Western Futures Fund (Chicago, IL)	1-800-621-0757

FINDING A COMMODITY ADVISER

A. T. A. Research Inc. Dallas, TX 1-214-373-7606	Managed Account Reports New York, NY 1-212-213-6202
Barclay Trading Group Fairfield, IA 1-515-472-3456	Trading Adviser, Inc. Denver, CO 1-303-433-3202

COMMODITY ADVISERS

One response investors have made to the trading scandal in Chicago is to hire professionals to do the trading for them. The advisers must be registered with the Commodity Futures Trading Commission. They charge in one of two ways: a percentage, usually 6%, of the funds turned over to them, or an incentive fee, typically 15% of any profits generated by the adviser.

$ HINT: Select an adviser who has an annual rate of return of at least 25% for a minimum of 3 years.

Burlington Hall Asset Management, in Hackettstown, NJ, offers a software program, called "La Porte Asset Allocation System," that evaluates trading advisers. Call 1-908-852-1694.

FOR FURTHER INFORMATION

"Commodity Traders Consumer Report"
1731 Howe Avenue
Sacramento, CA 95825
1-800-999-CTCR
Bimonthly; $198 per year plus $3 shipping

Dwight A. Jackson, *The Individual Investor's Guide to Commodities* (Chicago: Probus, 1991).

22 | PRECIOUS METALS

Some say it's a hedge against inflation; doomsayers swear it's our only protection against the inevitable downfall of our entire economic system. And in between are those who believe in diversification. Precious metals have a place in every portfolio *as long as one realizes they are a volatile long-term holding.*

Here's how to invest:

- *Bullion.* You can buy the bullion itself through larger banks, brokerage firms, and major dealers.

$ HINT: Bullion coins should not be confused with rare coins. Bullion coins have very little value as a collectible; their price is based on their gold content. Rare coins purchased at auction or from dealers have numismatic value that is based upon their age, rarity, and popularity.

- *Certificates.* Unless you want to fill up your living room with bars or coins, buy certificates. The minimum is $1,000. They are sold at roughly 3% over the price of the metal, and have an annual storage fee of about 1%.
- *Mutual funds.* Funds specializing in precious metals are the easiest way to invest. However, this is not a "pure play"—you are buying partial shares of stocks of companies that mine metals. Your profit will depend on how well the fund is managed.
- *Stocks.* Another route is to purchase the individual stocks of mining companies. Stocks offer potential price appreciation and dividend income, yet leave you subject to market risks, political upheavals, and mining strikes.
- *Futures and options.* This is the riskiest because it involves betting on the future direction of prices. With a gold, silver, or platinum futures contract, you agree to

buy or sell a certain quantity at a specified future price. You are required to put up 5% to 10% of the value of the contract as "margin." So, you control a large amount of metal for very few dollars, but you can lose your entire investment if your bet is incorrect.

The true gold bug shuns mutual funds and certificates, maintaining that if the world caves in, only the real tangible metals will be valuable. If you're less of a purist, then you may be content with a certificate or shares of stock or a fund.

☐ CAUTION: Put no more than 5% to 8% of your portfolio in precious metals.

GUIDELINES FOR BUYING

Here are the key facts to keep in mind:

GOLD
To enhance your potential profits in gold, watch for changes in these leading indicators:

- Political situation in South Africa
- The trend of inflation and the Consumer Price Index
- Movement of interest rates
- Direction of the dollar
- Third-world debt and related banking problems
- Changes in gold production

Remember, gold vies with the dollar as the world's safest currency. When the dollar is strong, gold tends to be low in price and vice versa.

SILVER
Silver is primarily an industrial metal; its price is directly related to supply and demand and less (as is the case with gold) to inflation, interest rates, and politics. Silver is

225

BEFORE BUYING A PRECIOUS METAL

Follow these guidelines and heed these warnings:
- Paper trade for at least 1 month. Make decisions, calculate margins, set stop-loss prices, and monitor how well you are doing in theory.
- Never commit more than half of your risk capital to metals. If you are trading contracts, keep the balance in a money market account to meet any margin calls.
- Read the commodity columns in the *Wall Street Journal* and *Barron's*. Ask several dealers to send you their research reports.
- Track the direction of interest rates, inflation, and the spot prices of the metals. (Spot price is the cash price for metals that are delivered at once.)
- Never give discretionary powers to anyone in the business.
- Never place an order over the phone with someone who has called you cold.

used in coins, jewelry, and silverware, but its greatest demand is in the photographic, electronic, dental, and medical fields. Its industrial uses are so great, in fact, that the world consumes as much silver as is mined.

The American silver bullion coin is called the Silver Eagle.

PLATINUM
Although platinum has generally been considered more valuable than gold or silver because of its limited availability, it

LEADING GOLD COINS

American Gold Eagle	Canadian Maple Leaf
Mexican 50 Peso	Mexican Onza
Austrian 100 Corona	Australian Nugget
Hungarian Corona	Chinese Panda

has never been as popular with investors. Its primary uses are in the electronics, chemical, and automobile industries. It is an essential ingredient in the production of catalytic converters for pollution control in cars. During the past decade, the world generally consumed more platinum than it produced.

Platinum coins include the Noble, Canadian Maple Leaf, and Australian Koala.

BUYING METALS BY PHONE

Although you should never succumb to a high-pressure salesman, you can buy bullion bars and coins by phone from reliable dealers; however, check prices and fees first.
- *Wilmington Trust Refined Investments* allows clients to use their VISA or MasterCard to buy precious metals, provided you store the metals with them. Call: 1-800-223-1080. Their 24-hour Quoteline gives the latest spot prices: 1-302-427-4700.
- *Merrill Lynch's "Blueprint"* program has a minimum purchase of only $500 with $50 thereafter. Call: 1-800-637-3766.
- *Benham Certified Metals* has a discount brokerage division. The minimum for silver is $1,000 and $2,000 for gold and platinum. Call: 1-800-447-4653.
- *Rhode Island Hospital Trust National Bank* of Providence sells coins, bars, and certificates. It also has an accumulation account for only $100 per month. Call: 1-800-343-8419.

FOR FURTHER INFORMATION

Dow Theory Letters
P.O. Box 1759
La Jolla, CA 92038
1-619-454-0481
$250 per year

Your Introduction to Investing in Gold and *Your Introduction to Investing in Silver*
The Gold and Silver Institute
1112 16th Street NW
Washington, DC 20036
1-202-835-0185
$5 each

23 | FUTURES AND MARKET INDEXES

FINANCIAL FUTURES

If trading corn and pork bellies is too tame, you can move along to another type of commodity: interest-bearing securities, such as Treasury bonds and notes, CDs, and Ginnie Maes. For amateurs, financial futures and stock indexes are just about the riskiest areas of Wall Street. Yet professional money managers use them as investment tools, as a way to hedge their portfolios. Just as agribusinesses rely on commodities futures, so money managers and others use financial futures to protect their profits.

Financial futures trading requires an ability to predict correctly the short-term or intermediate movements of interest rates, because futures involve debt issues whose values move with the cost of money; that is, with interest rates. With tiny margins (as small as $800 to control $1 million), a shift of ½% in the interest rate can double your money—or lose most of your capital.

The swings of financial futures are often dramatic, but the forecast of higher interest rates by only one financial guru can send these contracts down as fast as a punctured balloon.

If you are a modest investor, skip this chapter. If you have over $100,000 in a portfolio, read it rapidly. If you are a speculator who can afford to lose half your stake, study the explanations and then deal with an experienced broker.

HOW FINANCIAL FUTURES WORK

Basically, these are contracts that involve money. They are used by major investors, such as banks, insurance companies, and pension fund managers, to protect positions by hedging: What they gain (lose) in the cash market will be offset by the loss (profit) in the futures market.

The terms and rules of trading are set by the exchanges.

A financial futures contract is in essence a contract on an interest rate. The most popular are Treasury bills, bonds, and notes; Ginnie Maes; and CDs. They are sold through brokers or firms specializing in commodities. Contract sizes vary with the underlying security and the exchange, but they range from approximately $20,000 to $1 million. However, since margin requirements are low, sometimes only 5% to 10% of total value, your actual outlay is surprisingly little, relatively speaking.

The value of a financial futures contract is determined by interest rates:

- When rates rise, the price of fixed-income securities and the futures based on them *fall*.
- When rates decline, these investments *rise* in value.

§ HINT: Place stop orders with your broker. These provide instructions to close out your position when the price falls to a certain level, which will help limit any potential losses.

U.S. TREASURY BOND FUTURES

Since their introduction in 1977, U.S. T-bond futures have become the most actively traded futures contract worldwide. Although there are various other financial futures traded, we will illustrate the principle with T-bonds and T-notes. ("For Further Information" at the end of this chapter lists more in-depth studies of trading financial futures.)

Like all futures contracts, T-bond futures contracts are standardized (see box on page 227). Their only variable is the price, which is established on the floor of the Chicago Board of

Trade. Bond prices, of course, move in inverse relationship to interest rates: When rates rise, bond prices fall. Speculators and others use T-bonds to take advantage of anticipated interest rate changes; hedgers focus more on reducing and managing risk for their portfolios.

➤ IF YOU EXPECT INTEREST RATES TO FALL Such an expectation implies that bond futures will rise. This means you'll want to take a long position in order to take advantage of the potentially rising bond market (to be long on a contract is to buy it; to short a contract is to sell). For example, if bond futures are now trading at 72% of par, you go long one $100,000-face-value bond contract. If bond prices then rise to 74% of par, you offset your original long position by going short for a profit of 2 points, or $2,000.

Long one contract @ 72 or $72,000
Short one contract @ 74 or $74,000
Profit: $2,000

➤ IF YOU EXPECT INTEREST RATES TO RISE You then take a short position. Then when bond prices fall to 69, you can offset your original position by going long for a $3,000 profit.

Short one contract @ 72 or $72,000
Long one contract @ 69 or $69,000
Profit: $3,000

➤ SPREADS Speculators usually trade financial futures by going long on one position and short on another with both contracts due in the same month. But you can also use spreads: buying one contract month and selling another. This technique is used when there's an abnormal relation between the yields and thus the prices of two contracts with different maturities. These situations don't come often, but when they do, they can be mighty rewarding, because the gains will come from a restoration of the normal spread.

Example: An investor notes that June T-bonds are selling at 80-11 (each $\frac{1}{32}$% equals $3.125 of a standard $100,000 contract) and that September's are at 81-05. The basis for quotations is an 8% coupon and 15-year maturity.

U.S. TREASURY BOND FUTURES

Trading unit: $100,000 face value of U.S. T-bonds

Deliverable: U.S. Treasury bonds with a nominal 8% coupon maturing at least 15 years from delivery date if not callable; if callable, not for at least 15 years from delivery date

Delivery method: Federal Reserve book entry wire transfer system

Par: $1,000

Price quote: Percentage of par in minimum increments of $\frac{1}{32}$ point, or $3.125 per "tick," e.g., 74-01 means 74$\frac{1}{32}$% of par

Daily price limit: $\frac{64}{32}$ or $2,000 per contract above or below the previous day's settlement price

Delivery months: March, June, September, or December

Ticker symbol: US—traded on Chicago Board of Trade

Based on experience, he decides that this $\frac{26}{32}$ difference ($81\frac{5}{32} - 80\frac{11}{32} = \frac{26}{32}$) is out of line with normal pricing. He *sells* the September contract and *buys* the June one. In a couple of weeks, prices begin to normalize: The September contract edges up to 81-08 and the June one surges to 80-24. Now he starts to cash in: He loses $\frac{3}{32}$ ($93.75) on the September contract but gains $\frac{13}{32}$ ($406.25) on the June one: $312.50 profit minus commission.

RULES TO FOLLOW

If you have money you can afford to lose, time enough to keep abreast of developments in the financial world, strong nerves, and a trustworthy, knowledgeable broker, trading in financial futures may be rewarding and surely will be exciting. Of course, if you're involved with substantial holdings, you probably are already familiar with hedging, so you can stick to protective contracts. Otherwise, follow these rules:

- *Make dry runs on paper for several months.* Interest rates change slowly. Pick different types of financial futures each week and keep practicing until you get a feel for the market and risks and, over at least a week, chalk up more winners than losers.
- *Buy long when you look for a drop in interest rates.* With lower yields, the prices of all contracts will rise.
- *Sell short when you expect a higher cost of money.* This will force down the value of the contracts, and you can cover your position at a profit.
- *Set a strategy and stick to it.* Don't try to mix contracts until you are comfortable and making money.

$ HINT: Set stop and limit orders, not market orders. A market order is executed immediately at the best possible price. A stop order, to buy or to sell at a given price, becomes a market order when that price is touched. A limit order is the maximum price at which to buy and the minimum at which to sell.

OPTIONS ON FUTURES

Another way to participate in the futures market is through options (see Chapter 17). A futures option is a contract that gives you the right to buy (call) or sell (put) a certain futures contract within a specified period of time for a specified price (called the premium).

➤ OPTIONS ON COMMODITIES Options are traded on futures for agricultural commodities, oil, livestock, metals, etc. Quotes are listed in the newspaper under "Futures Options." These involve far less money than contracts do: roughly, $100 for an option compared to $1,800 for a futures contract. There are no margin calls, and the risk is limited to the premium. But these are for professionals and gamblers. If you ride a strong market trend, you can make a lot of money with a small outlay and rapid fluctuations, or you can make a modest profit by successful hedging. *Be cautious and limit your commitment.* It's easy to con yourself into thinking you're a genius when you hit a couple of big winners fast, but unless you bank half of those profits, you will lose money over a period of time if only because of the commissions.

➤ OPTIONS ON FINANCIAL FUTURES Options are also traded on some interest-bearing securities, such as Treasury bills and notes. T-bond options, for example, are traded on the Chicago Board of Trade. The T-bond futures contract underlying the option is for $100,000 of Treasury bonds, bearing an 8% or equivalent coupon, which do not mature and are noncallable for at least 15 years. When long-term interest rates fall, the value of the futures contract and the call option increases while the value of a put option decreases. The opposite is true when long-term rates rise.

Premiums for T-bond futures options are quoted in $1/64$ths of 1% (1 point). Thus $1/64$ point equals $15.63 ($100,000 $\times$ 0.01 $\times$ $1/64$). A

CONTRACT SPECIFICATIONS OF FUTURES				
	U.S. TREASURY BONDS	10-YEAR U.S. TREASURY NOTES	GNMA-CDR	GNMA II
Basic trading unit	$100,000 face value	$100,000 face value	$100,000 principal balance	$100,000 principal balance
Price quotation	Full points (one point equals $1,000) and 32nds of a full point			
Minimum price fluctuation	$1/32$ of a full point ($3.125 per contract)			
Daily price limit	$64/32$ (2 points or $2,000) above or below the previous day's settlement price			
Date introduced	Aug. 22, 1977	May 3, 1982	Oct. 20, 1975	1984
Ticker symbol	US	TY	M	GT

SOURCE: Chicago Board of Trade.

premium quote of 2–16 means $2^{16}/_{64}$, or [(2 × 64) + 16] × $15.63, or $2,250.72 per option.

The profit is the premium you receive when the option is sold minus the premium paid when you purchased the option.

➤ SETTING UP HEDGES Options provide excellent opportunities to set up hedges if you plan your strategy and understand the risks and rewards. Here's an example cited by Stanley Angrist in *Forbes.*

In March, the June T-bond contract is selling at 72–05 (72⅝). Calls at 72, 74, and 76 are quoted at premiums of 2–06, 1–20, and 0–46, respectively; puts at 68, 70, and 72 are available at 0–30, 0–61, and 1–54. You think that the market will remain stable, so you make these paper projections of hedges with a margin of $3,000:

Sell June 72 call	$2,093.75
Sell June 72 put	1,843.75
Total income	$3,937.50

If the T-bond is still worth 72 on the June strike date, both options will expire worthless, so you have an extra $3,937.50 minus commissions.

GOVERNMENT INSTRUMENT FUTURES CONTRACTS

COMMODITY	SYMBOL	ONE CONTRACT EQUALS
U.S. Treasury bonds	US	Face value at maturity: $100,000
10-year T-notes	TY	Face value at maturity: $100,000
GNMA	M	$100,000 principal balance
30-day Treasury repo	—	$2.5 million face value
90-day Treasury repo	—	$1 million face value
Zero coupon T-bonds	—	Discounted
Zero coupon T-notes	—	Discounted

SOURCE: Chicago Board of Trade.

Sell June 74 call	$1,312.50
Sell June 70 put	953.13
Total income	$2,265.63

This is less risky, and less profitable, because both options will expire worthless if the last-day price is between 70 and 74.

Sell June 76 call	$ 718.75
Sell June 68 call	468.75
Total income	$1,187.50

If the final price is between 68 and 76, you will do OK. You swap a lower income for a broader price range.

STOCK INDEXES

You can also trade options on stock index futures. Both index options and index futures options are available.

These are the fastest-growing area of speculations and make it possible to play the market without owning a single share of stock. They combine the growth potential of equities with the speculative hopes of commodities.

With a stock index, you are betting on the future price of the composite of a group of stocks: *buying* if you anticipate a rise soon, *selling* if you look for a decline. You put up cash or collateral equal to about 7% of the contract value vs. 50% for stocks. All you need is a little capital and a lot of nerve. A minor jiggle can produce sizable losses or gains. And there are also options that require even less money.

To emphasize the speculative nature of indexes, some brokerage firms advise their brokers to limit trading to individuals with a net worth of $100,000 (exclusive of home and life insurance).

These stock indexes currently have futures contracts and/or options on futures available:

- **Standard & Poor's 500 (SPX):** stocks of 500 industrials, financial companies, utilities, and transportation issues, all listed on the NYSE. They are weighted by market value. This means each stock is weighted so that changes in the stock's price influence the index in proportion to the stock's representative market value. Contracts are valued at 500 times the index. They are traded on the Chicago

Mercantile Exchange. Generally, this is the index favored by big hitters, as contracts are extremely liquid and it's widely used to measure institutional performance. *Options* on the SPX trade only on the Chicago Board of Options Exchange (CBOE).

■ **Standard & Poor's 100:** a condensed version of the S&P 500 index (known as OEX). It is weighted by capitalization of the component corporations, all of which have options traded on the CBOE. The value is 100 times the worth of the stocks.

■ **Value Line Composite (XVL):** an equally weighted geometric index of about 1,700 stocks actively traded on the NYSE, AMEX, and OTC. Contracts are quoted at 500 times the index. This tends to be difficult to trade because of a thin market on the small Kansas City Board of Trade. Options trade on the Philadelphia exchange.

■ **AMEX Market Value Index (XAM):** measures the changes in the aggregate market of over 800 AMEX issues. The weighting is by industry groups: 32% natural resources, 19% high technology, 13% service, 11% consumer goods. No one company accounts for more than 7% of the total.

■ **Major Market Index (XMI):** based on 20 blue chip NYSE stocks and price-weighted so that higher-priced shares have a greater effect on the average than lower-priced ones. Options trade on the American exchange.

■ **AMEX Oil & Gas Index (XOI):** made up of the stocks of 30 oil and gas companies with Exxon representing about 17%. Options trade on the AMEX.

■ **Computer Technology Index (XCI):** stocks of 30 major computer companies, with IBM accounting for about half and Hewlett-Packard, Digital Equipment, and Motorola another 16%. Options trade on the American.

■ **NYSE Composite Index (NYA):** a capitalization-weighted average of about 1,500 Big Board stocks. Options trade on the New York Stock Exchange.

■ **Standard & Poor's Computer & Business Equipment Index (OBR):** a capitalization-weighted average of a dozen major office

and business equipment companies, with IBM about 75%, Digital Equipment, Wang, and NCR about 18%.

■ **Technology Index (PTI):** a price-weighted index of 100 stocks of which 45 are traded OTC. Very volatile. Options trade on the Philadelphia Stock Exchange.

■ **Gold & Silver Index (XAU):** options trade on the Philadelphia Stock Exchange.

■ **National OTC Index (NCMP):** options trade on the Philadelphia Stock Exchange.

■ **NYSE Beta Index (NHB):** options trade on the New York Stock Exchange.

GUIDELINES FOR SUCCESS

■ *Follow the trend.* If the price of the index is higher than it was the day before, which in turn is higher than it was the previous day, go long. If the reverse, sell short.

■ *Set stop-loss prices at 3 points below cost.* If they are too close, one erratic move can stop you out at a loss even though the market may resume its uptrend soon.

■ *Recognize the role of the professionals.* To date, most contracts have been traded by brokerage houses active in arbitrage and spreads and in hedging large block positions. Only a handful of institutional managers have done more than experiment. So the amateur is competing with top professionals who have plenty of capital and no commissions to pay and who are in positions to get the latest information and make quick decisions.

■ *Study the price spreads.* Contracts for distant months are more volatile. In a strong market, buy far-out contracts and short nearby months; in a weak market, buy the closer months and short the distant ones.

■ *Be mindful that dividends can distort prices.* In heavy payout months, these discrepancies can be significant.

■ *Use a hedge only when your portfolio approximates that of the index:* roughly a minimum of $250,000 (very rarely does a major investor buy only 100 shares of a stock). In most cases, any single portfolio has little resemblance to that of the index.

OPTIONS ON STOCK INDEXES

These are the ultimate in speculations. For a few hundred dollars, you can control a cross section of stocks worth $75,000 or so. The action is fast and exciting. The options, both calls and puts, have expiration dates every 3 months, they are quoted at intervals of 5 points, and their premiums reflect hopes and fears, the time premiums declining with the approach of the strike date. There are no margin calls, and the risks are limited.

Example: An investor has $60,000 worth of quality stocks and anticipates a drop in the overall stock market. The Standard & Poor's 500 index is at 151.50. She sells short one September contract. By mid-September the index is up to 153, so she didn't need the protection. She paid $150 for insurance, but the value of her holdings was up about $600.

With volatile stocks, options on the special indexes can be useful. You're bullish (but hesitant) on high-tech stocks. Here's what to do, according to *Indicator Digest:*

- In January the XCO options index is at 100.79. You buy a March 100 call at 4⅜ and sell a March 105 call at $1^{13}/_{16}$: a net cost of $2^9/_{16}$ points, or $256.25 (not counting commissions).
- If the XCO trades at 105 or above at expiration (about +4%), you make 2¼ points ($225)—more than an 80% gain. The maximum loss will be the cost of the spread if the index trades at 100 or less at expiration.

With all options on indexes, settlements are made in cash. When the option is exercised, the holder receives the difference between the exercise price and the closing index price on the date the option is exercised.

☐CAUTION: This can be far from the price the day the assignment notice is received. A hedge can lose on both the long and short side!

FOR FURTHER INFORMATION

Al Gietzen, *Real-Time Futures Trading* (Chicago: Probus Publishing Co., 1992).

Mark J. Powers, *Inside the Financial Futures Markets* (New York: John Wiley & Sons, 1991).

Edward W. Schwartz, *Financial Futures* (Homewood, IL: Dow Jones–Irwin, 1986).

William and Susan Nix, *The Dow Jones–Irwin Guide to Stock Index Futures and Options* (Homewood, IL: Dow Jones–Irwin, 1984).

Contact the following exchanges for pamphlets on futures trading:

The Options Exchange
La Salle at Van Buren
Chicago, IL 60605
1-312-786-5600

Chicago Board of Trade
Literature Services Department
141 West La Salle, at Jackson
Chicago, IL 60604
1-312-435-3500

Chicago Mercantile Exchange
30 South Wacker Drive
Chicago, IL 60606
1-312-930-1000

Chicago Mercantile Exchange
67 Wall Street
New York, NY 10005
1-212-363-7000

24 | SPLITS, SPIN-OFFS, SMALL CAPS, STUBS, AND STOCK BUY-BACKS

This catchall chapter is simultaneously geared to experienced investors and those with money set aside for speculation. Opportunities are investments and speculations. The definition depends on the type of security, the quality of the corporation, and the trading techniques used.

- **Splits.** Companies that split their stocks can be excellent investments when these splits are justified by profitable growth. The techniques used in buying and selling, however, can be speculative: That is, when it appears that a company may split its stock, the price of its shares will usually rise rapidly and, after the split, fall sharply. The long-term investor who bought the shares when undervalued will probably benefit automatically. The speculative investor, however, buys as the prospects of a split catch Wall Street's fancy and sells at a quick profit right after the announcement.
- **Spin-offs.** When a company divests itself of a subsidiary, the investor in the parent company automatically owns stock in the new company as well. This provides possible price appreciation.
- **Small caps.** Companies with a small number of shares can be investments when you know, and have confidence in, the owners, but they are speculations when there are problems because of limited capital, poor management, or threats of acquisition.
- **Stubs.** Stubs are mini-stocks left over after the company paid a special high dividend. They often rise quickly in price.
- **Bankrupt companies.** Bankrupt stocks offer speculative investors an opportunity to make money if the company pulls itself together or restructures successfully.
- **Stock buy-backs.** Companies often buy

back their own shares to maintain control. This procedure often boosts the stock's price.

COMPANIES THAT SPLIT THEIR STOCKS FREQUENTLY

One of the most rewarding and exciting investments can be a corporation that increases the number of its shares of common stock: issuing 1, 2, 3, or more shares for each outstanding share. Such splits usually occur when:

- The price of such a stock moves to a historic high so that individual investors are unwilling or unable to buy shares. Psychologically, a stock trading at 50 will attract far more than double the number of investors who are willing to pay 100.
- A small, growing company, whose shares are traded OTC, wants to list its stock on an exchange where the rules for listing are far tougher. The NYSE, for example, requires a minimum of 1.1 million common shares and at least 2,000 shareholders with 100 shares or more. Such a listing broadens investment acceptance as many institutions prefer the liquidity of an established market, and more individuals can use the shares as collateral for margin loans.
- A corporation seeks to make an acquisition with minimal cash or debt.
- The price of the stock reaches $75 per share. The most attractive range for most investors is $20 to $45 a share, so few splits are declared when the stock price is that low.
- Management becomes fearful of an unfriendly takeover. When the top officials hold only a small percentage of the outstanding shares, a stock split will make

more shares available at a lower price and thus, it is hoped, lessen the likelihood of a raid.

- Earnings are likely to continue to grow, which means that the price of the shares will keep rising. With more stock, the per-share profits will appear smaller—for a while.

- The company has a record of stock splits. This indicates that the directors recognize, and are familiar with, the advantages of adding shares to keep old stockholders and attract new ones.

SPIN-OFFS

These take place when the parent company divests itself of a division, which may be unrelated to the rest of the business or may not fit into the parent company's future plans. The new division becomes an independent company. The parent company then issues shares in this new corporation to shareholders of the parent company in proportion to their original investment. Now they hold shares in two companies instead of one.

The theory behind a spin-off is that the division will be better off operating independently and that the parent company will be better off without this particular division. A prime example: General Mills' spin-off of its fashion and toy divisions. Similarly, after Allied Corp. and Signal Corp. merged, the parent company selected a number of businesses in which it was less interested and spun these off as an entity called Henley Group. Thus shareholder value was maintained and the parent company's objectives were met.

If you have a good sense of timing, you may be able to cash in on spin-offs. Most follow a fairly similar pattern:

- After the new spin-off stock is issued, it falls in price.

- It then tends to move back up within several months.

That corporate spinoffs create shareholder wealth has been verified by several studies. The Pennsylvania State University's Department of Finance found that performance of parent companies' shares outpaced the benchmark indexes, and in one out of seven cases, the spinoffs eventually attracted premium-priced takeover

bids. A University of Texas Graduate School of Business study found that shares of spinoffs fell 4% to 10% during the first days of trading and then moved up. That time period is obviously optimum buying time.

§ IF YOU DARE: Buy spin-off shares after they decline, if you have faith in the company, and hold for the long term or until they have rebounded close to their initial price.

SMALL CAP OR SECOND-TIER STOCKS

Small cap companies typically have a capitalization of $150 million or less. With blue chips up in price, small caps, like OTC issues, offer a defensive position against a market correction, as well as an alternative to paying high premiums for quality stocks. They have outperformed larger stocks in the early stages of the last eight bull markets.

Second-tier stocks have been pushed to the foreground because of the diminishing supply of moderately priced blue chips due to the large number of takeovers and leveraged buyouts that took place in the late 1980s. This trend removed common shares from the trading arena.

Small caps are not without their problems, however. They are not heavily followed by Wall Street pros, which means little readily available research, but that also means they're often undiscovered and still low in price.

When corporations have a limited number of shares, their stock prices can move sharply: up when there's heavy buying, down when there's concerted selling. Theoretically, when a company has fewer than 500,000 shares, it should be an excellent speculation. Typically, the price-earnings ratios are low and the dividends sometimes relatively high. These firms are often targets for merger or acquisition and thus profitable long-term speculations.

If you prefer to have a professional select small cap stocks, then investigate one of the mutual funds that specialize in these companies (see box page 235).

David Alger, manager of the Alger Small Capitalization Portfolio (a top-ranking mutual fund) selects companies with market capitalization of less than $1 billion that are successful in their own small market niches. Alger looks for companies that will generate annual earnings growth of at least 30% per share. The Alger portfolio typically is turned over 3 or 4 times a year, with the manager often buying and selling the same stock several times, depending on market conditions.

The fund is about 80% invested in common stocks. Among those in the portfolio as of summer 1992 were:

BIO-TECHNOLOGY
- Centocor Inc.
- Immune Response Corp.
- MedChem Products, Inc.
- Somatogen Inc.

COMPUTER & BUSINESS
- BMC Software Inc.
- Chipcom Corp.
- Exabyte Corp.
- Linear Technology Corp.
- Parametric Technology Corp.
- Systems Software Associates
- Wellfleet Communications

ELECTRONICS
- Altera Corp.
- Maxim Integrated Products

- Trimble Navigation
- Xilinx, Inc.

FINANCIAL SERVICES
- Advanta Corp.

FOOD & BEVERAGES
- Clearly Canadian Beverages Corp.
- Smith Food & Drug Centers

HEALTH CARE
- Critical Care of America
- Employee Benefit Plans, Inc.
- HEALTHSOUTH Rehabilitation Corp.
- HealthCare Compare Corp.
- Medical Care International
- Sierra Health Services, Inc.

LEISURE & ENTERTAINMENT
- International Game Technology

MEDICAL PRODUCTS & SERVICES
- Beverly Enterprises Inc.
- Foundation Health Corp.
- HMO America, Inc.
- Molecular Biosystems Inc.
- Ramsay-HMO Inc.
- Vencor Inc.

MEDICAL TECHNOLOGY
- Isomedix Inc.

TWELVE TOP COMPANIES
SMALL CAP

COMPANY	BUSINESS	SALES $ MIL	EARNINGS $ MIL	PRICE	P/E
Artisoft	Computer soft/hardware	64.3	10.8	$26	39
Platinum Technology	IBM compatible software	32.1	5.5	16	59
Outback Steakhouse	Southern chain	66.2	7.2	29	43
Score Board	Baseball cards	58.6	6.0	28	22
Technology Solutions	Computer systems	63.2	10.6	24	25
Danek Group	Orthopedic goods	48.7	7.9	27	58
Video Lottery Technologies	Gaming equipment	32.2	4.1	31	68
Parametric Technology	Egineering Software	61.3	14.4	36	69
Environmental Elements	Pollution control systems	97.6	6.0	16	18
Cambex	IBM memory equipment	46.2	8.3	13	13
Checkers Drive-In Restaurants	Southern chain	51.1	5.2	26	79

Prices as of May 15, 1992.

SMALL-COMPANY GROWTH MUTUAL FUNDS

	TOTAL RETURN (1/1/92 TO 3/31/92)
Shearson Lehman Small Capital (call local office)	−1.75%
Colonial Small Stock Index (1-800-248-2828)	+17
Ariel Growth (1-800-368-2748)	+2.41
Vanguard Small Cap Stock Fund (1-800-662-7447)	+7.96
Quasar Associates (1-800-221-5672)	+2.2
Fidelity Low Price Stock Fund (1-800-544-8888)	+12.49
Alger Small Cap Fund (1-800-992-FUND)	−8.61

- Lifeline Systems, Inc.
- Syncor International Corp.
- U.S. Bioscience, Inc.

POLLUTION CONTROL
- Chambers Development Co., Inc.
- Mid-America Waste Systems Inc.
- O.I. Corp.

RETAILING
- Best Buy Company
- Circuit City Stores
- Fabric Centers of America
- The Good Guys
- Value Merchants
- QVC Network

STUBS

This relatively new vehicle can be potentially profitable, provided you are in the right place at the right time.

Stubs, as their name implies, are small stocks, the result of a takeover attempt. Stubs are the company's leftover stock after it has issued a special, one-time, high dividend to shareholders in order to defend itself from an unwanted takeover.

A classic example is Kroger. When the nationwide supermarket chain was threatened with a takeover, management decided to take preventive measures. It issued a special $40 dividend to existing shareholders. The result: The stock soared in price.

Following the dividend payout, the regular shares of Kroger were still in existence, but now as stubs, and sold at about $10 per share. Approximately a year later, the stubs had recovered somewhat and had been as high as $18. In May 1992, the stubs were trading again at $18.

How do stubs fend off corporate raiders? They reduce the stock's appeal because they are full of debt, which an acquirer does not want to assume. Take the case of Kroger. It raised its debt level to $4.6 billion to pay its special dividend to shareholders. Then to reduce its new debt, the corporation had to sell assets—in this case, a large number of its stores and warehouses.

STOCKS SELLING BELOW BOOK VALUE

As explained on page 169, book value is the net worth per share of common stock: all assets minus all liabilities. When the stock price is

TIPS FOR BUYING STUBS

You can participate in stubs:
- Automatically, if you own stock in a company that is restructuring and if that company issues a cash dividend for your existing shares
- By purchasing existing stubs of corporations you feel offer substantial growth potential

Existing stubs: Harcourt Brace Jovanovich, Holiday Corp., Owens-Corning, Kroger.

below book value, it is at a bargain level in that: (1) the corporation may be worth more dead than alive: if it were liquidated, shareholders would get more from the sale of assets than the current value of the stock; and (2) the company may be a candidate for a takeover.

The usefulness of book value as a criterion depends on the type of corporation. Steel firms and manufacturers of heavy machinery have huge investments in plants and equipment, so they usually have a high book value. But they rarely make much money.

By contrast, a drug manufacturer or retailer will have a low book value but will often have excellent earnings. The trick in using book value effectively is to find a company whose stock is trading below that figure and is making a comeback that has not yet been recognized in the marketplace.

In such a situation, you will get a double plus: buying assets at a discount, and a higher stock price due to better profits. Just make sure that the assets are real and that the earnings are the result of management's skill, not accounting legerdemain.

BANKRUPT COMPANIES

When corporations fall upon hard times, their misfortunes can signal investment opportunities for the strong willed. Before these companies revive, their stocks and bonds are often available at bargain prices. What are your chances for success? Edward Altman, professor of finance at New York University's business school, released a report in early 1990 showing that investors who bought bonds of companies that

TEN SELECTED STOCKS SELLING WELL
BELOW BOOK VALUE

COMPANY	PRICE	% PRICE TO BOOK VALUE
CalFed, Inc.	$ 3	9%
Allied Prod.	2	28
Travelers	20	43
British Steel	15	45
Luria & Son	6	47
Nat'l. Standard	3	48
Preston Corp.	7	48
Brown & Sharpe	8	49
Hartmarx	6	51

SOURCE: Value Line, May 1992.

STOCK DIVIDENDS

Stock dividends are extra shares issued to current shareholders, usually on a percentage basis: That is, a 5% stock dividend means that 5 new shares are issued for every 100 old shares. Such a policy can be habit-forming, and most companies continue the extra distributions year after year because it conserves cash, keeps shareholders happy, and provides an easy, inexpensive way to expand the number of publicly owned shares and, usually, stockholders.

It's pleasant to receive such a bonus, but be sure that the payout is justified. The actual dollar profits of the corporation should keep rising. If they stay about the same or decline, stock dividends may be more for show than growth. To evaluate a stock dividend in terms of a company's earning power and the stock's current price:

1 Find the future earnings yield on the current stock price. Use anticipated earnings per share for the current year. If the projected profits are $3 per share and the current price of the stock is 50, the earnings yield is 6%: $3 ÷ 50 = 0.06.

2 Add the stock dividend percentage declared for the current year to the annual cash dividend yield. If the stock dividend is 5% and the cash dividend is 2%, the figure is 7%—the total dividend yield.

If the second figure (7%) exceeds the first (6%), a shareholder faces earnings dilution and probable price weakness *unless* the corporate prospects are strong.

But if the profits are $5 per share, the earnings yield is 10%. Since this is more than the total dividend yield (7%), the stock dividend is not excessive.

declared bankruptcy or defaulted on meeting their payments averaged nearly 30% in compounded annual returns over the past 4 years.

$ HINT: You can invest in bankrupt companies through Fidelity Special Situations, 1-800-544-8888, a mutual fund that puts about 10% of its assets in distressed companies.

If you'd like to select your own stocks, begin by looking at management. If a company has gone through restructuring and the new team is competent, the value of the stock will rise. It takes time for the improved performance to be recognized.

- *Look for corporations that have resources and a strong position in their field.* The broader the customer base, the greater the chance of success.

- *Diversify with at least three holdings.* If you're lucky, one will prove to be a winner, the second will stay about even, and the loss on the third will be small. Hopefully, that right choice will pay off well enough to make all the risks worthwhile.

- *Buy soon after emergence from Chapter 11.* At that point, there's the greatest uncertainty and maximum risk but also a low base for future gains.

According to the National Institute of Business Management, investors can identify a company preparing for a strong comeback by looking for these traits:

- A large tax loss carryforward that can be written off against future earnings, thus sharply boosting after-tax profits

- Substantial salable assets relative to debt, indicating that the securities will appreciate even if the company is partially or completely liquidated

- A new management team, especially one with turnaround experience

- Selling off of unprofitable divisions or buying of profitable new ones

- Restructuring of debt to improve cash flow

- Reduced leverage

$ IF YOU DARE: Since many institutions shy away from stocks of troubled companies, individual investors willing to assume the

high degree of risk involved can sometimes make large profits in turnaround situations. To be on the safe side of an unsafe situation, wait until the company has announced a reorganization plan, or buy secured debt of the company.

STOCK BUY-BACKS

A corporate action that has become more prevalent than in the past is the stock buy-back. Like spin-offs and stubs, the buy-back bears study because it reflects the shifting action on the part of companies to protect themselves. Many companies, in an effort to raise their earnings per share and the price of their stock, have been buying back their common shares, either by making public tender offers or by simply going into the open market.

The motives are often clear. Managements, fearing a hostile takeover, try to give their stockholders nearly the same benefits as a takeover by raising their own stock's price.

Here again, as in the case of takeovers, cash flow and high asset values provide the money for corporate buy-backs of stock. When cash flow per share is high, cash is obviously available for common stock buy-backs.

Large understated assets may enable a corporation to raise cash from sales of those same assets and use the cash to buy back its own stock, thus closing some of the gap between market price and breakup value.

Companies with high NAV and strong cash flows tend to benefit stockholders because they have the capability to buy back their own shares. The three main reasons behind a stock buy-back are (1) to fend off hostile takeovers, (2) to boost shareholder values, and (3) to increase earnings per share. Therefore, investors are well advised to search for companies already embarked on buy-back programs.

FOR FURTHER INFORMATION

David Alger, *The Raging Bull: How to Invest in the Growth Stocks of the 90s* (Homewood, IL: Business One Irwin, 1992).

PART FIVE

YOU AND YOUR ACCOUNT

You might think you've done enough once you've learned what investments are best and when to buy and sell them. Yet surprisingly, your education will not be complete then. After you've set your financial goals, selected various securities, and worked out a balanced portfolio, you need to correctly implement your plan, to put it into action in the most effective way possible.

The financial planner or broker you select, the firm you use, and the type of account you have make the difference between success and failure, between being in charge of your money or merely letting someone else, often a stranger, pull the strings. So, before you start trading securities, read this section carefully, or if, unfortunately, you are in the midst of a situation you're displeased with, study the suggestions for changing brokers and arbitrating disputes.

In this section you will learn:

- How to find, interview, and select the best professionals
- How to settle discord with your broker
- Whether to use a full-service broker or a discount broker
- The advantages of regional stockbrokers
- How to change brokers
- The type of brokerage account that's best for you
- What types of orders to use and when
- Easy ways to build a profitable portfolio
- Whether or not to have a margin account
- How to do your own research
- Dividend reinvestment plans
- Dollar cost averaging

FINDING THE BEST PROFESSIONAL HELP

Many people who are willing to spend some time in research and analysis, to adhere to principles such as are outlined in this guide, and to use common sense can be successful investors. But there are times when professionals can be useful: for *direction* when you are starting out, for *confirmation* when you become more experienced, and for *management* when you have substantial assets.

Be slow to let anyone else manage your money without understanding your goals. It's yours; you worked hard to earn it, and in most cases, you know your risk tolerance and needs better than anyone else does.

There are three general categories of people whose job it is to help you with your investments. There are also various institutional planning departments.

STOCKBROKERS

These are representatives or agents who act as an intermediary between a buyer and a seller of securities. Brokers, who receive commissions for their services, are sometimes partners in a brokerage firm, but if not, they are called registered representatives (reps) and are regular employees. Brokers and registered reps must first be employed by a member firm of the National Association of Security Dealers (NASD) and then pass a comprehensive exam. Only upon successful completion of the exam is the broker registered and allowed to buy and sell securities for customers.

INVESTMENT ADVISERS

This all-inclusive term covers pension fund managers, publishers of investment newsletters, and personal money advisers who provide in-

vestment advice for a fee. The SEC requires all investment advisers to register, although it does not impose any special training or qualifications to register. The SEC does ask, however, that advisers disclose all potential conflicts of interest with their recommendations, that is, if the adviser owns the security that he or she is recommending or selling to customers.

Investment advisers are individuals or groups; some operate independently, but most are associated with other financially oriented organizations. Roughly, their fees are 2% of portfolio value with a minimum of $500 a year. Above $1 million, the fees are scaled down. Small accounts, under $250,000, are usually handled through standard portfolios designed for various investment objectives. Larger holdings receive personal attention.

➤ ADVISERS' BIGGEST PLUS You have someone to talk to, someone who can keep you up to date on economic and financial developments, back up recommendations with research reports, and explain the pros and cons of various opportunities or options.

➤ THE TEAM APPROACH It is essential to *use advisers in related areas:* a competent lawyer to set up a retirement plan or trust, a tax expert to make certain that you are taking advantage of legitimate ways to reduce taxes, and an experienced accountant to prepare complicated tax returns. A professional money manager can be valuable when you are involved with large sums in a fiduciary capacity, but for personal and pension savings, the primary role of the investment adviser should be to establish a system that will enable you to make your own decisions. Once you have a sound base, you can decide whether you want to handle your savings directly or with help, or to turn management over to someone else—for a fee.

Ask your lawyer, accountant, or stockbroker

for names of reliable investment advisers. You can also get a list by writing to:

Investment Counsel Association of America
20 Exchange Place
New York, NY 10005
1-212-344-0999

FINANCIAL PLANNERS

These generalists, who theoretically help you develop an overall financial plan and then implement it with you, are not licensed or regulated by the government. Most work independently or in a small practice. They usually charge a fee for drawing up a written plan for what you should do, covering your budget, insurance, savings, investments, taxes, and overall goals. This is then reviewed periodically. Planners receive a fee for their services, which can range from $150 to several thousand dollars, depending on the size of your portfolio. Almost anyone can be a financial planner, although planners tend to be insurance salespeople, brokers, bankers, or lawyers. They may or may not have taken special courses. Unless a planner is a stockbroker, he or she does not advise on stocks and bonds. Instead, the planner favors mutual funds or refers you to a broker.

At least 200,000 people call themselves financial planners according to the Consumer Federation of America, but only 15% to 20% have ever completed a course in the field. With no federal regulations and no nationwide accreditation requirements, it's not easy to weed through the crop. Before you turn your money over to a planner, read this section carefully. There are three basic categories of financial planners—determined by what they charge clients.

➤ FEE-ONLY These planners charge either an annual fee, based on your assets and investment activity, or an hourly fee, ranging from $75 to $250+. Fee-only planners give advice but may or may not sell products; therefore they are not burdened by potential conflict of interest in promoting a particular investment, such as stocks, insurance, or limited partnerships. However, you still have to pay for any securities you eventually purchase, and of course you are charged for the plan, whether you follow it or not.

➤ COMMISSION ONLY Some planners do not charge a fee but receive a commission on the investments they sell—for example, on a mutual fund or insurance product. With a commision-only planner, you benefit from one-stop shopping. Since any financial plan entails investments with a commission, you can do it all with the same person. However, the commission-only planner may have a vested interest in selling particular commission products. If you have a good relationship with your planner, this need not be a problem.

➤ FEE PLUS COMMISSION Many planners charge a fee for their overall plan and a commission on investments you purchase. In many cases the commission is lower than with a commission-only planner, simply because under this arrangement the adviser also receives a fee. In addition, the fee is almost always lower than with a fee-only planner.

$ HINT: Always get a written estimate of what services you can expect for what price before making a commitment to a planner.

SELECTING A PLANNER OR ADVISER

Don't use a financial planner, broker, or investment adviser who:

- Has a criminal record or a history of securities-related complaints. Check with your state Securities Agency, or contact The National Association of Securities Dealers, P.O. Box 9401, Gaithersburg, MD 20898 (1-202-728-8000), and ask for an information request form.

- Has no staff or operates from a post office box or telephone answering service. Insist on visiting the office, and then check out the person's ties with other professionals. No one planner can master the U.S. Tax Code, pension laws, stocks, bonds, real estate, and insurance.

Unless you know an exceptional financial planner personally, confine your search to those who have demonstrated their seriousness by obtaining one of the several designations offered in the field. For example, those who have the designation CFP after their names have studied and been awarded this certification by the International Board of Standards & Practices for Certified Financial Planners. Other degree programs and designations are listed below. Although meeting the requirements is not a guarantee of brilliance, it does represent dedication to the field.

- **CFP** (Certified Financial Planner). Has an average of 3 years' experience and has completed 2 years of classes and passed a comprehensive exam. Course covers financial planning, risk management, investments, taxes, retirement, employee benefits, and estate planning. It is given at colleges registered through:

    International Board of Standards & Practices for Certified Financial Planners
    1660 Lincoln Street
    Denver, CO 80264
    1-303-830-7543

- **ChFC** (Chartered Financial Consultant). An outgrowth of the Chartered Life Underwriter course for insurance agents, this is a correspondence course or may be taken locally if offered. It consists of 8 required parts plus 2 electives, with 10 2-hour exams.

    American College
    270 Bryn Mawr Avenue
    Bryn Mawr, PA 19010
    1-215-526-1000

- **CLU** (Chartered Life Underwriter). An insurance agent who has completed course work at the American College (see ChFC).

- **MSFS** (Master of Science in Financial Services). Granted by the American College to those who complete an advanced course in financial planning.

- **RFP** (Registered Financial Planner). Presented by The International Association of Registered Financial Planners to members who prove they have had 4 years full-time practice as a planner and have either a BA or graduate degree in business or economics or another comparable degree, plus a brokerage securities license and an insurance license. Members must devote 40 hours per year to continuing education. Only about 1,000 financial planners qualify as RFPs.

    International Association of Registered Financial Planners
    305 East Franklin Avenue
    El Paso, TX 77901
    1-800-749-7947

- **RIA** (Registered Investment Advisor). Indicates registration with the SEC. Has provided written information about fees, types of clients, investment specialties, education, industry affiliation, and compensation. No formal training required.

FINDING THE BEST

Select a financial adviser the same way you do your doctor: with great care and caution. Your financial well-being is second only to your physical health. Don't be tempted by tips you hear at cocktail parties or Little League baseball games. By following these steps you will find the person best suited to guide your financial future.

Step 1 Ask for names from friends and colleagues whose business judgment you respect.

Step 2 Ask your lawyer and accountant for referrals.

Step 3 If you have a contact at a particular firm, ask the manager or president for the names of two or three brokers.

The number one consideration in choosing any type of investment adviser is comfort: Select someone you respect, whose advice you are willing to follow, who operates in a professional manner (with integrity, intelligence, and information), who answers your questions and eases your doubts and fears.

These criteria eliminate brokers hustling for commissions; salespeople who make quick recommendations without considering your assets, income obligations, and goals; and everyone who promises large, fast returns.

Look for the following:

➤ PERFORMANCE OVER THE LONG TERM Select someone with at least 5 years' experience in order to cover both bull and bear markets. Anyone can be lucky with a few stocks for a few years, but concentrate on an individual or firm whose recommendations have outpaced market averages by at least 2 percentage points: higher in *up* markets, lower in *down* periods. This applies to total returns—income plus appreciation or minus depreciation—and refers primarily to stocks but is a sound guideline for debt securities. A minimum expectation of return on investment from an investment adviser should range between 15% and 20% including income and appreciation. The cost of this advice, including commissions and fees, will be at least 2%, according to veteran money manager Harold C. (Bill) Mayer of New York City.

Superior performance should be a continuing criterion. Every 6 months, compare the returns on your investments with those of a standard indicator: for *bonds,* the Dow Jones Bond Average or, for tax-frees, the Dow Municipal Bond Average; for *stocks,* Standard & Poor's 500 (which is broader and more representative than the Dow Jones Industrial Average). Then subtract the commissions you paid to see whether you're getting your money's worth.

➤ REPUTATION Comments from old customers are most valuable for helping you learn how you are likely to be treated, including promptness and efficiency of service and reports. Is extra cash moved quickly into a money market fund? Are orders executed promptly and correctly? Are dividends posted immediately? Are monthly reports issued on time?

➤ COMPATIBILITY Choose an adviser whose overall investment philosophy matches your objectives of income or growth. If you're conservative, stay away from a swinger who constantly comes up with new issues, wants you to trade frequently, suggests speculative situations, and scoffs at interest and dividends.

If you're aggressive, look for someone who keeps up on growth opportunities and is smart enough to recognize that no one should always be fully invested in equities and not to recommend bonds or liquid assets under unfavorable stock market conditions.

➤ STRATEGIES AND TECHNIQUES Find out by asking questions such as these:

- **Where do you get investment ideas?** From in-house research or from brokerage firms?

- **What are your favorite stock-picking strategies?** Out-of-favor stocks with low price-earnings ratios? Small company growth stocks? Larger corporations whose shares are now undervalued according to predictable earnings expectations?

- **How diversified are the portfolios?** Do you shoot for big gains from a few stocks or seek modest profits from a broader list?

➤ WILLINGNESS TO SELL Successful investing relies on two factors: how much you make and how little you lose. Check the composition of several portfolios for the past 5 years. If they are still holding glamor stocks bought at peaks and now near lows, move on! Don't stick with professionals who ignore their losses.

➤ SAY NO After you've made a choice, **don't be afraid to say no** if you don't understand or if you lack confidence in the recommendations. Nothing is more important than trust when you are dealing with money. You can forgive a few mistakes, but if they mount up, cancel the agreement. Remember, it is your money and you have every right to call the shots.

INTERVIEWING POTENTIAL ADVISERS AND BROKERS

Whatever you do, don't select someone to help you with your investments by walking into a firm cold off the street. And never sign on with the first person you talk with. Set up interviews with several candidates. Go to the interview prepared with a series of questions and compare how each of your potential advisers answers them.

Jay J. Pack, a broker and author of *How to Talk to a Broker,* suggests the following six basic questions:

- What do you suggest that I do with my $25,000 (or whatever amount you have)? Beware of the person who suggests you put it all in one product.

- How long have you been in business? With this firm?

- Will you give me several references so that I may check on your record?

- What will it cost me to use your help? Get specifics about fees and commissions, in writing.

- What sort of return can I expect from my investment?

- What research materials do you rely on?

Any good planner, adviser, or broker should:

- Be willing to meet with you in person for a free consultation

- Provide you with references or sample portfolios
- Ask you about your net worth, financial goals, and tolerance for risk
- Offer you several alternatives and explain them
- Be able to refer you to other professionals for specific help
- Set up a schedule for reviewing your securities, assets, and overall financial picture
- Answer your phone calls promptly

$ HINT: The NASD will tell you if a broker or his or her firm has been slapped with a disciplinary action or convicted of a crime. Unresolved complaints are not provided. Call: 1-800-289-9999.

SETTLING DISPUTES: ARBITRATION

As with all businesses, there are individuals who either deliberately or carelessly give poor advice. In the brokerage business, integrity is paramount—all the exchanges have strict rules, and most firms have compliance officers whose responsibility it is to monitor trading, make sure that full information is provided to all clients, and act promptly when there are deviations.

The trouble comes when the customer does not understand an investment or when the broker is not clear about all the facts or has not made them clear to the client. When the price of the securities goes down, recriminations start. If you take a flier, you can't blame the broker for your mistake. But brokers may be at fault if they cross the line between optimism and misrepresentation.

The areas in which problems most often arise are options, commodities, and margin accounts, or what are called "other, esoteric" investments. Every broker is required to know each customer and not put any customer in an inappropriate, high-risk investment. A client's net worth, income, investment objectives, and experience help determine what is suitable.

If you have a problem with your broker, begin by trying to settle it informally with your broker. If the problem remains unresolved, take the following action:

Step 1: Talk to the broker's supervisor or

BEFORE YOU UNDERTAKE ARBITRATION . . .

Arbitration is a long and often unpleasant procedure and should never be entered into casually.

According to Jay J. Pack, author of *How to Talk to a Broker:*

- The odds for an arbitration settlement in your favor are typically 50-50.
- You will improve your chances if you are prepared ahead of time. Gather proper documentation and other evidence to support your case.
- In 1987 the SEC ruled that arbitration results are binding. Therefore, if you decide to go to arbitration and the case is not decided in your favor, you cannot turn around and sue your broker.
- Act immediately if you are planning to go to arbitration. Arbitrators won't look favorably upon your complaint if you wait to see whether the investment in question goes up in price.

For further information, see sources listed at the end of this chapter.

---

branch manager. Brokerage firms do not want to earn bad reputations with the public or have a number of vociferous, complaining clients.

Step 2: Write a letter of complaint to the broker and the firm's compliance officer, with a copy to the branch manager. Request a written response from the compliance officer.

Step 3: Send a copy of the letter to the state securities administrator. The North American Securities Administrators Association is the national organization for all 50 state securities officials. Call NASAA for the person in your state: 1-202-737-0900.

Step 4: Contact the SEC, Office of Consumer Affairs, 450 5th Street NW, Washington, DC 20549. If your problem involves a commodities or futures contract, a copy of the complaint letter should go to the Commodity Futures Trading Commission, Office of Public Information, 2033 K Street NW, Washington, DC 20581.

HOW TO PROTECT YOURSELF

- Keep track of all your trades, including monthly statements.
- Note all important conversations with your broker in a diary.
- Contact your firm's manager if there's a problem—the company wants to keep, not lose customers.
- If you're not satisfied, contact an experienced lawyer; ask about fee structure.
- Figure out your brokerage losses plus the lawyer's fee. Is it worth taking the next step?

Step 5: Finally, send a copy to the exchange involved (see Appendix E for addresses).

Step 6: If you cannot resolve your complaint through phone calls and letters—and if it involves a great deal of money, you probably can't—the next step is arbitration.

When you opened your brokerage account, you signed a customer's agreement form of some sort. Many forms specify which arbitration body will hear a case if there is a dispute. Contact that body.

Arbitration panels sponsored by the industry's self-regulatory bodies consist of three people, and only one can be affiliated with the securities industry. Arbitrators have awarded punitive damages of as much as $1 million. They often also award attorneys' fees.

By contrast, the American Arbitration Association has absolutely no connection to the brokerage industry. Check your brokerage agreement. Although it may be more impartial, filing with the AAA is also more costly—from $300 for a dispute involving $20,000 or less to $3,750 for disputes of $500,000 or more. At the National Association of Security Dealers, it is $30 for $1,000 or less and $1,250 for amounts over $500,000.

$ HINT: In May 1990, the U.S. Supreme Court upheld a ruling that allows securities dealers to refuse to open accounts for clients who do not agree in advance to settle disputes through arbitration rather than by suing. Arbitration is generally quicker and less costly than a long court battle. See "For Further Information" at the end of this chapter.

DISCOUNT STOCKBROKERS

If you like to make your own buy-and-sell decisions, do your own research, and can operate independently of a full-service brokerage firm, it is possible to save between 30% and 80% on your commissions by using a discount broker.

These no-frills operations are able to offer lower rates because they do not provide research, they hire salaried order clerks and not commissioned brokers, and they maintain low overheads. Yet many have a surprisingly complete line of investment choices available: In addition to stocks and bonds, many handle Treasury issues, municipals, options, and mortgage-backed securities and will set up self-directed IRAs or Keoghs. The country's largest discounter, Charles Schwab & Co., also offers to trade mutual fund shares. Shearman Ralston and Securities Research have distinguished themselves in the field by publishing a monthly market report newsletter and offering modest amounts of research free to customers.

Several discounters have also moved into the computer field: Quick & Reilly, Charles Schwab, and Fidelity Brokerage Services market software programs enabling customers to place trades from their home computers, to receive stock quotes, and even to evaluate their portfolios.

As a general rule, you will be able to save $25 to $75 when doing a 300-share trade. But discounters set up varying schedules, so it definitely pays to shop around when selecting a firm. With some—called value brokers—the rates escalate with both the number of shares and their price. With others—called share brokers—rates are tied solely to the number of shares traded. You will save more with lower-priced shares if you use a value broker and with higher-priced stocks if you use a share broker.

As guidelines, use a discount broker if you:
- Have a portfolio of $100,000
- Trade at least twice a month in units of 300 shares or more
- Feel so confident of your stock market skill

DISCOUNTERS

Baker & Co., Cleveland, OH
(1-800-321-1640; 1-800-362-2008 in
Ohio); $40 minimum

Fidelity, Boston, MA (1-800-544-3939; 1-
800-544-6767 in Massachusetts); $38
minimum

Pacific Brokerage Services, Los Angeles,
CA (1-800-421-8395);
$25 + $3 service fee minimum

Quick & Reilly, New York, NY
(1-800-221-5220; 1-800-522-8712 in
New York); $37.50 minimum

Charles Schwab & Co., San Francisco, CA
(1-800-435-4000); $39 minimum

Shearman Ralston, Inc., New York, NY (1-
800-221-4242; 1-212-248-1160 in New
York); $40 minimum

Securities Research, Inc., Vero Beach, FL
(1-800-327-3156); $35 minimum

Muriel Siebert & Co., New York, NY
(1-800-872-0711); $37.50 minimum

StockCross, Inc., Boston, MA
(1-800-225-6196; 1-800-392-6104 in
Massachusetts); $25 plus 8.5¢ per share
minimum

Max Ule, New York, NY (1-800-223-6642;
1-212-809-1160 in New York); $35
minimum

Wilmington Brokerage Services, Wilmington, DE (1-800-345-7550;
1-302-651-1011); $39 minimum

SHOULD YOU USE A DISCOUNT BROKER?

YES, IF:
- You have investment savvy.
- You enjoy following the stock market and have time to do so.
- You have clear ideas about what to buy and sell, and when.
- You subscribe to an investment service or to serious professional periodicals.
- You follow technical indicators.
- You read market news on a regular basis.
- You trade often.
- You are not afraid to make mistakes.

NO, IF:
- You cannot decide what to buy and sell.
- You require investment advice.
- You are too busy to follow the market.
- You are nervous about things financial.
- You are inexperienced.

SOURCE: Jay J. Pack, *How to Talk to a Broker* (New York: Harper & Row, 1985).

If you are a heavy trader, play it both ways: Get information from your regular broker, and handle large deals through the discount house.

Don't assume that all discount firms are alike. Always ask what services are offered in addition to buying and selling stocks at a discount. For example, Charles Schwab & Co., headquartered in San Francisco, makes it possible for clients to:

- Purchase any of 600 no-load and low-load mutual funds through any of its 175 branch offices
- Place buy and sell orders 24 hours a day
- Purchase fixed-income securities, including Treasuries, municipals, and corporate bonds
- Receive independent research reports by fax, phone, and mail
- Trade your account by modem and access stock market research through its Equalizer software package, available to those with an IBM-compatible computer

that you do not want someone else to monitor or question your decisions
- Are sure that the savings in commissions are worthwhile: at least 20% below rates negotiated with regular stock brokerage firms
- Are not involved with special securities such as convertibles, options, or warrants, where accurate information is difficult to obtain

COMMISSIONS: FULL-RATE FIRMS VS. DISCOUNT BROKERS

	200 SHARES @ 25	300 SHARES @ 20	500 SHARES @ 18	1,000 SHARES @ 14
Merrill Lynch	129.50	157.00	214.50	293.60
Shearson	128.00	154.25	222.25	347.75
Prudential	140.92	167.08	232.60	348.95
Dean Witter	122.13	145.52	205.86	322.82
Charles Schwab	81.00	87.00	96.00	111.00
Fidelity Brokerage	80.75	86.75	95.75	110.75
Quick & Reilly	60.50	65.00	81.50	94.00
Olde Discount	60.00	60.00	80.00	105.00

- Get a no-fee CMA-type account, called the Schwab One Account, free checking, and a VISA debit card
- Trade stocks, get price quotes, and check on your account through TeleBroker, an automated service available to customers with touch-tone phones

REGIONAL STOCKBROKERS

Regional brokerage firms, those with home bases outside New York, are recognized for their personal touch, local knowledge, and independent nature. Many are excellent in picking stocks. That's because regional brokers are in positions to spot promising unnoticed stocks and bonds of local companies, ones Wall Street firms either ignore or do not follow closely. For investors, this means a chance to buy a stock before the rest of the investment world becomes bullish.

The regionals also pride themselves on better service. Brokers tend to stay longer at these firms, which lessens the chances of a rookie or broker-of-the-day handling your account. They also have the freedom to sell products of other firms—mutual funds, unit investment trusts, limited partnerships, and so forth.

$HINT: To check out a regional firm, read the annual report to see if it's been profitable during bull and bear cycles (see list on pages 248–249).

GETTING YOUR BROKER'S RESEARCH

The advantage of a full-service broker is access to investment research that separates companies on the rise from those that are heading down. Reports on individual companies as well as industry groups are prepared by analysts. Assigned to follow a particular industry, analysts interview corporate executives, study financial reports, and identify trends, potential problems, and new developments. Their reports are the basis of investment decisions made by your broker.

Reports produced by analysts are a mixed bag—some are financial tables of little use to individuals, while others contain useful comments on a company's stock. Some are brilliant; most are ordinary. Many analysts tend to run with the pack. To overcome this tendency, take the advice to "hold" a stock and interpret it as "OK to sell."

If your broker recommends a stock, always ask for the most recent report on the company. Or, if you hear about a potentially interesting buy, find out if the firm has taken a position on it. If you are a regular customer, your broker should send you the firm's weekly or monthly roundup reports, which cover a number of

---

BEWARE OF THE PONZI SCHEME

Every year, intelligent people are taken in by seemingly attractive, smart embezzlers through the Ponzi scheme—a swindle in which the first few investors are paid interest out of the proceeds of later investors. The latter end up with zero when the balloon breaks and the swindler pockets the remaining money. Ponzi schemes masquerade as tax shelters, deals in precious metals, gold and diamonds, real estate, and collectibles.

A sure sign: a guarantee of far higher interest rates or returns than the prevailing market is paying.

REGIONAL BROKERAGE FIRMS

FIRM	NUMBER OF BRANCHES	TELEPHONE
Advest Inc. 280 Trumbull Street Hartford, CT 06103	84	1-203-525-1421 1-800-243-8115
Blunt Ellis & Loewi 111 East Kilbourn Avenue Milwaukee, WI 53202	72	1-414-347-3400 1-800-558-1055
J. C. Bradford & Co. 330 Commerce Street Nashville, TN 37201	74	1-615-748-9000 1-800-251-1060
Alex Brown & Sons Co. 135 East Baltimore Street Baltimore, MD 21202	21	1-301-727-1700 1-800-638-2596
Crowell, Weedon & Co. 624 South Grand Avenue Suite 2800 Los Angeles, CA 90017	7	1-213-620-1850
Dain Bosworth Inc. Dain Bosworth Tower 60 South 6th Street Minneapolis, MN 55402	50	1-612-371-2711
D. A. Davidson & Co. P.O. Box 5015 Great Falls, MT 59403	13	1-406-727-4200 1-800-332-5915
Edward D. Jones & Co. 201 Progress Parkway Maryland Heights, MO 63043	1,700	1-314-851-2000
A. G. Edwards & Sons, Inc. One North Jefferson Avenue St. Louis, MO 63103	455	1-314-289-3000

stocks. If your broker resists sending these to you, maybe you should look for another broker. (However, don't expect the firm's best reports if you make only a handful of trades a year.)

A publication that merits reading by serious investors is *Wall Street Transcript*, which taps into the research departments of nearly every brokerage firm and investment house. It often reprints in full their major reports and summarizes many others each week. Brokers regularly read the "roundtable" feature, which covers discussions among three or four analysts who follow a single industry. There is one roundtable per issue. Since a one-year subscription now costs $1,890, you may want to read the copy at your library or broker's office.

ON-LINE RESEARCH

If you have a computer, then yet another way to tap brokerage research is InvesText, offered by Compu-

REGIONAL BROKERAGE FIRMS

FIRM	NUMBER OF BRANCHES	TELEPHONE
Interstate/Johnson Lane 121 West Trade Street Charlotte, NC 28202	54	1-704-379-9000
Janney Montgomery Scott Inc. 1601 Market St. Philadelphia, PA 19103	41	1-215-665-6000 1-800-526-6397
Legg Mason Wood Walker 111 South Calvert Street Baltimore, MD 21202	79	1-301-539-0000 1-800-368-2558
McDonald & Co. 2100 Society Building Cleveland, OH 44114	28	1-216-443-2300 1-800-553-2240
Piper, Jaffray & Hopwood 222 South 9th Street Minneapolis, MN 55402	92	1-612-342-6000
Prescott, Ball & Turben 1331 Euclid Avenue Cleveland, OH 44115	154	1-216-574-7300
Raymond James & Associates 880 Carillon Parkway St. Petersburg, FL 33716	41	1-813-573-3800 1-800-248-8863
Rauscher Pierce Refsnes, Inc. Plaza of the Americas 2500 RPR Tower Dallas, TX 75201	22	1-214-978-0111
Sutro & Co. 201 California Street San Francisco, CA 94111	15	1-415-445-8500 1-800-652-1030
Van Kasper & Co. 50 California Street San Francisco, CA 94111	3	1-415-391-5600 1-800-652-1747
Wheat First Securities Box 1357 Richmond, VA 23211	92	1-804-649-2311 1-800-627-8625

Serve, Dow Jones News/Retrieval, and the Source Information Network. InvesText provides brokerage reports from a number of Wall Street, regional, and foreign brokerage firms and investment companies. It includes reports by institutional firms such as Morgan Stanley, Dillon Read, and First Boston that are not usually available to individuals. You pay by the minute.

THE BIG THREE

If you decide to do your own research or supplement that offered by your stockbroker or adviser, three publication services will be enormously helpful. They are expensive, so you may want to use them at your library or broker's office before buying your own copies.

MOODY'S

Moody's Investors Service
99 Church Street
New York, NY 10007
1-212-553-0300
1-800-342-5647

A leading research and information service aimed primarily at the business community, Moody's (a Dun & Bradstreet Corporation company) is known throughout the world for its bond ratings and factual publications. It is not an investment advisory service.

➤ MOODY'S MANUALS The company publishes 8 manuals on an annual basis. Each is continually updated, some as often as twice a week. The manuals cover 20,000 U.S. and foreign corporations and 15,000 municipal and government entities. Each one gives financial and operating data, company histories, product descriptions, plant and property locations, and lists of officers. The 8 are:

- *Bank and Finance.* Covers 14,000 financial institutions, including insurance companies, mutual funds, banks, and real estate trusts.
- *Industrial.* Covers every industrial corporation on the NYSE and AMEX plus 500+ on regional exchanges.
- *OTC Industrial.* Covers 3,200 industrial companies traded on NASDAQ or OTC.
- *OTC Unlisted.* Covers 2,000 hard-to-find companies not listed on NASDAQ's National Market System.
- *Public Utility.* Covers every publicly held U.S. gas and electric utility, gas transmission, telephone, and water company.
- *Transportation.* Covers airlines, railroads, oil pipelines, bridge and tunnel operators, bus and truck companies, and auto and truck rental and leasing firms.

- *International.* Covers 5,000+ international corporations in 100 countries.
- *Municipal and Government.* Covers 15,000 bond-issuing municipalities and government agencies; includes bond ratings.

➤ MOODY'S HANDBOOKS These soft-cover books, published quarterly, give concise overviews of 2,200 corporations. Useful for instant facts and financial summaries. They are called *Handbook of Common Stocks* and *Handbook of OTC Stocks.*

➤ OTHER PUBLICATIONS *Moody's Dividend Record.* Detailed reports on current dividend data of 18,300 stocks; updated twice weekly.

Moody's Industry Review. Ranks 4,000 leading companies in 145 industry groups.

Moody's Bond Record. Monthly guide to 56,000 fixed-income issues including ratings, yield to maturity, and prices.

Moody's Bond Survey. Weekly publication on new issues.

➤ A WORD ABOUT MOODY'S BOND RATINGS Their purpose is to grade the relative quality of investments by using 9 symbols ranging from Aaa (the highest) to C (the lowest). In addition, each classification from Aa to B (for corporate bonds) sometimes has a numerical modifier: The number 1 indicates that the security ranks at the highest end of the category; the number 2, in the middle; and the number 3, at the lower end.

STANDARD & POOR'S

Standard & Poor's Corp.
25 Broadway
New York, NY 10004
1-212-208-8000
1-800-221-5277

For over 120 years Standard & Poor's has been providing financial information, stock and bond analysis, and bond rating and investment guidance. Its materials are used by investors as well as the professional and business community.

➤ MAJOR PUBLICATIONS
- *Corporation Records.* Seven volumes covering financial details, history, and products of 12,000 corporations. One volume, *Daily News,* provides continually updated information 5 days a week about these publicly held corporations.

- *Stock Reports.* Analytical data on 4,000 corporations. Includes every company traded on the NYSE and AMEX plus 1,500 over-the-counters. There are 2-page reports on each company.
- *Industry Surveys.* This 2-volume looseleaf is continually updated and covers 20 leading U.S. industries. Surveys cover all aspects of an industry including market trends, earnings, and government regulations.
- *Stock Guide.* A small paperback containing 48 columns of statistical material on 5,100 stocks. A broker's bible.
- *The Outlook.* A weekly advisory newsletter covering the economic climate, stock forecasts, industry predictions, buy-and-sell recommendations, etc. Presents a "master list of supervised stocks" with 4 separate portfolios: long-term growth, promising growth, cyclical and speculative stocks, and income stocks.
- *Trendline Publications.* Publishes marketing behavior charts providing investors with a visual look at a company's performance. Includes charts of indexes and indicators.

➤ OTHER PUBLICATIONS *CreditWeek, Bond Guide, Commercial Paper Ratings Guide, Standard & Poor's Register of Corporations, Directors and Executives and Security Dealers of North America.*

➤ A WORD ABOUT STANDARD & POOR'S FIXED-INCOME RATINGS Standard & Poor's rates bonds from AAA (the highest) to D (bonds in default). Those with ratings between AAA and BBB are considered of investment quality. Those below BBB fall into the speculative category. Ratings between AA and CCC often have a + or − to indicate relative strength within the larger categories.

VALUE LINE

Value Line, Inc.
711 Third Avenue
New York, NY 10017
1-212-687-3965
1-800-634-3583

An independent investment advisory, Value Line, Inc., publishes one of the country's leading investment advisory services, the *Value Line Investment Survey*, as well as several other publications and the Value Line index.

➤ MAJOR PUBLICATION *The Value Line Investment Survey*, begun in 1935, is a weekly advisory service published in a 2-volume looseleaf binder. It covers reports on each of 1,700 common stocks divided into 94 industry groups.

➤ OTHER PUBLICATIONS *The Value Line OTC Special Situations Service.* Covers fast-growing smaller companies. Published 24 times a year.

Value Line Options. Evaluates and ranks nearly all options listed on the U.S. exchanges. Published 48 times a year.

Value Line Convertibles. Evaluates and ranks for future market performance 580 companies and 75 warrants. Published 48 times a year.

FOR FURTHER INFORMATION

ARBITRATION

Director of Arbitration
New York Stock Exchange
20 Broad Street
New York, NY 10005
1-212-656-3000

Director of Arbitration
National Association of Security Dealers
33 Whitehall Street
New York, NY 10004
1-212-480-4881

Office of Consumer Affairs
Securities & Exchange Commission
450 Fifth Street NW
Washington, DC 20549
1-202-272-7440

American Arbitration Association
140 West 51st Street
New York, NY 10020
1-212-484-4000

Coping with the Crash: A Step-by-Step Guide to Investor Rights
North American Securities Administrators Association
555 New Jersey Avenue NW
Washington, DC 20001
1-202-737-0900

Lists telephone numbers and addresses of state administrators and federal agencies.

BROKERS

Jay J. Pack, *How to Talk to a Broker* (New York: Harper & Row, 1985).

The 1992 Discount Brokerage Surveys (rates 150 brokers)

> Mercer, Inc.
> 80 Fifth Avenue
> New York, NY 10011
> 1-212-807-6800
> $29.95

> *Tips on Selecting a Stockbroker*
> Council of Better Business Bureaus, Inc.
> Publications Dept.
> 4200 Wilson Boulevard, 8th floor
> Arlington, VA 22203
> 1-703-276-0100
> $1 plus SASE with 87¢ postage

FINANCIAL PLANNERS

> *Consumer's Guide to Financial Independence*
> International Association of Financial Planning
> 2 Concourse Parkway
> Atlanta, GA 30328
> Free

Selecting a Qualified Financial Planning Professional
Institute of Certified Financial Planners
7600 East Eastman Avenue
Denver, CO 80231
Free

Tips on Financial Planners
Council of Better Business Bureaus, Inc.
Publications Dept.
4200 Wilson Boulevard, 8th floor
Arlington, VA 22203
1-703-276-0100
$1 plus SASE with 87¢ postage

Fee-only Planners
National Association of Personal Financial Advisors
1130 Lake Cook Road
Buffalo Grove, IL 60089
1-800-366-2732
Free

Investment Swindles: How They Work and How to Avoid Them
National Futures Association
Public Affairs Dept.
200 West Madison Street
Chicago, IL 60606
1-312-781-1300
Free

26 | MANAGING YOUR BROKERAGE ACCOUNT

In the previous chapter you learned how to select a top-notch pro to help you buy and sell securities and manage your overall portfolio. Once you've lined up this adviser, you're not off the hook. You still have some decisions to make— such as what type of account to use, what types of orders to place, and the degree to which you want to be involved in running your account, all topics covered in this chapter.

YOUR ACCOUNT

First you must decide between a *margin account* and a *cash account.* Most investors should and do use a cash account. In a cash account you pay for your securities within 5 business days after the transaction.

A margin account is not only more risky, since it involves borrowing, but it can lead to actual dollar losses if you do not monitor your position on a regular basis. Margin accounts are discussed in detail later in this chapter.

➤ DISCRETIONARY OR NONDISCRETIONARY AC-COUNTS If you are just beginning to work with your broker, do not, repeat, *not* sign a discretionary account agreement. This type of account gives the broker the power to buy and sell securities without consulting you first. Discretionary accounts should be used only with brokers you have worked with for a number of years and you trust more than your own mother. Not surprisingly, discretionary accounts often cause problems—customers think the broker is churning their accounts (executing too many trades merely to rack up commissions) or not buying the right types of securities. The customer may or may not be right. Mismanagement of an account is hard to pinpoint, but it does happen. So don't let it become a possibility— stick with a cash account instead.

➤ IN STREET NAME Your broker will also ask you if you want your securities held in "street name"—that is, held with the firm—or if you want them registered in your own name with the certificates sent directly to you. If you decide to take physical possession of your securities, you will have to wait several weeks for them to arrive. If they are in street name, they become simply a computerized book entry at your firm, and your dividends and any stock splits are automatically collected and recorded for you.

$ HINT: If securities are in the broker's custody, transfer of shares when you sell them is easier than if the stock is registered in your name. Then you have to deliver the actual certificates to the broker's office.

➤ JOINT ACCOUNTS Before you open your account, check with your lawyer, especially if you are involved in estate planning. You may want to establish a joint account.

In a *joint tenancy with the rights of survivorship,* if one person dies, the other receives all the securities and cash in the account. The assets bypass probate and go directly to the survivor, although estate taxes may have to be paid.

In a *tenancy-in-common account,* the deceased's share of the account goes to the deceased's heirs, not to the joint account holder. The survivor must then open a new account.

If you have children, you may want to open a *Uniform Gifts to Minors account.* Whoever establishes the account names a "custodian" for the minor—very often they name themselves. All trading activity is then done by the custodian for the child's benefit. When the child reaches majority (age 18 or 21) he or she can legally take control of the account.

HOW TO SWITCH BROKERS

One of the most time-consuming and sometimes awkward tasks investors face is switching brokers. Transferring assets from one firm to another ought to be easy, but it often occurs at a tortoise-like pace. Delays sometimes last weeks or months, and occasionally investors lose money because securities dropped in value during the transit process.

Here's how to head off delays and trouble.

- Your new broker will ask for a list of what's held in your old account. Have that ready. Under the rules of the National Association of Securities Dealers and the New York Stock Exchange, the old broker must deliver the holdings in 5 to 10 days.
- If that deadline cannot be met, the old brokerage firm must send the new one cash equaling the market value of the securities under what is called a "fail-to-deliver contract." This money enables the customer to trade. When the securities arrive, the money is returned. (Fail-to-deliver contracts are required by the NASD under a 1986 ruling adopted because of the number of customer complaints about transfers.)

➤ HANDLING SNAGS Problems, of course, do arise. The key reasons are that (1) assets cannot be moved quickly, such as an IRA that requires a change of custodians or proprietary investments, such as a mutual fund run by the transferring brokerage firm; (2) the account has assets with virtually no value—bankrupt companies or companies with other technical problems; or (3) the old broker stalls—he or she may be annoyed that you're leaving, on vacation, or no longer with the firm. Talk first with the old broker, then with the supervisor. Ask why there is a hang-up. Prod gently, then firmly.

➤ SOLUTIONS If a serious delay occurs, you can complain to your old broker's supervisor, the NASD, and the SEC. Complaints to the NASD should be filed with the district office nearest the receiving broker. Contact the NASD in Gaithersburg, MD (1-301-590-6500) for the address of its nearest office. The SEC will contact the brokers and ask for an update. To complain, contact the Office of Consumer Affairs, SEC, 450 Fifth Street NW, Washington, DC 20549 (1-202-272-7440).

If you lose money because of a delay and your former broker won't help out, your only recourse is to use the NASD's arbitration service. For the proper forms, write to the NASD's Arbitration Office, 33 Whitehall Street, New York, NY 10004 (1-212-858-4488). Expect to spend between $30 and $1,250, depending on the amount involved. Cases take about 6 to 10 months to complete, and the decision is binding.

TYPES OF STOCK MARKET ORDERS

Once you have opened your account you're ready to trade. Although both dividend reinvestment plans and dollar cost averaging, discussed later on, are sensible ways to buy shares of stocks or mutual funds, they only work for securities you already own. When adding to your holdings or selling stocks, you need to know what type of order to place.

Most investors simply call their broker and place an order, called a market order, to buy or sell a security, leaving it up to the broker to get the best price possible. However, there are several other ways to go about it. Armed with a little more information, you can place a specific type of order and thereby protect your portfolio.

➤ MARKET ORDER This is the most common type of order. It tells your broker to buy or sell at the best price obtainable at the moment, or at the market. If the order is to buy, the broker must keep bidding at advancing prices until a willing seller is found. If the order is to sell, the broker bids at increasingly lower prices. With a market order, you can be certain that your order will be executed.

➤ LIMIT ORDER Usually a market order is sufficient, but when prices are fluctuating, it is wise to enter a limit order, which tells the broker the maximum price you're willing to pay, or if you're selling, the minimum you'll accept. For example, if you put in a limit order to buy a stock at 20 when the stock is trading at 22, your order will not go through unless the stock falls to 20.

➤ DAY ORDER This is an order to buy or sell that expires unless executed or canceled the same day it is placed. All orders are day orders unless you indicate otherwise. The key exception is a "good until canceled order."

➤ GOOD UNTIL CANCELED ORDER Also known

as an open order, this is an order that remains in effect until executed or canceled. If it remains unfilled for long, the broker generally checks to see if the customer is still interested in the stock should it reach the designated or target price.

➤ SCALE ORDER An order to buy or sell specified amounts of a security at specified price increments. For example, you might want to buy 5,000 shares but in lots of 500 each in stages of ¼ points as the market falls. Not all brokers will accept scale orders since they involve so much work.

➤ STOP AND LIMIT ORDER Both full and discount brokers will execute stop and limit orders, but they may refuse to do so for odd lot orders—those of less than 100 shares. (Orders consisting of 100 shares are called round lots.) And, depending upon your broker, you may or may not be able to set stop and limit orders on OTC securities.

➤ STOP-LOSS ORDERS An order that sets the sell price below the current market price. Stop-loss orders protect profits already made or prevent further losses if the stock falls in price.

☐ CAUTION: Both the New York and American stock exchanges have the power to halt stop orders in individual stocks to prohibit further sell-off in a declining stock. However, they very rarely use this power and in fact did not do so during the 1987 market crash.

HOW TO USE STOP ORDERS

Stop orders basically provide protection against the unexpected by forcing you to admit your mistakes and thus cut your losses. In effect, they say that you will not participate above or below a certain price. For example, if you bought a stock 6 months ago at $50 per share and it's now at $75, you can set a stop-loss order to sell at $60. Then, should it fall in price, you know that your broker will sell you out at $60. Stop orders are useful for the following purposes.

➤ TO LIMIT LOSSES ON STOCKS YOU OWN You buy 100 shares of Allied Wingding at 50 in hopes of a quick gain. You are a bit queasy about the market, so at the same time you enter an order to sell the stock at 47⅜ stop. If AW drops to 47⅜, your stop order becomes a market

order and you've limited your loss to 2⅝ points per share.

Traders generally set their loss targets at 10% below cost or recent high. Those who are concerned with long-term investments are more cautious and prefer a loss figure of about 15%: say, 42⅜ for a stock bought at 50.

$ HINT: For best results, set stop prices on the down side and have courage enough to back up your decisions. Once any stock starts to fall, there's no telling how far down it will go. Cut losses short and let your profits run.

➤ TO ENSURE A PROFIT A year ago you bought 100 shares of a stock at 42 and it is now at 55. You are planning a vacation trip and do not want to lose too much of your paper profit, so you give your broker an order to sell at 51 stop, good until canceled. If the market declines and the sale is made, you will protect most of your 9-point-per-share gain.

Similarly, the stop order can protect a profit on a short sale. This time, you sell short at 55. The price falls to 40, so you have a $15-per-share profit. You look for a further price decline but want protection while you're away. You enter a buy order at 45 stop. If the stock price does jump to 45, you will buy 100 shares, cover your short position, and have a $1,000 profit (assuming that the specialist is able to make the purchase on the nose).

➤ TO TOUCH OFF PREDETERMINED BUY, SELL, AND SELL-SHORT ORDERS If you rely on technical analysis and buy only when a stock breaks through a trend line on the up side and sell or sell short when it breaks out on the down side, you can place advance orders to "buy stop," "sell stop," or "sell short stop." These become market orders when the price of the securities hits the designated figure.

Example: Your stock is at 48¾ and appears likely to shoot up. But you want to be sure that the rise is genuine, because over the years there's been resistance at just about 50. You set a *buy stop order* at 51⅜. This becomes a *market order* if the stock hits the price 51⅜.

HOW TO SET STOP PRICES

Broadly speaking, there are two techniques to use:

➤ SET THE ORDER AT A PRICE THAT IS A FRACTION OF A POINT ABOVE THE ROUND FIGURE At 50⅛, for example. Your order will be executed before the stock drops to the round figure (50), which most investors will designate.

☐ CAUTION: There is no guarantee that your stock will be sold at the exact stop price. In a fast-moving market, the stock may drop rapidly and skip the stop price, and thus the sale will be at a lower figure than anticipated.

➤ RELATE THE STOP PRICE TO THE VOLATILITY OF THE STOCK This is the *beta*. In making calculations, the trader uses a base of 1, indicating that the stock has historically moved with the market. A stock with a beta of 1.1 would be 10% more volatile than the overall market; one with a beta of 0.8 would be 20% less volatile than the market. If your stop price is too close to the current price of a very volatile stock, your order may be executed prematurely.

Use these guidelines for relating your stop order to the volatility or beta of your stock:

- Under 0.8, the sell price is 8% below the purchase price.
- Between 0.8 and 1, the stop loss is set at 10% below the cost or recent high.
- 1.1 to 1.3: 12% below
- 1.4 to 1.6: 14% below
- Over 1.6: 16% below

Example: XYZ stock is acquired at 50. Its beta is 1.2, so the stop loss is set at 44: 12% below 50. If the market goes up, the stop is raised for every 20% gain in the stock price. At 60, the sell order would be 53: 12% below 60.

The lower the price of the stock, the greater the probable fluctuations; the higher the price of the stock, the smaller the swings are likely to be.

Thus Teledyne, at 150 with a 1.1 beta, would normally have a stop-loss price of 132, but because of its high price, it would probably be about 139.

SELLING SHORT

Selling short is a technique that seeks to sell high and buy low—or reverse the order of what most investors seek to do. It's speculative but can be used as a protective device. You sell stock you do not own at the market price in antici-

pation of a drop in price. You borrow the stock from your broker, who either has it in inventory, has shares in the margin account of another client, or borrows the shares from another broker. If the stock drops to a lower price than the price at which you sold it short, you buy it, pocket the profit, and return the stock you borrowed to your broker.

Example: The stock of Nifty-Fifty, a high-technology company, has soared from 20 to 48 in a few months. A report from your broker questions whether NF can continue its ever-higher earnings. From your own research—of the company and the industry—you agree and decide that after the next quarter's report, the price of the stock will probably fall sharply. You arrange with your broker to borrow 500 shares and sell these shares at 48.

Two months later, the company announces lower profits, and the stock falls to 40. Now you buy 500 shares and pocket a $4,000 profit (less commissions). Or if you're convinced that the price will continue to go down, you hold out for a lower purchase price.

This technique seems easy, but short selling is one of the most misunderstood of all types of securities transactions and is often considered un-American and dangerous, as indicated by the Wall Street aphorism "He who sells what isn't his'n buys it back or goes to pris'n." Yet when properly executed, selling short can preserve capital, turn losses into gains, defer or minimize taxes, and be profitable.

⑤ HINT: With few exceptions, the only people who make money with stocks in a bear market are those who sell short.

Here's another example. Say that in anticipation of a bear market, you sell short 100 shares of AW at 50. To reduce your risk if you are wrong and the market rises, you enter an order to buy 100 shares of AW at 52⅞ stop. If the stock price advances that high, you'll limit your loss to $287.50 (plus commissions).

With a stop-limit price, you specify a price below which the order must *not* be executed. This is useful with a volatile stock in an erratic market. Then if the price of the stock slips past the stop price, you won't be sold out.

Say you enter an order to sell 100 AW at 50 stop, 50 limit. The price declines from 50½ to 50. At that point, your order becomes a *limit* order at 50, *not a market order.* Your stock will *not* be sold at 49⅞, as can happen with a stop order at 50.

Short selling is not for the faint of heart or for those who rely on tips instead of research. You may have some nervous moments if your timing is poor and the price of the stock jumps right after you sell short. But if your projections are correct, the price of that stock will fall— eventually. You must have the courage of your convictions and be willing to hang on.

RULES AND CONDITIONS FOR SELLING SHORT

Because it's a special technique, short selling of all securities is subject to strict operational rules:

➤ MARGIN All short sales must be made in a margin account, usually with stock borrowed from another customer of the brokerage firm under an agreement signed when the margin account was established. If you own stock, you can sell "against the box," as will be explained. The minimum collateral must be the greater of $2,000 or 50% of the market value of the shorted stock.

§ HINT: For those who want to feel more comfortable with a short sale, it's best to maintain a margin balance equal to 90% of the short sale commitment. This will eliminate the necessity for coming up with more cash.

➤ INTEREST There are no interest charges on margin accounts.

➤ PREMIUMS Once in a while, if the shorted stock is in great demand, your broker may have to pay a premium for borrowing, usually $1 per 100 shares per business day.

➤ DIVIDENDS All dividends on shorted stock must be paid to the owner. That's why it's best to concentrate on warrants and stocks that pay low or no dividends.

➤ RIGHTS AND STOCK DIVIDENDS Because you are borrowing stock, you are not entitled to rights or stock dividends. You must return all stock rights and dividends to the owner.

If you know or suspect that a company is going to pass or decrease its payout, you can get an extra bonus by selling short. The price of the stock is almost sure to drop. *But be careful:* The decline may be too small to offset the commissions.

➤ SALES PRICE Short sales must be made on the uptick or zero tick: that is, the last price of the stock must be higher than that of the previous sale. If the stock is at 70, you cannot sell short when it drops to 69⅞ but must wait for a higher price: 70⅛ or more.

Exception: The broker may sell at the same price, 70, provided that the previous change in the price was upward. There might have been three or four transactions at 70. A short sale can be made when the last different price was 69⅞ or lower. This is called selling on an even tick.

CANDIDATES FOR SHORT SALES

In choosing stocks for short sales, professionals use computers to analyze economic, industry, and corporate factors—plus guesswork based on experience. Amateurs must rely on simpler indicators such as these:

- **Insider transactions.** That is, if officers and directors of the corporation have sold stock in the previous few months. The assumption is that when the number of insiders selling exceeds the number buying, the stock is at a high level and these knowledgeable people believe a decline is ahead.

- **Volatility,** as measured by the beta of the stock. This is the historical relation between the price movement of the stock and the overall market. A stock that moves with the market has a beta of 1.0; a more volatile issue is rated 1.5 because it swings 50% more than the market.

  The more volatile the stock, the better it may be for short selling. You can hope to make your profit more quickly.

- **Relative strength,** or how the stock stacks up with other companies in the same or similar industries. This calculation takes into account the consistency and growth of earnings and whether the last quarter's profits were lower or higher than anticipated by Wall Street. These data are available from statistical services such as Value Line and Standard & Poor's Earnings Forecast.

  When corporate earnings are lower than the professional forecasts, the stock will almost always fall sharply. Helene Curtis Industries stock dropped over 11 points, even though its annual earnings rose to $1.96 from $1.40, simply because this was below expectations. Catching such a situation so that you can sell short early will depend on your own projections, which can be based on news stories or information that you have gleaned from your personal contacts.

WHAT TO SELL

As a rule of thumb, the best candidates for short selling are (1) stocks that have zoomed up in a relatively short period; (2) one-time glamour stocks that are losing popularity; after reaching a peak, these stocks will be sold rapidly by the institutions, and since these "professionals" follow the leader, the prices can drop far and fast; (3) stocks that have begun to decline more than the market averages; this may be an indication of fundamental weakness; (4) warrants of volatile stocks, which are selling at high prices.

WHAT NOT TO SELL

The least attractive stocks for short selling are (1) thin issues of only a few hundred thousand outstanding shares; a little buying can boost their prices, and you can get caught in a squeeze and have to pay to borrow, or buy back, shares; (2) stocks with a large short interest: more than the volume of 3 days' normal trading; they have already been pressured downward, and when the shorts are covered, this extra demand will force prices up.

SELLING AGAINST THE BOX

This is a favorite year-end tactic that can freeze your paper profits and postpone taxes. You sell short against shares you own. The short sale brings in immediate cash and the profit (loss) is deferred until the short position is covered—next year. Here's how it works:

On March 1, Mary buys 100 shares of XYZ Corp. at 40. By July the stock is at 60, but the market is weakening and Mary gets nervous. She sells short 100 shares of XYZ with her own shares as collateral.

Her long position (the 100 shares bought at 40) remains in a margin account, where it represents collateral.

Her short position is made in a different "short account."

What are Mary's choices?

1   If the stock stays around 60, she may elect to deliver her stock against her short sale, which was made at 60, after January 1. This will postpone taxes until the new year and will also give her a 20-point profit (60 − 40 = 20).

2   If the stock drops from 60 to 50, she can deliver her stock and take a 20-point profit (60 − 40 = 20) as in choice 1, or she can take a 10-point profit by buying back her short sale. In this case she remains an investor in the company with the original stock at a cost of 40.

Commissions should be considered in selling against the box; they become a factor.

Under the wash sale rule (see page 317), there will be no tax loss if the short sale is covered by buying the same or identical securities within 30 days before or after the date of the original short sale. In other words, if Mary sells short at 60 and then her stock moves up in price within a short period of time and she covers the short sale by purchase within 30 days, the loss is *not* a tax loss; it is simply added to her original cost (40 per share). If she covers the short sale by purchase after 31 days, the loss is valid for tax purposes.

SOURCE: Joel Fein, ISI Group, Inc.

GUIDELINES FOR SUCCESSFUL SHORT SELLING

DON'T buck the trend. Do not sell short unless both the major and intermediate trends of the market—or, on occasion, those of an industry—are down. Make the market work for you. You may be convinced that an individual stock is overpriced, but do not take risks until there is clear, confirmed evidence of a fall in the market and in your target stock.

DON'T sell short at the market when the stock price is heading down. Place a limit order at the lowest price at which you are willing to sell short.

DO set protective prices. *On the up side,* 10% to 15% above the sale price, depending on the volatility of the stock. In most cases, a quick small loss will be wise.

Be careful with stop orders. You may be picked off if the stock price rises to the precise point of the stop order and then declines.

DON'T short several stocks at once until you are experienced and have ample funds and time enough to check daily. Start with one failing stock; if you make money, you will be ready for further speculations.

DO rely on the odd-lot selling indicator. This is available from several technical advisory services or can be set up on your own. It is calculated by dividing the total odd-lot sales into the odd-lot short sales and charting a 10-day moving average. When the indicator stays below 1.0 for several months, it's time to consider selling short. When it's down to 0.5, start selling.

Conversely, when the indicator rises above 1.0, do not sell short and cover your positions. And if you hesitate, cover all shorts when a 1-day reading bounces above 3.0.

DO set target prices but be ready to cover when there's a probability of an upswing. There will usually be a resistance level. If this is maintained with stronger volume, take your profit. You can't afford to try to outguess the professionals.

BREAKING EVEN

Before you hang on to a stock in hopes that its price will rise so that you can break even, check

IF A STOCK DROPS THE FOLLOWING PERCENTAGE	IT NEEDS TO RISE THIS PERCENTAGE FOR YOU TO BREAK EVEN
5% (100 to 95)	5% (95 to 100)
10% (100 to 90)	11% (90 to 100)
15% (100 to 85)	17% (85 to 100)
20% (100 to 80)	25% (80 to 100)
25% (100 to 75)	33% (75 to 100)
30% (100 to 70)	42% (70 to 100)
40% (100 to 60)	66% (60 to 100)
50% (100 to 50)	100% (50 to 100)
60% (100 to 40)	150% (40 to 100)
75% (100 to 25)	300% (25 to 100)

the following table. A stock must rise 100% to correct a 50% decline! If your stock declines from 100 to 50, it has dropped 50%. But it will take a doubling in price (a 100% increase) to rise from 50 back to 100. *Moral:* Take losses early; set stop orders to protect profits; stop dreaming.

PROGRAM TRADING

An ongoing situation individual stock investors should be aware of is "program trading," a complicated strategy used by institutions whereby computers trigger buy and sell orders. During the past 5 years it has added to market

---

THE TRIPLE WITCHING HOUR

Four times a year, three "items" expire on the same day: stock index futures, index options, and stock options. Program traders take offsetting positions, and a huge burst of buying and selling takes place, sometimes just before the market closes. There's no way to determine if the result will push the market up or down. This occurs on the third Friday of March, June, September, and December.

volatility and was blamed for much of the market's drop in October 1987.

Program trading is the result of the introduction of index options, index futures, and computers to Wall Street. It takes advantage of the price gap between index futures and option prices and the market value of the stocks making up the indexes.

The trader uses computers to follow the price differentials and then to sell automatically at a specified point. When a number of big institutions follow the same strategy, the market swings can be large. Here are two typical trading situations:

- If the value of the S&P 500 futures contract drops below the market price of the stocks that make up the index and the spread (or price gap) becomes wide enough, computers send out automatic signals to sell stocks. This huge sell order can lead to a drop in the price of the stocks.

- If the prices of the S&P 500 stocks fall behind the futures on the index, the computers will signal to buy these stocks and sell the futures when the spread reaches a certain amount. This can lead to a rise in stock prices.

SPACE YOUR TRADES

If you are making a large investment (500 shares or more) in any one stock, consider spacing out your purchases over a period of several days or even weeks. The commissions will be higher, but you'll gain a time span in which to review your investment decisions without committing all your funds. And if you decide that your choice was wrong, you can cancel the rest of the order.

EX-DIVIDEND DATE

Always check the ex-dividend dates before you sell. This will ensure extra income benefits.

Ex-dividend means without dividend. On the stock tables, this is shown by the symbol "x" after the name of the company in the "sales" column.

The buyer of a stock selling ex-dividend does not receive the most recently declared dividend. That dividend goes to the seller. With Consolidated Edison, the date is shown in Standard & Poor's *Stock Guide* as below.

Once a dividend is paid, it is no longer ex-dividend. Shareholders then look to the next dividend.

Going ex-dividend is actually a two-step process. The new dividend is payable to those who are "holders of record" as of a certain date. To be a holder of record, one must buy the stock at least 5 business days before the record date. On the 4th business day prior to the record date, the stock trades ex-dividend; that is, without dividend. Step two involves payment of the dividend by the corporation to the holders of record. This payment occurs 2 or 3 weeks after the official record date.

Once you have decided to sell a stable stock, you may want to delay the sale until a few days after the ex-dividend date, so you can earn the dividend. On the ex-dividend date, the stock will usually drop by the amount of the dividend but will tend to make it up in the following few days.

Ex-rights means without rights. As outlined in Chapter 18, rights offer stockholders the opportunity to buy new or additional stock at a discount. The buyer of a stock selling ex-rights is not entitled to this bargain after the announced date.

BUILDING YOUR PORTFOLIO

The simplest, easiest way to buy shares of a stock—once you own it, that is—is through a *dividend reinvestment plan,* so we'll discuss that approach first. *Dollar cost averaging* is another automatic way to add to your portfolio holdings. Neither dividend reinvestment nor

NAME OF ISSUE	DECLARED	EX-DIV.	RECORD	PAYMENT
Consolidated Edison	4/28	5/7	5/13	6/15/1992

AVOID ODD-LOT TRANSACTIONS

When you deal with odd lots of stocks—fewer than 100 shares—you may have to pay a premium, typically ⅛ point. This goes to the specialist handling the transaction. However, you may not be penalized if the issue is handled directly by the broker and it involves shares of a company for which the firm makes a market.

dollar cost averaging requires a great deal of work or thought on your part once you've actually purchased the stock or mutual fund for your portfolio.

DIVIDEND RE-INVESTMENT

In this plan, offered by most blue chip companies, dividends are automatically reinvested in shares of a company's stock without a brokerage fee. A number also offer a 5% price discount on new stock purchases. This service is offered by corporations to strengthen stockholder relations and raise additional capital at low cost; for investors, it is a handy, inexpensive means for regular saving. It avoids the nuisance of small dividend checks and forces regular investments. It's good for growth but not for current income, because you never see the dividend check. Many corporations permit extra cash deposits, ranging from $10 to $3,000 each dividend reinvestment time. There is usually an annual cap ranging anywhere from $10,000 to $100,000 per year.

Under such a plan, all dividends are automatically reinvested in the company's stock. The company then credits the full or fractional shares and pays dividends on the new total holdings.

Because these cash dividends are reinvested automatically at regular quarterly intervals, they resemble dollar cost averaging and turn out to be a way to buy more shares of a stock when its price is low. Full as well as fractional shares are credited to your account.

☐ CAUTION: You must pay income taxes on the dividends reinvested just as though you had received cash. If you buy the stock at a discount from its current market price, the difference is regarded as taxable income.

$ HINT: For more information, read *Buying Stocks Without a Broker* by Charles B. Carlson; published by McGraw-Hill; $16.95 + $3 shipping from: Dow Theory Forecasts, Inc. 7412 Calumet Avenue, Hammond, IN.

SOME CORPORATIONS WITH DIVIDEND REINVESTMENT PLANS: 1992

AT&T	Indiana Energy
Bell South	Kellogg
Bristol-Myers Squibb	Kroger Co.
Citicorp	McDonald's
Clorox	MMM
Commonwealth	Morgan (J.P.)
Edison	NYNEX
Duke Power	PepsiCo
DuPont	Piedmont Nat. Gas
Exxon	Raytheon
General Electric	Sears, Roebuck
Green Mountain	Southwestern Bell
Power	Texas Utilities
Hawaiian Electric	United Water Resources
Ind.	Universal Foods
Heinz	Wells Fargo
IBM	WPL Holdings
Illinois Power	Xerox Corp.

DOLLAR COST AVERAGING (DCA)

This, the most widely used direct-investment formula plan, eliminates the difficult problem of timing when to buy and sell. You purchase a fixed dollar amount of stocks at specific time intervals: 1 month, 3 months, or whatever time span meets your savings schedule. Consequently, your average cost will always be lower than the average market price. This is because lower prices always result in the purchase of more shares.

For example, if you invest $100 per month regardless of the price of the shares, the lower the market value, the more shares you buy. The stocks you buy fluctuate in price between 10 and 5 over 4 months. The first month you buy

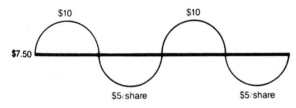

$10 $10

$7.50

$5/share $5/share

Total invested: $400
40 shares @ $5 = $200
20 shares @ $10 = 200
                  $400

STOCKS FOR DOLLAR COST AVERAGING: 1993

Aetna	Long Island Lighting
Archer-Daniels-Midland	Long's Drug Stores
Becton Dickinson	Luby's Cafeterias
Caterpillar	Merck & Co.
Clorox Co.	PepsiCo, Inc.
Coca-Cola	Pfizer, Inc.
Disney (Walt)	Pitney-Bowes
Dow Jones	Procter & Gamble
Eastman Kodak	Reader's Digest
Exxon	Rockwell Int'l.
General Electric	Rollins, Inc.
Goodyear Tire	Rubbermaid, Inc.
Hanson plc	Scott Paper
IBM	Upjohn Co.
Iowa Gas & Electric	Winn Dixie Stores
Kimberly-Clark	Wrigley (Wm.)
Lilly (Eli)	Xerox Corp.

10 shares at $10 each for a total of $100. The second month you buy 20 shares at $5 each, and so on. At the end of 4 months you have acquired 60 shares for your $400 at an average cost of $6.67 per share (400 ÷ 60). *Note:* During this same period, the average price was $7.50.

With DCA, the type of stock acquired is important. You want quality stocks that have these general characteristics:

- **Volatility** . . . but not too much. Preferably, the 10-year-high price should be 2½ times the low. These swings are more common with cyclical stocks such as motors, machinery, and natural resources, but they can also be found with industries whose popularity shifts: drugs, electronics, and food processors.

  In bear markets, your dollars buy more shares, but your paper losses on stock already held will be high, so you will have to have a stout heart and confidence enough to maintain your commitment. That's where quality counts.

- **Long-term growth.** These are stocks of companies that can be expected to continue to boost revenues and earnings and outperform the overall stock market. If your stock fails to keep pace with the market comeback, you will lose the main advantage of DCA. Look for stocks that are more volatile on the up side than on the down side.

- **Steady, ample dividends.** It is true that dividends, as such, have little to do with formula plans, but they can help to provide regular sums needed for periodic investments, especially when you find it difficult to scrape up spare cash.

With the right stocks and modest commitments, you may find that in a few years, the dividends will be enough to meet those periodic payments.

When you use margin, you can buy more shares with the same savings, but you will have to pay interest on your margin account. However, the interest charged will be partially offset by the dividends you receive.

$ HINT: Start your program a week or two before the date you expect to receive a dividend check from the company whose stock you plan to buy.

- **Better than average profitability.** The average profit rate of the company over a decade should be at least 10%. It's fine to be able to buy more stock when the price is low, but there's little benefit if its value does not move up steadily over the years. Corporations able to show consistent profitable growth will always be worth more in the future. With DCA, you are striving to accumulate greater wealth. This can always be done best by buying stocks of companies that make better than average profits.

REVERSE DOLLAR COST AVERAGING

SHARE PRICE	$100 PER MONTH: NO. SHARES SOLD	10 SHARES PER MONTH: INCOME
10	10	$100
5	20	50
10	10	100
20	5	200
10	10	100
5	20	50
	75	$600
Average redemption price per share	$8	$10

- **Good quality.** This means stocks of companies rated A− or higher by Standard & Poor's. With such criteria, you will avoid companies with high debt ratios and, usually, those whose prices swing sharply.

$ HINT: Shares of mutual funds are excellent vehicles for DCA. They provide diversification, generally stay in step with the stock market as a whole, and usually continue to pay dividends.

REVERSE DCA
This is a technique that is best used after retirement when you begin to liquidate shares of a mutual fund. Instead of drawing a fixed dollar amount (as most retirees do), you sell a fixed number of shares. The average selling price will come out higher that way.

For illustration only, the table above shows the values of fund shares that fluctuate widely over a 6-month period. To get $100 income, you must sell 10 shares in the first month, 20 in the second, etc. Over the half-year, you liquidate 75 shares at an average price of $8.

But if you sell a fixed number (10) of shares each month, your income will vary: $100 in month 1, $50 in month 2, $200 in month 4. Overall, you will cash in only 60 shares at an average redemption price of $10.

This can be dangerous for two reasons: (1)

You won't get the same dollars every month, but over the same period of time you will receive as much and have more shares still invested. Yet when the price of the shares drops, you will have to unload more shares and will have fewer assets invested in the fund. (2) You cannot know in advance the correct number of shares to sell; if you have to change the formula, you may be in trouble.

$ HINT: This system is arithmetically correct but may be difficult for people who do not have additional income to live on in months when fund per-share price is low.

➤ ADVANTAGES Over the years, the average cost of all shares will be less than the average price at which you bought them. But you lose the fun and pride of judgment-based investing.

☐CAUTION: When stock prices are falling, consistent purchases are a form of averaging down—generally a poor policy unless you are convinced that there will be a turnaround soon.

➤ DISADVANTAGES Formula plans sound simple, but they can be difficult to maintain. Most investors cannot convince themselves to sell when things are going well and to buy when the market action is unfavorable. These plans will seldom let you achieve a big killing, but they can stop you from being killed.

ONE-STOP INVESTING

If you have a brokerage account, a money market fund, and a major credit card, as well as some type of checking account, you may find it useful and economical to wrap it all together and put it into a combo, or central assets, account. In this way, all your financial transactions will be handled under one roof—at a bank or brokerage firm—which saves you time, red tape, and sometimes money, too.

A typical central assets account consists of one versatile package that can include stocks, bonds, your IRA, a money market fund, and credit or debit card transactions. But you must be able to meet the minimum amount set by the brokerage firm or bank, which ranges from $5,000 to $20,000.

For a yearly fee (zero to $200) the sponsoring bank or brokerage firm will provide unlimited checkwriting privileges on a money market account; an American Express, VISA, or MasterCard account; a line of credit; a securities brokerage account; and an all-inclusive monthly statement. An important additional benefit, known as the "sweep" feature, automatically transfers or sweeps any idle cash (from the sale of a security, from a CD that matured, or from dividends) into a high-paying money market fund. This system not only relieves you of keeping track of the money but, more important, prevents any loss of interest between transactions.

A central asset account comprises seven basic ingredients:

- A brokerage account in which securities can be bought and sold at regular commissions
- Automatic investment of idle cash into money market funds
- A checking account, usually with free checks; minimum amounts vary
- A debit or credit card that can be used for purchases, loans, or cash

- A line of credit, that is, the privilege of borrowing against your credit or debit card
- Quick loans secured by the margin value of the securities held in the account, with interest charged at slightly above the broker call rate
- Composite monthly statements showing all transactions and balances

Here's how a central assets account works. Let's say you have 300 shares of Eastman Kodak that you want to sell. You call your broker with directions to make the transaction. Money from the sale is immediately invested in a money market fund, where it earns around 4%. The transfer of money from your securities account to the money market fund is done automatically by computer.

Then a few weeks later you write a check for $800. You do so against your money market fund, leaving a balance of several thousand dollars. You felt this was an adequate balance—and it was, until you had a sudden emergency and needed to use that amount plus $1,500. So your broker arranged for a loan using your remaining securities as collateral. This was done in your margin account. By having an umbrella account, you avoided hours of time and miles of red tape that are customarily involved in obtaining a bank loan.

Many of the larger brokerage firms offer customers one of several funds in which to park their idle cash: a regular money market fund; a U.S. government fund, which is slightly safer but also has lower yields; and a tax-free money fund for those in high-tax brackets.

The traditional monthly statement includes:
- A list of securities held in the account
- Securities bought or sold with an indication of profit or loss
- Amount of commission paid to the broker
- Dividends received
- Interest received from the money market fund
- Number of money market fund shares
- Amount of margin loans either advanced or paid off
- Credit and debit card transactions
- Data required in preparing your income tax returns

Before you leap into a central assets account, check out the following:

- Minimum required to open the account
- Annual fee
- Commission charged
- Margin loan rate (explained below)
- Method for handling debit and credit card transactions
- Frequency of sweeps into money market funds
- Number of money market funds to choose from
- Minimum amount for writing checks
- Clarity of monthly statements
- Any extras offered

You should also keep in mind some of the disadvantages of this type of account. First of all, most components of a combo account are available elsewhere. Credit card holders already have credit lines and cash advances. Debit cards can be a disadvantage, because they provide a shorter "float period"—that is, less free credit time than for a standard credit card. With the latter, you can stretch your credit or payment time up to at least 30 days, sometimes 60 or 90.

Some investors find that such easy access to money and loans makes it possible for them to spend more than they should. If you fall into this category, steer clear of the central assets account.

The Better Business Bureau in many areas has free material on central asset accounts, banks, and brokerage services. Contact your local office.

MARGIN ACCOUNTS

Leverage—using borrowed funds to supplement your own commitments—is a key factor in making money make money. With *real estate*, it's making a small down payment and having a large mortgage; with *securities*, it's buying on margin: using cash, stocks, convertibles, bonds, etc. as collateral for a loan from your broker. When the borrowing is kept at a reasonable level and the interest costs are modest, buying on margin can enhance profits, because your money is working twice as hard since you put up only part of the cost. Margin, then, is trading on credit and a way of using borrowing power to take a larger position in the stock market.

Leverage in the stock market is not as simple as it sounds. Successful use of margin requires sophistication, sufficient resources to absorb substantial losses when the prices of the securities decline, and the temperament to handle debt.

THE RULES

When you open a margin account and sign a margin agreement and loan consent, you are giving your broker permission to lend the securities in your account.

Your stocks in a margin account are held "in street name," which means in the broker's firm. Therefore, you cannot put your stock certificates in your vault. You may also be subject to "margin call" if you use the assets in your account to the point where you have no more credit, or if the value of your portfolio falls below a minimum amount. Then your broker will ask you to reduce some of the loan. If you cannot come up with the cash or additional securities, your broker may have to sell some of your remaining stock.

Margin accounts are governed by the Federal Reserve Board's Regulation T, the New York Stock Exchange, the National Association of

---

EXCHANGE AND FEDERAL MARGIN REQUIREMENTS

Assuming you put up cash in the amount of $10,000 in each case, you could buy on margin:
- $20,000 worth of *marginable stocks*
- $20,000 worth of *listed corporate convertible bonds*

You can invest on margin in nearly every issue on the New York and American stock exchanges and in nearly 2,000 over-the-counter securities. To open an account, you must sign a margin agreement that includes a consent to loan securities. The margin account agreement states that all securities will be held "in street name"; that is, by the broker. The consent to loan means that the broker can lend your securities to others who may want them for the purpose of selling short.

Securities Dealers, and individual brokerage house rules.

1. Under the rules set forth by the Federal Reserve Board, the initial requirement for margin on stocks is 50%. So to buy $10,000 worth of securities you must put up at least $5,000. Greater leverage is allowed on government bonds, where you can borrow up to 95%.
2. The New York Stock Exchange, however, has stricter requirements. It asks members to demand that investors deposit a minimum of $2,000 in cash or its equivalent in securities in order to open a margin account. That means that if you want to buy $3,000 in stock, your initial margin requirement is actually 66⅔%, or $2,000, rather than the $1,500, or 50%, that the Federal Reserve Board requires.
3. Some brokers set even higher requirements.

All brokers hold securities purchased on margin in "street name."

The New York Stock Exchange also requires that the equity in the account be maintained at 25% to 30% at all times. This is called a "minimum maintenance margin." When the value of your portfolio drops below this level, your broker will issue a margin call, and you

---

DO NOT HAVE A MARGIN ACCOUNT IF:

- You lack the temperament.
- You are dealing in small amounts of money.
- You cannot absorb a loss.
- Your portfolio consists primarily of income equities.
- You tend to buy and hold stocks.

TO MINIMIZE RISKS:

- Set stop orders above the 30% loss point.
- Borrow less than the maximum.
- Buy on margin only in a bull market.
- Watch for increases in the broker loan rate.
- Check the prices of your margined stock at least once a week to avoid a surprise margin call.

CALCULATING YOUR YIELD WHEN BUYING ON MARGIN

To determine exactly what yield you get by buying on margin, you must ascertain the return on your actual investment: the *margin equivalent yield*. You can calculate this from the accompanying formula.

The *cash yield percent* (CY%) is the return on securities bought outright. The same formulas can be used for both pre-tax and after-tax yields.

$$MEY = \left(\frac{100}{\%M} \times CY\%\right) - \left[\left(\frac{100}{\%M} - 1\right) \times DI\%\right]$$

where MEY = margin equivalent yield
    %M = % margin
    CY% = cash yield %
    DI% = debit interest %

Example: You are on a 50% margin base, receive 12% cash yield from dividends, and pay 20% in your debit balance.

$$MEY = \left(\frac{100}{50} \times 12\right) - \left[\left(\frac{100}{50} - 1\right) \times 20\right]$$

$$MEY = (2 \times 12 = 24)$$
$$- [(2 - 1 = 1) \times 20 = 20]$$

$$MEY = 24 - 20 = 4\%$$

Thus the 12% return, with margin, dwindles to 4%.

---

will have to come up with more cash or the broker will sell enough securities in your account to bring it up to the required level.

Example: Let's say you want to buy 200 shares of a $50 stock. In a regular cash account, you would put up $10,000 ($50 × 200 = $10,000). But in a margin account, you only have to put up 50% of the purchase price, or $5,000 plus commission. Your broker lends you the other $5,000 and charges you interest on it.
➤ LOAN RATE Mounting interest charges can take a big chunk out of profits in a margin account, especially if you hold your stocks a long time. You are charged interest daily based on the *broker call rate*, the rate the banks

---

MARGIN CALL

If your firm requires a 30% minimum maintenance rather than 25%, to find out if you're approaching a call, multiply the price of the stock at the time you purchased it by 0.71. If it's reached that price, your phone will ring.

---

charge brokers for money. The interest the broker then charges you may run from 0.5% to 2.5% above the broker loan rate, which is currently ranges from 6¼ to 7¼%. The more active and the larger your account, the lower the rate is likely to be. Dividends, of course, can help offset some of the interest.

$ HINT: The interest you pay on your margin account is tax-deductible to the extent that it is offset by investment income—dividends and capital gains. So to deduct $2,000 in interest, you must report at least $2,000 in investment income.

□CAUTION: The New York Stock Exchange may set special margin requirements calling for more cash or securities or require full cash payments in very volatile stocks.

➤ SPECIAL MISCELLANEOUS ACCOUNT If you have excess cash or equity in your margin account, this is known as a special miscellaneous account (SMA). It is created by the deposit of more than 50% of the purchase price of stocks or securities bought on margin, by the accumulation of dividends, or by a rise in the value of the margined portfolio. As long as the value of your margined portfolio is at or above the minimum maintenance margin, you may use your SMA to buy additional securities, but if your account is below the minimum margin maintenance requirement your broker will use your SMA to meet the margin call.

$ HINT: If you use margin, don't let your equity fall below 50%. In a volatile market, you can get in trouble very fast.

ADDITIONAL REGULATIONS

- Margin rules have been extended to some mutual funds.
- Individuals are allowed to have more than one margin account at the same brokerage house under certain circumstances, which vary from firm to firm. Check with your broker.
- Not all securities traded over the counter are marginable. Stocks under $5 usually cannot be margined.
- The NYSE sets special loan limits for individual issues that show unusual volume, price fluctuations, or rapid turnover, to discourage undue speculation.
- Customers whose accounts show a pattern of "day trading" (purchasing and selling the same marginable issues on the same day) are required to maintain appropriate margin before the transactions are made.
- Each brokerage firm sets its own margin requirements for nonconvertible bonds, municipal bonds, and U.S. government bonds.

$ HINT: You may use your margin account to borrow from your broker for purposes other than to buy stocks and bonds. The rates are almost always lower than a consumer bank loan, and there is no monthly repayment of the loan payments.

PART SIX

FINANCING YOUR LIFE-STYLE

Whether you're a baby boomer, an empty nester, single, or in the senior citizen category, you need to arrange your finances to suit your life-style. In this section we look at the most important areas of financial planning as they relate to your particular needs:

- Housing in today's real estate market
- Mortgages
- REITs
- Family finances throughout your life: raising young children; paying for education costs; adjusting to adult children returning to the family homestead; providing financial help to aging parents; and going back to school yourself
- Retirement and pension plans
- Retirement living
- IRAs, Keoghs, 401(k)s, and Social Security
- GICs
- Insurance and annuities

27 HOUSING

The recession brought about a sharp decline in real estate values in many parts of the country. At the same time, mortgage interest rates are favorable. And, until prices approach their highs of the 1980s, there are still excellent opportunities.

WHAT TO DO IN THIS REAL ESTATE MARKET

1 *If you want to buy, start looking.* The slump in residential and commercial property has led to a large number of distress sales. The real estate auction, once a rarity, is gaining in popularity as a big inventory of foreclosure properties comes to market. Public notices of default sales are posted at some city halls and frequently announced in local newspapers. And due to the savings and loan debacle, the federal government is now one of the country's biggest real estate brokers and is auctioning thousands of homes through the Resolution Trust Corporation (RTC).

$ HINT: For a free list of repossessed properties in your area, call 1-800-782-3006. For other RTC publications, call 1-800-431-0600.

Government agencies and mortgage lenders also often list with local brokers; many accept smaller than usual down payments.

$ HINT: For a list of foreclosed properties offered by Fannie Mae (Federal National Mortgage Association), write to: Foreclosures, Box 13165, Baltimore, MD 21203

When investing in rental property, pick a location within a day's drive; it's easiest to be a landlord if your property is nearby.

2 *What about refinancing?* With lower interest rates, the question of refinancing your mortgage pops up. The rule of thumb is do not refinance unless the new rate is at least 2 percentage points lower than the old one. This guideline, however, overlooks a critical factor: how long you plan to stay in your home. The sooner you intend to move, the greater the rate differential between the two loans must be for refinancing to pay off. Why? You will probably pay 3% to 4% of the total loan in points and closing fees on a new loan, and it will take 2 to 4 years to recoup the up-front charges.

3 *Try a lease option.* If you own a house you would like to sell but haven't been able to, or if you want to buy but can't quite afford the down payment, a "lease-option" plan may solve the problem. Under this arrangement, the potential buyer moves into the house as a tenant, paying monthly rent. The rent, however, is considerably higher than normal, sometimes even double. The extra is credited toward the down payment. Some landlords also require an up-front cash payment. At the end of a specified time, typically 1 to 4 years, the tenant finds a mortgage and buys the house. If he cannot, the owner keeps the extra payments. Most of these arrangements are made through ads in local newspapers.

☐ CAUTION: Make certain the lease includes an exclusive contract that the property will be sold to the tenant for a set price when the lease expires and states whether or not the deposit is refundable. An option to buy could prove worthless unless a sales contract is attached to the lease and the contract has been signed in advance by the seller.

4   *Buying in an unknown area.* Whether it's rental property or a home for yourself, get a "destination appraisal" before buying in unfamiliar territory. Otherwise you might move in and find out six months later that an office building is going to be built nearby. Prepurchase appraisals range in price from $200 to $400. They let buyers know about hidden problems as well as give them an idea of the going prices.

$ HINT: To find a qualified appraiser, call the Society of Real Estate Appraisers at 1-312-335-4100 and request *Directory of Designated Members.*

$ HINT: *To find the lowest mortgage rate,* contact HSH Associates, 1-800-873-2387 or 1-201-838-3330. This firm tracks mortgage listings for most areas of the country. One survey costs $20.

5   *Real estate investment trusts.* REITs own properties or mortgages on them. Their shares sell on the stock exchanges. In 1991, REITs posted a total return (capital appreciation plus reinvested dividends) of 35.6% versus 30.5% for the Standard & Poor 500's. Although REITs are not universally sound investments, they tend to be safer and easier than direct ownership of commercial properties.

Health care REITs are among the best current investments in this category. Top performers include:

Nationwide Health Properties	$25	8.6%
Meditrust	27	9.1
Health & Rehabilitation Properties	12	10

6   *Stocks.* In January 1992, Engle Homes, a key builder in rapidly growing Florida housing markets, issued its first public offering at $11½ per share; as of May the stock was at $14¾.

American Strategic Income Portfolio is a closed-end fund invested primarily in participation mortgages of the Resolution Trust Corp., the Federal Deposit Insurance Corp., and non-troubled banks and savings and loans, as well as in mortgage-backed securities, such as those issued by the Government National Mortgage

Association (Ginnie Mae). As of mid-May, this stock was selling at $16¼ with a yield of 8.5%.

7   *ARMS.* Adjustable rate mortgage mutual funds are a relatively new and fast-growing type of investment vehicle that invests primarily in adjustable rate mortgage securities issued by Ginnie Mae, Fannie Mae, and Freddie Mac (see Chapter 12). Because the rates on ARM securities are adjusted periodically, prices are less volatile than fixed-income securities. However, some investment uncertainty is created by the varying patterns of mortgage prepayment by property owners.

The yield on ARM securities generally tracks the ebb and flow of short-term interest rates, but is typically 1.5% to 2% higher.

Two ARM mutual funds that impose no sales charges are Benham's Adjustable Rate Government Securities (1-800-472-3389) with a 6.62% yield, and T. Rowe Price's Adjustable

---

CALCULATING BENEFITS OF REFINANCING

If you have a $150,000 mortgage payable over 30 years at 10.5%, your monthly payments are $1,372. If after 3 years you refinance the mortgage balance, about $147,400, at 8.5% payable over 27 years, your monthly payments will be reduced by $210, to $1,162. However, you also must account for administrative fees and other costs: refinancing $147,400 will probably cost $2,710 ($500 in fees plus $2,210 for 1.5 points, a percentage of the loan amount).

Balance that against what you save in monthly payments: those refinancing costs will be recovered in about a year ($2,710 divided by $210 = 12.9 months). After that, your gross monthly cash flow is improved by $210 and your total interest paid over the life of the mortgage is reduced significantly.

Example courtesy of Thomas Hakala, partner of KPMG Peat Marwick in New York City.

Rate U.S. Government (1-800-541-8832) with a 7.02% yield.

YOUR HOME AS A TAX SHELTER

Once you own a home, you can use it to shelter taxes.

First, you can postpone gains made on the sale of your principal residence as long as you buy another that costs at least as much as the one you sold within 2 years of the sale date. If your new home costs less, you must pay taxes on the lesser of either the house sale profits or the difference between the prices of the old and new homes.

Second, you can continue to defer these taxes, provided you do not move more frequently than once every 2 years, unless the move is job related.

Third, when you reach age 55, you can take advantage of a special one-time tax break: a $125,000 capital gains exemption from your taxes. You must have lived in the home for 3 out of the past 5 years, unless you've been living in a nursing home. In that case, you must have lived at home for just one of the previous 5 years to escape tax on a sale. You can claim the $125,000 exclusion only once, and a married couple cannot claim the break when one spouse has already used his or her exclusion before the marriage. However, only one spouse must be over 55 to claim the exclusion on a jointly held home. When the home is not jointly owned, the spouse whose name is on the deed must be over 55 at the time of sale.

To make certain you whittle down the size of any eventual tax bill, keep good records. When your home is sold at a profit, the difference between the net sale price and the seller's "basis" in the property is the amount that is subject to tax. The basis is calculated as the price paid for the property plus closing costs, such as title insurance, incurred in making the purchase. Add to this expenses for capital improvements made over the years, but subtract any depreciation or casualty losses claimed. A capital improvement is anything that adds to the value of the property, for example, replacing a roof, fences, gates, central air conditioning, or

a burglar alarm. Painting and repairs are maintenance expenses, however, and do not increase the owner's basis in the property. So keep canceled checks, copies of invoices relating to capital improvements, and notices of co-op apartment assessments.

$HINT: Call the IRS at 1-800-TAX-FORM to get a copy of Publication 523, *Tax Information On Selling Your Home.*

HOME EQUITY LOANS

Interest on up to $100,000 of a home equity loan or a home equity line of credit is fully deductible as long as the loan is secured by your principal home or a second home that you own.

The elimination of deductibility of personal interest (on credit card loans, for example) has added to the appeal of home equity loans. And because this type of loan is secured by your home, interest rates are often lower than those charged on other borrowing.

$HINT: Call the IRS at 1-800-TAX-FORM to get a copy of Publication 963, *Home Mortgage Interest Deduction.*

Home equity lines of credit—basically a repackaging of a second mortgage loan—have grown in popularity since the 1986 Tax Reform Act was passed. Because the deductibility of interest on most consumer loans has been eliminated and because interest paid on debt secured by your personal residence is deductible, banks are promoting these "credit line" types of loans to pay for big-ticket items such as cars, college education, and vacations.

☐CAUTION: Use a home equity line of credit only if necessary. Your home could be repossessed if you fail to make payments.

With a home equity line of credit, the bank allows borrowers to apply for a loan, pay closing costs just once, and then borrow money as needed. You can usually borrow up to 80% of the home's appraised value minus any existing mortgages. Interest is higher than on first loans, but it is assessed only on money you actually draw. Fees and closing costs tend to be low because of lender competition.

$HINT: Interest rates are usually tied to prime, so look for a loan with an interest rate cap.

GETTING RENTAL INCOME

Rental property, whether it's a condo in Florida, a ski house in Montana, or a center-hall colonial in the suburbs, if purchased after January 1, 1987, does not fare as well as before. It must be depreciated over a much longer period of time. The write-off period, formerly 19 years on residential property, has been stretched out to 27½ years (31½ years for commercial property). In the past, as a landlord, you could deduct the total value of your investment over 19 years, writing off greater amounts in the first years, but now you must take deductions in equal amounts each year over 27½ years. *Note:* Depreciation can only be taken on the cost of the buildings, not on the underlying land.

If property produces rent, the income or losses generated are considered "passive," which means you cannot offset salary or investment income with these rental losses, with one exception: If your adjusted gross income is under $100,000 ($50,000 for married couples filing separately), the tax law allows you to write off up to $25,000 a year in rental property tax losses against other income, including your salary—*provided you actively manage the property.* This special $25,000 allowance is phased out as you become wealthier; if your adjusted gross income exceeds $150,000 ($75,000 for married couples filing separately), there is no such break.

§ HINT: Recalculate the return you receive on any property. If your property generates a loss *and* your income is less than $150,000, make certain you satisfy the IRS requirement of being an "active" participant in order to get the loss allowance.

DEDUCTIONS YOU MAY TAKE ON
RENTAL PROPERTY

- Maintenance   - Utility bills
- Depreciation   - Insurance
- Repairs

To be considered an active manager, you must own 10% of the property involved as well as make decisions on repairs, rents, and tenants. If you hire a manager but provide guidance, you will still be considered active provided you can document your involvement to the IRS.

In considering rental property, keep in mind that the restrictions for deducting losses mean you must invest in property that produces a positive cash flow; that is, rents must be greater than costs.

If you make more than $150,000 annually, you can still reap some benefits, because the changes pertain to tax reporting, not to your cash flow. This means that if your rental income covers mortgage payments, the only plus you've lost is the tax shelter aspect. In the meantime, keep a running account of your losses and apply them when you eventually sell the property or to offset passive income from limited partnerships or other rental income.

VACATION HOMES FOR PROFIT

If you do not rent out your vacation home, you can deduct interest on your mortgage up to the original purchase price plus the cost of improvements.

Your vacation home is considered a "residence" *if you use it personally for more than 14 days a year or more than 10% of the time you rent it out* (at a fair market rate), whichever is greater. Time that you spend on repairs and upkeep does not count toward personal or rental use. Deductions for rental expenses on a "residence" are for the most part limited to the income received. The IRS formula is precise; check with your accountant.

§ HINT: If you rent out for no more than 14 days a year, the income is tax-free and you are not even required to report it, but the expenses, other than property taxes and interest, are not deductible.

If you rent out more than 14 days or 10% of the time, the house is classified as rental (not residential) property. If the property was placed in service prior to January 1, 1987, you can still use the 19-year accelerated depreciation schedule, which allows larger deductions in

SEAFARING LOOPHOLE

Although tax reform eliminated interest deductions on most consumer credit loans, yacht owners and houseboat dwellers got a break. If your boat qualifies as a personal residence by having a head, galley, and sleeping facilities, you can probably deduct interest on any loan you take out to buy the floating home. Have your accountant check Code section 163(h) 5(A) (i) II, which governs interest deductions for qualified residences.

WHERE TO FIND BARGAINS IN RENTAL REAL ESTATE

- Someone desperate to sell—who has already moved, is being transferred, or has purchased another piece of property.
- An REO (real estate owned), also known as a foreclosure. Local bankers maintain listings. Prices are often well below market.
- Estate liquidations and family breakups.
- Distressed properties sold through sheriff's sales, IRS seizures for back taxes, and other forced sales.
- Discounted mortgages. These are existing loans sold by the lender for less than the balance owed. Check with real estate brokers, or place an ad in the newspaper. Review state foreclosure laws carefully.

early years. Otherwise, you must use the 27½-year depreciation schedule. Rental expenses cannot be used to offset regular income since they are considered passive losses. Under the 1986 law, these expenses can be deducted only from passive income from other rental properties or from limited partnerships and *not* from your wages, salary, or portfolio income. *Note:* There is an exception for those whose adjusted gross income is $150,000 or less, as explained earlier.

§ HINT: If your income is too high to benefit from the $25,000 active rental allowance, you may be better off converting a "rental" vacation home into a "residential" property and writing off the full amount of the mortgage interest.

TIME-SHARES

Time-sharing, which combines vacationing with a very small degree of investing, should be viewed cautiously if not with complete skepticism. When you buy a time-share, you purchase the right to use a studio, apartment, or house in a vacation complex year after year. Time-shares are usually 1- to 4-week periods. For example, you may purchase a 2-week time slot in Aspen for a fixed period, say the first 2 weeks in January, or for a floating period that changes from year to year.

The primary advantage is cost. It's an affordable way to vacation—1 week can range from $2,000 to $25,000+ depending on the location, season, and facilities. There is often an

annual maintenance fee as well. You pay only for the days you use your space, and in most situations you can sublet if you are unable to occupy your time-share. The interest on your mortgage is tax-deductible.

Many time-share investors have been disappointed that their property did not escalate in value as much as traditional real estate. The resale potential of time-shares depends on their location, how well they're managed, and the market.

The concept of time-sharing is less popular today than when it first came to the public's attention more than 20 years ago. Since then it has suffered as a result of industry mismanagement and a period when dishonest operators were more common than they are now. Federal and state regulations now protect the investor, so it is possible that time-sharing will regain some popularity. However, with the widespread trend toward co-ops and condos, this remains a less than timely investment.

☐ CAUTION: Buy a time-share for vacationing, not primarily as an investment.

THE MORTGAGE MAZE

One thing that has not changed over the years is the fact that getting a mortgage is one of the largest financial commitments most people make. To help get through the mortgage maze, review these most popular types.

➤ FIXED-RATE MORTGAGE The old standby, the 30-year fixed-rate mortgage, remains the most popular type of real estate loan. Interest rate and monthly payments are fixed for the life of the loan, which protects buyers from increased monthly payments when interest rates rise. On the other hand, when rates drop, it often pays to refinance this type of mortgage in order to get lower monthly payments.

$ HINT: Shop carefully for a fixed-rate mortgage, because even a small rate difference affects your monthly payments.

This mortgage is generally considered a good choice for those planning to remain in their houses a number of years. The borrower knows what the payments will be, and equity builds up steadily over time.

A variation on this theme is the *15-year fixed-rate mortgage.* The good news here is that the debt is paid off in half the time it would be with a 30-year mortgage, and the total interest cost of the loan is lower. The bad news: Monthly payments are higher. On a $100,000 loan, for instance, the monthly payment would be $1,106 on a 15-year mortgage at 10.5% versus $953 on an 11%, 30-year loan. The major advantage of a 15-year mortgage is that you build equity faster and save on interest costs. This makes it a logical choice for those near retirement who want to be free of mortgage payments and/or those with sufficient disposable income to handle higher monthly payments.

➤ BIWEEKLY MORTGAGE This is another way to build equity more quickly and reduce interest costs. Instead of paying down your mortgage on a monthly basis, you do so every 2 weeks. The biweekly payments are half of what a monthly payment would be, but there's the equivalent of one more monthly payment per year. In other words, 26 biweekly payments equal 13 monthly payments. Most lenders require that biweekly payments be automatically deducted from your bank account.

➤ ADJUSTABLE-RATE MORTGAGES Called ARMs for short, this mortgage generally offers lower initial rates than fixed-rate home loans, but the interest rate and the monthly payment are adjusted periodically according to terms specified by the lender. Most peg the rate to an index

---

HOW TO AVOID DROWNING IN A MORTGAGE

1 *Shop around.* Call several banks and mortgage companies and find out what they are offering. Compare details carefully. Don't rely only on your real estate broker's recommendation.

2 *Do your math.* You must figure out the exact amount you will pay each month for each type of mortgage. When doing the numbers for ARMs, assume interest rates will rise the maximum.

3 *Look for hidden traps.* Read the mortgage document before signing on. Among the traps to look for in the fine print: a bank that requires permission for borrowers to obtain a second mortgage or a home equity line of credit; a clause requiring you to sell your old house before the bank will let you close on a new one; any add-on charges and fees.

4 *Make extra payments.* Assume a mortgage only if it lets you make payments above the stated required amount. This reduces the length of your mortgage and will save you thousands of dollars in interest, since the prepaid amount is applied to the principal.

---

based on short-term Treasury bill rates. Many ARMs are adjusted annually, semiannually, or once every 3 years over a 5-year period, and thereafter remain fixed. With others, the rate remains fixed for one or more years and then is adjusted annually. In most cases, the increase in interest is capped and cannot be adjusted by more than 2 points over the life of the loan. Some ARMs have a conversion feature allowing borrowers to convert (for a fee) to a fixed-rate mortgage, usually between the second and fifth year.

$ HINT: ARMs are particularly well suited to young people who anticipate growth in income and those who do not plan to stay in the same home for more than a few years.

➤ SEVEN-YEAR TWO-STEP It may sound like a dance, but it's a mortgage with fixed monthly payments for the first 7 years at a rate ¼ to ½ a percentage point less than those on a 30-year fixed. After 7 years, the rate is adjusted to market level.

§HINT: This mortgage is suggested for buyers who are fairly confident they will be moving.

TIPS ON MORTGAGES

While the purpose of this chapter is to discuss real estate as an investment, a key part of successful investing is leverage—that is, your mortgage. For current rates and information, keep up to date by reading the popular press and talking to bank loan officers. To help you make informed decisions, consult these sources.

➤ FINDING A MORTGAGE
HSH Associates
1200 Route 23
Butler, NJ 07405
1-800-UPDATES

This group operates a mortgage hotline (1-201-838-8197), which lists the national average rates on a variety of mortgages. For $18 to $20 HSH will send you a listing of mortgage rates in your area plus a planning kit. HSH covers 50 metropolitan areas.

➤ REFINANCING Tables to determine if you should refinance or pay off your mortgage early appear in *Consumer's Guide to Refinancing Your Mortgage.*

Mortgage Bankers Association of America
1125 15th Street NW, 5th Fl.
Washington, DC 20005
1-202-861-6500

➤ PREPAYMENT Design your own mortgage prepayment plan with *The Banker's Secret.* The book ($14.95 plus $3 handling) or book software package ($39.95 plus $3 handling) is available from:

Good Advice Press
Post Office Box 78
Elizaville, NY 12523
1-914-758-1400; 1-800-255-0899

➤ ADJUSTABLE-RATE MORTGAGES For a copy of *Introducing a New ARM for Today's Homeowner,* contact:

Public Information
Federal Home Loan Bank Board
3900 Wisconsin Avenue NW
Washington, DC 20016
1-202-752-7124

➤ VACANT LOTS Know your legal rights and avoid problems by reading the Department of Housing and Urban Development's brochure *Buying Lots from Developers.*

HUD
Program Information
451 7th Street SW
Washington, DC 20410
1-202-708-1420
Free

☐CAUTION: Make certain that any "points" you pay in connection with your mortgage are for interest (1 point equals 1% of the loan amount). As long as you pay points up front, with a separate check, they are tax-deductible in the year you buy the property. Points that are really origination fees are not deductible until you sell your property for a profit. Points paid for refinancing a mortgage are not deductible in full in the year they were paid. They must be deducted over the term of the mortgage. This is particularly important now, because lenders are sending reports to the IRS.

SWAPPING PROPERTY

The 1986 tax law gave a boost to a rather obscure yet legal technique that allows real estate investors (in theory) to sell one piece of investment property and buy another while deferring capital gains taxes. In fact, you can swap any number of times and not pay taxes until you actually sell for cash. The exchange must be completed within 180 days.

§HINT: Discipline yourself to invest the money that would have gone to pay the capital gains tax.

To qualify for this tax deferral you must:
- Exchange like pieces of property.
- Use the property for business or hold it as

an investment; your home does not qualify, nor does an interest in a real estate limited partnership.

If the two pieces of property involved in a swap are not of equal monetary value, cash or an additional piece of property is used to make up the difference. *Note:* The cash or extra property is a taxable transaction.

HOW TO REDUCE YOUR PROPERTY TAXES

Experts estimate that 60% of all homeowners pay too much property tax. Take time to study your taxes and if you suspect you're being overcharged, file a challenge.

➤ THE MOST COMMON MISTAKES Errors in paperwork and/or math are widespread. So go in person to the tax assessor's office and ask to see the worksheet used when your property was evaluated. You have a legal right to examine this document. Check for:

1   *Typographical errors.* The assessment amount on the worksheet should match the assessment on the tax bill.
2   *Measurements.* Dimensions and square footage should be accurate.

After checking out the figures, look at how your property was evaluated. The assessed value of property, adjusted by the local tax assessment office, is almost always lower than the market value. To find out if you are being overassessed, ask what the *adjusted* assessment value is plus what *multiplier* was used to make the adjust-

ment. For instance, if your tax bill shows an assessed value of $100,000 and the multiplier is 2, then your home is really assessed at $200,000. If you believe your home is worth less than $200,000, challenge the assessment by following these steps:

1   Find out the assessed values of comparable property in your neighborhood. This is public information.
2   Get the actual selling prices of similar homes in the"Recorder of Public Deeds" office at your town hall.
3   Find copies of any existing professional appraisals of your property. (Your bank is likely to have this document.)
4   Get a new appraisal to document the fact that the value of your home is lower than its appraised value.

Present these facts to the assessor. If your appeal is denied, you can present your case to a board of review for an impartial opinion. Ask the assessor for an appeal form and the filing deadline.

FOR FURTHER INFORMATION

National Timeshare Council
1220 L Street NW, 5th floor
Washington, DC 20005
1-202-371-6700

Julian Block, *The Homeowner's Tax Guide* (Runzheimer International, 1992).

FAMILY FINANCES

THE HIGH COST OF CHILDREN

For many people, nothing is ever as exciting as having a baby—or as expensive. It's certainly one of life's most costly endeavors. Depending on where you live and how extravagant you want to be, raising a child from birth to age 18 can set you back anywhere from $47,000 to $120,000. And, if you want to indulge your son or daughter, add on another $50,000. That's before college bills. So there's no question that having a baby will drastically change your financial life.

The best way to enjoy parenthood is to have enough money to care for your child, to maintain the life-style you and your spouse had before baby made three, and to minimize as many financial sacrifices as possible. The biggest sacrifice for most couples is the loss of the mother's income, since the majority of women take 3 to 6 months off for the first child. Yet, armed with a sensible financial plan, you can minimize the dollar drain and fully enjoy the newest member of your family.

➤ PRENATAL TO AGE 2 As soon as you know you'll be having a baby, both you and your spouse should find out what your respective firms offer in terms of maternity leave, including possible benefits for the father. Then check your health coverage. Whether you have a private policy or one sponsored by your firm, determine precisely what medical costs for the first 2 years are covered.

$ HINT: Borrow maternity and baby clothes as well as equipment from friends, or buy from second-hand shops, discount stores, and outlets. And don't be shy: Encourage baby showers. Your family and friends may pitch in and purchase some of the

big-ticket items for you. Use family members to baby-sit or join a baby-sitting cooperative and share the task with other parents.

Build up your savings as soon as you know you'll be having a baby. Stash all or part of one salary in a money market fund and practice living on one salary, which will be the case when the baby arrives.

If you already have a nest egg, divide it into two categories: Put half into a money market fund so you can draw on it to pay immediate bills when the baby is born, and put the remainder into a revolving certificate of deposit program, purchasing CDs with staggered maturity dates. Save all cash gifts the baby receives. You'll need to get the baby a Social Security number to put them in his or her name.

➤ AGES 2 TO 5 Now that the start-up costs of having a baby have been absorbed, use these

SAVINGS BONDS PAY FOR COLLEGE

The earlier you start saving, the more you will have when your child is ready for college.

CHILD'S AGE	VALUE AT AGE 18, BASED ON MONTHLY DEPOSITS OF:	
	$50	$100
1	$17,356.08	$34,712.16
6	10,328.96	20,657.92
10	6,025.72	12,051.44
12	4,226.88	8,453.76

Assumes an annual interest rate of 6%, the current minimum rate on bonds held 5 years.

SOURCE: U.S. Treasury.

years to replace or add to your savings, especially if you plan to move to a larger home. If you have not done so, you and your spouse should try to put at least 3% to 5% of your take-home pay in safe investments, such as Treasuries. You'll also need this money if you have a second child. Make certain you have adequate life and disability insurance to provide for your child, up to and through college. Finally, make out your wills and name guardians for the baby.

➤ ELEMENTARY SCHOOL YEARS When your child reaches age 6, you have approximately 12 years left in which to save money for college. Begin immediately adding to the college fund established when he or she was born. An early start will pay off. For example, a zero coupon Treasury that matures in 18 years can be purchased for approximately $150. When it comes due you will receive $1,000.

➤ JUNIOR AND SENIOR HIGH SCHOOL Encourage your child to earn his or her own money. Do not pay for everything. Instead, teach your child how to save and pay for certain items. And remember, children learn by what they see regularly—make sure you are not living off credit and neglecting to save while encouraging your child to do so. Start to investigate financial aid for college by ordering a free copy of "Planning for College" from the Investment Company Institute, 1600 M Street NW, Washington, DC 20036.

PAYING FOR COLLEGE

Most children have plenty of toys, clothes, bikes, and even cars, but very few have a nest egg to pay for one of life's biggest expenses: a college degree. It takes more than good grades to get through school: During the 1980s, the average cost of attending college doubled, with tuition, room and board, and books increasing almost 10% a year. And there's no sign that it will slow down.

Early planning certainly eases the pain, as the time value of money works to everyone's advantage. For instance, if parents want to accumulate $35,000 by the time their child reaches age 18, based on a fixed interest rate of 9%, compounded monthly, they must save $73.08 per month, if the child is now 1 year old. If they wait until the child is 14, that figure jumps to $608.48 a month.

Yet the picture's not all that hopeless. There are a number of ways to stockpile money and find financial aid. Here's what parents and grandparents can do to meet college costs.

➤ STEP ONE Know who should own the nest egg. Money earmarked for college can be held in an adult's name, in the child's name, or in trust with the child named as beneficiary. Putting the money in the adult's name is, of course, the easiest, and it gives the adult complete control over the money and how it is used. It's also advantageous when it comes to seeking financial help: Most financial aid formulas require the student to contribute 35% of his or her assets to college costs annually, while parents are expected to contribute far less, usually only 5%.

☐CAUTION: All the income and capital gains in the account are taxed at the parent's rate, which is almost always higher than the child's rate.

Money can also be transferred to the child through the Uniform Gifts to Minors Act (UGMA), adopted in almost all states, and the Uniform Transfers to Minors Act (UTMA), available in over 30 states. The key difference between them is the type of property an adult can transfer to a child. UTMA allows any kind of property—real estate, personal property, securities, cash—to be given as a custodial gift, whereas UGMA restricts custodial gifts to bank deposits, securities (including mutual funds), and insurance policies.

Both are simple to set up and administer. Almost any bank, mutual fund company, stockbroker, or attorney can do so. The custodian, who can be a parent or someone else named by the person funding the trust, controls the money until the child becomes of legal age (18 or 21, depending on the state). The custodian can invest, manage, or even dispose of the gifted property on the minor's behalf.

☐CAUTION: At age 18 or 21, the money must be turned over to the child, who can then use it any way at all—to buy a car, join the circus, or, ideally, pay for college.

There are other types of tax-advantaged trusts for sizable amounts of money that an accountant or attorney can explain.

➤ STEP TWO Understand the tax law. The so-called kiddie tax seriously affects college nest eggs. Study the box below and talk to an accountant or tax lawyer before deciding who should hold the assets for college. For example, if the child is under age 14, it's advantageous to put the money in the child's name only as long as the income it earns does *not* exceed the annual $1,000 income cap.

➤ STEP THREE Consider gifts. A parent, grandparent, or anyone else can give a child up to $10,000 a year without paying gift taxes. If parents or grandparents have sizable estates that they plan to leave to the family, such a gift reduces future estate taxes. Grandparents can also make cash gifts in any amount and pay no gift tax *as long as* the gift goes for tuition and is paid directly to the college. And a grandparent can give an additional $10,000 free of gift tax to pay for room and board.

➤ STEP FOUR Set up a savings plan. Save a certain amount every month. Parents who find this difficult or who lack the discipline to do so on their own can establish an automatic payroll-deduction plan at work so that a set amount is taken out of paychecks on a regular basis and is used to purchase EE savings bonds or is transferred to a high-yielding money market fund. Both are low in risk. The current yield on money market funds is around 5.58% and is effective through October 31, 1992. EE bonds pay a guaranteed minimum rate of 6% if held at least 5 years. After that the rate is adjusted every 6 months. Although the interest on these bonds has always been exempt from state and local taxes, it's now exempt from federal taxes if the bonds are purchased after January 1, 1990, and are used to pay college tuition. However, the parents' total income must fall below a certain dollar amount when the bonds are cashed in. This income cap is adjusted annually for inflation. Bonds purchased in this tax-free education plan cannot be held in the child's name.

$HINT: For details, send 50¢ for *U.S. Savings Bonds: Now Tax-Free for Education*, #449Y, to: Consumer Information Center, Pueblo, CO 81002.

➤ STEP FIVE Consider other investments. Certain investments are particularly suited for a college nest egg because they grow in value over time. One of the most popular is zero coupon bonds, described on page 149. Growth stocks and mutual funds are suitable for long-term investments. Conservative choices include certificates of deposit and Treasury bonds and notes. Deferred

annuities can be purchased so that they start paying out income when tuition bills come due. An added advantage: Earnings inside an annuity grow tax-deferred until the money is paid out.

➤ STEP SIX Look into baccalaureate bonds. A growing number of states offer special municipal zero coupon bonds to help parents. They are sold at a discount from face value and do not pay interest until they mature. At that time, the bondholders receive the principal plus earned interest in one lump sum. Their great advantage: Parents know exactly how much money is coming due on a certain date. Some states even pay a cash bonus when the bonds mature if the child attends a state college. These bonds are exempt from federal taxes and, for state residents, from state and local taxes. Call your stockbroker or your state's treasury department for current details.

➤ STEP SEVEN Investigate special college deals. Tuition prepayment plans allow parents to pay a flat one-time dollar amount that is guaranteed to cover the cost of schooling later on. These plans eliminate the risk that inflation will boost tuition bills out of sight.

$HINT: Before signing up, ask the following questions: Can the money be transferred to another member of the family? What does the plan cover—tuition only, or other costs? Is the plan insured or guaranteed? Is there an on-campus residency requirement? Is the money available in an emergency? What if the child elects to go to another school?

Many schools will also arrange for bills to be paid on an installment basis, typically with monthly payments over a 10-month period, for a nominal fee.

➤ STEP EIGHT Apply for financial aid. Although it's tough to get, some financial aid is available, even to middle-income families. When visiting college campuses or writing for catalogs, ask each school about its financial aid packages. A statement of the family's financial resources must be submitted along with the application.

☐CAUTION: Keep in mind that shifting money into a child's name may jeopardize aid.

Many people assume incorrectly that they won't qualify for financial aid. The three most common misconceptions are: (1) The money I've saved in my retirement account will count against my child's chances of getting aid. *Wrong:*

Money from 401(k)s, IRAs, and Keoghs is *not* counted in the formula for determining aid. (2) If one child was rejected, the other will be too. *Wrong:* Families with more than one child in school often have a better chance than those with just one in college. (3) Older people returning to college or those who are going for the first time aren't financial aid candidates. *Wrong:* Older students are just as eligible as traditionally aged students.

➤ STEP NINE Borrow if you have to. Meeting the staggering costs may mean borrowing. Check these three relatively low-cost sources first: (1) Many companies allow employees to borrow from their 401(k) retirement plans to pay college bills. The major advantage: Interest payments are made into the account, not to a bank. (2) Borrow against a universal life insurance policy. Policyholders pay premiums to the company, which are then invested in an account where they grow tax-deferred. When it's time to pay tuition, policyholders can withdraw the cash balance or borrow against it. Loan rates are almost always lower than bank rates. (3) Home equity loans offer a tax break in that the interest is tax deductible.

$ HINT: For a free brochure on using home equity loans, send a stamped, self-addressed envelope to: Home Equity, Public Relations Dept., Credit Union National Association, Inc., Box 431, Madison, WI 53701.

PLUS (Parent Loan for Undergraduate Students) loans do not require parents to show financial need, although they must have a good credit history. These loans are made by private financial institutions, not the government. Other similar loans are available. The college financial aid office will give you information on them.

➤ STEP TEN Have the student help out. Encourage children to shoulder some of the expenses by saving money from jobs or working part time. Another cost-cutting choice: Attend a school that offers a work-study program in which students alternate working and attending classes, so they earn money as they go along. Among the leading such schools are Drexel in Philadelphia, the University of Detroit, and Northeastern University in Boston. Students can also commute and eliminate the cost of room and board, or attend a community college for the first two years, where the tuition is much lower than at

a four-year school. Military schools supported by the government, such as West Point, Annapolis, or the Air Force Academy, provide free education if, in return, the student pledges a certain number of years of military service. These schools are difficult to get into, but most other colleges and universities offer ROTC, which is open to all and covers most school expenses.

FOR FURTHER INFORMATION

- *How to Pay for Your Children's College* and *The College Guide for Parents* are available, along with other publications on financial planning, from: The College Board, 1-212-713-8150.
- *Don't Miss Out; The Ambitious Student's Guide to Financial Aid* (Alexandria, VA: Octameron Press, 1993–94).
- *Paying for College: A Step by Step College Planning Guide,* is free from T. Rowe Price, 1-800-638-5660.

BOOMERANG KIDS OR ADULT CHILDREN COME HOME

Your child may wend his or her way back home after college, bringing the stereo, posters, and a pile of dirty clothes. He or she may plan to stay just for the summer or longer—until landing an apartment, a job, a spouse, or all three. Or your child may have no plan at all. You face a philosophical decision about money at this point: Should you be an indulgent parent and provide free housing, a car, spending money, a lavish

---

HOW A CHILD'S MONEY IS TAXED

IF THE CHILD IS:	THEN
Under age 14	The first $500 of income is tax-free; $501 to $1,000 of income is taxed at the child's tax rate, usually 15%
Age 14 or older	All income is taxed at the child's rate

wardrobe? Even though you say it's because you're a loving parent, such moves actually encourage dependence and continue to keep your son or daughter in the role of child. Alternatively, you can treat the stay as you would that of any other adult boarder: charging room and board, drawing up a simple contract, and encouraging adult behavior and self-reliance.

Check insurance coverage for adult children living at home:

- *Medical.* If the plan where you work does not include grown dependents, then your child will need individual coverage, unless he or she is working and is covered there.
- *Automobile.* Drivers under age 25 typically add to the premium costs of family vehicles.
- *Personal liability.* You may want to take out an umbrella policy that will supplement your coverage for accidents around the house as well as in the family car.

From time to time, even when the nest is empty, you may receive requests for additional financial help—for graduate school, a downpayment on a car or house, or a wedding. If your child has a trust fund or a secure job, encourage the child to use his or her own money, perhaps with some help from you. If you're in a quandary about how much to help, set dollar and time limits and divide the responsibility. You may want to make a no- or low-interest loan. At this point, you must also think about your own financial needs, about saving for retirement or to help your elderly parents if they need it. Although you want to be supportive, emotionally and financially, you also want to encourage self-reliance—what you set out to do when you taught your toddler how to cross the street and tie shoelaces.

These judgment calls are not easy to make; they are filled with emotion. It's particularly hard to say no to your own children. But keep in mind that setting limits is sensible and reasonable, for both of you. Regardless of the choice you make, when you make a loan you should get a written IOU spelling out the amount of the loan, interest, and terms of repayment.

$ HINT: If you need additional advice, read *Boomerang Kids: How to Live with Children Who Return Home*, by Jean Okimoto and Phyllis Steggal (Boston: Little, Brown and Co., 1987).

TRADING PLACES: HELPING YOUR PARENTS

When age or a serious illness hits one's parents, children must often step in and help out. But as in anything financial, the results will be far superior if some planning takes place before a crisis hits. Your parents have three sources of support: their own assets, help from their children or other relatives, and the government. Here's what you can do to make certain all three are fully used.

First, talk. While your parents are still fit, discuss their plans for the future. If you need help breaking the ice, refer to the pamphlet *Tomorrow's Choices: Preparing Now for Legal, Financial and Health Care Decisions* available free from the American Association of Retired Persons, AARP Fulfillment, 601 E Street NW, Washington, DC 20049. Hold any discussions on parent's turf or a neutral place, such as a lawyer's office. Among the topics to cover:

- *Assets and liabilities* Ask parents to make a complete list of bank accounts, stocks, bonds, mutual funds, CDs, life insurance policies, safe deposit boxes, real estate, and other holdings. Debts should be listed as well.
- *Income* Review sources of income: Social Security, investments, pensions. Is it enough?
- *Wills* Each parent should have a separate will and all wills should have been updated since the 1986 Tax Reform Act, following relocation to a new state, a death, divorce, or birth in the family.
- *Important papers* Where are documents stored? Who has the key to the safe deposit box? Get names and telephone numbers of attorney, accountant, stockbroker, insurance agent, financial planner, and clergy. Is there a burial plot? Where is the deed?
- *Insurance* Determine whether parents are adequately insured or overinsured. Parents 65 or older are eligible to enroll in Medicare, a federal health insurance program. Still, supplemental insurance may be required to fill in the gaps. For an explanation of benefits and exclusions under the Medicare program, ask your doctor for a copy of *Medicare: What It*

Will and Will Not Pay For, published by the American Society of Internal Medicine; or call the association at 1-202-289-1700.

- *Housing* Be prepared to help your parents move to a new, smaller home, a retirement community, or perhaps even a nursing home. Read *Choosing a Nursing Home: A Guide to Quality Care,* free with a self-addressed, stamped envelope from the American Association of Homes for the Aging, 901 E Street NW, Washington, DC 20004; (see also Chapter 28).

- *Incapacity* If no provisions are made for physical or mental incapacity, the court can declare parents incompetent and appoint a guardian or conservator. So get a lawyer to draw up one or more durable powers of attorney to ensure that a person the parents trust will manage their financial and medical welfare if they cannot. Parents can confer the power on each other and also name, as successor, one of their children. The powers can be broad or narrow: The appointed individual can manage all finances, for instance, or merely have checkwriting privileges. A medical durable power of attorney enables an appointed trustee to make health care decisions on the parents' behalf.

Short of getting power of attorney, a joint checking account, usually with a spouse or child, can provide funds for an incapacitated individual.

Discuss drawing up a living will that specifies medical measures to be taken or not taken in case of terminal illness.

Consult a knowledgeable attorney regarding joint ownership of property and various types of trusts. A revocable living trust, for example, in which a parent is the trustee but makes provisions for a successor trustee, provides money management in case the parent becomes mentally or physically disabled.

PROVIDING FINANCIAL HELP

Review these suggestions with a lawyer familiar with estate planning.

- *Hire parents* Children who own a business can hire parents to work on a part- or full-time basis. This is a good way to provide fit parents with income while receiving tax benefits.

- *Make tax-free gifts* Anyone can give as much as $10,000 ($20,000 if given jointly with a spouse) without incurring a gift tax. If parents don't want to accept a gift, try making a loan instead. The money can eventually be repaid from the estate or sale of their home.

- *Increase investment income* Money in low-yielding bank accounts or CDs should be transferred to higher yielding money market funds.

- *Tap equity in their home* (see page 272) One final note—you are not alone. Thousands of children face similar situations. Children of Aging Parents, Woodbourne Office Campus, 1602 Woodbourne Rd., Suite 302A, Levittown, PA 19057 will put you in touch with a support group in your area. Membership is $15 a year, or send $2 and a SASE. Call: 1-215-945-6900.

GOING BACK TO SCHOOL

Some say that youth is wasted on the young. The same might be said about a college education, which is one reason why so many adults return to school with enthusiasm, absorbing new information and skills. If you're planning to return to college or professional school, be prepared for the fact that tuition is probably higher than when you last sat in a classroom. And, keep in mind that raising money takes time; start as early as possible. Here are some tips for funding your schooling:

- Ask the school you're applying to about special tuition deals. Many state institutions reduce tuition for nontraditional and/or adult students.

- As soon as you're accepted into a program, contact the school's financial aid officer. This person typically knows the most about sources of money.

- Many states have loan programs for students pursuing careers as teachers, with "forgiveness" features for those who wind up in the classroom, as well as incentives for professionals the state needs—usually medicine, nursing, and special and bilingual education. Write to the appropriate state department of higher education. For addresses see: *Need a Lift? Educational Opportunities, Careers, Loans, Scholarships, Employment,* $2 from the American Legion, Box 1050, Indianapolis, IN 46206.

- *Perkins Loans* are available for both undergraduates and graduate students. They are distributed by the school's financial aid office.
- *Stafford Student Loans* are federally guaranteed student loans made by banks, S&Ls, and credit unions. Interest rates are 8% for the first four years, 10% thereafter. Get a loan application from a lender and send it to the college.
- *Supplemental loans.* Banks provide federally guaranteed loans of up to $4,000 per academic year to students who are not dependents. Obtain application from banks.

$HINT: For quick information about loans and procedures, call 1-800-4-FEDAID; for information about other public student loans, call the Student Loan Marketing Association at 1-800-831-5626.

- *Private loans,* unlike public funds, do not carry income limits or have needs tests provisions. Approval is based on the credit-worthiness of the applicant or, if necessary, on the participation of a

reliable cosigner. The three leading sources are:

- *Nellie Mae loans.* New England Education Loan Marketing Corp.; 1-800-634-9308.
- *PLATO.* Personal Loans for Accredited Teaching Organizations; 1-800-767-5626.
- *TERI.* The Education Resource Institute; 1-800-255-8374.

Also consult: *Directory of Financial Aids for Women* by Gail Schlachter, Reference Service Press, San Carlos, CA; 1-415-594-0743; and *Don't Miss Out: The Ambitious Student's Guide to Financial Aid* by Robert and Anna Leider (Octameron Press, Box 2748, Alexandria, VA 22301).

Those who are working or home with children will find "Weekend Colleges" designed to meet their needs. Classes are held on Friday evenings, Saturdays, and Sundays, depending upon the school. Some, like Trinity College in Washington, DC, provide on-campus babysitting and rent dorm rooms for only $15/night. Others, like The College of St. Catherine in St. Paul, MN, allow adult students to pay tuition using their Visa or MasterCard and spread out the bills over three payment periods—for which there is a small interest charge.

$HINT: Read IRS Publication #508, *Educational Expenses* to learn what expenses qualify as income tax deductions.

29 RETIREMENT LIVING

As retirement draws near, most people begin to reevaluate their housing needs. So should you, if you haven't already done so. The house you bought 20, 30, or 40 years ago may indeed be your most valuable asset, one that you can put to active use to provide income and security as well as shelter.

TO MOVE OR NOT TO MOVE

Your rambling three-story Victorian was probably perfect for raising a family, but now it may be empty most of the time. Perhaps you'd like to sell and move to smaller quarters, all on one floor, maybe in a warmer climate. Or you may be so attached that you don't want to move but would like to make better use of the space. Either way, you can profit from the fact that you own a valuable piece of property.

Among the investment-related alternatives to consider are:

- Selling and moving to a less expensive, smaller house or apartment
- Renting out part of your house
- Sharing your house with a friend or relative, especially if you live alone
- Remodeling to create a separate, self-contained apartment, either to live in or to rent
- Selling and moving to a retirement or planned community

If you're thinking of this last possibility, be certain that you want to live with people all the same age. If so, select a place where you have friends or can easily make new ones, where you are near work if you would like to work part-time or as a consultant, and where you have the kinds of activities you enjoy close at hand—golf, swimming, schools, etc. Adequate transportation and health facilities are also important when relocating.

If you buy into a community, select one that is accredited by the American Association of Homes for the Aging, preferably one that has a waiting list. Both are indications of a well-run establishment. Among the other points to check out before making a financial commitment are:

- Management's experience and reputation
- The corporation's balance sheet
- Potential price increases
- Restrictions on use of the property (pets, children, car space, visitors)
- Any deed restrictions

$ HINT: If you are age 55 or older, $125,000 of the proceeds of the sale of a house that is your primary residence is tax-free. This is a once-in-a-lifetime tax break.

FREEING UP THE ASSETS IN YOUR HOUSE

Here is a thumbnail sketch of techniques that can turn your house into a source of income. For more on each one, check the source list at the end of this chapter. And regardless of which path you take, consult your accountant or tax lawyer well in advance. Laws change, and state regulations vary widely.

➤ SELLING TO THE CHILDREN You can sell your house to your children and then lease it back, paying them a fair market value. This gives them the tax advantages associated with real estate as well as your rental money with which to meet their costs. You can invest the money from the sale, perhaps in an annuity or other vehicle that provides you with a steady stream of income.

➤ MOVE TO A RENTAL THAT MAY GO CO-OP OR CONDO Check the local and state laws first. In many areas, when a rental building converts to co-op or condo, tenants over a certain age can stay on forever as renters. This is known as a noneviction plan. If the rent is modest, this could be to your financial advantage.

➤ TAKE OUT A MORTGAGE ON YOUR HOME Then invest the proceeds. You can deduct the interest portion of your mortgage payments.

HINT: Be cautious about selling your home, especially to someone outside your family, and certainly if it is your only residence. Your house is immune from claims by the government, even if you or your spouse apply for Medicaid, particularly if one of you lives in it. Cash is not.

➤ GET A REVERSE MORTGAGE This is a home loan in reverse that allows you to take the equity in your home and turn it into regular monthly income without giving up your property. A reverse mortgage is designed to help elderly homeowners who are house rich but cash poor. The monthly amount is deducted with interest from the accumulated equity in the home. Each month the equity declines. The loan is paid off when the house is sold or the owner dies.

Nationally, about 150,000 home equity conversion loans have been made since they began in the early 1980s. Of these, about 10,000 have been made through private banks. Federally insured reverse mortgages are available in 41 states.

"Short-term" reverse mortgages tend to run 3 to 10 years, which can be a problem if you outlive the loan—you must repay the loan in full, refinance, or sell.

"Long-term" reverse mortgages establish payments until the owner dies or sells the house. The amount received monthly is based on the value of your home, your age, prevailing interest rates, and the percentage of future increases in the value of the house that you agree to share with the lender or bank. If, for example, you own a $100,000 house and are 65 years of age, depending upon the type of reverse mortgage you take out, your monthly check could range from $207 to $496.

CAUTION: Keep in mind that a reverse mortgage means leaving less for heirs.

Before signing any papers, have a lawyer and an accountant review all terms.

➤ CONTINUING CARE RETIREMENT COMMUNITIES If you are concerned that your parents, or you, may need nursing services but not a nursing home, consider CCRCs, a flexible, although fairly expensive, form of long-term care insurance. As of early 1992, about 250,000 people with an average age of 82 live in these communities. CCRCs offer a range of leisure activities as well as residential and nursing services.

In a typical CCRC, you do not purchase your home, but you pay a hefty entry charge plus a monthly fee. The fee covers nursing care for residents who need it. If you don't need the care, or if you move out, it is very unlikely that you will get your money back because you are *not* buying real estate as much as you are buying a service.

Examples: (call for up-to-date figures)

■ *Type A facility* provides unlimited nursing care. Median entry charge for a one-bedroom apartment is $70,529 with a monthly fee of $1,145. At the high end of the range: $195,000 to $250,000 for two bedrooms with a monthly fee of $4,100.

■ *Type B facility* provides specified level of long-term care, often 60 days a year; after that you pay $50 to $150 per day for care. Median entry charge is $50,830; monthly fee is $948.

■ *Type C facility* provides a "fee-for-service" plan with access to nursing facilities—but you pay full rate. Medicare will cover short-term care only. In some facilities, residents pay for meals. Median entry price: $41,766 plus a $766 monthly fee.

Predicting your illness or that of your parents is not easy to do. But your decision can be guided by other more "known" factors. For instance: Can you or your parents afford to pay the monthly fees for as long as the CCRC resident lives? Select a CCRC that's in sound financial shape; ask to see its audited financial statement and review it with a knowledgeable accountant. Know under what circumstances the monthly fees can rise, or if there are any refunds in the event you or your parents move or do not need long-term care. Determine what happens to the fee and the unit if one parent moves to the health center.

$ HINT: Choose a CCRC that has a seal of approval from the American Association of Homes for the Aging (AAHA). Of the 700 CCRCs in the United States, about 110 have been so accredited. For a list, send a SASE to: CCRC, 901 E Street NW, Washington, DC 20004.

➤ **IF YOU RETIRE EARLY, ARE FIRED, OR LAID OFF** In recent years a great many American corporations have eliminated thousands of blue- and white-collar jobs. No one, not even top executives, are immune to cutbacks. Those who planned to glide into retirement are cast adrift. Those on the fast track are suddenly being derailed. If you're one of the many Americans who has been "let go," you face a number of important financial decisions. Although it is beyond the scope of this book to guide you through this period in your life, the following financial tips may help make life a bit easier.

1 Make a realistic budget and stick to it. Prepare for leaner times. Cut back on luxury items, eating out, taxis, and the like.

2 Keep any severance pay in a liquid account, such as a money market fund. If you received a sizable amount, put half in a fund and half in a high yielding closed-end bond fund (see page 3 for a list).

3 If you are given the choice of taking severance in a lump sum or payments, it's generally best to opt for the lump sum and invest it so it starts earning interest. This way you won't need to worry about your ex-employer's financial condition. If it's near year-end, it may be better to schedule payments so you can defer income into the next year.

4 Do not make the common mistake of using the severance check to pay off the mortgage. You may need this money, and a mortgage is usually one of the lowest-rate loans around with interest tax deductible.

5 If you receive a large sum from your 401(k) or other retirement plan, try not to touch it. That money has never been taxed. If you take it out now, you will pay income tax on it plus a 10% penalty if you're under age 59½. In many cases,

profit sharing and stock option plans can be left with the company. However, if you suspect that your pension might be underfunded, take it with you. If you do take it with you, roll it over into an IRA within 60 days so it will continue to grow on a tax-deferred basis with no penalty. Keep this IRA money separate from any other IRAs; if you take a new job, you can roll it over into the new employer's plan.

6 Don't be too proud to take unemployment insurance if you were fired. (You cannot collect if you leave voluntarily.) You and your employer have helped fund this benefit over years; now you're certainly entitled to use it.

7 In a true emergency you may have to use some of your retirement savings.

8 Keep track of job hunting expenses; some of these may be deducted from your taxable income as "miscellaneous itemized deductions." Check with your accountant for details. Among the expenses to track are recruitment and agency fees, transportation, telephone calls, and resumé preparation.

9 Keep your health insurance. In 1986 a federal law was enacted requiring employers sponsoring group health plans to offer employees and their dependents the opportunity to extend their health coverage at group rates. This is called "continuation coverage" and it lasts for 18 months, longer if you are disabled. You will have to pay the costs, but they will be far less than taking out your own policy. If you are forced to take out your own policy, look into group rates offered by professional associations, unions, or an alumni association. If you are self-employed, look into membership in the National Association for the Self-Employed; call 1-817-589-2475 or 1-800-232-NASE.

10 Don't panic. Most problems have solutions and people willing to help you find them. Join a local group comprised of others who are out of work. There's much to be gained by sharing your situation with others. The worst thing you can do is to bury your head in the sand and hide from the reality of what has happened.

FOR FURTHER INFORMATION

For a list of reverse mortgage programs and a fact sheet, send a self-addressed, stamped envelope to the National Center for Home Equity Conversion. It also has a useful book, *Retirement Income on the House,* available at libraries or for $29.45 from the Center.

National Center for Home Equity Conversion
1210 East College Drive, Suite 300
Marshall, MN 56258
1-507-532-3230

HomeMade Money: Consumers' Guide to Home Equity Conversion
AARP Home Equity Information Center
601 E Street NW
Washington, DC 20049

American Association of Homes for the Aging
901 E Street NW
Washington, DC 20004
1-202-783-2242

Free literature plus a directory of member homes.

Continuing Care Retirement Communities
American Association of Retired Persons Resource Center
601 E Street NW
Washington, DC 20049
1-202-728-4880
Free

Discusses contacts, payment plans, and financial matters, plus how to evaluate communities

Tax Information for Older Americans
IRS Publication #554
1-800-TAX-FORM
Free

30   RETIREMENT AND PENSION PLANS

The time to start planning for a financially secure retirement is the day you receive your first paycheck, although few of us ever do. But don't agonize over the fact; just avoid further delays and start now. This chapter is not intended to be a complete retirement guide, but the information here will help you lay the financial groundwork that makes the difference between merely getting along and continuing life at full tilt.

HOW MUCH WILL YOU NEED?

Retirees are living much longer now—a person retiring in 1992 at age 60 is expected to live about another 25 years or more. This means that accumulating enough money to carry you through those years is critical. The combination of a pension and Social Security may equal only 40% to 60% of preretirement income, so the balance must come from personal savings and/or part-time work. In addition, the higher your annual earnings, the less percentage-wise may be replaced by Social Security. Inflation, too, will erode retirement funds: At 4% a year, $1,000 will be worth only $380 in 25 years.

SOCIAL SECURITY

In order to plan your retirement investments intelligently, start by taking a close look at your Social Security situation. Then build around this basic data. It may seem like a nuisance, but ignoring Social Security records could lead to lower benefits than you're legitimately entitled to, since benefits are based on the Social Security Administration's records of what you have earned. It's up to you, and not the Social Security Administration, to find out if your records are accurate. Serious errors could cost you thousands of dollars in benefits.

STEPS YOU MUST TAKE

➤ STEP 1   Request a written statement of earnings. Call the Social Security Administration, 1-800-772-1213, or visit your local office to get a copy of Form SSA-7004, "Request for Social Security Earnings and Benefit Estimate Statement." Fill it out, sign it, and mail it back. In a few weeks, you will receive a computerized statement showing all earnings credited to your account. It will give a year-by-year listing of earnings from 1983 on, with a lump-sum total for your working years.

Check the information for errors. If you suspect an error, contact your Social Security office. Provide them with copies of as much data as possible, including dates of employment, wages received, employer's name and address, copies of W-2 forms, and paycheck stubs. The most common error results from incorrect reporting by your employer, unreported name changes because of marriage, or clerical errors at the Social Security Administration.

$ HINT: If for some reason you cannot find your old W-2 forms, try to get copies from the employer you had at the time of the error. If you fail, you can get a certified copy of any tax return from the last six years for $4.25 by sending Form 4506 to the Internal Revenue Service Center where you filed your return.

In 1989, Congress virtually eliminated the three-year statute of limitations on errors, so you can now correct mistakes, even those the Administration previously refused to address.

➤ STEP 2 Request this statement periodically, especially if you have changed employers, or if you have more than one employer.

➤ STEP 3 File an application three months before you want retirement benefits to begin. You should file for disability or survivor benefits as soon as possible after disability or death occurs. Start any application by calling 1-800-772-1213. Social Security will not start sending your benefits until you file an application. Most applications can be taken by telephone. If you are late in filing an application, it's possible you may be paid only some of your benefits. Social Security seldom goes back more than 12 months, no matter how long ago you could have started receiving benefits had you filed on time.

Keep in mind these points about Social Security:

- Working spouses who pay Social Security taxes earn their own benefits.
- Nonworking spouses qualify for a retirement benefit that is equal to half what their retired spouses receive.
- You can supplement your retirement income by working, but any amount earned over $10,200 will reduce benefits for retirees aged 65 to 69; earnings above $7,440 reduce benefits for those under age 65. If you are 70, there is no limit. If your earnings go over these limits, Social Security withholds $1 in benefits for every $2 of earnings above the limits when you are under age 65. Between ages 65 to 69, $1 in benefits is withheld for every $3 of earnings.
- Social Security payments rise 3% for each year you delay collecting them. This credit escalates until it reaches 8% in 2008.

FOR ADDITIONAL HELP

Several hundred lawyers specialize in resolving Social Security problems related to disability benefits. They are members of the National Organization of Social Security Claimants' Representatives, which operates a nationwide referral service. For a member in your area, call 1-800-431-2804.

- Benefits may be taxed if your modified adjusted gross income exceeds the base amount: $32,000 for filers of joint returns, $0 for marrieds filing separately who lived with their spouse at any time during the year, and $25,000 for all other filers. The formula for determining how much is taxed is: the lesser of (1) one-half the net Social Security benefits or (2) one-half the amount by which modified adjusted gross income plus half the Social Security benefits exceeds the base amount.

Example: A married couple receives $10,000 in Social Security benefits, $30,000 in pensions, and $5,000 in tax-free municipal bond interest. Their modified adjusted gross income is $35,000 ($30,000 + $5,000). To that figure, add half their Social Security benefits, or $5,000, for a total of $40,000. Then subtract the base figure of $32,000 from $40,000 for $8,000. Half of $8,000 is $4,000, which is $1,000 less than half their Social Security benefits. Therefore, they must pay taxes on the $4,000.

Now that you know what you're likely to receive from Social Security, you're undoubtedly impressed with the fact that you will need a great deal more to continue a comfortable lifestyle after age 65! Other ways to build a retirement nest egg are covered later in this chapter.

WHEN TO BEGIN TAKING SOCIAL SECURITY

Are you wondering whether to start collecting Social Security benefits at age 62 or waiting until you're 65? If you begin taking checks as early as possible, your benefits will be reduced by 20% for life. Yet in some cases it pays to begin early. It takes about 12 years of bigger checks to catch up with the total payments made to the early retiree. And if you invest the early payments, the break-even point is still further away. According to a study done at Widener University in Chester, Pennsylvania, by Paul Marshall and Robert Myers:

- If you plan to work after age 62 and you expect to make more than the earnings limit for Social Security recipients, you are better off delaying benefits.
- The current tax law is in favor of waiting

HOW AN IRA CAN PAY OFF

If you invest $2,000 a year and you are in the 28% tax bracket, here's what you'll earn in an IRA versus in a taxable investment. The figures assume that you'll earn 7% annually on the money invested.

	IN AN IRA	IN A TAXABLE INVESTMENT
5 years	$12,306	$11,617
10 years	29,567	26,473
15 years	53,776	45,469
20 years	87,730	69,759
30 years	202,146	140,537

SOURCE: Chase Manhattan Bank.

for full benefits if your income, including half of your Social Security benefits, is high enough to trigger a tax on your benefits. If your income is over $32,000 on a joint return or $25,000 on a single return, as much as half of your benefits will be taxed.

■ Chances are you will live long enough to reap the money you passed up by not collecting benefits at age 62. You break even after 12 years of higher benefits, or at age 77. According to the National Center for Health Statistics, the life expectancies for 62-year-olds are as follows:

White females: 83.1 years
Black females: 81 years
White males: 78.9 years
Black males: 77.1 years

Obviously, as life expectancies for Americans increase, the advantage of taking lower benefits at age 62 diminishes.

INDIVIDUAL RETIREMENT ACCOUNTS (IRAs)

Whenever you work for yourself or a company, you can build a retirement nest egg with an IRA. In fact, if you've been stashing away $2,000 a year since 1981, when IRAs were made available to all workers even if they had

a pension plan, you have a sizable amount of money on hand. Your philosophy should be shifting too—away from thinking of your IRA as savings to be ignored or placed in a CD toward realizing that it's an investment requiring diversification and thoughtful management.

Where you should invest it depends on several factors: the current economic environment, your age, other sources of income, and your appetite for risk. The closer you are to retirement, of course, the less risk you should take. You must also decide if you are temperamentally suited to manage your account or if you need a professional. In general, high-yield conservative investments should form the basic core of most IRAs, but there are exceptions and variations. A part of your IRA should go into other vehicles such as growth stocks, which protect your nest egg from reduced returns when interest rates are low and yet take advantage of a rising stock market.

Only a few investments are excluded by law from IRAs: collectibles (such as gems, stamps, art, antiques, and Oriental rugs), commodities, and leveraged investments (those made with borrowed cash). The 1986 Tax Reform Act permits inclusion of U.S. legal tender gold and silver coins acquired after December 31, 1986, but they must be held by a custodian, not the IRA owner. You may borrow money to put in your IRA, but margined stocks, commodity futures, and mortgaged real estate are out. Among the tax-advantaged investments that make no sense in an IRA are municipal bonds, tax shelters, and deferred annuities.

Originally, the $2,000 annual deduction was available to all who earned at least that much in salary form. That's no longer true:

■ If your adjusted gross income (before IRA contribution) is over $50,000 ($35,000 for singles) *and* you or your spouse is an active participant in an employer's pension plan, you are no longer entitled to any IRA tax deduction, but you can make nondeductible contributions.

■ If your gross adjusted income (before IRA contribution) is between $40,000 and $50,000 ($25,000 to $35,000 for singles) *and* you or your spouse is an active participant in an employer's pension plan, your IRA deduction is reduced.

■ If you or your spouse is not an active

participant in such a plan, you can still deduct the full $2,000 IRA contribution.

■ Full $2,000 deduction is available to workers who are active participants in employer-maintained retirement plans only if their adjusted gross income is below $25,000 for singles and $40,000 for those filing jointly.

The following retirement programs disqualify you from making a fully deductible IRA contribution: Keogh, SEP, money-purchase pension plan, profit-sharing plan, defined-benefit plan, 401(k), employee stock option plan, government employee retirement plan, 403(b) (teachers' annuity), 457s (municipal employee retirement plan), and Taft-Hartley plan (union employee retirement plan).

$ HINT: Oppenheimer Fund Management has a free calculator that lets you determine the growth of an IRA depending on the size of annual contributions, the number of years contributions are made, and various assumed rates of return. Call: 1-800-525-7048.

SHOULD YOU HAVE AN IRA?

If you no longer qualify for the $2,000 tax deduction, you may decide it's not worth contributing to your IRA anymore. This is a mistake for most investors. Over the long run, your money will accumulate on a tax-deferred basis, more than offsetting the fact that it's not an immediate tax deduction. And, of course, it is a forced way of saving. In general, the higher the rate you earn on your IRA and the higher your tax bracket, the more valuable this shelter is. And there's no guarantee that Congress won't raise the tax brackets before you retire.

$ HINT: Contributions that do not qualify as a tax deduction should be paid into a separate IRA to avoid confusion.

Make your IRA contribution as early as possible in the new year—this will boost the value of your account in the long run. Most people delay until April 14 to fund their IRA because they either feel that they can't spare the $2,000 or they can't decide where to invest the money.

$ HINT: Use an automatic plan with a mutual fund or your stockbroker. Plan to deposit

$167 each month, even if it's into a money market fund. You will have accumulated $2,000 within a year, painlessly.

$ HINT: If you can only make nondeductible IRA contributions, you may want to consider a deferred annuity contract. These, too, allow you to accumulate interest and dividend earnings tax-free. Two added pluses: There is no limitation on the amount you can invest, and the early withdrawal penalty is usually less than the 10% for an IRA.

SELF-DIRECTED IRAs

When your IRA contains $5,000 to $10,000, you're ready to benefit from diversification. Consider doing so through a self-directed account, which can be set up at a brokerage firm for $25 to $35 plus a yearly fee. Designed for those who want to guide their own accounts, it allows you to invest in stocks, bonds, limited partnerships, options, Treasuries, zeros, or mortgage-backed securities. If you want advice on managing the portfolio, use a full-service broker; otherwise, save on commissions with a discount broker. A self-directed account takes time and vigilance on your part, yet it offers the greatest degree of flexibility along with the greatest potential for appreciation. It also involves the most risk.

☐ CAUTION: Avoid investments that are attractive largely for tax advantages, such as tax-exempt municipal bonds. Since IRAs are already sheltered from taxes, the exemption is wasted. In addition, all income, including tax-free yields, will be taxed when withdrawn.

$ HINT: The Cleveland Electric Illuminating Co. was the first company to establish an IRA for those who buy the stock through its dividend reinvestment plan. There are no brokerage commissions, and dividends can be automatically reinvested. Check with the electric utility company in your area.

YOUR IRA AND YOUR HEIRS

If you're blessed with sufficient income from other sources, you may want to leave IRA funds to your heirs. Although the IRS views IRAs primarily as a retirement benefit, not a death benefit, the new mortality tables

STOCKS FOR YOUR IRA: 1993

An IRA holds plenty of appeal for building retirement funds. These stocks combine good capital gains potential with attractive yields, dividend growth prospects, and above-average safety.

STOCK	REASON
American Home Products	Top dividend record
AT&T	Long-term growth
Bell South	Growing service region
Bristol-Myers Squibb	Attractive drug issue
Citizens Utilities B	Provides utility growth
Coca Cola	Solid overseas sales
Consolidated Natural Gas	Energy play
Kellogg	Recession-resistant company
Morgan (J.P.) & Co.	Leader in banking field
Royal Dutch Petroleum	Energy play; high yield
Southwestern Bell	Appeal of cellular business
WPL Holdings	Expanding via acquisition

help those who want to leave money behind by making it possible for them to withdraw less money from their IRAs. You must start withdrawing money by April 1 of the year after you turn 70½; otherwise, you face a stiff 50% excise tax on excess accumulations. Study the table on page 294 and check with your accountant or financial planner to determine your withdrawals.

□CAUTION: An IRA left to a beneficiary is fully taxable to the heir. If it is left to an heir under age 14, it is taxed at the parents' rate. These funds cannot be rolled over, and thus another tax benefit is eliminated.

IRA ROLLOVER

If you receive a partial or lump-sum distribution from a qualified retirement plan or tax-sheltered annuity, you may roll it over into an IRA. The amount you roll over may not include your after-tax contributions to the plan. But you may roll over all or only part (but at least 50%) of the distribution that would otherwise be taxable. Once in the IRA rollover, the savings continue to accumulate tax-free until payouts start—permissible after age 59½, mandatory at 70½.

The transfers must be made within 60 days after the distribution. Be extremely careful when rolling over or transferring these funds, especially if the transfer is to yourself. The safest method is from trustee to trustee.

AVOID PENALTIES

If for any reason you have inadvertently put too much money into your IRA, take it out immediately. For each year the excess remains in the account, a 6% excise tax is levied on both it and earnings. Earnings on the excess must be reported as income in the year earned. The excess and earnings on the excess may also be subject to a 10% penalty when withdrawn.

YOUR COMPANY PENSION PLAN

The next scheduled stop on your road map for an enjoyable retirement should be your company pension plan. The crash of '87 proved to all of us that the value of even the best-run pension plan can decrease, just as a personal portfolio can. So even if you have little or no control over where your plan is invested, you need the facts. Ask. Find out what you can expect to

IRA BASICS

- Annual contribution: $2,000 of earned income if under age 70½.
- You can wait until April 15 to make your contribution for the previous year.
- If you and your spouse both work, you may each have an IRA.
- You can contribute a total of $2,250 to a spousal account; this amount can be split between accounts as long as neither gets over $2,000.
- IRA money must be invested with an IRS-approved custodian, such as a bank, savings and loan, stockbroker, mutual fund, or insurance company.
- You can open as many IRA accounts as you like using a different custodian or investment each year and thus spreading out your risk.
- There is a 10% penalty for withdrawing money before you are 59½.
- Money withdrawn from IRAs funded by deductible contributions is taxed as ordinary income. (Only the earnings from IRAs funded by nondeductible contributions are taxed as ordinary income upon withdrawal.) If you withdraw before age 59½, you pay both the tax *and* the 10% penalty.
- You must withdraw money starting at age 70½ or be penalized.

CALCULATING MINIMUM IRA WITHDRAWALS

AGE AT WITHDRAWAL		DIVIDE ACCOUNT BALANCE BY:
MEN	**WOMEN**	
65	70	15.0
70	75	12.1
75	80	9.6
80	85	7.5
85	90	5.7
90	95	4.2
95	100	3.1

Note: Other figures are used for joint life expectancy.

SOURCE: Internal Revenue Service.

- What choices do I have about where my pension is invested? How many times a year can I move my money from one place (usually a mutual fund) to another?
- What are the penalties for early withdrawal?
- Can I borrow money from my plan? How much? At what rate?
- Can I make contributions to my plan to build up the dollar amount? How much? How often?
- How much is my plan worth today?
- How much do you estimate it will be worth when I retire?
- How will the benefits be paid out? What are the advantages and disadvantages of taking it in a lump sum?
- What happens if I become disabled? If I die?
- What happens to my pension if the firm is bought by another company or if the firm closes down?
- What is the estimated amount I will receive on a monthly basis when I retire?

$ HINT: If you have no pension plan, you're not alone. According to AARP, thousands of Americans are in this situation. The organization has two booklets that will help you: *Working Options* and *Planning Your Retirement*. Order from: AARP Fulfillment Office, 601 E Street NW, Washington, DC 20049.

receive. The answer will help you determine what additional savings you will need to live comfortably in your later years.

Here are 12 questions you should gather the answers to during the course of 1993:

- Am I eligible to receive retirement benefits? If not now, when will I be?
- What type of retirement plan do I have, defined benefit or defined contribution? (A defined-contribution plan gives you some flexibility regarding where the money is invested, but it doesn't guarantee you any set amount when you retire. A defined-benefit plan is less flexible, but it guarantees you a certain amount when you retire.)

There are several fundamental types of retirement programs available to employees. Programs for the self-employed—Keoghs and SEPs—are discussed later on in this chapter.

- *Defined-benefit plans.* These are the traditional type of pension plans that pay a fixed retirement benefit, such as 50% of your final salary, determined by a formula. The advantage here is that you know what your final pension will be.
- *Defined-contribution plans.* Popularly called profit-sharing plans. The company decides how much it wants to contribute each year. Amounts are contributed to individual employee accounts. The employee's final benefit is not determined in advance, but depends upon the amount of money accumulated in his or her account prior to leaving the company. In a self-directed plan, you, the employee, assume responsibility for whether the money is invested in stocks, bonds, or money market accounts.
- *Money-purchase plans.* The company contributes a fixed percentage of your salary into an individual benefit account. You decide how it should be invested.
- *401(k) plans.* You voluntarily contribute part of your own salary into individual accounts. The tax advantages are explained below. The company often supplements your contribution by matching a percentage of employee contributions.
- *Combination plans.* Your company may set up more than one plan, say, for example, a pension plan and a profit-sharing plan. The most common combination is a money-purchase plan to which the company makes an annual contribution equal to, say, 10% of salary, combined with a profit-sharing plan to which the company has the option of contributing up to another 15%.
- *Medical benefit plans.* Many companies pay medical benefits to retirees.
- *Employee stock ownership plans (ESOPs).* An ESOP is a retirement program that invests contributions in the company's own stock. The ESOP buys company stock with money obtained from a third-party lender, thus giving the company in effect

the proceeds of a bank loan. The bank loan is repaid through annual contributions to the ESOP.

401(k) PLANS

This plan, also called a "salary-reduction" plan, is offered by nearly four out of five major firms. Employers like it because it reduces the firm's pension costs by encouraging employees to save more themselves. The main attraction is the plan's tax break along with the fact that employers often add dollars to it for their employees.

HOW THEY WORK

1 Your employer sets up the plan with a regulated investment company, a bank trust department, or an insurance company.

2 You set aside part of your salary into a special savings and investment account. You have several options, typically a guaranteed fixed-rate income fund, a portfolio of stocks or bonds, or short-term money market securities. The amount set aside is *not* counted as income when figuring your federal income tax. For example, if you earn $50,000 and put $5,000 into a 401(k), you report only $45,000 compensation. In addition, earnings that accumulate in the 401(k) plan do so free of tax until withdrawn.

3 Many companies match employee savings, up to 5% or 6%. Most often a firm chips in 25¢ to 50¢ for each $1 the employee saves. Employer contributions can be up to 15% or $30,000, whichever is less.

4 The maximum you can contribute is $8,728, and there is a 10% penalty for withdrawing funds before age 59½. The maximum contribution is adjusted annually for inflation.

5 If you change jobs or take out the balance in a lump sum after age 59½, you can take advantage of 5-year averaging, another tax break. (You treat the total payout as though you received it in 5 annual installments.)

6 You can withdraw money without paying a penalty:

- When you reach 59½
- If you separate from service and you are age 55 when the distribution occurs
- If you are disabled
- If you need money for medical expenses that are greater than 7.5% of your adjusted gross income

TAKING MONEY OUT OF YOUR 401(k)

Regulations that went into effect January 1, 1989, make it tougher to take money out of your 401(k). Even if you meet the so-called hardship qualifications, you must have no other sources of income reasonably available, and you will still have to pay the 10% early withdrawal penalty unless the money is going for medical expenses that exceed 7.5% of your adjusted gross income. *Hardship reasons for borrowing that will satisfy the IRS are:*

- Medical expenses for you, your spouse, or dependents
- Down payment on your principal home
- Post-secondary tuition for you, your spouse, or dependents
- Prevention of foreclosure on or eviction from principal residence
- Funeral costs for a member of the family

BORROWING FROM YOUR 401(k)

Balances up to half the funding but not more than $50,000 can be borrowed under many plans. You pay interest on the loan to your own account, typically a percentage point less than what banks charge on secured personal loans, which, as we go to press, averages just below 13% nationally. By law, 50% of your balance must stay in the account as security against the loan. The loan must be repaid at least quarterly and fully within 5 years, unless the money goes for buying a principal residence.

☐ CAUTION: You lose tax-deferred compounding until you repay the loan, so if you own a home, get up to $100,000 from a tax-deductible home equity loan instead.

Whatever amount you borrow usually must be paid back within 5 years, although extensions are usually granted if the loan is helping you purchase your principal residence.

GUARANTEED INVESTMENT CONTRACTS (GICs)

Few people realize that the most popular investment in most 401(k) and company pension funds is a *guaranteed investment contract,* or GIC. GICs are fixed-rate, fixed-term debt instruments sold by insurance companies to corporate pension plans. They offer a stated, fixed rate of return for a specific period. They are the life insurance industry's equivalent of bank CDs, although they are not federally insured.

HOW THEY WORK

GICs run as long as the retirement manager likes, generally 1 to 10 years. The insurance company invests the cash it raises in a number of conservative investments, such as long-term bonds, public utility bonds, real estate and mortgages, and, to some extent, stocks. The rate of return is guaranteed by the issuer, but no specific pool of funds backs a GIC and most are not backed by federal insurance or government guarantees. Instead, the assets of the insurance carrier back the principal contract, so any default of an underlying issue or drop in interest rates is absorbed by the insurance company.

Most employees who select where to invest their retirement funds select GICs but know little about them, since the contracts are sold to institutions, not individuals. Make sure you learn about them. (They may also go by other names, such as "guaranteed fund," "stable return fund" or "benefit accumulation contract.")

If rates rise, as with any fixed-income vehicle, you are locked into a lower yield. If rates fall, you benefit.

CHECK THE QUALITY

As a member of a 401(k) plan you are legally entitled to at least annual reports from your plan manager on how your plan is performing. Check for the names of the insurance companies that sold the GICs. Then turn to A. M. Best Co., which publishes ratings of insurance companies, including those that sell GICs. In addition, Standard & Poor's and Moody's rank the insurance companies. Find out if the parent life insurance company or a pension subsidiary issues your GIC. If the subsidiary has any financial problems, will the parent company bail it out? Some states, including New York, have regulations requiring bailout of failed insurers. Call the state insurance commissioner in the state where the insurer is domiciled.

$ HINT: Call A. M. Best for information on a specific insurance company: 1-908-439-2200. Or call Weiss Research for information on judging creditworthiness: 1-800-289-9222.

☐ CAUTION: GICs guarantee only the interest rate; the ability to pay is not guaranteed and depends upon the creditworthiness of the insurance company.

During 1990, several insurers, most notably First Executive Corp. of California, ran into financial trouble because they had more than 5% of their assets in junk bonds. If you're concerned about your 401(k) plan in a GIC, find out exactly where that money is invested. Begin your inquiry with your plan administrator, usually your company's employee benefits department. Ask which insurance companies and banks are represented in the plan's GIC portfolio and what portion of the portfolio each insurer accounts for. Some plans place all fixed-income money with one insurer, but of course it's safer if it's spread among several insurers, which is more often the case with large companies than smaller ones.

The most important question to ask is how much of the money is in a portfolio of troubled junk bonds. The quality of an issuer's portfolio is reflected in its credit rating—the higher the rating the less likely the company and its GICs will run into trouble. Your plan administrator should be able to give you the credit rating of *each* issuer. Top-rated insurance companies will have an AAA rating. Beware of issuers with ratings below single A.

$ HINT: If you don't like what you learn, ask about making a change. Most plans allow investment choices to be changed several times a year. Although you probably cannot select among GICs, you can move money into stocks, bonds, and cash.

PLANS FOR THE SELF-EMPLOYED: KEOGHS AND SEPs

If you run an unincorporated business, either full time or as a moonlighter, you can reduce your income tax by saving for retirement. This is accomplished by putting some of these earnings each year into a Keogh plan or a simplified employee pension (SEP). In both you can defer federal income tax on your contributions and all the money accumulated from investment returns. The money is taxed when you withdraw it.

To qualify for a Keogh plan or a SEP, your earnings must come from your business or from fees for services you provided. The IRS will recognize you as self-employed if the companies that paid you send you Form 1099-MISC, which is used to report nonemployee compensation, instead of the Form W-2.

KEOGH PLANS

Keoghs work much like IRAs but have several added advantages. You can put away as much as $30,000 a year and, as with an IRA, your Keogh contribution is deductible from income when calculating your taxes. Earnings are not taxed until withdrawn. If you have a Keogh, you may also have an IRA.

To get your annual deduction, however, you must have the Keogh in place by the end of that year, although dollar contributions don't have to be completed until you file your income tax return.

One disadvantage to keep in mind: If you, as a self-employed person, establish a Keogh for yourself, you must extend its benefits to your employees. In fact, employees must get comparable benefits on a percentage basis: For example, if you put in 15% of earned income for yourself, you must match that 15% for each employee.

There are several types of Keoghs:

- *Defined-contribution plan.* In this type, you decide how much to put in. In other words, the annual contribution is predetermined and what you receive upon retirement is variable, depending on how well you've invested the deposits. You can contribute up to a maximum of 25% of compensation, not to exceed $30,000 a year.

- *Money-purchase plan.* The amount you can contribute is sometimes given as 20% of earned income or as 25% of compensation minus your Keogh contribution, which works out to 20% of net earnings. For example, if you make $100,000, you can contribute $20,000

($100,000 minus $20,000 contribution = $80,000 compensation; 25% of $80,000 = $20,000). In a money-purchase plan you must hew to this percentage no matter how hard-pressed you may be. In other words, the percentage contribution initially established must continue in the future. Although this plan gives you the most mileage by letting you determine the annual contribution at a fixed rate that is as high as 20% (25% of "net" income), you must stick to this percentage in lean years as well as prosperous ones.

- *Profit-sharing plan.* The most you can contribute and deduct here amounts to 13.043% of your net self-employed earnings. This plan gives you the flexibility to contribute less than the maximum or even nothing at all, from year to year.

- *Combination plan.* To keep your right to make maximum contributions without committing yourself to them every year, you can open two accounts: a profit-sharing and a money-purchase plan. Set your obligatory money-purchase plan at 7% of income. Then, in good years, you can put up to 13% in the profit-sharing plan.

- *Defined-benefit plan.* If you've only recently started to make a high income, you can shelter as much as it takes, up to 100% of self-employment income, in a defined-benefit plan. This plan is best for those with surplus income. For example, if you're earning $55,000 from a sideline business, you may be able to shelter it all from taxes. A defined-benefit plan is designed to pay a predetermined benefit each year after you retire. A pension actuary determines how much you need to deposit each year to provide for your benefits. This amount is adjusted for inflation. This type of Keogh is smart for those over 50, since there are fewer years left in which to put aside retirement funds.

➤ FEES AND FILINGS Starting and maintaining a defined-benefit Keogh plan is expensive. Pension specialists may charge several thousand dollars to set one up and then $750 or so a year to administer the plan. Profit-sharing and money-

purchase plans, on the other hand, may cost nothing or only a few dollars to set up and run.

If you have a Keogh plan with more than $25,000 in the plan or more than one participant, you must file a special tax form with the IRS on or before July 31 each year. If you work alone, this is not complicated—fill out the appropriate lines on Form 550EZ—but if your plan covers several employees, consult a tax pro.

- *Investment choices.* With a profit-sharing or money-purchase Keogh you have a number of investment choices available to you, just as you do with an IRA. Banks, mutual funds, stockbrokers, and life insurance companies all sponsor Keoghs. Use one that has a prototype plan on file so your paperwork will be limited.

  Defined-benefit Keoghs must be invested to meet the rules of the Employee Retirement Income Security Act (ERISA). You can still use a wide variety of investments, but they will be subject to scrutiny by federal regulations.

➤ WITHDRAWALS You must start taking money out of your Keogh or SEP by April 1 of the year after you turn 70½. (You can keep contributing after that date, however.) Lump-sum withdrawals from Keoghs after age 59½ (but NOT from

---

**HOW MUCH INCOME
YOU CAN PUT AWAY**

KEOGH DEFINED-CONTRIBUTION PLANS:
Money-purchase: The lesser of 20% or $30,000
Profit-sharing: The lesser of 13.043% or $30,000

KEOGH DEFINED-BENEFIT PLAN: as much as 100%

SEP
Regular plan: The lesser of 13.043% or $30,000
Salary-reduction plan: The lesser of 15% or about $8,000

SEPs) are eligible for 5-year forward averaging, which can reduce your tax bite. If you were born before 1936, you can use the even more advantageous 10-year averaging.

SIMPLIFIED EMPLOYEE PENSION PLANS (SEPs)

There is another type of tax-saving retirement plan for the self-employed that has received far less publicity than either the IRA or Keogh, yet it permits employer contributions greater than $2,000 a year. Called a *simplified employee pension plan* (SEP), it is suitable for small businesses and sole proprietors. Designed to cut red tape, it's considerably easier to set up and administer than a Keogh. Although its initial purpose was to encourage small and new firms to establish retirement programs, self-employeds without Keoghs can use it too. The deadline for setting up a SEP is April 15, just as it is with a regular IRA. (With a Keogh, the date is December 31.)

When an employer—which can be you as a sole proprietor—establishes a SEP, the employee then opens an IRA at a bank, mutual fund, or other approved institution. The employer can put up to 15% of an employee's annual earnings in the SEP, to a maximum of $30,000. The contributions made on your behalf are not included in total wages on your W-2, and no deduction for the amount contributed in your behalf is allowed.

ANNUITIES AND YOUR PENSION

If you're close to retirement or changing jobs, you're faced with the issue of how to handle the balance in your pension account. There are three basic choices: (1) cashing it in for a lump-sum distribution, (2) taking it in monthly payments, and (3) rolling it over into an IRA. Your accountant should be consulted prior to making a final decision.

- With a *lump-sum payment,* you will have control over your investment choices and you may also be able to take advantage of the 5- or 10-year averaging tax formula.
- If you decide on *monthly payments,* your employer uses your pension dollars to buy an annuity. As discussed on pages 308–314, annuity returns vary widely. Find out. Of course, you can also buy your own individual annuity.
- With an *IRA rollover,* your money will grow tax-free until withdrawn, starting no later than age 70½.

If you elect an annuity, you can specify how your pension savings will be invested: for *fixed income,* where the holdings will be bonds and mortgages to provide a set sum each month, or *variable income,* where the investments are split between bonds and stocks and the returns will vary, depending on how well the portfolio performs.

If you have a defined-benefit plan (see page 295), in which the amount of distribution is guaranteed, you will probably have these four choices:

1 *Straight-life (single-life) annuity.* This is the classic annuity in which you get a fixed monthly payment for the rest of your life, whether you live 5 days, 50 years, or more. *Best for:* singles with no dependents and people with dependents who are unlikely to outlive them. It offers

---

MOVING YOUR IRA, SEP, OR KEOGH

As your account grows or as market conditions change, you may want to invest your dollars elsewhere. The IRS has strict rules to follow.

A TRANSFER
- If you arrange for a direct transfer of funds from one custodian to another, there is no limit on the number of switches you can make.
- Plan on transfers taking at least a month. Banks, brokerage firms, and even some mutual funds are often backlogged with paperwork.
- Get instructions early on, ideally in writing, from both the resigning and accepting sponsor. Pay fees and notarize necessary papers immediately. Keep track of details as well as deadlines; don't depend on the institution to do this for you.

A ROLLOVER
- You may take personal possession of your money once a year for 60 days.
- If you hold the money longer than 60 days, you'll be subject to the 10% penalty.

the highest monthly payment. Some plans also offer a guaranteed minimum of 5 years of payment, which are made to your beneficiary if you die within 5 years of retiring.

2   *Joint and survivor annuity.* You get a fixed monthly payment during your lifetime, and if you predecease your spouse, he or she receives a set percentage of that monthly amount for the rest of his or her life. However, the younger your spouse and the higher his or her percentage, the smaller the current payment you'll receive. Since 1984, this plan is required by law to make a minimum 50% payment to the surviving spouse of married retirees. A married person can select a different option only if the spouse provides written consent within 90 days of the person's retirement date.

3   *Period-certain annuity.* This annuity makes payments for your entire life, but if you die within a certain number of years, your surviving dependent receives your full monthly pension for the remaining years. *Best for:* those who need to provide for a current dependent who will eventually become independent. Also ideal for people with spouses who are expected to live only a few years.

4   *Lump-sum certain.* Although this is not usually offered in defined-benefit plans, you should know its ramifications. Here you relieve your company of its legal obligation to pay you a lifetime monthly retirement benefit. In exchange, it gives you one large lump sum. This single payment is based on the average life expectancy for someone your age and a given interest rate. Of course, the older you are and the higher the rate, the lower the lump sum. *Best for:* retirees with other resources who are not terribly dependent on their pension, and for those in poor health who will not be receiving annuity payments for very long.

FINDING WORK

According to a 1990 study by the Commonwealth Fund, a New York philanthropic group, about 2 million retired Americans over age 50 want to work, but they're not looking for jobs—they think employers will say they're too old. Wrong! The study points out that certain employers are clamoring for mature workers.

- *Banks.* Older workers are excellent as tellers and customer service representatives. The Bank of America, Citibank, and others actively seek older workers.
- *Hotels.* Over one-third of Days Inn's employees are 55 and older. Their absentee rate is only 3%. Other chains, including Marriott, are following Days Inn's example.
- *Home health care.* Demand for home health aids is soaring—physical therapists, companions, preparation and delivery of meals.
- *Travel agencies.* Since one in four pleasure trips is taken by someone age 55 or older, the gray-haired employee is a plus in this industry. Take a six- to eight-week course at a travel agent school. And you get extra perks: reduced hotel rates and airfares.
- *Hardware stores.* Builders Emporium, Hechinger, and Home Depot all rely heavily on older employees who have fix-up experience.
- *Tax return preparers.* The IRS hires people during tax time; so do accounting firms.
- *Temp agencies.* Kelly, Adia, and Volt actively recruit employees over 55. Demand for accountants is strong during the first quarter of the year; engineers can land short-term projects; office assignments are unending.

$ HINT: If you work as a temp you can get around the fact that Social Security benefits are cut when annual wages are over $7,080 for someone under age 65 or $9,720 for someone age 65 to 69—when your income reaches that amount, you simply delay going to work until next year.

FOR FURTHER INFORMATION

Retirement Income Guide
A. M. Best Company
A. M. Best Road

Oldwick, NJ 08858
1-908-439-2200
Twice a year; $55 per year

Lauraine Snelling, *Start Your Own Business After 50—or 60—or 70!* (Bristol Publishing Enterprises, 1991), $8.95.

United Retirement Bulletin
United Business Service Inc.
101 Prescott Street
Wellesley Hills, MA 02181
1-617-235-0900
Monthly; $34 per year

"A Step By Step Guide to Planning Your Retirement"
(IRA Fact Kit)
Fidelity Investments
1-800-544-8888
Free

"Retirement Planning Kit"
T. Rowe Price
100 East Pratt Street
Baltimore, MD 21202
1-800-638-5660
Free

Deciding What to Do With Your Company Retirement Money
T. Rowe Price
1-800-IRA-5000
Free

Walter W. David, *The 50 Plus Guide to Retirement Investing*
(Homewood, IL: Business One Irwin, 1992).

Retirement Plans for the Self-Employed
IRS Publication #560
1-800-TAX-FORM
Free

31

INSURANCE AND ANNUITIES

It may never have occurred to you, but you can turn your life into a tax shelter. Certain types of life insurance double as an investment, a tax-deferred way to save, and as coverage on your life. That's because Congress preserved the tax-free buildup of savings (called "cash value") inside both insurance policies and annuities, making them one of the few ways left to defer taxes since the 1986 Tax Reform Act was passed.

There are other advantages to this type of tax shelter: In a crisis you can cash in your policy and get most of your money back. With some policies, you can withdraw part of your cash value or borrow against the policy at below market rates, save for future expenses, and, of course, provide for your beneficiaries.

In this chapter we concentrate on *insurance as an investment.* However, do not overlook health and disability coverage, both of which should be part of your overall financial planning. Both annuities and life insurance are long-term investments, and many impose heavy sales charges and early surrender fees. If you decide to purchase either life insurance or an annuity, deal only with a financially stable company, one rated A or A+ by A. M. Best Co., the nationwide rating service. Most libraries and all insurance salespeople have the A. M. Best rating service.

This is not idle advice: In 1991, First Executive Corp., a Los Angeles-based holding company that owns four life insurers with $18 billion in assets, failed and was taken over by the state of California.

TERM INSURANCE

There are two basic types of life insurance plans—*term* and *cash.* Term, which is not an investment, provides pure life insurance protec-

tion for a specified time, usually 1, 5, 10, or 20 years or up to age 65. It has absolutely no savings feature. When the policyowner dies, the beneficiary of a term policy receives the full face value of the policy.

Term insurance must be renewed every term, generally once a year. If you stop paying premiums, then the insurance coverage also stops. Premiums are relatively low when you are young but move up significantly with your age. Although there is no cash buildup inside a term policy, a "convertible" term policy can be converted, for a higher premium, into a cash value policy without requiring you to meet new medical standards. Term is initially cheaper than other types of policies for the same protection. It is best for those who need coverage for a certain time period—parents of young children, home buyers, etc.

$ HINT: Make certain any term policy you buy has a "renewable" provision. Then you do not have to prove you are insurable each time.

CASH VALUE OR WHOLE LIFE INSURANCE

Cash value policies, also called straight or permanent life, are part insurance and part investment since they have a savings feature. You pay a premium based on your age when you purchase the policy, and this amount remains fixed as long as the policy is in effect. Premiums are paid monthly, annually, or quarterly. During the early years, the premium exceeds the insurance company's estimated cost of insuring your life. Then after several years the surplus and interest are channeled into a cash or surplus fund. You do not select where your cash value is invested—the insurance company does—usually in conservative, fixed-rate, long-term bonds

---

GETTING THE BEST RATES

Insurance Information, Inc., will do a search of term rates for a $50 fee. It guarantees it will save you at least $50 over your current policy or the $50 will be refunded. Call: 1-800-472-5800.

---

and mortgages and blue chip stocks. The insurance company uses part of this cash fund to pay administrative costs and any agent's commission. If you cancel your policy, you receive the cash value (or most of it) in a lump sum.

Because of the cash reserve feature, premiums for whole life insurance are generally higher than those for term.

TYPES OF WHOLE LIFE INSURANCE

- *Modified life:* Premium is relatively low in the first several years but escalates in later years. Designed for those who want whole life but need to pay lower premiums when they are young.
- *Limited-payment whole life:* Provides protection for the life of the insured, but the premiums are payable over a shorter period of time. This makes the premiums higher than for traditional whole life.
- *Single-premium whole life:* Provides protection for the insured's life, but the premium is paid in one lump sum when you take out the policy.
- *Combination plans:* Policies are available that combine term and whole life within one contract. Generally premiums for combination plans do not increase as you get older.
- *Universal life:* Can pay premiums at any time in virtually any amount subject to certain minimums.
- *Variable life:* The cash value fluctuates according to the yields earned by the fund in which the premiums are invested.

☐CAUTION: Keep in mind that sales charges are high, consuming 50% or more of the first year's premium.

When the policyowner dies, the beneficiary receives *only* the face value of the policy and not the cash reserve. This face value is a predetermined amount, selected when you buy the policy. The latter is used to pay off the claim. For example, if the face value of your policy is $200,000, but the cash value has built up to $175,000, the insurance company needs to put up only $25,000 to pay off the claim.

You can borrow from your cash reserve, typically at low rates, currently in the neighborhood of 5% to 8%, and still be insured. The loan is repaid either prior to death or is deducted from the death benefit.

Taxes on your cash reserve are deferred until it is withdrawn or surrendered, and then you pay only on the amount of cash that exceeds the total amount of premiums you paid in.

TERM VS. CASH

When purchasing life insurance, keep in mind that commissions are highest for whole life. Agents, aware of this fact, may try to steer you away from term, saying it is really only a temporary solution. However, term almost always provides the most insurance coverage for the price and is initially cheaper.

Yet term premiums become extremely expensive as you get older. If your family is adequately covered by your pension and other sources of income, you could conceivably drop term in your later years.

Term tends to be best for those who need large amounts of coverage for a given time span: parents of young children, for example, or homeowners.

$HINT: Purchase a term policy that is convertible *and* renewable. Then switch to whole life as your age and family circumstances change.

UNIVERSAL LIFE

Universal life, a fairly new form of whole life, has grown in popularity because of its unique and flexible features:

1 The death benefit, i.e., the face value, can be increased or decreased.

2 The premium payments can vary, subject to a basic minimum. You can elect to pay annually, quarterly, or monthly.

3 You can use money from your cash buildup value to meet premium payments.

4 You can borrow against the cash value at low interest rates.

5 You can cash in the policy at any time and receive most of your savings.

With universal life, part of each premium is used to cover sales commission and administrative fees; this is called a load charge. The rest of your premium is invested in various low-risk vehicles. With some universal life policies you can designate how much you want to go for insurance and how much into savings. The company, however, determines the rate of return, which is often tied to an index, such as the Treasury bill rate. Rates generally are guaranteed for 1 year but when changed will not fall below the minimum stated in the policy—about 4% to 5%.

Some companies now offer a variable universal life plan that lets you switch your investments among several mutual funds sponsored by the insurance company.

At the present time, standard universal life policies are paying between 7½% and 9%, although the yield is actually less after fees and commissions are deducted.

☐CAUTION: Sales fees and other costs can eat up as much as 50% of your first year's premium and between 2% and 5% annually thereafter. So plan to hold your policy at least 10 years.

No-load universal life is now being offered by some companies. The premiums are less because, of course, there are no commissions. However, you must buy your policy through a salesperson, such as a financial planner, who receives a fee. No load, however, does not mean no cost. There are still administrative costs and other fees.

VARIABLE LIFE

Another relatively recent type of cash value insurance is variable life. Its premiums are fixed; however, the death benefits and the cash value vary based on how successfully your cash reserve is invested. Most companies offer a number of choices, including stocks, bonds, and money market funds, as well as the opportunity to switch from one to another.

With this type of insurance, you have the potential of a far greater return than with other types of cash value policies, but there is also substantially more risk.

☐CAUTION: If your investment choices turn out to be poor, you could conceivably wind up with less cash value in a variable policy than with other types of insurance.

There are two types of variable: scheduled premium and flexible premium. Premiums in the scheduled premium plans are fixed, both in timing and dollar amount. With a flexible premium plan, you can change both the timing and the amount.

TIPS FOR INVESTING IN LIFE INSURANCE

A recent study by the Federal Trade Commission concluded that (1) life insurance is so complicated that the public is practically unable to evaluate the true costs of various policies; (2) the savings portions of cash value policies that do not pay dividends offer an extremely low rate of return; (3) prices for similar policies vary widely; and (4) the public loses large amounts of money when they surrender cash value policies within the first 10 years.

As a result of these FTC conclusions, the National Insurance Consumer Organization (NICO), an independent consumer advocacy group, devised these guidelines for selecting an insurance policy.

- *Don't buy if you don't need it.* If you are without dependents you probably don't need life insurance, and don't buy a policy to cover your children's lives.

- *Buy only annual renewable term insurance.* If you buy term, purchase only this type.

- *Don't buy credit life insurance.* This pays off your loan when you die and is way overpriced in most states, although New York is an exception.

- *Don't buy mail-order life insurance* unless you compare its price to annual renewable term and find it less expensive.

- *Don't let an agent talk you into dropping*

RATING THE INSURANCE COMPANIES

The insolvencies of several companies have highlighted the importance of dealing with an A-rated company. Check with these sources.
- *Best's Insurance Reports*
  A. M. Best Co.
  Oldwick, NJ 08858
- *List of Ratings*
  Insurance Forum
  P.O. Box 245
  Ellettsville, IN 47429
  $10
- *Standard & Poor's Insurance Rating Service*
  25 Broadway
  New York, NY 10004
- *Weiss Safety Hotline*
  1-800-289-9222

an old policy. If it still pays dividends you may be better off borrowing out any cash value and reinvesting it elsewhere at higher rates.

Weiss Research, based in West Palm Beach, Florida, was the first rating agency to give Executive Life, a subsidiary of the failed First Executive Corp, a negative rating. In August 1989, while A. M. Best and Standard & Poor's were still giving Executive Life top ratings, Weiss gave the company a C–. In early 1990, Weiss downgraded Executive Life to a D. In April 1991, Weiss gave the following three insurers a D+ rating because of their substantial junk bond holdings and excessive interest rate guarantees:

    Equitable Life Assurance Society of the U.S.
    Kemper Investors Life
    First Capital Life Insurance Company

$ HINT: Consumers can obtain a rating over the phone for $15 per company, a 1-page *Personal Safety Brief* for $25, or an 18-page *Personal Safety Report* for $45 from: Weiss Research, Inc., 2200 North Florida Mango Road, West Palm Beach, FL 33409; 1-800-289-9222.

HOW MUCH INSURANCE DO YOU NEED?

When you decide to buy any kind of insurance, don't automatically rely on an agent's advice. They have an inherent desire to sell you as much coverage as possible. Instead, begin with these general guidelines and then adapt them to your particular situation. Keep in mind that the amount of life insurance you should have is related to other coverage.

➤ LIFE Depends upon how many people need your financial help. If you have several small children, you want enough coverage to support them until they are 18 or through college, but if you are single, put your money elsewhere. The rule of thumb is 65% to 75% of the breadwinner's income—but this does not all have to come from life insurance. Because insurance needs are so individual, even the old formula—which said your coverage should equal 5 times your total annual take-home pay—no longer holds. Instead, assess your assets, liabilities, and income requirements using the worksheet in *A Consumer's Guide to Life Insurance*, available free from American Council of Life Insurance, 1-202-624-2000.

➤ HEALTH You need a major medical policy

INSURANCE TIPS

DO:
- Take the maximum deductible you can afford.
- Ask if you qualify for a discount.
- Get coverage through a group when possible; it's cheaper.

DON'T:
- Buy narrow policies; they frequently duplicate coverage you may have in other policies.
- Switch from one policy to another without studying the costs; fees and commissions are high.
- Use life insurance only for an investment; your first goal is coverage, then investment.

that covers at least 80% of doctor and hospital bills above your deductible. Avoid a policy that has exclusions for expensive diseases such as cancer.

➤ DISABILITY Get a policy that replaces 60% to 80% of your net income. Select one that will pay out when you cannot work at your *own* occupation, not when you cannot do any type of work.

➤ AUTO Meet these minimums: $100,000 for one injury; $300,000 total per accident, and $50,000 for property damage. If your car has lost at least one-third of its initial value, consider canceling collision. Your state may require you to be covered against uninsured motorists. Ask if discounts are available for safe drivers, non-smokers, honor-roll students, graduates of driver education courses, and owners of cars with airbags.

➤ HOMEOWNERS Be covered for at least 80% of the replacement cost of your home, not including land value, plus a minimum of $100,000 for liability. Ask if discounts are available for those with smoke alarms, deadbolt locks, and fire extinguishers.

➤ UMBRELLA POLICY If your assets are above $100,000, you have a swimming pool, throw lots of parties, race cars, or are vulnerable to lawsuits, take out an umbrella policy for $1 million.

BORROWING AGAINST LIFE INSURANCE

Although your agent may say you can borrow up to 95% of the cash value of your policy at below market rates, the true cost of the loan is not always clear. (The cash value is the sum by which the premiums and the dividends earn money above the insurer's estimated cost of coverage.) Read the fine print first, and watch in particular for dividend cuts. Some policies continue paying the same dividends on the entire cash value, but many cut earnings on that portion of cash equal to the loan amount. This is known as a "two-tier" dividend treatment.

☐CAUTION: You do not have to pay back a policy loan, but generally all outstanding loans plus interest are deducted from the amount paid to the beneficiary.

NO-LOAD UNIVERSAL LIFE POLICIES

The following companies have no-load universal policies. This list is not an endorsement but serves merely to start you on your search for information.
- American Life of New York (1-212-581-1200)
- Ameritas Life Insurance (1-800-255-9678)
- USAA Life (1-800-531-8000)

Loans taken out against single-premium life policies are called "zero percent loans." Because you pay a large single premium up front ($5,000 to $100,000+), you begin earning large dividends immediately; consequently, the policy has a high cash value sooner than other types of life insurance. These loans are "wash loans," because the insurer charges the same rate for the loan as it pays on the policy—if you borrow against the earnings.

☐CAUTION: This money of course is not earning interest while being borrowed. Single-premium policies have many twists, so check the prospectus carefully for penalties and other restrictions.

To determine the actual cost of borrowing from your life insurance policy, subtract the after-loan rate from the rate you earned before the loan. Add to that figure the stated policy loan rate. This is the true cost of borrowing.

Preloan rate − Postloan rate

  12%   −   6.5%

                     + Policy loan rate = Loan cost

                   +   8%   =   13.5%

SWITCHING YOUR LIFE INSURANCE POLICY

Before changing your policy, take time to compare the death benefit, annual premium, initial rate of cash buildup, and, most importantly, the net yield—what your money earns after all charges and fees.

For help analyzing the rate of return, write:

National Insurance Consumer Organization
121 North Payne Street
Alexandria, VA 22314
1-703-549-8050

For $35 for the first proposal and $25 for each additional one, NICO will analyze the rate of return on your current cash value policy.

MEDIGAP INSURANCE

This supplemental policy is designed to fill the gaps between your medical bills and what Medicare covers. Before you buy such a policy, be clear about what Medicare now covers:

- Hospital stays after a deductible and copayments; check for limitations
- Up to 100 days in a skilled nursing facility; with some copayments
- Hospice-care benefits for the terminally ill; check for certain limitations
- Home health care
- 80% of approved doctor's charges after a $100 deductible

(*Note*: The rulings are continually being revised.)

INSURANCE QUOTE FIRMS

Insurance quote firms provide four or five of the lowest-cost policies in their computer files. Most deal only with highly rated companies. Some operate in all states; others are licensed only in certain areas.

Insurance Information
Cobblestone Court #2, Rte. 134
South Dennis, MA 02660
1-800-472-5800

Insurance Quote
3200 North Dobson Road, Building C
Chandler, AZ 85224
1-800-972-1104

SelectQuote
140 Second Street, 5th floor
San Francisco, CA 94105
1-800-343-1985

$ HINT: "The Medicare Handbook" has complete explanation of coverage. Call: 1-800-772-1213 for a copy.

Whether or not you need a Medigap policy depends on what other coverage you already have. Review your existing policies carefully, and take full advantage of the "free look" provision recommended by the National Association of Insurance Commissioners (NAIC), which gives you 30 days to change your mind after purchasing a policy. Most states have adopted this provision. Follow these guidelines:

- Buy one comprehensive policy, not several with possible overlapping coverage.
- Buy a policy that is renewable for life.
- Find out about exclusions for preexisting conditions and waiting periods.
- Turn down any policy that says it is government sponsored or guaranteed; it's not.
- Write a check only to the insurance company, not the agent. If your policy does not arrive in 30 days, call your state insurance office.

A Medigap policy is not worth the premiums to anyone who uses doctors who accept "Assignment"—that is, doctors who agree to take whatever Medicare approves as their full payment. Ask your doctor.

WHO NEEDS COVERAGE: If you have assets between $100,000 and $1 million, excluding your home *and* you want to pass it on to heirs. If you have more than $1 million you can pay for care yourself; under $100,000; Medicaid will pay after your money runs out.

Heed the words of Robert Hunter, president of the National Insurance Consumer Organization in Alexandria, VA, "I wouldn't pay more than $700 a year for a Medigap policy."

NURSING HOME INSURANCE

As you (or members of your family) approach your late 60s or 70s, part of retirement planning should deal with long-term care. Depending on your financial situation, you may want to consider this new type of insurance. According to the American Health Care Association, the national average for nursing home costs are $80 a

---

NURSING HOME INSURANCE PROVIDERS

COMPANY	TELEPHONE
CNA Box 593925 Orlando, FL 32859	1-800-327-2430
AMEX Life Assurance Co. Box 2060 San Rafael, CA 94912	1-800-456-7766
Prudential AARP P.O. Box 7000 Allentown, PA 18175	1-800-245-1212

---

day, or over $30,000 a year. Many senior citizens incorrectly believe that Medicare will pick up the total bill. It does not.

Although an insurance policy may initially seem the logical solution, this particular field is complex and riddled with problems. Read the brochures listed at the end of this chapter before purchasing a policy.

More than 100 companies now sell long-term care coverage, according to the Health Insurance Association of America. And although the National Association of Insurance Commissioners has issued guidelines for policies, insurers are not legally forced to abide by them. This means you must do some serious research before purchasing a long-term care policy. The companies listed in the box above may be a good place to begin gathering information, as are the sources listed at the end of this chapter. Before taking out a policy, discuss the matter with your insurance agent or financial planner and study at least two, preferably three, different plans before making a final decision.

The downside of long-term health care policies is that if you never need this care, the premiums paid are not recoverable. However, a new type of policy, which uses the structure and guarantees of whole life insurance, recently came onto the market. With a single premium of $10,000 or more, you can purchase a death benefit that also doubles as an account for paying for the cost of long-term care. It is

available on a single life or joint basis, and if an insured needs nursing home care, the policy will pay up to 2% (4% for both insureds) of the death benefit for these costs. It is available from the Golden Rule Insurance Company in Lawrenceville, IL (1-800-950-4474).

The National Association for Retired Credit Union People offers these suggestions regarding nursing home insurance:

- More than half of those admitted to nursing homes die or go home within 90 days. About 40%, however, stay at least 2½ years.
- For those qualifying, Medicare may pay the costs of up to 100 days of skilled nursing or rehabilitation care in a nursing home following hospitalization.
- The poor and those who have depleted most of their assets in paying for nursing home care are likely to be eligible for Medicaid. Federal law permits the spouse of the person receiving nursing home care under Medicaid to retain some assets, including the car and home.

TIPS FOR EVALUATING INSURANCE POLICIES

Select a policy that:
- Covers these three areas: skilled, intermediate, and custodial care.
- Does not require being hospitalized before receiving long-term care. Those with Alzheimer's, for instance, are not usually hospitalized before entering a home.
- Covers long-term care in the home.
- Guarantees renewability for life.
- Covers "organically based mental conditions" (e.g., Alzheimer's).
- Has an inflation clause—you want to have your benefits ride up with the cost of living.
- Covers any type of health-care facility, not just a Medicare-certified nursing home.

ANNUITIES: A SAVINGS ALTERNATIVE

If you'd like to stockpile tax-deferred savings for your retirement years, then take a close look at an annuity—it's one of the few investment vehicles that survived the 1986 Tax Reform Act relatively unscathed. Annuities have all the benefits of an IRA, but no $2,000 cap on annual contributions, and with most you can continue to invest on an after-tax basis beyond age 70. The minimums are low, often only $1,000, and with most you can invest as much as you like. However, annuities are complicated, riddled with fees, charges, rules, and restrictions, so do your homework first.

THE BASICS

An annuity is simply a contract between you and an insurance company in which you pay a sum of money and in return receive regular payments, for life or for a stated period of time. The money grows on a tax-deferred basis until you begin receiving it, typically after age 59½. At that point you can postpone the tax bite by annuitizing; that is, converting your assets into a monthly stream of income. Then, only that portion of the payout representing growth or interest income is taxed.

Annuities are often confused with life insurance. They are not the same. An annuity provides a steady stream of income while you are alive, while a life insurance policy pays off upon your death and benefits your heirs.

There are two basic types of annuities: fixed and variable.

➤ FIXED ANNUITIES With a fixed annuity the premiums are invested in fixed-rate instruments, usually bonds or mortgages. Your money earns a fixed rate of return that is guaranteed for a certain time period, anywhere from 1 to 5 years, occasionally longer. After the guarantee period is over, your assets are automatically rolled over for a new time period at a new rate. The new rate will have moved up or down, depending upon the general direction of interest rates. Fixed annuities are best in times of high interest rates, when you can lock in good yields.

Most fixed annuities have a "floor" or guaranteed rate below which your return will not drop. This floor, often tied to the T-bill rate or other index, lasts the life of the annuity.

▢CAUTION: Watch out for any plan that entices investors with an initially high teaser rate and then reduces it drastically when the guarantee period is up. And make certain when you roll over that the new rate is equal to that being paid to new customers.

➤ VARIABLE ANNUITIES A variable annuity, which works rather like a tax-deferred mutual fund, has more pizzazz as well as more risk. Your premiums are invested in stocks, bonds, real estate, money market instruments, and managed portfolios, thus offering the potential of a higher return than with a fixed annuity. You can direct your assets among portfolios (or have the insurance company do so for you). Your return varies, depending upon the portfolio's performance, hence the name variable annuity.

PAYING FOR AN ANNUITY

You can select either a single-premium annuity, in which case you make a one-time payment, or an installment or flexible premium, which you pay for in stages over time. You can also purchase an annuity long before you retire, which is known as a deferred annuity, or close to retirement, known as an immediate annuity. An immediate annuity, in which payments begin almost at once, is often used by those who

---

QUESTIONS TO ASK YOUR INSURANCE COMPANY

Before purchasing an annuity, read the contract, have your accountant or financial adviser review it as well, and make certain you know the answers to these questions:

- What is the current interest rate?
- What were the rates for the last 3 to 5 years?
- How long is the rate guaranteed for?
- How is the rate determined?
- What are the bond ratings in the portfolio? (Select a policy with bonds rated A or above.)
- How long has the insurance company been selling this particular annuity?
- What is the company's A. M. Best rating? (Again, it should be A or above.)

VARIABLE ANNUITIES WITH GOOD RESULTS FOR 1991

COMPANY/INSURER (CONTRACT NAME) TELEPHONE	*S&P RATING	INVESTMENT VEHICLE INVESTMENT MANAGER	FIRST OFFERED	INV. OBJ.
MFS/Sun Life (N.Y.) (Compass 2-NY-VA) 1-800-343-2829	AAA	Managed Sectors MFS	5/88	AG
Northbrook Life Ins. (Dean Witter Var Annuity) 1-212-392-2550	AAA	Equity Dean Witter	3/84	G
American Skandia Life (LifeVest-VA) 1-800-752-6342	AA	AA Small Capitalization Fred Alger Mgt., Inc.	9/88	SC
Anchor Nat'l Life Ins (ICAP II-VA) 1-800-922-0876	AA	Aggressive Growth Wellington	3/87	AG
Hartford Life Ins. (The Director-VA) 1-800-862-6668	AAA	Aggressive Growth Hartford/Wellington	4/84	AG
Guardian Ins. & Annuity (Guardian Investor-VA) 1-800-221-3253	AAA	Value Line Centurion Value Line, Inc.	5/90	G
Keyport Life Ins. (KEYFLEX 4-VA) 1-800-437-4466	A+	Managed Growth Stk. Fd. Stein Roe & Farnham	5/90	G
Putnam/Hartford Life Ins. (Putnam Capital Mgr-VA) 1-800-862-6668	AAA	Voyager Fund Putnam Mgt. Co.	2/88	G
Union Central Life (Carillon Account-VA) 1-513-595-2600	A−	Equity Portfolio Carillon Advis/Bartlett	6/85	G
Nationwide Life Ins. (Best of Amer 2, 3 & 4-VA) 1-800-321-6064	AAA	Fidelity VIPF-Growth Fidelity Mgt. & Res.	12/87	G

*S&P insurance claims-paing ability ratings; AAA—Superior, AA—Excellent, A—Adequate, BBB—Good, + indicates positive implications, BB and lower ratings not considered secure investments. AG—Aggressive Growth. G—Growth. SC—Small Capitalization. †Mortality and expense fees. ‡Unit value is the value of a separate account after deducting mortality charges and expense fees. NA—Not available. *SOURCE:* S&P's Stock Guide.

FEES & EXPENSES				‡GROWTH OF UNIT VALUE (%)		
†INS. FEES %	FUND MGMT. %	ADMINISTRATION, SURRENDER, SALES CHARGES	TOTAL ASSETS 9/30/91 ($ MIL.)	1989	1990	1991
1.30	1.25	ADMIN: $30 annual contract fee. SUR: 5% yrs. 1 through 5	49.8	+43.6	−11.6	+60.1
1.35	0.62	ADMIN: $30 annual contract fee. SUR: 6% yr. 1, scale down 1% per yr. through yr. 6.	49.9	+17.7	−4.6	+57.5
1.40	1.50	ADMIN: $30 annual contract fee, SUR: 7% yr. 1, scale down 1% per yr. through yr. 7.	37.1	+62.9	+7.2	+55.4
1.40	1.00	ADMIN: $30 annual contract fee. SUR: 5% yr. 1, scale down 1% per yr. through yr. 6.	41.1	+23.4	−17.5	+54.1
1.32	0.96	ADMIN: $25 annual contract fee. SUR: 7% yr. 1, scale down 1% per yr. through yr. 7.	57.7	+22.6	−12.0	+52.2
1.15	0.54	ADMIN: $35 annual contract fee. SUR: 6% yr. 1 & 2, scale down 1% per yr. through yr. 7.	245.0	NA	+6.4	+50.5
1.40	1.50	ADMIN: $30 annual contract fee. SUR: 7% yr. 1, scale down 1% per yr. through yr. 7	30.7	NA	−3.0	+46.0
1.31	0.88	ADMIN: $25 annual contract fee. SUR: 7% yr. 1, scale down 1% per yr. through yr. 7.	113.5	+30.5	−3.4	+44.0
1.45	0.82	ADMIN: $25 annual contract fee. SUR: 7% yrs. 1 & 2, scale down 1% per yr. through yr. 8.	19.7	+10.2	−17.0	+44.0
1.30	0.88	ADMIN: $30 annual contract fee. SUR: 7% yr. 1, scale down 1% per yr. through yr. 7.	NA	+29.7	−12.9	+43.7

receive a lump-sum payment from a company pension plan. In a deferred payment annuity, no payments are made until at least a year or more after you've paid your premium.

All annuities have two phases: accumulation and payment.

GETTING YOUR MONEY BACK

When you reach 59½ your money is returned to you in one of several ways: in a lump sum, in regular monthly payments, or as lifetime income for you and your spouse. Pay-

---

SPONSORS OF HIGH-RATED ANNUITIES

—FIXED RATE ANNUITIES—

COMPANY	MINIMUM	CURRENT FIXED RATE (MAY 1992)
American Investors & Life Insurance Topeka, KA Guarantor 5 1-800-255-2405	$ 5,000	5.5%
Lincoln Benefit Life Lincoln, NB 1-800-525-9287	5,000	6.1%
USAA Annuity and Life Insurance San Antonio, TX 1-800-531-8000	1,000	6.5%

—VARIABLE ANNUITIES—

COMPANY	MINIMUM	
Keyport Co. Insurance Boston, MA 1-800-367-3653 1-617-457-1400	$ 5,000	
Guardian Investor Services New York, NY 1-800-221-3253	5,000	
National Home Life c/o Vanguard Annuity Plan Valley Forge, PA 1-800-522-5555	5,000	
Northwestern National Life Insurance Minneapolis, MN c/o Fidelity Growth Portfolio Boston, MA 1-612-372-1896	2,500	
Western Capital Financial Group The Specialty Manager Los Angeles, CA 1-213-556-5499 1-800-423-4891	10,000	

ments vary depending on the amount you have contributed, your age, the length of time your money has been compounding, and the rate of return on the portfolios. Taxes must be paid on all payouts.

□ CAUTION: If you withdraw money before age 59½ there is a 10% IRS tax penalty.

SURRENDER CHARGES

Cashing in your annuity early is expensive. As mentioned above, there's a 10% IRS penalty for money taken out before you reach 59½. In addition, most insurance companies let you take out only up to 10% of your assets before they impose a surrender charge. Go beyond that 10% and you'll be slapped with a fee, typically 6% of the withdrawal during the 1st year, going down to 0% by the 7th year. (One plan, The Specialty Manager from Western Capital Financial in Los Angeles, lets you cash out up to 15% with no fee. Another, Colonial Liberty/John Hancock Variable Annuity, has waived all surrender fees by reducing broker's commissions to 2% from 4%.)

The combination of surrender charges and a 10% penalty means an annuity *must* be viewed as a long-term investment.

□ CAUTION: Look for a plan that has a "bailout" clause so you can cash out with no surrender charge *if* the insurer lowers the renewal rate by more than 1% below the initial rate.

SELECTING AN ANNUITY

Annuities are not federally protected or guaranteed. If you need that type of security, you should purchase a bank CD, which is covered by FDIC insurance, or Treasury securities, which are backed by the full faith and credit of the U.S. government. With an annuity, you must depend on the financial strength of the insurance company. It should have an A or A+ A. M. Best rating. (Most large libraries carry this rating book, or you can ask the insurance company what its rating is.)

It's a good idea to check the ratings periodically, since insurance companies can be downgraded. Remember, Baldwin United, which filed for bankruptcy just over 6 years ago, once had an A+ rating! (The company had approxi-

mately $3.4 billion in annuities. The investors did not lose their principal, but a great many did not have access to it for several years.)

$ HINT: If your company's rating drops, you can make a tax-free exchange into another annuity. Called a 1035 exchange, it is similar to a tax-free IRA rollover.

Additional protection is provided in all 50 states—but not in Washington, DC. If one insurer goes bankrupt, the state fund assesses charges against other insurance companies in the state to cover investor losses. Call your state insurance commission to determine if you live in one of these states. Coverage is generally limited to $300,000 per life insurance policy or $100,000 per annuity—*Find out!*

The current rates for over 180 fixed annuities are tracked by Comparative Annuity Reports (P.O. Box 1268, Fair Oaks, CA 95628). A copy of the monthly newsletter, which provides an overview of the top ten programs is $10. Returns on variable annuities are tracked by Lipper Analytical Services of Summit, NJ, and reported weekly in *Barron's*. Since Lipper does not take into account sales charges, you may want to consult the latest monthly survey by Variable Annuity Research & Data Services (VARDS) of Miami. VARDS, which tracks the total returns of 700 annuity funds, subtracts management fees in calculating performance figures. Call: 305-252-4600.

The tax-deferred advantages of an annuity do not come cheap. Sales charges, surrender fees, management costs, and other expenses can eat away at your return. You can reduce some of these costs by purchasing a no- or low-load annuity, such as the Vanguard plan (see box on page 312).

FOR FURTHER INFORMATION

INSURANCE

Glenn Daily, *The Individual Investor's Guide to Low-Load Insurance Products*. (International Publishing Corp., 1991), $19.95.

For a copy of *A Consumer's Guide to Life Insurance*, contact:

The American Council of Life Insurance Company Services

1001 Pennsylvania Avenue NW
Washington, DC 20004
1-202-624-2000
Free

For the organization's list of publications, as well as "Rate of Return" data, contact:

NICO
121 North Payne Street
Alexandria, VA 22314
1-703-549-8050

For details and an evaluation of rates, bailout provisions, and suitability of over 30 insurance companies offering single-premium whole life, single-premium annuities, term, and universal life insurance, contact:

Tax Planning Seminars
Frank Miller
2 Echelon Plaza, Suite 220
Voorhees, NJ 08043
1-800-445-6914

LONG-TERM CARE INSURANCE

Long Term Care: A Dollars and Sense Guide
United Seniors Health Cooperative
1331 H Street NW
Washington, DC 20005
1-202-393-6222
$10

How Do I Pay for My Long-Term Care?
Berkeley Planning Associates
440 Grand Avenue, Suite 500
Oakland, CA 94610
1-510-465-7884
$7.77

Consumer's Guide to Long Term Care Insurance
Health Insurance Association of America
1025 Connecticut Avenue NW
Washington, DC 20036
1-202-223-7780
Free

The Association will also send you a list of private insurers offering long-term health care policies in your state.

MEDIGAP INSURANCE

Guide to Medigap Policies
The Health Insurance Association of America
1025 Connecticut Avenue NW
Washington, DC 20036
1-202-223-7780

Medigap (#D13696)
AARP Fulfillment
601 E Street NW
Washington, DC 20049

Guide to Health Insurance for People with Medicare
Consumer Information Center
Box 100
Pueblo, CO 81002
$1

PART SEVEN

TAXES AND YOUR INVESTMENTS

The U.S. Congress is continually overhauling the tax code. Unless you master its basic points, you could unwittingly lose hundreds of dollars to the IRS. It is particularly crucial that every financial decision you make be made only after reading the following two chapters and consulting with your tax adviser.

These chapters explain the pertinent parts of the law and how it relates to investments and also shows you how to take advantage of these changes. Among the topics covered are:

- Margin loans
- AMT
- Your investments
- Sources of tax-free income
- Last-minute tax savers

32

DEALING WITH YOUR TAXES

After months of negotiations, Congress finally passed the Omnibus Budget Reconciliation Act of 1990 on October 27, 1990. The goal: to reduce the deficit by about $500 billion over 5 years. Here's how it affects you and your taxes:

- Beginning in 1992, if you are a married individual filing a joint return with taxable income in excess of $86,500, or a single individual with income over $51,900, you will pay tax at a marginal rate of 31%. (Before, there were theoretically two tax rates: 15% and 28%.)
- Your capital gains will be taxed at a marginal rate of no more than 28%.
- The alternative minimum tax (AMT) has been increased to 24%, up from 21%.
- If your adjusted gross income (AGI) is over $105,250 or $52,625 for married filing separately, certain itemized deductions are reduced.
- From now on, if you are claiming an exemption for a 1-year-old dependent, you must include that dependent's Social Security number on your tax return. (You can get a Social Security number by filing Form SS-5 with the Social Security Administration.) Previously, Social Security numbers were required starting at age 2.
- Starting after 1990, the cost of cosmetic surgery not necessary to ameliorate a deformity arising from or directly related to a congenital abnormality, a personal injury resulting from an accident or trauma, or a disfiguring disease is no longer a deductible medical expense. That means there is no deduction for nose jobs, face-lifts, or hair transplants.
- Personal exemptions have been phased out for taxpayers with adjusted gross incomes exceeding $105,250 for single and $157,900 for joint returns.

- A new luxury tax of 10% has been imposed on purchases of what Congress calls "luxury" goods.

This chapter and the next are designed to show you *as an investor* ways to save on taxes, and, at the same time, invest profitably. Tax considerations are clearly important when it comes to investing, but they should never be allowed to eclipse the basics.

THE ALTERNATIVE MINIMUM TAX

This tax was designed to make certain that Americans with high incomes and high deductions would still have to pay at a rate of 21% on their alternative minimum taxable income (AMTI). The Omnibus Budget Reconciliation Act of 1990 increased the alternative minimum tax (AMT) to 24%. So no matter how rich you are, no matter how many loopholes or tax shelters your accountant finds for you, if you have a high income, you may still have to pay some federal income tax.

You can easily determine if you are subject to the alternative minimum tax by following these steps:

1   Add all your preference items and adjustments (see following list) to your taxable income.
2   From this amount, subtract $40,000 if you are married and filing jointly, $30,000 if you are single, or $20,000 if you are married and filing separately. If AMTI exceeds $150,000 (married filing jointly), $112,500 (single), or $75,000 (married filing separately), the $40,000, $30,000, or $20,000 must be reduced by 25% of the excess over the $150,000, $112,500, or $75,000.

3 Multiply this amount by a flat 24%. The result is your minimum tax.

If your standard tax is less than this figure, you must pay the alternative minimum tax. The AMT is imposed only when it is greater than the regular tax, reduced by certain credits.

Certain preference items and adjustments (line items that get favorable treatment on your regular income) increase your chances of being vulnerable to the AMT. Among the key items are:

- Accelerated depreciation on real property you own that was placed in service before 1987
- Certain costs often associated with tax shelters, such as research and development costs and intangible drilling costs
- State and local income tax, real estate and personal property tax
- Tax-exempt interest on newly issued private activity bonds
- Untaxed appreciation on charitable contributions of appreciated property
- Excess of fair market value of stock acquired by exercising an incentive stock option over the amount paid, unless you sell the stock in the same year
- Deductible portion of passive activity losses

Deductions that reduce your AMT are:
- Depletion
- Medical expenses that exceed 10% of your gross income. (Do not confuse this limit with the 7.5% limit for regular tax purposes.)
- Charitable contributions, generally up to 50% of your adjusted gross income
- Casualty losses in excess of 10% of adjusted gross income and the $100 floor
- Interest costs on your home
- Certain estate taxes
- Interest costs to the extent that they do not exceed your net investment income, refigured for AMT

$ HINT: Since 1985 the IRS has required taxpayers to make estimated tax payments to cover taxes due under the AMT category. If you have substantial tax shelter write-offs, figure your AMT liability using IRS Form 6251 and then make certain this amount is covered through withholding or quarterly estimated tax payments, if appropriate.

BORROWED MONEY AND BONDS

In the past, the IRS allowed you to borrow money to buy bonds, and to the extent that the interest rate on your loan exceeded the interest income from the bond, you had a deduction. This deduction could then be used to offset other current income. Excess interest expense that is equal to the discount and interest accruing, but not includable in income, is *not* deductible. The excess interest is deductible when includable interest exceeds interest expense or when disposition occurs.

This ruling killed one of the most popular year-end tax-saving strategies of all time. In the past, you could borrow money to buy a Treasury bond or note that matured after the end of the year. The interest on the borrowed money was deductible in the current year, yet you were not taxed on it until you sold the T-bill in the next year.

Now, however, to the extent that you have unrealized income on the T-bill, you are not allowed to deduct the interest expense. Your deduction is deferred until you sell or redeem the T-bill. This also applies to other debt instruments.

TIMELY MOVES: WISE YEAR-END INVESTMENT STRATEGIES

TAX STRATEGIES

- If you have been buying or selling commodities, a different set of tax rules applies. Check with your accountant, as this ruling is extremely complicated.
- If you own stock in a corporation whose long-term outlook is favorable but whose stock has dropped in price, you may want to take a loss for tax purposes but not give up your position entirely. You can buy more stock now at the lower price and sell your original holdings 31 days later. (You must wait the 31 days in order to avoid the "wash sale rule," which prevents loss deductions on sale and repurchase transactions made within 31 days. You

can buy it back after 31 days.) The risk involved is of course that the stock could continue to fall in price.

■ If you own stock that has gone way up in price since you purchased it and you feel it is near its peak and you want to lock in your profit but not pay taxes this year, you can "sell short against the box" (see page 258). In other words, you can keep your stock until the covering date next year, when you will be taxed. This is known as "closing the transaction." The gain is always taxed in the year the transaction is closed.

BOND SWAPS

Another year-end strategy that can help save on taxes is a bond swap. You'll find that under certain circumstances it pays to sell bonds worth less than their initial cost in order to set up a tax loss and then reinvest that same money in a similar bond. By converting a paper loss to an actual loss, you can offset any taxable gains earned in more profitable investments. In the process of swapping, you may also be able to increase your yield.

If you're thinking of a bond swap, don't wait until the last days of the year. It may take your broker several weeks to locate an appropriate bond.

Bond swaps involve two steps:
1 Selling bonds that have declined in price
2 Replacing these assets with similar (but not substantially identical) bonds

By immediately purchasing similar bonds for approximately the same price as the ones you sold, you restore your market position and your income.

➤ TAX BREAKS Even if you didn't make a killing in the market this year, if you took some investment profits, a bond swap can help reduce your tax bite. Here's how it works:

If you own bonds purchased when interest rates were lower, they are probably worth less in the secondary market today. If you sell them, you can take a loss that can be used, dollar for dollar, to offset any capital gains. If you have no long- or short-term capital gains, the loss can be used to offset up to $3,000 of taxable income, on a dollar-for-dollar basis. If your loss is greater

DEDUCTIONS FOR THE INVESTOR

You can deduct the amount over 2% of adjusted gross income for certain expenses incurred to produce and collect income and to manage or maintain property held to make income. Among these deductible-as-itemized deductions are:
■ Subscriptions to investment publications
■ Cost of books on investing and taxes
■ Clerical expenses
■ Insurance on investment property
■ Safe deposit box rent or home safe if used to hold securities
■ Fees for accounting or investment advice and for legal advice if related to tax or investment matters
■ Expenses directly related to tax (but not investment) seminars, including transportation
■ Travel expenses to visit your broker, your safe deposit box, and your tax accountant or lawyer for investment or income-tax purposes
■ Computers: The cost of a computer used in managing your investments is sometimes deductible. (If you use your computer for business over 50% of the time, you can depreciate it over 5 years.)
■ IRA or Keogh account custodial fees

than that, it can be carried over into the next year.

A bond swap enables you to keep your position by buying comparable bonds selling for approximately the same price.

In order for the IRS to recognize a loss for tax purposes, you must buy bonds of a different issuer or with a substantially different maturity date or coupon.

➤ STATE INCOME TAX A bond swap is also useful if you move from a state with no income tax to one that has an income tax. Buy municipal bonds issued by the new state that are not subject to state taxes.

➤ SWAPPING COSTS Unlike stocks and most other securities, where commissions are noted separately from the purchase or sale price, municipal bonds have their commission included in the price of the bond. Commissions range from $5 to $20 per $1,000-face-value bond, which means that a swap involving $50,000 worth of bonds could entail a commission somewhere between $500 and $2,000.

SHIFTING INCOME TO CHILDREN

According to the new tax law, unearned income of a child aged 14 or less, regardless of the source, is taxed at the parent's rate when this income exceeds $1,157 per year. But the first $578 is not taxed, and the next $539 is taxed at the child's rate. If the child is over 14, all income is taxed at the child's rate, presumably lower than the parent's.

The new law has in effect put an end to the value of the Clifford trust, which was one of the most popular ways to reduce taxes by transferring assets to children.

If you wish to give money to your children but you don't want it to be taxed at your rate, you are limited to a handful of choices. One, of course, is tax-free municipal bonds. Another is U.S. EE savings bonds. In the latter case, interest is not taxed until the bonds are cashed in. Then, when your child turns 14, you can change the portfolio mix and periodically cash in the bonds, since the income will then be taxed at the child's rate.

§ HINT: Earnings in Clifford trusts set up after March 1, 1986, will be taxed to the donor regardless of the beneficiary's age.

If you have already transferred investments to a child under age 14, you may want to put these investments into municipals or zero coupon bonds.

§ HINT: You can still make a tax-free loan up to $10,000 ($20,000 for a couple) to each member of your family per year. It is also possible to loan up to $100,000 if tax avoidance is not one of the principal purposes. Imputed interest is then limited to the borrower's investment income. This is a popular way for parents to help children buy property.

If you are involved in income shifting, keep careful records indicating that you have separate accounts for your children.

LAST-MINUTE TAX MANEUVERS

Despite New Year's resolutions and other good intentions, most people put off organizing their tax return materials until the first week in April. If you're serious about reducing your tax bite, you should start at the end of the year. Here are 10 last-minute moves that will pay off:

- *Shift income.* You have until December 31 to shift money to reduce your taxable income and at the same time avoid the gift tax. The law allows you to give anyone up to $10,000 a year ($20,000 for a married couple) tax free. Although there is no gift tax on the transfer, there will be income tax on any earnings the gift generates. Note: The recipient of the income must have immediate access to the funds transferred. Check with your accountant for exceptions.

- *Set aside retirement money.* If you have income from your own business or from free-lance work, set up a Keogh retirement account at a bank or brokerage firm. The dollar amount you contribute is tax deductible directly from your taxable income and the principal grows on a tax-deferred basis. You must open your Keogh before the end of the year but you do not need to make a dollar contribution until you actually file your tax return.

- *Contribute early to your IRA.* Put aside money now to fund your IRA or Keogh plan. Tax is deferred on the income earned from the day you contribute until withdrawal. If you delay making your 1993 contribution until the last minute, you are giving up months of compounded tax-deferred income.

- *Add up your deductions.* Take time to determine if you have spent enough on tax-deductible items to qualify for write-offs. Miscellaneous deductible expenses must be greater than 2% of your adjusted gross income in order to be itemized. Unreimbursed medical expenses must add up to more than 7.5% of your AGI to be deductible. If you are still far away from these minimums (known as "floors"), try to postpone these expenses until next year when you may have enough to deduct then. On the other hand, if you are near these thresholds, consider making additional expenditures that will lift you above the floor. *Note:* Some municipal bonds are subject to the AMT; check with your accountant.

- *Establish a charitable remainder trust.* The philanthropic should consider a remainder trust in which you give appreciated securities, such as stocks, bonds, or property, to a charity in exchange for a qualified annuity. As the donor, you receive an immediate charitable deduction. The amount is determined by IRS tables. This type of annuity is not subject to premature withdrawal penalties or new pension excise tax. Since rulings are complex, work out this particular tax move with a knowledgeable accountant.
- *Defer capital gains tax on property.* Until Congress decides otherwise, you can still swap one piece of investment property for another, deferring capital gains tax until the property is sold for cash. The pieces exchanged must be comparable and used for business or investment purposes. (Your home does not qualify.) If the two properties are not of equal value, and cash or an additional piece of property has been included in the swap to make up the difference, both are taxable.
- *File correct estimates.* If you underestimate this particular tax, you face a penalty, but if you overestimate you lose the earning power of that money. To be safe, estimate 100% of last year's tax liability—the actual amount reported on your return or, if required, 90% of current liability. Check with your accountant. Then, even if your income goes up, you will not be penalized.

- *Pre-pay property and state and local income taxes by December 31.* If you pay 100% of your state tax liability by December 31 you can deduct it on this year's federal income tax return.
- *Make charitable contributions with appreciated investments.* If you are considering making a charitable contribution, do so by December 31, and use appreciated investments, such as stocks or bonds. Your capital gains tax will be forgiven and you can get a deduction.
- *Defer income.* Delay receipt of self-employment income or year-end bonuses; or delay billing customers so payments are made to you after December 31.

☐CAUTION: If you are subject to the alternative minimum tax, check with your accountant first before using this option.

OTHER RULES TO KEEP IN MIND

➤ STATE AND LOCAL TAXES Except for sales tax, these taxes continue to be fully deductible.

➤ INVESTMENT EXPENSES These, including tax planning, the cost of this book, tax-return preparation, investment publications, and other miscellaneous items are deductible only for amounts in excess of 2% of your adjusted gross income.

➤ CHARITABLE DEDUCTIONS Unless you itemize, you cannot deduct your charitable contributions.

➤ MEDICAL EXPENSES You can deduct unreimbursed medical expenses only to the extent that they exceed 7.5% of your adjusted gross income.

SOURCES OF TAX-FREE INCOME

By carefully planning your investment strategies, you can easily increase the amount of tax-free or tax-deferred money you receive every year. Here are 10 ways to do just that:

- *IRAs.* You don't pay any tax on the earnings in an individual retirement account until you withdraw the funds. Interest earned is reinvested and thus continues to compound on a tax-deferred basis.

- *Life insurance.* As with an IRA, the interest income earned inside a life insurance investment is tax-deferred until you cash in the policy.
- *Disability insurance.* If you paid your own disability insurance premium, the benefits from accident or health insurance policies are tax-free. However, if your employer paid the premiums, any income you receive from the policy is taxable.
- *Municipal bonds.* Interest earned on muni bonds is free from federal income tax. You may have to pay a state tax if you purchase bonds in a state where they have not been issued—for example, if you live in Minnesota and purchase a bond for New York State, you may have to pay Minnesota tax on the income.
- *Real estate.* Some real estate investments yield depreciation deductions over the life of the property.
- *Savings plans, annuities, and pension plans.* Any investment made with after-tax income is tax-free when you withdraw it or when you receive a payment that represents the return of your investment. Or, to state it another way, the principal is tax-free, although the income earned on the principal is generally taxed.
- *Social Security.* Disability, retirement, or surviving spouse income may be tax-free, depending on your other income. Taxpayers with income greater than $32,000 ($25,000 for singles) have to pay tax on half of their Social Security income. A minimum of half of this income is tax-free.
- *Tax-deferred annuities.* Sometimes called single-premium deferred annuities. The money invested with an insurance company in this type of annuity and the interest earned is deferred until you cash in and receive that income.
- *Tax-free money market funds.* Mutual funds whose portfolios consist of very short-term municipal notes offer tax-free income.
- *U.S. Treasury issues.* Treasury bonds, notes, bills, and savings bonds are exempt from tax at the state level no matter what state you live in. However, there is a federal tax due on these investments.

FOR FURTHER INFORMATION

These publications are available free of charge at your local IRS office or by calling 1-800-TAX-FORM (3676). For a complete list of all IRS brochures, ask for publication 910, *Guide to Free Tax Services.*

523 Tax Information on Selling Your Home
527 Residential Rental Property
530 Tax Information for Home Owners including Condominiums and Cooperative Apartments
550 Investment Income and Expenses
554 Tax Information for Older Americans
560 Retirement Plans for the Self-employed
564 Mutual Fund Distributions
575 Pension and Annuity Income
590 Individual Retirement Arrangements (IRAs)
915 Social Security Benefits

33

ALPHABETICAL DIRECTORY OF YOUR INVESTMENTS AND THEIR TAX STATUS

The information that follows is general in scope and intended as an introductory explanation of how taxes affect your investments. Remember, the IRS recognizes three types of income:

- *PORTFOLIO or INVESTMENT: dividends and interest*
- *ACTIVE INCOME: salaries, wages, fees, commissions, and personal services*
- *PASSIVE INCOME: From businesses you don't actively manage and from rental property. Note: Passive losses cannot offset active or portfolio income; they can offset only passive income.*

You should always consult your accountant about specific problems.

ANNUITIES

- Interest earned can accumulate tax-free until withdrawn. When it is withdrawn, only the interest earned is taxed, not your initial investment.
- If you withdraw money prior to age 59½, there is a 10% tax penalty. With qualified employer-sponsored annuities, there is no 10% penalty if you immediately transfer the money to a qualified annuity with another company.
- For other rulings, check your policy.

ANTIQUES, ART, COINS, GEMS, STAMPS, AND OTHER COLLECTIBLES

- Profits made upon sale are subject to federal income tax at the regular rate of 15%, 28%, or 31%. The purchase price is subject to state and local sales tax.

BONDS (AGENCY ISSUES)

- Interest income is subject to federal tax.
- Interest income on some agency issues is exempt from state and local taxes. Ask your broker or accountant.

BONDS (CORPORATE)

- Interest income is subject to federal, state, and local taxes.
- Gains made when bonds are sold are taxed at regular rates, but this is under review.
- Losses can be used to offset other net gains you may have, plus up to $3,000 of wages, salary, and other "ordinary" income.

BONDS (MUNICIPAL)

- Interest earned on most munis is exempt from federal income tax and from state and local taxes for residents of the state where the bonds are issued.
- Most states tax out-of-state bonds.
- Bonds issued by the Commonwealth of Puerto Rico and the District of Columbia are exempt from taxes in all states.
- Interest earned on certain "private-activity" bonds that were issued after August 7, 1986, is a tax preference item to be included in the calculation of the alternative minimum tax (see page 316). If you are not subject to the AMT, you will not pay taxes on these particular bonds.
- Some bonds are now subject to federal tax but remain exempt at the state and local levels—these include bonds to help finance convention centers.

- Illinois, Iowa, Kansas, Oklahoma, and Wisconsin tax any municipal bonds issued in their state.
- Interest earned on fully tax-exempt bonds can have a tax cost when held by retired people receiving Social Security. If you are retired and if your adjusted gross income plus half your Social Security plus tax-exempt interest income is over $25,000 for a single return or $32,000 for a joint return, interest earned on the tax-exempt bonds *is* effectively taxable.

BONDS (PREMIUM)

- If you purchase a bond at a premium, you can only use any amortizable premium to offset your interest income. In other words, you can no longer use the premium as a deduction against other types of income. The amortized premium is subtracted directly from the interest you earn on the bond, rather than deducted as a separate expense subject to the investment interest expense limitations.

BONDS (ZERO)

- Taxes must be paid on the so-called imputed interest that accrues annually, even though, of course, no interest is actually paid to the bondholder.
- Because you must pay tax as though you had received interest, zeros are well suited for IRAs and Keoghs where interest income is deferred from taxes until withdrawn and for children over 14 not subject to the kiddie tax.
- Zero coupon municipals are usually exempt from federal taxes and from state and local taxes when bonds are issued in the investor's state.
- Zero coupon Treasuries are exempt from state and local taxes.

CERTIFICATES OF DEPOSIT (CDs)

- Any interest earned is subject to federal, state, and local taxes.
- Interest is taxed in the year it is available for withdrawal without substantial

penalty. Interest can be deferred on a CD with a term of 1 year or less. If you invest in a 6-month CD before July 1, the entire amount of interest is paid 6 months later and taxable in the year of payment. However, if you invest in a 6-month CD after June 30, only the interest actually paid or made available for withdrawal without penalty is taxable in the year issued. The balance is taxable in the year of maturity. The interest, however, must specifically be deferred to the year of maturity by the terms of the CD.

CHILDREN'S INVESTMENTS

- This tax applies only to children under age 14 with investment income over $1,157. Such children must compute their tax on Form 8615 at their parent's top rate unless the parent elects to report the income directly on his or her own return. In other words, the kiddie tax is based on the parent's taxable income. Income in custodial accounts is treated as the child's income and is subject to the kiddie tax, but income the child earns from wages or self-employment is not subject to the kiddie tax.

COMMERCIAL PAPER

- Any interest earned is subject to federal, state, and local taxes.
- *Exception:* Commercial paper issued by state and local governments is usually, but not always, exempt from federal as well as state and local taxes.

COMMODITIES AND FUTURES CONTRACTS

- Profits are taxed at 60/40 rates: 60% long-term and 40% short-term. However, this currently makes no difference.
- Profits become taxable at the end of the year, even if you have not closed out your position. The IRS, in effect, will tax you on your paper profits.
- In some cases, you can deduct paper losses, even of positions still open. These

rules may apply to contracts subject to the mark-to-the-market rule. Check with your accountant.

CONVERTIBLE STOCKS AND BONDS

- There is no gain or loss when you convert a bond into a stock or preferred stock into common stock of the same corporation, IF the conversion privilege was granted by the bond or preferred stock certificate.

CREDIT UNION ACCOUNTS

- Even though depositors are actually shareholders of the credit union and the money earned is known as a dividend, your earnings are regarded as interest and subject to federal, state, and local taxes.

DIVIDEND INCOME

Dividends and interest you receive are reported to the IRS by the company on various versions of form 1099: dividends on Form 1099-DIV, interest on Form 1099-INT, and original issue discount on Form 1099-OID. You also will receive copies from the company and must report the amounts shown on your tax return. The IRS will use its forms to check the income you report.

- *Cash dividends.* If you receive dividends from IBM, GE, Pepsi, or any other corporation, the amount is reported by the company directly to the IRS. You, in turn, receive Form 1099-DIV from each corporation telling precisely how much you received for the year.
- *Stock dividends.* If you own common stock in a company and receive additional shares as a dividend, it is usually not taxable. Exceptions: if you can take either stock or cash or if it is a taxable class of stock. Your company will notify you if it is taxable.
- *Dividend reinvestment plans.* If you sign up to have your dividends automatically reinvested in the company's stock and if you pay fair market value for these shares, the full cash dividend is taxable. The IRS maintains that since you could

have had cash but elected not to, you will be taxed the same year you receive the dividend.

- *Return of capital.* Corporations sometimes give a return of capital distribution. If this is the case it will be so designated on your 1099 slip. Most return of capital is not taxed; however, your basis of stock must be reduced by whatever the amount is. If a return of capital exceeds basis, the excess is taxable and the basis is reduced to zero.
- *Insurance dividends.* Any dividends you may receive on veterans' insurance are *not* taxed, and dividends received from regular life insurance are generally not taxed. However, if you are in doubt, check with your accountant or insurance company.
- *Other types of dividends.* Money market mutual funds pay what is called a dividend, and you should list it as such on your tax return.

If you have an interest-bearing checking account with a savings and loan or a credit union, you may collect interest, although it is sometimes referred to as dividend income. Be aware: If this interest is reported on the 1099 slip as dividends, you too should report it as dividend income.

EQUIPMENT-LEASING PARTNERSHIPS

- Income is subject to federal, state, and local taxes.
- Deductions generated by the partnership will help shelter some of the income derived from lease payments. The key deduction is depreciation for the cost of the equipment. If the partnership borrows to pay for the equipment, interest may also be deductible.
- When deductions are greater than income, resulting losses cannot be used to shelter your salary, wages, interest, and dividend income or profits made in the stock market. The partnership losses can only be used to shelter income from other passive activities.
- If you do not have passive income (i.e., interest in a partnership or S corporation where you do not actively participate in

the business), you can carry these losses forward and use them when the equipment-leasing deal has excess income or when the investment is disposed of.
- If the partnership is publicly traded, income and loss require special treatment; check with your accountant.

FOREIGN CURRENCY

- If you have a foreign bank account or a foreign securities account, you must indicate this on Form TDF 90-22.1 if the value of the accounts at any time during the year was over $10,000.

GINNIE MAE, FREDDIE MAC, AND FANNIE MAE CERTIFICATES

- The interest portion of the monthly payments you receive is subject to federal, state, and local taxes.
- Profits from the sale of any mortgage-backed security are taxed as well.

GOLD AND SILVER

- If you buy gold or silver coins or bullion, most states impose state and local sales tax. In many cases you can sidestep this tax if you do not take delivery but leave the metal with the dealer and buy certificates instead.
- Profits from the sale of gold and silver are taxed at regular rates, generally as capital gains, but this is under review.
- Dividends from precious metals stocks and mutual funds are taxed at regular rates, in the same manner as other dividends.
- Profits from futures and options: see "Commodities."
- An exchange of gold for gold coins or silver for silver coins usually qualifies as a tax-free exchange of like-kind investment property—for example, if you exchange Mexican pesos for Austrian coronas. However, exchanging silver for gold is not tax-free.

HISTORIC REHABILITATION

- The credit is 20% or 10%, depending on the building (10% for nonresidential buildings put into service prior to 1936 and 20% for all certified historic structures).
- The tax credit is not a deduction: It provides a dollar-for-dollar reduction in the actual amount of income tax you owe.
- The tax credit is applicable only to depreciable buildings—those used in a trade or business or held for the production of income, such as a commercial or residential rental property. A nondepreciable building may qualify as a certified historic structure *if* it is the subject of charitable contributions for conservation purposes.
- A *certified historic structure* is any structure that is listed individually in the National Register of Historic Places, maintained by the Department of the Interior, *or* located in a registered historic district and certified by the Secretary of the Interior.
- A *registered historic district* is any district that is listed in the National Register of Historic Places *or* designated under a state or local statute that has been certified by the Secretary of the Interior as "containing criteria which will substantially achieve the purpose of preserving and rehabilitating buildings of significance to the district."

INVESTMENT CLUBS

- If the club is considered a corporation, it reports and pays a tax on the club's earnings. As an individual, you report dividend distributions made by the club to you. If the club is a partnership, the club files a partnership return that includes the tax consequences of its transactions and the shares of each member. The club does not pay a tax. You and the other members pay tax on your shares of dividends, interest, capital gains, and any other income earned by the club. You report your share as if you earned it personally.

Note: You may deduct as itemized deductions your share of the club's investment expenses, subject, of course, to the 2% AGI floor.

IRAS AND KEOGHS

- See Chapter 30.

LAND

- Any profits made when land is sold are taxable.
- Rental income is subject to regular income tax, although it may be partially offset by deductible expenses, property costs, and mortgage interest payments.
- Land does not qualify for depreciation deductions.
- Check with your accountant regarding the status of income-producing land vis-à-vis the current passive loss rules, as these rulings are complex.

LIFE INSURANCE

- When you purchase whole life insurance, part of your premium goes toward the purchase of insurance; the rest is an investment. The earned income on the investment portion builds up tax-deferred until you cash in the policy. If you die before you cash in, and the benefits are paid to your children or spouse, this buildup becomes completely income tax–free, not just tax-deferred.

☐CAUTION: Single-premium annuities or life insurance policies, where you pay only one premium, no longer qualify for this tax-deferred treatment.

- If you purchase a single-premium contract after June 30, 1988, and you borrow from the contract, the loan is treated as a distribution of income on which you must pay regular income tax and, in most cases, a 10% penalty on the taxable portion. (There's no 10% penalty if distributions are made after you reach 59½ or if you are disabled or if the distribution is part of a life annuity.) The same rules apply to a partial surrender of the contract, a cash withdrawal, or the distribution of

dividends that are not retained by the insurance company as a premium if received on or after the annuity starting date. If received before the annuity starting date, special rules apply. Check with your accountant.

- These rules generally apply also to any life insurance plans ("modified endowment contract") that you fund with fewer than seven annual payments of equal size.
- You must also pay income tax on distributions from single-premium contracts purchased on or after June 21, 1988, to the extent that the distributions exceed your contract investment. Distributions of less than $25,000 made after your death to cover your burial are not taxed.

LOW-INCOME HOUSING

- Tax credits are available to those who buy, build, or rehabilitate low-income housing.
- The credits can offset regular income tax, subject to certain limits, but are phased out if your adjusted gross income is over $200,000. If your income exceeds $250,000, there are no credits.
- For newly constructed properties not federally subsidized, the annual credit is 9%. For acquisition of existing buildings and/or where federal subsidies are used, it is 4%.

☐CAUTION: This can be a high-risk investment and should be examined carefully by a knowledgeable professional. Avoid projects of inexperienced developers.

- Low-income and rehab participation also entitles you to a $25,000 exemption. This benefit is phased out for those with adjusted gross incomes between $100,000 and $150,000. It's available whether or not you actively participate.

These new rules have hurt the real estate industry, which traditionally financed development via limited partnerships that provided tax losses to those who invested during the first years of a project. But the new rules affect others as well—no one who invests in a business without participating in its operations "on a regular, continuous, and substantial basis" can take losses to offset other income.

MARGIN LOANS

- Interest you pay on money borrowed from your broker for investment purposes is deductible only to the extent that it is offset by investment income (from dividends, capital gains, interest income, and royalties). For example, if you want to deduct $1,500 worth of interest on your margin loan, you must report at least $1,500 of investment income to the IRS.
- You must use the money borrowed to make an investment in order to deduct the interest. Keep careful records to document the fact that you used the money for an investment.
- ☐CAUTION: If you borrow to hold municipal bonds or any other tax-exempt investment, interest (or margin) expense is *not* deductible.

MONEY MARKET DEPOSIT ACCOUNTS

- Interest earned is subject to federal, state, and local income taxes.

MONEY MARKET MUTUAL FUNDS

- Interest is subject to federal, state, and local taxes.
- With tax-exempt money market funds, interest is exempt from federal tax and possibly from state and local tax if the fund buys securities in the investor's state.

MUTUAL FUNDS

- Dividend income and capital gains distributions are usually taxed at federal, state, and local levels, except for tax-free or municipal bond funds.
- Income from municipal bond funds is exempt from federal tax and is also exempt from state and local taxes if the securities in the portfolio are issued in the taxpayer's state.

- Mutual fund companies must send investors a year-end statement documenting all distributions and their tax status (Form 1099 and/or Form 1099-B).
- A dividend declared in December by a mutual fund is taxable in the year declared IF it is paid before February 1 of the following year.

Income received from a tax-exempt municipal bond fund is usually tax-free, but capital gains distributions are taxable. Tax-free dividends are not shown on Form 1099-DIV, but capital gains are shown on Form 1099-DIV and must be reported. When selling shares in a tax-exempt bond fund, you make a taxable sale on which you realize a capital gain or loss.

- When you sell your fund shares at a profit, this gain is taxed at the applicable income rate of either 15%, 28%, or 33%.
- Losses can be used to offset gains and up to $3,000 in salary, wages, and ordinary income.
- You must also pay taxes on your share of the fund's investment advisory fees. (Prior to tax reform, this was merely deducted from earnings.) The amount is indicated on Form 1099. You may be able to claim a deduction for this as an investment expense—provided that you itemize and your investment expenses and other miscellaneous itemized expenses exceed 2% of your adjusted gross income. Check with your accountant. The rules regarding these deductions have changed several times.

OIL AND GAS PARTNER-SHIPS

- In year 1 of a drilling program, investors may receive a write-off for 60% to 90% of their investment. This deduction is derived from "intangible drilling costs"—labor, fuel, chemicals, nonsalvageable items.
- If oil is found, deductions are also derived from capital expenditures for materials and equipment (pumps, tanks, etc.). These deductions must be written off over the lifetime of the assets.
- When oil is found, income earned from the partnership is subject to regular tax rates. However "depletion" deductions may

shelter 15% of the gross income of the property, subject to certain limitations.

- In an oil and gas limited partnership, you cannot use losses or write-offs in excess of income to shelter your salary or portfolio income. You can, however, use write-offs against income from this or another tax-sheltered partnership. You can also carry the write-offs forward to a year when the partnership has excess income.
- However, when the partnership interest is ended or when you dispose of your investment, any tax losses can be used to offset other income.
- *Exception:* Investors with "working interests" in oil and gas partnerships (as opposed to a limited partnership investment) can use tax losses to shelter wages, salary, and ordinary income. The risk, of course, is that your entire net worth is exposed. In a limited partnership, your risk is limited to the amount you invest.
- Deductions for intangible drilling costs and depletion are preference items and used in calculating the AMT. Check with your accountant.

OPTIONS

- Profits are taxed at regular rates.
- If your option expires and is therefore worthless, this loss can be used to offset gains and up to $3,000 of salary, wages, and ordinary income.
- If you do not exercise your option, the premium income you receive is taxed.
- If you do exercise the option, the premium is added on to the sales proceeds of the stock. It is then taxed, based on the sale of the stock.

POINTS

- See "Real Estate."

PREFERRED STOCKS

- See "Stocks."

PUBLIC LIMITED PARTNER-SHIPS

- If a limited partnership trades publicly, income earned is not passive but is considered portfolio income, and current losses cannot be used to offset income from other public partnerships.
- Most funds make their largest distributions at the end of the year; call the 800 number to verify. Avoid buying fund shares just before major distributions. The fund's NAV or share price immediately drops by the amount of the distribution. By waiting for a fund to go ex-dividend, you can buy in at a lower share price and avoid paying tax. Consult IRS Publication 564, "Mutual Fund Distributions."

REAL ESTATE

- Until tax reform, the absolute deductibility of mortgage interest was viewed as an inalienable benefit of home ownership. But the 1986 Act and rules passed since then have changed all that. There are now two kinds of mortgage debt: acquisition indebtedness and home equity indebtedness.
- *Acquisition debt.* This is money used to purchase or substantially improve a residence. You may deduct all mortgage interest costs on up to a total of $1 million in acquisition debt for primary and secondary residences purchased or refinanced after October 13, 1987.
- *Home equity debt.* This is money you borrow using your home as collateral. You may deduct interest on home equity loans up to $100,000. The proceeds of this loan can be used for any purpose.
- *Points.* Lenders charge "points" above the regular interest rate to increase their fees and get around state limits. Whether points are deductible as interest depends on what the charge covers. You may deduct points if the payment is solely for your use of the money and not for services performed by the lender, which are separately charged. Points do *not* include fees for services such as appraisal fees,

notary fees, and recording fees. Points should be paid separately by check. Points associated with refinancing a loan are not fully deductible in the year paid but must be deducted ratably over the life of the loan.

- Gain on the sale of your principal residence may be deferred if the proceeds are invested in another principal residence that you buy or build within a time period beginning 2 years before the date of the sale and ending 2 years after the sale date. To defer the full amount of the gain, the cost of the new residence must be at least equal to the adjusted sales price of the old residence.
- *The $125,000 capital gains exclusion.* This has been expanded, so that if you are age 55 or older and you sold your home after September 30, 1988, you may be able to exclude up to $125,000 of the capital gain from your income even if you did not use the house as a principal residence for 3 of the 5 previous years. New rules offer an exception for a homeowner who, because of physical or mental handicaps, lived in residential care facilities, provided he or she lived in the principal residence for 1 of the 5 years before it was sold.

REAL ESTATE INVESTMENT TRUSTS (REITs)

- Although REITs generally do not pay taxes themselves, you as an investor do. Most dividends are taxable, even those that represent capital gains distributions from the sale of property.
- There is an exception: Dividends paid out of the shareholders' equity and treated as a return of your original investment are not taxed.
- When you sell your REIT stock, any gains realized are taxed at regular rates, but this is under review.
- Losses from a REIT stock can be used to offset gains, plus up to $3,000 of salary, wages, and ordinary income.

REAL ESTATE LIMITED PARTNERSHIPS (RELPs)

- Partnerships generate deductions based on depreciation, operating expenses, and interest, but they can be used by investors to shelter only income from this partnership or from another passive activity, not ordinary income.
- Excess deductions cannot be used to offset taxes you owe on your salary, wages, interest and dividend income, or stock market profits.
- Income from a partnership that is greater than the deductions allowed is taxed at regular rates.
- Profits made from the sale of property are taxed at regular rates.
- Low-income housing and historic rehabilitation partnerships are exceptions to the rules. If your adjusted gross income is $200,000 or less, you can use the special tax credits offered by two types of deals to offset tax of up to $25,000 of other income. The $25,000 amount is reduced for those with higher incomes; if your income is $250,000 or above, the credit is phased out entirely.

RENTAL REAL ESTATE

- Rental income and profits when property is sold are taxed at regular rates.
- Much rental income can be sheltered by deductions and expenses, such as mortgage interest, property taxes, depreciation, maintenance, repairs, and travel to and from the property. You can write off the cost of residential properties over a period of 27½ years, or 31½ years for commercial property.
- Up to $25,000 per year in tax losses can be used to offset your wages, salary, and other income, provided that your adjusted gross income is under $100,000. This $25,000 cap is reduced 50¢ for each dollar by which your adjusted gross income exceeds $100,000. By the time your income hits $150,000, the cap is at zero. You must, however, pass the active participation test to receive this benefit.
- If your adjusted gross income is over $150,000, you can use tax deductions only up to the amount of rental income received that year. If there are any excess losses, they can be carried over until such time as you have excess income. These

losses, however, can be used to offset income from other passive activities.

- To claim losses, you cannot have less than a 10% ownership in rental property.

SAVINGS ACCOUNTS

- Interest earned is taxable even though you do not present your passbook to have the interest entered. *Note*: Dividends on deposits or accounts in some institutions are reported as interest income: mutual savings banks, cooperative banks, domestic building and loan associations, and savings and loan associations.

SAVINGS BONDS

- Interest is exempt from state and local taxes.
- Federal income tax can be deferred on Series EE bonds until the bond is redeemed or matures.
- If you roll over your Series EEs into Series HHs, federal tax on the accrued interest can again be deferred until the HH bonds either mature or are redeemed.
- Interest earned on Series HH bonds is taxed each year.
- If you elect to pay the federal tax due each year on Series EE bonds, you pay on the annual increase in redemption value of the bond. However, once you begin paying, you must continue doing so for the bonds you presently own plus any new ones you buy.
- *Children's accounts.* If a child is under age 14 the first $578 of investment income is not taxed. The next $539 is taxed at the child's rate. Any investment income over $1,000 per year is taxed at the parent's tax rate, which is presumably higher. Starting at age 14, the income is taxed at the child's lower rate. By timing bonds to come due after the child turns 14, you can save on taxes.
- EE savings bonds purchased after January 1, 1990, by a bondholder at least 24 years old, and used to pay college tuition for yourself, your spouse, or dependent children, are free from federal income tax provided you fall within recently

established income guidelines. Since the guidelines are inflation-indexed, check with your tax adviser to see if you can take advantage of this tax break.

STOCK INDEX OPTIONS AND FUTURES

- Profits are generally taxed at regular rates.
- Profits on futures and options become taxable at the end of the year, even if you have not closed out your position. In effect, the IRS will tax you on paper profits.
- In some cases you can deduct paper losses, even of positions still open. Check with your accountant.

STOCK RIGHTS

- If you sell your rights, the profit is taxed.
- If you exercise the rights, you will eventually pay tax, but not until you sell the new stock.
- If you receive stock rights (as opposed to purchasing them in the market) and then let them expire, you cannot claim a deduction for the loss.
- If you purchase rights in the market and let them expire as worthless, you can deduct the loss.

STOCK SPLITS

- Stock splits are not dividends; they do not represent a distribution of surplus funds as do stock dividends. Therefore, stock splits are not taxable.

STOCKS

- Profits from the sale of stocks and dividends earned are taxed at regular rates, but this is under review.
- Losses from sales may be used to offset any gains you have plus up to $3,000 of salary, wages, and other ordinary income.
- Interest on margin loans may be claimed as an itemized deduction. Check with your accountant.
- Gain on the exchange of common stock for other common stock (or preferred for other

preferred) of the same company is not taxable. An exchange of preferred stock for common, or common for preferred, in the same company, is generally not tax-free, unless the exchange is part of a tax-free recapitalization.

- You may deduct as a capital loss the cost basis of securities that became worthless during the year. *Note*: It is deductible *only* in the year it became completely worthless. To support this deduction, you must show that it had some value the previous year and that it became worthless in the current year—showing that the company went bankrupt, stopped doing business, or is insolvent. Check with your stockbroker.

STOCKS (FOREIGN)

- If you have foreign tax withheld from dividends of a foreign stock, you are entitled to a credit. To determine how much, divide your taxable foreign income by your total income, then multiply by the amount of U.S. tax. *Example:* You receive taxable foreign income of $5,000 and your total taxable income is $100,000. Divide $5,000 by $100,000 and multiply that by $28,000 (the estimated U.S. tax on $100,000). The maximum tax credit you could claim would be $1,400. Your credit would be the lesser of the amount withheld and the maximum credit calculated. Any amount disallowed in the current year may be carried forward.
- You can also list foreign taxes as an itemized deduction on line 7 of Schedule A. But you must choose one method or the other.

TREASURY BILLS

- Interest income is subject to federal tax but not state and local taxes.
- The income earned is subject to taxation the year in which it matures or in which you sell it.
- With T-bills, the dollar difference between the original price and the amount you receive when you redeem the bill is regarded as the interest income.

- You can defer income from one year to the next by purchasing a T-bill that matures in the new calendar year.

TREASURY BONDS

- Interest is subject to federal tax but free from state and local tax.
- Losses from sales can be used to offset any capital gains you have plus up to $3,000 of salary, wages, and other ordinary income.

TREASURY NOTES

- Interest income is subject to federal income tax but exempt from state and local tax.
- Any profit made when T-notes are sold is taxed.
- Any losses from sales can be used to offset any gains you have plus up to $3,000 of salary, wages, and ordinary income.

VACATION HOMES

- *If a home is solely for personal use,* you can deduct mortgage interest and real estate taxes, as you can with your principal residence. Mortgage interest is not deductible on third or fourth homes unless they are rental properties.
- You can deduct mortgage interest on loans up to the amount of your original purchase price plus improvements. Special rules apply to refinancing.
- *If a home is used for pleasure and rental,* your tax liability varies, depending on how long you rent it out and how long you use it. If you rent it out for no more than 14 days per year, there is no tax on the rental income. You do not even have to report it.
- If you use your home more than 14 days a year or 10% of the number of days rented, whichever is greater, your property qualifies as a second home. Mortgage interest and property taxes become deductible. Rental expenses can be deducted, but only up to the amount of rental income. If you have excess expenses, they can be carried forward.

- If your personal use of your house is 14 days or less a year or 10% of the number of days the house is rented out, whichever is greater, the house is a rental property (see "Rental Real Estate"). Remember, you cannot deduct more than the rental income received, nor can you deduct mortgage interest in excess of rental income, because that is allowed only if the home falls under the second home category. (This is a simplification of a fairly complicated rule. Consult an accountant.)

- When you sell a vacation home, profits are taxed at regular rates. But they do not qualify for the preferential treatment that your primary residence does. With a primary residence, taxes on the profits of a sale can be deferred as long as the profits are reinvested in a principal residence that costs at least as much as the sale price of the previous home. The special one-time $125,000 exemption of gains from the sale of a primary residence available to those age 55 or older is not extended to the sale of vacation homes. Losses from sales of vacation homes are not deductible.

WARRANTS

- Profits made when warrants are sold are taxed at regular rates.

- If your warrant expires worthless, the cost of the warrant can be used to offset capital gains plus up to $3,000 of salary, wages, and other ordinary income.

- If the warrant is converted to stock shares, no taxes are due on the transaction.

PART EIGHT

YOUR CUSTOMIZED PORTFOLIO

You've now read over 300 pages about investing, provided you started at the beginning and plowed straight through to this point. Yet all reading and no action won't make you rich. It's now time to actually pick specific investments that will work for you. In this special section you will find suggestions for what to buy— and why. Although we've divided the sample portfolios by lifestyle, you should read all of them and mix and match investments that seem right to you. If you're worried or nervous about making a move, resist sitting on the sidelines. It may seem safe, but earning 3 to 4% in a savings account is not safe since it barely equals the current rate of inflation. Calm your investment jitters by heeding the advice of the great Cowboy-Humorist Will Rogers: "Even if you're on the right track, you'll get run over if you just sit there."

Sample portfolios follow for those who are:
- Just out of school
- Newly married, or living with a significant other
- Raising a family
- Empty nesters
- Retired, or just about to be
- Have, or are starting, a small business

Plus, how to protect your portfolio during tough economic times.

YOUR CUSTOMIZED PORTFOLIO

Whether you're in your twenties or your eighties, or somewhere in between, certain investments are just right for you.

The following sample portfolios contain investment ideas that are geared toward the various stages of your life. Many of them, particularly the stocks, should be held at least a year or more. The portfolios are divided into five lifestyle categories: investors who are just out of school, those who are newly married, those having a family, the empty nesters, and finally, those approaching or in retirement. Even though all the suggestions are above average in quality, major world events, market conditions and interest rates shift rapidly, so actively monitor your portfolio year-round and discuss your stock and bond selections with a reliable pro.

IF YOU'RE JUST OUT OF SCHOOL

This is a time for new beginnings—you're on your own, perhaps for the first time in your life, and although your income is probably modest, it's likely to increase quite quickly. Your responsibilities are limited—perhaps only to you and your cat—so you can focus your financial attention on building up a solid cash base. Follow these 10 steps to achieve financial independence:

Step 1. Set financial goals (see suggestions in the box on page 335).

Step 2. Open a bank account. If you're new in the area, try the same institution your company uses.

Step 3. Get a credit card and pay all bills on time to establish a good credit rating.

Step 4. Open a money market mutual fund. A list of high-yielding funds appears on page 43.

Step 5. Sign up for the automatic payroll savings plan where you work and have 3% to 5% of your paycheck transferred into your money market fund.

Step 6. After you've accumulated cash to cover three months' worth of living expenses you're ready to invest. (Aim to keep housing costs to 30% or less of take-home pay.) Begin by purchasing several short-term CDs with different maturities, either at a local bank for convenience or with an out-of-the-area bank that has higher rates. Check *Barron's* (a weekly) or Friday's *Wall Street Journal* for a list of the nation's top-yielding CDs.

Step 7. Purchase 100 shares of stock in the company you work for, if you have faith in its future, using the company's stock purchase plan, if one exists. You'll avoid a broker's commission and you may be able to buy shares at a discount.

Alternative: Buy 100 shares of a company whose product you use or like, or one that is within the industry where you work. *Suggestions:* Ben & Jerry's, Apple Computer, Nike, PepsiCo, Club Med, J.P. Morgan, and Kellogg's. Use this as a learning experience, as your introduction to the stock market.

Step 8. Study the financial condition of your local electric or gas utility company. Read the annual report and check the rating in *Value Line.* If the utility is rated #1 or #2 in safety, add 100 shares to your portfolio. If your particular utility is not a smart investment, select one of those listed in Chapter 16 on utilities.

Step 9. After a year or two you can afford to take greater risks with your money. Consider the sample portfolios that follow and incorporate those choices that you find appealing, keeping in mind that it is essential to diversify—between types of investments as well as types of industries.

Step 10. Open an IRA so fifty years from

PORTFOLIO FOR THE RECENT GRAD

INVESTMENT	AMOUNT	DETAILS
Money market account	3-months' living expenses	Add cash gifts, bonuses, freelance income
Certificates of deposit	Due in 3, 6, and 12 months	Roll over if rates go up
Company you work for	100 shares	Use employee stock purchase plan
or		
Ben & Jerry's, Apple Computer, Nike, PepsiCo, Club Med, J.P. Morgan, Kellogg's	100 shares	Monitor carefully and reinvest dividends
Electric utility	100 shares	Reinvest dividends
IRA	$2,000	Stock, CD, Treasuries

now you'll have a sizeable retirement fund. Put in $2,000 all at once or in smaller monthly or quarterly payments.

§ HINT: Look into a "Smart Loan" Account which enables college grads to consolidate their student loans into a single loan. Payments in the first four years (when interest is typically higher) are cut by nearly 40%. Students can stretch repayment term from 10 to 15 years. INFO: Sallie Mae (Student Loan Marketing Association) 1-800-524-9100.

IF YOU'RE NEWLY MARRIED OR LIVING WITH A SIGNIFICANT OTHER

Now that you've added someone else to your life, review and revise your financial goals. Draw up a new set of your own as well as some joint goals. Just because you are part of a team doesn't mean that all your goals must match. Some can be his or hers, and some should be

---

GOALS FOR THE RECENT GRAD

- Pay off college loans
- Build up a cash nest egg
- Buy a car
- Save for a vacation
- Save for graduate school or an advanced degree

---

united. Decide whether to invest jointly or separately or do a little of both, keeping in mind that your dual incomes give you doubled investing and saving power.

Step 1. Review the portfolio for the recent grad. All suggestions there should be part of your financial life, too.

Step 2. Focus on the housing issue. You've probably been renting, but now together, by putting aside 3% to 5% of both your salaries, you can save a sizable amount for a down payment on a house or co-op. Begin by purchasing Treasury notes with two- to four-year maturities. Put the semiannual monthly interest payments in your money fund. This cash plus your CDs can be combined with your Treasuries when the latter come due.

Alternative: Treasury zeros require less cash to purchase. For example, those with a 8.2% coupon due February 1997 are priced at just 73. You'll receive $1,000 per note in 1997 (but no interim interest payments). However, you must pay federal taxes each year as if you received the income.

Step 3. Because you have a lot of time to build assets, securities should be primarily for growth, not income, at this point in your life. Check the list of suggested stocks in the box. Regard them as long-term holdings, yet monitor earnings trends regularly and be prepared to sell.

Step 4. If you are in the 28% tax bracket, put 10% to 15% of your investments in municipal bonds or a tax-free unit investment trust.

Step 5. If you and your spouse spend weekends going to flea markets, auctions, or garage

PORTFOLIO FOR THE NEWLY COUPLED

INVESTMENT	AMOUNT	DETAILS
Company you work for	100 shares	Use employee purchase plan, when available
Electric utility company	100 shares	Reinvest dividends
U.S. Treasury notes or zeros	$5,000 minimum	Hold until maturity
Municipal bonds or UIT	$1,000 minimum	Hold until maturity
Neuberger & Berman Partners Fund	$1,000 minimum	Call 1-800-367-0770
IRA	$2,000	Stock, CDs, Treasuries
PepsiCo	100 shares	Price: $37
		Yield: 1.4%
Sysco Corp.	100 shares	Price: $25
		Yield: 1.0%
Montgomery Street Income Securities, Inc.	200 shares	Price: $21
		Yield: 8.3%
H.J. Heinz	100 shares	Price: $40
		Yield: 2.7%
Marvel Entertainment	100 shares	Price: $33
		Yield: none

Prices are as of August 7, 1992.

sales, consider becoming a knowledgeable collector. Every year the "Investor's Almanac" section of this book contains ideas for building a savvy collection. Check your library for previous editions.

➤ PEPSICO. (PEP) This leading soft drink company continues to report increased earnings. It is well positioned overseas to reap benefits of the growing international market for its products and in Mexico, where it is the largest food company. It has a solid balance sheet and strong management.

➤ SYSCO CORP. (SYY) This company distributes food to restaurants, hospitals, hotel/motel chains, and educational institutions. The largest company of its type in the U.S., Sysco is virtually recession-proof.

➤ MONTGOMERY STREET INCOME SECURITIES, INC. (MTS) A closed-end diversified investment company with 74% of assets in high-quality debt instruments. These shares, with their impressive 8.3% yield, are suitable for the most conservative investors, regardless of age.

➤ H. J. HEINZ (HNZ) A well-balanced food company with known brands: Starkist Tuna, Heinz ketchup, and Weight Watchers frozen foods. HNZ is a low-cost producer in many product areas, with growing overseas sales.

➤ MARVEL ENTERTAINMENT (MRV) Derives earnings from sale of comic books and baseball and other trading cards. Recent purchase of Fleer Corp., a producer of baseball cards and gum, makes Marvel a leader in the field.

IF YOU HAVE A FAMILY

Nothing is ever quite as exciting or expensive as raising a family. Depending upon where you live and how extravagant you are, raising a child from birth to 18 can set you back between $50,000 and $100,000+. Then add college expenses, currently running $4,000 to $28,000 per year, and the total bill for four years is more than the cost of many houses.

Step 1. As soon as you know you're going to have a family, check your firm's maternity leave and possible benefits for the father as well as your health coverage.

Step 2. Put all or part of the mother-to-be's

salary in a money market fund or other liquid investment and practice living on one salary, which may be the case when the baby arrives, at least at the beginning.

Step 3. Then put half of your money market fund into a series of CDs, staggered to come due at various dates, for example, one every two months after the baby is born. This will provide an influx of much-needed cash.

Step 4. Start a college education fund before the baby leaves the hospital's nursery. Begin by putting all gifts of cash or securities the baby receives in a custodial account under the Uniform Gifts to Minor Act in the baby's name. You'll need to get your child a Social Security number. When he or she reaches adulthood (18 or 21, depending upon the state), this money must be turned over to the child. (See Chapter 32 for tax implications.)

Step 5. At this stage your portfolio should be both income- and growth-oriented—income, to cover extra costs of the family, and growth, to make it possible to move into a larger home, add on to your present one, save for college tuition, and finance any expansion of your family. See the suggested stocks and bonds in the table.

§ HINT: If you have a teenager who is working summers or part-time, consider putting up to $2,000 of his earnings into an IRA and reimburse him with spending money. This provides a small tax deduction on your child's tax return and you will have started him on a smart savings program. But explain that he cannot use the IRA money for college education or a downpayment on a future house since withdrawing money before age 59½ incurs a penalty.

➤ AMERICAN CAPITAL BOND FUND (ABC) This diversified closed-end management fund states its investment objective to be income and conservation of capital. ABC invests solely in non-convertible debt securities. Approximately 82% of its assets are in high-quality instruments. These shares, with their 8.2% yield, should be held for income.

➤ WASTE MANAGEMENT (WMX) A leader in gar-

PORTFOLIO FOR THOSE WITH A FAMILY

INVESTMENT	AMOUNT	DETAILS
Company you work for	100 shares	Use employee purchase plan
Electric utility company	100 shares	Reinvest dividends
Municipal bonds or UIT	$1,000 minimum	Hold until maturity
Neuberger & Berman Partners Fund	$1,000 minimum	Sell when you've reached your profit point
U.S. Treasury notes	$5,000 minimum	Use if needed to purchase house or pay child expenses
IRA	$2,000	Stocks, CDs, Treasuries
American Capital Bond Fund	200 shares	Price: $20½ Yield: 8.2%
Waste Management	100 shares	Price: $34 Yield: 0.5%
Archer Daniels Midland	100 shares	Price: $27 Yield: 0.4%
Pacific Telesis	150 shares	Price: $44 Yield: 5.0%
Wrigley (Wm)	100 shares	Price: $86 Yield: 1.2%

Prices are as of August 7, 1992.

bage collection and waste disposal, earnings from industrial waste should increase as we come out of the recession.

➤ ARCHER DANIELS MIDLAND (ADM) This well-managed Illinois firm processes and sells agricultural commodities. Its chemical division, which produces ethanol, will reap big gains from the new Clean Air Act requiring 42 cities to improve their air quality.

➤ PACIFIC TELESIS (PAC) This company has strong telephone operations in California, as well as a foothold in the cellular business that is growing at a rate of over 50% annually. Any dividend increases can easily be covered by strong cash flow. Its yield of 5% is high for a common stock.

➤ WRIGLEY (WM) The world's largest manufacturer of chewing gum. The company has no debt, no pension liability, and a steady growth rate. William Wrigley and family own about 27% of the stock. Conservatively managed and in a recession-proof business.

IF YOU'RE AN EMPTY NESTER

These are the peak payout years of your life, whether you are married or single, with or without adult children. You can now afford to focus on maintaining a comfortable life-style,

caring for your own aging parents, fueling an expanding business or career. During this period your income is probably the highest it will ever be, which enables you to make more aggressive investments than when you were footing the bill for college education or just getting started. Look at a second home or rental property, additional growth-oriented stocks, precious metals, and even some junk bonds. Fund your 401(k) or Keogh plan to the fullest and set up a tax-deferred annuity, keeping in mind that tax-free issues are all-important at this stage.

➤ STUDENT LOAN MARKETING (SLM) Sallie Mae is a federally chartered corporation that purchases and services student loans. Its loans are regarded as federal agency paper and high in safety. Its business grows along with the rising cost of college.

➤ WAL-MART STORES (WMT) Regarded now as the best retail store in the country—it surpasses Sears in sales. Earnings were up 21% last year. Sam's Wholesale Clubs are adding to the company's impressive cash flow. Death of the founder has given the company additional publicity.

➤ MEDITRUST (MT) One of the nation's largest health care REITs (real estate investment trust), it owns 116 properties, including nursing homes. Well managed, it has steady cash flow from its holdings and investments. The dividend has

PORTFOLIO FOR AN EMPTY NESTER

INVESTMENT	AMOUNT	DETAILS
IRA	$2,000	Stocks, CDs, Treasuries
Student Loan Marketing	150 shares	Price: $68
		Yield: 1.5%
AT&T 8.80s 2005, 101	5 to 10 bonds	Reinvest income or use to purchase real estate
Wal-Mart Stores	100 shares	Price: $57
		Yield: 0.4%
Con Edison 8.4s 2003, 96	5 to 10 bonds	Reinvest income
Government zeros	5 to 10 bonds	Plan to mature when retired
Meditrust	200 shares	Price: $29
		Yield: 8.7%

Prices are as of August 7, 1992.

ALTERNATIVE PORTFOLIO SUGGESTIONS FOR ALL AGES

- *Buy Embassy Suites bonds*, 10⅞s, due 2002, selling at 105. Five bonds at 105 each will cost $5,250. Annual income from these junk bonds will be approximately $544.
- *Buy Puerto Rico aqua and sewer municipal bonds*, 7.00s, due 2019, priced at $100. Total cost for ten bonds is $10,000. Annual income will be approximately $700. Puerto Rican municipals are exempt from local, state, and federal taxes in all 50 states.
- *Buy government zeros*, due August 2003, with a yield of 7.1%. Cost per bond is $470. Total cost for $10,000 worth of bonds is $4,700. In the year 2002 you will receive the full $10,000.
- *Dreyfus Strategic Gov't Fund (DSI)*. This closed-end bond fund trades on the NYSE and invests in U.S. and foreign government debt. Its shares in August 1992 were $12 for an 8.5% yield.

been raised for the last 24 quarters. Note the solid yet high yield.

IF YOU'RE RETIRED OR ABOUT TO BE

Now the emphasis should be on income plus some growth. Safety should be paramount unless you have sufficient money from an inheritance or sale of your home. Top-rated bonds, blue chip stocks, and high-yielding securities are most appropriate during these years. In addition to the specific suggestions that appear in the table, take a look at these investments:

- *Treasury bonds.* As we go to press, U.S. Treasury bonds with the longer maturities, i.e., those due in 30 years, are yielding a little under 7.5%.
- *High-yield bonds.* If you are willing to assume some risk, put a small portion (up to 5%) in a high-yield or junk bond mutual fund or select your own.
- *Zero coupon bonds* to mature at or soon after your retirement date. Put these in your tax-sheltered pension plan, where taxes are deferred. Remember, zeros do not pay annual interest, but you must pay annual taxes on the imputed income.

PORTFOLIO FOR THOSE RETIRED OR ABOUT TO BE

INVESTMENT	AMOUNT	DETAILS
American Electric Power	200 shares	Price: $33 Yield: 7.2%
AT&T 7⅛s, 2002 at 102	5 to 10 bonds	Use interest income or reinvest
Mutual of Omaha Interest Shares	200 shares	Price: $15½ Yield: 7.5%
1838 Bond Deb. Fund	150 shares	Price: $25 Yield: 7.3%
Bristol-Myers Squibb	100 shares	Price: $70 Yield: 3.9%
Oryx Corp. 10⅜s 2018, 106	5 to 10 bonds	Monitor these junk bonds
Long Island Lighting pfd Z	100 shares	Price: $28 Yield: 8.5%
Giant Food	100 shares	Price: $27 Yield: 2.3%

Prices are as of August 7, 1992.

FOR ANY PORTFOLIO
The Top Yielding Stocks in the Dow

At any time when you have accumulated enough cash, use this simple strategy that almost always beats the market: On a given day, say January 2nd, buy equal amounts of the 10 highest-yielding stocks in the Dow Jones industrial average. Then, on that same date each year, replace any that have fallen out of the top ten. In 1991, for example, this technique returned 34.4% compared with 34.3% for the Dow as a whole.

STOCK	PRICE	YIELD
Westinghouse	$17	4.2%
General Motors	39	4.1
IBM	92	5.3
Sears	40	5.0
Texaco	63	5.1
Union Carbide	14	5.3
American Express	22	4.4
Chevron	71	4.6
Exxon	64	4.5
Eastman Kodak	44	4.5

Prices as of August 7, 1992.

- *Ginnie Maes or Fannie Maes* that pay high yields (7 to 8½%) through monthly checks. Most pass-throughs are fully paid out in less than 15 years, so time your certificate purchase to coincide with your retirement. If you are younger, look into CMOs, a similar investment with more predictable payout dates, described in Chapter 12.
- *Bristol-Myers Squibb.* A leading pharmaceutical company with solid earnings both domestically and abroad.
- *Oryx Energy.* These bonds are issued by a large producer of gas and oil. It also explores for oil in the U.S. and Europe. These bonds, rated BBB−, fall into the high junk bond category.
- *Giant Food (GFSA).* An outstanding regional food chain which is relatively immune to economic swings. Has about 50% of market share in Washington, DC, Virginia, and Maryland. Has an ambitious expansion program. Conservatively financed; long-term debt is 29% of capital.

IF YOU HAVE OR ARE STARTING A SMALL BUSINESS

It may not seem logical but an economic slump can be a good time to start a business. Lowered interest rates and a plentiful labor pool with people willing to work for reasonable salaries can be viewed in a positive light. If you already own a business and your credit is good, it's also an advantageous time to borrow and expand, with interest rates lower than they have been in some time. Despite what you may hear, banks are willing to grant loans to solid businesses. Before doing either, take these steps.

Step 1. Address personal financial needs. No one should be in business for themselves if there's any question about where money for the kids' education or the next mortgage payment is coming from. We increase our nest egg suggestion for business owners: you should have enough money set aside in a money market fund or CDs to cover at least one year's worth of personal living expenses. (Ordinarily that time frame is six or nine months, depending upon the economy and one's age.)

Step 2. Take care of personal medical and disability insurance. Under federal law, you have the right to continue medical coverage for eighteen months after leaving a job, at your expense. Since premiums for a group policy are lower than for individual coverage it is wise to arrange to continue coverage by paying the premiums yourself. Then you're on your own. Bear in mind that various benefits—health, life and disability insurance plus paid vacations, make up almost one-third of most employees' annual salaries. So for you to stay even, your business must generate more than just your salary.

Your portfolio should be geared to provide income to weather any downturns in your business and to provide collateral should you wish to use part of it to obtain a loan. (There are two ways to finance a business: debt financing consists of loans that the business must

---

PORTFOLIO FOR BUSINESS OWNERS

INVESTMENT	DETAILS
Money market account	9-months' living expenses
and/or	
Certificates of deposit	9-months' living expenses
IRA ($2,000/annually)	Stocks, CDs, Treasuries

Discuss these high yield choices with your investment advisor. Be certain to diversify, ideally with stocks and bonds both represented.

American Capital Bond Fund (NYSE: ACB)	Price: $20½
	Yield: 8.2%
American Electric Power (NYSE: AEP)	Price: $33
	Yield: 7.2%
AT&T 7⅛s due 2002 selling at 102	Solid utility bond
Long Island Lighting pfd Z	Price: $28
	Yield: 8.5%
1838 Bond Deb. Fund (NYSE: BDF)	Price: $25
	Yield: 7.3%
Gen Corp. 12⅜s due 2003; selling at 103	One of the better junk bonds
General Electric 8½s due 2004; selling at 101	Top rated corporate bond
Meditrust (NYSE: MT)	Price: $29
	Yield: 8.7%
Montgomery Street Income Securities (NYSE: MTS)	Price: $21
	Yield: 8.2%
Mutual of Omaha Interest Shares (NYSE: MUO)	Price: $15
	Yield: 7.5%
Putnam Premier Income Trust (NYSE: PPT)	Price: $8
	Yield: 10%*

* Some of this yield is actually a return of capital. Portfolio has some high risk holdings.
Prices as of August 7, 1992.

---

repay; equity financing consists of money given to a business in exchange for an ownership share in the business. In most cases, a balance between the two is ideal. Too much debt necessitates a huge cash flow to pay the interest on the loans and too much equity means you've given away control and perhaps too much ownership.)

The suggestions in the box above are aimed primarily at providing income as well as securities that can be used as collateral for a loan or sold if you should need an infusion of capital. Please note that the first 3 securities suggestions should be taken care of before attempting the rest.

$ HINT: Order IRS publication #334, Tax Guide for Small Businesses, free, by calling 1-800-829-3676

#583, Taxpayers Starting a Business
Free
#917, Business Use of a Car
Free

PROTECTING YOUR PORTFOLIO DURING HARD TIMES

The recession has affected virtually every American: some have lost jobs, others have failed to see wages materialize or have had their hours or salaries frozen, even cut back. Just about everyone is worried about finances. Whether or not you've been hit by the recession, it's prudent to know what steps to take to protect your family's money during tough times.

BUILD UP YOUR NEST EGG

If you're worried about your job security, start now to build up a sufficient nest egg to see you through hard times. Set aside a monthly sum immediately after paying the rent or mortgage. Don't wait to save until later. Useful steps:

1 Use automatic savings plans. Sign up for payroll deduction programs. Arrange for automatic transfers from checking to savings or to money market funds. Purchase EE Savings Bonds this way as well.

2 Pay cash for purchases. Avoid using credit cards, which often leads to overspending, debt buildup, and high interest rate charges.

3 Use retirement plans for forced savings. Voluntary contributions to 401(k) plans, IRAs, Keoghs and others not only defer taxes but they are tax-advantaged ways to save, since contributions may be funded with pre-tax dollars.

4 Increase tax withholding. Get a bigger tax refund by boosting salary withholding. Then use the refund for savings.

☐ CAUTION: Overwithholding operates like an interest-free loan to the government, since no interest is paid on the refund check.

OTHER STRATEGIES

If you are already experiencing financial difficulties:

1 Go on a crash budget.

2 Review avenues of income and fixed and variable expenses.

3 Trim variables, such as entertaining, travel, eating out, dry cleaning.

4 Stop outrageous spending.

5 Talk to the children. If you or your spouse has lost a job or has a sudden cutback in income, it's important to let children know the truth, but without frightening them. After all, they will be affected too. Reassure them that recessions are cyclical and hard times won't last forever.

6 Claim benefits. If you are laid off and entitled to unemployment compensation, do not be embarrassed to collect. After all, you've been paying to fund the system for many years.

7 Trim debt. Paying off high-rate loans, such as credit card debt, is critical. Be certain to pay all credit card balances within 30 days to avoid interest charges. And, consolidate high-rate debt to obtain a more favorable interest rate.

8 Ease up on savings. Delay contributions to 401(k) and other voluntary savings plans if cash is tight.

9 Pinch pennies. Conspicuous consumption, so in vogue during the 1980s, is out and sensible spending for the 1990s is in.

10 Eat home more. Or, if dining out, have drinks and dessert at home.

FINDING EXTRA CASH

You may discover that you need extra cash to tide yourself over. Here are some suggestions:

1 Review your portfolio and first sell securities that are not performing well. If need be, slowly sell other securities, holding until last the best performers.

2 Consider a home equity line of credit.

☐ CAUTION: It is virtually impossible to get this type of loan when you are out of work. If you fear losing your job, process the loan now. There's no obligation to use it, although you will incur some expense in setting it up.

3 Borrow against the cash value in any life insurance policies.

4 As a last resort, borrow from 401(k) plans. Hold off tapping this source as long as possible because it's hard to replace these funds, which you will need upon retirement. Most companies let employees borrow up to 50% of the amount vested, or $50,000, whichever is less. Typically you repay the money in installments through payroll deductions. Finance charges are based on current market rates—expect to pay prime plus one or two percentage points. Terms vary, so check with your benefits officer.

☐ CAUTION: Don't withdraw money from your IRA or Keogh plan if you are under age 59½. Not only is there regular income tax on such withdrawals, but there's a 10% penalty on top of that.

INVESTMENT ANALYSIS AND INFORMATION SOURCES

Now that you are well acquainted with the various types of investments available, the next step, of course, is deciding which ones to select for your personal portfolio. Do you want common stocks? If so, which ones? Perhaps you would benefit from bonds or convertibles. Yet selecting the best and avoiding the worst require skill and knowledge. That's where investment analysis enters the picture.

In this section you will learn the various techniques used by the experts in selecting all types of securities. You will come to know how to recognize the potential profit in stocks, bonds, and mutual funds and how to spot the winners and avoid the losers. Among the topics covered are:

- Reading a company's balance sheet and annual report
- Getting the most out of statistics
- Following technical analysis
- Studying the charts
- Using investment newsletters

In Parts Three and Four we explained the various types of stocks and the analytical tools for evaluating securities. You may want to review these points as you now learn precisely how to select top-quality securities on your own, including:

- Knowing the stock exchanges, indexes, and averages

USING AND EVALUATING INVESTMENT NEWSLETTERS

LEARNING FROM THE GURUS

Promises of 100% annual returns on your investments, guarantees of market success, predictions of great riches—these and other flamboyant bits of advertising have tempted more than a million people to subscribe to one of the hundreds of investment newsletters on the market. Are they worth the price of subscription? Some are, but many are not. Yet a well-written, carefully selected newsletter, along with other sources of information, can boost your investment awareness and consequently your performance.

Today, when the need for sound financial advice is so crucial, you're apt to be bombarded by a barrage of newsletters, each one claiming to be the answer to making a killing on Wall Street. Here are guidelines to help avoid the charlatans and opportunists and cash in on the wiser, more seasoned advisers.

A key factor to keep in mind is that from year to year, the performance success of all newsletters changes. And the selection of one or two securities or funds that either take off or bomb has enormous impact on the performance of a newsletter.

Before plunking down full price for any newsletter, take out a trial subscription to several (see suggested lists), which will cost from $25 to $65. Compare them and see if any suit your investment philosophy *and* income level. Ask your stockbroker, banker, accountant, or a reliable friend for recommendations. During the trial period, keep a record of the recommendations made.

Newsletters that do not represent a brokerage firm are no longer required to register as investment advisers with the SEC.

Often newsletters will twist their material to make it appear as though they've made a winning prediction. If the editor claims to have called a market change or picked an outstanding stock, go back to the issue and make certain this really was the case.

Although last year's success does not automatically guarantee the same for the next 12 months, it's one of the few benchmarks available. Try to determine a newsletter's overall track record.

Another way to study the newsletter industry is to read the reports of those who rank the publications or provide summaries of their contents. These include the following:

Hulbert Financial Digest
316 Commerce Street
Alexandria, VA 22314
1-703-683-5905
$135 per year; $37.50 for 5-month trial subscription; $67.50 special for first-time subscribers.

Tracks 120 newsletters based on their stock recommendations.

Timer Digest (Jim Schmitt, ed.)
P.O. Box 1688
Greenwich, CT 06836
1-203-629-3503; 1-800-356-2527
$225 per year

Follows 90 to 100 market timers.

BEST BETS

Among the newsletters that have been successful in either predicting the market or giving financial advice are:

Cabot Market Letter
P.O. Box 3044
Salem, MA 01970
1-508-745-5532; 1-800-777-2658
$230 per year

POINTS TO CONSIDER

DOES THE NEWSLETTER:
- Contradict itself from one issue to the next?
- Explain changes in recommendations?
- Evaluate its mistakes?
- Update its mistakes?
- Take credit for predictions it did not make?
- Present stale news, dated prices and statistics?
- Offer a hotline service?
- Include commissions and fees in its performance results?
- Leave you feeling confused—or is the advice clear, especially sell decisions?
- Provide sample portfolios with instructions, rather than just lists of equities with no advice?

Dessaurer's Journal
P.O. Box 1718
Orleans, MA 02653
1-508-255-1651
$195 per year; $35 for 2 months

Dow Theory Forecasts
7412 Calumet Avenue
Hammond, IN 46324
1-219-931-6480
$233 per year

Dow Theory Letters
P.O. Box 1759
La Jolla, CA 92038
1-619-454-0481
$250 per year

Growth Stock Outlook
Box 15381
Chevy Chase, MD 20825
1-301-654-5205
$195 per year

Investech Mutual Fund Advisor
2472 Birch Glen
Whitefish, MT 59937
1-406-862-7777
$160 per year; $59 for 3 months

Investors Intelligence
30 Church Street
New Rochelle, NY 10801
1-914-632-0422
$175 per year; $30 for 3 months

MPT Review
Box 5695
Incline Village, NV 89450
1-702-831-7800
$245 per year; $59 per 2 months

Mutual Fund Specialist
P.O. Box 1025
Eau Claire, WI 54702
1-715-834-7425
$95 per year

The Oberweis Report
841 North Lake Street
Aurora, IL 60506
1-708-897-7100
$99 per year; $25 for 3 months

The Option Advisor
P.O. Box 46709
Cincinnati, OH 45246
1-513-589-3838; 1-800-922-4869
$99 per year; $66 for 6 months

Princeton Portfolio
301 North Harrison, Suite 229
Princeton, NJ 08540
1-609-497-0362
$225 per year
Sent, by computer only, every Tuesday; more frequently depending upon market activity

Professional Tape Reader
P.O. Box 2407
Hollywood, FL 33022
1-800-868-7857
$350 per year; $59 for 5 months

Prudent Speculator
P.O. Box 1767
Santa Monica, CA 90406
1-213-315-9888
$225 for 17 issues

Systems & Forecasts
150 Great Neck Road
Great Neck, NY 11021
1-516-829-6444
$195 per year; $65 for 3 months; nightly telephone hotline

Your Window Into the Future
P.O. Box 22400
Minneapolis, MN 55422
1-612-537-8096
$99 per year; $1 for 1 issue
(with a business-size SASE)

The Zweig Forecast
P.O. Box 360
Bellmore, NY 11710
1-516-785-1300; 1-800-633-2252
$265 per year; $55 for 3 months

TRACKING INSIDER TRADING

The sales and purchases of any company's stock by the firm's officials can be an indication of stock price trends. It's not foolproof, but if you have time to do the research, you may unearth some interesting situations. A handful of newsletters chart this so-called insider trading.

The Insiders (Norman Fosback, ed.)
3471 North Federal Highway
Fort Lauderdale, FL 33306
1-305-563-9000; 1-800-327-6720
$49 for first year

Value Line
711 Third Avenue
New York, NY 10017
1-800-634-3583
$525 per year; 10-week introductory offer
  $65

Street Smart Investing (Wendy Boehm, ed.)
13-D Research
Southeast Executive Park
100 Executive Drive
Brewster, NY 10509
1-914-278-6500
$350 per year

Emerging & Special Situations
(Robert Natale, ed.)
Standard & Poor's Corp.
25 Broadway
New York, NY 10005
1-212-208-8000
$223.50 per year

FOR FURTHER INFORMATION

The best way to check out any newsletter is to ask for a sample issue or a trial subscription. Or take advantage of a special sample offer:

Select Information Exchange
244 West 54th Street, 7th Floor
New York, NY 10019
1-212-247-7123
25 services for $19

Mark Hulbert, *The Hulbert Guide to Financial Newsletters,* 4th ed. (Alexandria, VA: Mark Hulbert Publishing Co., 1991).

B | BEHIND THE SCENES: How to Read Annual Reports

Some are flashy, some are plain; some are fat and some are thin; but all annual reports are the single most important tool in analyzing corporations to decide whether to buy, hold, sell, or pass by their securities. In a few minutes, you can check the corporation's quality and profitability and, with closer study, learn a great deal about the character and ability of management, its methods of operation, its products and services, and, most important, its future prospects. If you own securities of the corporation, you will receive a copy of the annual report about 4 months after the close of its operating year. If you are considering becoming a shareholder, get a copy from your broker or by writing the company (get the address from Standard & Poor's, Value Line, Moody's, or other reference books at your library).

First, skim the text, check the statement of income and earnings to see how much money was made and whether this was more than that of previous years, and review the list of officers and directors for familiar names. Later, if you're still interested, you can follow up the points of interest.

The statements will always be factually correct, but the interpretations, especially those in the president's message, will naturally be the most favorable within legal and accounting limits.

If you are considering a stock to buy, look at 3 years' annual reports. Here's what to be aware of:

➤ TRENDS In sales, earnings, dividends, accounts receivable. If they continue to rise, chances are that you've found a winner. *Buy* when they are moving up; *review* when they plateau; *consider selling* when they are down.

➤ INFORMATION *From the tables:* corporate financial strength and operating success or failure. *From the text:* explanations of what happened during the year and what management projects for the future. If you don't believe management, do not hold the stock.

➤ POSITIVES New plants, products, personnel, and programs. Are the total assets greater and liabilities lower than in previous years? If so, why—tighter controls or decreases in allocations for R&D, marketing, etc.?

If the profits were up, was the gain due to fewer outstanding shares (because of repurchase of stock), to nonrecurring income from the sale of property, or to higher sales and lower costs?

➤ NEGATIVES Plant closings, sales of subsidiaries, discontinuance of products, and future needs for financing. Not all of these will always be adverse, but they can make a significant difference with respect to what happens in the next few years.

If the profits were down, was this because of the elimination of some products or services? Price wars? Poor managerial decisions?

➤ FOOTNOTES Read these carefully because they can point up problems. Be cautious if there were heavy markdowns of inventory, adverse governmental regulations, rollovers of debt, and other unusual events.

➤ BALANCE SHEET To see whether cash or liquid assets are diminishing and whether accounts receivable, inventories, or total debts are rising. Any such trend can serve as a yellow flag, if not a red one.

➤ FINANCIAL SUMMARY Not only for the past year but for the previous 5 years. This will provide an overall view of corporate performance and set the stage for an analysis of the most recent data.

In the stock market, *past is prologue.* Few companies achieve dramatic progress or fall on hard times suddenly. In most cases, the changes have been forecast. The corporation with a long, fairly consistent record of profitable growth can be expected to do as well, or better, in the years ahead and thus prove to be a worthwhile holding. The erratic performer is likely to move from high to low profits (or losses). And the faltering company will have signs of deterioration over a 2- or 3-year period.

READING THE REPORT

When you review the text, you will get an idea of the kind of people who are managing your money, learn what they did or did not do and why, and be able to draw some conclusions about future prospects.

➤ BEGIN WITH THE SHAREHOLDERS' LETTER This message from the chairman outlines the company's past performance and its prospects. Compare last year's letter with this year's facts. Did the company meet its previously stated goals? Beware of the chairman who never mentions any problems or areas of concern. If there were failures, there should be logical explanations. Management is not always right in its decisions, but in financial matters, frankness is the base for confidence. If previous promises were unfulfilled (and that's why you should keep a file of past annual reports), find out why. If the tone is overly optimistic, be wary. If you are skeptical, do not hold the stock or buy.

➤ WATCH FOR DOUBLE-TALK Clichés are an integral part of business writing, but they should not be substitutes for proper explanations. If you find such meaningless phrases as "a year of transition" or some of the locutions listed in the box on page 349, start getting ready to unload. There are better opportunities elsewhere.

➤ STUDY THE BALANCE SHEET This presents an instant picture of the company's assets and liabilities on the very last day of the fiscal year. Divide the current assets by the current liabilities to get the current ratio. A ratio of 2:1 or better signals that there are enough assets on hand to cover immediate debts. (We return to balance sheets in Appendix C.)

➤ LOOK AT LONG-TERM DEBT Divide long-term debt by long-term capital (i.e., long-term debt plus shareholders' equity). If it is below 50%, the company is probably solid, but, of course, the more debt, the less cash to help weather rough times.

➤ REVIEW ACCOUNTS RECEIVABLE Listed under current assets, this figure reflects the payments for products or services that the company expects to receive in the near future. If receivables are growing at a faster pace than sales, it may indicate that the company is not collecting its bills fast enough.

➤ LOOK AT CURRENT INVENTORIES If inventories are rising faster than sales, the company is creating or producing more than it can sell.

➤ LOOK AT NET INCOME PER SHARE Note if this figure, which reflects earnings, is trending up or down.

➤ COMPARE REVENUES AND EXPENSES If expenses are greater than revenues over time, management may be having trouble holding down overhead. Discount earnings increases that are due to a nonrecurring event, such as sale of a property or division. Nonrecurring items should be explained in the footnotes. The footnotes also reveal changes in accounting methods, lawsuits, and liabilities.

➤ STUDY THE QUALITY AND SOURCE OF EARNINGS When profits are entirely from operations, they indicate management's skill; when they are partially from bookkeeping, look again. But do not be hasty in drawing conclusions. Even the best of corporations may use "special" accounting.

Examples: In valuing inventories, LIFO (last in, first out) current sales are matched against the latest costs so that earnings can rise sharply when inventories are reduced and those latest costs get older and thus lower. When oil prices were at a peak, Texaco cut inventories by 16%. The LIFO cushion, built up over several years, was a whopping $454 million and transformed what would have been a drop in net income into a modest gain.

Such "tricks" are one reason why stocks fall or stay flat after annual profits are reported. Analysts are smart enough to discover that earnings are more paper than real.

➤ READ THE AUDITOR'S REPORT If there are hedging phrases such as "except for" or "subject to," be wary. These phrases can signal the inability to get accurate information and may forecast future write-offs.

➤ LOOK AT FOREIGN CURRENCY TRANSACTIONS These can be tricky and often difficult to understand. Under recent revisions of accounting rules, it's possible to recast them retroactively when, of course, they can be favorable. One major firm whose domestic profits had been

---

HOW TO TRANSLATE THE PRESIDENT'S MESSAGE

Here are some of the techniques used in writing annual reports to phrase comments in terms that tend to divert the reader's attention away from problems.

WHAT THE PRESIDENT SAYS	WHAT THE PRESIDENT MEANS
"The year was difficult and challenging."	"Sales and profits were off, but expenses (including executive salaries) were up."
"Management has taken steps to strengthen market share."	"We're underselling our competitors to drive them out of the market."
"Integrating the year's highs and lows proved challenging."	"Sales were up; profits went nowhere."
"Management worked diligently to preserve a strong financial position."	"We barely broke even but were able to avoid new debts."
"Your company is indebted to the dedicated service of its employees."	"We don't pay 'em much, but there's not much else to cheer about."

CONSOLIDATED STATEMENT: FRED MEYER, INC.

FISCAL YEAR ENDED ($ IN THOUSANDS EXCEPT PER-SHARE AMOUNTS)

	JANUARY 31, 1991	FEBRUARY 1, 1991	FEBRUARY 2, 1991 (53 WEEKS)
Net sales	$1,688,208	$1,583,796	$1,449,108
Cost of merchandise sold	1,200,379	1,135,836	1,053,689
Gross margin	487,829	447,960	395,419
Operating and administrative expenses	430,469	397,841	354,914
Income from operations	57,360	50,119	40,505
Interest expense, net of interest income of $1,679, $2,983, and $3,090	11,945	17,652	19,565
Income before income taxes and extraordinary items	45,415	32,467	20,940
Provision for income taxes	21,350	13,000	8,000
Income before extraordinary items	24,065	19,467	12,940
Extraordinary items	(1,530)		2,649
Net income	$ 22,535	$ 19,467	$ 15,589
Earnings per Common Share			
Income before extraordinary items	$ 1.15	$ 1.06	$ .73
Extraordinary items	(.07)		.15
Net income	$ 1.08	$ 1.06	$ .88
Weighted average number of common shares outstanding	20,870	18,355	17,790

lagging went back 4 years with its overseas reports and boosted its per-share profits to $7.08 from the previously reported $6.67 per share.

Most international corporations have elaborate systems for hedging against fluctuations in foreign currencies. These are relatively expensive, but they tend to even out sharp swings in the value of the dollar.

➤ CHECK FOR FUTURE OBLIGATIONS You may have to burrow in the footnotes, but with major companies, find out about the pension obligations: the money that the firm must pay to its retirees. One way to boost profits (because this means lower annual contributions) is to raise the assumed rate of return on pension fund investments.

➤ CALCULATE THE CASH FLOW Add after-tax earnings and annual depreciation on fixed assets and subtract preferred dividends, if any. Then compare the result with previous years. Cash flow is indicative of corporate earning power because it shows the dollars available for profits, new investments, etc.

➤ BEWARE OF OVERENTHUSIASM ABOUT NEW PRODUCTS, PROCESSES, OR SERVICES Usually, it takes 3 years to translate new operations into sizable sales and profits. And the majority of new projects are losers.

➤ PAY SPECIAL ATTENTION TO THE RETURN ON EQUITY (PROFIT RATE) This is the best measure of management's ability to make money with your money. Any ROE above 15% is good; when below, compare the figure with that of previous years and other firms in the same industry. Some industries seldom show a high rate of return: for example, heavy machinery because of the huge investment in plants and equipment, and utilities because of the ceiling set by public commissions.

➤ WATCH OUT FOR EQUITY ACCOUNTING Where earnings from other companies, which are more than 20% owned, are included in total profits. There are no cash dividends, so the money cannot be used for expansion or payouts to shareholders. This maneuver can massage the reported earnings, but that's about all. Teledyne, a major conglomerate, reported $19.96 per share profits, but a close examination revealed that $3.49 of this was from equity accounting— phantom, not real, earnings.

FOR FURTHER INFORMATION

How to Read a Financial Report, 1990 (pamphlet), free from any Merrill Lynch office.

George T. Friedlob and Ralph E. Welton, *Keys to Reading an Annual Report* (Hauppauge, NY: Barron's Educational Series, 1989).

BALANCE SHEETS MADE SIMPLE

DETERMINING VALUE

The idea is to buy low and sell high. This sounds easy, but it isn't. You must determine what is *low* and, to a lesser degree, what is *high.* That's where value comes in. The surest way to make money in the stock market is to buy securities when they are undervalued and sell them when they become fully priced. *Value shows the range in which a stock should be bought or sold and thus provides the base for investment profits.*

Value itself is based on financial "facts," as stated in the corporate reports. Projections, by contrast, are based on analyses of past performance, present strength, and future progress. When you select quality stocks on the basis of value (or undervaluation), you will almost always make money—perhaps quickly with speculative situations, more slowly with major corporations. You can identify value *if* you understand the basics of financial analysis, our next step.

HOW TO ANALYZE FINANCIAL REPORTS

Financial analysis is not as difficult as you may think, and once you get into the swing of things, you can pick the few quality stocks from the thousands of publicly owned securities. If you are speculation-minded, you can find bargains in securities of mediocre or even poor corporations.

Several basic figures and ratios show the company's current and prospective financial condition, its past and prospective earning power and growth, and therefore its investment desirability or lack of desirability.

Publicly owned corporations issue their financial reports on an annual, semiannual, or quarterly basis. Most of the information impor-tant to the investor can be found in (1) the balance sheet; (2) the profit and loss, or income, statement; and (3) the change in financial position or "flow of funds" data. In each of these three sections you should look for:

- *The key quantities:* net tangible assets, changes in working capital, sales costs, profits, taxes, dividends, etc.
- *The significant rates and ratios:* price-earnings multiples, profit rates, growth in net worth, earnings, dividends, etc.
- *The comparison of a corporation with a standard:* that of its industry, the stock market, the economy, or some other broader base.

The following data and explanations are digested from *Understanding Financial Statements,* prepared by the New York Stock Exchange. They do not cover every detail but will get you started. For a copy, write to the address given on page 74, or ask your broker for one.

INCOME AND RETAINED EARNINGS

Here's where you find out *how the corporation fared for the past year* in comparison with the two previous annual reporting periods: in other words, how much money the company took in, how much was spent for expenses and taxes, and the size of the resulting profits (if any), which were available either for distribution to shareholders or for reinvestment in the business. Income and retained earnings are the basis for comparisons, both between years for this company and between firms in the same or similar business.

SALES

How much business does the company do in a year? With public utilities, insurance firms, and service organizations, the term "revenues" is often used instead of sales.

In the past year, corporate sales in the sample corporation shown were up $5.8 million, a gain of 5.3%, not quite as good as the 5.5% rise the year before. Net income per share (middle) was also just slightly better: $0.4 million (to $9.9 from $9.5), +4.2%. Check these figures against those of the industry and major competitors. They may be better than they appear.

COSTS AND EXPENSES

➤ COST OF GOODS SOLD The dollars spent to keep the business operating. The $3.2 million more was less than the $5.8 million increase in sales.

➤ SELLING, GENERAL, AND ADMINISTRATIVE EXPENSES The costs of getting products or services

to customers and getting paid. These will vary with the kind of business: high for consumer goods manufacturers and distributors because of advertising; lower for companies selling primarily to industry or government.

➤ DEPRECIATION A bookkeeping item to provide for wear and tear and obsolescence of machinery and equipment, presumably to set aside reserves for replacement. The maximum calculations are set by tax laws. Typically, a straight-line accounting method might charge the same amount each year for a specified number of years.

With companies in the natural resource business, the reduction in value is called depletion, and it too is calculated over a period of years.

By changing the type of depreciation, a

STATEMENT OF INCOME AND RETAINED EARNINGS ($ millions)
"Your Company"

| | DECEMBER 31 YEAR-END | | |
	CURRENT YEAR	PREVIOUS YEAR	2 YEARS AGO
SALES	$115.8	$110.0	$104.5
Less:			
COSTS AND EXPENSES			
Cost of goods sold	$ 76.4	$ 73.2	$ 70.2
Selling, general, and administrative expenses	14.2	13.0	12.1
Depreciation	2.6	3.5	2.3
	$ 93.2	$ 89.7	$ 84.6
OPERATING PROFIT	$ 22.6	$ 20.3	$ 19.9
Interest charges	1.3	1.0	1.3
Earnings before income taxes	$ 21.3	$ 19.3	$ 18.6
Provision for taxes on income	11.4	9.8	9.5
Net income (per common share for year: current, $5.24; last, $5.03; 2 years ago, $4.97)*	$ 9.9	$ 9.5	$ 9.1
RETAINED EARNINGS, BEGINNING OF YEAR	42.2	37.6	33.1
Less dividends paid on:	$ 52.1	$ 47.1	$ 42.2
Preferred stock ($5 per share)	(.3)	(.3)	—
Common stock (per share: this year, $3.00; last year, $2.50; 2 years ago, $2.50)	(5.4)	(4.6)	(4.6)
RETAINED EARNINGS, END OF YEAR	$ 46.4	$ 42.2	$ 37.6

* After preferred share dividend requirements.

company can increase or decrease earnings, so always be wary when this happens.

OPERATING PROFIT

Operating profit consists of the dollars generated from the company's usual operations without regard to income from other sources or financing. As a percentage of sales, it tells the profit margin: a rising 19.5% in the last year compared with 18.5% the year before.

➤ INTEREST CHARGES The interest paid to bondholders. It is deductible before taxes. The available earnings should be many times the mandated interest charges: in this case, a welcome 17 times before provision for income taxes (i.e., $22.6 \div \$1.3 = 17$).

➤ EARNINGS BEFORE INCOME TAXES The operating profit minus interest charges. When companies have complicated reports, this can be a confusing area.

➤ PROVISION FOR TAXES ON INCOME The allocation of money for Uncle Sam—a widely variable figure because of exemptions, special credits, etc., from about 5% for some companies to 34% for industrial corporations.

➤ NET INCOME FOR THE YEAR *The bottom line.* This was 4.2% better than the year before— about the same as recorded in the previous period. This was no record breaker and works out better on a per-share basis: $5.24 vs. $5.03.

One year's change is interesting, but the true test of management's ability comes over 5 years.

Use this figure to make other comparisons (against sales: 8.5% vs. 8.6% the year before) and then relate this to returns of other companies in the same industry. The average manufacturing corporation earns about 5¢ per dollar of sales, but supermarkets are lucky to end up with 1¢ against shareowners' equity: the profit rate (PR). Here, the PR was a modest 13%.

To find the earnings per share, divide the net income (less preferred dividend requirements) by the average number of shares outstanding during the year. This is the key figure for most analysts. It is also used to determine the price-earnings (P/E) ratio: divide the market price of the stock by the per-share profits. If the stock was selling at 30, the P/E would be 10—slightly above the average of most publicly owned shares.

➤ RETAINED EARNINGS The dollars reinvested for future growth, always an important indica-

tion of future prospects. If the company continues to boost this figure, its basic value will increase. At the same PR, earnings will increase, and eventually so will the value of the common stock.

Here the company keeps plowing back more: $4.6 million in the current year vs. $4.5 million the year before. (Subtract the retained earnings at the beginning of the year from retained earnings of the previous year: $37.6 − \$33.1 = \$4.5$.)

➤ DIVIDENDS The amount paid out to shareholders for the use of their money. The $5 per share paid on the preferred stock is fixed. The payments for the common move with profits: last year up 50¢ per share to $3.00 from the flat $2.50 of the 2 prior years.

Note that this statement shows earnings retained as of the beginning and end of each year. Thus the company reinvested $46.4 million for the future.

BALANCE SHEET ITEMS

Now that you know what happened in the last year, it's time to take a look at the financial strength (or weakness) of the corporation. On page 354 is a typical balance sheet. Use it as the basis for reviewing annual reports of the companies in which you own, or plan to own, securities. The headings may vary according to the type of industry, but the basic data will be similar—and just as important.

CURRENT ASSETS

Items that can be converted into cash within 1 year. The total is $48.4 million this year, $4.2 million more than last year.

➤ CASH Mostly bank deposits, including compensating balances held under terms of a loan— like keeping a savings account to get free checking.

➤ MARKETABLE SECURITIES Corporate and government securities that can be sold quickly. In the current year, these were eliminated.

➤ RECEIVABLES Amounts due from customers for goods and services. This is a net amount after a set-aside for items that may not be collected.

➤ INVENTORIES Cost of raw materials, work in process, and finished goods. Statements and foot-

BALANCE SHEET ($ millions)
"Your Company"

ASSETS	DEC. 31 CURRENT YEAR	DEC. 31 PRIOR YEAR
Current Assets		
Cash	$ 9.0	$ 6.2
Marketable securities	—	2.0
Accounts and notes receivable	12.4	11.4
Inventories	27.0	24.6
Total current assets	$ 48.4	$ 44.2
Property, Plant, and Equipment		
Buildings, machinery, and equipment, at cost	104.3	92.7
Less accumulated depreciation	27.6	25.0
	$ 76.7	$ 67.7
Land, at cost	.9	.7
Total property, plant, and equipment	$ 77.6	$ 68.4
Other Assets		
Receivables due after 1 year	4.7	3.9
Surrender value of insurance	.2	.2
Other	.6	.5
Total other assets	$ 5.5	$ 4.6
Total Assets	$131.5	$117.2

LIABILITIES AND STOCKHOLDERS' EQUITY	DEC. 31 CURRENT YEAR	DEC. 31 PRIOR YEAR
Current Liabilities		
Accounts payable	$ 6.1	$ 5.0
Accrued liabilities	3.6	3.3
Current maturity of long-term debt	1.0	.8
Federal income and other taxes	9.6	8.4
Dividends payable	1.3	1.1
Total current liabilities	$ 21.6	$ 18.6
Other Liabilities		
Long-term debt	3.6	2.5
5% sinking-fund debentures, due July 31, 1990	26.0	20.0
Stockholders' Equity		
5% cumulative preferred stock ($100 par: authorized and outstanding, 60,000)	6.0	6.0
Common stock ($10 par: authorized, 2,000,000; outstanding, 1,830,000)	18.3	18.3
Capital surplus	9.6	9.6
Retained earnings	46.4	42.2
Total stockholders' equity	$ 80.3	$ 76.1
Total Liabilities and Stockholders' Equity	$131.5	$117.2

notes describe the basis, generally cost or current market price, whichever is lower. To handle the additional business, these were up over those of the previous year.

PROPERTY, PLANT, AND EQUIPMENT

The land, structures, machinery and equipment, tools, motor vehicles, etc. Except for land, these assets have a limited useful life, and a deduction is taken from cost as depreciation. With a new plant, the total outlays were $11.6 million more, with depreciation up $2.6 million.

OTHER ASSETS

Identifiable property is valued at cost. Intangibles such as patents, copyrights, franchises, trademarks, or goodwill cannot be assessed accurately, so they are omitted from the computation of tangible net worth or book value.

If an increase in sales does not follow an increased investment, management may have

STATEMENT OF CHANGES IN FINANCIAL POSITION ($ millions)
"Your Company"

	DEC. 31 CURRENT YEAR	DEC. 31 LAST YEAR	DEC. 31 2 YEARS AGO
FUNDS PROVIDED			
Net income	$ 9.9	$ 9.5	$ 9.1
Changes not requiring working capital:			
Depreciation	2.6	3.5	2.3
Increase in other liabilities	1.1	2.0	1.4
Funds provided by operations	$13.6	$15.0	$12.8
Proceeds from long-term debt	7.0	—	—
Proceeds from sale of 5% cumulative preferred stock	—	6.0	—
Total funds provided	$20.6	$21.0	$12.8
FUNDS USED			
Additions to fixed assets	$11.8	$ .5	$ 6.2
Dividends paid on preferred stock	.3	.3	—
Dividends paid on common stock	5.4	4.6	4.6
Payments on long-term debt	1.0	15.0	—
Increase in noncurrent receivables	.8	.1	.3
Increase in other assets	.1	—	.2
Total funds used	$19.4	$20.5	$11.3
Increase in working capital	$ 1.2	$ .5	$ 1.5
CHANGES IN COMPONENTS OF WORKING CAPITAL			
Increase (decrease) in current assets:			
Cash	$ 2.8	$ 1.0	$ 1.1
Marketable securities	(2.0)	.5	.4
Accounts receivable	1.0	.5	.8
Inventories	2.4	1.0	1.3
Increase in current assets	$ 4.2	$ 3.0	$ 3.6
Increase in current liabilities:			
Accounts payable	$ 1.1	$ .9	$ .6
Accrued liabilities	.3	.5	.2
Current maturity of long-term debt	.2	.1	.5
Federal income and other taxes	1.2	1.0	.8
Dividends payable	.2	—	—
Increase in current liabilities	$ 3.0	$ 2.5	$ 2.1
Increase in working capital	$ 1.2	$ .5	$ 1.5

misjudged the ability to produce and/or sell more goods, or the industry may have reached overcapacity. If a company's plant and equipment show little change for several years during a period of expanding business, the shareholder should be cautious about the company's progressiveness. In this example, both fixed and total assets grew steadily.

LIABILITIES
Divided into two classes: current (payable within a year) and long-term (debt or other obligations that come due after 1 year from the balance sheet date).

➤ ACCOUNTS PAYABLE Money owed for raw materials, other supplies, and services.

➤ ACCRUED LIABILITIES Unpaid wages, salaries and commissions, interest, etc.

➤ CURRENT LONG-TERM DEBT Amount due in the next year. This usually requires annual repayments over a period of years.

➤ INCOME TAXES Accrued federal, state, and local taxes.

➤ DIVIDENDS PAYABLE Preferred or common dividends (or both) declared but not yet paid. Once declared, dividends become a corporate obligation.

➤ TOTAL CURRENT LIABILITIES An increase of $3 million needed to finance expansion of business.

➤ LONG-TERM DEBT What's due for payment in the future less the amount due in the next year. Although the total was reduced to $20 million, an additional $6 million of debentures was issued.

STOCKHOLD-ERS' EQUITY (or CAPITAL)
All money invested in the business by stockholders as well as reinvested earnings.

➤ PREFERRED STOCK Holders are usually entitled to dividends before common stockholders and to priority in the event of dissolution or liquidation. Dividends are fixed. If cumulative, no dividends can be paid on common stock until the preferred dividends are up to date.

Here each share of preferred was issued at $100, but its market value will move with the cost of money: up when interest rates decline, down when they rise.

➤ COMMON STOCK Shown on the books at par value, an arbitrary amount having no relation to the market value or to what would be received in liquidation.

➤ CAPITAL SURPLUS The amount of money received from the sale of stock in excess of the par value.

➤ RETAINED EARNINGS Money reinvested in the business.

➤ TOTAL STOCKHOLDERS' EQUITY The sum of the common par value, additional paid-in capital, and retained earnings less any premium attributable to the preferred stock: what the stockholders own. The increase of $4.2 million is a rise of about 5%—not bad, but not as much as should be the mark of a true growth company.

CHANGES IN FINANCIAL POSITION

This presents a different view of the financing and investing activities of the company and clarifies the disposition of the funds produced by operations. It includes both cash and other elements of working capital—the excess of current assets over current liabilities.

The balance sheet shows that the working capital has increased by $1.2 million (current assets of $48.4 million exceeded current liabilities of $21.6 million by $26.8 million at the end of the year vs. $25.6 million the year before).

Sales and net income were up; the contribution to working capital from operations decreased to $13.6 million vs. $15 million the year before. This was narrowed to $.4 million by the proceeds of the $7 million in long-term debt, $1 million more than the proceeds from the sale of preferred stock the year before.

The difference between the funds used last year and the year before was $1.1 million, reflecting a heavier investment in productive capacity against a larger repayment of long-term debt the year before.

With increased capacity, the company should be able to handle higher sales. The additional cash may be a good sign, but when too much cash accumulates, it may indicate that management is not making the best use of its assets. In financially tense times, cash is still always welcome.

SEVEN KEYS TO VALUE

1   **Operating profit margin (PM)** The ratio of profit (before interest and taxes) to

KEYS TO VALUE

	CURRENT YEAR	PRIOR YEAR
1 Operating profit margin	19.5%	18.5%
2 Current ratio	2.24	2.38
3 Liquidity ratio	41.7%	44.1%
4 Capitalization ratios:		
Long-term debt	19.7%	20.8%
Preferred stock	6.0	6.3
Common stock and surplus	80.3	72.9
5 Sales to fixed assets	1.1	1.2
6 Sales to inventories	4.3	4.5
7 Net income to net worth	12.3%	12.5%

sales. As shown on the statement of income and retained earnings, the operating profit ($22.6) divided by sales ($115.8) equals 19.5%. This compares with 18.5% for the previous year. (Some analysts prefer to compute this margin without including depreciation and depletion as part of the cost, because these have nothing to do with the efficiency of the operation.)

When a company increases sales substantially, the PM should widen, because certain costs (rent, interest, property taxes, etc.) are pretty much fixed and do not rise in proportion to volume.

2 Current ratio The ratio of current assets to current liabilities is calculated from the balance sheet: $48.4 ÷ $21.6 = 2.24:1. For most industrial corporations, this ratio should be about 2:1. It varies with the type of business. Utilities and retail stores have rapid cash inflows and high turnovers of dollars, so they can operate effectively with low ratios.

When the ratio is high, say 5:1, it may mean that the company has too much cash and is not making the best use of these funds. They should be used to expand the business. Such corporations are often targets for takeovers.

3 Liquidity ratio Again referring to the balance sheet, the ratio of cash and equivalents to total current liabilities

($9 ÷ $21.6 = 41.7%). It should be used to supplement the current ratio, because the immediate ability of a company to meet current obligations or pay larger dividends may be impaired despite a high current ratio. This 41.7% liquidity ratio (down from 44.1% the year before) probably indicates a period of expansion, rising prices, heavier capital expenditures, and larger accounts payable. *If the decline persists, the company might have to raise additional capital.*

4 Capitalization ratios The percentage of each type of investment as part of the total investment in the corporation. Though often used to describe only the outstanding securities, capitalization is the sum of the face value of bonds ($26.0) and other debts *plus* the par value of all preferred and common stock issues ($18.3 + 6.0 = $24.3) *plus* the balance sheet totals for capital surplus ($9.6) and retained earnings ($46.4).

Bond, preferred stock, and common stock ratios are useful indicators of the relative risk and leverage involved for the owners of the three types of securities. For most industrial corporations, the debt ratio should be no more than 66⅔% of equity, or 40% of total capital. Higher ratios are appropriate for utilities and transportation corporations.

In this instance, looking at the balance sheet, the long-term debt plus preferred stock ($26.0 + $6.0 = $32.0) is 87.2% of the $27.9 equity represented by the common stock ($18.3) and surplus ($9.6), and 30.1% of total capital.

5 Sales-to-fixed-assets ratio Using both the statement of income and retained earnings and the balance sheet, this ratio is computed by dividing the annual sales ($115.8) by the year-end value of plant, equipment, and land before depreciation and amortization ($104.3 + $0.9 = $105.2). The ratio is therefore 1.1:1. This is down from 1.2:1 the year before.

This ratio helps to show whether funds used to enlarge productive facilities are being spent wisely. A sizable expansion in facilities should lead to larger sales volume. If it does not, there's something wrong. In this case, there were delays in getting production on stream at the new plant.

6   **Sales-to-inventories ratio**   Again referring to both statements, you can compute this ratio by dividing the annual sales by year-end inventories: $115.8 ÷ $27 = 4.3:1. The year before, the ratio was 4.5:1.

This shows inventory turnover: the number of times the equivalent of the year-end inventory has been bought and sold during the year.

It is more important in analyzing retail corporations than in analyzing manufacturers. A high ratio denotes a good quality of merchandise and correct pricing policies. A declining ratio may be a warning signal.

7   **Net-income-to-net-worth (return on equity) ratio**   One of the most significant of all financial ratios. Derived by dividing the net income from the statement of income and retained earnings ($9.9) by the total stockholders' equity from the balance sheet ($80.3). The result is 12.3%: the percentage of return that corporate management earned on the dollars entrusted by shareholders at the beginning of each year. Basically, it's that all-important PR (profit rate).

This 12.3% is a slight decrease from the 12.5% of the prior year. It's a fair return: not as good as that achieved by a top-quality corporation but better than that of the average publicly held company. *The higher the ratio, the more profitable the operation.* Any company that can consistently improve such a ratio is a true growth company. *But be sure that this gain is a result of operating skill, not of accounting legerdemain or extraordinary items.*

RATIOS AND TRENDS

Detailed financial analysis involves careful evaluation of income, costs, and earnings. But it is also important to study various ratios and trends, both those within the specific corporation and those of other companies in the same industry. Analysts usually prefer to use 5- or 10-year averages. These can reveal significant changes and, on occasion, point out special values in either concealed or inconspicuous assets.

➤ OPERATING RATIO   The ratio of operating costs to sales. It is the complement of *profit margin* (100% minus the PM percentage). Thus if a company's PM is 10%, its operating ratio is 90%. It's handy for comparing similar companies but not significant otherwise.

PMs vary with the type of business. They are low for companies with heavy plant investments (Ingersoll-Rand) and for retailers with fast turnovers (The Limited) and high for marketing firms (Gillette).

➤ INTEREST COVERAGE   The number of times interest charges or requirements have been earned. Divide the operating profit (or balance available for such payments before income taxes and interest charges) by the annual interest charges.

According to the statement of income and retained earnings, the interest (fixed charges) was covered 17.4 times in the past year and 20.3 times in the previous year. This is a high, safe coverage. If earnings declined to only 6% of the past year's results, interest would still be covered. As a rule, a manufacturing company should cover interest 5 times; utilities, 3 times.

Keep in mind that when a company (except utilities or transportation firms) has a high debt, it means that investors shy away from buying its common stock. To provide the plants, equipment, etc., that the company needs, management must issue bonds or preferred shares (straight or convertible to attract investors). There are some tax advantages in following such a course, but when the debt becomes too high, there can be trouble during times of recession. All or most of the gross profits will have to be used to pay interest, and there will be nothing or little left over for the common stockholders.

By contrast, speculators like high-debt situations when business is good. With hefty profits, interest can be paid easily, and the balance comes down to the common stock. Typically, airlines with heavy debt obligations for new planes do well in boom times. An extra 10% gain in traffic can boost profits by as much as 30%.

➤ PAYOUT RATIO   The ratio of the cash dividends to per-share profits after taxes. Fast-

---

COMPANIES WITH STRONG EARNINGS
GROWTH

Advanced Micro Dev.	MAPCO Inc.
Bard (C.R.)	Nevada Power
Blockbuster Entertainment	Nordstrom Inc.
	Philip Morris
Browne & Co.	Phillips-Van Heusen
Caesars World	Pioneer Hi-Bred
Cooper Tire & Rubber	Int'l.
	Premark
First Union	International
Fleet Financial Group	RJR Nabisco
General Signal	St. Jude Medical
Guilford Mills	Sears, Roebuck
Illinois Power	Springs Industries
Lam Research	Tyco Laboratories
Leslie Fay Cos.	Western Publishing
Limited Inc.	Whirlpool Corp.
Lotus Development	

Source: The Outlook, July 1, 1992.

---

growing corporations pay no or small dividends because they need money for expansion. Profitable companies pay out from about 25% to 50% of their profits. Utilities, which have almost assured earnings, pay out more. But be wary when those dividends represent much more than 70% of income.

It's pleasant to receive an ample dividend check, but for growth, look for companies that pay small dividends. The retained earnings will be used to improve financial strength and the operating future of the company. *And they are tax-free.*

➤ PRICE-TO-BOOK-VALUE RATIO The market price of the stock divided by its book value per share. Since book value trends are usually more stable than earnings trends, conservative analysts use this ratio as a price comparison. They check the historical over- or undervaluation of the stock, which in turn depends primarily on the company's profitable growth (or lack of it).

Because of inflation, understatement of assets on balance sheets—and, in boom times, the enthusiasm of investors—often pushes this ratio rather high. On the average, only stocks of the most profitable companies sell at much more than twice book value. Investors believe that these corporations will continue to achieve ever-higher earnings. But if the stock prices rise too high, their decline, in a bear market, can be fast and far.

➤ PRICE-EARNINGS (P/E) RATIO Calculated by dividing the price of the stock by the reported earnings per share for the past 12 months. Such projections can be made *only* for stocks of quality corporations with long, fairly consistent records of profitable growth. They will not work for shares of companies that are cyclical, erratic, or untested. There can be no guarantee that these goals will be attained as soon as anticipated. Wall Street is often slow to recognize value and always takes time to come to intelligent decisions.

➤ CASH FLOW A yardstick that is increasingly popular in investment analysis. Reported net earnings after taxes do not reflect the actual cash income available to the company. Cash flow shows the earnings after taxes *plus* charges against income that do not directly involve cash outlays (sums allocated to depreciation, depletion, amortization, and other special items).

A company might show a net profit of $250,000 plus depreciation of $1 million, so cash flow is $1,250,000. Deduct provisions for preferred dividends (if any), and then divide the balance by the number of shares of common stock to get the cash flow per share.

Two types of cash flow are important:

- *Distributable cash flow:* the amount of money that the company has on hand to pay dividends and/or invest in real growth. If this is negative, there are problems. If it's positive, fine, *unless* the company pays out more than this figure in dividends and is thus liquidating the firm.

- *Discretionary cash flow:* distributable cash flow minus dividends, that is, how much money is left to grow with, after allocations for maintenance and dividends. Companies do not actually set aside such funds, but they must ultimately have the money in some form—cash savings or borrowing.

HOW TO DETERMINE A PRUDENT P/E RATIO

Analysts usually justify their recommendations by adjusting the multiple of the price of the stock by estimated rate of future growth or by cash flow per share rather than by reported earnings. In both cases, these are attempts to justify a predetermined decision to buy. The projections appear plausible, especially when accompanied by tables and charts and computer printouts. But in most cases, they are useful only as background and not for the purpose of making decisions on the proper level to buy or later to sell. The calculations depend a good deal on market conditions and your own style, but here's one approach for those "supergrowth" stocks that will be suggested by your friends or broker.

Example: According to your financial adviser, the stock of a "future" company now selling at 40 times its recent earnings will be trading at "only 16 times its projected earnings 5 years hence *if* the company's average earnings growth is 20% a year." (See price evaluator, page 361.)

If you are speculating with this type of "hot" stock, you should compare it with other opportunities and on some basis decide how reasonable this projection really is.

A handy formula is

$$\text{Prudent P/E ratio} = GRTQM$$

G = growth
R = reliability and risk
T = time
Q = quality
M = multiple of price to earnings

➤ GROWTH The company's projected growth in earnings per share over the next 5 years. The basic compound interest formula is $(1 + G)^5$, where G is the projected growth rate, as shown in the price evaluator and prudent P/E multiples table. This omits dividend yields because they are usually small in relation to the potential capital appreciation.

➤ RELIABILITY AND RISK Not all projected growth rates are equally reliable or probable. A lower projected growth rate is likely to be more reliable

than a very high projected one (30% to 50% a year).

Logically, you can assign a higher reliability rating to a noncyclical company (utility, food processor, retailer) than to a corporation in a cyclical industry (aluminum, machinery, tools).

➤ TIME Another factor is the assumed length of the projected growth period. If you can realistically anticipate that the company will continue its rate of growth for the next 10 years, a 10% rate for its stock is more reliable than a 15% rate for a company whose growth visibility is only 3 to 5 years.

If you are uncertain about the corporation's consistency, you should assign it the greater risk.

➤ QUALITY As you know, this is the single most important investment consideration.

➤ MULTIPLE OF PRICE TO EARNINGS This is a comparative measurement. The first step is to determine the P/E for an average quality nongrowth stock. This is done by relating the current yield on guaranteed, fixed-income investments (savings accounts, corporate bonds) to the P/E multiple that will produce the same yield on the nongrowth stock.

$$P/E = \frac{D}{IR}$$

P/E = price/earnings ratio
D = dividend as percentage payout of earnings
IR = interest rate

Thus a stock yielding 8% on a 70% payout of profits must, over a 5-year period, be bought and sold at 7 times earnings to break even on capital and to make as much income as could be obtained over the same period via the ownership of a fixed-income investment continually yielding 10%:

$$P/E = \frac{7}{10} = .7$$

Note: This is *not* a valid comparison in terms of investment alone. Since the nongrowth stock carries a certain amount of risk in comparison to the certainty of a bond or money market fund, the stock should sell at a lower multiple, probably 5 to 6 times earnings.

Other key items used in analysis are:
➤ EARNINGS GROWTH RATE A formula that gives the rate at which a company's profits have

PRUDENT PRICE-EARNINGS MULTIPLES FOR GROWTH STOCKS

IF YOU PROJECT EARNINGS PER SHARE (AFTER TAXES) TO GROW IN NEXT 5 YEARS AT AN AVERAGE COMPOUNDED RATE OF:	WITH THESE QUALITY RATINGS* THESE ARE APPROXIMATE PRUDENT MULTIPLES THAT REPRESENT THE MAXIMUM CURRENT PRICE TO PAY:				
	B	B+	A−	A	A+
5%	12.0	12.9	13.7	15.0	16.7
6%	12.5	13.4	14.3	15.8	17.4
7%	13.0	14.0	14.9	16.5	18.2
8%	13.6	14.5	15.6	17.1	18.9
9%	14.1	15.1	16.2	17.8	19.7
10%	14.6	15.7	16.8	18.5	20.4
15%	17.4	18.7	20.1	22.0	24.5
20%	20.2	21.8	23.4	25.7	28.6
25%	23.0	24.7	26.6	29.3	32.7
30%	25.2	27.3	29.4	32.5	36.2
35%	28.5	31.0	33.5	37.1	41.5
40%	31.9	34.8	37.7	41.7	46.7

*Standard & Poor's designations. If not rated, use B; if a new, untested firm, use a conservative rating based on comparison with similar companies, preferably in the same industry.

increased over the past several years. You can find the earnings growth rate in annual reports or from your broker. Then divide it by the P/E and compare this number with the Standard & Poor's 500 to decide whether to buy or sell. Keep in mind that in good years the average growth rate for the Standard & Poor's 500 stock index has been 16% and the average P/E 8, so the index for the purposes of this formula should be divided by 2.

For example, let us assume that Company XYZ has an earnings growth rate of 40% per year. Its P/E is 20; its index is therefore 2, only equal to the Standard & Poor's average—nothing to get excited about.

Another company, the LMN Corporation, has an earnings growth rate of 40% also; however, its P/E is 15, so its index comes out to be 2.6. Because this ratio is above the Standard & Poor's index of 2, it is an apparent bargain.

➤ PERCENTAGE BUYING VALUE This is a variation of the formula developed by John B. Neff of the Windsor Fund. It uses the current yield plus the rate of earnings growth divided by the current P/E ratio. If the result is 2 or more, the stock is worth buying:

CY = current yield
EG = earnings growth
P/E = price-earnings ratio
PBV = percentage buying value

$$\frac{CY + EG}{P/E} = PBV$$

$$\frac{1.4 + 20}{22} = 9.7\% = buy$$

$$\frac{8.6 + 2}{7.7} = 1.32\% = sell\ or\ do\ not\ buy$$

➤ RETURN ON EQUITY AND P/E: TOTAL RETURN Most investors tend to think about their gains and losses in terms of price changes and not dividends, whereas those who own bonds pay attention to interest yields and seldom focus on price changes. Both approaches are mistakes. Although dividend yields are obviously more important if you are seeking income, and changes in price play a greater role in growth stocks, knowing the *total return* on a stock makes it possible for you to compare your investment in a stock with a similar investment in a corporate bond, municipal, Treasury, mutual fund, etc.

To calculate the total return, add (or subtract) the stock's price change and the dividends received for 12 months and then divide that number by the price at the beginning of the 12-month period.

Example: An investor bought a stock at $42 per share and received dividends for the 12-month period of $2.50. At the end of 12 months, the stock was sold at $45. The total return was 13%.

Dividend	$2.50
Stock price change	$3.00
	$5.50 ÷ $42 = 13%

➤ CORPORATE CASH POSITION Developed by Benjamin Graham, granddaddy of fundamentalists.

■ Subtract current liabilities, long-term debt, and preferred stock (at market value) from current assets of the corporation.

- Divide the result by the number of shares of common stock outstanding to get the current asset value per share.
- If it is higher than the price per share, Graham would place the stock on his review list.

CHECKPOINTS FOR FINDING UNDERVALUED STOCKS

- A price that is well below book value, asset value, and working capital per share
- Ample cash or liquid assets for both normal business and expansion
- A current dividend of 4.5% or more
- Cash dividends paid for at least 5, and preferably 10, years without decrease in dollar payout
- Total debt less than 30% of total capitalization
- Minimum current dividend protection ratio of at least 1:4 ($1.40 earnings for each $1.00 in dividends), preferably higher
- A P/E ratio lower than that of prior years and preferably below 10 times projected 12-month earnings
- A company that sells at 4 or 5 times cash flow and that generates excess cash, which can be used to expand or repurchase its stock
- Inventories that are valued lower than their initial cost or their immediate market value (check Value Line or S&P for figures)

LOW P/Es PAY OFF

Investors often get excited about stocks with high P/Es. They figure the stocks are so popular that their prices will keep on rising. But the facts prove

otherwise: Stocks with low P/Es (seemingly those with the worst prospects) outperform those with high multiples.

Low P/Es are often found in mature industries, in low-growth and blue chip companies. In general, low-P/E companies pay higher dividends, although there are many exceptions.

High P/Es, by contrast, tend to be found in newer, aggressive growth companies, which are far riskier than those with lower P/Es.

$ HINT: Look for companies with high sales per share in cyclical industries (auto, aluminum, rubber) that are temporarily depressed. When industry conditions change and profit margins increase, the turnaround in earnings can be dramatic.

COMPANIES REPURCHASING THEIR STOCK

When corporations set up a program to buy back their shares, it's a bullish sign. Over a 12-month period, one survey showed, 64% of such stock outpaced the market.

Repurchase of a substantial number of shares automatically benefits all shareholders: Profits are spread over a smaller total, there's more money for dividends and reinvestments, and there's a temporary price increase for the stock in many cases.

FOR FURTHER INFORMATION

Charles H. Brandes, *Value Investing Today* (Homewood, IL: Dow Jones–Irwin, 1989).

Rose Marie Bukics, *Financial Statement Analysis* (Chicago: Probus Publishing Co., 1992).

D USING TECHNICAL INDICATORS

Technical analysis (TA) is a way of doing securities research using indicators, charts, and computer programs to track price trends of stocks, bonds, commodities, and the market in general. Technical analysts use these indicators to predict price movements.

If you understand the basics of both technical and fundamental analysis, you'll have a great advantage as an investor.

TA is neither as complex nor as esoteric as many people think. It's a tell-it-as-it-is interpretation of stock market activity. The technician glances at the fundamental values of securities but basically concentrates on the behavior of the market, industry groups, and stocks themselves—their price movements, volume, trends, patterns; in sum, their supply and demand.

Basically, TA is concerned with what *is* and not with what *should be*. Dyed-in-the-wool technicians pay minimal attention to what the *company* does and concentrate on what its *stock* does. They recognize that over the short term, the values of stocks reflect what people *think* they are worth, not what they are really worth.

Technical analysts operate on the assumption that (1) the past action of the stock market is the best indicator of its future course, (2) 80% of a stock's price movement is due to factors outside the company's control and 20% to factors unique to that stock, and (3) the stock market over a few weeks or months is rooted 85% in psychology and only 15% in economics.

THE DOW THEORY

There are a number of technical theories, but the granddaddy is the Dow theory. It is the oldest and most widely used. As with all technical approaches, it is based on the belief that stock prices cannot be forecast accurately by fundamental analysis but that trends, indicated by price movements and volume, can be used successfully. These can be recorded, tracked, and interpreted because the market itself prolongs movements: Investors buy more when the market is rising and sell more when it's dropping.

This follow-the-crowd approach enables the pros to buy when the market is going up and to sell or sell short when the market turns down. For amateurs, such quick trading is costly because of the commissions involved and the need for accurate information. But when properly used, TA can be valuable in correctly timing your buy and sell positions.

The Dow theory is named after Charles H. Dow, one of the founders of Dow Jones & Company, Inc., the financial reporting and publishing organization. The original hypotheses have been changed somewhat by his followers, but broadly interpreted, the Dow theory signals both the beginning and end of bull and bear markets.

Dow believed the stock market to be a barometer of business. The purpose of his theory was not to predict movements of security prices but rather to call the turns of the market and to forecast the business cycle or longer movements of depression or prosperity. It was not concerned with ripples or day-to-day fluctuations.

The Dow theory basically states that once a trend of the Dow Jones Industrial Average (DJIA) has been established, it tends to follow the same direction until definitely canceled by *both* the Industrial and Railroad (now Transportation) Averages. The market cannot be expected to produce new indications of the trend every day, and unless there is positive evidence to the contrary, the existing trend will continue.

Dow and his disciples saw the stock market as made up of two types of "waves": the *primary wave*, which is a bull or bear market cycle of

TECHNICAL VS. FUNDAMENTAL ANALYSIS

Technical analysis focuses on the changes of a company's stock as illustrated on daily, weekly, or periodic charts. Volume or number of shares traded is included, and from this "technical" information future price movements are forecast.

Fundamental analysis of industries and companies, by contrast, centers on the outlook for earnings and growth. Analysts study such factors as sales, assets, earnings, products, services, potential markets, and management.

several years' duration, and the *secondary* (or *intermediary*) *wave,* which lasts from a few weeks to a few months. Any single primary wave may contain within it 20 or more secondary waves, both up and down.

The theory relies on similar action by the two averages (Industry and Transportation), which may vary in strength but not in direction. Robert Rhea, who expanded the original concept, explained it this way: "Successive rallies, penetrating preceding high points with ensuing declines terminating above preceding low points, offer a bullish indication . . . (and vice versa for bearish indication). . . . A rally or decline is defined as one or more daily movements resulting in a net reversal of direction exceeding 3% of either average. Such movements have little authority unless confirmed by both Industrial and Transportation Averages . . . but confirmation need not occur in the same day."

Dow did not consider that his theory applied to individual stock selections or analysis. He expected that specific issues would rise or fall with the averages most of the time, but he also recognized that any particular security would be affected by special conditions or situations.

These are the key indicators of the Dow theory:

- **A bull market is signaled as a possibility** when an intermediate decline in the DJIA stops above the bottom of the previous

intermediate decline. This action *must be confirmed* by the action of the Transportation Average (DJTA). A bull market is confirmed after this has happened and when on the next intermediate rise *both* averages rise above the peaks of the last previous intermediate rise.

- **A bull market is in progress** as long as each new intermediate rise goes *higher* than the peak of the previous intermediate advance and each new intermediate decline stops *above* the bottom of the previous one.
- **A bear market is signaled as a possibility** when an intermediate rally in the DJIA fails to break through the top of the previous intermediate rise. A bear market is *confirmed* (1) after this has happened, (2) when the next intermediate decline breaks through the low of the previous one, and (3) when it is confirmed by the DJTA.
- **A bear market is in progress** as long as each new intermediate decline goes *lower* than the bottom of the previous decline and each new intermediate rally fails to rise as high as the previous rally.

A pure Dow theorist considers the averages to be quite sufficient to use in forecasting and sees no need to supplement them with statistics of commodity prices, volume of production, car loadings, bank debts, exports, imports, etc.

➤ INTERPRETING THE DOW THEORY The Dow theory leaves no room for sentiment.

A primary bear market does not terminate until stock prices have thoroughly discounted the worst that is apt to occur. This decline requires three steps: (1) "the abandonment of hopes upon which stocks were purchased at inflated prices," (2) selling due to decreases in business and earnings, and (3) distress selling of sound securities despite value.

Primary bull markets follow the opposite pattern: (1) a broad movement, interrupted by secondary reactions averaging longer than 2 years, where successive rallies penetrate high points with ensuing declines terminating above preceding low points; (2) stock prices advancing because of demand created by both investors and speculators who start buying when business conditions improve; and (3) rampant speculation as stocks advance on hopes, expectations, and dreams.

§ HINT: A new primary trend is not actually confirmed by the Dow theory until *both* the DJTA and the DJIA penetrate their previous positions.

➤ CRITICISM There are analysts who scoff at the Dow theory. They point out that the stock market today is vastly different from that in the early 1900s when Dow formulated his theory. The number and value of shares of publicly owned corporations have increased enormously: In 1900, the average number of shares traded *annually* on the NYSE was 59.5 million. Now that's the volume on a very slow *day.*

The sharpest criticism is leveled against the breadth, scope, and significance of the averages. The original Industrial index had only 12 stocks, and today's 30 large companies do not provide a true picture of the broad, technologically oriented economy. Critics point out that the Transportation Average is also unrepresentative, because some of the railroads derive a major share of their revenues from natural resources, and the airlines and trucking companies are limited in their impact. Add the geographic dispersal of industry, and Transportation is no longer a reliable guide to the economy.

Finally, the purists argue that government regulations and institutional dominance of trading have so altered the original concept of individual investors that the Dow theory can no longer be considered all-powerful and always correct.

To most investors, the value of the Dow theory is that it represents a sort of think-for-yourself method that will pay worthwhile dividends for those who devote time and effort to gaining a sound understanding of the principles involved.

➤ WHAT'S AHEAD In July 1992, Richard Russell, publisher of the newsletter *Dow Theory Letters,* and the leading authority on the Dow theory, stated, "In driving down short-term interest rates, the Fed has gone a long way towards re-liquefying the banks. But while short rates have collapsed, the long rates have held high. Meanwhile, the banks have been having a picnic, paying little for money (Have you checked what your local bank is paying you on your passbook or for a CD?). At the same time,

the prime rate has remained relatively high, and the banks are almost reluctant to make loans. But the banks have been buying government bonds. Since our foreign friends have been cutting way back on buying U.S. paper, the banks have been taking up the slack. . . . Personally, I don't think the current stock market is a great place in which to make money. I prefer the currencies and bonds . . . Deutschemarks and ECUs . . . General Electric paper (rated AAA) . . . the Benham European Government Bond Fund with its 8.42% yield."

Russell also suggests for "those who like to ignore all trends and like formula investing" that they buy the top-yielding Dow stocks once every six months or once a year. As of July 1992, the top yielders were: IBM (5.4%), Kodak (5%), Texaco (4.91%), Sears (4.89%), Chevron (4.61%), Exxon (4.48%), American Express (4.23%), Woolworth (4.15%), Westinghouse (3.95%), J.P. Morgan (3.93%). "Woolworth is the newest addition to the top ten yielders. Exxon has been on the top ten list for the longest time—141 months." (Source: *Dow Theory Letters.*, P.O. Box 1759, La Jolla, CA 92038; $250 per year.)

PSYCHOLOGICAL INDICATORS

Keeping in mind that the stock market is rooted 15% in economics and 85% in psychology, some analysts predict the future by using such technical indicators as these:

➤ BARRON'S CONFIDENCE INDEX (BCI) This is published weekly in the financial news magazine *Barron's.* It shows the ratio of the yield on 10 highest-grade bonds to the yield on the broader-based Dow Jones 40-bond average. The ratio varies from the middle 80s (bearish) to the middle 90s (bullish).

The theory is that the trend of "smart money" is usually revealed in the bond market before it shows up in the stock market. Thus, *Barron's Confidence Index* will be *high* when shrewd investors are confident and buy more lower-grade bonds, thus reducing low-grade bond yields, and *low* when they are worried and stick to high-grade bonds, thus cutting high-grade yields.

If you see that the BCI simply keeps going back and forth aimlessly for many weeks, you can probably expect the same type of action from the overall stock market.

➤ OVERBOUGHT-OVERSOLD INDEX (OOI) This is a handy measure, designed by *Indicator Digest,* of a short-term trend and its anticipated duration. Minor upswings or downturns have limited lives. As they peter out, experienced traders say that the market is "overbought" or "over-sold" and is presumably ready for a near-term reversal.

➤ GLAMOUR AVERAGE Another *Indicator Digest* special, this shows what is happening with the institutional favorites, usually trading at high multiples because of their presumed growth potential and current popularity (in a bull market). By and large, this is a better indicator for speculators than investors.

➤ SPECULATION INDEX This is the ratio of AMEX-to-NYSE volume. When trading in AMEX stocks (generally more speculative) moves up faster than that in NYSE (quality) issues, speculation is growing. It's time for traders to move in and for investors to be cautious.

BROAD-BASED INDICATORS

➤ ODD-LOT INDEX This shows how small investors view the market, because it concentrates on trades of fewer than 100 shares. The small investor is presumably "uninformed" (a somewhat debatable assumption) and so tends to follow established patterns: selling as the market rises; jumping in to pick up bargains when it declines. The signal comes when the odd lotter deviates from this "normal" behavior.

When the small investor distrusts a rally after a long bear market, that investor gives a bullish signal: Initial selling is normal, but when this continues, it's abnormal and a signal to the pros to start buying.

➤ MOVING AVERAGE LINES You can also watch the direction of a stock by comparing its price to a *moving average* (MA). A moving average is an average that's periodically updated by dropping the first number and adding in the last one. A 30-week moving average, for example, is determined by adding the stock's closing price for the current week to the closing prices of the previous 29 weeks and then dividing by 30. Over time, this moving average indicates the trend of prices.

A long-term moving average tends to smooth out short-term fluctuations and provides a basis against which short-term price movement can be measured.

Moving averages can be calculated for both individual stocks and all stocks in a group— say, all those listed on the NYSE or all in a particular industry. Technical analysts use a variety of time frames: 10 days, 200 days, 30 weeks, etc. In most cases they compare the moving average with a regular market average, usually the Dow Jones Industrial Average. For example:

■ As long as the DJIA is *above* the MA, the outlook is bullish.

■ As long as the DJIA is *below* the MA, the outlook is bearish.

■ A confirmed downward penetration of the MA by the base index is a *sell* signal.

■ A confirmed penetration of the MA is a *buy* signal.

Beware of false penetrations, and delay action until there is a substantial penetration (2% to 3%), upward or downward, within a few weeks. In other words, don't be in a hurry to interpret the chart action.

MAs are vulnerable to swift market declines, especially from market tops. By the time you

MOST ACTIVE ISSUES, NYSE, MAY 20, 1992

NYSE	VOLUME	CLOSE	CHANGE
Gen. Motors	16,923,200	39	− ¼
Disney (Walt)	5,224,000	39⅜	−1½
RJR Nab. Hldg.	2,961,200	10	+ ¼
Limited Inc.	2,401,700	20⅝	− ¼
Adv. Micro Dvc.	2,395,600	14⅞	−1⅛
BankAmerica	2,222,900	48⅞	+1
Humana Inc.	2,142,400	23	−2¼
Alcatel Alsthom	2,006,800	23¾	· · ·
Coca-Cola Co.	1,630,100	44½	+ ⅝
McDonald's	1,596,200	46⅛	+1⅜
Phil. Elec.	1,416,000	x26	· · ·
Nuveen (John)	1,353,900	18	· · ·
AT&T	1,338,400	44	+ ⅝
Ford Motor Co.	1,323,300	44¼	− ¼
Heinz (H. J.) Co.	1,318,000	37⅞	+ ½

SOURCE: Wall Street Journal, May 20, 1992.

get the signal, you may have lost a bundle, because prices tend to fall twice as fast as they rise.

If you enjoy charting, develop a ratio of the stocks selling above their 30-week MA. When the ratio is over 50% and trending upward, the outlook is bullish. When it drops below 50% and/or is trending down, there's trouble ahead.

$ HINT: The longer the time span of the MA, the greater the significance of a crossover signal. An 18-month chart is more reliable than a 30-day one.

➤ BUYING POWER Buying power basically refers to the amount of money available to buy securities. It is determined by the cash in brokerage accounts plus the dollar amount that would be available if securities were fully margined. The bottom line: The market cannot rise above the available buying power.

The principle here is that at any point investors have only so much money available for investments. If it's in money market funds and cash, their buying power is stored up and readily available, not only to move into stocks but to push up prices. By contrast, if most investor buying power is already in stocks, there's little left for purchasing more stocks. In fact, in this situation investors could actually push the price of stocks down should they begin to sell.

Buying power is shown by these indicators:
- Rising volume in rallies. Investors are eager to buy, so the demand is greater than the supply, and prices go up.
- Shrinking volume on market declines. Investors are reluctant to sell.

With this technical approach, volume is the key indicator: It rises on rallies when the trend is up and rises on reactions when the trend is down.

$ HINT: Volume trends are apt to reverse before price trends. Shrinking volume almost always shows up before the top of a bull market and before the bottom of a bear market.

One other measure of buying power is the percentage of cash held in mutual funds. The Investment Company Institute in Washington, D.C., publishes this figure every month. In general, the ratio of cash to total assets in mutual funds tends to be low during market peaks, because this is the time when everyone is eager to buy stocks. The ratio is high during bull markets.

$ HINT: When cash holdings, as compiled by the Investment Company Institute, are above 7%, it's considered favorable; 9% to 10% is out-and-out bullish.

➤ MOST ACTIVE STOCKS This list is published at the top of daily or weekly reports of the NYSE, AMEX, and NASDAQ, and it gives the high, low, and last prices and change of 10 to 15 volume leaders. Here's where you can spot popular and unpopular industry groups and stocks.

Forget about the big-name companies such as Exxon, GE, and IBM. They have so many shares outstanding that trading is always heavy. Watch for repetition: of one industry or of one company. When the same names appear several times in a week or two, something is happening. Major investors are involved: buying if the price continues to rise, selling if it falls.

Watch most-actives for:
- *Newcomers,* especially small- or medium-sized corporations. When the same company pops up again and again, major shareholders are worried (price drop) or optimistic (price rise). Since volume requires substantial resources, the buyers must be big-money organizations. Once they have bought, you can move in, *if* the other fundamentals are sound.
- *Companies in the same industry.* Stocks tend to move as a group. Activity in computer retailers such as IBM and Apple *could* signal interest in this field.

➤ PERCENTAGE LEADERS This list is published weekly in several financial journals. It's primarily for those seeking to catch a few points on a continuing trend.

Although the value of the percentage leaders list has diminished recently because of the high gains scored by takeover or buyout candidates, it is still a way to spot some potential winners and to avoid losers. If you're thinking about making a move, check this list first. You may find several yet undiscovered stocks moving up in price.

➤ ADVANCES VERSUS DECLINES (A/D) This is a measure of the number of stocks that have advanced in price and the number that have declined within a given time span. Expressed as a ratio, the A/D illustrates the general direc-

PRICE PERCENTAGE GAINERS . . .   . . . AND LOSERS

NYSE	CLOSE	CHANGE	% CHANGE	NYSE	CLOSE	CHANGE	% CHANGE
Milestone Prpty	3¼	+ ½	+18.2	Rlty Refund Tr	11	−2⅝	−19.3
Baltimore Bncp	6⅞	+1	+17.0	Hall (F.B.) pf B	50½	−7	−12.2
El Paso Rfnry	9⅜	+1¼	+15.4	Live Entmt	2	− ¼	−11.1
Glenfed Inc	4½	+ ½	+12.5	Hancock Fab	11⅜	−1⅛	− 9.0
Rhone Plnc.wt	2½	+ ¼	+11.1	Humana Inc	23	−2¼	− 8.9
Western Digit	5⅛	+ ½	+10.8	Westpac Bkng	13⅝	−1¼	− 8.4
Alaska Air Grp	21	+1⅞	+9.8	Mickelberry	3¼	− ¼	− 7.1
Intl Family En	14	+1¼	+9.8	Adv Micro Dvc	14⅞	−1⅛	−7.0
Orbital Engine	22½	+2	+9.8	Lone Star Ind	3⅜	− ¼	−6.9
Salomon Inc	33½	+2⅞	+9.4	Duty Free Intl	37⅛	−2⅝	−6.6
Hm Shop Ntwk	5⅞	+ ½	+9.3	Reliance Grp	5⅜	− ⅜	−6.5
Mesa	4¾	+ ⅜	+8.6	Anacomp Inc	3¾	− ¼	−6.3
SFE Engy Ptnr	3¼	+ ¼	+8.3	MHI Group Inc	1⅞	− ⅛	−6.3
GRC Intl	3⅜	+ ¼	+8.0	Trammell Cr	1⅞	− ⅛	−6.3
Biocraft Labs	23	+1⅝	+7.6	Savin Corp	1⅞	− ⅛	−6.3
Aileen Inc	9	+ ⅝	+7.5	Coachmen Ind	7¾	− ½	−6.1
Prudntl Rlty	3⅝	+ ¼	+7.4	Southern Natl	17	−1	−5.6
Storage Tech	37½	+2½	+7.1	Am Ship Bldg	2⅛	− ⅛	−5.6
Grace Enrg	18¾	+1¼	+7.1	Hanson.wt	4⅜	− ¼	−5.4
Clarcor Inc	17⅛	+1⅛	+7.0	Jamesway	4½	− ¼	−5.3
NASDAQ NMS				**NASDAQ NMS**			
Security Tag	2¾	+ ⅝	+29.4	SANBORN.wt	2¼	−1	−30.8
Natl Vision	18¼	+2¾	+17.7	Fidelity Med	2⅞	− ¾	−20.7
Embrex.wt	2½	+ ⅜	+17.6	Rheometrics	2	− ½	−20.0
CA Short Intl	5¼	+ ¾	+16.7	Lifeline Sys	3½	− ¾	−17.6
Printronix Inc	5¼	+ ¾	+16.7	Sun Sportswear	5	−1	−16.7
Everex Sys	6½	+ ⅞	+15.6	Staar Surgical	7¾	−1½	−16.2
IIVI Inc	2⅞	+ ⅜	+15.0	Medicis Pharm	1¹¹⁄₁₆	− ⁵⁄₁₆	−15.6
CU Bncp	5¾	+ ¾	+15.0	Quarex Indus	4½	− ¾	−14.3
Alliance Imag	7¾	+1	+14.8	Essex Corp	3	− ½	−14.3
Auto Sec Hldgs	5	+ ⅝	+14.3	Abaxis	3⅞	− ⅝	−13.9
Dreco Enrg.clA	14	+1¾	+14.3	Osteotech	8	−1¼	−13.5
DNX Corp	6	+ ¾	+14.3	Kirschner Med	8¼	−1¼	−13.2
Great Cntry Bk	3	+ ⅜	+14.3	Clevetrust Rlty	2½	− ⅜	−13.0
Sunrise Bcp (Ca)	4	+ ½	+14.3	Sprouse-Reitz	3½	− ½	−12.5
AMEX				**AMEX**			
Cagle's.clA	9½	+1⅛	+13.4	B&H Maritime	3½	− ½	−12.5
Dataram Corp	15½	+1¾	+12.7	B&H Ocean	5¼	− ¾	−12.5
Wells-Gardner	6¼	+ ⅝	+11.1	Barr Labs	9⅜	− ⅞	−8.5
Helionetics	6¾	+ ⅝	+10.2	Essex Fncl	5½	− ½	−8.3
System Indus	2¾	+ ¼	+10.0	1st Natl Corp C	3½	− ¼	−6.7

SOURCE: Wall Street Journal, May 21, 1992.

tion of the market: When more stocks advance than decline on a single trading day, the market is thought to be bullish. The A/D can be an excellent guide to the trend of the overall market and, occasionally, of specific industry or stock groups. The best way to utilize A/D data is with a chart where the lines are plotted to show the cumulative difference between the advances and the declines on the NYSE or, for speculative holdings, on the AMEX. The total can cover 1 week, 21 days, or whatever period you choose, but because you're looking for developing trends, it should not be too long.

The table on page 370 shows a week when the advance/decline ratio was approximately 10 to 7, generally a positive trading day. On Wednesday, declines outnumbered advances by a small percentage, but new highs outnumbered new lows by a greater amount than on the prior day.

Many analysts prefer a moving average (MA) based on the net change for the week: 3,484 advances and 4,403 declines, for a net difference of 919. To make plotting easier, you can start with an arbitrary base, say 10,000, so the week's figure would be 9,081 (10,000 − 919).

The following week there's a net advance of 1,003, so the new total would be 10,084, etc. When you chart a 20-week MA, divide the cumulative figure by 20. When you add week 21, drop week 1. *Result:* a quick view of market optimism or pessimism.

To spot trouble ahead, compare the A/D chart with that of the DJIA. If the Dow is moving up for a month or so but the A/D line is flat or dropping, that's a negative signal. Watch out for new highs and lows on the A/D chart. Near market peaks, the A/D line will almost invariably top out and start declining before the overall market. At market lows, the A/D line seldom gives a far-in-advance warning.

Be cautious about using the A/D line alone. Make sure that it is confirmed by other indicators or, better yet, confirms other signals.

➤ VOLUME Trading volume, or the number of shares traded, is an important indicator in interpreting market direction and stock price changes. Changes in stock prices are the result of supply and demand, that is, the number of people who want to buy a stock and the number who want to sell. The key point here is that a rise or fall in price on a small volume of shares traded is far less important than a move supported by heavy volume. When there's heavy trading on the up side, buyers control the market, and their enthusiasm for the stock often pushes its price even higher.

§ HINT: Volume always precedes the direction of a stock's price.

➤ MOMENTUM This indicator measures the speed with which an index (or stock) is moving rather than its direction. Index changes are seldom if ever abrupt, so when an already rising index starts to rise even faster, it is thought likely to have a longer continuing upward run.

To measure momentum effectively you need to compare current figures to an index or previous average such as a 30-week moving average or the S&P 500.

➤ NEW HIGHS OR LOWS Every day the newspaper prints a list of stocks that hit a new price high or low for the year during the previous day's trading activity. Technical analysts use the ratio between the new highs and the new lows as an indication of the market's direction. They believe that when more stocks are making new highs than new lows, it's a bullish indication. If there are more lows than highs, pessimism abounds.

§ HINT: You should not use these figures as an absolute prediction of the future course of the market, because for a while a number of the same stocks will appear again and again. Also, the further into the year it is, the more difficult it is for a stock to continually post new highs.

LONDON'S *FINANCIAL TIMES* INDEX

The *Financial Times* Index is a British version of the Dow Jones Industrial Average. It records data on the London Stock Exchange: prices, volume, etc. Because it reflects worldwide business attitudes, it's a fairly reliable indicator of what's ahead, in 2 weeks to 2 months, for the NYSE.

There are, of course, temporary aberrations due to local situations, but over many years it has been a valuable technical tool. Since London is 5 hours ahead of New York, early risers benefit the most.

NYSE ADVANCES AND DECLINES:
HIGHS AND LOWS

NYSE	WED	TUE	WK AGO
Issues traded	2,267	2,282	2,268
Advances	821	1,010	883
Declines	881	698	829
Unchanged	565	574	556
New highs	72	62	91
New lows	13	19	10

SOURCE: *Wall Street Journal*, May 21, 1992.

These figures are most effective when converted to a chart and compared with a standard average. As long as the high and low indicators stay more or less in step with the Dow Jones Industrial Average or the S&P 500, they are simply a handy confirmation. But when the high-low line starts to dip while the average moves up, *watch out:* Internal market conditions are deteriorating.

This index of highs and lows exposes the underlying strength or weakness of the stock market, which is too often masked by the action of the DJIA. In an aging bull market, the DJIA may continue to rise, deceptively showing strength by the upward moves of a handful of major stocks; but closer examination will usually reveal that most stocks are too far below their yearly highs to make new peaks. At such periods, the small number of new highs is one of the most significant manifestations of internal market deterioration. The reverse is the telltale manner in which the total number of new lows appears in bear markets.

USING THE INDICATORS

Never rely on just one technical indicator. Only rarely can a single chart, ratio, average, MA, or index be 100% accurate. When an indicator breaks its pattern, look for confirmation from at least two other guidelines. Then wait a bit: at least 2 days in an ebullient market, a week or more in a normal one. This won't be easy, but what you are seeking is confirmation. These days a false move can be costly.

This emphasis on consensus applies also to newsletters, advisory services, and recommendations. If you select only one, look for a publication that uses—and explains—several indicators. Better yet, study two or three.

CHARTS: A VALUABLE TOOL FOR EVERYONE

Charts are a graphic ticker tape. They measure the flow of money into and out of the stock market, industry, or specific stock. They spotlight the highs and lows and point up how volume rises and falls on an advance or decline, illustrating the long-term patterns of the market and individual stocks.

Charting is simple, but interpretation can be complex. Even the strongest advocates of technical analysis (TA) disagree about the meaning of various formations, but they all start with three premises: (1) what happened before will be repeated, (2) a trend should be assumed to continue until a reversal is definite, and (3) a chart pattern that varies from a norm indicates that something unusual is happening. More than almost any other area of TA, chart reading is an art and a skill rather than a solid body of objective scientific information. It is an aid to stock analysis but not an end.

Charts are not surefire systems for beating the market, but they are one of the quickest and clearest ways to determine and follow trends. But all charts provide after-the-fact information.

The best combination for maximum profits and minimum losses is fundamental analysis supplemented by graphic technical analysis. Charts report that volume and price changes occur. Proper interpretation can predict the direction and intensity of change, because every purchase of every listed stock shows up on the chart.

Watch the bottom of the chart as well as the progress lines. This shows volume, and *volume precedes price.* A strong inflow of capital eventually pushes up the price of the stock; an outflow of dollars must result in a decline. To the charted results, it makes no difference who is doing the buying or selling.

Keeping in mind that charts are not infallible. Use them to:

■ **Help determine when to buy and when to sell** by indicating probable levels of support and supply and by signaling trend reversals

- **Call attention, by unusual volume or price behavior,** to something happening in an individual company that can be profitable to investors
- **Help determine the current trend:** up, down, or sideways, and whether the trend is accelerating or slowing
- **Provide a quick history of a stock** and show whether buying should be considered on a rally or a decline
- **Offer a sound means for confirming or rejecting** a buy or sell decision that is based on other information

$ HINT: Charts are history. By studying past action, it is often possible to make a reasonably valid prediction of the immediate future.

WIDELY USED CHARTS

The most commonly used types of charts are point-and-figure (P&F) and bar charts. For best results, they should be constructed on a daily or weekly basis.

If you have time, charting can be fun and highly educational. All you need is a pad of graph paper: plain squares for P&F charts, logarithmic or standard paper for bar charts.

P&F CHARTS
P&F charts are one-dimensional graphics. They show only price changes in relation to previous price changes. There are no indications of time or volume. The key factor is the change in price direction.

Some professionals think that P&F charts are oversimplified and consider them useful only as short-term guides and as a quick way to choose between two or three selections.

In making a P&F chart, the stock price is posted in a square: one above or below another, depending on the upward or downward movement of the price. As long as the price continues in the same direction, the same column is used. When the price shifts direction, the chartist moves to the next column.

In the chart shown here, the stock first fell in a downward sequence from 68 to 67 to 66. Then it rose to 67, so the chartist moved to column 2. The next moves were down to 62, up to 63 (new column), and so on. Most chartists

POINT AND FIGURE CHART

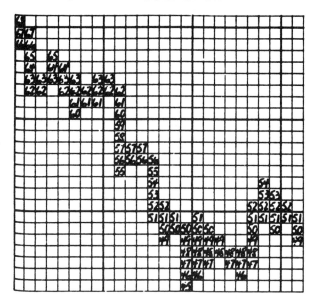

start the new column only when there is a distinct change, typically 1 point, but for longer projections, 2 or 3 points.

Note how a pattern is formed with various resistance levels where the price of the stock stayed within a narrow range (57–56 and later 48–47). The chart signals each shift from such a base: down from 56 to 51; up from 47 to 52.

The best way for an amateur to learn about P&F charts is to copy them. Take a stock that has been plotted for many years and slowly recopy its action on a piece of graph paper. Then draw in the trend lines: the uptrend line on the high points, the downtrend line along the low points. Then draw your channels, which are broad paths created by the highs and lows of a definite trend. (Without a trend your channel will be horizontal.)

P&F charts have disadvantages: They do not portray intraday action or consider volume. The financial pages report only the high (62), low (59¼), and close (61½). This does not show that the stock might have moved up and down from 60 to 62 several times during the day.

Despite the omission of volume on P&F charts, many technical analysts feel that volume should always be checked once there is a confirmed trend on the chart. Rising volume on upward movements and dwindling sales on the downside usually indicate that the stock has

BAR CHART

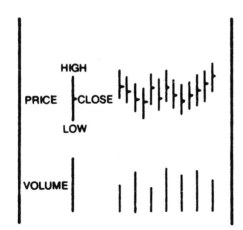

HEAD-AND-SHOULDERS CHART

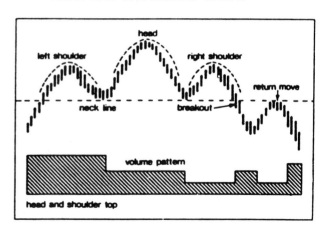

ample investor support. It's always wise to be on the same side as volume.

BAR CHARTS

These graphics record changes in relation to time. The horizontal axis represents time—a day, week, or month; the vertical coordinates refer to price. To follow volume on the same chart, add a series of vertical lines along the bottom. The higher the line, the greater the volume. On printed charts, adjustments are made so that everything fits into a convenient space.

In plotting a bar chart, enter a dot to mark the highest price at which the stock was traded that day; add another dot to record the low. Draw the vertical line between the dots to depict the price range, and draw a short horizontal nub to mark the closing price. After a few entries, a pattern will begin to emerge.

HEAD-AND-SHOULDER CHARTS

Almost every chartist has favorite configurations. They include such descriptive titles as the rounding bottom, the flag, the pennant, the tombstone top, the Prussian helmet formation, the megaphone top, and the lattice formation. One of the most popular formations is *head and shoulders* (H&S).

Oversimplified, the head-and-shoulders chart portrays three successive rallies and reactions, with the second reaching a higher point than either of the others. The failure of the third rally to equal the second peak is a warning that a major uptrend may have come to an end.

Conversely, a bottom H&S, formed upside down after a declining trend, suggests that an upturn lies ahead.

➤ LEFT SHOULDER This forms when an upturn of some duration, after hitting a climax, starts to fall. The volume of trading should increase with the rally and contract with the reaction. *Reason:* People who bought the stock on the uptrend start to take profits. When the technical reaction takes place, people who were slow to buy on the first rally start buying on the technical reaction.

➤ HEAD This is a second rally that carries the stock to new highs and is followed by a reaction that erases just about all the gain. Volume is high on the rally, yet lower than when forming the left shoulder. *Reason:* Investors who missed both the earlier actions start buying and force new highs.

This is followed by another drop as those who hesitated earlier see the second reaction and start acquiring the stock as it is sold by early buyers.

➤ RIGHT SHOULDER The third rally fails to reach the height of the head before the reaction. This is a sign of weakness. Watch the volume. If it contracts on a rally, it's likely that the price structure has weakened. If it increases, beware of a false signal.

➤ BREAKOUT This occurs when the stock price falls below the previous lows. At this point, most of the recent buyers have sold out—many of them at a loss.

No H&S should be regarded as complete

until the price breaks out below a line drawn tangent with the lows on the left and right shoulders. This is called the neckline.

INTERPRETING CHARTS

The charts from Securities Research Company (SRC) shown below and on page 374 are typical of those available from technical services. They can be valuable tools to improve the selection of securities and especially the timing of purchases and sales. Similar graphics are available for industry groups and stock market averages.

Do *not* buy any stock when the chart shows a confirmed downtrend. Buy *up* stocks in *up* groups in an *up* market. And unless you are holding for the long term, consider selling when there's a downtrend in the stock, the industry, and the market.

SRC offers two books of charts on stocks: blue for long-term trends over 12 years, red for short-term trends over 21 months. By using both, you get a better idea of the character, history, and probable performance of the stock.

LONG-TERM CHARTS

Ⓐ CAPITALIZATION Information on the corporation: dollars of bonds and preferred stocks (in millions); number of common shares outstanding (in thousands); and book value per common share.

Ⓑ EARNINGS AND DIVIDENDS Per-share data scaled from $1.40 to $5.50.

Ⓒ DIVIDENDS The annual rate of interim dividend payments. The circles mark the month in which the payments were made. Extra or irregular payouts (not shown) are typed in.

Ⓓ EARNINGS On a per-share 12-month-ended basis as shown by the solid black line. Dots indicate whether the company issues quarterly, semiannual, or annual earnings reports.

Ⓔ MONTHLY RANGES Shows the highest and lowest prices for the stock each month. Crossbars indicate the closing price.

Ⓕ PRICE SCALE This shows the dollar price of the stock, against which the monthly ranges are plotted.

Ⓖ RATIO-CATOR A guideline used by SRC. The plottings are obtained by dividing the closing price of the stock by the closing value of the DJIA on the same day. The resulting percentage is multiplied by a factor of 4.5 to bring the line close to the price bars and is read from the right-hand scale. The plotting indicates whether the stock has kept pace, outperformed, or lagged behind the general market.

Ⓗ VOLUME The number of shares traded, in thousands, each month on an arithmetic scale. Volume comes before price.

SHORT-TERM CHARTS

Here the data are similar to those of the longer-term charts but cover the action for only 21 months.

➤ EARNINGS For the last 12 months. Read from the left border to find the changes in dollar-per-share profits.

➤ DIVIDENDS On an annual basis; × indicates the ex-dividend date, ○, the dividend payment date.

➤ MOVING AVERAGE FOR 39 WEEKS Each dot represents the average of the closing prices of the 39 most recent weeks. When used with the price bars, it helps you determine trends as well as buying and selling points.

➤ RATIO-CATOR Shows the relative performance of the stock. It is calculated by dividing the closing price of the stock by the closing value of the DJIA on the same day and then multiplying by 7.0.

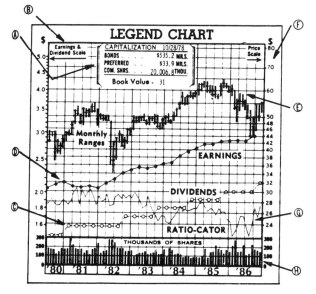

SOURCE: Securities Research Company, A Division of United Business Service Company, 208 Newbury Street, Boston, MA 02116.

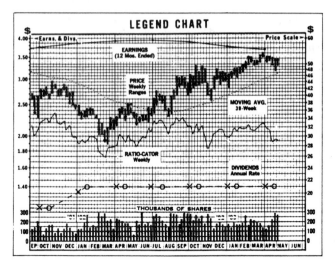

SOURCE: Securities Research Company, A Division of United Business Service Company, 208 Newbury Street, Boston, MA 02116.

Note: In plotting the short-term chart, the price range, earnings, and dividends are shown on a uniform ratio scale: that is, the vertical linear distance for a 100% move is the same any place on the chart regardless of whether the rise was from $5 to $10 or from $20 to $40. Thus all charts of all stocks are comparable.

USING TREND LINE CHARTS

The key to the successful use of charts, and most technical analysis, is the premise that *a trend in force will persist until a significant change in investor expectations causes it to reverse itself*—or as Martin Pring puts it, "on the assumption that people will continue to make the same mistakes they have made in the past." To discern that trend, the chartist draws lines connecting the lowest points of an upward-moving stock and the highest points of a downward-moving stock. This trend line is a reliable indicator about 80% of the time, because it predicts the immediate action of the stock or market.

The shrewd investor rises with the trend: buying when there's a confirmed upward move, considering selling when there's a definite downswing. Generally, the stock will move along that line—regardless of the direction. There will be interim bounces or dips, but most stocks hold to that pattern until there is a clear change.

Trend lines establish bases. The uptrend line becomes a support level below which an upward-moving stock is not likely to fall. The downtrend line marks a resistance level above which the stock is not likely to rise.

§ HINT: Before you invest—or speculate—in any stocks, check the chart and draw trend lines. Buy when the trend is up; hold or do not buy when it is moving down. The best profits always come when you buy an up stock in an up industry in an up market—clearly evident from trend lines on charts. And, of course, when you sell short, it's the opposite.

Technical analysis, especially charts, can be a valuable aid to timing if you remember these three points:

- Unless you are extremely optimistic and can afford to tie up your money for a while, *never* buy any stock until its chart is pointing up.

- *Always* check the chart action before you sell. You may think that the high has been reached, but the chart may disagree and make possible greater gains.

- If the chart shows a downtrend, consider selling. If it's a good investment, you can buy the stock back later at a lower price. If it's not, you'll save a lot of money.

Properly employed, technical analysis can be an important adjunct to fundamental investing and, more often than not, it will keep you humble!

FOR FURTHER INFORMATION

Robert D. Edwards and John Magee, *Technical Analysis of Stock Trends* (Boston: John Magee, Inc., 1992).

Martin Pring, *Technical Analysis Explained,* 3rd ed. (New York: McGraw-Hill, 1991).

T.H. Stewart, *How Charts Can Make You Money: Technical Analysis for Investors,* 2nd ed. (Chicago: Probus Publishing, 1990).

Robert W. Colby and Thomas A. Meyers, *The Encyclopedia of Technical Indicators* (Homewood, IL: Business One Irwin, 1992).

WHERE, WHAT, WHEN:
Exchanges, Indexes, and Indicators

In keeping with Wall Street jargon and financial reporting, initials are used frequently. Here are some of the most widely used:

EXCHANGES

➤ NYSE: NEW YORK STOCK EXCHANGE 11 Wall Street, New York, NY 10005; 1-212-656-3000. This is the oldest and largest exchange in the United States. To be listed, a corporation must:

- Demonstrate earning power of $2.5 million before federal income taxes for the most recent year and $2 million pre-tax for each of the preceding 2 years
- Have net tangible assets of $18 million
- Have market value of publicly held shares of $18 million
- Report a total of 1.1 million common shares publicly held
- Have 2,000 holders of 100 shares or more

➤ AMEX: AMERICAN STOCK EXCHANGE 86 Trinity Place, New York, NY 10006; 1-212-306-1000. These corporations are generally smaller and less financially strong than those on the NYSE. The firm must have:

- Pre-tax income of at least $750,000 in its last fiscal year or in two of the last three
- Stockholders' equity of $4 million
- 500,000 shares of common, exclusive of holdings of officers or directors
- 800 public stockholders or a minimum public distribution of 1 million shares together with a minimum of 400 holders of 100 or more shares
- Market price of $3 minimum with $3 million market value

➤ OTC: OVER THE COUNTER This is the market for securities that are not listed on major exchanges. The trading is conducted by dealers who are members of NASD (National Association of Securities Dealers, 1735 K Street NW, Wash-

ington, DC 20006; 1-202-728-8000) and who may or may not be members of other exchanges. Trading is by bid and asked prices. The primary market is NASDAQ (National Association of Securities Dealers Automated Quotations), which consists of about 4,700 of the most actively traded issues. Some 11,000 other stocks are quoted in daily financial summaries.

➤ CBOE: CHICAGO BOARD OPTIONS EXCHANGE La Salle at Van Buren, Chicago, IL 60005; 1-312-786-5600. The major auction market for calls and puts, primarily on NYSE stocks, and recently for special types of options such as those on Treasury bonds and on the S&P 100 and 500.

➤ ACC: AMEX OPTIONS EXCHANGE 86 Trinity Place, New York, NY 10006; 1-212-306-1000. The division of AMEX that trades puts and calls, almost entirely on NYSE-listed and OTC stocks.

➤ CBT: CHICAGO BOARD OF TRADE 141 West Jackson Boulevard, Chicago, IL 60604; 1-312-435-3500. A major market for futures contracts: commodities, interest rate securities, commercial paper, etc.

➤ CME: CHICAGO MERCANTILE EXCHANGE 30 South Wacker Drive, Chicago, IL 60606; 1-312-930-1000. Futures contracts for commodities.

➤ COMEX: COMMODITY EXCHANGE (FORMERLY NEW YORK COMMODITY EXCHANGE) 4 World Trade Center, New York, NY 10048; 1-212-938-2900. Futures and options of a limited number of commodities and metals (gold, silver, and copper).

➤ NYCE: NEW YORK COTTON EXCHANGE 4 World Trade Center, New York, NY 10048; 1-212-938-2650. Trading in futures in cotton and orange juice.

➤ IMM: INTERNATIONAL MONETARY MARKET; 1-312-930-1000. A part of the Chicago Mercantile Exchange. Trades in futures of foreign currency and U.S. Treasury bills.

OTHER STOCK EXCHANGES

U.S.

Boston Stock Exchange	1-617-723-9500
1 Boston Place, 38th floor	
Boston, MA 02108	
Cincinnati Stock Exchange	1-513-621-1410
36 E. 4th Street, Suite 906	
Cincinnati, OH 45202	
Midwest Stock Exchange	1-312-663-2222
440 S. LaSalle Street	
Chicago, IL 60605	
Pacific Stock Exchange	1-415-393-4000
301 Pine Street	
San Francisco, CA 94104	
or	
233 South Beaudry Avenue	1-213-977-4500
Los Angeles, CA 90012	
Philadelphia Stock Exchange	1-215-496-5000
1900 Market Street	
Philadelphia, PA 19103	

CANADIAN

Alberta Stock Exchange	1-403-262-7791
300 Fifth Avenue SW	
Calgary, Alberta T2P 3C4	
Montreal Stock Exchange	1-514-871-2424
800 Victoria Square	
Montreal, Quebec H4Z 1A9	
Toronto Stock Exchange	1-416-947-4700
Exchange Tower	
2 First Canadian Place	
Toronto, Ontario M5X 1J2	
Vancouver Stock Exchange	1-604-643-6590
609 Granville Street	
Vancouver, British Columbia	
V7Y 1HY	
Winnipeg Stock Exchange	1-204-942-8431
2901 One Lombard Place	
Winnipeg, Manitoba R3B	
0Y2	

➤ KCBT: KANSAS CITY BOARD OF TRADE 4800 Main Street, Suite 303, Kansas City, MO 64112; 1-816-753-7500. Trades in futures of commodities and Value Line futures index.

➤ NYFE: NEW YORK FUTURES EXCHANGE 20 Broad Street, New York, NY 10005; 1-212-656-4949.

A wholly owned subsidiary of the NYSE that trades in the NYSE Composite Index futures contract.

➤ NYME: NEW YORK MERCANTILE EXCHANGE 4 World Trade Center, New York, NY 10048; 1-212-938-2222. Trading in futures of petroleum, platinum, and palladium.

FEDERAL AGENCIES

➤ SEC: SECURITIES AND EXCHANGE COMMISSION 450 Fifth Street NW, Washington, DC 20549; 1-202-272-7440. A federal agency established to help protect investors. It is responsible for administering congressional acts regarding securities, stock exchanges, corporate reporting, investment companies, investment advisers, and public utility holding companies.

➤ FRB: FEDERAL RESERVE BOARD 20th and C Streets NW, Washington, DC 20551; 1-202-452-3000. The federal agency responsible for control of such important investment items as the discount rate, money supply, and margin requirements.

➤ FDIC: FEDERAL DEPOSIT INSURANCE CORPORATION 550 17th Street NW, Washington, DC 20429; 1-800-424-5488. An agency that insures bank deposits.

➤ SAVINGS ASSOCIATION INSURANCE FUND 550 17th Street NW, Washington, DC 20429; 1-800-424-5488. An agency that insures deposits with savings and loan associations.

➤ CFTC: COMMODITY FUTURES TRADING COMMISSION 2033 K Street NW, Washington, DC 20581; 1-202-254-6387. This is a watchdog for the commodities futures trading industry.

STOCK MARKET AVERAGES

AVERAGES VS. INDEXES

➤ DOW JONES AVERAGES The most popular indicators of the direction of the stock market, these were devised in 1884 by Charles H. Dow, a founder and first editor of the *Wall Street Journal*. The makeup of the Dow Jones averages appears in the box on page 377. Each is simply an average price of the stocks in the group, derived by adding up the prices and dividing

STOCKS IN DOW JONES AVERAGES AS OF MAY 1992

Industrials (DJIA)

Alcoa	International Business
Allied Signal	Machines
American Express	International Paper
AT&T	McDonald's Corp.
Bethlehem Steel	Merck & Co.
Boeing	Minnesota Mining &
Caterpillar	Mfg.
Chevron	J.P. Morgan
Coca-Cola	Philip Morris Co.
Disney	Procter & Gamble
Du Pont, E.I.	Sears, Roebuck
Eastman Kodak	Texaco, Inc.
Exxon Corporation	Union Carbide
General Electric	United Technologies
General Motors	Westinghouse Electric
Goodyear Tire	Woolworth (F.W.)

Transportation (DJTA)

Airborne Freight	Federal Express
Alaska Air Group	Norfolk & Southern
American President	Roadway Service
Lines	Ryder Systems
AMR Corp.	Santa Fe Southern
Burlington Northern	Pacific
Carolina Freight	Southwest Air
Consolidated Freightways	UAL Corp.
Consolidated Rail	Union Pacific Corp.
CSX Corp.	U.S. Air Group
Delta Airlines	XTRA Corp.

Utility (DJUA)

American Electric Power	Niagara Mohawk Power
Arkala	Pacific Gas & Electric
Centerior Energy	Panhandle Eastern Corp.
Commonwealth Edison	Peoples Energy
Consolidated Edison	Philadelphia Electric
Consolidated Natural Gas	Public Service
Detroit Edison	Enterprises
Houston Industries	SCE Corp.

by the number of stocks represented. Initially the divisor was 11; then in the 1920s it became 30 when the number of stocks was increased from 11 to 30; today it's .559. Each average measures the stocks' performance during one day. When one of the companies in the average declares a stock split or dividend, the divisor is reduced in size to accommodate the change.

For many years the Dow Jones Industrial Average hovered around 100, peaking at 386 in 1929 just prior to the crash. After the crash it climbed back up slowly, never moving much past 200 until World War II, when it hit 700. In 1966 it reached 1000. It fell again to 570 in 1974 only to return to 1000 two years later. In August 1987 the Dow posted an all-time high of 2722.42, but 2 months later, on October 19, it plunged a record 508 points to 1738.74. Since then there have been numerous ups and downs. In early July 1988 it reached 2158.61, the highest point since the October crash. A year later, in July 1989, it was 2456.56. As we go to press, it is 3368.88.

The Dow is often criticized for the fact that a high-priced stock, such as IBM, has a greater impact on the index than lower-priced issues. In other words, the stocks are *not* equally weighted, so on any given day, a fluctuation of significance in one or two high-priced stocks can distort the average. As a result, the Dow is useful for tracking the direction of the market over the long term but is often less reliable on a daily or even weekly basis. With only 30 stocks, it is also thought to be too small.

➤ STANDARD & POOR'S 500 INDEX This index addresses some of the criticism of the Dow and has challenged its premier position. The S&P 500, devised in 1957, is weighted according to the market value of each stock in the index. Covering 500 stocks, it is computed by multiplying the price of each stock by the number of shares outstanding. This gives larger and more influential corporations more weight.

Despite their different approaches, the averages and the index move together most of the time, especially on major swings.

$ HINT: Keep in mind that the Dow figure is about 10 times larger than the S&P 500. That's because S&P tried to devise an index that was more nearly comparable to the average dollar price of all stocks traded on the NYSE.

➤ DOW JONES INDUSTRIAL AVERAGE (DJIA) The oldest and most widely used stock market average. It shows the action of 30 actively traded blue chip stocks, representing about 15% of NYSE values, on a weighted basis: for example,

MARKET INDICATORS, INDEXES, AND AVERAGES

Whether you're bullish, bearish, or uncertain, you can get a reading on the direction of the market, interest rates, and the overall economy by following some of the key statistics (or indicators) regularly churned out by Wall Street and Washington. These should be regarded not as gospel but rather as tools to help you make informed and intelligent decisions about your investments and for timing moves between stocks, bonds, and cash equivalents. Make a point of jotting down these numbers on your own chart and track the trends. You will see definite patterns between the market, interest rates, and the money supply. (The indicators are presented in alphabetical order.)

ECONOMIC INDICATOR	COMPOSITION	WHAT IT PREDICTS
Consumer price index (CPI)	The average price of consumer goods and services	The direction of inflation and changes in the purchasing power of money
Dollar index	The value of the dollar as measured against major foreign currencies	Domestic corporate profits and multinational earning power
Dow Jones Industrial Average (DJIA)	30 major companies whose stock is held by many institutions and individuals; index is price-weighted so that moves in high-priced stocks exert more influence than those of lower-priced stock	Action of the stock market, which in turn anticipates future business activity
Employment figures and payroll employment	Number of people working or on company payrolls	Potential consumer spending, which in turn affects corporate profits
Gross domestic product (GDP)	Total goods and services produced in United States on an annual basis; inflation can distort the accuracy of this figure, so subtract inflation from GDP to get "real" GDP	General business trends and economic activity
Index of industrial production (IIP)	Shown as a percentage of the average, which has been tracked since 1967; base is 100	Amount of business volume
Money supply:		
M1	Currency held by the public plus balances in checking accounts, NOW accounts, traveler's checks, and money market funds	Extent of consumer purchasing power and liquidity of public's assets, used by Federal Reserve as a gauge for predicting as well as controlling the pace of the economy; when M1 shows a big increase, the Fed usually reduces the money supply, which sends interest rates up; Fed reduces M1 by selling Treasuries; tightening of M1 serves to curb inflation; an increase in M1 fuels inflation
M2	M1 plus time deposits over $100,000 and repurchase agreements	
M3	M2 plus T-bills, U.S. savings bonds, bankers' acceptances, term Eurodollars, commercial paper	

ECONOMIC INDICATOR	COMPOSITION	WHAT IT PREDICTS
Standard & Poor's 500 stock index	Indexed value of 500 stocks from NYSE, AMEX, and OTC; more useful than the Dow Jones Industrial Average because it's broader; includes 400 industrials, 40 public utilities, 20 transportations, and 40 financials; stocks are market-value weighted; that is, price of each stock is multiplied by the number of shares outstanding	Direction of the economy and the market; good leading indicator because the market tends to anticipate future economic conditions
Three-month Treasury bill rate	Interest rate paid to purchasers of T-bills	General direction of interest rates; gives indication of the Federal Reserve system's fiscal policy; for example, during a recession, the Fed increases the amount of currency in circulation, which serves to lower the T-bill rate; during inflation, currency is reduced and the T-bill rate rises; rising interest rates tend to reduce corporate profits because of the increased costs of borrowing; therefore, a continual rise in T-bill rates presages a decline in the stock market; falling rates help stock and bond prices
Wage settlements	Percentage changes in wages that come about because of new labor contracts	Price changes for goods and services; sharply higher wage settlements result in higher inflation rates

IBM at 110 carries more than 3 times the weight of Woolworth at 35.

The DJIA is determined by dividing the closing prices by a divisor that compensates for past stock splits and stock dividends. The average is quoted in points, not dollars.

➤ DOW JONES TRANSPORTATION AVERAGE (DJTA) This is made up of the stocks of 20 major transportation companies.

➤ DOW JONES UTILITY AVERAGE (DJUA) This consists of 15 major utilities to provide geographic representation. With more firms forming holding companies to engage in oil and gas exploration and distribution, its value is greater as a point of reference than as a guide to the market's evaluation of producers of electricity and distributors of gas.

➤ DOW JONES COMPOSITE INDEX Also called the 65 Stock Average, this combines the other three indexes and consists of 30 industrials, 20 transportation, and 15 utility stocks. It is not widely followed.

➤ STANDARD & POOR'S COMPOSITE INDEX OF 500 STOCKS A market-value-weighted index showing the change in the aggregate value of 500 stocks, it consists mainly of NYSE-listed companies with some AMEX and OTC stocks. There are 400 industrials, 60 transportation and utility companies, and 40 financial issues. It represents about 80% of the market value of all issues traded on the NYSE but actually reflects the action of a comparatively few large firms. Options on this index trade on the Chicago Board Options Exchange and futures on the Chicago Mercantile Exchange.

➤ STANDARD & POOR'S 400 MIDCAP INDEX Introduced in June 1991, this index is comprised of 400 domestic companies. The median market capitalization of stocks in the index is $610 million vs. about $2.2 billion for stocks in the S&P 500. It is a market-weighted index (stock price times shares outstanding).

➤ STANDARD & POOR'S 100 STOCK INDEX This consists of stocks for which options are listed on the Chicago Board Options Exchange. Options on the 100 Index are listed on the Chicago Board Options Exchange and futures on the Chicago Mercantile Exchange.

➤ WILSHIRE 5000 EQUITY INDEX This is a value-weighted index derived from the dollar value of 5,000 common stocks, including all those listed on the NYSE and AMEX and the most active OTC issues. It is the broadest index and thus is more representative of the overall market. Unfortunately, it has not received adequate publicity. The Wilshire is prepared by Wilshire Associates in Santa Monica, Calif. No futures or options are traded on the Wilshire.

➤ NYSE COMPOSITE INDEX A market-value-weighted index covering the price movements of all common stocks listed on the Big Board. It is based on the prices at the close of trading on December 31, 1965, and is weighted according to the number of shares listed for each issue. The base value is $50. Point changes are converted to dollars and cents to provide a meaningful measure of price action. Futures are traded on the NYFE and options on the NYSE itself.

➤ NASDAQ-COMPOSITE INDEX This represents all domestic OTC stocks except those having only one market maker. It covers a total of 3,500 stocks and is market-value weighted. No futures or options are traded.

➤ VALUE LINE COMPOSITE INDEX This is an equally weighted index of 1,700 NYSE, AMEX, and OTC stocks tracked by the *Value Line Investment Survey*. Designed to reflect price changes of typical industrial stocks, it is neither price- nor market-value weighted. Options trade on the Philadelphia Exchange and futures on the Kansas City Board of Trade.

➤ AMEX MAJOR MARKET INDEX Price-weighted, which means that high-priced stocks have a greater influence than low-priced ones, this is an average of 20 blue chip industrials. It was designed to mirror the Dow Jones Industrial Average and measure representative performance of these kinds of issues. Although produced by the AMEX, it includes stocks listed on the NYSE. Futures are traded on the Chicago Board of Trade.

➤ AMEX MARKET VALUE INDEX This is a capitalization-weighted index that measures the collective performance of more than 90% of AMEX-listed companies, including ADRs, warrants, and common stocks. Cash dividends are assumed to be reinvested. Options are traded on the AMEX.

➤ DOW JONES BOND AVERAGE This consists of bonds of 10 public utilities and 10 industrial corporations.

➤ BARRON'S CONFIDENCE INDEX Weekly index of corporate bond yields published by *Barron's*, the financial newspaper owned by Dow Jones. It shows the ratio of the average yield of 10 high-grade bonds to the Dow Jones average yield on 40 bonds. The premise is that when investors feel confident about the economy they buy lower-rated bonds.

➤ BOND BUYER'S INDEX Published daily, it measures municipal bonds.

GLOSSARY: WALL STREET JARGON MADE SIMPLE

amortization: Gradual reduction of a debt by a series of periodic payments. Each payment includes interest on the outstanding debt and part of the principal.

arbitrage: Profiting from price differences when a security, currency, or commodity is traded on different markets. Also, to buy shares in a company that is about to be taken over and sell short the shares of the acquiring company.

asset: A possession that has present and future financial value to its owner.

ATMs: Automated teller machines, located primarily at banks. Upon insertion of a magnetically coded bank identification card, the computer-controlled machine will dispense cash that you request or deposit money to your account and indicate the status of your account on a viewing screen. No teller is necessary, and the majority of ATMs are open 24 hours.

blue chip: The common stock of a well-known national company with a history of earnings growth and dividend increases, such as IBM or Exxon.

bond: A security that represents debt of an issuing corporation. Usually, the issuer is required to pay the bondholder a specified rate of interest for a specified time and then repay the entire debt (also known as face value) upon maturity.

bull and bear cycles: The up-and-down movements of the stock market. A bull believes that prices will rise and buys on that assumption. A bull market is a period when stock prices are advancing. A bear believes that security or commodity prices will decline. A bear market is marked by declining prices.

call: A feature of many bonds giving the issuer the right to call in or redeem the bonds before their maturity date.

capital: Also called capital assets; property or money from which a person or business receives some monetary gain.

cash equivalents: The generic term for assorted short-term instruments such as U.S. Treasury securities, CDs, and money market fund shares, which can be readily converted into cash.

central asset or combo account: Brokerage, money market fund, and checking account combined with a credit card. Offered by both banks and brokerage houses, some central asset accounts include forms of life insurance, mortgages, traveler's checks, and other special features.

certificates of deposit: Also called CDs or "time certificates of deposit"; official receipts issued by a bank stating that a given amount of money has been deposited for a certain length of time at a specified rate of interest. CDs are insured by the U.S. government for up to $100,000.

charts: Records of price and volume trends as well as the general movement of stock and bond markets, economic cycles, industries, and individual companies, updated continually. Chartists believe that past history as expressed on a chart gives a strong clue to the next price movement. They "read" the lines to determine what a stock has done and may do.

combo account: See *central asset or combo account.*

commodities: Goods, articles, services, and interest rates in which contracts for future delivery may be traded. These range from precious metals, food, and grain to U.S. Treasury securities and foreign currencies.

common stock: See *stock, common.*

compound interest: The amount earned on

the original principal plus the accumulated interest. With interest on interest plus interest on principal, an investment grows more rapidly.

convertibles: Bonds, debentures, or preferred stock that may be exchanged or converted into common stock.

correction: A reverse downward in the prices of stocks, bonds, or commodities.

credit card: A plastic card issued by a bank or financial institution that gives the holder access to a line of credit to purchase goods or to receive cash. Repayment may be required in full in 30 days or in installments. Compare *debit card.*

credit union: A nonprofit financial institution formed by a labor union, company employees, or members of a cooperative. Credit unions, which offer a range of financial services, tend to pay higher interest rates than commercial banks.

debit card: A deposit access card that debits the holder's bank account or money market account immediately upon use in purchasing. There is no grace period in which to pay; payment is transferred immediately and electronically at the moment of purchase. Compare *credit card.*

discount rate: The interest rate the Federal Reserve charges member banks; it provides a floor for interest rates banks charge their customers. See also *prime rate.*

disinflation: A reduction in the rate of ongoing inflation.

DJIA (Dow Jones Industrial Average): Price-weighted average of 30 blue chip stocks, representing overall price movements of all stocks on the New York Stock Exchange.

effective annual yield: Rate of return earned on your savings if you do not incur service charges or penalties.

face value: Value of a bond or note when issued. Corporate bonds are usually issued with $1,000 face value; municipals with $5,000; T-bills with $10,000. Also called par value.

FDIC (Federal Deposit Insurance Corporation): An independent agency of the U.S. government whose basic purpose is to insure bank deposits. Depositors are covered up to $100,000, at an insured bank.

financial futures: Contracts to deliver a spec-ified number of financial instruments at a given price by a certain date, such as U.S. Treasury bonds and bills, GNMA certificates, CDs, and foreign currency.

financial planner: A person who handles all aspects of your finances, including stocks, bonds, insurance, savings, and tax shelters.

front running: A trader knowing in advance of a block trade that will affect the price of a security and buying to profit from the trade.

futures: See *commodities.*

government or municipal bonds: Contracts of indebtedness issued by the U.S. Treasury, federal agencies, or state and local governments, which promise to pay back the principal amount plus interest at a specified date.

index: A statistical yardstick that measures a whole market by using a representative selection of stocks or bonds. Changes are compared to a base year. Futures are now sold on stock indexes, such as the S&P 500.

index arbitrage: Profiting from the difference in prices of the same security. In program trading, traders buy and sell to profit from small price discrepancies, using computers that monitor both the S&P 500 stock index and futures contracts on the index. When there is a larger than normal gap, the computers notify the traders to sell.

index future: A contract to buy or sell an index (Standard & Poor's, for example) at a future date. An index is a statistical yardstick that measures changes compared to a base period. The New York Stock Exchange Composite Index of all NYSE common stocks is based on a 1965 average of 50. *Note:* An index is not an average.

inflation: An increase in the average price level of goods and services over time.

institutions: Organizations that trade huge blocks of securities, such as banks, pension funds, mutual funds, and insurance companies.

interest: Money paid for the use of money. See also *discount rate; prime rate.*

junk bonds: High-risk, high-yielding bonds, rated BB or lower.

LBO (leveraged buyout): The purchase of a corporation by using a large amount of debt, much of it short-term bank loans secured by the assets of the company being acquired. After the buyout is completed, the acquired company issues bonds to pay off a portion of the debt taken on in the takeover.

liability: A debt; something owed by one person or business to another.

limited partnership: Investment organization in which your liability is limited to the dollar amount you invest; a general partner manages the project, which may be in real estate, farming, oil and gas, etc.

liquid: Cash or investments easily convertible into cash, such as money market funds or bank deposits.

liquidity: The ability of an asset or security to be converted quickly into cash.

"Mae" family: Various mortgage-backed securities either sponsored or partially guaranteed by a handful of government agencies or by private corporations, such as the Government National Mortgage Association (GNMA, or "Ginnie Mae") and the Federal Home Loan Mortgage Corporation ("Freddie Mac").

margin: The amount a client deposits with a broker in order to borrow from the broker to buy stocks.

mark to the market: The value of any portfolio based on the most recent closing price of the securities held.

mature: To come due; to reach the time when the face value of a bond or note must be paid.

money market fund: A mutual fund that invests only in high-yielding, short-term money market instruments such as U.S. Treasury bills, bank certificates of deposit, and commercial paper. Shareholders receive higher interest on their shares than in a bank money market account.

money market instruments: Short-term credit instruments such as Treasury bills, commercial paper, bankers' acceptances, CDs, and bank repurchase agreements.

municipal bonds: Also known as "munis"; debt obligations of state and local entities. For the most part, the interest earned is free from federal taxation and often from state and local taxes as well.

mutual fund: An investment trust in which an investor's dollars are pooled with those of thousands of others; the combined total is invested by a professional manager in a variety of securities.

net asset value (NAV):   The price at which you buy or sell shares of a mutual fund. To determine NAV, mutual funds compute their assets daily by adding up the market value of all securities owned by the fund, deducting all liabilities, and dividing the balance by the number of shares outstanding. The NAV per share is the figure quoted in the papers.

net worth: Total value (of cash, property, investments) after deducting outstanding expenses or amounts owed.

option: The right to buy (call) or sell (put) a certain amount of stock at a given price (strike price) for a specified length of time.

over-the-counter (OTC) stock: A security not listed or traded on a major exchange. Transactions take place by telephone and computer network rather than on the floor of an exchange.

points: A measure of a price change. With a stock, a point change means a change of $1; with a bond, with a $1,000 facevalue; it refers to a $10 change.

portfolio insurance: When the stock market falls by a certain amount, computers notify money managers, who then protect their portfolios by selling a stock index future (a contract on a basket of stocks). The cash raised from this sale helps offset the drop in the value of the portfolio.

preferred stock: See *stock, preferred.*

prime rate: Rate banks charge their largest and best customers. See also *discount rate.*

program trading: Computerized institutional buying or selling of all stocks in a program or in an index on which options and futures are traded.

prospectus: A summary of data on an issue of securities that will be sold to the public, enabling investors to evaluate the security and decide whether or not to buy it. The SEC regulations determine what basic information must be set forth in every prospectus.

put: An options contract giving the investor the right to sell a specified number of shares by a certain date at a certain price.

SAIF (Savings Association Insurance Fund):   An independent agency of the U.S. government that insures deposits held in the savings institutions of members for up to $100,000.

SEC (Securities and Exchange Commission):   A federal agency with power to enforce federal laws pertaining to the sale of securities and governing exchanges, stockbrokers, and investment advisers.

sharedraft: Interest-bearing checking account at a credit union.

SIPC (Securities Investor Protection Corporation): An independent agency established by Congress to provide customers of most brokerage firms with protection similar to that provided by the FDIC for bank depositors, in the event that a firm is unable to meet its financial obligations.

stock, common: A security that represents ownership in a corporation.

stock, preferred: A stock that pays a fixed dividend and has first claim on profits over common stocks for the payment of that dividend. The dividend does not rise or fall with profits.

stock right: A short-term privilege issued by a corporation to its existing stockholders granting them the right to buy new stock at a stated price.

stockbroker: An agent who handles the public's orders to buy and sell securities, commodities, and other properties. A broker may be a partner of a brokerage firm or a registered representative, who is an employee of a brokerage firm. Brokers charge a commission for their services.

strike price: The dollar amount per share at which an option buyer can purchase the underlying stock or a put option buyer can sell the stock. Also called the exercise price.

takeover: When the controlling interest of a corporation is taken over by a new company. Takeovers can be friendly or hostile.

takeover candidate: A company that may be acquired by another corporation.

tax bracket: The point on the income tax rate schedules where one's taxable income (income subject to tax after exemptions and deductions) falls. It is expressed as a percentage to be applied to each additional dollar earned over the base amount for that bracket. The current tax brackets for individuals in the United States are 15%, 28%, and 31%.

tax shelter: An investment that allows an investor to realize significant tax benefits by reducing or deferring taxable income.

total return: Dividend or interest income plus any capital gain; a better measure of an investment's return than just dividends or just interest.

Treasury securities: Bonds issued by the U.S. Treasury and federal agencies that are sold at half their face value, beginning at $25 for a $50 bond. The term includes U.S. savings bonds; Treasury bills, which have a face value of $10,000, are sold at a discount, and mature in 1 year or less; Treasury notes, which have a face value of $1,000 or $5,000 and mature in 1 to 10 years; and Treasury bonds, which mature in 10 to 30 years and have a face value of $1,000. Interest on Treasuries is exempt from state and local income taxes.

triple tax-exempt bonds: Municipal bonds exempt from federal, state, and local taxes for residents of the states and localities that issue the bonds.

vested interest: The nonforfeitable dollar amount in a pension plan. You will not lose that portion of your benefit should you leave the job.

warrant: A security, usually issued with a bond or preferred stock, giving the owner the privilege of buying a specified number of shares of a stock at a fixed price, usually for a period of years.

yield: The income paid or earned by a security divided by its current price. For example, a $20 stock with an annual dividend of $1.50 has a 7.5% yield.

zero coupon bond: A bond that pays no current interest but is sold at a deep discount from face value. At maturity, all compounded interest is paid and the bondholder collects the full face value of the bond (usually $1,000). EE savings bonds are zeros.

INDEX

INDEX OF SECURITIES

(Note: Closed-end funds that trade on the exchanges are listed here as securities, not with open end mutual funds.)

MUTUAL FUNDS

(Note: For closed end bond funds that trade on stock exchanges, see Equities Index.)